EDUCATIONAL VALUES
AND COGNITIVE INSTRUCTION:
IMPLICATIONS FOR REFORM

EDUCATIONAL VALUES AND COGNITIVE INSTRUCTION: IMPLICATIONS FOR REFORM

EDITED BY

LORNA IDOL
Institute for Learning and Development

BEAU FLY JONES
North Central Regional Educational Laboratory

LAWRENCE ERLBAUM ASSOCIATES, PUBLISHERS
1991   Hillsdale, New Jersey   Hove and London

This publication is based in part on work conducted under Contract No. 400-86-0004 with the Office of Educational Research and Improvement (OERI), U.S. Department of Education.
The opinions expressed do not necessarily reflect the position or policy of OERI and no official endorsement should be inferred.

Lawrence Erlbaum Associates, Inc., Publishers
365 Broadway
Hillsdale, New Jersey

Library of Congress Cataloging-in-Publication Data

Educational values and cognitive instruction : implications for reform
   / edited by Lorna Idol, Beau Fly Jones.
        p.   cm.
      "North Central Regional Educational Laboratory."
      Companion volume to Dimensions of thinking and cognitive
   instruction.
      Includes bibliographical references and indexes.
      ISBN 0-8058-0364-5
      1. Thought and thinking—Study and teaching.   2. Teaching.
   3. Critical thinking.   I. Idol, Lorna.   II. Jones, Beau Fly.
   III. North Central Regional Educational Laboratory (U.S.)
   IV. Dimensions of thinking and cognitive instruction.
   LB1590.3.E35   1990
   371.1'02—dc20   90-43963
                                                      CIP

Printed in the United States of America
10 9 8 7 6 5 4 3 2 1

Contents

Introduction

THE FIRST VOLUME –
DIMENSIONS OF THINKING AND COGNITIVE
INSTRUCTION: IMPLICATIONS FOR REFORM

The first volume of this series examined the dimensions of thinking and cognitive instruction. *Dimensions of Thinking* was originally a book (Marzano et al., 1988) that provided a comprehensive framework for classifying and understanding various processes, skills, and other elements of thinking. The framework included these dimensions of thinking: metacognition, critical and creative thinking, thinking processes, core thinking skills, and the relationship of content-area knowledge to thinking. The chapters in the first volume were organized around these dimensions, yet they also offer an expansion to include discussion of the cognitive processes as they occur in a variety of learning contexts. Emphasis is placed on an expanded view of thinking, linking cognition with the affective, social, and physical contexts of learning. Perusal of the chapters should convince nearly any reader that a need for educational reform is both eminent and massive, as little of what is described is currently being taught in schools.

In Volume 1, the chapter authors examined the various types of metacognitive and cognitive processes thought to be used in human cognition. Included were examinations of metacognition as a mean of improving both academic learning and instruction (Paris & Winograd), and an exploration of the interdependence and influence of metacogni-

1

tion, attributions, and self-esteem on self-regulated cognition (Borkowski, Carr, Rellinger, & Pressley).

Furthermore, cognitive processes were presented as including the
abilities to conceptualize, communicate with reasoning, comprehend,
compose, solve problems, inquire, and make decisions. Klausmier offered
a complete and complex explanation of what the process of conceptualizing might look like, as well as how it might be taught. Roth explained
how conceptualizations are developed as students study science education. Kline and Delia offered a new dimension to our understanding of
cognition by describing how reasoning takes place as communication
skills are developed.

Specific to basic skills instruction, Pearson and Raphael described
thinking as it has begun to be understood in the reading comprehension
process, placing particular emphasis on the assimilation and accommodation of prior knowledge with newly acquired information gleaned from
textual reading. Hayes explored new ground by describing thinking as
it occurs in writers as they compose, setting a new stage for the advancement of writing instruction. Research on problem solving and inquiry
was examined within the context of mathematical and scientific problem
solving by Silver and Marshall and within the context of science education
by Tweney and Walker. Finally, the processes of cognition were described, within the context of how instructors think and make decisions
as they are teaching, by Borko and Shavelson. These various chapters
are intertwined and offer a rich and welcome addition to our understanding of how students might think during the learning process, as well as
how teachers might aid them in this process.

The latter, cognitive instruction itself, was explored in more detail in
the first volume as Derry described learning strategies used for knowledge acquisition, placing emphasis on teaching students how to use strategies for improving their learning processes. Bransford, Vye, Kinzer, and
Risko offered an integrated approach to teaching creativity within a
particular content area.

The volume continues with a stirring analysis of the nature and nurture of thinking by Perkins. This was followed by Paul's philosophical
perspective on how critical and reflective thinking are modeled and
shaped by the perspective of cognition that is taken, be it a psychological
perspective or a philosophical perspective. Paul provided an interesting
discussion and illustration of how thinking might be taught from a philosophical perspective, emphasizing reflection and critical examination.

The commonality of themes woven across these various chapters offers
the reader an opportunity to integrate seemingly disparate views of
human cognition, as represented by the various disciplines studying human cognition and the individual perspectives taken by the various au-

thors. *Dimensions of Thinking and Cognitive Instruction* sets a precedent as a pioneering effort that begins to develop a truly interdisciplinary understanding of how humans think and learn.

THE SECOND VOLUME —
EDUCATIONAL VALUES AND COGNITIVE
INSTRUCTION: IMPLICATIONS FOR REFORM

Equally innovative in the breaking of new ground is any effort to begin to understand the implications for instruction. As these understandings develop, the impact on educational reform is inevitable. However, in the case of cognitive instruction, the outcomes of related educational reform have the potential to be far more outreaching than earlier reform movements have been. Such reform would impact not only on specific content instruction, but on instructional practice in general; it also would certainly impact on how curricular materials are developed and how teachers are prepared. Because of the far-reaching implications, such reform must be brought about thoughtfully and carefully. The authors of the chapters in *Educational Values and Cognitive Instruction* pave the way for such a conscious movement.

The general theme of this volume is directed toward implications for educational reform. The volume is organized into three major areas: (a) cognitive instruction as it currently exists with implications for the future, (b) consideration of contextual factors that are likely to influence the teaching of thinking skills, and (c) a discussion of the implications for attempting to bring about change.

Cognitive Instruction

Six chapters appear in the first section of this volume, entitled *Cognitive Instruction*. The lead chapter sets the tone for the entire volume as the authors (Kennedy, Fisher, and Ennis) discuss both historical and current perspectives on critical thinking, calling for a change in both school and research agendas. This comprehensive review spans the disciplines of cognitive psychology, philosophy, human development, curriculum development, and educational psychology. The authors view critical thinking as being "reasonable, reflective thinking that is focused on deciding what to believe or do" (Ennis, 1985, p. 46). They point out that critical thinking consists of both skills (or abilities) and dispositions (attitudes). The inclusion of both skills and attitudes in the Ennis definition coincides nicely with the specific types of metacognitive and cognitive processes (or skills) presented in the first volume, as well as with the similarity between dispositions or attitudes and Paul's commentary on the impact of philosophy on thinking (see the final chapter in the first volume).

The second chapter, by O'Flavahan and Tierney, explores the relationships among reading, writing, and critical thinking, making the case that reading and writing are powerful ways to promote critical thinking, because of the synergistic nature of integrated reading and writing activities and the multiplicative effects they have on learning. These authors view critical thinking as including the following: (a) self-initiated and self-directed exploration of ideas, (b) critical examination of one's own ideas, (c) pursuit of multiple perspectives, including a perspective on these perspectives, (d) creation of appropriate environments in which to orchestrate such examination, and (e) ongoing consideration of the quality of these examinations. They go on to describe approaches for creating literate environments where cognitive instruction focuses on teaching meaningful applications of thinking skills and independent learning in functional contexts, with particular emphasis placed on the development of self-initiated learning.

In the third chapter, Idol, Jones, and Mayer describe some of the general characteristics of thinking versus some characteristics that are specific to particular subject areas, such as language arts, science, and mathematics. This discussion is critical to our understanding of the issues related to whether thinking should be taught in a separate curriculum or within an integrated curriculum. These authors present a detailed and comparative analysis of curricular programs for teaching thinking skills separately versus some promising instructional strategies that can be used within reading and content area instruction. Attention is given to issues such as availability of efficacy research and efforts to teach generalized learning, as well as to a number of critical aspects of the feasibility of program implementation. The authors also place emphasis on the various types of teaching roles that are relevant for cognitive instruction, including the teacher as a manager and executive; as a guide, directing students' thoughts explicitly; as a mediator of student cognitive processing; and as a model for exemplifying the thinking process.

In the fourth chapter of *Cognitive Instruction*, Collins brings to us the notion of cognitive apprenticeship as a means of teaching thinking. He reminds us that the apprenticeship system of learning was a commonly used method of teaching in earlier times and demonstrates how the idea of apprenticeships can be applied to the development of apprenticeship learning environments, placing emphasis on the development of cognition rather than on physical skills as it was used in earlier days. Collins' premise is that cognitive apprenticeships can be very effectively applied to the development of an instructional technology that has been used in computerized classroom, resulting in technological instruction that is an innovative extension of our old and traditional practice of teaching via apprenticeships. Collins describes six characteristics of cognitive apprenticeship for which technology provides particular leverage, including situated learning; modeling and explaining; coaching; reflection on performance; articulation, or requiring students to explain and think about what they are doing; and exploration, or urging students to try out different hypotheses, methods, and strategies.

In the fifth chapter, Feuerstein, Rand, Egozi, and Shachar-Segey provide an indepth description of the Instructional Enrichment Program, initially designed for low-functioning students in Israel. The students for whom this curriculum was intended were originally thought of by many as being low-functioning and even as mentally retarded; however, based on the reactions and achievements of students receiving this instruction, it has become increasingly more apparent that these students were high-risk, disadvantaged students who, despite the limiting circumstances into which they were born, had potential to develop and achieve. In the chapter, its authors describe a carefully constructed framework for developing conceptual frameworks for children who have been unaccustomed to using such mental operations.

As a means of drawing together the chapters in the section on *Cognitive Instruction*, Linn explores the implications for assessment and testing that are raised as a result of placing emphasis on teaching thinking. He addresses several pertinent concerns about test construction that must be taken into consideration: overemphasis on factual knowledge, the constraints of multiple-choice tests, and the inadequacy of current tests as targets that will enhance thinking. Linn reminds us that standardized achievement tests are quite efficient at measuring a student's accumulation of declarative knowledge, as well as being a mean of measuring success in applying established procedures to solve problems with specified characteristics; in contrast, he points out their present inadequacies for assessing higher order thinking processes that a student is using or in diagnosing misconceptions or particular sources of difficulty a student may be having. He builds a case for the need to develop alternative assessment procedures that measure specific higher order thinking skills and that provide information about thinking processes. These include: (a) the formation of problem representation, (b) the construction of a mental model, (c) the generation of hypotheses, (d) the planning of steps to solve problems, (e) the self-monitoring of the application of a solution strategy, and (f) the yielding of diagnostic information that can help guide instruction. Some of the alternatives include teacher-directed assessment,

assessment of reading for understanding, assessment of critical thinking skills, use of open-ended test responses, use of diagnostic testing, and use of computer simulations in assessment testing.

Influence of Contextual Factors

The second section of this volume is about the influence of contextual factors (i. e., grouping for instruction, student motivation, influence of policy and regulations, student diversity, use of language in the classroom) on thinking itself, as well as how thinking is taught. The first chapter, by Barr and Anderson, is a cogent review of the research on ability grouping. Barr raises serious questions about the impact of such practice on at-risk, and often culturally different and/or economically disadvantaged, students who are often assigned to low-ability groups with few opportunities to rise to higher functioning groups. These authors capture for us the complex decision-making process that is entailed when classroom, school, or district personnel decide to use a particular grouping configuration for instruction. These processes are illustrated by examination of an elementary school district where instructional grouping practices were studied by a committee consisting of three primary teachers, three intermediate teachers, two principals, the curriculum coordinator of the district, and the assistant superintendent. If this committee can be viewed as a microcosm of a larger social system, then insights can be gained by examining how this committee went about evaluating the effectiveness of their 'grouping practices and establishing a policy on grouping.

Ames and Ames have written a chapter concerned with the impact of student motivation on school achievement, as a means of helping teachers eliminate some factors that commonly elicit negative student motivation in the classroom. They describe several strategies to enhance positive motivation in students. Their view of motivation focuses on certain qualitative aspects of how students think about the learning process, such as how students place different values on various goals, how they process and attend to information, and how the different beliefs and evaluations they have about themselves affect their performances. Ames and Ames examine these various aspects of motivation and then describe several effective teaching practices to enhance student motivation.

Another important group of contextual factors has to do with the development of policies and regulations and the influences they have on instruction. In chapter 9, Allington writes of the impact of such factors in the development of cognitively based programs of instruction in reading and, in particular, instruction for students at risk for school failure.

The emphasis is on the explanation that children are more likely to learn what they are taught than what they are not, and that at-risk students receive a limited type of instruction. His review of current instructional practices in the education of low-achievement learners includes examination of instructional time allocations, instructional tasks that are set, and the nature of the teaching offered to these children. This is followed by an interpretation of how federal, state, district, and building policies and regulations that constrain these programs shape the nature of the instruction that is offered. Concerns are raised about issues like the following: how higher order thinking skills should be taught to poor readers, how to best offer individualized instruction, how to appropriately implement federal and state policies, examination of the relationship between reimbursement of excess costs associated with remedial or special education interventions and higher classification of eligible youth, the influences of program regulations on instructional content of programs, the influences of segregated instruction on fragmented and inconsistent programs of instruction, and the overemphasis on and inconsistency of use of psychometric procedures for determining special program eligibility.

Another contextual factor, particularly critical to the education of at-risk students, is that of student diversity as discussed in Secada's chapter on student diversity and mathematics education reform. Secada provides us with an overview of the current educational status of minorities in mathematics education, indicating broad-based disparities among groups as defined by demographic characteristics along various indicators, such as gender disparities, ethnic disparities, socioeconomic disparities, and language proficiency characteristics. Relationships have been found among these disparities and characteristics and the types of courses students take, the affect in the classroom, overall academic achievement, academic degrees, and careers related to mathematics. Secada calls for mathematics curriculum reform that is responsive to the changing population of students in America, as well as to changing job market demands. Secada then goes on to examine the need to rethink our basic assumptions about mathematics education of minorities, including how the learner is viewed (drawing distinctions between cultural *differences* versus cultural *deficiencies*), limited English proficiency, and over-representation of minority students in compensatory education programs. Consideration is given to reform of classroom practice to include use of direct instruction, cooperative learning, the concept of the zone of proximal development drawn from the work of Vygotsky, as well as revision of teachers' attitudes and beliefs about students.

The final chapter in the section on *Contextual Factors, Thinking, and the Teaching of Thinking* is written by Green, Kantor, and Rogers and explores the complexity of language and learning in the life of the classroom. They describe a body of knowledge about language learning and the influence of language on learning that stems from the language-related disciplines of anthropology, linguistics, literary theory, psychology, and sociology. They place emphasis on the need to locate language in the stream of everyday life and to explore its influence both on learning and on functioning and participation in life, literally extending our understanding of how children learn through language both in and out of school. These authors offer a conceptual framework for considering the role and place of language in everyday social life as a means of exemplifying the complexities that exist between language and learning. Their perspective is largely influenced by three complementary perspectives: an anthropological view of culture, an interactive sociolinguistic conceptualization of face-to-face interaction, and a sociological perspective on the social accomplishment of everyday life. These perspectives are merged in an attempt to understand the classroom as a social setting and a culture, a life that is constructed by teachers and students as they interact with and build on each others' behaviors, actions, messages, and intentions, and the influence that the language they use has on learning.

Implications for Change

Reading about the types of cognitive instruction that are needed in our schools and the contextual factors that must be taken into consideration for the instruction to be effective will ignite a passion in most readers to think about what kinds of changes really need to be made in American education. In the section on *Implications for Change*, three chapters explore what some of these implications might be.

In the first chapter, Florio-Ruane describes instructional conversations as they occur between teachers and students. The intent is to help us understand the instructional limits of the teacher–student conversations typically held in classrooms and the impact these may have on the processes of students learning to write and teachers learning to teach. Central to understanding teacher–student conversations are two popular images described by cognitive scientists: expert–novice conversations as a means of fostering cognitive development and use of instructional scaffolding to support and extend learners' intellectual growth. These authors explore these two images as they might apply to the process of teaching writing, although the implications for the need to change how teachers teach in general is very important. Paramount to this exploration is the impact of the teacher's knowledge base on the quality of the instruction itself, leading us to consider issues in need of change: (a) the conditions for learning as they currently exist, and (b) questions about how teachers are being prepared to teach. A key point in this chapter is the idea that it is important for teachers to draw from research on the talk of mothers and children as a means of gaining insights into the conditions under which social life serves to support intellectual development.

The second chapter, concerned with bringing about change, is Levine and Cooper's analysis of the change process and the implications of this for the teaching of thinking. These authors have reviewed the literature on successful implementation of innovations in schools and other organizations, placing emphasis on innovation geared toward the teaching of higher order thinking skills. They discuss four fundamental issues that should be considered when undertaking a significant innovation: (a) critical factors for instructional adaptation, (b) a comparison of "top-down" versus "bottom-up" mandates within the organizational structure of schools, (c) use of packaged versus locally developed curricula, and (d) design and implementation plans that take into consideration both appropriate program scope and an adequate phasing processes. They have identified ten prerequisites that have been well-established in the literature but that often go unrecognized in practice. Considerable discussion is given to the development of innovation that is manageable for teachers and "implementable" in the real world of schools and classrooms. They are quick to point out that research and observation consistently confirm that successful innovation requires substantial resources and administrative support, as well as clarity in goals, role definitions, and technical procedures.

An appropriate final chapter to the section, *Implications for Change*, as well as to the entire volume, is Marzano's chapter on creating an education paradigm centered on learning through teacher-directed, naturalistic inquiry. Marzano describes for us why so many attempts at educational reform have failed: those such as programmed instruction, open classrooms, the Platoon System, differentiated staffing, new math, and flexible scheduling. He maintains that the problem lies in the lack of fit between theoretical paradigms constructed by theoreticians, academicians, and researchers and the predominant educational culture of the schools. For decades now we have talked of the need to bridge the gap between theory/research and practical implementation. Marzano says that this lack of transfer is because what innovators create does not necessarily match with the needs, levels of acceptance, value, and beliefs of educators in the field. What is needed, he says, is the development of educational paradigms by practitioners (hopefully working collaboratively with theoreticians and researchers), rather than theoretical paradigms developed solely by academicians. In such a new world, teachers would learn to use naturalistic inquiry in the classroom to determine efficacious methods of teaching. Such inquiry would require their thinking not only about what they teach but how they think as they teach and how they teach. This shift would, in fact, bring empowerment to teachers. Marzano describes five types of thinking that appear to be characteristic of effective learning experiences, which could be considered by teachers: (a) thinking that establishes and maintains the context for learning, (b) thinking that gives rise to the structuring of content, (c) thinking that generates the representation of content in long-term memory, (d) thinking that changes existing knowledge structures, and (e) dispositional thought; parts of these components are adapted from a framework developed earlier by Marzano and Marzano (1988). Marzano maintains that such teacher-directed, naturalistic inquiry about the learning process can result in the most powerful shift in education in recent decades.

As a reader, you have the opportunity to explore the wealth of information contained in *Educational Values and Instructional Reform,* where you will find several key issues woven throughout the chapters. The issues include: (a) whether or not to teach thinking skills in a separate or an integrated curriculum, (b) whether or not thinking skills taught separately will transfer or generalize to new and relevant contexts, (c) the influence of particular student characteristics on cognitive instruction, (d) the influence of the classroom atmosphere and other contextual factors on cognitive instruction, (e) the need for the future preparation of teachers to teach thinking skills, and (f) critical areas to consider in bringing about change in American schooling. We return to a discussion of these issues in the Epilogue.

The readings that follow will stretch your imagination and your standards for what America's schools could become. Please join us in the process of merging knowledge from a truly interdisciplinary base, as exemplified by the various chapters in this book, and developing an educational experience for our children that is appropriate to the changing society for which they must be prepared.

Lorna Idol
Beau F. Jones

REFERENCES

Marzano, R. J., Brandt, R. S., Hughes, C. S., Jones, B. F., Presseisen, B. Z., Rankin, S. C., & Suhor, C. (1988). *Dimensions of thinking: A framework of curriculum and instruction.* Alexandria, VA: Association for Supervision and Curriculum Development.
Marzano, R. J., & Marzano, J. S. (1988). A cognitive model of commitment and its implications for therapy. *Psychotherapy in Private Practice, 6*(4), 69–81.

Critical Thinking: Literature Review and Needed Research

Mellen Kennedy
Michelle B. Fisher
Robert H. Ennis
University of Illinois at Urbana-Champaign

Critical thinking in education is an enduring and controversial topic. A plethora of articles, books, and studies exist in the field, particularly from recent years, making a fully comprehensive review of the literature virtually impossible. It is a broad topic overlapping with many areas of study in various disciplines, including cognitive psychology, philosophy, human development, curriculum development, and educational psychology, to name a few. An effort is made in this review to cover a wide range of issues relevant to critical thinking as well as the most important and controversial works.

To start, we discuss the movement in critical thinking followed by definitions and theories of critical thinking. We then present an overview of efforts in curriculum and instruction related to the teaching and learning of critical thinking, as well as a discussion of the issues involved in teacher training. The testing and evaluation of critical thinking capacities is then discussed. Finally, we make some suggestions for further research that is needed.

THE MOVEMENT IN CRITICAL THINKING

At the beginning of this century, John Dewey (1933), a major figure in American education, asserted that reflective thinking is a basic principle for organizing the curriculum. "Processes of instruction," he wrote, "are unified in the degree in which they center in the production of good habits of thinking" (1916, p. 163). Similarly, in *General Education in a Free Society*, the Harvard Committee proposed three educational abilities that "should be sought above all others," one of which is "to think effectively" (1945, p. 65). In 1961, the Educational Policies Commission of the National Education Association advocated teaching for rational thinking, particularly as a route to responsible citizenship: "The purpose which runs through and strengthens all other educational purposes—the common thread of education—is the development of the ability to think" (pp. 11–12).

The 1980s have witnessed a burst of interest in critical thinking. There is a concern for a capable, thinking electorate as a basis for a functioning democracy. In addition, the complexity and rapid rate of change that characterizes our modern world also motivates the renewed emphasis on thinking abilities. The Carnegie Task Force on Teaching as a Profession (1986) and the Holmes Group (1986) have assessed the need for education to respond to modern circumstances, in part by preparing students and teachers alike to think for themselves. In the same vein, higher problem-solving skills were deemed a necessary basic competency in *Educating Americans for the 21st Century* (National Science Board Commission on Precollege Education in Mathematics, Science, and Technology, 1983). The Commission on the Humanities (1980), the College Board (1983), the Panel on the General Professional Education of the Physician and College Preparation for Medicine (1984), the National Education Association (Futrell, 1987), and the American Federation of Teachers (1985) similarly advocate the central role of thinking skills in education.

Ernest Boyer, the current president of the Carnegie Foundation for the Advancement of Teaching, proposed as the first of four essential educational goals that "the high school help all students develop the capacity to think critically and communicate effectively through language" (1983, p. 66). Theodore Sizer (1984), in *Horace's Compromise: The Dilemma of the American High School*, also pressed for the need for direct teaching of thinking skills.

Much of the current interest in the teaching of critical thinking has arisen from evidence of the current *lack* of thinking ability among American students. In reference to the performance of students on the "assessment items requiring explanations of criteria, analysis of text, or defense of a judgment or point of view," the National Assessment of Educational Progress report found that "few students could provide more than superficial responses to such tasks, and even the 'better' responses showed little evidence of well-developed problem-solving strategies or critical thinking skills" (1981, p. 2). In *A Nation at Risk*, the National Commission on Excellence in Education reported that: "Many 17-year-olds do not possess the 'higher order' intellectual skills we should expect of them. Nearly 40% cannot draw inferences from written material; only one-fifth can write a persuasive essay; and only one-third can solve a mathematics problem requiring several steps" (1983, p. 9).

The current interest in critical thinking has arisen from the reasons mentioned above, that is, the lack of higher-order thinking ability among students and the need for students to be able to think critically in order to both meet the demands of the modern world and participate fully in our democratic society. This has resulted in a movement where educators have been asked to promote critical thinking in the classroom. It is necessary, however, to know what critical thinking is before we attempt to teach it or assess it in the classroom. It would be helpful, then, to look at some prominent theories and definitions of critical thinking.

THEORIES AND DEFINITIONS
OF CRITICAL THINKING

"Critical thinking," along with "higher cognitive skills," "metacognition," "creative thinking," "reasoning," and "problem solving," to name but a few, are now buzz words in education. Cuban (1984) asserts that schoolteachers, principals, and administrators use these terms interchangeably and that "distinctions that psychologists make on the basis of their perspectives are often lost in the crucible of the classroom" (p. 677).

Just what is meant by critical thinking is not a matter of total agreement. As the recent dialogue on critical thinking has developed, educators have often turned to two particular figures in history as guides. One of these, previously mentioned, is John Dewey, an early advocate and pioneer in the study of thinking. He used the term "reflective thinking" to refer to "the kind of thinking that consists in turning a subject over in the mind and giving it serious consecutive consideration" (1933, p. 3). He stressed the idea of a problem-solving focus to learning. He also emphasized the necessity for education to go beyond the teaching of subject matter alone and to address the teaching of thinking.

Another major historical source on critical thinking has been Bloom's cognitive taxonomy of educational objectives (Bloom, Englehart, Furst, Hill, & Krathwohl, 1956). The top three categories (analysis, synthesis, and evaluation) are often equated with critical thinking. Some educators have been dissatisfied with Bloom's taxonomy, however, because it does not offer much useful, practical guidance for instruction (Ennis, 1981a; Furst, 1981; Nelson, 1981; Paul, 1985; Seddon, 1978).

Critical thinking has been defined both broadly and narrowly. McPeck has offered this broad definition: "The propensity and skill to engage in an activity with reflective skepticism" (1981, p. 8). Ennis' broad definition of critical thinking, "reasonable, reflective thinking that is focused on deciding what to believe or do" (1985a, p. 46) has replaced his narrower definition, "the correct assessing of statements" (1962, p. 6), which, by and large, excluded creative thinking from critical thinking. Current

usage of the term "critical thinking" generally reflects Ennis' broad definition.

Critical thinking, so conceived, is composed of both skills and dispositions (Ennis, 1987b). Skills (or abilities) are the more cognitive aspect of
critical thinking, whereas dispositions (or attitudes) are the more affective
aspect.

Across the various lists and descriptions of critical thinking skills, the
following frequently appear: identifying assumptions, both stated and unstated, both ones' own and others; clarifying, focusing, and staying relevant
to the topic; understanding logic (including inference, deduction, and induction); and judging sources, their reliability and credibility. Ennis' taxonomy of critical thinking dispositions and abilities which has developed
over a period of years (1962, 1980, 1981b, 1985a, 1987b), encompasses
many of the skills (as well as the dispositions discussed below) found in
various elaborations of critical thinking (see Figure 1.1, p. 31).

The importance of dispositions has been heavily stressed in the literature (Ennis, 1987b; Nickerson, 1984; Norris, 1985; Passmore, 1972; Paul,
1984; Scheffler, 1973; Siegel, 1980; Sternberg, 1985). A person may
possess thinking skills and yet not be disposed or inclined to exhibit or
use them. The lists and conceptions of specific dispositions differ more
than the lists of critical thinking skills. Some dispositions commonly mentioned include: being open-minded and considerate of other people;
staying relevant; being impartial; suspending judgment and taking a
stance when warranted; questioning one's own views; and using one's
critical thinking skills.

Nickerson's list of characteristics of a "Good Thinker" (1987) contains
some important dispositions not mentioned frequently in other lists.
They include the tendency to transfer learning to new situations, and
recognition that real-world problems are complex and not solved with
one simple answer. Glaser portrays dispositions as part of a way of life:
"Persons who have acquired a disposition to *want* evidence for beliefs,
and who have acquired an attitude for reasonableness have also acquired
something of a way of life which makes for more considerate and humane
relationships among [others]" (1941, p. 6).

The merit of a theory or definition is often ascertainable when it is
applied in practice. Hence, we now turn to the teaching of critical thinking in the classroom.

THE TEACHING OF CRITICAL THINKING

The overarching question "Can students' thinking improve through instruction?" has been answered in the affirmative by the research. It is
apparent that students who undergo thinking instruction generally do
score better on outcome measures than their controls (Chance, 1986;

Nickerson, 1984; Nickerson, Perkins, & Smith, 1985; Sternberg & Kastoor, 1986). The remaining task, and it is a large one, is the refinement of our understanding of what aspects of thinking can be learned, by whom, under what conditions, in what settings, and using what methods.

Subject Matter Specificity and Instruction

One debate is focused on whether critical thinking is the same across disciplines, whether all critical thinking abilities are specific to disciplines, or whether the truth lies somewhere in between. McPeck (1981) contends that generalizable thinking skills do not exist. He holds that thinking is always about a subject, so general thinking ability detached from a subject cannot conceptually exist. This is the conceptual version of the subject-specificity view. The epistemological version is also advocated by McPeck, who holds that in different subject areas, different things "constitute good reasons for various beliefs" (McPeck, 1981, p. 21). McPeck concludes that critical thinking must, therefore, vary from subject area to subject area. The empirical version of the subject-specificity view is held by many contemporary cognitive psychologists (e.g., Glaser, 1984). They hold that it is empirically unlikely that general critical thinking skills can be taught and transferred to other domains, or in other words, critical thinking is domain-specific. Ennis (1989) has elaborated these three versions of subject specificity and two teaching approaches based on subject specificity: infusion and immersion. Infusion calls for thinking in subject areas together with explicit attention to general principles of critical thinking that apply in the subject area. Immersion calls only for thinking in the subject area.

At the other extreme, we have the view that there are general principles of critical thinking and that these should be taught separately from the standard subject areas. Proponents of this view include those who advocate "instrumental enrichment" (Feuerstein, Jensen, Hoffman, & Rand, 1985), "lateral thinking" (deBono, 1983), "structure of the intellect" (Meeker, 1969), "philosophy for children" (Lipman, 1982), and informal logic courses for college students.

The third and often overlooked view is that critical thinking is a combination of using a set of general dispositions and abilities, along with specific experience and knowledge within a particular area of concern—in school, often the subject-matter area. This view might lead to the teaching of general critical thinking principles (e. g., conflict of interest, denial of the consequent) both as a separate course (or within an existing course sequence such as English or social studies), and as infused into the existing subject-matter instruction, where general dispositions and abilities would be applied.

It is not known which approach is most effective. The numerous attempts at infusion or immersion include content areas such as social studies, chemistry, geometry, general science, and the physical sciences. They have generally yielded higher experimental group gains in critical thinking ability, and sometimes even in content areas (Blair & Goodson, 1939; Cousins, 1962; Fawcett, 1938; Rickert, 1967; Ulmer, 1939).

Project IMPACT (Winocur, 1985) in California is an example of a systematic attempt at thinking instruction infused in the content areas of mathematics, reading, and language arts in middle and high schools. In this approach, teacher training is well-structured. Although complete evaluation results are forthcoming, the interim results have been positive.

Examples of separate instruction include courses in philosophy, informal logic, and programs such as Philosophy for Children (Lipman, 1982). Generally, studies of these courses have also revealed gains in thinking test scores (Chance, 1986; Glaser, 1941). Ross and Semb (1981) compared undergraduate students taking a philosophy course with those not taking one. They reported that the philosophy students scored significantly higher on a critical thinking post-test than the non-philosophy students. Annis and Annis (1979) also studied college students taking various kinds of philosophy courses (i. e., philosophy, ethics, and logic) with a control group who studied none of these subjects. They found that the philosophy students scored significantly higher on certain aspects of critical thinking than did the controls.

Ennis (1985b) and Sternberg (1987) have pointed out that each approach has its advantages. They have argued for a "mixed model" (Sternberg, 1987, p. 225) of providing both a separate course or part of an existing course in critical thinking and concurrently infusing or immersing critical thinking into other courses. Theoretically, this approach will provide ample opportunity for practice in a variety of contexts, and will serve to reinforce the skills taught.

Transfer

Whether critical thinking skills will transfer from one context to another is the subject of much debate. Transfer refers to the carry-over and use of skills and knowledge to domains other than the ones in which they were taught. There is general agreement in the literature that transfer of critical thinking from one domain to another is desirable and that teaching approaches should be designed to optimize this by teaching critical thinking in a variety of domains and by emphasizing transfer

(Belmont & Butterfield, 1977; Michenbaum, 1985; Nickerson, 1987; Pingry, 1951; Sternberg, 1987; Taba, 1962). However, before this advice can be applied, a definition of *domain* is needed that will enable us to tell in the areas of prospective application whether two activities are in the same or different domains (Ennis, 1989). Transfer across domains, broadly defined, can mean transfer across academic disciplines or from the academic to the nonacademic world of the student. Narrowly defined, transfer across domains can mean transfer from one task or situation to another within a particular subject area (e. g., from a bending rods task to a pendulum task in physical science).

Measuring transfer is a difficult task. Data on the issue is often anecdotal (Chance, 1986). Osborn, for example, studied students' ability to resist propaganda following an informational unit on the "direct study of the tricks and techniques of propaganda" (1939, p. 4). The skills covered in the unit were related to critical thinking and included making judgments and assessing arguments. Osborn concluded that in this study, the information on propaganda did not transfer into use in evaluating a written propaganda piece. The experimental group did not differ from the control in ability to resist propaganda following their training.

Nickerson, Perkins, and Smith (1985) state that in the concrete operations stage, students cannot easily transfer knowledge learned in one context into a new one because, before formal operations, they cannot generalize or handle abstract ideas. Taba (1962), in her review of the literature, states that transfer is not automatic as was once believed, but must be specifically taught. She concludes that the understanding of basic principles as well as practice in both abstracting and using them in different contexts are essential for transfer to be achieved.

It has been found that unless transfer of thinking skills is specifically taught, it rarely occurs (Belmont & Butterfield, 1977). Instruction that emphasizes executive or metacognitive skills shows evidence of achieving transfer (Michenbaum, 1985). These skills include the student's setting goals, planning, and self-monitoring. Sternberg (1987) suggests practice in a variety of contexts, both academic and real life, as helpful in promoting transfer.

Classroom Atmosphere

The manner in which a classroom is structured is a vital issue in regard to the teaching of critical thinking and its transfer to other domains. Discussion is often suggested as a preferred method (Eisner, 1983; Ennis, 1985c, 1985d; Lipman, 1985; Passmore, 1972; Paul, 1985; Perkins, 1987; Siegel, 1985; Taba, 1962). Dillon (1984) distinguishes between recitation and discussion, with discussion calling for higher cognitive skills than recitation. He states, however, that there is little empirical research on discussion. Bridges (1979) points out the necessity of dispositions such as openness and respect for others as necessary conditions for a discussion.

Experts have also suggested that classwork should include the addressing of real-world problems, as opposed to focusing solely on artificial exercises (Eisner, 1983; Paul, 1985; Scriven, 1985). This could be accomplished through the use of materials other than the standard texts (e. g., newspaper editorials, magazine articles, advertisements, and television programs).

Group work, cooperation, and teacher questioning have all been proposed as important components of teaching critical thinking (Dillon, 1984; George, 1984; Hallam, 1979). Smith (1977) studied college classroom environments and found critical thinking to be related to peer interaction, teacher support, and teacher questioning. In a review of studies of wait-time (i. e., the time that elapses between the teacher's asking and the student's answering of a question) in elementary, middle, and high school classrooms, Tobin (1987) reports that the teacher's increase in wait-time has been related to higher student achievement scores. He points out that it seems to be a necessary, but not sufficient, condition for encouraging the use of higher cognitive skills. He stresses that there may be circumstances under which increased wait-time is inappropriate, such as during memorization drills. In addition, he points out that is it not known whether different groups of students benefit differently from increased wait-time.

In a meta-analysis of teacher questioning, Redfield and Rousseau (1981) conclude that higher cognitive questioning yields higher student achievement. They define higher cognitive questions as those "requiring that students mentally manipulate bits of information previously learned to create or support an answer with logically reasoned evidence" (1981, p. 237). They looked at experiments of teacher training and the teaching of skills. In both, the positive effect of higher cognitive questioning on student achievement was evident.

THE LEARNING OF CRITICAL THINKING

Developmental Readiness

Typically, experts agree that students' ability to understand and master critical thinking varies with their ages. They also concur that teaching needs to be tailored to the developmental level of the students and that even young children can benefit from critical thinking training (Bruner, Goodnow, & Austin, 1976; Passmore, 1972; Perkins, 1987; Taba, 1962).

The theories of Jean Piaget, the forerunner of research on child development, have been formative for much thinking in this area. In a review of the literature, however, Gelman concludes that Piagetian stage theory is not accurate: ". . . evidence from recent research on the nature of cognitive development in preschoolers calls into question the idea that they have structures that differ fundamentally from those of older children, or that they lack pieces of mental structures that older children have" (1985, p. 537). Gelman concludes that "young children's competencies are more like older children's than once assumed . . . cast[ing] serious doubt on the hypothesis that age differences in performance reflect fundamental characteristics" (1985, p. 538).

Even if we adhere to Piagetian stage theory, there is substantial evidence that many college-age students have not attained this formal operations stage of thinking (Blasi & Hoeffel, 1974; Kohlberg & Gilligan, 1971; Nickerson, Perkins, & Smith, 1985). Yet this kind of thinking, which entails being able to deal with abstract concepts, is necessary for successful endeavors. Students' natural progression through developmental stages cannot be assumed.

Lehman (1963) studied changes in critical thinking, attitudes, and values in college students. He concluded that there was a significant change in these areas between freshman and senior year. In addition, students were less dogmatic and more open-minded at the end of the time period. He noted, however, that most of the change occurred in the freshman and sophomore years. Whether the change is due to college attendance or is a result primarily of maturation is not ascertainable from this study. Nevertheless, it is interesting to note that significant development can occur during this time period.

It is not clear, however, just what developmental constraints exist for different groups of students, and in what ways teaching can attend to them. We do know that very young children are capable of some forms of propositional logic causal inference (Carey, 1985; Ennis, 1971, 1982). Yet, in testing cognitive abilities, children's knowledge of and familiarity with the topic and the materials with which they were tested determine the success of their performance to a large extent. What were previously considered limitations in children's cognitive performance due to developmental constraints are now attributed by some—at least in part—to lack of specific knowledge (Carey, 1985; Nickerson, Perkins, & Smith, 1985).

Prior Knowledge

There is general agreement that an individual's familiarity with the subject matter plays an important part in the person's performance on thinking tasks in that area (Glaser, 1984; Norris, 1985; Passmore, 1972; Siegel, 1980; Sternberg & Baron, 1985). Nickerson, Perkins, and Smith

(1985) describe knowledge and thinking skills as interdependent. Bereiter and Scardamalia (1985) call attention to the problem of "inert
knowledge," which is knowledge that students possess but cannot access
or apply. Dewey (1938) similarly points out that if students do not reflec-
tively think about the content they are studying, the knowledge cannot
be useful. Some advocates of critical thinking have claimed that teaching
for thinking enhances the learning of content knowledge (Dewey, 1933;
Walsh & Paul, 1985). In a study of conditional reasoning, Markovits
(1986) found that for a college student sample, as familiarity with the
content area increased, so did scores in a conditional reasoning test in
that area.

Traditional education has emphasized mastering and memorizing
content knowledge almost to the point of completely ignoring the development of critical thinking. Sizer (1984) holds that teaching has been too
focused on routine memorization of content. Glaser commented that "as
individuals acquire knowledge, they also should be empowered to think
and reason" (1984, p. 103).

Most advocates of the teaching of critical thinking do not suggest the
neglect of teaching subject matter. Dewey (1938) calls for the teaching
of thinking as part of the progressive development of subject matter.
Passmore (1972) quite clearly calls for a balance of direct instruction in
teaching content and encouragement of critical thinking. Swartz (1987)
calls for the infusion of critical thinking in subject matter instruction, as
do Ennis (1985b) and Sternberg (1987) in their mixed model approach.

Student Characteristics

The issue of the effects of prior knowledge on the learning of critical
thinking is closely linked to characteristics of learners in that students'
socioeconomic and cultural background influences their prior knowledge. Developmental level, intellectual ability, gender, and cultural and
socioeconomic background are factors that have been investigated in
relation to the degree to which different groups of students exhibit
facility or difficulty in mastering critical thinking. We will discuss each
one of these factors in turn.

Intellectual ability.   Some critical thinking programs are intended specifically as remedial, whereas others are for average ability students, and
still others are intended for the gifted. There is some indication that
students of all intellectual ability levels can benefit from critical thinking
instruction (Chance, 1986; Nickerson, Perkins, & Smith, 1985). Ulmer
(1939) taught reflective thinking in high school geometry and found that,

in the experimental group, students at all three IQ levels made large gains in the reflective thinking ability scores and did significantly better overall than the controls. Rickert (1967) studied the teaching of critical thinking in freshman physics and found that, in the experimental group, all three intellectual ability levels did better than the controls. The greatest gains were made by the low-ability students in the experimental condition.

Gender differences.   In a literature review on cognition and gender differences, Halpern (1986) concludes that gender differences in performance on cognitive tests turn up consistently. In the areas of quantitative and visual/spatial abilities, males usually outperform females; and in the area of verbal skills, females outperform males. It has been found, however, that with instruction in spatial skills, the gender differences disappear (Halpern, 1986). This indicates that, perhaps, females' lower performance is a result of their having fewer experiences requiring the use of these skills. Edwards (1950), who developed a test of critical thinking in high school science, found that females did better on judging and males did better on applying principles. Hallam (1979), on the other hand, found no gender differences in his study of the development of logical thinking in history. Lehman (1963), in a study of changes in critical thinking and attitudes of college students, discovered no gender differences from freshman to senior year in the critical thinking scores. Ennis, Millman, and Tomko (1985) report no gender differences on the two Cornell critical thinking tests.

In terms of dispositions, it has been verified consistently in the literature that sex-role stereotyping exists (Bem, 1974; Halpern, 1986). For example, it is typically believed that males are and should be independent and competitive, whereas females are and should be emotional and warm. It has also been demonstrated that even very young children are aware of their own gender and of the gender-typed dispositions ascribed to them (Halpern, 1986). It seems likely that, to the extent that critical thinking dispositions are gender-typed traits or are related to gender, it will be more difficult for students to acquire those dispositions that are opposite gender-typed. Possible sex-role stereotyping of critical thinking dispositions needs more study.

Socioeconomic and cultural differences.   Socioeconomic and cultural differences among students are closely associated with differences in prior knowledge. This issue has received little attention in the critical thinking literature, though much more in related literature. For example, Simmons (1985) has emphasized the importance of the cultural contexts in which activities take place and the variation of performance of individuals on tasks as it relates to their familiarity with these cultural contexts. Franklin (1985) has demonstrated that the low performance of minority students on organizational tasks disappears, or even reverses, when the material of the task is familiar. Williams (1987) reports on the Cognitive Instruction Project, an urban district-wide effort in Paterson, New Jersey, where 90% of students are minorities: The results of the project, although not complete, suggest a general trend approaching significant increases in student achievement scores over its 5-year history.

TEACHER TRAINING

There is general agreement in the literature that teachers need to be trained in critical thinking dispositions and skills in order to be able to teach thinking effectively (Johnson, 1987; Lipman, 1985; Nickerson, 1987; Swartz, 1987; Taba, 1950; Walsh & Paul, 1985; Winocur, 1985). There is some anecdotal evidence to support this view. Ulmer (1939), in a study of teaching high school geometry to enhance reflective thinking, noted that the two teachers in the experimental condition whose classes had the highest outcome scores, had themselves participated in a course on teaching logic in geometry just prior to the study. In addition, the teacher in the experimental condition whose class scored lowest, had joined the study late and had not had the full training.

George (1967), in a study of student teachers, compared the critical thinking abilities of science education majors with non-science education majors. He found that the science education majors scored significantly higher on the Watson-Glaser Critical Thinking Test than did all the other education students with the exception of the mathematics education students. It was concluded that the disciplines of science and mathematics foster the development of critical thinking more than do other subject areas. An alternative interpretation, however, is that better critical thinkers tend to go into mathematics and science teaching. Whether the critical thinking scores of the science and mathematics teachers will carry over into the classroom and improve their teaching was not investigated.

In an attempt to discover which skills are difficult to teach, Fox (1962) surveyed teachers of high school social studies who maintained the teaching of critical thinking as one of their goals. They reported that the higher order thinking skills are the most difficult to teach. In response to why it was difficult, 28% indicated lack of interest or apathy on the part of students, 10% indicated not enough time, and just over 30% indicated immaturity and lack of training of students. Not only were students unprepared for that level of challenge, but the system itself was not supportive of the goal, as indicated by the lack of time. Possibly, the teachers did not know how to engage students' interest or how to work with them at their level. Fox also reported that more experienced teachers found it more difficult to teach some of the particular subskills than did the newer teachers. Fox proposed that perhaps teacher training was better preparing new teachers for the task of fostering critical thinking.

Thinking programs (cf. Chance, 1986) typically require that teachers who are new to the programs be specially trained. Examples are Feuerstein's Instrumental Enrichment Program (Feuerstein, Jensen, Hoffman, & Rand, 1985), Philosophy for Children (Lipman, 1984), and Project IMPACT (Winocur, 1985). For other programs, the training of teachers is optional, for example CoRT Thinking (deBono, 1976) and Productive Thinking (Covington, Crutchfield, Davies, & Olton, 1974). Project IMPACT (Winocur, 1985) involves a systematic and long-range plan for introducing critical thinking to middle and secondary teachers, training them, and providing ongoing support as they incorporate the teaching of thinking into their classrooms. The preliminary results are encouraging.

TESTING AND EVALUATION

Although the teaching and learning of critical thinking has received a good deal of attention, its assessment and evaluation have been sorely neglected. According to Norris and Ennis (1989), the only general-knowledge critical thinking tests currently commercially available in North America are the following:

Multi-aspect Tests:
  machine-scorable tests:
  Cornell Critical Thinking Test, Level X (Ennis & Millman, 1985);
  Cornell Critical Thinking Test, Level Z (Ennis & Millman, 1985);
  New Jersey Test of Reasoning Skills (Shipman, 1983);
  Ross Test of Higher Cognitive Processes (Ross & Ross, 1976);
  Watson-Glaser Critical Thinking Appraisal (Watson & Glaser, 1980).
  non-machine-scorable tests:
  Ennis-Weir Critical Thinking Essay Test (Ennis & Weir, 1985).

Aspect-Specific Tests:
  Cornell Class-Reasoning Test, Form X (Ennis, Gardiner, Morrow, Paulus, & Ringel, 1964);
  Cornell Conditional-Reasoning Test, Form X (Ennis, Gardiner, Guzzetta, Morrow, Paulus, & Ringel, 1964);

Judgment: Deductive Logic and Assumption Recognition (Shaffer & Steiger, 1971);
Logical Reasoning (Hertzka & Guilford, 1955);
Test on Appraising Observations (Norris & King, 1983).

Another comprehensive test that is specific to science and social studies is published in Australia: *Test of Enquiry Skills* (Fraser, 1979).

This list demonstrates the shortage of commercially-available tests, considering the importance of critical thinking. The focus on machine-scorability, the total absence of tests for use below the 4th-grade level, the dearth of aspect-specific tests, and the lack of subject-specific critical thinking tests are features of this shortage that are particularly acute.

Subject-specificity

If critical thinking is viewed as subject-specific (according to the conceptual version discussed above), one would only be able to construct subject-matter specific critical thinking tests. Furthermore, (according to either the conceptual or empirical versions) success on a critical thinking test item would indicate a critical thinking disposition or ability only in the subject domain of the item or test, not in general nor in some other domain. Here, again, we confront the problem of defining what constitutes a domain, that is, whether it is limited to the particular topic at hand (such as a particular science experiment on growing plants) or if it encompasses an entire subject area (such as botany, or even science). If we cannot ascertain whether two test items are supposed to represent the same or different domains, then we cannot even ask the empirical question of whether success on one item is supposed to indicate success on another item in the same domain (discussed in greater detail in Ennis, 1989).

Machine-scorability and Other Approaches

Approaches to and problems in critical thinking testing are examined by Ennis and Norris (in press) and Norris and Ennis (1989). They point out that the reasons for the heavy emphasis on pencil-and-paper, machine-scorable tests are understandable: They are more economical (than, for example, essay tests) in that they are easier to administer to large groups of students and are easier and quicker to score. In addition, they do not require a researcher or practitioner trained in critical thinking in order to administer and score, as do other methods of evaluation. However, there are also disadvantages to relying solely on this one approach. The evaluation of critical thinking dispositions, such as one's disposition to be open-minded, cannot be easily assessed by multiple-choice questions. An examinee knows that he or she is being tested and might deliberately exhibit the appropriate behavior without having the underlying disposition. For example, an individual might know that trying to be well-informed is considered to be a critical thinking disposition and answer the test items accordingly, but not really be disposed to be well-informed.

Currently available machine-scorable tests also have the disadvantage of testing only the judgments, not the reasoning behind the judgments. Sometimes, students give answers that are not the keyed answers, perhaps because they have different background assumptions about the world and yet have done very sound reasoning. It seems unfair to penalize students who think well but have different background assumptions from those of the test constructors.

This problem can be addressed by offering students, in a multiple-choice format, a number of alternative justifications of the judgment they make, and then scoring them on the combination of answer and justification—an evaluation methodology used in the Eight Year Study (Progressive Education Association, 1939). Another way to address this problem is to use topics where there is common background knowledge in the tested population so that everyone brings nearly the same background assumptions to the test—as would occur in subject-matter specific critical thinking tests. A third way, advocated by Norris and King (1984), is to interview a number of representative students from the targeted population to find out how they think about the items and what kinds of justifications they offer. Even then, the test would be applicable only to the population from which the representative students were selected, and perhaps not to other populations.

Essay tests leave the students more room for justifying the judgments they make. Informal interviews, though very expensive, would be even better in enabling the interviewer to seek justification whenever something seems unclear. A compromise between these two methods would be a repeat-test format, where students would be initially tested with an essay test, then retested or interviewed on those items or issues that were unclear or vague. Perhaps even the multiple-choice test could be used as the initial test where an essay test or interview would take place for those items in which the student's answer did not match the keyed answer. This would allow the student to justify his/her answers.

NEEDED RESEARCH

Over two decades ago, Ennis (1963) assessed the state of knowledge about critical thinking and found a number of areas in need of research, including: the "further refinement and definition of the concept ['critical thinking']" (p. 18); the development and comparison of "teaching methods and curriculum organization" (p. 20); "discovering the learning capabilities of children" (p. 19); and the "development of critical thinking tests" (p. 18). Despite the interest in and importance of critical thinking, these areas are still in need of further investigation.

Definition

Although there is considerable agreement as to what constitutes critical thinking, the picture is not complete. How broadly or narrowly should critical thinking be defined? Is critical thinking, narrowly defined, completely distinct from creative thinking? As broadly defined, to what extent does critical thinking overlap with creative thinking? What is the relationship of critical thinking to problem solving, reflective thinking, and higher order thinking? What common critical thinking vocabulary is most fruitful across fields? There is disparity in usage of such terms as "valid," "connotation," "assumption," "induction," and "credibility."

Issues concerning epistemological subject-specificity are still unresolved. For instance, what are the differences and similarities among the fields as to what counts as a good reason? To what extent do general rules hold across fields? How much variation is there within fields? Are differences within fields greater than differences across fields? Research on these issues is needed.

The Teaching of Critical Thinking

How should the classroom itself be structured so as to promote the exercise of critical thinking? What factors promote discussion in the classroom (e. g., "wait-time")? What should classwork focus on: real-world, artificial problems, or a combination of both? Further research is needed to determine what role each of these elements plays in fostering critical thinking in the classroom.

Should critical thinking be added to the existing curriculum as a separate course, infused or immersed throughout the subject areas, or a combination of both (a mixed model)? Do these approaches interact with other factors, such as school size, general ability level, or socioeconomic status? Is the teaching of some critical thinking abilities more effective with one of these approaches than another? Do some existing subject areas lend themselves more to one of these approaches than the others? How effective are these approaches at different grade levels? These three approaches need to be examined and compared over a long period of time (not just the usual 1-shot, 2-week, 6-week, or 2-month interventions but over 4- to 12-year periods of time) using teachers who are familiar with and good at the respective approaches.

Under what conditions do individuals apply general critical thinking instruction to specific situations other than those in which it was first taught? To what extent does transfer occur from academic disciplines to the nonacademic world of the student? What specific factors foster transfer? Are some aspects of critical thinking more readily transferable than others? As with reading, writing, and arithmetic, it seems probable that there are some generalizable critical thinking skills that can be utilized throughout many domains, although existing research in critical thinking, not unequivocally, suggests that this generalizability is difficult to attain. We need to determine to what extent and which aspects of critical thinking are generalizable. On a more basic level, in order to make predictions regarding transfer from one domain to another, we need a clearer definition of "domain," one that will tell us how to distinguish one domain from another. These topics need further exploration.

The Learning of Critical Thinking

To what extent do factors such as age, gender, socioeconomic background, cultural background, and intellectual ability influence the development of critical thinking? Exactly what role does prior content knowledge play in learning to think critically? Does limited prior knowledge restrict the development of critical thinking abilities and dispositions? It certainly restricts their employment. Does critical thinking bolster the learning of content? What are students at different age levels capable of doing? Are there cognitive gender differences that foster or inhibit the learning of the different aspects of critical thinking? Are some dispositions or abilities "gender-typed"? That is, are girls, for instance, more open-minded or sensitive to the feelings and background of others than are boys? To what extent does one's socioeconomic and cultural background affect the development of critical thinking? Are some dispositions or abilities "culture- or SES-typed"? Questions such as these need to be addressed if we are to understand which individual differences impede and which ones foster the learning of critical thinking. We shall elaborate.

Developmental readiness.   The factors affecting developmental readiness and their interrelationships are not fully understood. What are students of different ages capable of doing? What factors determine one's developmental level? At what developmental level do children learn each aspect of critical thinking? To what extent does the limited content knowledge of younger children constrain their development of critical thinking? Do students of different abilities do better in an infused, immersed, separate, or mixed approach? Are students of different abilities able to master different aspects of critical thinking at different ages? How can critical thinking instruction serve as a remedial approach for low ability students? How should instruction differ for students of different ability levels?

Gender. Gender differences in critical thinking need to be further researched. What are the implications of cognitive gender differences for the teaching of critical thinking? Do gender differences make a difference in the learning of critical thinking? To the extent that they do, can instruction minimize their presence? Do boys and girls have different needs in terms of how they learn critical thinking and what abilities they can master? In terms of dispositions, the question of gender differences does not seem to have been addressed. To what extent are dispositions gender-typed? Are there gender differences in the development of dispositions? If there are differences, can instruction improve the development of dispositions?

Socioeconomic and cultural differences. To what extent are prior knowledge differences factors in the employment of critical thinking abilities for students of various socioeconomic and cultural backgrounds? What instructional approaches can attend to these differences? Are the differences more problematic for acquiring particular dispositions or abilities? This issue cannot be overlooked if critical thinking instruction is to be effective, and moreover, equitable.

Teacher Training

Should teachers take preparatory critical thinking courses that are subject-specific, general, or both? Do teachers need additional methods courses to ensure effective teaching of critical thinking in their subject-matter areas? Methods such as fostering discussion, higher-level questioning, and encouraging group work are not typically taught in the traditional teacher training programs.

Both the Carnegie report (Carnegie Task Force on Teaching as a Profession, 1986) and the Holmes report (Holmes Group, 1986) have mentioned critical thinking as desirable for teachers. But the question of how we can help teachers acquire critical thinking abilities and dispositions has not really been investigated. How can the transition be facilitated for experienced teachers to go from the traditional classroom approach to the critical thinking approach? How different or alike is the critical thinking approach from the traditional approach? Winocur (1985) has done work in this area, but more research of this kind is needed.

Testing and Evaluation

Agreement on a definition of and a vocabulary for critical thinking is needed in order to get a better idea of what should be assessed by critical thinking evaluation instruments. Up until now, the assessment of critical thinking has been restricted, for the most part, to abilities. Inexpensive techniques need to be developed to evaluate critical thinking dispositions as well.

Currently, there are very few critical thinking tests readily available. As of 1989, there seem to be only 6 general content, multi-aspect critical thinking tests (5 multiple choice, 1 essay) and only 5 aspect-specific tests commercially available in English from North American sources (Norris & Ennis, 1989). There is a need for further test development of more general-content, multi-aspect and aspect-specific tests, and especially of subject-specific, multi-aspect and aspect-specific tests. These tests need to be developed at all levels. There is currently nothing commercially available under the 4th-grade level. There is also a need to develop evaluation devices other than the prevalent paper-and-pencil multiple-choice tests. The evaluation of critical thinking dispositions, such as one's disposition to be open-minded, cannot be assessed by multiple-choice questions. Naturalistic evaluation methods, such as observation and interviewing, have not yet been widely explored, although the essay test approach has received limited attention. We are not advocating the replacement of one approach by another; we are only pointing out that the current evaluation methods are insufficient by themselves if we want to adequately assess the abilities and dispositions essential to critical thinking.

Earlier we mentioned the need to determine the effect of prior content knowledge on the development of critical thinking. In regard to testing, we need to determine how the effect of content knowledge can be neutralized when assessing generalized critical thinking abilities and dispositions. As a way of addressing this problem, Baron (1987) proposes including both questions that test solely content knowledge and questions that require applying critical thinking to that content knowledge. Further research is needed to test the effectiveness of this approach and to explore other avenues.

CONCLUSION

We hope we have shown that there is still much to be learned in the area of critical thinking research. Although we know that there is some brilliant and creative teaching going on in our schools, we need to make the techniques and variables that allow for such instruction known to educators so that the teaching of critical thinking to our students becomes the rule and not the exception. We currently have many critical thinking programs and procedures that are enthusiastically endorsed; we need to be able to distinguish between those that justifiably deserve our support and those that do not. We need to move ahead in each area of needed research concurrently, attending to conceptual clarification of what critical thinking is and at the same time dealing with questions of what makes for effective instruction, what individual characteristics affect the learning of critical thinking, how to train our teachers to teach critical thinking effectively in the classroom, and how to assess and evaluate the acquisition of the various critical thinking abilities and dispositions. There is much to be done.

ACKNOWLEDGMENTS

This is an expanded version of a paper delivered at the annual meeting of the American Educational Research Association, April, 1987, in Washington, D. C. We wish to express appreciation for support provided by the Spencer Foundation, the Center for Advanced Study in the Behavioral Sciences, and the College of Education of the University of Illinois, U-C. We also wish to thank Adrian Fisher for his careful reading of the paper and his valuable suggestions.

FIG. 1.1.   Goals for a Critical Thinking Curriculum

Assuming that critical thinking is reasonable and reflective thinking that is focused on deciding what to believe or do, here is a set of goals for a critical thinking curriculum. This list can also serve as a basis for a table of specifications for a critical thinking test or evaluation procedure. Elaboration of this set of proposed goals may be found in Ennis (1962, 1969, 1980, 1981b, 1985a, 1987a, and 1987b).

A. *Dispositions:*
    1.   Seek a statement of the thesis or question
    2.   Seek reasons
    3.   Try to be well informed
    4.   Use credible sources and mention them
    5.   Take into account the total situation
    6.   Try to remain relevant to the main point
    7.   Keep in mind the original and/or basic concern
    8.   Look for alternatives
    9.   Be open-minded
         a.   Consider seriously other points of view than one's own
         b.   Reason from premises with which one disagrees—without letting the disagreement interfere with one's reasoning ("suppositional reasoning")
         c.   Withhold judgment when the evidence and reasons are insufficient
    10. Take a position (and change a position) when the evidence and reasons are sufficient to do so
    11. Seek as much precision as the subject permits
    12. Deal in an orderly manner with the parts of a complex whole
    13. Employ one's critical thinking abilities
    14. Be sensitive to the feelings, level of knowledge, and degree of sophistication of others [This is not strictly speaking a critical thinking disposition. Rather it is a social disposition that is desirable for a critical thinker to have.]

B. *Abilities* (classified under these categories: Elementary Clarification, Basic Support, Inference, Advanced Clarification, and Strategy and Tactics):
    Elementary Clarification
    1.   Focusing on a question
         a.   Identifying or formulating a question
         b.   Identifying or formulating criteria for judging possible answers
         c.   Keeping the situation in mind
    2.   Analyzing arguments
         a.   Identifying conclusions
         b.   Identifying stated reasons
         c.   Identifying unstated reasons
         d.   Seeing similarities and differences
         e.   Identifying and handling irrelevance
         f.   Seeing the structure of an argument
         g.   Summarizing
    3.   Asking and answering questions of clarification and/or challenge, for example:
         a.   Why?
         b.   What is your main point?

FIG. 1.1. *Continued*

    c.   What do you mean by _____?
    d.   What would be an example?
    e.   What would not be an example (though close to being one)?
    f.   How does that apply to this case (describe the case, which might well appear to be a counter-example)?
    g.   What difference does it make?
    h.   What are the facts?
    i.   Is this what you are saying?
    j.   Would you say more about that?

Basic Support
    4.   Judging the credibility of a source; criteria:
        a.   Expertise
        b.   Lack of conflict of interest
        c.   Agreement among sources
        d.   Reputation
        e.   Use of established procedures
        f.   Known risk to reputation
        g.   Ability to give reasons
        h.   Careful habits
    5.   Observing, and judging observation reports; criteria:
        a.   Minimal inferring involved
        b.   Short time interval between observation and report
        c.   Report made by observer, rather than someone else (i.e., not hearsay)
        d.   The use of records. If report is based upon a record, it is generally best that:
            (1)   The making of the record was close in time to the observation
            (2)   The record was made by the observer
            (3)   The record was made by the reporter
            (4)   The statement was believed by the reporter, either because of a prior belief in its correctness or because of a belief that the observer was habitually correct
        e.   Corroboration
        g.   Possibility of corroboration
        h.   Competent employment of technology, if technology is useful
        i.   Satisfaction by observer (and reporter, if a different person) of the credibility criteria (#4 above)

Inference
    6.   Deducing and judging deductions
        a.   Class logic—Euler circles
        b.   Conditional logic
        c.   Interpretation of statements
            (1)   Double negation
            (2)   Necessary and sufficient conditions
            (3)   Other logical words: "only", "if and only if", "or", "some", "unless", "not", "not both", etc.

FIG. 1.1. *Continued*

7. Inducing, and judging inductions
   a. Generalizing
      (1) Typicality of data: limitation of coverage
      (2) Sampling
      (3) Tables and graphs
   b. Inferring explanatory conclusions and hypotheses
      (a) Causal claims
      (b) Claims about the beliefs and attitudes of people
      (c) Interpretations of authors' intended meanings
      (d) Historical claims that certain things happened
      (e) Reported definitions (see 9b1a)
      (f) Claims that something is an unstated reasons or unstated conclusion
      (2) Investigating
         (a) Designing experiments, including planning to control variables
         (b) seeking evidence and counterevidence
         (c) seeking other possible explanations
      (3) Criteria: Given reasonable assumptions,
         (a) The proposed conclusion would explain the evidence (essential)
         (b) The proposed conclusion is consistent with known facts (essential)
         (c) Competitive alternative conclusions are inconsistent with known facts (essential)
         (d) The proposed conclusion seems plausible (desirable)
8. Making and judging value judgments
   a. Background facts
   b. Consequences
   c. *Prima facie* application of acceptable principles
   d. Considering alternatives
   e. Balancing, weighing, and deciding

Advanced Clarification
9. Defining terms, and judging definitions; three dimensions:
   a. Form
      (1) Synonym
      (2) Classification
      (3) Range
      (4) Equivalent expression
      (5) Operational
      (6) Example—nonexample
   b. Definitional strategy
      (1) Acts
         (a) Report a meaning ("reported definition")
         (b) Stipulate a meaning ("stipulative definition")
         (c) Express a position on an issue ("positional" (including "programmatic" and "persuasive") definition)

FIG. 1.1.   *Continued*

    (2)   Identifying and handling equivocation
        (a)   Attention to the context
        (b)   Possible types of response
            i)   "The definition is just wrong" (the simplest type of response)
            ii)   Reduction to absurdity: "According to that definition, there is an outlandish result"
            iii)   Considering alternative interpretations: "On this interpretation there is this problem; on that interpretation there is that problem. These are the only plausible interpretations."
            iv)   Establishing that there are two meanings of the key term, and a shift in meaning from one to the other
            v)   Swallowing the special meaning
    (3)   Content
10. Identifying assumptions
    a.   Unstated reasons
    b.   Needed assumptions; argument reconstruction

Strategy and Tactics
11. Deciding on an action
    a.   Define the problem
    b.   Select criteria to judge possible solutions
    c.   Formulate alternative solutions
    d.   Tentatively decide what to do
    e.   Review, taking into account the total situation, and decide
    f.   Monitor the implementation
12. Interacting with others
    a.   Employing and reacting to "fallacy" labels (including)

(1) Circularity	(12) Conversion
(2) Appeal to authority	(13) Begging the question
(3) Bandwagon	(14) Either-or
(4) Glittering term	(15) Vagueness
(5) Namecalling	(16) Equivocation
(6) Slippery slope	(17) Straw person
(7) Post hoc	(18) Appeal to tradition
(8) Non sequitur	(19) Argument from analogy
(9) Ad hominem	(20) Hypothetical question
(10) Affirming the consequent	(21) Oversimplification
(11) Denying the antecedent	(22) Irrelevance

    b.   Logical strategies
    c.   Rhetorical strategies
    d.   Presenting a position, oral or written (argumentation)
        (1)   Aiming at particular audience and keeping it in mind
        (2)   Organizing (common type: main point, clarification, reasons, alternatives, attempt to rebut prospective challenges, summary—including repeat of the main point)

REFERENCES

American Federation of Teachers (1985, September). Critical thinking: It's a basic. *American Teacher*, p. 21.

Annis, L. F., & Annis, D. B. (1979). The impact of philosophy on students' critical thinking ability. *Contemporary Educational Psychology, 4*, 219–226.

Baron, J. B. (1987). Evaluating thinking skills in the classroom. In J. B. Baron & R. J. Sternberg (Eds.), *Teaching thinking skills: Theory and practice* (pp. 221–247). New York: Freeman.

Belmont, J. M., & Butterfield, E. C. (1977). The instructional approach to developmental cognitive research. In R. Kail & J. W. Hagen (Eds.), *Perspectives on the development of memory and cognition*. Hillsdale, NJ: Lawrence Erlbaum Associates.

Bem, S. L. (1974). The measurement of psychological androgyny. *Journal of Consulting and Clinical Psychology, 42*(2), 155–162.

Bereiter, C., & Scardamalia, M. (1985). Cognitive coping strategies and the problem of "inert knowledge." In S. F. Chipman, J. W. Segal, & R. Glaser (Eds.), *Thinking and learning skills: Vol. 2. Research and open questions* (pp. 65–80). Hillsdale, NJ: Lawrence Erlbaum Associates.

Blair, G. M., & Goodson, M. R. (1939). Development of scientific thinking through general science. *School Review, 47*(9), 695–701.

Blasi, A., & Hoeffel, E. C. (1974). Adolescence and formal operations. *Human Development, 17*, 344–363.

Bloom, B. S., Engelhart, M. D., Furst, E. J., Hill, W. H., & Krathwohl, D. R. (1956). *Taxonomy of educational objectives. Handbook I: Cognitive domain*. New York: Longmans, Green.

Boyer, E. L. (1983). *High school: A report on secondary education in America*. New York: Harper & Row.

Bridges, D. (1979). *Education, democracy, and discussion*. Windsor, Berkshire, England: National Foundation for Educational Research in England and Wales.

Bruner, J. S., Goodnow, J. J., & Austin, G. A. (1976). *A study of thinking*. New York: John Wiley & Sons.

Carey, S. (1985). Are children fundamentally different kinds of thinkers and learners than adults? In S. F. Chipman, J. W. Segal, & R. Glaser (Eds.), *Thinking and learning skills: Vol. 2. Research and open questions* (pp. 485–518). Hillsdale, NJ: Lawrence Erlbaum Associates.

Carnegie Task Force on Teaching as a Profession. (1986). *A nation prepared: Teachers for the 21st century*. New York: Carnegie Forum on Education and the Economy.

Chance, P. (1986). Introduction: The thinking movement. In P. Chance & R. S. Brandt (Eds.), *Thinking in the classroom: A survey of programs* (pp. 1–9). New York: Teachers College Press.

College Board (1983). *Academic preparation for college: What students need to know and be able to do*. New York: College Entrance Examination Board.

Commission on the Humanities. (1980). *The humanities in American life*. Berkeley, CA: University of California Press.

Cousins, J. E. (1962). *The development of reflective thinking in an eighth grade social studies class*. Unpublished doctoral dissertation, Indiana University.

Covington, M. V., Crutchfield, R. S., Davies, L., & Olton, R. M., Jr. (1974). *The productive thinking program: A course in learning to think*. Columbus, OH: Charles E. Merrill.

Cuban, L. (1984). Policy and research dilemmas in the teaching of reasoning: Unplanned designs. *Review of Educational Research, 54*(4), 655–681.

deBono, E. (1976). *Teaching thinking*. London: Maurice Temple Smith.

deBono, E. (1983). The direct teaching of critical thinking. *Phi Delta Kappan, 65*, 703–708.

Dewey, J. (1916). *Democracy and education.* New York: Free Press.

Dewey, J. (1933). *How we think.* Boston: D. C. Heath.

Dewey, J. (1938). *Experience and education.* New York: Collier Books.

Dillon, J. T. (1984). Research on questioning and discussion. *Educational Leadership, 42*(3), 50–56.

Educational Policies Commission. (1961). *The central purpose of American education.* Washington, D. C.: National Educational Association.

Edwards, T. B. (1950). Measurement of some aspects of critical thinking. *Journal of Experimental Education, 18,* 263–278.

Eisner, E. W. (1983). The kinds of schools we need. *Educational Leadership, 41,* 48–55.

Ennis, R. H. (1962). A concept of critical thinking. *Harvard Educational Review, 32,* 81–111.

Ennis, R. H. (1963). Needed: Research in critical thinking. *Educational Leadership, 21*(1), 17–20.

Ennis, R. H. (1969). *Logic in teaching.* Englewood Cliffs, NJ: Prentice-Hall.

Ennis, R. H. (1971). Conditional logic and primary school children: A developmental study. *Interchange, 2*(2), 126–132.

Ennis, R. H. (1980). A conception of rational thinking. In J. R. Coombs (Ed.), *Philosophy of education 1979: Proceedings of the thirty-fifth annual meeting of the Philosophy of Education Society* (pp. 3–30). Bloomington, IL: Philosophy of Education Society.

Ennis, R. H. (1981a). Eight fallacies in Bloom's taxonomy. In C. J. B. Macmillan (Ed.), *Philosophy of education 1980: Proceedings of the thirty-sixth annual meeting of the Philosophy of Education Society* (pp. 269–273). Normal, IL: Philosophy of Education Society.

Ennis, R. H. (1981b). Rational thinking and educational practice. In J. Soltis (Ed.), *Philosophy and education: Vol. 1* (pp. 143–183). Chicago: National Society for the Study of Education.

Ennis, R. H. (1982). Children's ability to handle Piaget's propositional logic: A conceptual critique. In S. Modgil & C. Modgil (Eds.), *Jean Piaget: Consensus and controversy* (pp. 101–130). London: Holt, Rinehart, & Winston. (Reprinted from *Review of Educational Research, 45*(1), 1–41.)

Ennis, R. H. (1985a). A logical basis for measuring critical thinking skills. *Educational Leadership, 43,* 44–48.

Ennis, R. H. (1985b). Critical thinking and the curriculum. *National Forum, 65,* 28–31.

Ennis, R. H. (1985c). Goals for a critical thinking curriculum. In A. L. Costa (Ed.), *Developing minds: A resource book for teaching thinking* (pp. 54–57). Washington, D. C.: Association for Supervision and Curriculum Development.

Ennis, R. H. (1985d). Tests that could be called critical thinking tests. In A. L. Costa (Ed.), *Developing minds: A resource book for teaching thinking* (pp. 303–304). Washington, D.C.: Association for Supervision and Curriculum Development.

Ennis, R. H. (1987a, Summer). A conception of critical thinking—with some curriculum suggestions. *American Philosophical Association Newsletter on the Teaching of Philosophy,* 1–5.

Ennis, R. H. (1987b). A taxonomy of critical thinking dispositions and abilities. In J. B. Baron & R. J. Sternberg (Eds.), *Teaching thinking skills* (pp. 9–26). New York: Freeman.

Ennis, R. H. (1989). Critical thinking and subject specificity: Clarification and needed research. *Educational Researcher, 18*(3), 4–10.

Ennis, R. H., Gardiner, W. L., Guzzetta, J., Morrow, R., Paulus, D., & Ringel, L. (1964). *Cornell Conditional-Reasoning Test, Form X.* Champaign, IL: Illinois Critical Thinking Project, University of Illinois.

Ennis, R. H., Gardiner, W. L., Morrow, R., Paulus, D., & Ringel, L. (1964). *Cornell Class-*

Reasoning Test, Form X. Champaign, IL: Illinois Critical Thinking Project, University of Illinois.

Ennis, R. H., & Millman, J. (1985). *Cornell Critical Thinking Test, Level X.* Pacific Grove, CA: Midwest Publications.

Ennis, R. H., & Millman, J. (1985). *Cornell Critical Thinking Test, Level Z.* Pacific Grove, CA: Midwest Publications.

Ennis, R. H., Millman, J., & Tomko, T. N. (1985). *Cornell Critical Thinking Tests Level X. & Level Z—Manual* (3rd ed.). Pacific Grove, CA: Midwest Publications.

Ennis, R. H., & Norris, S. P. (in press). Critical thinking testing and other critical thinking evaluation: Status, issues, needs. In S. Legg. & J. Algina (Eds.), *Alternative testing strategies.* Princeton, NJ: Ablex.

Ennis, R. H., & Weir, E. (1985). *Ennis-Weir Critical Thinking Essay Test.* Pacific Grove, CA: Midwest Publications.

Fawcett, H. P. (1938). *The nature of proof* (13th Yearbook of the National Council of Teachers of Mathematics). New York: Teachers College, Columbia University.

Feuerstein, R., Jensen, M., Hoffman, M. B., & Rand, Y. (1985). Instrumental enrichment, an intervention program for cognitive modifiability: Theory and practice. In J. W. Segal, S. F. Chipman, & R. Glaser (Eds.), *Thinking and learning skills: Volume 1. Relating instruction to research* (pp. 43–82). Hillsdale, NJ: Lawrence Erlbaum Associates.

Fox, R. B. (1962). Difficulties in developing skill in critical thinking. *Journal of Educational Research, 55,* 335–337.

Franklin, A. J. (1985). The social context and socialization variables as factors in thinking and learning. In S. F. Chipman, J. W. Segal, & R. Glaser (Eds.), *Thinking and learning skills: Vol 2. Research and open questions* (pp. 81–106). Hillsdale, NJ: Lawrence Erlbaum Associates.

Fraser, B. J. (1979). *Test of Enquiry Skills.* Hawthorn, Victoria, Australia: Australian Council for Educational Research.

Furst, E. J. (1981). Bloom's taxonomy of educational objectives for the cognitive domain: Philosophical and educational issues. *Review of Educational Research, 51*(4), 441–453.

Futrell, M. H. (1987, December 9). A message long overdue. *Education Week, 7*(14), 9.

Gelman, R. (1985). The developmental perspective on the problem of knowledge acquisition: A discussion. In S. F. Chipman, J. W. Segal, & R. Glaser (Eds.), *Thinking and learning skills: Vol. 2. Research and open questions* (pp. 537–544). Hillsdale, NJ: Lawrence Erlbaum Associates.

George, D. (1984). Creating contexts: Using the research paper to teach critical thinking. *English Journal, 73*(5), 27–32.

George, K. D. (1967). A comparison of the critical-thinking abilities of science and non-science majors. *Science Education, 51*(1), 11–18.

Glaser, E. M. (1941). *An experiment in the development of critical thinking.* New York: Teachers College, Columbia University.

Glaser, R. (1984). Education and thinking: The role of knowledge. *American Psychologist, 39*(2), 93–104.

Hallam, R. N. (1979). Attempting to improve logical thinking in school history. *Research in Education, 21,* 1–23.

Halpern, D. F. (1986). *Sex differences in cognitive abilities.* Hillsdale, NJ: Lawrence Erlbaum Associates.

Harvard Committee. (1945). *General education in a free society.* Cambridge, MA: Harvard University Press.

Hertzka, A. F., & Guilford, J. P. (1955). *Logical Reasoning.* Orange, CA: Sheridan Psychological Services.

Holmes Group (1986). *Tomorrow's teachers.* East Lansing, MI: author.

Johnson, T. W. (1987). Philosophy for children and its critics—Going beyond the information given. *Educational Theory, 37*(1), 61–68.

Kohlberg, L., & Gilligan, C. (1971). The adolescent as a philosopher: The discovery of the self in a post-conventional world. *Daedalus, 100,* 1051–1086.

Lehman, I. J. (1963). *Critical thinking, attitudes, and values in higher education.* East Lansing, MI: Michigan State University.

Lipman, M. (1982). Philosophy for children. *Thinking, 3,* 35–44.

Lipman, M. (1984). The cultivation of reasoning through philosophy. *Educational Leadership, 42*(1), 51–56.

Lipman, M. (1985). Philosophical practice and educational reform. *Journal of Thought, 20*(4), 21–36.

Markovits, H. (1986). Familiarity effects in conditional reasoning. *Journal of Educational Psychology, 78*(6), 492–494.

McPeck, J. (1981). *Critical thinking and education.* New York: St. Martin's.

Meeker, M. (1969). *The structure of intellect: Its interpretation and uses.* Columbus, OH: Charles E. Merrill.

Michenbaum, P. (1985). Teaching thinking: A cognitive-behavioral perspective. In S. F. Chipman, J. W. Segal, & R. Glaser (Eds.), *Thinking and learning skills: Vol. 2. Research and open questions* (pp. 407–426). Hillsdale, NJ: Lawrence Erlbaum Associates.

National Assessment of Educational Progress (1981). *Reading, thinking and writing: Results from the 1979–80 national assessment of reading and literature.* Princeton, NJ: Educational Testing Service.

National Commission on Excellence in Education (1983). *A nation at risk: The imperative for educational reform* (Report No. 065-000-00166- Z). Washington, D. C.: U. S. Government Printing Office.

National Science Board Commission on Precollege Education in Mathematics, Science, and Technology. (1983). *Educating Americans for the 21st century.* Washington, D. C.: National Science Board Commission.

Nelson, B. K. (1981). Hierarchy, utility and fallacy in Bloom's taxonomy. In C. J. B. Macmillan (Ed.), *Philosophy of education 1980: Proceedings of the thirty-sixth annual meeting of the Philosophy of Education Society* (pp. 260–268). Normal, IL: Philosophy of Education Society.

Nickerson, R. S. (1984). Kinds of thinking taught in current programs. *Educational Leadership, 42*(1), 26–36.

Nickerson, R. S. (1987). Why teach thinking? In J. B. Baron & R. J. Sternberg (Eds.), *Teaching thinking skills* (pp. 27–37). New York: Freeman.

Nickerson, R. S., Perkins, D. N., & Smith, E. E. (1985). *The teaching of thinking.* Hillsdale, NJ: Lawrence Erlbaum Associates.

Norris, S. P. (1985). Synthesis of research on critical thinking. *Educational Leadership, 43,* 40–45.

Norris, S. P., & Ennis, R. H. (1989). *Evaluating critical thinking.* Pacific Grove, CA: Midwest Publications.

Norris, S. P., & King, R. (1983). *Test on Appraising Observations.* St. John's, Newfoundland, Canada: Institute for Educational Research and Development, Memorial University of Newfoundland.

Norris, S. P., & King, R. (1984). *The design of a critical thinking test on appraising observations.* St. John's, Newfoundland: Institute for Educational Research and Development, Memorial University of Newfoundland.

Osborn, W. W. (1939). An experiment in teaching resistance to propaganda. *Journal of Experimental Education, 8*(1), 1–17.

Panel on the General Professional Education of the Physician and College Preparation for Medicine. (1984). *Physicians for the twenty-first century: The GPEP report.* Washington, D. C.: Association of American Medical Colleges.

Passmore, J. (1972). On teaching to be critical. In R. F. Dearden, P. H. Hirst, & R. S. Peters (Eds.), *Education and the development of reason* (pp. 415–433). London: Routledge & Kegan Paul.

Paul, R. W. (1984). Critical thinking: Fundamental for education in a free society. *Educational Leadership, 42*, 4–14.

Paul, R. W. (1985). Critical thinking research: A response to Stephen Norris. *Educational Leadership, 44*, 46.

Perkins, D. N. (1987). Thinking frames: An integrative perspective on teaching cognitive skills. In J. B. Baron & R. J. Sternberg (Eds.), *Teaching thinking skills: Theory and practice* (pp. 41–61). New York: Freeman.

Pingry, R. E. (1951). Critical thinking—What is it? *Mathematics Teacher, 44*, 466–470.

Progressive Education Association. (1939). *Test 5.11: Application of Certain Principles of Logical Reasoning*. Chicago: author, Evaluation in the Eight Year Study, University of Chicago.

Redfield, D. L., & Rousseau, E. W. (1981). A meta-analysis of experimental research on teacher questioning behavior. *Review of Educational Research, 51*(2), 237–245.

Rickert, R. K. (1967). Developing critical thinking. *Science Education, 51*(1), 24–27.

Ross, G., & Semb, G. (1981). Philosophy *can* teach critical thinking skills. *Teaching Philosophy, 4*(2), 111–122.

Ross, J. D., & Ross, C. M. (1976). *Ross Test of Higher Cognitive Processes*. Novato, CA: Academic Therapy Publications.

Scheffler, I. (1973). *Reason and teaching*. New York: Bobbs-Merrill.

Scriven, M. (1985). Critical for survival. *National Forum, 65*(1), 9–12.

Seddon, G. M. (1978). The properties of Bloom's taxonomy of educational objectives for the cognitive domain. *Review of Educational Research, 48*(2), 303–323.

Shaffer, E., & Steiger, J. (1971). Judgment: Deductive logic and assumption recognition. Los Angeles: Instructional Objectives Exchange.

Shipman, V. (1983). *New Jersey Test of Reasoning Skills*. Upper Montclair, NJ: IAPC, Test Division, Montclair State College.

Siegel, H. (1980, November). Critical thinking as an educational ideal. *Educational Forum, 44*, 7–23.

Seigel, H. (1985). Educating reason: Critical thinking, informal logic, and the philosophy of education. *Informal Logic, 7*, 69–81.

Simmons, W. (1985). Social class and ethnic differences in cognition: A cultural practice perspective. In S. F. Chipman, J. W. Segal, & R. Glaser (Eds.), *Thinking and learning skills: Vol. 2. Research and open questions* (pp. 519–536). Hillsdale, NJ: Lawrence Erlbaum Associates.

Sizer, T. R. (1984). *Horace's compromise: The dilemma of the American high school*. Boston: Houghton Mifflin.

Smith, D. G. (1977). College classroom interactions and critical thinking. *Journal of Educational Psychology, 69*(2), 180–190.

Sternberg, R. J. (1985). A statewide approach to measuring critical thinking skills. *Educational Leadership, 43*, 40–43.

Sternberg, R. J. (1987). Questions and answers about the nature and teaching of thinking skills. In J. B. Baron & R. J. Sternberg (Eds.), *Teaching thinking skills: Theory and practice* (pp. 251–259). New York: Freeman.

Sternberg, R. J., & Baron, J. B. (1985, April). *A triarchic approach to measuring critical thinking skills: A psychologist's view*. Paper presented at the annual meeting of the American Educational Research Association, San Francisco.

Sternberg, R. J., & Kastoor, B. (1986). Synthesis of research on the effectiveness of intellectual skills programs: Snake oil remedies or miracle cures? *Educational Leadership, 44*(2), 60–67.

Swartz, R. (1987). Teaching for thinking: A developmental model for the infusion of thinking skills into mainstream instruction. In J. B. Baron & R. J. Sternberg (Eds.), *Teaching thinking skills: Theory and practice* (pp. 106–126). New York: Freeman.

Taba, H. (1950). Problems in developing critical thinking. *Progressive Education*, 45–48, 61.

Taba, H. (1962). *Curriculum development: Theory and practice*. New York: Harcourt, Brace & World.

Tobin, K. (1987). The role of wait-time in higher cognitive level learning. *Review of Educational Research*, 57(1), 69–95.

Ulmer, G. (1939). Teaching geometry to cultivate reflective thinking: An experimental study with 1239 high school pupils. *Journal of Experimental Education*, 8(1), 18–25.

Walsh, D., & Paul, R. W. (1985). *The goal of critical thinking: From educational ideal to educational reality*. Washington, D. C.: American Federation of Teachers.

Watson, G., & Glaser, E. M. (1980). *Watson-Glaser Critical Thinking Appraisal*. San Antonio, TX: The Psychological Corporation.

Williams, B. (1987). Implementing thinking skills in instruction in an urban district: An effort to close the gap. *Educational Leadership*, 44(6), 50–53.

Winocur, S. L. (1985). Project IMPACT. In A. L. Costa (Ed.), *Developing minds* (pp. 210–211). Alexandria, VA: Association for Supervision and Curriculum Development.

2

Reading, Writing, and Critical Thinking

J. F. O'Flahavan
University of Maryland, College Park

Robert J. Tierney
The Ohio State University

In this chapter, we make the case that reading and writing are powerful ways to promote critical thinking. In doing so, we adopt a view of critical thinking that entails a commitment to the following: (a) self-initiated and self-directed exploration of ideas; (b) critical examination of one's own ideas; (c) the pursuit of multiple perspectives, including a perspective on these perspectives; (d) the creation of appropriate environments in which to orchestrate such examinations; and (e) the ongoing consideration of the quality of these examinations.

Our view of critical thinking is not unique. For example, we view the end goals of critical thinking (i. e., the products of learning) as consistent with Ennis' (1987) definition: "Critical thinking is reasonable reflective thinking that is focused on deciding what to believe or do" (p. 10). Our commitment to the scrutiny of ideas from multiple perspectives is consistent with the need to adopt a variety of dispositions toward ideas (Ennis, 1987; Norris, 1985; Paul, 1984; Siegel, 1980; Sternberg, 1985; see also chapter 1, this volume). Our belief in the attainment of a perspective on perspectives is consistent with the idea of *production* that Norris (1985) has discussed:

> One must also be *productive*, in the sense of conceiving of alternative courses of action and candidates for belief, before critically appraising which alternative to choose. People must be able to produce reliable observations, make sound inferences, and offer reasonable hypotheses. (p. 40)

Though others have not designated it as a requisite component of critical thinking, we believe that one's reasoning ability is best developed in conjunction with learning situations that nurture student initiative. Empowering learners with the *inalienable right* to guide their own learning is an important aspect of our view of critical thinking; without this, the behaviors associated with independent learning (e. g., intrinsically driven involvement in their own learning) may fail to emerge.

Strategic control and regulation of one's own skill is allied to student initiative. All of the reading and writing strategies we address in this chapter, for example, depend on successful control and regulation by the learner. In the literature, the types of control processes necessary for such monitoring and regulation have been referred to as *metacognition* (Brown, 1978; Flavell, 1978; Paris, Lipson, & Wixson, 1983). Realizing the need to help students develop and take responsibility for this dimension of the ability to learn, a number of current curricula designed to enhance thinking ability in the context of integrated language arts instruction cite metacognitive strategy instruction as an important pedagogical goal (Jones, Palincsar, Ogle, & Carr, 1987; Jones, Tinzman, Friedman, & Walker, 1987; Marzano, et al., 1988).

Throughout the chapter, our focus relates to reading and writing as productive vehicles through which the learner decides "what to believe or do." We begin by reviewing some of the relevant findings from research pertaining to the *reading/writing connection*, a line of research that has recently established the shared and unique characteristics of reading and writing. We make a case for exploiting the *symbiotic* as well as the *synergistic* nature of extended, integrated reading and writing engagements.

For illustrative purposes, two characterizations of the reading/writing connection are summarized: how the composing acts of reading and writing vary with respect to the cognitive operations either elicits and how reading and writing, in various combinations, contribute to critical thought.

The second part of this chapter serves to extend the current notion of what it means to connect reading and writing in the classroom. We explore how and why a learner depends on the acts of reading and writing while engaged in complex learning situations, such as the process of creating a research paper or preparing for a seminar. It is in these situations that the disposition and the ability to think critically is nurtured best and needed most.

Finally, we explore issues regarding research and instruction. We begin with the idea of self-initiated, complex learning situations as the ultimate goal of instruction and explore the type of learning environment needed to help learners achieve increased levels of independent learning.

THE READING/WRITING CONNECTION:
SYMBIOSIS, SYNERGY, OR BOTH?

Numerous theorists have characterized reading and writing as generative, composing processes. The proposed theories highlight the role of the thoughtful, active learner while engaged in the acts of reading and writing. The reading process, for example, has been shown to be one that begins with a transaction between a reader's existing knowledge and the ideas residing within the text (Goodman, 1976; Iser, 1978; Rosenblatt, 1978; Smith, 1982). Within this transaction, recursive negotiation of meaning via the orchestration of *declarative, strategic,* and *conditional* knowledge leads to the products of comprehension (Anderson & Pearson, 1984; Collins, Brown, & Larkin, 1980; Langer, 1986; Rumelhart, 1984; Spiro, 1980).

What are the key reading abilities a learner requires in order to read or write successfully? The theme running through *strategic* or *cognitive* approaches to teaching relates to successful integration of new knowledge with a learner's prior knowledge at the same time that declarative, procedural, and conditional knowledge is developed (Collins, Brown, & Newman, 1989; Jones, Tinzmann, et al., 1987; Jones, Palincsar, et al., 1987; Marzano, et al., 1988).

With respect to reading, these approaches tend to make a clear distinction between the types of strategies a reader should invoke under different conditions. The most frequently cited conditions are *before reading, during reading,* and *after reading.* For example, before reading, an able reader will define a purpose for reading. This may involve the use of such strategies as previewing textual features (i. e., headings, subheadings, graphics, etc.), ascertaining genre type or organizational pattern, activating relevant prior knowledge, generating predictions or questions, and utilizing any information reduction techniques available (i. e., notetaking strategies, advance organizers, etc.)

During reading, an able reader will actively construct a mental representation of the text and attempt to assimilate that representation into existing knowledge. Successful assimilation will involve strategies such as summarizing local portions of the text and the text as a whole, confirming or rejecting predictions made at the outset of the reading engagement or throughout the act of reading, generating new questions en route, and connecting, organizing, and synthesizing ideas.

During the third phase, post-reading, an able reader will consolidate a wholistic representation of the text, assimilate that consolidation into existing knowledge, and assess the efficacy of his or her own performance (i. e., "Did I accomplish the purpose for reading this particular text?").

This may include further summarization, confirmation of predictions, identification of confusion or misinterpretations, rehearsal of information, further study, and so on.

The three phases are, by and large, artifacts of pedagogy. The reading process is not linearly sequenced (with the exception of guided reading activities, perhaps). A reader may recursively invoke so-called post-reading strategies while reading (i. e., notetaking, jotting notes in a journal) and may do so to revise the previously defined purpose for learning, which is most often labelled a pre-reading strategy.

Writing has also been touted as a powerful vehicle for thinking. The writing process has been described as a recursive act that includes identifiable yet amorphous stages, such as planning, translating, and reviewing (cf. Flower & Hayes, 1981). Writing affords the learner an opportunity to gain access to, organize, and analyze existing knowledge, while also synthesizing new information with existing knowledge representations (Emig, 1977; Flower & Hayes, 1980; Gage, 1986; Irmscher, 1979; Odell, 1980).

What are the key writing abilities required by a learner with respect to planning, translating, and reviewing? It has been suggested that an able writer will plan his or her text by envisioning what Witte (1985) has referred to as *pre- text*, an abstract, mental representation of the writer's text before it is actually written. For example, during planning, an able writer may define the rhetorical goal (i. e., journal entry, letter, memo, literary essay, etc.), consider the intended audience (i. e., teacher, peer, self, etc.), generate ideas (i. e., via brainstorming, free-writing, interviewing, conference, etc.), and organize information (i. e., notetaking, outlining, mapping, listing, etc.).

During translating, the writer translates his or her ideas into text. An able writer negotiates the syntactic and semantic demands of the linguistic system, as well as his or her intentions pertaining to tone, audience, and style. Additionally, able writers know when to turn the internal editor off in order to increase writing fluency while drafting.

Reviewing entails the ongoing or post hoc inspection of the grammatical, syntactic, semantic, and rhetorical features of the text that the writer has produced.

Similar to stage theories of reading, the linear representations of the writing process are artificial characterizations of the writing process as exhibited by actual writers in actual writing situations. Writing does not move from the planning stage to the translating stage in every situation, nor does a writer wait until the entire text has been composed to revise. Rather, the writer monitors text production throughout the process of writing and may engage in planning, translating, and reviewing behaviors at any time (Flower & Hayes, 1981; Scardamalia & Bereiter, 1986).

Due to the cognitive emphasis in reading and writing research, comparisons between reading and writing as processes were inevitable. Tierney & Pearson (1983), for example, made an argument for reading as a recursive composing process involving planning, drafting, aligning, revising, and monitoring: "We believe that at the heart of understanding reading and writing connections one must begin to view reading and writing as essentially similar processes of meaning construction" (p. 568). This view and others like it eventually gave rise to research that examined the *connection* between the two composing acts.

Two complementary characterizations of the reading/writing connection have emerged. The first relates to the symbiotic nature of reading and writing: The two processes, in effect, dip into the same pool of cognitive resources and, therefore, have moderate effects on one another (Galda, 1984; Shanahan, 1980, 1984, 1988; Shanahan & Lomax, 1986; Stotsky, 1983; Tierney & Leys, 1986).

However, upon closer examination, the similarities between reading and writing begin to dissipate. In a study that demonstrates the shared and unique qualities of reading and writing and their related effects on learning, Langer (1986) examined the think-aloud protocols of children as they read and wrote. She claimed that both processes exhibited evidence of purposeful, meaning-based behavior. Yet, based on the comments that the students made while comprehending or composing, Langer concluded further that reading engaged students in dissimilar patterns of cognitive operations than writing.

Involvement in reading, for example, yielded more use of schemata and a deeper concern for supporting and validating interpretations that writing. Involvement in writing, on the other hand, elicited greater attention to the generation of hypotheses and metacomments about the evolving text (Langer, 1986).

The second characterization of the reading/writing connection relates to the *synergistic* nature of integrated reading and writing activities: Reading and writing have multiplicative effects on learning when the two are juxtaposed within a larger, purposeful task.

One of our recent studies provides support for the synergistic effects of integrated reading and writing activity on critical thinking (Tierney, Soter, O'Flahavan, & McGinley, 1989). We asked undergraduate students ($N = 138$) to engage in various combinations of reading and writing activities so that we might ascertain the effects of these particular combinations on critical thinking. Students began by drafting their opinions (letters to a fictional newspaper editor) on one of two controversial issues (whether discrimination against women in the movie industry existed or not; whether implanting a baboon's heart in Baby Fae was ethical or not). Different groups of students then progressed through one of the following combinatorial tasks: read an article that defended a position related to the argument; read an article and answered multiple- choice and open-ended questions; answered just the questions; or moved immediately from initial draft to revision. All students were given the chance to revise if they felt compelled to do so. Figure 2.1 depicts each of the possible sequences of engagements.

We hypothesized that the quality of the drafts and the types and frequencies of revisions would allow us to judge how critically the students were thinking during each of the tasks. Based on our analyses, reading and writing in combination with each other contributed to a wider range of revisions (i. e., additions, deletions, substitutions, etc.) and higher quality drafts than reading or writing alone. The results suggest

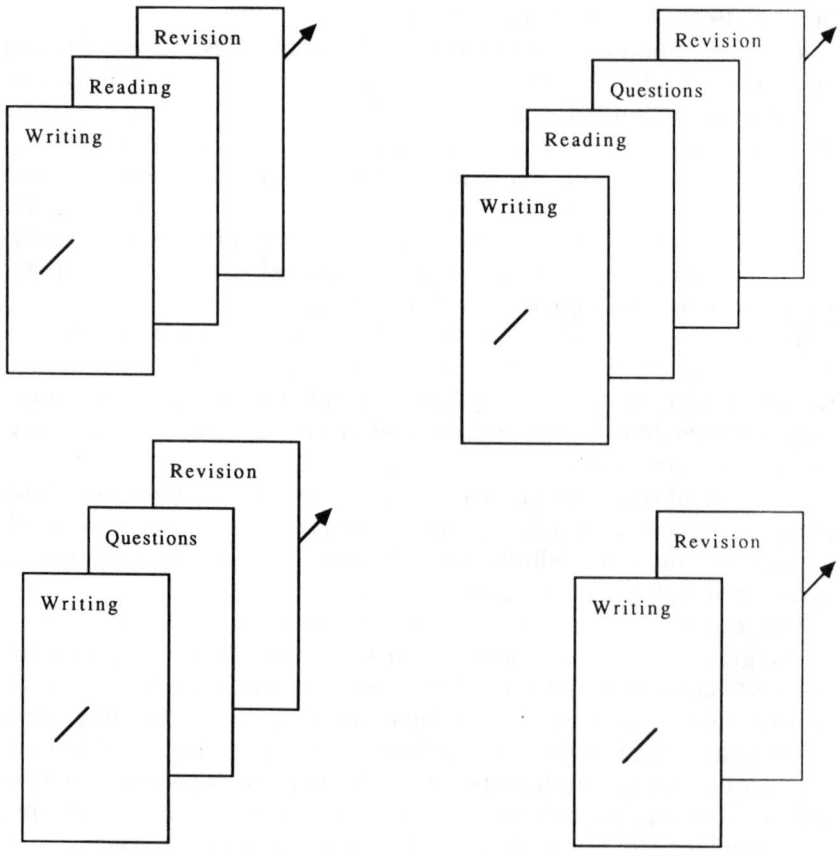

FIG. 2.1.   Sequences of engagements (from Tierney, Soter, O'Flahavan, & McGinley, 1989).

that reading and writing in combination are more likely to promote critical thinking than when reading is separated from writing. We believe the learner has the opportunity to engage in either a dialectical or dialogical exchange *with the self*: Reading may serve as the requisite partner in this exchange, as a resource of opposing views or further elaborations on an idea; writing may serve as a mode through which the learner might resolve disputes or allow ideas to come to fruition.

We also asked the students to reflect upon how the various reading, writing, and questioning activities influenced their thinking throughout the task. These comments shed some light on how the students perceived the unique purposes that both reading and writing served in their thinking.

For example, the following comments relate to the impact of writing upon their thinking as they wrote the first draft of the letter:

(Writing) made me choose an opinion on the issue and bring up all the facts and opinions.

The letter forced me to choose [a position]—against or for it—[and] polarized my opinion more than it had been originally.

I had to get my thoughts and opinions together on the subject, and also try to find out how much I knew about it.

It helped me to understand the topic more and my feelings about it as I saw what I wrote. I had to think before I wrote to organize my thoughts. The more I thought about it, the more I began to understand it.

In each of the four comments, we see the mobilizing effect of writing, the generative process of accessing knowledge, followed by an attempt to organize this knowledge into communicable form. In addition, we also see the beginnings of one side of the dialectic in statements such as, "(writing) made me choose an opinion," and "the letter forced me to choose—against or for it—polarized my opinion." Further, writing helped these students elaborate on their "sides" of the argument: "It helped me understand the topic more and my feelings about it as I saw what I wrote."

Once the students mobilized their arguments, they were asked to read an article concerning the topic. In some cases, the article corroborated their own views; in others, the article served as an opposing view. In either case, reading served mainly as a way of examining perspectives (pro vs. con) and, perhaps, acquiring new knowledge about the topic:

This had an influencing effect! I could imagine if I was given an article with the opposite views supported, I would have probably made a few more changes in the letter itself!

(Reading) opened me up to other opinions on the subject—presented different points of view.

. . . made me think twice about my viewpoint . . .

Allowed me to educate myself on the issues involved.

Reading helped me see the topic in a clearer perspective, but only one side of it. There was another direction I could've chosen, but I chose not to.

Just as in a constructive debate, where dialectic partners attempt to enlighten the opposing party, the reader can engage in a dialogue with the author of the text. If the reader enters this dialogue with an open mind and a willingness to continually update his or her understanding of a number of perspectives, reading will serve the purposes of reflection, examination, and acquisition.

Inasmuch as it has been suggested that metacognition is an integral part of comprehension (Baker & Brown, 1984) and, more specifically, critical thinking (Jones, Palincsar, et al., 1987; Jones, Tinzmann, et al., 1987; Marzano et al., 1988), one might hypothesize that integrated engagements in reading and writing would require some metacognitive awareness as to how one's thinking via reading might be affecting one's subsequent thinking via writing, and vice versa. Two effects are worthy of note here. First, when one moves between reading and writing in the act of problem solving, one may *sense the depth and breadth of one's knowledge*:

I became aware of how much I don't know about the topic. It's true that I can form opinions by what I see in the movies, but I need to do more reading on the topic.

I feel it was a bit reactionary and I would want to know more before I really wrote a letter.

If the learner is trying to fashion a solution to some problem, then this awareness may lead to further involvements in reading or writing, depending on the person's need at the time. For instance, both of the preceding comments may lead to further engagements in reading. Further engagement in writing may allow the learner to generate an even deeper understanding of his or her knowledge.

A second type of metacognitive control has to do with the act of *moving in and out of the reading and writing modes* themselves. McGinley & Tierney (Tierney & McGinley, 1987; McGinley & Tierney, 1989) suggested that reading and writing enable a learner to "traverse" topics, experiences, or problems (after Spiro, Vispoel, Schmitz, Samarapungavan, & Boerger, 1987). This type of awareness is crucial for the person who willingly engages in this type of dialectic. The learner has to have some inkling as to when it is time to *stop* one mode and *move* to another.

> After reading the article, I wrote my editorial more thoroughly. I referred back to the article and thought about what parts of the article I was aware of—did I see actresses being exploited? Was age a factor?

> (Reading) helped me a lot in writing because I could see which stands I agreed with.

Referring back to the genesis of an idea, and knowing both how and when reading or writing will aid one's thinking are illustrations of the requisite, metacognitive knowledge needed in such reader–author transactions.

The final stage in the reading–writing sequence was revision. The students had already mobilized a perspective and then entered in an exchange with another writer about the issue. Afterwards, they had the opportunity to return to their initial positions and revise that stance, if they felt compelled to do so.

> (Revision) allowed me to re-evaluate my position in light of what I had just learned.

> Revision allowed me to focus my argument more rationally—made me cut out superfluous things.

> I could rethink the issue, after organizing a few ideas and thinking about my reactions.

> I went back over and analyzed and organized my thoughts.

These comments are examples of the entire critical thinking process in operation. The learner is at the helm; he or she must initiate the line of inquiry, monitor and control movement along that line, learning all the while on the unique and cumulative contributions that reading and writing offer.

In summary, examinations of the nature of reading and writing suggest two interrelated conclusions. First, reading and writing involve similar underlying processes, though engagement in each produces unique arrays of these underlying processes. Second, by virtue of these similarities and differences, reading and writing together afford the learner the opportunity to develop multiple perspectives. Reading and writing are the vehicles with which learners may examine and re-examine ideas, consider explanations, make comparisons, and reflect upon various views.

What implications does this have for instruction? Whether the goal is to develop critical thinking ability or depth of knowledge in a particular discipline, we believe that instruction should capitalize on the symbiotic and synergistic nature of reading and writing. Two general guidelines are noteworthy at this point in our discussion. First, instructional designs should optimize the composing nature of both reading and writing equally (Shanahan, 1988). Second, instruction should simultaneously emphasize the unique contributions that reading and writing can offer.

Achieving these two goals will involve providing or allowing for a variety of writing experiences for different purposes and audiences, in conjunction with a variety of related reading experiences. For example, one approach has been to emphasize reading instruction with the support of writing. This can be accomplished by juxtaposing writing to reading as either a pre-reading or post-reading activity. Likewise, one may decide to improve the quality of written prose by juxtaposing reading with writing as either a pre-writing or a between-drafts activity (for a review of these initiatives, refer to McGinley & Tierney, 1989; Tierney & McGinley, 1987).

Instructional designs that juxtapose reading and writing engagements, however, should vary in length according to goals set forth by the learner or the teacher. Consider the tasks completed by the students in the study (Tierney, et al., 1989). Each was typical of those in the reading/writing connection vein—they were juxtapositional in nature. For the sake of illustration, we will name each of the types. The first type, a *zero-order* juxtaposition, is one where a learner engages in only one activity, such as reading or writing. There were none in the portion of the study reported here. However, there were higher order juxtapositions. For example, the next highest order juxtaposition would be one where one activity is juxtaposed with another. In this case, the *first-order* juxtapositions were writing followed immediately by revision. The *second-order* juxtapositions were writing followed by reading, followed by revision, and so on. The highest order juxtaposition in the study, a *third-order* juxtaposition, was writing followed by reading, questions, and revision.

We have developed this nomenclature to make a point. Current perspectives of the reading/writing connection must be extended beyond zero-order juxtapositions to what we refer to as *extended engagements*; these are higher order juxtapositions that exploit both the symbiotic and synergistic natures of integrated reading and writing engagements. Most first-order juxtapositions (and many higher order juxtapositions, too) are usually designed, initiated, monitored, and evaluated by the teacher. Thus, teachers often find themselves caught in the quintessential paradox of teaching: The objectives of the lesson might ultimately be met as a result of such connections, but the long-term goals of developing strategic and metacognitive learning behavior may be in jeopardy.

EXTENDED ENGAGEMENTS: HIGHER ORDER
READING AND WRITING CONNECTIONS

Much of what happens in classrooms runs counter to having students assume responsibility for their own learning. Because of pre-established curricula, pacing schedules, and the like, students are often told what they are expected to learn; students' reading is guided; students are asked questions that "check" their comprehension, rather than helping them "go beyond" the text at hand; students are offered a range of topics from which to choose when they write; and, most of the products of students' learning are evaluated based on whether or not key facts were remembered or coherent and accurate reports were produced. In the end, students separate themselves from what they are learning, satisfied to be informed by someone else rather than to search for themselves, and satisfied to be tested by others rather than to evaluate their own thinking (Applebee, 1981; Tierney, Lazansky, & Schallert, 1980; Tierney & O'Flahavan, 1989). In short, someone else may do the bulk of their thinking.

In this section, we explore how and why a self-initiating learner depends on the acts of reading and writing while engaged in complex learning situations. Consider the following extended engagement and one of its many possible solutions as an illustration:

> Imagine for the moment that a well-known hospital administrator has been invited to deliver a keynote address for an upcoming conference. She has been asked to address the debate involving the need for socialized medicine in the United States. She begins by reading a few journal articles by authors who hold opposing positions so that she might reacquaint herself with the current perspectives pertaining to nationalized health insurance. These texts spark some new ideas and help her access some old ones, and she jots some notes. Eventually, a thesis is born for her address, and she quickly moves to a draft.

The hospital administrator in this example has to consider three dimensions to the task that lays in front of her: the rhetorical goal (a speech); the anticipated context (a conference of peers); and, the content (socialized medicine in the United States). Each of these dimensions can be combined into what we call "the line of inquiry."

The first dimension, the rhetorical goal, requires knowledge of genre-specific conventions. The second dimension requires knowledge of audience. The last dimension posits an awareness of one's current state of understanding regarding the content. In this case, the administrator requires knowledge of the types of speeches made by keynote speakers at these types of conferences, an understanding of the audience's expectation of a keynote address regarding this topic, and the current state of her own knowledge regarding socialized medicine. Additionally, the administrator will need to capitalize on her abilities as a reader and writer and on her ability to get help from people in her environment.

Figure 2.2a depicts the sequence of reading and writing engagements that the hospital administrator invoked while preparing her address. Notice that the line of inquiry slices through the various engagements she consciously sequenced for herself in order to complete the task; in effect, an awareness of the multidimensional problem enabled her to capitalize on the symbiotic and synergistic nature of reading and writing.

Figures 2.1, 2.2a, and 2.2b (and others like them) are not to be misconstrued as linear representations of the reading and writing processes, nor of thought processes in general. *Within each engagement*, the thoughts and problem-solving processes are recursive. What we are trying to represent here are the *footprints* left behind by a literate person in the wake of critical inquiry. Learners virtually switch engagements when they perceive it is time to do so, for whatever reasons, and, as a result, a sequence of engagements, or footprints, is left behind.

Let us imagine for the moment that we have asked our administrator to describe the decisions she made as she moved along the line of inquiry.

> Once I agreed to give the address, the wheels started turning. I sat down one night to think about what I knew about socialized medicine. Had the issues changed substantially? What were some of the "experts" saying? Were there any model programs to critique? I realized that the details had become fuzzy, so I went to the library the next day and got some articles by whom I remembered to be experts on the subject.
>
> The next night, I read the articles, one after another. It wasn't until afterwards that I wished I had jotted some notes while I read, because I had to go back and refresh myself on all of the details of their arguments. The reading made me think about who might be in the audience—it could very well be that the authors I'd just read would be there, so I would have to be precise. Quote them, too, maybe. Anyway, I made some notes after reading, and pulled together what I thought was the beginning of an outline.
>
> The next day, I started writing; it took a long time. I'd forgotten how difficult it was. I wasn't too concerned with it, though, because I wanted the talk to be somewhat extemporaneous—jokes and stuff—so I only half-planned the talk; I didn't write out the whole thing word for word . . .

Guided by a meaningful goad, the administrator successfully enlisted reading and writing as vehicles of thought, and each, in its own way, enabled her to think about "what to believe or do" (Ennis, 1987). As

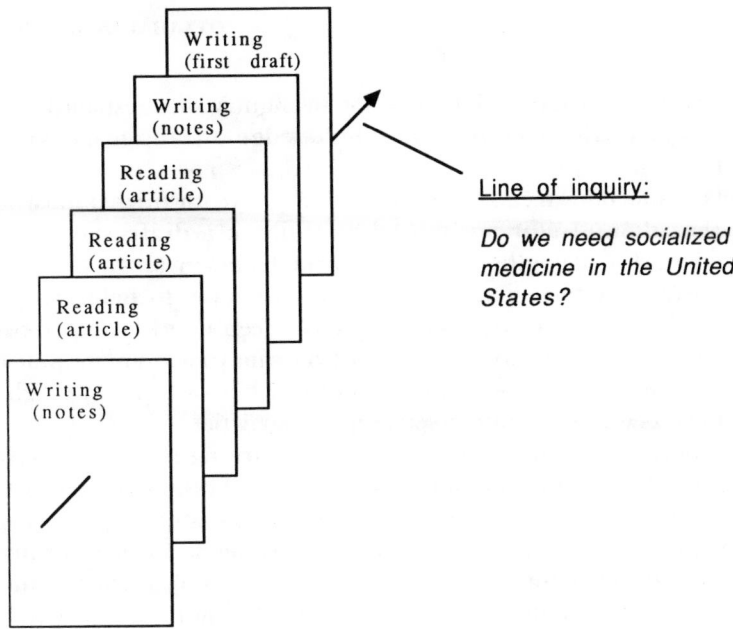

FIG. 2.2A.   Hospital administrator.

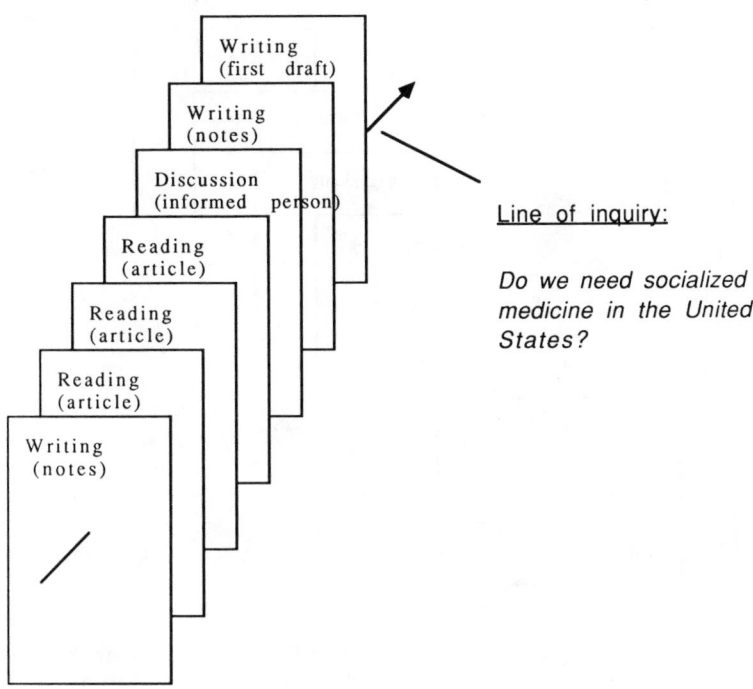

FIG. 2.2B.   Hospital administrator.

she monitored progress along the line of inquiry she'd established, new information was linked with existing knowledge, and the goal was eventually attained.

Let us entertain an equally plausible alternative for further illustration. Had the administrator not moved so easily to a draft, she may have entered into a dialogue with an informed person (e. g., a colleague, journalist, or state legislator) regarding the topic to help clarify her position. This informed person may have been one whose perspective was similar to her own, or the administrator may have sought out someone whose perspective was the antithesis of her own. Figure 2.2b may then have been the resulting sequence of activities.

A general way of looking at this type of learning experience is shown in Fig. 2.3. First, a line of inquiry is established. The line of inquiry could be a query or a problem, much like the query found in the hospital administrator example. Once the line is established, the learner invokes the requisite skills, thought processes, and modes of discourse through which he or she might move along the line of inquiry. Every text, every draft, every discussion is salient to that particular line of inquiry. The

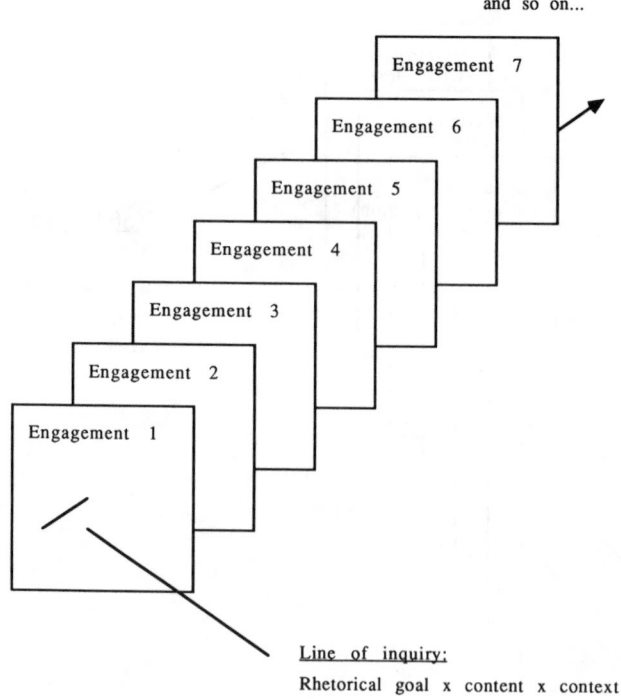

FIG. 2.3.   Extended engagements.

learner defines the purpose for invoking a particular skill, thought process, or discourse mode, and monitors his or her progress through the sequence. Inherently, the sequence of activities becomes self-sustaining.

As might be inferred from the preceding examples, initiative is a central tenet to this view of critical thinking. Critical thinkers must *have* and *take* the initiative in order to move along a line of inquiry. Critical thinkers must recognize the value of initiating an engagement at an appropriate time. They must have an understanding of the unique purposes of reading and writing, as well as the combinatorial power of the two. The hospital administrator, for example, knew that writing was the best mode through which to organize her thoughts after having read three journal articles.

Additionally, one must be disposed to think and act critically in complex learning situations such as these. How, when, and why one juggles the resources available depends on what disposition is guiding the person's mindset at any particular time (Sternberg, 1985). For example, close-mindedness tends to terminate any active engagement in creative or critical thought, whereas open-mindedness may take a person through an endless journey of reading, writing, speaking, and listening activities before a reasonable judgment is achieved.

At this point, it is important to make the distinction between *self-sanctioned* learning and *self-directed* learning. Self-sanctioned learning is learning that is initiated and directed by the learner. Topics are selected, lines of inquiry are created, goals are established, resources are hunted down, progress is monitored, and the products of learning are evaluated along the way.

In self-directed learning, only selected portions of the activity are governed by the learner. The task is negotiated or parsed by the teacher (or whomever) for the learner in order to reduce the complexity of the task, and to perhaps highlight learning in one particular phase of the task. However, it is important to note that the portions of the task that the learner is directing are meaningful. For example, the teacher may constrain the task by limiting the range of topics or number of resources available to the learner. Similarly, the teacher may decide to take responsibility for 75% of the task, leaving 25% for the learner, then gradually increase the proportion of responsibility for the learner over time (Pearson & Gallagher, 1983). From the learner's point of view then, self-sanctioned learning involves both initiative and direction, whereas self-directed learning may only require a portion of the total responsibility of the task.

In summary, we believe that the reading–writing connection should include a variety of juxtapositional tasks, each related to relevant purposes for learning. Additionally, we believe self-sanctioned learning is the goal in this type of learning. Inherent within these goals are the reconceptualization of classroom learning environments, a topic to which we now turn.

IMPLICATIONS FOR INSTRUCTION

The question, "How should we teach critical thinking?" has plagued educators for some time. Because this chapter relates to the possibilities of integrating reading, writing, and critical thinking ability, we concern ourselves with initiatives aiming to do just that. Two recent approaches to integrating thinking skills instruction with instruction in the four modes of language maintain that the trend should be away from isolated skills instruction and toward an approach that fosters meaningful application of thinking skills and independent learning in functional contexts (Marzano et al., 1988; Jones, Palincsar, et al., 1987; Jones, Tinzman, et al., 1987). We concur with this directive, although we add one other goal: self-sanctioned learning. The purpose of this section is to address issues regarding the type of learning environment needed in which such a philosophy can be realized.

A helpful rubric for such a discussion is found in Fig. 2.4. This figure depicts the elements of what we believe to be the type of complex environment in which the symbiotic and synergistic nature of reading and writing

---

A supportive, literate, thinking community

    modular space and time
    socially functional learning activity

Role of the learner within this community: Initiator

    decision-maker
    apprentice to prpocess and product
    collaborator to peers
    facilitator for peers
    monitor of self

Role of the teacher in this community: Informed Opportunist

    mentor
    collaborator
    facilitator
    monitor

FIG. 2.4.   Elements of a literate environment.

might flourish and in which students as decision-makers might be supported.

A supportive, literate thinking community is probably the most important element in the environment. It is a community where learners are free to hypothesize and test their theories; to take risks and reflect upon others' risks; and, to both challenge and accept divergent perspectives. When operating at its peak potential, it is a community where writers find readers, readers meet willing discussion partners, and self-sanctioned learners confront problems, pose questions, and seek solutions. It is the place where language is incessantly shaped and reborn.

One of the pedagogical realizations that precedes such a community involves a reevaluation of classroom space and time. Teachers who wish to optimize the effects of their methods might approach the physical space within their classroom much like the interior designer approaches space when attempting to establish an intended ambience. A teacher might use different physical arrangements to evoke the appropriate mood for different tasks. Because the walls cannot be easily moved, the modular pieces in the room are arranged and rearranged so as to minimize the space limitations and maximize the room's potential.

Consider this metaphor of community further, and consider it from a literate person's point of view. A literate person requires and utilizes certain resources within the community. For example, the existence of a *library* has a range of purposes; it is a resource that is valuable to the person who relies on print. The *office supply store* is an important resource for one who writes, as is the *publishing house*. These manifestations of the metaphor exist in many classrooms already.

However, the metaphor can be extended to include other meaningful community resources—resources to which many students do not have regular access. Consider the *local theater*, where local playwrites may produce the latest piece; the *sidewalk cafe*, where writers meet to discuss in-progress work, or where readers congregate, over coffee, to talk about a favorite author's latest book; or, the *local newspaper*, where daily columns or occasional letters to the editor might appear. These are manifestations of the community outside of the school that should exists in classroom communities, at the classroom, building, or district level. These metaphors are a key step in building perceptions of the relevance of literacy. They could be conceptualized as learning centers, and these centers could be introduced at strategic times throughout the year.

Desk space is also key. If students are to connect reading and writing they need space for books, notes, and other resources as they write, as well as the space to write as they read. A manifestation of the community metaphor with respect to desk space is what we have come to call *The Workbench* (Tierney & O'Flahavan, 1989). Much like the workbench found in many garages or workshops, this metaphorical workbench has around it tools for the trade, such as the raw materials used for construction (i. e., books, pencils, paper, magazines, a dictionary, a thesaurus, a word processor, etc.). The workbench is the hub of activity, a place where numerous combinations of activities can come together as a product takes shape. Activities such as notes from library research, ideas collated from multiple readings, reflective thoughts from journals, new discoveries from peer discussions, and a helpful tip from a knowing teacher are all examples of the activities one would find at the workbench.

Time is another factor. Learning that involves extended engagements in reading and writing often requires involvement in different tasks for variable amounts of time. Learners need time to reflect upon why they are doing what they are doing, time to interact with peers, time to read and ponder, to gain distance, to achieve and maintain involvement, and to extend the development of their own ideas. Most importantly, learners need to learn how to operate within an allotted time block (e. g., a pre-specified language-arts block per day) by setting appropriate goals and managing their on-task performance.

The other categories within the framework involve the roles of student and teacher. Inevitably, we would hope that every student would evolve into an initiator and a decision-maker. The student might function in the community as collaborator to fellow peers, facilitator for peers, monitor of his or her own learning, as well as apprentice to mentors or experts. The learner should be given the opportunity to initiate, direct, and assess his or her own learning. This does not entail a student working in total isolation or without any teacher or peer support. Students learn from others as they facilitate their own learning and others' learning by sharing, offering support, suggesting possibilities, and evaluating ideas in a social context involving communities of learners who are doing the same. In this way, a student is not only an initiator; the student may be a collaborator, partner, and apprentice, whenever strategically appropriate.

The teacher's role is similarly dynamic. Teachers should consider themselves *informed opportunists*. They need to decide when it is appropriate to become the center of the environment and when it is best to retreat to the sidelines or dissolve into the group, as a fellow member. Teachers need to judge when it is time to reduce their authority or input, step back from the center, and provide support. Essentially, teachers might view themselves as active facilitators of the decision-making of others. While teachers might step into the center of the environment and actively model the subtleties of various reading and writing strategies and skills, they must be careful not to sabotage student learning by taking away the students' decision-making power.

In summary, this type of literate environment supports interactions among thinkers who utilize reading and writing (as well as discussion) as vehicles for critical thought. Such an environment suggests the need for collaborations between class members not unlike those amidst an active community; this entails opportunities to discuss, solicit input, and solve problems with others.

How might such an environment be created? Essentially, there are two major decisions required of the teacher in an ongoing fashion, sometimes moment-to-moment: task choice and locus of control. Learning begins with task choice. *Task choice* involves the selection of a line of inquiry and a game plan for immersion into the task. From there, any number of literacy engagements may occur in any sequence: reading a test; writing an essay; jotting some thoughts in a journal; interviewing an expert; brainstorming with a peer; to name but a few. Where the inquiry begins and what mode the learner first invokes is not of paramount concern— there is no correct first step, although some will appear to be more advantageous than others in certain circumstances.

The second decision relates to *locus of control*: How much control should the teacher retain over the complexity of the overall task? At some point, the inevitable goal for all teaching is that the student will exhibit the sort of independence and initiative such as that displayed by the hospital administrator. Therefore, the teacher has to make a decision regarding the degree to which he or she reduces the complexity of the problem facing the learner.

To illustrate how pedagogical decisions regarding task choice and locus of control might interact, we return to the Workbench. At some point, the teacher must decide whether or not to (a) initiate the line of inquiry for the learner, (b) constrain the types of resources found at the workbench, (c) sequence the various engagements for the learner, or (d) relinquish all of these responsibilities to the learner.

Salvatori, for example, created a series of reading, writing, and discussion activities designed to help basic reading and writing students begin to see the values of integrated literacy activity. Interspersed within the writing activity were reading engagements and seminars. As Salvatori (1985) wrote:

> Our course description defines BRW [Basic Reading and Writing] as a "seminar." And seminar it is, in the sense that the group does engage in "original research" under the guidance of two teachers who meet regularly with students for reports and discussion; but it is also a "seminary," that is, a "place," an "environment" where the conditions conducive to such discussion are introduced, nurtured and ultimately carried away by the students. (p. 151)

To accomplish this, Salvatori made some critical decisions, and there were ramifications for each of these decisions. Firstly, she established most of the lines of inquiry for each task. Secondly, she regulated the students' movement in and out of the reading, writing, and seminar experiences along the various lines of inquiry. Lastly, she did not constrain the students' movement within each of the reading, writing, and seminar experiences; in fact, she was a participant. In this last case, due to the nature of group discussion, students were responsible for detecting and monitoring the consistency of peer statements and arguments, and the accuracy of details used for support of an argument. Salvatori tried to establish "mediation" with her basic readers and writers, rather than remediation. Instead of compensatory education, her class became exploratory. Because of their low levels of success in past literacy efforts, she believed they required the type of guidance she provided.

As a result, these basic reading and writing students were able to carry on both private and public dialogues with their evolving texts, the texts they read, and with their peers in the class. In essence, the students and their texts became the driving forces within an open forum. In such a learning environment, critical dispositions are nurtured, acquired, and reinforced over time. More importantly, in such environments, there is a higher probability that in similar situations, the learner will be disposed towards initiating or addressing increasingly challenging tasks.

Salvatori also made some of the key decisions related to metacognitive development. Although she would inevitably like to see her BRW students making it for themselves, she knew that they would find more success, at first, if she managed movement back and forth from reading to writing to seminar.

At what point is the responsibility for extended engagements turned over to the student? In Ohio, the Columbus City Schools developed a framework for developing increased levels of student decision-making while simultaneously nurturing integrated reading and writing skill (Tierney & O'Flahavan, 1989). In conjunction with discussions of short stories by well-known authors, teachers invited students to consider experiences they had had that related to certain themes and topics. After some brainstorming, students might be given the opportunity to write their experiences and then share their stories with classmates. After hearing several of these stories, students were introduced to one or more stories on the same theme or topic, written by a professional author. Again, students discussed the stories, were encouraged to compare them to their own, and then were invited to work again on new stories. Lastly, students were asked to reflect upon the interpretations they had constructed as well as to evaluate their efforts.

Throughout, a great deal of emphasis was given to student decision making. Students were encouraged to make their own decisions with regard to what they would write, how they would share, what changes they would entertain, to share their view of what they had learned, as well as evaluate their own work.

CONCLUSION

In this chapter, we have argued that reading and writing have the potential to be powerful vehicles for critical thinking. We are not so foolish to believe that any and all reading and writing experiences will promote critical thinking, however. In fact, we expect that a number of classroom practices that inhibit critical thinking exist. For example, we speculate that critical thinking is less likely to emerge in those classes where more emphasis is placed on retrieval of ideas, accuracy of interpretation, test performance, and teacher-sanctioned inquiry.

Indeed, a concern for the following has pervaded our discussion of reading, writing, and critical thinking: (a) reading and writing should be viewed as vehicles for achieving multiple perspectives; (b) educators should cultivate a commitment to self-sanctioned learning by students; and (c) educators should create environments that support these possibilities.

What we see as essential for moving forward in terms of these concerns are research and development efforts that examine the thought processes engaged by learners as a result of various reading and writing initiatives they pursue, in the context of different literate environments. McGinley (1989) is currently pursuing a detailed analysis of the cognitive operations and knowledge shifts that occur in conjunction when learners move back and forth from reading to writing to notetaking, and so on. His preliminary data suggest that able learners are consciously aware of when movement from one vehicle of thought to another is necessary for purposes of achieving the goal prescribed by the learner.

We need to understand the reasons why learners of all abilities decide to read or write, in what sequences, and for what purposes. We need to investigate the perceptions students possess about the relevancy of reading and writing they have developed as a result of membership in different types of learning environments.

In the interim, we need to establish as our agenda goals for learning that place a premium on engendering in students a passion for thinking critically. In this regard, our view of the learner is not unlike Paul's recent description (Paul, 1986):

> A passionate drive for clarity, accuracy, and fair-mindedness, a fervor for getting to the bottom of things, to the deepest root issues, for listening

sympathetically to opposite points of view, a compelling drive to seek out evidence, and intense aversion to contradiction, sloppy thinking, inconsistent application of standards, a devotion to truth against self-interest— these are essential components of the rational person. (p. 1)

Critical thinkers are those who can avail themselves of the shared and unique powers of reading and writing in order to achieve these benefits.

REFERENCES

Anderson, R. C., & Pearson, P. D. (1984). A schema-theoretic view of the basic processes in reading comprehension. In P. D. Pearson (Ed.), *Handbook of reading research* (pp. 255–291). New York, NY: Longman.

Applebee, A. N. (1981). *Writing in the secondary school: English and the content areas.* Urbana, IL: National Council of Teachers of English.

Baker, L., & Brown, A. L. (1984). Metacognitive skills and reading. In P. D. Pearson (Ed.), *Handbook of reading research* (pp. 353–394). New York, NY: Longman.

Brown, A. L. (1978). Knowing when, where, and how to remember: A problem of metacognition. In R. Glaser (Ed.), *Advances in instructional psychology.* Hillsdale, NJ: Lawrence Erlbaum Associates.

Collins, A., Brown, J. S., & Larkin, K. M. (1980). Inference in text understanding. In R. J. Spiro, B. C. Bruce, & W. F. Brewer (Eds.), *Theoretical issues in reading comprehension.* Hillsdale, NJ: Lawrence Erlbaum Associates.

Collins, A., Brown, J. S., & Newman, S. (in press). Cognitive apprenticeships: Teaching students the craft of reading, writing, and mathematics. In L. B. Resnick (Ed.), *Cognition and instruction: Issues and agendas.* Hillsdale, NJ: Lawrence Erlbaum Associates.

Emig, J. (1977). Writing as a mode of learning. *College Composition and Communication, 28,* 122–127.

Ennis, R. H. (1987). A taxonomy of critical thinking dispositions and abilities. In J. Baron & R. Sternberg (Eds.), *Teaching for thinking.* New York, NY: D. H. Freeman.

Flavell, J. H. (1978). Metacognitive development. In J. M. Scandura & C. J. Brainerd (Eds.), *Structural/process theories of complex human behavior.* Netherlands: Sijthoff and Noordoff.

Flower, L., & Hayes, J. R. (1980). The dynamics of composing: Making plans and juggling constraints. In L. W. Gregg & E. R. Steinberg (Eds.), *Cognitive processes in writing.* Hillsdale, NJ: Lawrence Erlbaum Associates.

Flower, L., & Hayes, J. R. (1981). Plans that guide the composing process. In C. H. Frederiksen & J. F. Dominic (Eds.), *Writing: The nature, development and teaching of written communication. Vol 2: Writing: Process, development and communication.* Hillsdale, NJ: Lawrence Erlbaum Associates.

Gage, J. (1986). Why write? In D. Bartholomea & A. Petrosky (Eds.), *The teaching of writing.* Chicago: National Society for the Study of Education.

Galda, L. (1984). The relations between reading and writing in young children. In R. Beach & L. Bridwell (Eds.), *New directions in composition research.* New York, NY: Guilford Press.

Goodman, K. (1976). Reading: A psycholinguistic guessing game. In H. Singer & R. Ruddell (Eds.), *Theoretical models and processes of reading* (2nd ed). Newark, DE: International Reading Association.

Iser, W. (1978). *The act of reading: A theory of aesthetic response.* Baltimore, MD: Johns Hopkins Press.

Jones, B. F., Palincsar, A. S., Ogle, D. S., & Carr, E. G. (1987). *Strategic instruction: Cognitive instruction in the content area.* Alexandria, VA: Association for Supervision and Curriculum Development.

Jones, B. F., Tinzmann, M., Friedman, L. B., & Walker, B. J. (1987). *Teaching thinking skills: English/language arts.* Washington, D. C.: National Education Association.

Langer, J. A. (1986). Reading, writing, and understanding: An analysis of the construction of meaning. *Written Communication, 3,* 219–267.

Marzano, R. J., Brandt, R. S., Hughes, C. S., Jones, B. F., Presseisen, B. Z., Rankin, S. C., & Suhor, C. (1988). *Dimensions of thinking: A framework for curriculum and instruction.* Alexandria, VA: Association for Supervision and Curriculum Development.

McGinley, W. M. (1989). *A study of college students' dynamic use of reading and writing to learn.* Unpublished manuscript. University of Michigan, Ann Arbor.

McGinley, W., & Tierney, R. J. (1989). *Traversing the topical landscape: Reading and writing as ways of knowing. Written Communication 6,* 3, 243–269.

Norris, S. P. (1985). Synthesis of research on critical thinking. *Educational Leadership, 43,* 40–45.

Odell, C. (1980). The process of writing and the process of learning. *College Composition and Communication, 31,* 1, 42–50.

Paris, S. G., Lipson, M. Y., & Wixson, K. K. (1983). Becoming a strategic reader. *Contemporary Educational Psychology, 8,* 293–316.

Paul, R. W. (1984). Critical thinking: Fundamental to education for a free society. *Educational Leadership, 42,* 4–14.

Paul, R. W. (1986). *Program for the Fourth International Conference on Critical Thinking and Educational Reform.* Rohnert Park, CA: Sonoma State University, Center for Critical Thinking and Moral Critique.

Pearson, P. D., & Gallagher, M. C. (1983). The instruction of reading comprehension. *Contemporary Educational Psychology, 8,* 317–344.

Rosenblatt, L. M. (1978). *The reader, the text, the poem.* Carbondale, IL: The Southern Illinois University Press.

Rumelhart, D. E. (1984). Understanding understanding. In J. Flood (Ed.), *Understanding reading comprehension: Cognition, language and the structure of prose* (pp. 1–20). Newark, DE: International Reading Association.

Salvatori, M. (1985). The dialogical nature of basic reading and writing. In D. Bartholomea & A. Petrosky (Eds.), *Facts, artifacts, and counterfacts* (pp. 137–166). NJ: Boyton/Cook Publishers.

Scardamalia, M., & Bereiter, C. (1986). Written composition. In M. Wittrock, *Handbook of research on teaching* (3rd ed.) (pp. 321–384). Chicago, IL: Rand McNally.

Shanahan, T. (1980). The impact of writing instruction in learning to read. *Reading World, 19,* 357–368.

Shanahan, T. (1984). The nature of the reading–writing relationship: An exploratory multivariate analysis. *Journal of Educational Psychology, 76,* 466–477.

Shanahan, T. (1988). The reading–writing relationship: Seven instructional principles. *The Reading Teacher, 41,* 7, 636–647.

Shanahan, T., & Lomax, R. (1986). An analysis and comparison of theoretical models of the reading–writing relationship. *Journal of Educational Psychology, 78,* 116–123.

Siegel, H. (1980). Critical thinking as an educational ideal. *Educational Forum, 45,* 1, 7–23.

Smith, F. (1982). *Understanding reading.* New York: Holt, Rinehart & Winston.

Spiro, R. J. (1980). Constructive processes in prose comprehension and recall. In R. J. Spiro, B. C. Bruce, and W. F. Brewer (Eds.), *Theoretical issues in reading comprehension* (pp. 245–278). Hillsdale, NJ: Lawrence Erlbaum Associates.

Spiro, R. J., Vispoel, W. L., Schmitz, J. G., Samarapungavan, A., & Boerger, A. E. (1987). Knowledge acquisition for application: Cognitive flexibility and transfer in complex content domains. In B. C. Britton & S. Glynn (Eds.), *Executive control processes* (pp. 177–199). Hillsdale, NJ: Lawrence Erlbaum Associates.

Sternberg, R. J. (1985). *Beyond IQ: A triarchic theory of human intelligence.* New York: Cambridge University Press.

Stotsky, S. (1983). Research on reading/writing relationships: A synthesis and suggested directions. *Language arts, 60,* 627–643.

Tierney, R. J., LaZansky, J., & Schallert, D. (1980). Secondary students' use of social studies bilogy texts. In D. Schallert & R. J. Tierney (Eds.), *Learning from expository text: The interaction of text structure and reader characteristics* (pp. 13–36). Final report NIE-6-79-0167, US Office of Education.

Tierney, R. J., & Leys, M. (1986). What is the value of connecting reading and writing? In B. Peterson (Ed.), *Convergences: Transactions in reading and writing* (pp. 94–111). Urbana, IL: National Conference of Teachers of English.

Tierney, R. J., & McGinley, W. (1987). Exploring reading and writing as ways of knowing. In *Language and literacy learning* (pp. 19–31). *Proceedings of the 13th Annual Australian Conference on Literacy,* (pp. 19–31). Gosford, NSW: Ashton-Scholastic.

Tierney, R. J., & O'Flahavan, J. F. (1989). Literacy, learning, and student decision-making: Establishing classrooms in which reading and writing work together. In D. Lapp, J. Flood, & N. Farnan (Eds.), *Content area reading and learning* (pp. 297–303). Englewood Cliffs, NJ: Prentice-Hall.

Tierney, R. J., & Pearson, P. D. (1983). Toward a composing model of reading. *Language arts, 60,* 568–581.

Tierney, R. J., Soter, A., O'Flahavan, J. F., & McGinley, W. (1989). The effects of reading and writing upon thinking critically. *Reading Research Quarterly,* 24, 2, 134–173.

Witte, S. P. (1985). Revising, composing theory, and research design. In S. W. Freedman (Ed.), *The acquisition of written language: Response and revision* (pp. 250–284). Norwood, NJ: Ablex.

Classroom Instruction: The Teaching of Thinking

Lorna Idol
Institute for Learning and Development

Beau Fly Jones
North Central Regional Educational Laboratory

Richard E. Mayer
University of California

> *It has always seemed to me that the ability to think critically and creatively is the prime cause for every important discovery that man has made.*
>
> —Albert Einstein

COGNITIVE INSTRUCTION

Rationale

Statistical reports from the U.S. Department of Education (Livingston, 1985; Miller & Linn, 1986; National Assessment of Educational Progress, 1978; 1980; 1983; 1985) reveal disturbing trends in student progress in thinking, particularly as it relates to school performance in reading, mathematics, science, and writing. Although students were reading better in 1984 than they were in 1971, 40% of 13-year-old students and 16% of 17-year-old students had not acquired intermediate reading skills, and they have had difficulty reading the range of academic materials they encountered in school. The majority (61%) of 17-year-old students were unable to perform at the adept level, and few (5%) had advanced reading skills. (Definitions of rudimentary, basic, intermediate, adept, and advanced reading skills are presented in Table 3.1.)

Equally disturbing are the outcomes of student performance for fourth-, eighth-, and eleventh-grade students in writing achievement. On the average, students at all grade levels were unable to express them-

TABLE 3.1
Definitions of Rudimentary, Basic, Intermediate, Adept,
and Advanced Reading Proficiency Levels

Rudimentary— The ability to carry out simple, discrete reading tasks, including selecting
words, phrases, or sentences to describe a simple picture and
interpreting simple written clues to identify a common object.

Basic   — The ability to understand specific or sequentially related information,
including locating and identifying facts, combining ideas, and making
inferences from simple informational paragraphs, stories, and news
articles.

Intermediate— The ability to search for specific information, interrelate ideas, and
generalize from relatively lengthy passages dealing with literature,
science, and social studies.

Adept   — The ability to find, understand, summarize, and explain relatively
complicated information in literary and information passages, including
material about topics studied at school and less familiar material.

Advanced   — The ability to synthesize and learn from specialized reading materials,
such as scientific materials, literary essays, historical documents, and
materials similar to those found in professional and technical working
environments.

Note: From National Assessment of Educational Progress (1985).

selves well enough to ensure that their writing would accomplish its
intended purposes. For any of the three grade levels, average writing
skills were never rated above a minimal performance. (Refer to Table
3.2 for definitions of how writing samples were scored.)

Another content area that should be impacted upon by application of
various thinking and problem-solving skills is in the teaching of science.
Between 1970 and 1973, science performance has shown an overall
decline for 9-year-olds, 13-year-olds, and 17-year-olds; since 1973, de-
clines have been less severe for the younger groups but still declining
substantially for 17-year-olds.

Similarly, mathematics performance has continued to decline for 17-

TABLE 3.2
Definitions for Scoring of Writing Samples

Unsatisfactory — Failed to reflect a basic understanding of the task.

Minimal   — Recognized the elements needed to complete the task, but were not
managed well enough to insure the intended purpose.

Adequate   — Included features critical to accomplishing the purpose of the task and
were likely to have the intended effect.

Elaborated   — Beyond adequate, reflecting a higher level of coherence and
elaboration.

Not rated   — Illegible or otherwise unscorable.

Note: From National Assessment of Educational Progress (1986).

year-olds, although performances have remained relatively stable for 9-year-olds and have improved for 13-year-olds. Perhaps most disturbing about mathematics achievement are the results of international comparative studies of student performance in the developed and developing countries of Belgium (Flemish and French), Canada (British Columbia and Ontario), England and Wales (combines), Finland, Hungary, Japan, New Zealand, Scotland, Sweden, and the United States. American students lagged behind not only high-scoring Japan, but also behind the average of all participating developed countries. It has been pointed out that disappointing performances of American students is likely due to differences in how mathematics are taught in the United States versus in Japan (Travers & McKnight, 1985), with the Japanese placing much more emphasis on conceptual problem solving as opposed to teaching students to simply perform the necessary calculations. These various data all contribute to the growing national concern that American students are lacking in thinking skills, as exemplified in such areas as inferential comprehension in reading, expression of complex ideas in writing, and application of problem-solving skills in reading, mathematics, and science. In order to prevent such disturbing data trends in the future, constructed models and paradigms must be carefully constructed to aid us in offering our nation's children quality instruction to help them think and solve problems more effectively.

This chapter is organized around three central areas of emphasis pertaining to the teaching of thinking. The first section describes the general characteristics of cognitive instruction, as well as those characteristics that are specific to the study of selected content areas. The second area is a discussion of the role teachers play in the delivery of cognitive instruction. Teacher role is described in terms of four metaphors: (a) the teacher as a manager and an executive; (b) the teacher as a guide, directing students' thoughts explicitly; (c) the teacher as a mediator of student cognitive processing; and (d) the teacher as a model for exemplifying the thinking process. The third and final area is a critical analysis of several well-known programs for teaching thinking skills, as well as promising approaches for teaching within the context of learning from text.

Some General Definitions

Broadly stated, *cognition* refers to all aspects of human mental functions (Resnick, 1987). This includes knowledge acquisition, knowledge production, and self-knowledge (Dillon & Sternberg, 1986). *Cognitive instruction*, as defined here, refers to any effort in teaching or in designing instructional materials to help students process information in meaningful ways and to become independent learners. This definition includes efforts to help students construct meaning from text, solve problems, select and develop effective thinking strategies, and take responsibility for their own learning, as well as to transfer skills and concepts to new situations. Accordingly, this definition encompasses research on cognition and instruction in the following areas: composing, concept development, comprehension instruction in reading and content areas, problem solving, decision making, critical and creative thinking, memory, expert teaching, and metacognition.

Cognitive instruction has the *potential* to alter substantially the capability of the learner, especially the low-achieving learner, perhaps as much as microchips have radically altered the capability of the computer. It is therefore imperative to extend the existing educational reform movement to include a major national thrust focusing on cognitive instruction.

GENERAL CHARACTERISTICS OF COGNITIVE INSTRUCTION

Research and theory on thinking has generated a number of key concepts that should be central to cognitive instruction. The following is our effort to define the general characteristics of this emergent movement.

A Model of Learning

Cognitive instruction is based on a model of learning that is emerging from cognitive science, which Resnick (1987) has defined as a loose confederation of psychology, linguistics, and computer science. Each of these fields studies the processes by which humans acquire, transform, and use information (Cole & Scribner, 1974).

In the last decade, there has been an extraordinary confluence of ideas regarding how knowledge acquisition and learning take place. From schema theory, comprehension is understood as an active and constructive process in which the learner is constantly reviewing what is known, linking new information to prior knowledge, forming and testing hypotheses about the meaning of what is read or the problem to be solved, assessing appropriate strategies, and revising concepts as new information is acquired (see Anderson & Pearson, 1985; Rumelhart, 1980; Spiro, 1980).

Parallel concepts have emerged in recent learning theory. We can no longer conceptualize learning as the result of rote memory and mnemonic strategies that merely link meaningless bits of information to one another. To the contrary, memory requires thinking with various levels of processing information for both short-term and long-term storage of information (Jenkins, 1974; Shuell, 1986). In general, the deeper the level of processing, the higher the level of immediate and delayed recall (Craik & Lockhart, 1972; Mayer, 1984).

Additionally, the effective learner uses a repertoire of specific thinking and study strategies to interact with the instructional materials before, during, and after reading or problem solving (Anderson, 1980; Derry, 1990; Schoenfeld, 1985; also see chapter 2, this volume). Novices and poor readers apparently do not develop this repertoire spontaneously (Derry, 1990; Pearson & Raphael, 1990; Rohwer, 1971; also see chap. 5, this volume). Also, low-achieving students are hampered by strongly held misconceptions (Anderson & Smith, 1987; Larkin, 1983; Roth, in press), lack of flexibility (Bransford, Vye, Kinzer, & Risko, in press; Brown, 1980), failures in error detection (Maria & McGinitie, 1982), and ineffective problem-solving strategies (Larkin, 1983).

At the same time, this body of literature on reading and thinking suggests that the capability to learn can be significantly improved by appropriate instruction. By this we mean instruction that (a) builds on the student's existing knowledge base, (b) extends the individual's repertoire of cognitive and metacognitive strategies, and (c) corrects specific learning problems. Metacognitive research, for example, indicates that a major component of effective learning involves planning, comprehension monitoring, and selecting appropriate strategies, as well as effective management of stress and time (Borkowski, Carr, Rellinger, & Pressley, 1990; Paris & Winograd, 1990; Weinstein & Mayer, 1986).

This model of learning differs with traditional instruction, which assumes that the learner is an "empty vessel" into which the teacher must "pour" information. Thus, in traditional instruction, the learner is passive, and meaning is somehow conveyed by teachers' words, not constructed by the learner.

The Goals of Cognitive Instruction

The overall goals of cognitive instruction differ from traditional instruction. In cognitive instruction, the overall goals are (a) to teach for understanding in all subject areas and (b) to help students learn how to learn (Novak & Gowin, 1984). Regarding the first goal, there is much emphasis on helping the learner link the new information to prior knowledge. Where misconceptions are involved, this goal also means striving for conceptual change, that is, changing information and ideas that conflict with the disciplinary view. Regarding the second goal, learning how to learn refers not only to independent application of specific strategies but also to self-appraisal and self-regulation of the process of learning, including efforts to set learning goals and assess what has been learned. These characteristics of cognitive instruction contrast with traditional instruction which, at worst, focus on content covered and, at best, consider transfer and application of specific skills.

The Organization of Skills Instruction

Among proponents of cognitive instruction, there is much debate about the focus and location of skills instruction. On the one hand, the strategy/skills approach argues that it is difficult for most students, and especially for low-achieving students, to learn complex content and skills at the same time (see chap. 5, this volume). Therefore, this approach provides explicit instruction of strategies and skills, usually as an adjunct course, with some thrust, at least nominally if not functionally, to "bridge" or transfer learning to the content areas. This is the approach of the best of the commercial thinking-skills programs reviewed in the final section of this chapter (see also Borkowski et al., 1990; Chance, 1986; Holley & Dansereau, 1984c; Nickerson, Perkins, & Smith, 1985; Perkins, 1990; Pressley & Levin, 1983; Weinstein, Goetz, & Alexander, 1988). It is also the rationale of those using cognitive strategy modification (e.g., Meichenbaum, 1977).

On the other hand, the "dual agenda" approach argues for a focus on content and skills (Jones, Palincsar, Ogle, & Carr, 1987). According to this view, the primary objectives should be content objectives, taught by the content teacher but buttressed by a repertoire of objectives for specific strategies that will help students learn particular content objectives (Paul, Pearson, & Raphael, 1990; Silver & Marshall, 1990; Schoenfeld, 1985; Tierney, Readence, & Dishner, 1985. Proponents of this approach argue that skills and strategies necessarily have content-specific components, that learning takes on a functional meaning and purpose which are lacking when skills are taught as ends in themselves, and that strategies and skills should be taught as means to learning the content objectives.

What distinguishes both approaches to cognitive instruction from traditional instruction is the focus on tasks and skills objectives. Specifically, both the thinking skills approach and the dual agenda approach select tasks that will help students think in order to be able to transform and use information productively as well as to assess and regulate their own learning. Unfortunately, traditional instruction focuses on recall of isolated facts and skills as ends in themselves.

Alignment of the Variables of Instruction

Most proponents of cognitive instruction are careful to align the main variables of instruction: the characteristics of the learner, the characteristics of the instructional materials, the teaching/learning strategies, and the critical tasks (Brown, Campione, & Day, 1981). This characteristic can be seen throughout the chapters in Volume 1 as well as in most chapters in this volume. This alignment is sadly missing from traditional instruction. Too often, low-achieving students are assigned instructional materials and tasks that are too difficult or too easy and simplistic, and the instruction is poorly addressed to helping them build on their prior knowledge, conceptualize what they learn, or become independent learners. Moreover, in cognitive instruction, there is typically more emphasis on informal testing through interviews, conferences, observations, questioning, self-assessment, and coaching rather than the use of standardized tests that may be poorly aligned with instruction.

Phases of Instruction

Noting that the model reader engages in different cognitive activities *before, during,* and *after* focused learning, Anderson (1980) argued that instruction should address each phase of learning. Mayer (1984) labeled these phases of learning and instruction *selection, organization,* and *integration,* respectively. He showed how the teacher can help students to use various features of the instructional materials such as objectives, reviews, and summaries as aids for each phase: to select what is important from prior knowledge and transfer it to working memory, to build connections between important parts (to represent relationships), and to integrate the new information with prior knowledge (see also Weinstein & Mayer, 1986).

These arguments have influenced much of our thinking about quality cognitive instruction. Jones and her colleagues have argued that teachers can sequence teaching/learning strategies for each phase of learning (Jones, 1985a; 1985b; Jones et al., 1987; Jones, Pierce, & Hunter, 1988). That is, teachers can select and sequence specific strategies to help learners prepare for learning, to help them understand and monitor comprehension during focused instruction, and to help them consolidate and extend learning after focused instruction. Thus, the strategic teacher's repertoire of instructional strategies should be, in part, the mirror image of the repertoire of thinking strategies used by the strategic learner (see also Collins, Brown, & Larkin, 1980; Derry, 1990; Tierney, 1983; and Weinstein & Mayer, 1986, for definitions for the repertoire of learning strategies during various phases of learning (see Alvermann, 1987; Anderson, 1987; Beach, 1987; and Lindquist, 1987, for specific strategies in each phase for learning in specific content areas). Additionally, several state and school initiatives purporting to teach the new definition of reading have incorporated this notion of the phases of instruction (Michigan State Department of Education, 1986; Orange County Public Schools, 1988; Wisconsin Department of Public Instruction, 1986; 1989). (For a description of the teaching/learning strategies at each phase, see chap. 2, this volume.)

This notion, that instruction has phases yet is recursive and nonlinear, differs sharply with traditional instruction, which at worst still consists of preteaching specified vocabulary, whether it is important or not (Mezynski, 1983), oral or silent reading, and comprehension assessment (Durkin, 1978–1979). However, many of the recent basals, especially those that purport to teach the whole language approach, may incorporate these phases and iterative cycles of reading, writing, and thinking.

The New Definition of Direct Instruction

Direct instruction is a key feature of most approaches to cognitive instruction, but the definition given to it by cognitive scientists is different from the definition contributed by research on effective teaching. Initially, the term *direct instruction* was part of the acronym for DISTAR (Direct Instruction Systems for Teaching Arithmetic and Reading). Then, Rosenshine (1983; 1986) and others (e.g., Carnine & Silbert, 1979) sought to provide generic definitions based largely on "process/product" research on effective teaching. Rosenshine's definition seems to be the most widely used, emphasizing reviews, checks for understanding and reteaching if necessary, teacher explanations, guided practice, and independent practice (see Rosenshine, 1983, p. 60). The chief limiting factor of this definition for applicability to cognitive instruction is that, in his model and others like it, the focus of instruction is largely on teaching basic skills in reading and mathematics (Brophy, 1988).

More recently, however, direct instruction has been redefined by Pearson and Leys (1985) and others (e.g., Borkowski et al., in press; Paris & Winograd, 1990; Garner, Hare, Alexander, Haynes, & Winograd, 1984; Paris, Lipson, & Wixson, 1983; Schallert, Alexander, & Goetz, 1985; Winograd & Hare, 1988). These new definitions emphasize (a) explicit strategy or skills instruction, namely, teacher explanations regarding *what* the strategy is and *when, where,* and *how* to use it, as well as *why* it should be used; (b) the gradual transfer of responsibility for learning from the teacher to the student; (c) the focus on constructing meaning and problem solving; and (d) both cognitive and metacognitive instruction.

These aspects of direct instruction have emerged from experimental training studies of explicit strategy instruction (see Winograd & Hare, 1988) and very recently have been linked to research on effective teaching by Rosenshine, Harnischfeger, and Walberg (1985) and Brophy (1988). Clearly, there is much overlap between the two definitions of direct instruction, but they have profoundly different implications for curriculum and the role of the teacher especially (Jones & Friedman, 1988).

This is not to say that all cognitive instruction models use either definition of direct instruction. For example, the "reading in the content area" model developed by Herber (1978; 1985) and others (e.g., Singer & Donlan, 1985; Smith, Smith, & Mikulecky, 1978) constitutes an approach to cognitive instruction, but it does not emphasize explicit strategy instruction or transfer of responsibility that are fundamental to the other concept of direct instruction or to the new cognitive strategy/skills concept of instruction. Similarly, the language experience approach developed by Stauffer (1970) and others is a cognitive approach, but it does not focus on direct strategy instruction.

The New Definition of Metacognition

In broad terms, metacognition refers to two dimensions of learning: self-appraisal and self-regulation. This term, too, has been recently redefined (Paris & Winograd, 1990). In the past, metacognition was defined largely as an individual behavior and was not initially linked to motivation. Now, it is defined as shared behavior (thinking aloud), and it includes the learners' beliefs, judgments, attitudes, motivation, and self-concept. Therefore, it is vital for teachers to address beliefs and misconceptions about time and stress management, effective and ineffective strategy use, and so on. Additionally, teachers might focus on direct instruction and coaching to help learners plan, monitor, evaluate, and revise their learning as well as to set goals and evaluate their own learning.

SPECIFIC CHARACTERISTICS OF COGNITIVE INSTRUCTION

This chapter is concerned with the teachability of thinking. In particular, we want to know what teachers can do to help their students become better problem solvers. When students are faced with new problems, we want them to be able to use their knowledge creatively to come up with novel situations.

The history of research on teaching and thinking is a disappointing one, marked by cycles of strong claims and corresponding curricular changes, followed by failure of students to demonstrate transfer and corresponding reaction against meaningful instruction (Detterman & Sternberg, 1982; Mayer, 1987a). From the Latin School movement of the 1700s to the Head-Start Program of the 1960s, the search for teachable aspects of problem solving has generally failed to uncover evidence that students transfer what they have learned to new domains (Mayer, 1987a).

The recently emerging cognitive approach to teaching students how to think, however, offers new techniques for conceptualizing and implementing the teaching of thinking (Chipman, Segal, & Glaser, 1985; Mayer, 1987b, in press; Nickerson et al., 1985; Segal, Chipman, & Glaser, 1985). In particular, this approach requires that teachers address several questions about the characteristics of effective programs of cognitive instruction. The characteristics concern what, how, where, who, and when to teach.

What to Teach?   Instead of the traditional view of thinking as a single general intellectual ability, the cognitive approach views thinking as supported by a collection of many small skills (Gardner, 1983; Sternberg, 1986). This changing conception of intelligence rejects the idea that intellectual ability is a fixed monolithic entity that is not affected by instruction. Instead, for any to-be-taught material, such as arithmetic word problems or the concept of electrical flow in science, specifically relevant skills can be successfully taught (Mayer, in press). For example, in reading, students can learn how to locate main ideas, how to organize main ideas into a coherent outline, and how to relate the main ideas to prior knowledge; in writing, students can learn how to plan, organize, and revise; in mathematical problem solving, students can learn skills for how to represent problems and how to devise and monitor solution plans; and in science, students can learn how to generate and test hypotheses.

To make use of the cognitive approach to intellectual abilities, teachers must change their conceptions of intelligence. Instead of focusing on how much is learned or how much intelligence can be increased, teachers should focus on what is learned and which specific kinds of intellectual skills can be enhanced. Instead of developing techniques to make students smarter in some general sense, teachers should determine the specific cognitive and metacognitive skills that are needed for students to succeed in problem solving for specific target tasks. Thus, a major characteristic of cognitive instruction is that competent skills for specific tasks must be targeted.

How to Teach? Instead of the traditional focus on generating a correct final answer (i.e., the product of problem solving), the cognitive approach emphasizes the process of problem solving by which answers can be developed (Bloom & Broder, 1950; Lochhead & Clement, 1979). A particularly effective technique for teaching problem-solving process is modeling, in which expert problem solvers describe their thought processes for a given problem and the students compare their processes to those of the expert models (Bloom & Broder, 1950; Schoenfeld, 1985). In addition to learning how to use a particular skill, students must learn metacognitive skills such as self-monitoring to determine whether or not a particular skill has helped to solve a problem. Thus, a major characteristic of cognitive instruction is emphasis on teaching the process of thinking.

Where to Teach? Instead of the traditional attempts to teach domain-free thinking, the cognitive approach opts for embedding thinking within specific subject domains (Dillon & Sternberg, 1986; Sternberg, 1985). The emphasis on cognitive instruction within subject domains is particularly relevant for classroom instruction, because it suggests that problem solving should be integrated across the curriculum, rather than segregated into a "general problem-solving ghetto." For example, teaching of problem representation skills must be adapted separately within mathematics, science, writing, and reading.

Similarly, research on problem solving indicates that transfer from one domain to another is rare (Mayer, 1987b). Instead, when teachers teach for transfer, they should expect transfer to occur most strongly for domains that are similar to the target material. Thus, a major characteristic of cognitive instruction is its domain specificity.

Who to Teach? Instead of using meaningful instruction for higher aptitude students and rote methods for lower aptitude students, the cognitive approach suggests helping lower aptitude students to acquire the prerequisite knowledge they need to benefit from meaningful methods of instruction. Students most likely to benefit from cognitive instruction are lower aptitude students who would not acquire the skills under normal instructional methods (Snow & Lohman, 1984). Indeed, Lohman (1986) has found that teaching a thinking skill to a student who has mastered the skill may actually hinder the student's performance. Thus, a major characteristic of cognitive instruction is its appeal for students with special needs (Cermak, 1983).

When to Teach? Instead of regarding students as empty vessels that can be filled with new skills, the cognitive approach recognizes that students come to the learning situation with existing knowledge and skills that may affect the effectiveness of cognitive instruction. Scientific problem solving, for example, depends on replacing students misconceptions with more useful conceptions (McCloskey, Caramazza, & Green, 1980). Further, for any to-be-taught skills, the teacher must determine the relevant prerequisite skills and knowledge. For example, if the teacher wants to teach how to plan and organize a written essay, prerequisites include that the student be able to write legibly and spell correctly. If a student lacks the prerequisites, the teacher should make sure that the student automates the prerequisite skills before moving on to higher thinking skills—such as drilling the student on spelling and handwriting—or somehow remove the constraints imposed by the prerequisites—such as asking students to dictate their essays rather than handwrite them. When students are close to having the prerequisite skills, it makes sense to provide instruction to prerequisite skills before teaching higher skills. When students are years away from possessing prerequisites or when developmental constraints on information processing capacity exist, it makes sense to teach higher skills in a developmentally appropriate way that minimizes or removes the constraints (Case, 1985; Siegler, 1978). Thus, a final characteristic of cognitive instruction is a sensitivity to the existing cognitive skills and capacities of the learner.

In summary, cognitive instruction for thinking focuses on teaching component skills integrated within the context of subject domains. Active methods of instruction are used to aim at students who lack the skills but who have the capacity to acquire them.

CONTEXTUALIZED INSTRUCTION

A theme of this chapter is that cognitive instruction for thinking skills should be *contextualized*—that is, cognitive instruction should be conducted within subject matter areas and within the context of tasks that have meaning for students. For example, this approach suggests that instruction in planning skills such as how to break a problem down into parts, should be adapted to specific subject areas, such as mathematics, science, or language arts—rather than teaching of planning as a general skill that is independent of content area. Further, the principle of contextualization suggests that, within each subject area, planning skills should be taught within the context of substantial tasks, such as how to solve real mathematics problems, how to conduct a scientific experiment, or how to compose an essay—rather than as an isolated skill independent of a larger, meaningful goal. In this section, we present examples of some cognitive skills involved in aspects of mathematics, science, and language arts.

Cognitive Instruction for Mathematics

Mayer (1987) has argued that students need instruction in four major components of mathematical problem solving: problem translation, problem integration, solution planning/monitoring, and solution execution.

The first component, problem translation, involves building an internal, mental representation of each major statement in the problem description. For example, elementary school students have considerable difficulty in comprehending simple relational statements such as, "Tom has five more marbles than Joe" (Riley, Greeno, & Heller, 1982), and college students make errors in representing, "There are six times as many students as professors at this university" (Soloway, Lochhead, & Clement, 1982). Direct training in how to mentally represent relational statements can improve students' mathematical problem-solving performance (Lewis, in press; Lewis & Mayer, 1987).

The second component, problem integration, involves putting the problem information together in order to build a coherent mental representation of the problem. Experienced problem solvers possess schemas for problem types that support problem integration, whereas inexperienced students rely on key words and surface characteristics to categorize problems (Hinsley, Hayes, & Simon, 1977; Lewis & Mayer, 1987; Mayer, 1981, 1982; Riley et al., 1982; Silver, 1981). This research suggests that students need practice recognizing whether a problem can be solved in a way that is similar to a previously solved problem.

The third component involves devising a plan that consists of smaller subgoals and continually monitoring whether one is making progress in carrying out the plan. For example, Polya (1945) and Schoenfeld (1985) have demonstrated how problem-solving heuristics can be explicitly taught to mathematics students.

The fourth component is problem execution—carrying out the needed computations. Although most mathematics instruction focuses on building the skills of problem execution, students often acquire procedures that contain bugs (Brown & Burton, 1978; Sloboda & Rogers, 1987). This work suggests that instruction should focus on helping students to identify and fix the specific bugs that they have in their computational procedures.

Cognitive Instruction for Science

Cognitive instruction for science requires teaching both scientific principles, such as the physical laws of motion, and scientific thinking, such as how to test a theory. Cognitive instruction for scientific principles is based on the idea that students come to the science classroom with preconceptions about the way the world works. For example, students in physics courses may already possess intuitive physics, such as the idea that force is required to keep an object moving (Clement, 1982; McCloskey, 1983; McCloskey et al., 1980). Instruction must help students recognize that their preconceptions lead to incorrect predictions (Champagne, Gunstone, & Klopfer, 1985). However, science instruction must be related to events in the real world so that students do not learn one set of rules for school science and another for outside of school (West & Pines, 1985).

Cognitive instruction for scientific thinking is based on the idea that students often come to the science classroom without scientific reasoning skills. For example, most science students use unscientific approaches to problems involving control of variables or proportional reasoning (Karplus, Karplus, Formisano, & Paulsen, 1979; Thornton & Fuller, 1981). However, direct instruction in the use of scientific reasoning skills, such as control of variables and proportion reasoning, has been effective in improving student performance (Lawton & Snitgen, 1982).

Cognitive Instruction for Language Arts

Based on an examination of how students write essays, Hayes and Flower (1980) have identified three processes in writing: planning, translating, and reviewing. The first process, planning, involves using information from the assignment and from one's long-term memory to establish a plan for producing text. The planning process includes retrieving relevant information, selecting and organizing the most important information, and setting goals. Research on writing shows that, in many cases, writers spend most of their time planning (Gould, 1978a, 1978b, 1980; Scardamalia, Bereiter, & Goelman, 1982). One way to improve the planning process is to insure that students possess accessible knowledge about the topic (Voss & Bisanz, 1985).

The second process, translating, involves producing text that corresponds to the plan. Nystrand (1982) has identified several constraints that can interfere with the translation process including graphic constraints, such as needing to write legibly and syntactic constraints. Such constraints may require such a heavy load on working memory that little cognitive capacity is left over for paying attention to the organization and effectiveness of the text. One instructional approach to improving writing quality is to remove as many constraints as possible—such as allowing students to ignore initially the rules of spelling and grammar as well as the principles of good penmanship (Read, 1981; Scardamalia et al., 1982; Glynn, Britton, Muth, & Dogan, 1982). For example, when students are instructed to get their ideas down on a first draft without worrying about spelling and punctuation rules or proper sentence formation, they ultimately produced higher quality second drafts as compared to students who were asked to write a polished first draft (Glynn et al., 1982).

The third process, reviewing, involves identifying problems in the text and correcting them. Research on writing shows that writers devote little effort to review and often fail to detect errors in their writing (Bartlett, 1982; Gould, 1978b). However, de Beaugrande (1982) provided some promising examples of how students can be given training in how to detect and correct various types of errors. Similarly, computerized reviewing aids may ultimately also come to play a role in improving students reviewing process (Macdonald, Frase, Gingrich, & Keenan, 1982).

THE ROLE OF THE TEACHER IN COGNITIVE INSTRUCTION

As with metacognition and direct instruction, the role of the teacher has undergone significant enrichment in recent years. Although many metaphors capture critical features of various teaching functions, we think the following are most useful.

The Teacher as Manager and Executive

As a manager, the teacher keeps track of student records and attends to issues of time on-task, discipline, and interpersonal relationships within the classroom (Fisher et al., 1978; Good & Brophy, 1984). As an executive, the teacher makes decisions about such classroom issues as diagnosis and prescription, the use of instructional time, the specific content to be covered, lesson plans, and homework assignments, as well as the matching of student levels of achievement to levels of text, pacing, and grouping (Berliner, 1984, 1986; Fisher et al., 1978). Both of these roles are vital to good instruction, as stated earlier; yet, they do not define the knowledge and behaviors for teachers to help students develop strategies and skills, to construct meaning, or to learn how to learn. For these, we must turn to other concepts.

The Teacher as Guide in Explicit Instruction

This role has been defined differently by different researchers. For example, the Beginning Teacher Evaluation Study (BTES) model focuses on presenting the content or instruction, providing student activities, monitoring, and giving feedback (Fisher et al., 1978). Other descriptions include utilizing questioning strategies (Berliner, 1986) and communicating teacher expectations (Good & Brophy, 1984). Rosenshine (1983; 1986) has identified teaching functions that have proven to be successful in experimental and correlational research on teaching: review of the previous day's work and homework, presentation of new content, guided student practice, feedback and correctives, and review of weekly and monthly work. Rosenshine referred to these teaching functions as *direct instruction* (see also Gersten & Carnine, 1986).

The Teacher as Strategist

Jones, Palincsar, Ogle, and Carr (1987) have argued that strategic teaching is a hallmark of cognitive instruction. Strategic teaching has many dimensions. First, the strategic teacher is a *thinker and decision maker.* Expert teachers have well-developed knowledge structures for (a) planning and correcting homework assignments, (b) linking new information and instruction to previous lessons and to prior knowledge of the students, (c) making sure that students understand "why", and (d) anticipating difficulties in learning (Berliner, 1986; Leinhardt, 1986). Additionally, teachers have complex thought processes for making decisions in the classroom that draw upon established routines and frames (Clark & Peterson, 1986).

Second, strategic teachers draw on a *rich knowledge base* to decide what is important, how best to organize and represent the concepts given the prior knowledge of the students, and what works in terms of teaching and learning. Berliner (1986), Leinhardt (1986), and others (e.g., Duffy, Roehler, & Rackliffe, 1985) have documented that expert teachers have internalized repertoires of principles, procedures, and patterns pertaining to the content and to lesson planning in the content that are not available to novices.

Third, the strategic teacher is a *mediator.* Feuerstein and Jensen (1980) have argued that a central function of the teacher in cognitive instruction is to mediate the learner's experiences by interpreting and organizing external stimuli and by guiding the thinking of the student to appropriate learning goals, always aiming toward independent learning. More specifically, mediated learning experiences (MLE) might include helping students observe, select what content is important, represent information, select and plan to use specific cognitive and metacognitive strategies, compare and contrast, monitor understanding, and assess the use of a strategy. This concept of the teacher as mediator in Feuerstein's philosophy also includes a strong emphasis on interactive teaching with much student–teacher dialogue and collaboration with increasing transfer of responsibility for learning.

Feuerstein and Jensen (1980) have maintained that a major difference between low- and high-achieving students is that high-achieving students have had access to mediated learning experiences, whereas low-achieving students typically have not. Much of Feuerstein's work is devoted to refining the concept of the teacher as mediator in helping students represent, interpret, and organize what they perceive.

Similarly, research on student cognitive processing argues that "mediate" refers to the teacher's guidance of students through the thinking processes that are needed for constructing meaning and learning independently (Winne & Marx, 1983; Wittrock, 1983; 1986). Duffy, Roehler, and Rackliffe (1985), for example, have identified some of the ways in which effective teachers help students to construct meaning. Especially important are the teacher's skills in (a) linking new information to prior knowledge, (b) conceptualizing skills and strategies as means to learning the content and not as isolated ends in themselves, (c) focusing on information processing skills, and (d) explaining how ideas are related. Mediation also involves helping students to set standards of excellence for learning objectives. Thus, the teacher serves as "mediator" between the task and the students.

Fourth, the strategic teacher is a *model*. In some descriptions of modeling, it is defined as showing the student how or why to do something in an organized, refined presentation—what would now be referred to as "explaining." More recently, modeling has been defined largely in terms of thinking aloud to express the thoughts, feelings, and attitudes of teachers as they figure something out—with all the stops and starts, puzzlements, revisions, and on-line processing of thinking as it occurs in reality. Modeling of thinking aloud is particularly important in teaching students how to construct meaning (especially because of the nonlinear aspect of thinking), how to monitor one's own thinking, and how to answer a question through reasoning. Modeling also demonstrates how different people may construct somewhat different meanings because they have different prior knowledge and different perspectives about a singular topic (Davey, 1983; Palincsar & Brown, 1985). Therefore, modeling is most effective when two or more persons do it in teacher-student pairs or in small groups.

Fifth, the strategic teacher *plans for student misconceptions*. This concept comes largely from research in science, but it is a powerful concept and one that we predict will be a key concept in other areas of strategic teaching of thinking skills. Anderson and Smith (1987) and Roth (1990) have studied the teaching of science to middle-grade students for several years. A major problem in student achievement in science is that most learners hold very tenacious misconceptions about how the world works. These misconceptions are so strong that they essentially prevent conceptual change from taking place. Even high-achieving students, for example, can master tests on such concepts as photosynthesis and motion, and still not really comprehend that plants make their own food through the process of photosynthesis and that objects do not acquire motion when thrown.

These misconceptions persist largely because (a) they are meaningful to students and (b) the instruction allows students to regurgitate information in multiple-choice questions without any real learning. The primary instructional strategy that facilitates conceptual change is for teachers to confront the misconception directly throughout the instruction in various ways. Before focused instruction, teachers might ask students to give their own explanations of scientific phenomena. During instruction, the teacher provides very explicit explanations and textual materials that require students to understand the correct explanation. Later, the teacher guides the student to compare the new conception to the old misconception in order to render the misconception meaningless and to articulate what was learned. Thus, the concept of direct instruction takes on yet another meaning—specifically, the need to articulate directly what ideas have changed.

Scaffolded Instruction and Mentoring for Apprentices

Collins, Brown, and Newman (in press) have analyzed what they perceive as the most successful models that exemplify excellence in teaching: reciprocal teaching in reading (Palincsar & Brown, 1985), the methods of teaching writing developed by Scardamalia and Bereiter (1984), and the problem-solving approach of Schoenfeld (1985). The "hallmark" strategies that were critical in these approaches were: (a) modeling, especially thinking aloud about how to apply the strategy or skill; (b) coaching, which involves diagnosing problems, prescribing correctives, and providing feedback; (c) inquiry; (d) articulation (getting students to articulate their knowledge and thinking process); (e) reflection about the process of thinking; and (f) exploration (pushing students to extend their learning).

Equally important, Collins, Brown, and Newman (in press) define three *principles of sequencing instruction* that they think are critical for good teaching: scaffolding, increasing complexity, and increasing diversity. In their definition, scaffolding refers to the support the teacher gives to students by carrying out some part of the task initially until they can progress without these supports. These supports may be cues, such as providing frame categories and questions, teacher explanations, changing misconceptions, and coaching. However, fading or gradually removing these supports is essential if students are to become independent learners. Both the content and the task need to be made increasingly more complex and diverse.

Finally, we would like to emphasize a point that Collins, Brown, and Newman (in press) made but did not identify as a specific strategy (such as modeling). The instruction in each of their success models, either implicitly or explicitly, raises and confronts misconceptions about what it is that the model learner does. That is, Scardamalia and Bereiter (1984), for example, noted that children perceive of writing as "knowledge telling"; they write what they know with little reference to planning, revising, or other thinking processes. One reason why Scardamalia and Bereiter's methods work so well may be that they have confronted this misconception directly.

MODEL PROGRAMS/APPROACHES

In the earlier sections of this chapter, we presented our ideas on what constitutes the thinking process, as well as what the generic and specific characteristics of thinking might be. We have also described what the role of the teacher should be in the teaching of thinking skills. In this section, we describe selected model programs and approaches commonly used to teach various thinking skills. An historical precedent in education is that we, as educators, often implement curricular programs without sufficient demand for empirical evidence to support use of the same. As we venture into unmarked and often difficult-to-measure territories, such as the teaching of cognitive process, we would be well advised to halt the practice of widespread adoption without adequate field testing. We need to examine closely any possible evidence to justify use of a particular program or approach before widespread adoption is justified.

In this light, the following is a critique comparing programs using separate curricula to teaching approaches that are used within content area instruction. This critique should aid educators in the selection of model programs and approaches for the teaching of thinking. Particular attention is given to program evaluation, as well as to questions pertaining to the usefulness, adaptability, and predictive outcome of the various programs and approaches. The five programs and four approaches were selected according to two criteria: (a) the program or approach was fairly well known, and (b) the program/approach authors or other researchers/program evaluators have provided some evidence for its efficacy. Once selected, the programs and approaches were analyzed across 11 different criterial questions as described hereafter and as depicted by the categories in Table 3.3. Each program/approach is discussed in terms of how it appears in relation to these categories, examining both strengths and weaknesses of each program.

Criterial Questions

The questions that we used for critique of model programs and approaches included the following:

1. How much evidence of field-testing of the program is available? How much of these data are available to consumers.?

2. What are the specific thinking skills taught in the program or approach?

3. Who is the population that the program or approach is intended for?

4. How much guidance is available for teachers to be able to replicate the program? Is the guidance in the form of descriptive materials and/or training?

5. Are the examples of a varied type available for teachers to use in teaching the lessons?

6. Is there a specified endpoint or expected outcome for each of the subskills taught in the program or approach (Armbruster, Echols, & Brown, 1982)?

7. What is the nature of the materials used in the program or approach (Armbruster et al., 1982)?

8. What are the types of activities engaged in by learners (Armbruster et al., 1982)?

9. How many examples of a varied type are available for learners to practice concepts with?

10. Do the activities promote independent and generalized learning in students (Idol, 1987b; Idol, 1983)?

11. To what degree can the program or approach be fitted within the existing curriculum?

12. How well can the program or approach be fitted within a state or district guidelines for curricular content?

13. Is the program or approach cost effective as measured by actual cost?

14. How much time is necessary for implementation?

15. Is any additional equipment needed for teaching the program or approach?
16. Is staff development needed to prepare teachers to use the program or approach?

We analyzed five widely known and intact programs (Instrumental Enrichment Program, Structure of the Intellect Program, Odyssey Program, Cognitive Research Trust [CoRT], and Tactics for Thinking) and four promising approaches to teaching thinking (mapping strategies, networking strategies, reciprocal teaching, and the SPaRCS procedure). These programs/approaches are listed in the first column of Table 3.3, along with the references for the sources for each.

Efficacy Evidence

The second column of Table 3.3 contains the referential information for any efforts to develop empirical and supporting evidence for use of each program/approach. One program (Instrumental Enrichment) and two approaches (reciprocal teaching and mapping strategies) could be described as having developing beginning research bases. The Instrumental Enrichment Program offers a considerable amount of evaluative effort and one research study. A series of studies have been conducted with reciprocal teaching and networking strategies; three studies have been done with the mapping strategies. (Refer to Table 3.3 for all research and evaluative citations.) Three programs (Odyssey, CoRT, Tactics for Thinking) and one approach (SPaRCS) have only a single research study or a single evaluation effort. The remaining program (Structure of the Intellect) has only brief, anecdotal evaluation reports. With the exception of one program and three approaches, the majority of these programs/ approaches have a severely limited research/evaluation base to support their use.

Characteristic Thinking Skills

The thinking skills contained in each program/approach are listed in the third column of Table 3.3. In general, there is a tremendous amount of variety among the programs/approaches. The programs tend to cover a considerably large number of general thinking skills, whereas the approaches tend to focus on specific thinking skills tied to reading with understanding. In an attempt to summarize, we looked for overlapping areas across the programs/approaches and found that five out of nine programs/approaches focus on teaching reasoning skills (Structure of the Intellect; CoRT; Odyssey; Tactics for Thinking, networking strategies), four directly teach decision-making skills (Odyssey; all three approaches), and four focus on remediation of deficient functions (Structure of the Intellect and all three approaches). At least three out of the eight programs/approaches teach the basic concepts of thinking (Instructional Enrichment Program; Structure of the Intellect; CoRT), summarizing skills (all four approaches), metacognition (Tactics for Thinking; reciprocal teaching; SPaRCS), organizational thinking (mapping; CoRT; SPaRCS; networking strategies), and applying prior knowledge (reciprocal teaching; mapping; SPaRCS).

To our surprise, only two programs/approaches taught divergent/ convergent thinking (Structure of the Intellect; Odyssey), and two taught students how to ask questions (Structure of the Intellect and reciprocal teaching). Some other seemingly important thinking skills were only taught in one of the eight programs/approaches, such as creativity (CoRT), problem solving (Odyssey), and motivation and reflection (Structure of the Intellect). Consumers of such programs/approaches need to be certain of the types of skills they want to develop in an educational curriculum in order to select among these sometimes very diverse programs/approaches.

In returning to the general definition of cognition, provided earlier in this chapter, all of the general areas of thinking (composing, concept development, comprehension instruction in reading and content areas, problem solving, decision making, critical and creative thinking, memory, and metacognition) are taught within at least one of the programs/approaches, but no more than four of them offer instruction in more than one of these areas. Developers of new programs/approaches and authors planning to revise the existing programs/approaches would be well advised to develop new products that are more expansive across these general areas.

Targeted Population

Two programs were designed for use by learners of any age (Tactics for Thinking; Structure of the Intellect), and two more CoRT; Instrumental Enrichment Program) for school-aged to adult learners. The remaining program (Odyssey) was designed for middle-grade students. The reciprocal teaching approach has also been used primarily with middle-grade students, although it has also been used for students from age 8 to 18. The mapping approach has been used with students in grades 3 to 12; likewise, the SPaRCS procedure has been used at various grade levels with both low- and high-functioning students. The networking strategy has been used with undergraduate and graduate students.

Guidance for Program Use

Detailed information on provision of guidance is included in Table 3.2. Four of the five programs for teaching thinking are highly structured, with a scripted teacher's manual included. The remaining program (Instrumental Enrichment Program) is more dependent on specialized training in order to use the procedures correctly. All four approaches require modeling of the procedures; this information is available in the form of videotapes for reciprocal teaching and the SPaRCS Procedure. The procedures for the mapping and networking approaches are described within the research studies testing their efficacy.

Varied Examples

Determination of the degree of varied examples for teaching a concept is important, especially for building a series of examples that will lead to a generalization in learning. This is particularly important for teaching low-functioning students. The approaches to teaching thinking within the context of teaching reading rank superior to any prepared program, because the generic structures of the approaches lend themselves to generation of an infinite number of examples via new and varied reading assignments. When trying to build a program that meets this criterion, it is important not to confuse repetition (e.g., CoRT) with a rich variety of different examples (e.g., Odyssey). In general, the prepared programs suffer from a certain amount of inconsistency; some lessons provide a variety of examples, and others do not.

Expected Outcomes

In spite of the variability of the types of thinking skills taught across the programs/approaches, the expected outcomes for all are fairly common. Five of the nine programs and approaches are intended to correct cognitive deficiencies (Instructional Enrichment; Structure of the Intellect; mapping; reciprocal teaching; SPaRCS). Oddysey and CoRT are also intended to teach specific intellectual skills, but they are not necessarily intended as a being primarily corrective. Another commonality can be seen in that one program (Tactics for Thinking) and all four approaches are intended to strengthen student performance in school curricula.

Types of Learning Activities

All programs and approaches have a student application component with the majority requiring students to use pencil-and-paper activities; the prepared programs tend to require students to use workbooks, whereas the approaches require students to be engaged in the writing process, or in the diagramming process (in the case of the networking approach). Emphasis is placed on class discussion and/or dialogue in three of the programs (CoRT, Odyssey, Structure of the Intellect) and with all of the approaches (reciprocal teaching, mapping, networking, and SPaRCS).

Sufficient Practice Opportunity

In general, the prepared programs are constructed so that teacher demonstration is followed by several opportunities for practice. The number of opportunities per lesson varies both within and across programs, but in general, needed for all are more practice opportunities for the student who is difficult to teach. Such students require multiple opportunities for practice before a concept—particularly a difficult one—is acquired, maintained over time, and generalized to new situations or settings. Here, the strategy approaches have the advantage over the prepared programs. Because of the generic nature of the strategies being taught, the number of opportunities for practice is limited only by the amount of available reading materials.

Promotion of Independent and Generalized Learning

Of all of the criterial questions asked within this analysis, degree of promotion of independent and generalized learning is probably the most important. If students are unable to apply the concepts taught independently and in appropriate new learning situations, then the many hours devoted to direct instruction are wasted. Three of the programs (Structure of the Intellect; Odyssey; Tactics for Thinking) and all of the approaches take this essential aspect of learning into consideration. No explicit plan for independence and generalized learning could be found in the SOI program, and with the CoRT program spontaneous generalization is expected to occur. As with the importance of provision of multiple learning opportunities for slower learners, the importance of a planned program for independent application and generalized learning cannot be overstated. It is interesting to note that with the SPaRCS procedure students are required to demonstrate generalized learning as a part of strategy mastery. With the mapping strategies, students are taught to use them by use of a standard principle of direct instruction; that is, use of a teacher-model, teacher/student-lead, student-test teaching paradigm. To illustrate, first the teacher demonstrates the required skill, then the leader assists the students in using the skills, then the student is required to demonstrate independent mastery. With the networking strategy the teaching of modeling and demonstration and peer interactions are used.

Degree of Fit within The Existing Curriculum

None of the programs were designed for teaching thinking skills within any of the various content areas. Their authors have raised various arguments for this separatist approach to the teaching of thinking, such as that the intent of the program is to prepare the mind (Structure of the Intellect). The only exception is that the Tactics for Thinking program provides examples within content subject areas. In contrast, the approaches are designed for direct use with reading a variety of materials. The networking approach could be used outside of the context of reading, simply as a means of helping students understand the important elements in any lesson. The argument in favor of use of the approaches is obvious; the opposing argument is that the programs offer practice and mastery of a much broader range of generic thinking skills that should be generally applicable.

Cost Effectiveness

Four areas were examined in assessing the cost-effectiveness of the programs/approaches: cost, time requirements, necessary equipment, and necessary staff development time.

Cost. The costs of the programs are extremely varied, as indicated in Table 3.3, ranging from as little as $114 (Odyssey) to over $1,200 for an entire set of materials for 3 years (Structure of the Intellect). The reciprocal teaching program and the networking strategy require no additional costs, and the mapping and SPaRCS approaches require only reproduction costs for the story and critical-thinking maps and graphic outlines.

Time Required. Two programs are designed for long-term use over a 15-month to a 3-year period of time (Intellectual Enrichment; Odyssey; CoRT); other programs provide no time specification (Structure of the Intellect; Tactics for Thinking). None of the approaches are designed for a specified time period; they should be used as long as students benefit from them but no longer than is necessary to achieve mastery, independence, and generalized learning.

Additional Equipment. The amount of additional equipment required for use of any of the programs or approaches is quite minimal. The only exceptions are that some provide videotapes to assist with teacher preparation (Instrumental Enrichment; Tactics for Thinking; reciprocal teaching), and one (Structure of the Intellect) provides a computerized diagnostic service.

Staff Development. Although formal teacher preparation for use of any of the programs/approaches is certainly desirable, the range of training requirements across programs/approaches is considerable. Two programs require mandatory or necessary training (Instructional Enrichment; Structure of the Intellect), and two more recommend training (Odyssey; Tactics for Thinking). Training is unnecessary for the CoRT program. All authors of the four approaches would probably provide training upon request but do not describe it as being absolutely necessary.

Summary. Practitioners, decision makers, and teacher educators all over the nation are responding to the call of researchers and program builders to offer students instruction in cognition. The recommendations seem to fall into three general classes: (a) teach various reasoning skills directly in the classroom (e.g., Ennis, 1986), (b) teach specific strategies to enhance the reading process (e.g., Idol, 1987b; Jones, 1986; Palincsar & Brown, 1985), or (c) identify specific strategies for solving various types of problems (e.g., Bransford & Stein, 1984). The programs/approaches we have analyzed could be placed at various points across a continuum representing these three different recommendations. Some have a beginning research/evaluation base for use of their particular program/approach; others are just beginning to explore the efficacy question. As with all educational reform, practitioners and decision makers won't wait for researchers to offer them the very best plan of operation to use. They are currently responding to this call for direct teaching of cognition and will weigh the evidence as it currently stands.

RECOMMENDATIONS FOR CLOSING THE GAP

Our analyses of the literature, effective teaching practices, and the various programs and approaches have influenced us to favor cognitive instruction that presents immediate relevancy for students, that will aid in general school achievement, and that will enhance generalized application and learning. Such instruction is critical to improving student outcomes, regardless of the particular program or approach that is used, although the contextually related approaches seem to hold the most promise. To change the quality of instruction on a large scale, it is imperative that teacher education in preservice institutions, as well as textual materials and electronic media, focus on cognitive instruction. Such extensive change will not occur without:

1. National recognition of the limitations of existing instruction in schools and teacher education institutions.

2. Efforts in both preservice and inservice teacher development to prepare teachers to offer the kind of instruction described in this chapter.

3. Clarification of how cognitive instruction differs from traditional instruction, direct instruction, and mastery learning.

4. Widespread communication of recent research on cognition and cognition instruction.

5. The dissemination of alternative practices and guidelines for cognitive educators, policy makers, curriculum developers, textbook selection committees, and parents.

6. Assistance to practitioners in making choices from among alternative models.

7. Increased interest in and support for developing high-quality, research-based instructional materials for students to use in the classroom, as well as for teachers as part of their preservice and inservice training.

8. Greater use of cognitive research and researchers among all those groups that make decisions about schooling, teacher education, and publishing.

In summary, cognitive research offers new insights on the learner, the teacher, texts, and tests. This research effectively redefines the characteristics of the model learner, effective teaching, and the processes of reading, thinking, and writing. If educators apply cognitive instruction research and implement the recommendations for increased rigor in the schools, it is likely that all students will benefit, but especially low-achieving students. Moreover, we will come closer to a valued goal: providing quality education for all our nation's students.

TABLE 3.3
Analysis of Model Programs and Approaches to Teaching Cognition
Item One

Model Programs/Approaches	Efficacy Evidence
Instrumental Enrichment Program (Feuerstein, 1978)	Some serious evaluations attempts have been made and are reported in Feuerstein, Rand, Hoffman, & Miller (1980); some evidence that low-IQ students learn to perform the tasks as well as above-average students (Arbitman-Smith, Haywood, & Bransford, 1978)
Structure of the Intellect (SOI) (Guilford, 1967; Guilford & Hoepfner 1971); extended by Meeker (1969) into a design for educational application.	The SOI model was developed through factor-analytic research; the statistical analyses have been cricitized for not adequately separating the many cellular components (Horn & Knapp, 1973; Sternberg, 1977); limited brief reports on its efficacy for teaching are available from the SOI Institute.
Odyssey (Harvard University, Bolt Beranek and Newman, Inc., & the Ministry of Education of the Republic of Venezuela [in press])	One study is available (Harvard University, 1983) that is based on a Venezuelan version of the program; trained students ($n=450$) made substantially greater gains than comparison students ($n=450$) on specially constructed tests; modest gains were shown on standardized tests.
Cognitive Research Trust Thinking Lessons (CoRT) (de Bono, 1973)	Some evidence exists that students who have used CoRT improve on a CoRT curriculum-based assessment (CoRT 2 Teachers Manual, deBono, 1973; Edwards & Baldauf, 1973); no evidence of transfer to science exam scores although correlated gains were also positively correlated to IQ (Edwards & Baldauf, 1973); a study using a modified and expanded program (via more practice opportunities) evidenced limited transfer (de Sanchez & Astorga, 1983).
Tactics for Thinking (Marzano & Arredondo, 1986) (Secondary services include Marzano & Hutchins (1985) and Marzano & Marzano [no date].)	An evaluation study was conducted by the primary author (Marzano, 1986), using teacher-made tests with no reliability or validity data for the instruments. Eighteen thinking skills were evaluated with some effect changes shown for each skill; some field-testing has been done in Walla Walla, Washington (Arrendondo & Marzano, 1986).

Spatial Learning Strategies: Networking (Holley & Dansereau, 1984a; 1984b).

The authors have conducted a series of experiments to test the efficacy of teaching students to use networking (node-arc representations of long-term memory); the effects have been field-tested with college-age students in a series of six different experiments (Holley & Dansereau, 1984b); students have performed significantly better on text processing tasks (Dansereau et al., 1979; Holley, Dansereau, McDonald, Garland, & Collins, 1978). A variant of networking has been tested successfully with hearing-impaired students (Long & Aldersley, 1984).

Cognitive mapping strategies: Story Map and Critical Thinking Map (Idol, 1987a; 1987b; Idol & Croll, 1987).

Three applied research studies are available. The first tested the story map with learning-disabled elementary students (Idol & Croll, 1987); the second with heterogenous groups learning-disabled, low-achieving, and normally achieving students in a third-grade class (Idol, 1987a); the third the effects of using the critical thinking map with secondary-aged special education and remedial reading students (Idol, 1987b).

Reciprocal Teaching (Brown & Palincsar, 1982, in press; Palincsar & Brown, 1984, 1986)

A series of experimental studies has been conducted (see references in column one) and are summarized in Palincsar and Brown (1985)

SPaRCS Procedure (Jones, 1986).

The procedure was developed over a period of 5 years for the CIRCA (Collaboration to Improve Reading in the Content Area) Project (See Armbruster et al., in press; Jones et al., 1985. Field testing occurred in the Chicago Public Schools during this 5-year period; no controlled studies have been conducted.

Item Two

Model Programs/Approaches	Thinking Skills Contained in the Program/Approach
Instrumental Enrichment Program (Feuerstein, 1978)	The six subgoals of the program include: (1) correction of deficient cognitive functions;

(Continued)

TABLE 3.3
(*continued*)
Item Two

Model Programs/Approaches	Thinking Skills Contained in the Program/Approach
	(2) acquisition of certain basic concepts, labels, vocabulary, operations, and relationships for necessary for cognitive tasks; (3) production of intrinsic motivation; (4) production of reflective, insightful thinking; (5) creation of task-intrinsic motivation; (6) instillation in the self as an active generator of knowledge and information.
Structure of the Intellect (SOI) (Guilford, 1967; Guilford & Hoepfner 1971); extended by Meeker (1969) into a design for educational application.	Guilford's three-dimensional model of the structure of the intellect is classified into three general categories with specific sub-areas: (1) Operations a. cognition b. memory c. convergent thinking d. divergent thinking e. evaluation (2) Content a. figural b. semantic c. symbolic d. behavorial (3) Products a. units b. classes c. relations d. systems e. transformations f. implications.
Odyssey (Harvard University, Bolt Beranek and Newman, Inc., & the Ministry of Education of the Republic of Venezuela [in press])	The authors assume that intellectual performance depends on abilities, methods, knowledge, and attitudes. These are organized into six categories of training: (1) Foundations of Reasoning a. observation and classification b. ordering c. hierarchical classification d. analogies e. spatial reasoning and strategies

(2) Understanding Language
a. word relations
b. language structure
c. reading comprehension
(3) Verbal Reasoning
a. assertions
b. arguments
(4) Problem Solving
a. linear representations
b. tabular representations
c. representations by simulation and enactment
d. systematic trial and error
e. thinking out implications
(5) Decision Making
a. the nature of decisions
b. using information
c. analyzing complex situations
(6) Inventive Thinking
a. analyzing and improving designs
b. procedures as designs

Cognitive Research Trust Thinking Lessons (CoRT) (deBono, 1973)

(1) CoRT 1: Breadth—how to broaden thinking;
(1) CoRT 2: Organization—how to organize thinking;
(2) CoRT 3: Interaction—how to assess evidence;
(3) CoRT 4: Creativity—how to escape from imprisoning ideas, provocate new ideas, and define problems;
(4) CoRT 5: Information and Feeling—how to deal with information processes (e.g., clues, questions, guessing, belief, ready-made opinions, and misuses of information);
(5) CoRT 6: Action—Concerned with the total process of thinking.

Tactics for Thinking (Marzano & Arredondo, 1986) (Secondary services include Marzano & Hutchins [1985] and Marzano & Marzano [no date].)

(1) Learning to Learn Skills
(2) Content Thinking Skills
(3) Reasoning Skills

Spatial Learning Strategies: Networking (Holley & Dansereau, 1984a, 1984b).

The networking system is an interactive and spatial learning strategy composed of *primary* strategies, which are used to operate directly on the text material (e.g., comprehension and meaning strategies), and *support* strategies, which are used to maintain a suitable cognitive climate (e.g.,

(Continued)

TABLE 3.3
(*continued*)
Item Two

Model Programs/Approaches	Thinking Skills Contained in the Program/Approach
	concentration strategies) (Dansereau, 1978, 1980; Dansereau et al., 1977, 1979, Dansereau & Holley, 1982; 1984a; Holley et al., 1978, 1979).
Cognitive mapping strategies: Story Map and Critical Thinking (Idol, 1987a, 1987b, Idol & Croll, 1987).	The story map provides practice in organizational thinking to improve thinking and understanding while reading, exemplied by identifying basic/generic story components: (1) characters; (2) setting; (3) problem; (4) goals; (5) actions; (6) outcomes The critical thinking map provides practice in thinking to improve reading comprehension by combining new information with prior knowledge as exemplified by these components: (1) important events, points, or steps leading to the main idea/lesson; (2) the main idea/lesson; (3) other viewpoints and opinions of the reader; (4) reader's conclusions based on items (2) and (3) (5) any relevancy the reader perceives for contemporary situations.
Reciprocal Teaching (Brown & Palincsar 1982, in press; Palincsar & Brown, 1984, 1986)	Reciprocal teaching refers to an instructional activity that occurs in the form of a dialogue between teachers and students regarding segments of text and using four thinking skills: (1) summarizing (2) question generating (3) clarifying (4) predicting
SPaRCS Procedure (Jones, 1986).	The thinking skills taught with the procedure include: (1) surveying and predicting; (2) relating new information to prior knowledge; (3) summarizing

(4) confirming and refining predictions;
(5) self-monitoring of comprehension;
(6) brainstorming;
(7) clarifying; and
(8) organizing and categorizing

Item Three

Model Programs/Approaches	Targeted Population
Instrumental Enrichment Program (Feuerstein, 1978)	Low-functioning (low-achieving and mentally retarded) adolescents; designed for group instruction; ages 11 to adult, but suited for those below grade level (Chance, 1986).
Structure of the Intellect (SOI) (Guilford, 1967; Guilford & Hoepfner, 1971); extended by Meeker (1969) into a design for educational application.	Preschool to adult
Odyssey (Harvard University, Bolt Beranek and Newman, Inc., Ministry of Education of the Republic of Venezuela [in press])	Fourth- to Sixth-grade students who are able to read the materials.
Cognitive Research Trust Thinking Lessons (CoRT) (deBono, 1973)	Students aged 8 to 17 years across intellectual abilities (IQ 80 to 140); commonly used with students aged 9 to 12 years (Chance, 1986).
Tactics for Thinking (Marzano & Arrendondo, 1986) (Secondary services include Marzano & Nutchins [1985] and Marzano & Marzano [no date].)	Students in grades K–12
Spatial Learning Strategies: Networking (Holley & Dansereau, 1984a, 1985b).	Undergraduate and graduate students. (Holley & Dansereau 1984b).
Cognitive mapping strategies: Story Map and Critical Thinking (Idol, 1987a, 1987b; Idol & Croll, 1987).	School-aged students from grades 3 to 12, especially those with severe reading comprehension problems; remedial reading, learning-disabled and other mildly learning handicapped special-education students.
Reciprocal Teaching (Brown & Palincsar 1982, in press; Palincsar & Brown, 1984, 1986)	Experimental studies have been completed with middle-school students with poor comprehension enrolled in Chapter I reading programs, as well as with larger classes with group sizes ranging from 8–18 students.
SPaRCS Procedure (Jones, 1986).	The procedure was intended for whole-group instruction for students at various grade levels, including both high- and low-achieving students.

(Continued)

TABLE 3.3
(*continued*)
Item Four

Model Programs/Approaches	Guidance
Instrumental Enrichment Program (Feuerstein, 1978)	Use of the program requires a specially trained teacher, who is also involved in regular subject-matter instruction; the teacher leads discussion of the exercises.
Structure of the Intellect (SOI) (Guilford, 1967; Guilford & Hoepfner, 1971); extended by Meefer (1969) into a design for educational application.	SOI testing materials are obtained from the SOI Institute; materials are administered to students and then returned to the Institute for computerized grading analysis and diagnostic prescription; the prescription is tied to SOI sourcebooks.
Odyssey (Harvard University, Bolt Beranek and Newman, Inc., & the Ministry of Education of the Republic of Venezuela [in press]).	The teacher' manuals for each of the six books are detailed, including sample scripts for leading dialogue.
Cognitive Research Trust Thinking Lessons (CoRT) (de Bono, 1973)	Lessons are usually taught to groups; lessons are briskly paced; teacher's manual is provided for each of the lesson booklets.
Tactics for Thinking (Marzano & Arredondo, 1986) (Secondary services include Marzano & Hutchins [1985] and Marzano & Marzano [no date].)	Lessons are intended for general classroom instruction; each unit contains a definition of the thinking skill, relevant background information, a rationale for teaching skill, sample strategies, and classroom examples.
Spatial Learning Strategies: Networking (Holley & Dansereau, 1984a, 1984b).	Teacher modeling and demonstration is used to instruct learners.
Cognitive mapping strategies: Story Map and Critical Thinking (Idol, 1987a, 1987b, Idol & Croll, 1987).	In all three intervention studies, the teaching procedures are explicitly described, utilizing direct instruction teaching methodology (teacher modeling, teacher assisting, and student performing independently).
Reciprocal Teaching (Brown & Palincsar 1982, in press; Palincsar & Brown, 1984, 1986)	In the past, the reciprocal teaching program has been criticized for not providing potential consumers with sufficient information in the methology of instruction. Currently, several sources are available for providing teacher's guidance information (e.g., Palincsar, Ogle, Jones & Carr, 1986, which includes a video tape and training material.

SPaRCS Procedures (Jones, 1986).

Teacher demonstration and guidance is used to show students how to construct the frames. A start/stop process is used, especially for students who are having difficulty with the text. The process is that students read a segment of text, stop and assess what they have learned and understood, raise new questions and predictions for the next portion of the text, and then read the next text segment.

Item Five

Model/Approaches	Varied Examples
Instrumental Enrichment Program (Feuerstein, 1978)	Information not available
Structure of the Intellect (SOI) (Guilford, 1967; Guilford & Hoepfner, 1971); extended by Meeker (1969) into a design for educational application.	Each training exercise addresses one or more factors (i.e., combinations of categories from three dimensions); information on the variety of examples within the combinations was not available.
Odyssey (Harvard University, Bolt Beranek and Newman, Inc., & the Ministry of Education of the Republic of Venezuela [in press])	Concepts are taught through several examples.
Cognitive Research Trust Thinking Lessons (CoRT) (de Bono, 1973)	Lessons are organized around one or two related operations, with an occasional lesson for integration and review; examples are included; lesson subdivisions suggest different ways that the skill being taught can be applied; high amount of repetition among activities (Chance, 1986).
Tactics for Thinking (Marzano & Arredondo, 1986) (Secondary services include Marzano & Hutchins [1985] and Marzano & Marzano [no date].)	The number of examples varies from unit to unit, although in general a sufficient number of examples seems to be provided.
Spatial Learning Strategies: Networking (Holley & Dansereau, 1984a, 1984b).	An infinite number of examples are available within texts used and subject areas taught.
Cognitive mapping strategies: Story Map and Critical Thinking (Idol. 1987a, 1987b, Idol & Croll, 1987).	Due to the generic nature of the maps, an infinite number of examples can be applied; the examples are gleaned from the passages/stories/lessons read in school programs.

(Continued)

TABLE 3.3
(*continued*)
Item Five

Model Approaches	Varied Examples
Reciprocal Teaching (Brown & Palincsar 1982, in press; Palincsar & Brown, 1984, 1986)	Examples and definitions of each of the four thinking skills are provided, coupled with samples of dialogue between teacher and students to illustrate the reciprocal teaching process (e.g., Palincsar & Brown, 1984; 1986; Palincsar et al., 1986).
SPaRCS Procedure (Jones, 1986).	An infinite number of examples are available within the texts used; the SPaRCS procedure remains constant for all textual reading.

Item Six

Model Programs/Approaches	Expected Outcome(s)
Instrumental Enrichment Program (Feuerstein, 1978)	To correct cognitive deficiencies such as impulsivity and inaccuracy in student responses to learning.
Structure of the Intellect (SOI) (Guilford, 1967; Guilford & Hoepfner, 1971); extended by Meeker (1969) into a design for educational application.	To determine students' strengths and weaknesses on the various factors of the model and to provide instruction on factors on which performance of students is weak.
Odyssey (Harvard University, Bolt Beranek and Newman, Inc., Ministry of Education of the Republic of Venezuela [in press])	To teach students to perform intellectual tasks that require "careful observation, deductive reasoning, (in precise use of language, inferential use of information in memory, hypothesis generation and testing, problem solving, inventiveness and creativity, decision making and so on" (Nickerson & Adams, 1983, p.2)
Cognitive Research Trust Thinking Lessons (CoRT) (deBono, 1973)	To teach lateral thinking skills (i.e., learning to restructure the problem space) as opposed to vertical or logical thinking (i.e., sequential, predictable, and unconventional).
Tactics for Thinking (Marzano & Arredondo, 1986) (Secondary services include Marzano & Hutchins [1985] and Marzano & Marzano [no date].)	To teach and reinforce thinking skills with the curriculum; to improve a student's knowledge of content by teaching thinking skills.
Spatial Learning Strategies: Networking (Holley & Dansereau, 1984a, 1984b).	To teach students to identify important concepts or ideas in materials and represent their interrelationships and

structure in the form of a network map. Students are taught a set of named links that can be used to code the relationship between ideas.

Cognitive mapping strategies: Story Map and Critical Thinking (Idol, 1987a, 1987b; Idol & Croll, 1987).

Students are expected to eventually:
(1) use the maps independently,
(2) demonstrate maintained and improved comprehension (80% correct or better) without map use, and
(3) generalize improved comprehension to both similar and other types of reading assignments.

Reciprocal Teaching (Brown & Palincsar 1982, in press; Palincsar & Brown, 1984, 1986)

The primary purpose is to facilitate a group effort between teacher and students to bring meaning to text; it is especially intended for improving reading comprehension of poor comprehenders; final expected outcomes are to aid students in constructing meaning from text and to monitor their own reading to ensure that they understand what they read.

SPaRCS Procedure (Jones, 1986).

The goal of the CIRCA Project was to develop instructional materials for teachers and students in social studies that reflected recent research in reading. The SPaRCS procedure provides teachers and students with a repertoire of frames, question, categories, and outlines that can be applied in various content areas and across grade levels.

Item Seven

Model Programs/Approaches	Types of Materials
Instrumental Enrichment Program (Feuerstein, 1978)	An evaluation instrument is provided— the Learning Potential Assessment Device (LPAD), designed to assess learning potential by producing cognitive changes during the testing process (Feuerstein, Rand, & Hoffman, 1979); the program consists of a series of pencil-and-paper exercises clustered into 20 instruments; each instrument focuses on one or more cognitive functions.
Structure of the Intellect (SOI) (Guilford, 1967; Guilford & Hoepfner, 1971); extended by Meeker (1969) into a design for educational application.	An evaluation instrument is available that tests all 27 combinations of the model; instructional materials are available by prescription from the SOI Institute for all

(Continued)

TABLE 3.3
(*continued*)
Item Seven

Model Programs/Approaches	Types of Material
	model factors except the behavioral factor of the content category.
Odyssey (Harvard University, Bolt Beranek and Newman, Inc., & the Ministry of Education of the Republic of Venezuela [in press])	Ninety-nine 45-minute lessons organized into six books, organized by six categories of thinking (see column delineating the thinking skills). A teachers' manual accompanies each book and includes sections on rationale, lesson objectives, target abilities, materials, and classroom procedures.
Cognitive Research Trust Thinking Lessons (CoRT) (deBono, 1973)	Contains 63 lessons within six units, with some variation in format from lesson to lesson; materials include teacher handbook and notes and student textbook and notes.
Tactics for Thinking (Marzano & Arredondo, 1986) (Secondary services include Marzano & Hutchins [1985] and Marzano & Marzano [no date].)	Contains 22 units organized across three types of thinking skills (learning to learn, content thinking, and reasoning); included is a teacher's manual and teacher training opportunities.
Spatial Learning Strategies: Networking (Holley & Dansereau, 1984a, 1984b).	Any materials used for instruction.
Cognitive mapping strategies: Story Map and Critical Thinking (Idol, 1987a, 1987b; Idol & Croll, 1987).	Standard, fictional text from basal reading programs are used with the story map. Any type of fictional or biographical text can be used. Standard, expository text is used with the critical thinking map. The field-testing has been done with a social studies curriculum.
Reciprocal Teaching (Brown & Palincsar, 1982, in press; Palincsar & Brown, 1984, 1986)	Any reading material can be used.
SPaRCS Procedure (Jones, 1986).	Any reading material can be used.

Item Eight

Model Programs/Approaches	Types of Learning Activities
Instrumental Enrichment Program (Feuerstein, 1978)	The focus is on mediated learning experiences of two types: The sequence of instruction is: (1) the teacher defines the nature of the tasks, (2) the teacher presents necessary concepts, vocabulary, and operations,

Structure of the Intellect (SOI) (Guilford, 1967; Guilford & Hoepfner, 1971); extended by Meeker (1969) into a design for educational application.

Odyssey (Harvard University, Bolt Beranek and Newman, Inc., & the Ministry of Education of the Republic of Venezuela [in press])

Cognitive Research Trust Thinking Lessons (CoRT) (deBono, 1973)

Tactics for Thinking (Marzano & Arredondo, 1986) (Secondary services include Marzano & Hutchins (1985) and Marzano & Marzano [no date].)

Spatial Learning Strategies: Networking (Holley & Dansereau, 1984a, 1984b).

Cognitive mapping strategies: Story Map and Critical Thinking (Idol, 1987a, 1987b, Idol & Croll, 1987).

Reciprocal Teaching (Brown & Palincsar 1982, in press; Palincsar & Brown, 1984, 1986)

---

identifying rules, relationships, and strategies,
(3) students work independently with 1:1 teacher/student interaction,
(4) group discussion focusing on developing insight into functions and strategies useful for various tasks and applications of principles.

Specific teaching tasks have been developed for each cell in the SOI model (Meeker, Sexton, & Richardson, 1970), except the behavioral component.

The skills are taught through use of dialogue and written exercises.

Each lesson covers one stage in the total framework; there are two review lessons.

The activities include teacher demonstration and student application.

A networking process is taught that emphasizes the identification and representation of (a) hierarchies (type-part), (b) chains (tones of reasoning—temporal orderings—causal sequences, and (c) clusters (characteristics, definitions, analogies). While constructing the network maps, students are encouraged to paraphrase and/or draw pictorial representations of the important ideas and concepts for inclusion in the network.

The teaching/learning sequence is:
(a) the teacher models how to use the map (model),
(b) students are expected to use the map under teacher supervision (lead);
(c) students use the map without teacher assistance (test),
(d) students continue to complete reading assignments without use of maps to ensure that maintained learning has occurred.

The procedures include:
(1) the teacher and students read a passage silently.

(Continued)

TABLE 3.3
(*continued*)
Item Eight

Model Programs/Approaches	Types of Learning Activities
	(2) the teacher asks question, summarizes, predicts, and asks for clarification.
	(3) a student is selected to replicate the teacher role (described in No. 2).
	(4) turn-taking across students and the teacher, each practicing the teacher role; is continued with teacher guidance.
SPaRCS Procedure (Jones, 1986).	Use of frames and graphic outlining is emphasized; reading and writing are integrated.

Item Nine

Model Programs/Approaches	Sufficient Practice Opportunity
Instrumental Enrichment Program (Feuerstein, 1978)	Information not available.
Structure of the Intellect (SOI) (Guilford, 1967; Guilford & Hoepfner, 1971); extended by Meeker (1969) into a design for educational application.	Information not available.
Odyssey (Harvard University, Bolt Beranek and Newman, Inc., & the Ministry of Education of the Republic of Venezuela [in press])	Teacher demonstration is provided for each lesson followed by several opportunities for practice.
Cognitive Research Trust Thinking Lessons (CoRT) (de Bono, 1973)	Each lesson contains five practice items and three project items.
Tactics for Thinking (Marzano & Arredondo, 1986) (Secondary services include Marzano & Nutchins [1985] and Marzano & Marzano [no date].)	Opportunities are suggested for ways in which students can practice and apply skills; the Classroom Examples section in each unit provides such opportunities.
Spatial Learning Strategies: Networking (Holley & Dansereau, 1984a, 1984b).	The networking map and process can be constructed for an indefinite number of times or lessons.
Cognitive mapping strategies: Story Map and Critical Thinking (Idol, 1987a, 1987b; Idol & Croll, 1987).	Students practice on an unlimited number of readings until they meet a mastery criterion of 80% correct reading comprehension.
Reciprocal Teaching (Brown & Palincsar 1982, in press; Palincsar & Brown, 1984, 1986	There is opportunity for unlimited practice with students practicing the reciprocal process in groups, as well as

applying the four thinking skills as
individual learners.

SPaRCS Procedure (Jones, 1986).   The start/stop process can be used and
indefinite number of times within any
reading lesson or across a variety of
lessons.

Item Ten

Model Programs/Approaches	Promotion of Independent Generalized Learning
Instrumental Enrichment Program (Feuerstein, 1978)	Students are required to work independently with emphasis placed on teacher mediation of feelings of competency and on developing and maintaining motivation; skills are taught in isolated contexts; then bridging activities are presented that are intended to expedite transfer, although such activities don't always occur (Brandt, 1986); there is some research evidence that low-IQ students transfer learning to other kinds of tasks and to everyday problems (Arbitman-Smith et al., 1978).
Structure of the Intellect (SOI) (Guilford, 1967; Guilford & Hoepfner, 1971); extended by Meeker (1969) into a design for educational application.	There are no readily available reports of direct measures of the impact of the training or general school performance (Nickerson et al., 1985); automatic transfer of learned skills via training materials to classroom instruction can not be assumed.
Odyssey (Harvard University, Bolt Beranek and Newman, Inc., & the Ministry of Education of the Republic of Venezuela [in press])	After teacher demonstration, students are encouraged to use the materials independently; in some lessons there are activities called "challenges," where students are asked to apply a strategy on a process in an out-of-school context (Brandt, 1986).
Cognitive Research Trust Thinking Lessons (CoRT) (de Bono, 1973)	Transfer to other domains and subject matter is expected to occur spontaneously.
Tactics for Thinking (Marzano & Arredondo. 1986) (Secondary services include Marzano & Nutchins [1985] and Marzano & Marzano [no date].)	The Classroom Examples section of each session guides students in applying each thinking skill to a variety of content areas.

(Continued)

TABLE 3.3
(*continued*)
Item Ten

Model Programs/Approaches	Promotion of Independent Generalized Learning
Spatial Learning Strategies: Networking (Holley & Dansereau, 1984a, 1984b).	There is evidence (Holley & Dansereau, 1984b) that college students report using the networking strategy in their regular coursework without teacher assistance.
Cognitive mapping strategies: Story Map and Critical Thinking (Idol, 1987a, 1987b; Idol & Croll, 1987).	The Model-Lead-Test, direct instruction teaching methodology and the generic cognitive maps are designed to promote independent and generalized learning. Use of story maps has been reported to cause generalized and improved performance in writing in journals (Idol, 1987a); critical thinking maps have been reported to improve comprehension of similar materials for all tested students, and to different materials for four to six tested students (Idol, 1987b).
Reciprocal Teaching (Brown & Palincsar 1982, in press; Palincsar & Brown, 1984, 1986)	Generalized learning is a primary intent of this approach. The field studies typically include measurement of generalized learning; explicit instruction on how to generalize is not provided.
SPaRCS Procedure (Jones, 1986).	Students are encouraged to use the procedure within teacher assistance. Two types of generalization takes place: (a) generalization to new text segments, as the student continues to apply the same procedure to all new materials, and (b) in phase 3 students are required to summarize the contents of the graphic outline.

Item Eleven

Model Programs/Approaches	Degree of Fit within the Existing Curriculum
Instrumental Enrichment Program (Feuerstein, 1978)	This is a program that focused on preparing the mind to deal with school content later on. There is no effort to relate the skill to a subject-centered curriculum (Brandt, 1986); there is a problem with "bridging" the application of concepts, thinking skills, and strategies to specific learning situations in content instruction; teachers seemingly fail to apply the course's thinking skills and

Model Programs/Approaches	
	strategies to content area instruction; no direction is provided to do this.
Structure of the Intellect (SOI) (Guilford, 1967; Guilford & Hoepfner, 1971); extended by Meeker (1969) into a design for educational application.	The instructional materials have been selected to be relevant to mathematics, writing, and creativity; information on the basis of the selection is not available; there are no directives for applying the components of the SOI model to content area instruction.
Odyssey (Harvard University, Bolt Beranek and Newman, Inc., & the Ministry of Education of the Republic of Venezuela [in press])	The skills are taught independently of course work.
Cognitive Research Trust Thinking Lessons (CoRT) (de Bono, 1973)	Curriculum is taught in isolation from other subject matter.
Tactics for Thinking (Marzano & Arredondo, 1986) (Secondary services include Marzano & Hutchins [1985] and Marzano & Marzano [no date].)	The underlying assumption is that the teaching of thinking cannot be separated from the teaching of content.
Spatial Learning Strategies: Networking (Holley & Dansereau, 1984a, 1984b).	The procedure has been used for teaching a variety of content areas.
Cognitive mapping strategies: Story Map and Critical Thinking (Idol, 1987a, 1987b; Idol & Croll, 1987).	Available reading curricula and content area textbooks are used with the cognitive maps.
Reciprocal Teaching (Brown & Palincsar 1982, in press; Palincsar & Brown, 1984, 1986)	The existing reading curriculum is used to teach the reciprocal process.
SPaRCS Procedure (Jones, 1986).	The procedure has been used for teaching a variety of content areas, including social studies, mathematics foreign languages, and health sciences.

Item Twelve

Model Programs/Approaches	Cost
Instrumental Enrichment Program (Feuerstein, 1978)	Materials for the first year (including four instruments for 20 pupils) is $325; forthe second year (including six instruments for 20 pupils) the cost is $350; for the third year (including instruments for 20 pupils) it is $400. The teacher's guide is $40 for the first year, $50 for the second year, and $55 for the third year.
Structure of the Intellect (SOI) (Guilford, 1967; Guilford & Hoepfner, 1971);	Training materials include source books of lesson plans and teaching strategies

(Continued)

TABLE 3.3
(*continued*)
Item Twelve

Model Programs/Approaches	Cost
extended by Meeker (1969) into a design for educational application.	($12.00), ability training kits of self-instructional modules ($16.00 to $48.00), and memory training materials ($5.00 to $15.00). There is an introductory packet for $67.85.
Odyssey (Harvard University, Beranek and Newman, Inc., & the Ministry of Education of the Republic of Venezuela [in press])	Materials include six teachers' manuals ($15.00 each) and six students' books ($4.00 each).
Cognitive Research Trust Thinking Lessons (CoRT) (de Bono, 1973)	For each of the six lesson areas, the materials needed include the Teacher's Notes selling for $12.50 and the Student Workcards for $19.00. The general Teacher's Handbook is $19.00, and each Student's Text is $8.50. The total package costs $185.00.
Tactics for Thinking (Marzano & Arredondo, 1986) (Secondary services include Marzano & Nutchins [1985] and Marzano & Marzano [no date].)	The Teacher's Manual costs $12.00; the Training Manual costs $35.00. Videotapes are available for $545.00 (A special preview tape is available for 2-day loan for $20.00).
Spatial Learning Strategies: Networking (Holley & Dansereau, 1984a, 1984b).	The only cost is that of the curriculum used for applying the networking strategy.
Cognitive Mapping strategies: Story map and Critical Thinking (Idol, 1987a, 1987b; Idol & Croll, 1987).	The only cost is that of the curriculum used for reading and content area instruction.
Reciprocal Teaching (Brown & Palincsar 1982, in press; Palincsar & Brown, 1984, 1986)	The only cost is that of the curriculum used for reading and content area instruction.
SPaRCS Procedure (Jones, 1986)	The only cost is that of the curriculum used for reading and content area instruction.

Item Thirteen

Model Programs/Approaches	Time Required
Instrumental Enrichment (Feuerstein, 1978)	The tasks on the program take from 200 to 300 hours to complete to be used in a 2- or 3-year program; the program typically takes 5 hours per week.

Structure of the Intellect (SOI) (Guilford, 1967; Guilford & Hoepfner, 1971); extended by Meeker (1969) into a design for educational application.

Two half-hour lessons per week are recommended.

Odyssey (Harvard University, Beranek and Newman, Inc., & the Ministry of Education of the Republic of Venezuela [in press])

Three to four lessons per week over a 2-year period; each lesson lasts about 45 minutes.

Cognitive Research Trust Thinking Lessons (CoRT) (de Bono, 1973)

Each lesson takes about 35 minutes covering one lesson per week with a total of 63 lessons; according to one manual it would take about 15 months to complete the program at this pace; more time than this is probably needed; a second source (Chance, 1986) says it would take 2 years to complete the program.

Tactics for Thinking (Marzano & Arredondo, 1986) (Secondary services include Marzano & Nutchins [1985] and Marzano & Marzano [no date].)

The time for teaching each unit is not specified and will vary depending on how much of each unit is used.

Spatial Learning Strategies: Networking (Holley & Dansereau, 1984a, 1984b).

Not specified although type (textbook chapters) and length (passages of 2500 words or more) appear to be important variables.

Cognitive mapping strategies: Story map and Critical Thinking (Idol, 1987a, 1987b; Idol & Croll, 1987).

Field-tests studies averaged 30–40 minutes of instruction and independent reading per school day.

Reciprocal Teaching (Brown & Palincsar 1982, in press; Palincsar & Brown, 1984, 1986)

Most sessions reported in the studies had lessons of approximately 30 minutes each.

SPaRCS Procedure (Jones, 1986).

Indefinite depending on teacher discretion and student ability.

Item Fourteen

Model Programs/Approaches	Additional Equipment
Instrumental Enrichment (Feuerstein, 1978)	None described although several school districts (e.g., Detroit public schools) have developed video tapes to assist teachers in training.
Structure of the Intellect (SOI) (Guilford, 1967; Guilford & Hoepfner, 1971); extended by Meeker (1969) into a design for educational application.	Student use of materials is prescribed based on an diagnostic test; computer software gives analyses and prescriptions; these analyses are provided by the SOI for a fee.

(Continued)

TABLE 3.3
(*continued*)
Item Fourteen

Model Programs/Approaches	Additional Equipment
Odyssey (Harvard University, Beranek and Newman, Inc., & the Ministry of Education of the Republic of Venezuela [in press])	None required.
Cognitive Research Trust Thinking Lessons (CoRT) (de Bono, 1973)	None required.
Tactics for Thinking (Marzano & Arredondo, 1986) (Secondary services include Marzano & Nutchins [1985] and Marzano & Marzano [no date].)	Video tape player equipment and overhead projector.
Spatial Learning Strategies: Networking (Holley & Dansereau, 1984a, 1984b).	None required.
Cognitive mapping strategies: Story Map and Critical Thinking (Idol, 1987a, 1987b; Idol & Croll, 1987).	An overhead projector was used for group instruction of map usage (Idol & Croll, 1987).
Reciprocal Teaching (Brown & Palincsar 1982, in press; Palincsar & Brown, 1984, 1986)	None required.
SPaRCS Procedure (Jones, 1986).	The graphic outlines are presented in handouts or on a chalkboard.

Item Fifteen

Model Programs/Approaches	Staff Development Time
Instrumental Enrichment (Feuerstein, 1978)	Teacher training is mandatory; some say teachers need to be intelligent in order to facilitate the complexities of the program (Chance, 1986). Teacher training involves a minimum of 45 hours per year. Teacher training costs for an individual teacher is $300 plus the cost of the teacher's materials; for 10 or more teachers the cost is $250 plus materials cost.
Structure of the Intellect (SOI) (Guilford, 1967; Guilford & Hoepfner, 1971); extended by Meeker (1969) into a design for educational application.	All training is provided by the SOI Institute for a fee.
Odyssey (Harvard University, Beranek and Newman, Inc., the Ministry of Education of the Republic of Venezuela [in press])	Formal training is considered desirable and is offered & through the publisher; the teacher's manual provides detailed suggestions for conducting the lessons so

	that teachers could use the materials without formal training.
Cognitive Research Trust Thinking Lessons (CoRT) (de Bono, 1973)	No additional training is recommended, although it may be necessary to relate the separate curriculum to content area instruction.
Tactics for Thinking (Marzano & Arredondo, 1986) (Secondary services include Marzano & Hutchins [1985] and Marzano & Marzano [no date].)	It is recommended that formal training be offered to teachers who will use this curriculum. The cost of 3-day training sessions is $300.
Spatial Learning Strategies: Networking (Holley & Dansereau, 1984a, 1984b).	Teacher training is needed to develop skills in: (1) presentation of content strategy usage. (2) expert modeling. (3) interactive peer modeling (Holley & Dansereau, 1984b).
Cognitive mapping strategies: Story Map and Critical Thinking (Idol, 1987a, 1987b; Idol & Croll, 1987).	The information is not in the literature. (Personal communication: 2–4 hours of staff development time), training sometimes available upon request.
Reciprocal Teaching (Brown & Palincsar 1982, in press; Palincsar & Brown, 1984, 1986)	A major criticism is that teachers seem to need a lot of practice in learning to lead the dialogue and accompanying trainer's manual require approximately 60 mintues of time; in addition, discussion and practice are needed. Training sometimes available upon request.
SPaRCS Procedure (Jones, 1986).	

REFERENCES

Alvermann, D. (1987). Strategic teaching in social studies. In B. F. Jones, A. S. Palincsar, D. S. Ogle, & E. G. Carr (Eds.), *Strategic teaching and learning: Cognitive instruction in the content areas* (pp. 92–110). Alexandria, VA: Association for Supervision and Curriculum Development.

Anderson, C. W. (1987). Strategic teaching in science. In B. F. Jones, A. S. Palincsar, D. S. Ogle, & E. G. Carr (Eds.), *Strategic teaching and learning: Cognitive instruction in the content areas* (pp. 73–91). Alexandria, VA: Association for Supervision and Curriculum Development.

Anderson, C. W., & Smith, L. (1987). Teaching science. In V. Richardson-Koehler (Ed.), *The educator's handbook: A research perspective* (pp. 84–112). New York: Longman.

Anderson, R. C., & Pearson, P. D. (1985). A schema-theoretic view of basic processes in reading comprehension. In P. D. Pearson (Ed.), *Handbook of reading research* (pp. 255–292). New York: Longman.

Arbitman-Smith, R., Haywood, H. C., & Bransford, J. D. (1978). Assessing cognitive change. In C. M. McCauley, R. Pserber, & P. Brooks (Eds.), *Learning and cognition in the mentally retarded.* Baltimore, MD: University Park Press.

Armbruster, B. B., Anderston, T. H., Cox, B. E., Friedman, L. B., Jones, B. F., Karlin, S., Kazarian, M., Martin, B., Osborn, J., & Walker, B. J. (in press). *The collaboration to improve reading in the content area. The CIRCA project: A description.* (Tech. Rep.), Urbana, IL: University of Illinois, Center for the Study of Reading.

Armbruster, B. B., Echols, L. H., & Brown, A. L. (1982). The role of metacognition in reading to learn: A developmental perspective. *Volta Review, 84,* 46–56.

Arredondo, D. E., & Marzano, R. J. (1986). One district's approach to implementing a comprehensive K–12 thinking skills program. *Educational Leadership, May,* 28–30.

Bartlett, E. J. (1982). Learning to revise: Some component processes. In M. Nystrand (Ed.), *What writers know* (pp. 345–364). New York: Academic Press.

Beach, R. (1987). Strategic teaching in literature. In B. F. Jones, A. S. Palincsar, D. S. Ogle, & E. G. Carr (Eds.), *Strategic teaching and learning: Cognitive instruction in the content areas* (pp. 135–160). Alexandria, VA: Association for Supervision and Curriculum Development.

Berliner, D. C. (1984). The half-full glass: A review of research in teaching. In P. L. Hosford (Ed.), *Using what we know about teaching* (pp. 51–77). Alexandria, VA: Association for Supervision and Curriculum Development.

Berliner, D. C. (1986). In pursuit of the expert pedagogue. *Educational Researcher, 15,* 5–4.

Bloom, B. S., & Broder, L. H. (1950). *Problem solving processes of college students.* Chicago: University of Chicago Press.

Brandt, R. (1986). On creativity and thinking skills: A conversation with David Perkins. *Educational Leadership, May,* 12–18.

Bransford, J. D., & Stein, B. S. (1984). *The IDEAL problem solver.* New York: D. H. Freeman.

Brophy, J. (1988). Research linking teacher behavior to student achievement: Potential implications for instruction of Chapter 1 students. *Educational Psychologist, 23,* 235–286.

Brown, A. L. (1980). Metacognitive development and reading. In R. J. Spiro, B. C. Bruce, & W. F. Brewer (Eds.), *Theoretical issues in reading comprehension* (pp. 453–483). Hillsdale, NJ: Lawrence Erlbaum Associates.

Brown, A. L., Campione, J. C., & Day, J. (1981). Learning to learn: On training students to learn from texts. *Educational Researcher, 10,* 14–24.

Brown, A. L., & Palincsar, A. S. (1982). Inducing strategic learning from text by means of informed, self-control training. *Topics in Learning and Learning Disabilities, 2*(1), 1–17.

Brown, A. L., & Palincsar, A. S. (in press). Guided cooperative learning and individual knowledge acquisition. In L. B. Resnick (Ed.), *Cognition and instruction: Issues and agenda.* Hillsdale, NJ: Lawrence Erlbaum Associates.

Brown, J. S., & Burton, R. R. (1978). Diagnostic models for procedural bugs in basic mathematics skills. *Cognitive Science, 2,* 155–192.

Carnine, D., & Silbert, J. (1979). *Direct instruction reading.* Columbus, OH: Charles E. Merrill.

Case, R. (1985). A developmentally based approach to the problem of instructional design. In S. F. Chipman, J. W. Segal, & R. Glaser (Eds.), *Thinking and learning skills (Vol. 2): Research and open questions. Hillsdale, NJ: Lawrence Erlbaum Associates.*

Cermak, L. S. (1983). *Information processing deficits in children with learning disabilities. Journal of Learning Disabilities, 16,* 599–605.

Champagne, A. B., Gunstone, R. F., & Klopfer, L. E. (1985). Effecting changes in cognitive structure among physics students. In H. T. West & A. L. Pines (Eds.), *Cognitive structure and conceptual change* (pp. 61–90). Orlando, FL: Academic Press.

Chance, P. (1986). *Thinking in the classroom: A survey of programs.* New York: Teachers College Press.

Chipman, S. F., & Segal, J. W., & Glaser, R. (1985). *Thinking and learning skills (Vol. 2): Research and open questions.* Hillsdale, NJ: Lawrence Erlbaum Associates.

Clark, C. M., & Peterson, P. L. (1986). Teachers' thought processes. In M. C. Wittrock (Ed.), *Handbook of research on teaching* (pp. 235–296). New York: Macmillan.

Clement, J. (1982). Students' preconceptions in introductory mechanics. *American Journal of Physics, 50,* 66–71.

Cole, M., & Scribner, S. (1974). *Culture and thought: A psychological introduction.* New York: Wiley.

Collins, A., Brown, J. S., & Larkin, K. M. (1980). Inferences in text understanding. In R. J. Spiro, B. C. Bruce, & W. F. Brewer (Eds.), *Theoretical issues in reading comprehension* (pp. 385–410). Hillsdale, NJ: Lawrence Erlbaum Associates.

Collins, A., Brown, J. S., & Newmann, S. (in press). Cognitive apprenticeship: Teaching the craft of reading, writing, and mathematics. In L. Resnick (Ed.), *Knowing, learning, and instruction: Essays in honor of Robert Glaser.* Hillsdale, NJ: Lawrence Erlbaum Associates.

Craik, F. I. M., & Lockhart, R. S. (1972). Levels of processing: A framework for memory research. *Journal of Verbal Learning and Verbal Behavior, 11,* 671–684.

Dansereau, D. F. (1978). The development of a learning strategies curriculum. In H. F. O'Neil, Jr. (Ed.), *Learning strategies* (pp. 3–19). New York: Academic Press.

Dansereau, D. F. (1985). Learning strategy research. In J. W. Segal, S. F. Chipman, & R. Glaser (Eds.), *Thinking and learning skills: Relating instruction to research (Vol. 1)* (pp. 209–240). Hillsdale, NJ: Lawrence Erlbaum Associates.

Dansereau, D. F., & Holley, C. D. (1982). Development and evaluation of a text mapping strategy. In A. Flammer & W. Kintsch (Eds.), *Discourse processing.* Amsterdam: North-Holland.

Dansereau, D. F., McDonald, B. A., Collins, K. W., Garland, J. C., Holley, C. D., Diekhoff, G. M., & Evans, S. H. (1979). Evaluation of a learning strategy system. In H. F. O'Neil, Jr., & C. D. Spielberger (Eds.), *Cognitive and affective learning strategies* (pp. 3–44). New York: Academic Press.

Davey, B. (1983, October). Think aloud-modeling the cognitive processes of reading comprehension. *Journal of Reading, 27*(1), 44–47.

de Beaugrande, R. (1982). Psychology and composition: Past, present, and future. In M. Nystrand (Ed.), *What writers know.* (pp. 211–268) New York: Academic Press.

de Bono, E. (1973). *CoRT Thinking.* New York: Pergamon Press.

de Sanchez, M. A., & Astorga, M. (1983). *Pyroecto aprender apensar: Estudio de sus efectos sobre una muestra de estadiantes venezolanos.* Caracas, Venezuela: Ministerio de Educacion.

Detterman, D. K., & Sternberg, R. J. (1982). *How and how much can intelligence be increased?* Hillsdale, NJ: Lawrence Erlbaum Associates.

Dillon, R. F., & Sternberg, R. J. (1986). *Cognition and instruction.* New York: Academic Press.

Duffy, G. G., Roehler, L. R., & Rackliffe, G. (1985, April). *Student cognitive processing of teacher explanations during reading instruction.* Paper presented at the annual meeting of the American Educational Research Association, Chicago.

Durkin, D. (1978–1979). What classroom observations reveal about reading comprehension instruction. *Reading Research Quarterly, 15,* 481–533.

Edwards, J., & Baldauf, R. B. (1983). Teaching science in a secondary science. In W. Maxwell (Ed.), *Thinking: The expanding frontier.* Philadelphia: The Franklin Institute.

Ennis, R. H. (1986). A taxonomy of critical thinking dispositions and abilities. In J. Baron & R. Sternberg (Eds.), *Teaching for thinking.* New York: D. H. Freeman.

Feuerstein, R. (1978). *Just a minute . . . Let me think.* Baltimore, MD: University Park Press.

Feuerstein, R., & Jensen, M. R. (1980). Instrumental enrichment: Theoretical basis, goals, and instruments. *The Educational Forum, 46,* 401–423.

Feuerstein, R., Rand, Y., & Hoffman, M. (1979). *The dynamic assessment of retarded performers: The learning potential assessment device.* Baltimore, MD: University Park Press.

Feuerstein, R., Rand, Y., Hoffman, M., & Miller, R. (1980). *Instructional enrichment*. Baltimore: University Park Press.

Fisher, C., Berliner, D. C., Filby, N., Marliave, R., Cahen, L., Dishaw, M., & Moore, J. (1978). *Teaching and learning in elementary schools: A summary of the beginning teacher evaluation study*. San Francisco: Far West Laboratory.

Gardner, H. (1983). *Frames of mind*. New York: Basic Books.

Garner, R., Hare, V. C., Alexander, P., Haynes, J., & Winograd, P. N. (1984). Inducing use of a text lookback strategy among unsuccessful readers. *American Educational Research Journal 21*, 789–798.

Gersten, R., & Carnine, D. (1986). Direct instruction in reading comprehension. *Educational Leadership, 43*, 70–78.

Glynn, S. M., Britton, B. K., Muth, D., & Dogan, N. (1982). Writing and revising persuasive documents: Cognitive demands. *Journal of Educational Psychology, 74*, 557–567.

Good, T. L., & Brophy, J. E. (1984). *Looking in classrooms*. Cambridge, MA: Harper & Row.

Gould, J. D. (1978a). How experts dictate. *Journal of Experimental Psychology: Human Perception and Performance, 4*, 648–661.

Gould, J. D. (1978b). An experimental study of writing, dictating, and speaking. In J. Requien (Ed.), *Attention and performance VII*. (pp. 299–319). Hillsdale, NJ: Lawrence Erlbaum Associates.

Gould, J. D. (1980). Experiments on composing letters: Some facts, some myths, and some observations. In L. W. Gregg & E. R. Steinberg (Eds.), *Cognitive processes in writing* (pp. 97–127). Hillsdale, NJ: Lawrence Erlbaum Associates.

Guilford, J. P. (1967). *The nature of human intelligence*. New York: McGraw-Hill.

Guilford, J. P., & Hoepfner, R. (1971). *The analysis of intelligence*. New York: McGraw-Hill.

Harvard University. (1983). *Project intelligence: The development of procedures to enhance thinking skills*. Final Report, submitted to the Minister for the Development of Human Intelligence, Republica of Venezuela.

Harvard University, Bolt Beranek and Newman, Inc., & the Ministry of Education of the Republic of Venezuela. (in press). *Odyssey: A curriculum for thinking (Foundations of reasoning; Understanding language; Verbal reasoning; Problem solving; Decision making; Inventive thinking)*. Watertown, MA: Mastery Education Corp.

Hayes, J. R. & Flower, L. S. (1980). Identifying the organization of writing processes. In L. W. Gregg & E. R. Steinberg (Eds.), *Cognitive processes in writing*. (pp. 3–30). Hillsdale, NJ: Lawrence Erlbaum Associates.

Herber, H. L. (1978). *Reading in the content areas*. (Text for teachers). Englewood Cliffs, NJ: Prentice-Hall.

Herber, H. L. (1985). Developing reading and thinking skills in content areas. In J. W. Segal, S. F. Chipman, & R. Glaser, (Eds.), *Thinking and learning skills: Relating research to instruction* (Vol. 1, pp. 297–316). Hillsdale, NJ: Lawrence Erlbaum Associates.

Hinsley, D., Hayes, J. R., & Simon, H. A. (1977). From words to equations. In M. Just & P. Carpenter (Eds.), *Cognitive processes in comprehension* (pp. 89–108). Hillsdale, NJ: Lawrence Erlbaum Associates.

Holley, C. D., & Dansereau, D. F. (1984a). The development of spatial learning strategies. In C. D. Holley & D. F. Dansereau (Eds.), *Spatial learning strategies* (pp. 3–19). New York: Academic Press.

Holley, C. D., & Dansereau, D. F. (1984b). Networking: The technique and the empirical evidence. In C. D. Holley & D. F. Dansereau (Eds.), *Spatial learning strategies* (pp. 81–108). New York: Academic Press.

Holley, C. D., & Dansereau, D. F. (1984c). *Spatial learning strategies: Techniques, applications, and related issues*. New York: Academic Press.

Holley, C. D., Dansereau, D. F., McDonald, B. A., Garland, J. C., & Collins, K. W. (1978).

Networking as an information processing approach to classroom performance. Paper presented at the Southern Educational Research Association Annual Meeting, Austin, TX.

Holley, C. D., Dansereau, D. F., McDonald, B. A., Garland, J. C., & Collins, K. W. (1979). Evaluation of a hierarchical mapping technique as an aid to prose processing. *Contemporary Educational Psychology, 4,* 227–237.

Horn, J. L., & Knapp, J. R. (1973). On the subjective character of the empirical base of Guilford's structure-of-intellect mode. *Psychological Bulletin, 80*(1), 33–43.

Idol, L. (1983). *Special educator's consultation handbook.* Austin, TX: PRO-ED.

Idol, L. (1987a). Group story mapping: A comprehension strategy for both skilled and unskilled readers. *Journal of Learning Disabilities, 20,* 196–205.

Idol, L. (1987b). A critical thinking map to improve content area comprehension of poor readers. *Remedial and Special Education, 8*(4), 28–40.

Idol, L., & Croll, V. J. (1987). The effects of training in story mapping procedures on the reading comprehension of poor readers. *Learning Disability Quarterly, 10*(3), 214–230.

Jenkins, J. (1974). Remember that old theory of memory? Well, forget it! *American Psychologists, 29,* 785–795.

Jones, B. F. (1985a). Reading and thinking: In A. Costa (Ed.), *Developing minds: A resource book for teaching thinking* (pp. 108–113). Alexandria, VA: Association for Supervision and Curriculum Development.

Jones, B. F. (1985b). Response instruction. In T. L. Harris & E. J. Cooper (Eds.), *Reading, thinking, and conceptual development: Strategies for the classroom* (pp. 105–128). New York: The College Board.

Jones, B. F. (1986). SPaRCS procedure. In A. S. Palincsar, D. S. Ogle, B. F. Jones, & E. G. Carr (Eds.), *Facilitator's manual for teaching reading as thinking* (pp. 18–27). Alexandria, VA: Association for Supervision and Curriculum Development.

Jones, B. F., Amiran, M. R., & Katims, M. (1985). Teaching cognitive strategies and text structures within language arts programs. In J. Segal, S. F. Chipman, & R. Glaser (Eds.), *Thinking and learning skills: Relating instruction to research* (Vol. 1, pp. 259–296). Hillsdale, NJ: Lawrence Erlbaum Associates.

Jones, B. F., & Friedman, L. (1988). Active instruction for students on merging process–outcome and cognitive perspectives. *Educational Psychologist, 23,* 299–308.

Jones, B. F., Palincsar, A. S., Ogle, D. S., & Carr, E. G. (1987). *Strategic teaching and learning: Cognitive instruction in the content areas.* Alexandria, VA: Association for Supervision and Curriculum Development.

Jones, B. F., Pierce, J., & Hunter, B. (1988). Teaching students to construct graphic representations. *Educational Leadership, 46* (4), 20–25.

Karplus, R., Karplus, E., Formisano, M., & Paulsen, A. (1979). Proportional reasoning and control of variables in seven countries. In J. Lochhead & J. Clement (Eds.), *Cognitive process instruction: Research on teaching thinking skills* (pp. 47–104). Philadelphia: Franklin Institute Press.

Larkin, J. (1983). Research on science education. In A. M. Lesgold & F. Reif (Eds.), *Computers in education: Realizing the potential* (pp. 95–108). (Report of a research conference.) Washington, DC: Office of the Assistant Secretary for Educational Research and Improvement.

Lawton, A., & Snitgen, D. A. (1982). Teaching formal reasoning in a college biology course for preservice teachers. *Journal of Research in Science Teaching, 19,* 233–248.

Leinhardt, G. (1986). Expertise in mathematics teaching. *Educational Leadership, 43,* 23–27.

Lewis, A. B. (in press). Effects of training on students' representation of compare word problems. *Journal of Educational Psychology.*

Lewis, A. B., & Mayer, R. E. (1987). Students' miscomprehension of relational statements in arithmetic word problems. *Journal of Educational Psychology, 79,* 363–371.

Lindquist, M. M. (1987). Strategic teaching in mathematics. In B. F. Jones, A. S. Palincsar, D. S. Ogle, & E. G. Carr (Eds.), *Strategic teaching and learning: Cognitive instruction in the content areas* (pp. 111–134). Alexandria, VA: Association for Supervision and Curriculum Development.

Livingstone, I. D. (1985). *Perceptions of the intended and implemented mathematics curriculum.* A report of the Second International Mathematics Study prepared by the members of the International Association for the Evaluation of Educational Achievement for the U. S. Department of Education, Center for Statistics.

Lochhead, J., & Clement, J. (Eds.). (1979). *Cognitive process instruction.* Philadelphia: Franklin Institute Press.

Long, G., & Aldersly, S. (1984). In C. D. Holley & D. F. Dansereau (Eds.), *Spatial learning strategies* (pp. 109–126). New York: Academic Press.

MacDonald, N. H., Frase, L. T., Gingrich, P. S., & Keenan, S. A. (1982). The writer's workbench: Computer aids for text analysis. *Educational Psychologist, 17,* 172–179.

Maria, K., & McGinitie, W. H. (1982). Reading comprehension disabilities, knowledge structures, and non-accommodating text processing strategies. *Annals of Dyslexia, 32,* 33–59.

Marzano, R. J. (1986). *An evaluation of the McREL thinking skills program.* Aurora, CO: Mid-continent Regional Educational Laboratory (ERIC Document Reproduction Service No. ED 267 907)

Marzano, R. J., & Arrendondo, D. E. (1986). *Tactics for thinking.* Aurora, CO: Mid-continent Regional Educational Laboratory.

Marzano, R. J., & Hutchins, C. L. (1985). *Thinking skills: A conceptual framework.* Aurora, CO: Mid-continent Regional Educational Laboratory.

Marzano, R. J., & Marzano, J. S. (no date). *Contextual thinking: The most basic of the cognitive skills.* Denver, CO: Mid-Continent Regional Educational Laboratory.

Mayer, R. E. (1981). Frequency norms and structural analysis of algebra story problems into families, categories, and templates. *Instructional Science, 10,* 135–175.

Mayer, R. E. (1982). Memory for algebra story problems. *Journal of Educational Psychology, 74,* 199–216.

Mayer, R. E. (1984). Aids to text comprehension. *Educational Psychologist, 19,* 30–42.

Mayer, R. E. (1987a). The elusive search for teachable aspects of problem solving. In J. A. Glover & R. R. Ronning (Eds.), *Historical foundations of educational psychology* (pp. 327–347). Boston: Little, Brown & Co.

Mayer, R. E. (1987b). *Educational psychology: A cognitive approach.* Boston: Little, Brown.

Mayer, R. E. (in press). Teaching for thinking: Research on the teachability of thinking skills. In *G. Stanley Hall Lecture Series, Volume 8.* Washington, DC: American Psychological Association.

McCloskey, M. (1983). Intuitive physics. *Scientific American, 248*(4), 122–130.

McCloskey, M., Caramazza, A., & Green, B. (1980). Curvilinear motion in the absence of external forces: Naive beliefs about the motion of objects. *Science, 210*(4474), 1139–1143.

Meeker, M. N. (1969). *The structure of the intellect: Its interpretation and uses.* Columbus, OH: Charles Merrill.

Meeker, M. N., Sexton, K., & Richardson, K. (1970). *SOI abilities workbook.* Los Angeles: Loyola Marymount University.

Meichenbaum, D. M. (1977). *Cognitive behavior modification: An integrative approach.* New York: Plenum.

Mezysnki, K. (1983). Issues concerning the acquisition of knowledge: Effects of vocabulary training on reading comprehension. *Review of Educational Research, 53,* 253–279.

Michigan State Department of Education, and Michigan State Board of Education. (1986). *New decisions about reading.* Lansing, MI: Michigan State Board of Education.

Miller, D., & Linn, R. L. (1986). *Cross national achievement with differential retention rates.* Unpublished contractor report to the U. S. Department of Education, Center for Statistics.

National Assessment of Educational Progress. (1978). *Three national assessments of science: Changes in achievement, 1969–1977* (Report No. 08-S-00). U. S. Department of Education, Center for Statistics.

National Assessment of Educational Progress. (1980). *Mathematical technical reports: Summary Volume.* U. S. Department of Education, Center for Statistics.

National Assessment of Educational Progress. (1983). *Science assessment and research project. Images of science. A summary of results from the 1981–82 national assessment in science.* (Report No. 08-S-00). U. S. Department of Education, Center for Statistics.

National Assessment of Educational Progress. (1985). *The reading report card, Progress toward excellence in our schools.* (Report No. 15-R-01). U. S. Department of Education, Center for Statistics.

National Assessment of Educational Progress. (1984). *The writing report card. Writing achievement in American schools.* (Report No. 15-W-02). U. S. Department of Education, Center for Statistics.

Nickerson, R. S. (1984). *Teaching thinking: What is being done with what results?* Cambridge, MA: Bolt Beranek & Newman.

Nickerson, R. S., & Adams, M. J. (1983). Introduction. In *Project Intelligence: The development of procedures to enhance thinking skills, teachers' manual.* Cambridge, MA: Harvard University and Bolt Beranek and Newman, Inc.

Nickerson, R. S., Perkins, D. N., & Smith, E. E. (1985). *The teaching of thinking.* Hillsdale, NJ: Lawrence Erlbaum Associates.

Novak, J. D., & Gowin, D. B. (1984). *Learning how to learn.* New York: Cambridge University Press.

Nystrand, M. (1982). An analysis of errors in written communication. In M. Nystrand (Ed.), *What writers know* (pp. 57–74). New York: Academic Press.

Orange County Public Schools. (1988). *At-risk students: Reading, learning, and remembering.* Orlando, FL: Orange County Public Schools.

Palincsar, A. S., & Brown, A. L. (1984). The reciprocal teaching of comprehension-fostering and comprehension-monitoring activities. *Cognition and Instruction, 1*(2), 117–175.

Palincsar, A. S., & Brown, A. L. (1985). Reciprocal teaching: Activities to promote "reading with your mind." In T. L. Harris & E. J. Cooper (Eds.), *Reading, thinking, and concept development: Strategies for the classroom* (pp. 147–160). New York: The College Board.

Palincsar, A. S., & Brown, A. L. (1986). Interactive teaching to promote independent learning from text. *The Reading Teacher, 39*(8), 771–777.

Palincsar, A. S., & Ogle, D. S., Jones, B. F., & Carr, E. G. (1986). *Facilitator's manual for teaching reading as thinking.* Alexandria, VA: Association for Supervision and Curriculum Development.

Paris, S. G., Lipson, M. Y., & Wixson, K. (1983). Becoming a strategic reader. *Contemporary Educational Psychology 8,* 293–316.

Pressley, M., & Levin, J. R. (1983). *Cognitive strategy research: Educational applications.* New York: Springer-Verlag.

Polya, G. (1945). *How to solve it.* Princeton, NJ: Princeton University Press.

Read, C. (1981). Writing is not the inverse of reading for young children. In C. H. Frederiksen & J. F. Dominic (Eds.), *Writing, Volume 2.* Hillsdale, NJ: Lawrence Erlbaum Association.

Resnick, L. B. (1987). *Education and learning to think.* A special report prepared for the Commission on Behavioral and Social Sciences and Education, National Research Council.

Riley, M., Greeno, J. G., & Heller, J. (1982). The development of children's problem solving ability in arithmetic. In H. Ginsburg (Ed.), *The development of mathematical thinking* (pp. 153–200). New York: Academic Press.

Rosenshine, B. V. (1983). Teaching functions in instructional programs. *The Elementary School Journal, 83,* 335–351.

Rosenshine, B. V. (1986). Synthesis of research on explicit teaching. *Educational Leadership, 43,* 60–69.

Rosenshine, B. V., Harnischfeger, A., & Walberg, H. (1985, March). *Classroom programs for school improvement.* An advisory paper for the North Central Regional Educational Laboratory, Elmhurst, IL.

Rumelhart, D. E. (1980). Schemata: The building blocks of cognition. In R. J. Spiro, B. C. Bruce, & W. F. Brewer (Eds.), *Theoretical issues in reading comprehension* (pp. 33–58). Hillsdale, NJ: Lawrence Erlbaum Associates.

Scardamalia, M., & Bereiter, C. (1984). Teachability of reflective processes in written composition. *Cognitive Science, 8,* 173–190.

Scardamalia, M., Bereiter, C., & Goelman, H. (1982). The role of production factors in writing ability. In M. Nystrand (Ed.), *What writers know* (pp. 175–210). New York: Academic Press.

Schallert, D. L., Alexander, P. A., & Goetz, E. T. (1985). What do instructors and authors do to influence the textbook–student relationship? In J. A. Niles & R. V. Lalik (Eds.), *Issues in literacy: A research perspective.* Rochester, NY: National Reading Conference.

Schoenfeld, A. H. (1985). *Mathematical problem solving.* New York: Academic Press.

Segal, J. W., Chipman, S. F., & Glaser, R. (1985). *Thinking and learning skills (Vol. 1): Relating instruction to research.* Hillsdale, NJ: Lawrence Erlbaum Associates.

Siegler, R. S. (1978). The origins of scientific thinking. In R. S. Siegler (Eds.), *Children's thinking: What develops?* Hillsdale, NJ: Lawrence Erlbaum Associates.

Silver, E. A. (1981). Recall of mathematical problem information: Solving related problems. *Journal for Research in Mathematics Education, 12,* 54–64.

Singer, H. S., & Donlan, D. (1985). *Reading and learning from text.* Hillsdale, NJ: Lawrence Erlbaum Associates.

Sloboda, J. A., & Rogers, D. (1987). *Cognitive processes in mathematics.* Oxford: Oxford University Press.

Smith, C. B., Smith, S. L., & Mikulecky, L. (1978). *Teaching reading secondary content subjects: A bookthinking process.* New York: Holt, Rinehart, and Winston.

Snow, R. E., & Lohman, D. F. (1984). Toward a theory of cognitive aptitude for learning from instruction. *Journal of Educational Psychology, 76,* 347–376.

Soloway, E., Lochhead, J., & Clement, J. (1982). Does computer programming enhance problem solving ability? Some evidence on algebra word problems. In R. J. Seidel, R. E. Anderson, & B. Hunter (Eds.), *Computer literacy* (pp. 171–186). New York: Academic Press.

Spiro, R. J. (1980). Constructive processes in prose comprehension and recall. In R. J. Spiro, B. C. Bruce, & W. F. Brewer (Eds.), *Theoretical issues in reading comprehension* (pp. 245–278). Hillsdale, NJ: Lawrence Erlbaum Associates.

Stauffer, R. (1970). *The language-experience approach to the teaching of reading.* New York: Harper & Row.

Sternberg, R. J. (1977). *Intelligence, information processing, and analogical reasoning: The componential analysis of human abilities.* Hillsdale, NJ: Lawrence Erlbaum Associates.

Sternberg, R. J. (Ed.). (1985). *Human abilities: An information processing approach.* New York: Freeman.

Sternberg, R. J. (1986). *Intelligence applied.* San Diego: Harcourt Brace Jovanovich.

Thornton, M. C., & Fuller, R. G. (1981). How do college students solve proportional reasoning problems? *Journal of Research in Science Teaching, 18*(4), 335–340.

Tierney, R. J. (1983). *Learning from text* (Reading Education Rep. No. 37). Urbana, IL: University of Illinois, Center for the Study of Reading.

Tierney, R. J., Readence, J. E., & Dishner, E. K. (1985). *Reading strategies and practices: A guide for improving instruction.* Boston: Allyn and Bacon.

Voss, J. F., & Bisanz, G. L. (1985). Knowledge and processing of narrative and expository texts. In B. K. Britton & J. B. Black (Eds.), *Understanding expository text* (pp. 173–198). Hillsdale, NJ: Lawrence Erlbaum Associates.

Weinstein, C. E., Goetz, E. T., & Alexander, P. A. (1988). *Learning and study strategies: Issues in assessment, instruction, and evaluation.* New York: Academic Press.

Weinstein, C. E., & Mayer, R. E. (1986). The teaching of learning strategies. In M. C. Wittrock (Ed.), *Handbook of research on teaching* (3rd ed.) (pp. 315–327). New York: Macmillan.

West, L. H. T., & Pines, A. L. (1985). *Cognitive structure and conceptual change.* Orlando, FL: Academic Press.

Winne, P., & Marx, R. W. (1983). *Students cognitive processes while learning from teaching* (Vols. 1 & 2). Instructional Psychology Research Group, (NIE Final Report, Grant No. NIE-G-79-0098). Burnaby, British Columbia: Simon Fraser University.

Winograd, P. N., & Hare, V. C. (1988). Direct instruction of reading comprehension strategies: The nature of teacher explanation. In E. Goetz, P. Alexander, & C. Weinstein (Eds.), *Learning and study strategy research: Issues in assessment, instruction, and evaluation* (pp. 121–140). New York: Academic Press.

Wisconsin Department of Public Instruction. (1986). *A guide to curriculum planning in reading* (D. Cook, Ed.). Madison, WI: Wisconsin Department of Public Instruction.

Wisconsin Department of Public Instruction. (1989). *Developing strategic learners in content areas* (D. Cook, Ed.). Madison, WI: Wisconsin State Board of Education.

Wittrock, M. C. (1983). *Generative reading comprehension.* (Ginn Occasional Reports). Boston: Ginn.

Wittrock, M. C. (1986). Students' thought processes. *Handbook of research on teaching.* New York: Macmillan.

4

Cognitive Apprenticeship and Instructional Technology

Allan Collins
Bolt Beranek & Newman Inc.,
Cambridge, MA

In earlier times, practically everything was taught by apprenticeship: growing crops, running trades, administering governments. Schools are a recent invention that use many fewer teaching resources. But the computer enables us to go back to a resource-intensive mode of education, in a form we call cognitive apprenticeship (Collins, Brown, & Newman, 1989). As we argued in Collins, Brown, and Newman (1989), cognitive apprenticeship employs the modeling, coaching, and fading paradigm of traditional apprenticeship, but with emphasis on cognitive, rather than physical skills. My basic thesis in this chapter is that technology enables us to realize apprenticeship learning environments that were either not possible or not cost-effective before.

This chapter addresses the questions: What kind of leverage do we derive from computer technology, and what design criteria can we specify for building computational learning environments? We have developed a tentative set of characteristics (Collins, Brown, & Newman, 1989) that we think computational learning environments should have, based on analyzing what kinds of tutoring systems we see emerging, what we have learned from studies such as Lampert (1986), Palincsar and Brown (1984), Scardamalia, Bereiter, and Steinbach (1984), and Schoenfeld (1983, 1985), and what resource-rich learning environments (such as tennis coaches and graduate school instruction) are like.

This chapter discusses six characteristics of cognitive apprenticeship for which technology provides particular leverage. For each abstract characteristic, I address:

1. What the abstraction refers to.

2. The implications that technology has for realizing the abstraction in practice.

3. Why realizing the abstraction is of benefit to students.

4. An example of a computer system that embodies the abstraction.

SITUATED LEARNING

Situated learning is the notion of learning knowledge and skills in contexts that reflect the way the knowledge will be useful in real life. It is the sine qua non of apprenticeship; but it should be thought of in the most general way. In the context of math skills, they might be taught in contexts ranging from running a bank or shopping in a grocery store to inventing new theorems or finding new proofs. That is, situated learning can incorporate situations from everyday life to the most theoretical endeavors (Schoenfeld, in press).

The computer allows us to create environments that mimic situations in the real world that we cannot otherwise realize in a classroom (or home). One approach is through microworlds, but also through computer networks, data bases, graphic packages, and text editors (Collins, 1986). There are inherent dangers in microworlds, such as learning to make decisions based on a few variables rather than a rich set of variables (Dreyfus & Dreyfus, 1986), but potentially the benefits far outweigh the risks.

The benefits of situated learning include:

1. *Students learn conditions for applying knowledge.* By learning arithmetic, for example, in representative contexts such as grocery shopping or running a bank, the student ties the knowledge learned to specific contexts. Then when they are in novel situations, such as buying airline tickets or working in an accounting department, they will be able to see how the knowledge learned might apply in these new situations by analogy to the situations they learned about.

2. *Situations foster invention.* When students use their knowledge to deal with real problems and situations, they are forced to make inventions to apply their knowledge (Lampert, 1986). Thus, they are learning how to use their knowledge flexibly to deal with novel situations.

3. *Students see the implications of the knowledge.* When learning is embedded in context, then its uses are more apparent to students. They can actually see how the knowledge is used in different settings, and what

power it gives them to use the knowledge. It is not readily apparent to students how most of what they learn in school might be used.

4. *Context structures knowledge appropriate to its uses.* When students learn things for school, they often invoke suboptimal schemes for remembering the information. For example, they may infer that all arithmetic word problems with the word "left" (e.g., "Mary had 7 apples. She gave 3 to John. How many did she have left?") are subtraction problems (Schoenfeld, in press). Or they may memorize facts in a rather rote way so that they can be retrieved for a test (e.g., the capital of Oregon is Salem: with the *oar* in Oregon you can go *sail*). When knowledge is learned in the context of its uses, it is more likely to be stored in a form that is usable in novel contexts.

These may be the central issues as to why transfer of knowledge is so difficult: By learning in multiple contexts, students learn different ways that knowledge can be used, and they begin to generalize on these ways. This is opposed to the way we teach knowledge in an abstract way in schools now, which leads to strategies, such as depending on the fact that everything in a particular chapter uses a single method, or storing information just long enough to retrieve it for a test. Instead of trying to teach abstract knowledge and how to apply it in contexts (as word problems are supposed to do), we advocate teaching in multiple contexts and then trying to generalize across those contexts. In this way, knowledge becomes both specific and general.

An excellent example of a computer-based situated learning environment based on a microworld is *Geography Search* by Tom Snyder (Snyder & Palmer, 1986), which is one of five programs in the Search Series by McGraw Hill. It teaches history, math, planning, and problem solving. In this simulated microworld, groups of students sail ships from Europe to the New World about the time of Columbus, in order to look for treasure that is distributed around North and South America. Land and other ships come into view on the screen when the ship nears them. Students have to calculate their route using sextant and compass in the way sailors did of old. They must also keep track of food and supplies, so they don't run out while they are at sea. In this way, students are learning history and math in a context where novel problems continually arise.

Another example of situated learning is the reconvening of the Constitutional Convention among school students in the Boston area using a computer mail system (William Fitzhugh, personal communication). Different schools represent different delegations (e.g., Delaware, Virginia). The students prepare by reading about the concerns of their states in 1787. During the convention, they will try to negotiate a draft constitution to correct for the difficulties that were encountered with the Articles of Confederation. A similar kind of convention could be held to cope with the modern-day problems that have arisen with the Constitution (e.g., the budget process, the advent of media and its expenses, the disagreements over who controls foreign policy, the difficulties when presidents are disabled for any reason). Government and its structures become real in dealing with these kinds of questions.

History is typical of the information that schools teach in a nonsituated way. Schools try to pour in a lot of facts and theories and make no use of that knowledge other than recall. Computers give us enormous power to create situated learning environments where students are learning about reading, writing, math, science, and social studies in ways that reflect the kinds of activities they will need these for.

Modeling and Explaining

Modeling is showing how a process unfolds, and explaining involves giving reasons why it happens that way. It is the showing and telling that is so characteristic of apprenticeship.

Two kinds of modeling are important for education:

1. *Modeling of processes in the world.* For example, one might show how electrons move in circuits (Haertel, 1987) or how information coded in DNA is translated into protein molecules.

2. *Modeling of expert performance.* For example, in teaching reading, teachers might read in one voice and verbalize their thinking in another voice, like a slow-motion movie. They could verbalize what is confusing, what to do when you don't understand, any tentative hypotheses about what is meant and what will come later, any evidence as it comes in about these hypotheses, their summaries and integrations, their guesses as to the author's intentions, and evaluations of the structure and style of the writing—in short, all the thoughts of a skilled reader (Collins & Smith, 1982).

The computer makes it possible to represent processes in ways that books never could, and even in ways that people cannot. Computers can make the invisible visible: They let you see inside pipes or inside the body, how current changes in circuits based on electron flow, where the center of mass for a group of bodies is, how microscopic processes unfold. At the same time, they can make tacit knowledge explicit, by showing the strategies that experts use to solve problems that students set for them. To the degree that we can develop good process models of expert performance, we can embed these in technology, where they can be observed over and over for different details.

Computers can use multimedia (i.e., animation, voice, text, and graphics) to characterize different aspects of processes. Ways of integrating animation and voice are just beginning to be explored, but it is clear that they have enormous potential for making things clearer. For example, it is possible to highlight each component of a system while it is talked about. One can show both what happens and what does not happen. We can render unto voice what verbal description best transmits (e.g., reasons why, abstract ideas) and render unto animation what visual description best transmits (e.g., processes and relations between components, concrete ideas). We also achieve *simultaneous presentation* so that what is seen happening on the screen can be explained orally without looking elsewhere. Eventually, much of the information in text books and libraries will be in this form.

The benefits of modeling include:

1. *Seeing expert solutions to problems set by the student.* For the most part in school, students never see how experts solve problems—they see only worked-out solutions. Worked-out solutions do not show the false starts or dead ends that characterize real-world problem solving. If students can pick problems that raise issues in their mind, and watch how an expert computer program attacks the problem, then they will have a genuinely new kind of learning experience.

2. *Integrating what happens and why it happens.* Demonstrations in class or process descriptions in text have inherent limitations. Many demonstrations occur too fast to assimilate what is happening and why it is happening. In books, simultaneity can only be approximated with static diagrams and text explanation. The ability to see what is happening, in slow motion if need be, and hear at the same time a verbal explanation of why it is happening facilitates building an integrated understanding of processes.

3. *Making visible the parts of a process that are not normally seen.* Because much of what we want students to learn is not ordinarily seen, students must infer from end products and a few intermediate states how processes unfold. By revealing these processes in detail, many more students will have a chance to figure out what is happening.

I can illustrate modeling with a computer system called *Summit* (Feurzeig & White, 1984), designed for teaching addition and subtraction.

Summit combines visual animation with spoken explanation. The system had two representations for addition and subtraction: the standard algorithm and a bin-model representation, derived from Dienes blocks. In both representations, students can pose problems to the system to see what happens. Figure 4.1 illustrates how the system represents a simple addition problem (2593 + 9) in the two representations.

The bin model works as follows. Suppose that the ones bin has 3 icons in it and 9 more are added to it. The model first displays all 12 icons, stacked one on top of the other, in the ones bin. Next, the computer says, "Now there are too many ones. We have to take some to the tens." An empty box then appears in between the ones and tens bins. Next, 10 icons are removed from the ones bin, one at a time, and placed in the box. There is a counter displayed on the box. When there are 10 icons in the box, the box becomes a tens icon, which is added to the tens bin. This in turn leads to an overflow in the tens bin, and the process repeats itself.

Summit models the addition process for the standard algorithm in a similar way, saying: "Then we add the ones. Three plus 9 is 12, but 12

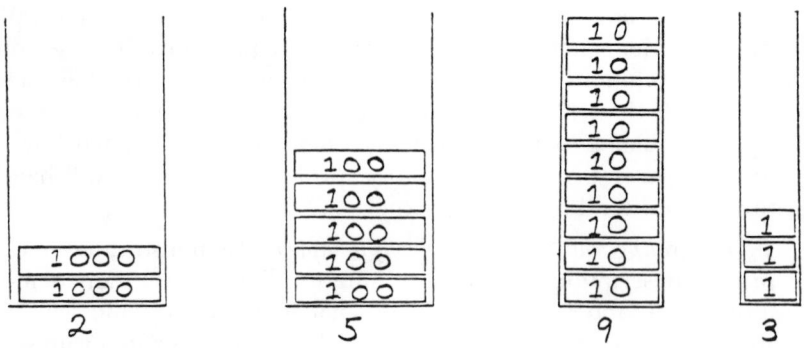

$$
\begin{array}{r}
1\ 1 \\
2593 \\
9 \\
\hline
2602
\end{array}
$$

FIG. 4.1.   Bin Model representation of 2593 and standard representation of the addition problem 2593 + 9 in Summit (from Feurzeig & White, 1984).

won't fit. So we write the 2 under the ones column, and take the 1 over to the tens column," writing it just above the tens column. "Then we add the tens. One plus 9 is 10, but 10 won't fit. So we write 0 in the tens column, and take the 1 over the hundreds column," and so on. Each of the actions appears on the screen as the voice explains it.

There are other systems, such as Sophie (Brown, Burton, & deKleer, 1982) and Quest (White & Frederiksen, 1989), in the electricity domain that not only model how a process unfolds, but how experts troubleshoot a faulty system, as well. In these systems, students can see an expert troubleshooting whatever faults they decide to set in the system. Thus, they can pick problems that are at the edge of their own competence in order to see how to extend their troubleshooting strategies.

COACHING

Computer systems have the ability to patiently observe students as they try to carry out tasks, providing hints or assistance when needed. This kind of personal attention is simply not feasible in most school classrooms.

Not only is the computer patient, it can remember perfectly what the student did before. It can consider multiple hypotheses about the difficulties the student is having (Burton, 1982), and it can observe over a period of time in order to tell what problems the student is really having. Moreover, a computer coach gives students a different perspective from which to understand their own performance.

The benefits of coaching include:

1. *Coaching provides help directed at real difficulties.* By observing students in a problem-solving situation, the coach can see what difficulties a particular student is having. Because teachers in school rarely have a chance to observe student problem solving, most of the help they give is not really directed at the problems students actually have.

2. *Coaching provides help at critical times.* Coaching provides help to students when they most need it: when they are struggling with a task and are most aware of the critical factors guiding their decisions. Thus, they are in the best position to use any help given.

3. *Coaching provides as much help as is needed to accomplish tasks.* Coaching enables students to do tasks they might not otherwise be able to complete. It gives them a sense that they can really do difficult tasks. As they become more skilled, the coach's role can fade, giving students more and more control over execution of the task.

4. *Coaching provides new eyeglasses for the student.* Coaching can help students see the process from an entirely different perspective. The coach can point out things that do not go as expected and explain why. Furthermore, a coach can introduce new terms, such as "forward chaining" and "thrashing" (discussed in the next section), that are critical to employing heuristic and metacognitive strategies.

The best example of a computer coach is the coach built by Burton and Brown (1982) for the computer game "How the West Was Won." Originally developed as part of the Plato system, the game, which is a variant on Chutes and Ladders, is designed to teach children basic arithmetic operations. It can be played either by one person against the computer or by two people against each other. Figure 4.2 shows a display of what the game board looks like to the players.

The rules of the game are as follows: When it is a player's turn, he or she must form an arithmetic expression from the three spinners using two different operations (e.g., $2 \times 1 + 2$), and after the player has formed such an expression he or she must input the value of the expression (in this case, 4). If the player miscalculates, he or she loses his or her turn; if the player is correct, he or she moves forward on the board the number

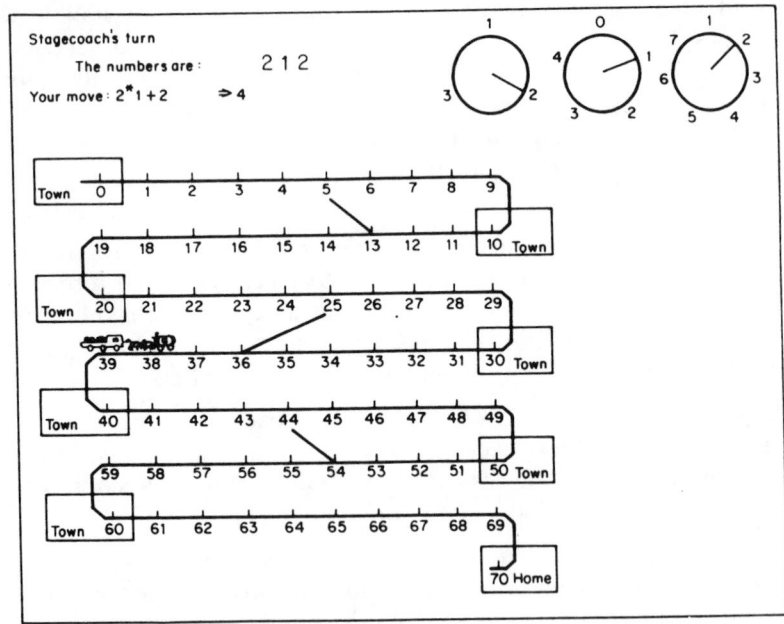

FIG. 4.2.   Screen used in "How the West was Won" game (from Burton & Brown, 1982).

of spaces calculated. The object is to reach the last town (which is 70) before your opponent, but, in order to reach the last town, you must form an expression that lands you exactly on the town (i.e., you cannot overshoot it). There are some special rules that make the game more challenging: (a) if you land on a town (every 10 squares), you advance to the next town; (b) if you land at the beginning of one of the short cuts (i.e., 5, 25, 44), you advance to the end of the shortcut (i.e., 13, 36, 54); and (c) if you land on your opponent, you send him or her back two towns.

These special rules make it advantageous to consider many possible different moves, which would require trying out different arithmetic expressions and calculating their values. But students playing the Plato game do not consider alternative moves: They tend, instead, to lock onto a particular strategy, such as multiplying the largest number times the sum of the other two numbers, which gives them the largest value they can make. Thus, they do not play very well or learn much arithmetic without coaching.

To remedy this situation, Burton and Brown (1982) built a computer coach that observes students as they play the game and gives them hints or advice at critical moments. The computer coach rank orders every possible move a player might make given the three spinner values. The rank order is constructed with respect to how far ahead of your opponent any move leaves you. This gives the coach a way to evaluate the effectiveness of any move.

The coach observes the player's moves by looking at certain "issues," for example, whether the student knows to land on towns or on the opponent when it is effective to do so, whether the student knows to use parentheses or the minus sign or the divide sign when it is effective to do so. If the student systematically fails to make moves that require understanding of any of these issues, then the coach will notice the pattern. The coach will then intervene with a hint about a particular issue when that issue is particularly salient to making a good move; that is, when the student's move is much inferior to the best move possible, taking into account that issue. The intervention by the tutor occurs just after the student's move: The system points out how using parentheses or a short cut, for example, would improve the player's position, and gives the student a chance to retake his or her turn. Thus, the coach tries to expand the student's awareness of how he or she might play the game more successfully.

There are other examples of computer coaches that help students when they are carrying out tasks. For example, Anderson, Boyle, and Reiser (1985) have developed computer coaches for plane geometry and computer programming that pose problems to students and offer advice when the student takes a step in working the problem that reflects a common misunderstanding or error. Similarly, the PROUST system of Johnson and Soloway (1985) recognizes common errors students make in computer programming and gives advice as to what the problem is. Computer coaches make it possible for students to spend their learning time actively carrying out tasks and projects, receiving personal help or guidance when they need it.

REFLECTION ON PERFORMANCE

Reflection refers to students looking back over what they did and analyzing their performance. There are four ways of permitting students to reflect on their performance (Collins & Brown, 1988): (a) imitation, (b) replay, (c) abstracted replay, and (d) spatial reification. These can be illustrated in the context of tennis. *Imitation* occurs when a tennis coach shows you how you swing your racquet, perhaps contrasting it with the way you should swing it. *Replay* occurs when the coach videotapes your swing, which you can compare to videotapes of experts. An *abstracted replay* might be constructed by using reflective tape on critical points— the elbows, wrist, end of racquet, and so on—so that the student can see how these points move with respect to each other in a videotaped replay. A *spatial reification* might be a plot of the trajectory of these points moving through space. In general, students should be given multiple views and be able to compare their performance to expert performance. Technology makes the last three forms of reflection possible, so this is a genuinely new teaching method emerging out of technology.

The benefits of reflection include:

1. *What the student did becomes an object of study.* The students begin to see their performance on tasks as data to be analyzed. They may never have taken what they did seriously before: Reflection encourages them to think about their processes from the point of view of how they might be different and what changes would lead to improved performance.

2. *Students can compare their performance to that of others.* Reflection lets students see how different students and more expert performers carry out the same task. This encourages them to form hypotheses about what aspects of a process are critical to successful and unsuccessful performance.

3. *Abstractions about the process can be used for characterizing strategies.* It is possible to describe various heuristics and metacognitive strategies (Schoenfeld, 1985) in terms of the process the student is reflecting on.

For example, in working geometry problems, it is possible to characterize forward chaining as working from the givens and backward chaining as working from the statement to be proved. A good heuristic strategy is to start forward chaining from each of the givens to see what they imply, and then switch to backward chaining to work out the problem solution.

4. *Spatial reification permits comparison of multiple performances to form abstractions.* If students can see a process laid out in graphic form, then they can compare different people's approaches and try to characterize what aspects of the process are critical to expert versus novice performance. The spatial representation permits them to see and even measure aspects of the process that are not apparent in a replay.

A good example of a spatial reification that permits reflection on a process is the problem-solving trace that Anderson, Boyle, and Reiser's (1985) Geometry Tutor constructs as the student works a problem. Figure 4.3 shows three views of the screen as a student works a problem. Initially, in the top view, the student sees a screen with the givens at the bottom and the statement to be proved at the top. In the middle screen, the student has worked part way through the problem, working both forward from the givens and backwards from the statement to be proved. The third screen shows the final problem solution, along with various dead ends (e.g., $<MDB=<MCA$) that the student never used in the proof.

As Anderson, Boyle, Farrel, and Reiser (1984) have pointed out, geometry proofs are usually presented in a fundamentally misleading way. Proofs on paper appear to be linear structures that start from a set of givens and proceed step by step (with a justification for each step) to the statement to be proved. But this is not how proofs are constructed by mathematicians or by anybody else. The process of constructing proofs involves an interplay between forward chaining from the givens and backward chaining from the goal statement. Yet, the use of paper and its properties encourage students to write proofs as if they were produced only by forward chaining—starting with the givens at the top of the page and working downward to the goal in a two-column linear format (left column for the derived statements, right column for the logical justifications). If students infer that they should *construct* proofs this way, they will fail at any long proof. Properly designed computational learning environments can encourage students to proceed in both directions, moving forward, exploring the givens, and moving backwards, finding bridges to the goals.

The representation in Geometry Tutor is an abstraction of the problem-solving process in terms of a "problem space." The system shows the states in the problem space that the student reached and the operators

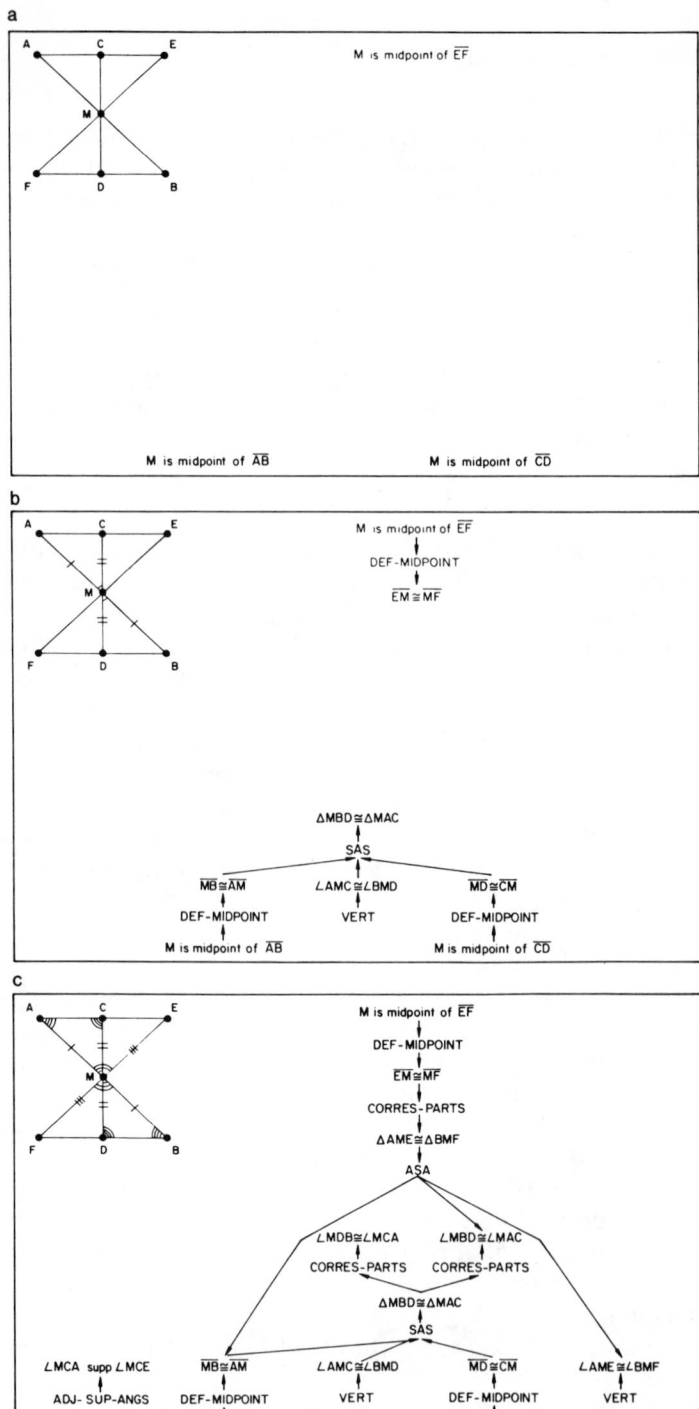

FIG. 4.3.   (a) The Geometry Tutor's initial representation of the problem; (b) a representation in the middle of the problem; and (c) a representation at the solution of the problem (from Anderson, Boyle, & Reiser, 1985).

used to reach each of those states. Simply seeing the steps toward a solution reified in this way helps to create a problem space as a mental entity in its own right. This, in turn, makes it possible, for both teachers and students, to characterize problem-solving strategies in terms of abstractions that *refer* to the properties concretely manifested in the reified problem space. For example, in geometry it is a good strategy to forward chain at the beginning of a problem in order to understand the implications of the givens. Similarly, if you are stuck backward chaining, and do not see a way to connect your backward chain to any of the givens, then either go back to forward chaining or go back to the goal state again and try backward chaining along a different path.

Videotape first made systematic reflection on performance possible. The computer extends this to abstracted replays and reifications that highlight critical aspects of performance. In this way, students can analyze their performance from different perspectives and compare themselves to other students and experts.

ARTICULATION

Articulation refers to methods for forcing students to explain and think about what they are doing, that is, making their tacit knowledge explicit. There are two ways that computers provide leverage for encouraging students to articulate their knowledge. First, computers make it possible for students to actually build their theories or ideas into artifacts that can be tested and revised. One challenge for their fellow students might be to show the limitations or failures of these theories. Second, computers can provide tools and settings where students try to articulate their ideas to other students, as in the Constitutional Convention convened on an electronic network in Boston (see Situated Learning, in the beginning of this chapter).

The benefits of articulation include:

1. *Making tacit knowledge explicit.* When knowledge is tacit, it can only be used in contexts that elicit the knowledge automatically, that is, that call up the knowledge because they are very similar to the conditions in which the knowledge was acquired. By forcing students to articulate their knowledge, it generalizes the knowledge from a particular context so that it can be used in other circumstances.

2. *Making knowledge more available to be recruited in other tasks.* Knowledge that is articulated as part of a set of interconnected ideas becomes more easily available. For example, if students acquire the idea of "thrash-

ing" in problem solving (i.e., the concept of moving through a problem space without getting closer to the goal), then they can learn to recognize thrashing when they see it in different circumstances and develop strategies for dealing with it when it occurs.

3. *Comparing strategies across contexts.* When strategies are articulated, students can begin to see how the same strategies apply in different contexts. For example, the strategy of decomposing complex problems into simpler problems takes the form of writing subroutines in computer programming, and proving lemmas in geometry.

4. *Articulation for other students promotes insight into alternative perspectives.* If students try to explain an idea (or problem) to other students, then they begin to see the idea from the other students' perspectives. If they get responses from other students, they can see what difficulties other students have with the idea and how other people view the same issue (as will occur with the Constitutional Convention mentioned earlier).

We can illustrate articulation by a computer program called Robot Odyssey, developed by the Learning Company. In it, students first learn how to wire robots to behave in different ways when they sense different conditions. The robots have bumpers that detect when objects or walls are encountered on different sides, and sensors that detect the direction of particular objects in the vicinity of the robot. The robots have thrusters that can send them in different directions and grabbers to pick up objects. Students can wire these robots in very complicated patterns to move around, explore, and pick up or avoid different objects. Thus, students can construct robots that behave in complicated ways and turn them loose in the world to see what happens. The challenge of Robot Odyssey is to use the robots to navigate through a complicated maze, as in an Adventure game, where there are puzzles to solve and enemies to avoid in order to come through successfully. This, then, is the test of how well students have wired their robots or, more generally, how deep their understanding is of how to build intelligent artifacts to deal with different situations.

Wiring robots is just one of many such enterprises. In languages like Logo (Goldenberg & Feurzeig, 1987) students can write programs that, for example, take any noun and generate a plural for it, or transform input sentences in active voice to passive voice. Thus, students can articulate their grammatical theories in forms that can be tested out.

In an entirely different vein, Sharples (1980) has developed a game kit that allows students to create computer adventure games for other students to play (where they explore caves looking for treasure, avoiding monsters, and trying to find the way out). This forces students to articulate their images of different caverns in a series of caves, and pose problems for others that are solvable but challenging.

These examples illustrate some of the different ways computers can be used to foster articulation by students. Although articulation is often encouraged by teachers in schools, computational articulation requires even more explicitness.

EXPLORATION

Exploration involves pushing students to try out different hypotheses, methods, and strategies to see their effects. This puts students in control of problem solving, but they need to learn how to explore productively. The computer provides powerful tools that allow students to explore hypotheses and solutions (i.e., problem spaces) faster, so they don't become frustrated.

The benefits of exploration include:

1. *Learning how to set achievable goals.* Many students set goals for themselves that are either too easily achievable or impossible to achieve (Atkinson, 1964). Studies of successful artists (Getzels & Csikszentmihalyi, 1976) have identified problem finding as the most critical skill for success; yet, very little effort in school goes into teaching students how to set reasonable goals and to revise their goals as they proceed deeper into a problem. Instead, school emphasizes giving students well-defined tasks, unlike anything in the real world.

2. *Learning how to form and test hypotheses.* One of the major goals of inquiry teachers (Collins & Stevens, 1982, 1983) is to teach students how to formulate hypotheses, rules, or theories and then how to test out whether or not they are correct. Making sense out of the world around us requires these skills, and unless students practice forming and testing hypotheses in many different domains with the help of expert guidance, they will not learn to do so effectively.

3. *Students will make discoveries on their own.* When students are put into an environment where they are making and testing hypotheses, they get a sense of what it is like to be a scientist. They will feel the joy of generating their own ideas and seeing if they are correct. They may even discover genuinely novel ideas. But even when they come up with old ideas, they will at least sense where the ideas came from and why they are important.

We can illustrate the potential for exploration with the science laboratories developed by TERC (Mokros & Tinker, 1987). In one laboratory, students can detect how far a moving object is from a sensor and plot velocity, distance, and acceleration. This enables them to discover Galileo's laws of falling objects. Or they can conduct experiments with balls hitting other balls to see how changes in direction affect velocity. There are many different phenomena that students can investigate, and with the immediate graphic plotting they can test out many different ideas quickly.

Another example of an exploratory computer-based environment is the economics simulation called Smithtown developed by Shute and Bonar (1986). In Smithtown students can manipulate different variables, such as the price of coffee, to see how they affect other variables, such as the amount sold. They are then encouraged to try to figure out the various laws that relate the different variables. Thus, they are discovering basic economic relationships. Similarly, students with a music or painting program can compose works quickly and with much less effort. Hence, they can explore many different techniques and see how effective they are. Computers provide powerful tools for exploration (Papert, 1980), and we are just beginning to investigate their potential.

CONCLUSION

As technology becomes cheaper, it gives us the capability to realize resource-intensive education once again. In particular, technology allows us to return to a kind of apprenticeship centered around modeling, coaching, and fading in situations that reflect the real-world uses of the knowledge gained. Moreover, technology enables us to create environments where new methods of learning—reflection, articulation, and exploration—are possible. This raises the question of what form education should take, given the capabilities and limitations of the technologies that are developing.

ACKNOWLEDGMENT

This research was supported by the Personnel and Training Research Programs, Psychological Sciences Division, Office of Naval Research under Contract No. N00014-C-85-0026, Contract Authority Identification Number, NR 667-540.

REFERENCES

Anderson, J. R., Boyle, C. F., Farrell, R., & Reiser, B. J. (1984). Cognitive principles in the design of computer tutors. In *Proceedings of the Sixth Annual Conference of the Cognitive Science Society* (pp. 2–9). Hillsdale, NJ: Lawrence Erlbaum Associates.

Anderson, J. R., Boyle, C. F., & Reiser, B. J. (1985). Intelligent tutoring systems. *Science, 228*, 456–468.

Atkinson, J. W. (1964). *An introduction to motivation.* Princeton, NJ: Van Nostrand.

Brown, J. S., Burton, R. R., & deKleer, J. (1982). Pedagogical natural language and knowledge engineering techniques in SOPHIE I, II, and III. In D. Sleeman & J. S. Brown (Eds.), *Intelligent tutoring systems* (pp. 227–282). New York: Academic Press.

Burton, R. R. (1982). Diagnosing bugs in a simple procedural skill. In D. Sleeman & J. S. Brown (Eds.), *Intelligent tutoring systems* (pp. 157–184). New York: Academic Press.

Burton, R. R., & Brown, J. S. (1982). An investigation of computer coaching for informal learning activities. In D. Sleeman & J. S. Brown (Eds.), *Intelligent tutoring systems* (pp. 79–98). New York: Academic Press.

Collins A. (1986). Teaching reading and writing with personal computers. In J. Orasanu (Ed.), *A decade of reading research: Implications for practice* (pp. 171–187). Hillsdale, NJ: Lawrence Erlbaum Associates.

Collins, A., & Brown, J. S. (1988). The computer as a tool for learning through reflection. In H. Mandl & Lesgold (Eds.), *Learning issues for intelligent tutoring systems* (pp. 1–18). New York: Springer.

Collins, A., Brown, J. S., & Newman, S. (1989). Cognitive apprenticeship: Teaching the crafts of reading, writing, and mathematics. In L. B. Resnick (Ed.), *Knowing, learning, and instruction: Essays in honor of Robert Glaser* (pp. 453–494). Hillsdale, NJ: Lawrence Erlbaum Associates.

Collins, A., & Smith, E. E. (1982). Teaching the process of reading comprehension. In D. K. Detterman & R. J. Sternberg (Eds.), *How much and how can intelligence be increased?* (pp. 173–185). Norwood, NJ: Ablex.

Collins, A., & Stevens, A. L. (1982). Goals and strategies of inquiry teachers. In R. Glaser (Ed.), *Advances in instructional psychology* (Vol. 2) (pp. 65–119). Hillsdale, NJ: Lawrence Erlbaum Associates.

Collins, A., & Stevens, A. L. (1983). A cognitive theory of interactive teaching. In C. M. Reigeluth (Ed.), *Instructional design theories and models: An overview* (pp. 247–278). Hillsdale, NJ: Lawrence Erlbaum Associates.

Dreyfus, H. L. & Dreyfus, S. E. (1986). *Mind over machine: The power of human intuition and expertise in the era of the computer.* New York: Free Press.

Feurzeig, W. & White, B. Y. (1984). *An articulate instructional system for teaching arithmetic procedures.* Cambridge, MA: Bolt Beranek and Newman, Inc.

Getzels, J., & Csikszentmihalyi, M. (1976). *The creative vision: A longitudinal study of problem finding in art.* New York: Wiley.

Goldenberg, E. P. & Feurzeig, W. (1987). *Exploring language with Logo.* Cambridge, MA: MIT Press.

Haertel, H. (1987). *A qualitative approach to electricity.* Palo Alto, CA: Xerox Corporation, Institute for Research on Learning.

Johnson, W. L. & Soloway, E. (1985). PROUST: An automatic debugger for pascal programs. *Byte, 10*, 179–190.

Lampert, M. (1986). Knowing, doing, and teaching multiplication. *Cognition and Instruction, 3*, 305–342.

Mokros, J. R. & Tinker, R. F. (1987). The impact of microcomputer-based labs on children's ability to interpret graphs. *Journal of Research in Science Teaching, 24*, 369–383.

Palincsar, A. S., & Brown, A. L. (1984). Reciprocal teaching of comprehension-fostering and monitoring activities. *Cognition and Instruction, 1,* 117–175.

Papert, S. (1980), *Mindstorms: Children, computers, and powerful ideas.* New York: Basic Books.

Scardamalia, M., Bereiter, C., & Steinbach, R. (1984). Teachability of reflective processes in written composition. *Cognitive Science, 8,* 173–190.

Schoenfeld, A. H. (1983). Problem solving in the mathematics curriculum: A report, recommendations and an annotated bibliography. *The Mathematical Association of America,* MAA Notes, No. 1.

Schoenfeld, A. H. (1985). *Mathematical problem solving.* New York: Academic Press.

Schoenfeld, A. H. (in press). On mathematics as sense-making: An informal attack on the unfortunate divorce of formal and informal mathematics. In D. N. Perkins, J, Segal, & J. Voss (Eds.), *Informal reasoning and education.* Hillsdale, NJ: Lawrence Erlbaum Associates.

Sharples, M. (1980). *A computer written language lab* (DAI Working Paper No. 134). Edinburgh: University of Edinburgh, Scotland, Artificial Intelligence Department.

Shute, V., & Bonar, J. (1986). Intelligent tutoring systems for scientific inquiry skills. In *Proceedings of the Eighth Annual Conference of the Cognitive Science Society* (pp. 353–370). Hillsdale, NJ: Lawrence Erlbaum Associates.

Snyder, T., & Palmer, J. (1986). *In search of the most amazing thing: Children, education, and computers.* Reading, MA: Addison-Wesley.

White, B. Y., & Frederiksen, J. (1989). Progressions of qualitative models as a foundation for intelligent learning environments. *Artificial Intelligence, 27.*

5

Intervention Programs for Retarded Performers: Goals, Means, and Expected Outcomes

Reuven Feuerstein
Ya'acov Rand
Bar Ilan University
Haddasah-Wizo Canada Research Institute, Jerusalem, Israel
Mildred B. Hoffman, Moshe Egozi, and Nilly Ben Shachar-Segev
Hadassah-Wizo Canada Research Institute, Jerusalem, Israel

Social services have long been plagued with "creaming up." Creaming up introduces inequities in the access to well-intentioned programs of social intervention due to their methods of helping the needy. This inequity is most clearly reflected in the fact that those individuals and groups who need help less are helped more, whereas those who are most in need of help are either not helped at all or are helped in a very limited and unsatisfactory way.

The creaming-up phenomenon, initially described in social welfare, is strongly paralleled in the field of education, in general, and in the development of programs that aim at the enhancement of intelligence, in particular. A number of programs oriented to various dimensions of thinking (e.g., problem solving, critical thinking, creative thinking) have been developed for generalized use with relatively advantaged students. These students simply need to learn to make better use of the opportunities offered to them within the traditional public school system. Among the better known of these programs are Meeker's Structure of the Intellect (1969); de Bono's CORT (1973); Philosophy in the Classroom developed by Lipman, Sharp, and Oscanyan (1980); Whimbey and Lockhead's Problem Solving and Comprehension (1980); Harvard University's Odyssey (1983); Marzano and Arrendondo's Tactics of Thinking (1986); and Sternberg's (1986) program for developing practical intelligence. These programs have been structured in a way that makes their accessibility contingent upon a number of prerequisites: cognitive, emotional, motivational, and functional basic school skills. The absence of these prerequisites in a given individual or group of individuals makes these interven-

tion programs inaccessible to them. Yet the very absence of the
prerequisites is often the determinant of the individual's failure to learn
and therefore makes an intervention program even more necessary.

We begin this chapter by giving several examples of the creaming-up
phenomenon to show its pervasiveness. The remainder of the chapter is
devoted to providing guidelines for developing programs that do address
the cognitive and metacognitive prerequisites for low-functioning performers. Thus, this chapter is not intended to be a systematic, comprehensive review of thinking skills programs or of existing programs for
retarded performers; rather, the purpose of the chapter is to provide a
broad-stroke discussion of the creaming-up phenomenon, generally, and
then a framework for analyzing current instructional programs and developing new ones. This framework emerges from over 20 years of
clinical research and experience with retarded performers. In our use of
the term "retarded performance," we differentiate between the manifest
level of performance and the potential for learning that has not yet
been actualized. It is the performance that is labeled "retarded," not the
individual.

THE CREAMING-UP PHENOMENON
IN EDUCATION

In Bourdieu and Passeron (1964), French sociologists, analyzed the effects of the open-gate policy that was instituted by the French higher
educational authorities. This open-gate policy allowed individuals who
usually would not have access to the university to enroll in courses there.
Their findings pointed out that only a few of the students from the
disadvantaged population were able to benefit from this policy; those
who made best use of it were those who would have "made it" in any
case. The limited success of this program, designed to help individuals
and groups in need of social promotion, was due to the lack of prerequisites possessed by the participants, which would have enabled them to
benefit from the program. Accordingly, Bourdieu and Passeron (1964)
concluded that an open-gate policy to higher education, unsupported by
adequate measures to render it effective, only gives rise to pessimism
about the role that education can play in the promotion of the disadvantaged. As the limited benefit of the opportunities offered to the disadvantaged becomes more evident the finger points to heredity as the major
determinant of achievement. Indeed, Bourdieu and Passeron called their
book *Les Heritiers,* hinting at the emphasis placed by certain behavioral
scientists on the decisive role attributed to heredity as compared with the
role played by education.

Similarly, a large number of intervention programs require that an individual show a minimal degree of initiative and resourcefulness in order to have access to them. However, the truly needy often lack this minimal capacity to create and persistently maintain conditions of inaccessibility to such programs. Thus, they are unable to make use of them. As with organisms under extreme conditions of hunger, they remain passive and in a state of torpidity that is not easily overcome, even at the sight of the most appealing food. A frequently observed reaction of many of the individuals and groups is that the programs are too late to be as helpful to them as to those whose conditions may make them less eligible, but whose power, motivation, and knowledge turn them into "up-and-comers."

Thus, for example, it is said that remedial programs for reading are not effective with retarded individuals. Remedial programs are structured to be useful for the learning-disabled, intelligent individual. Paradoxically enough, according to the clinical definition of retardation, the retarded performer does not suffer from learning disability. This view has kept thousands of children and youngsters out of remediational reading programs. Instead, they are offered some very inadequate and highly ineffective reading programs that are not considered (even by those who implement them) as giving these children a real chance to acquire reading skills. So, the most needy are once again left out. This is true for many other programs that, from the very beginning, serve only those persons who have the prerequisites necessary to benefit from them, rather than being constructed so as to accommodate various individual conditions. Thus, these programs are not helpful to all who might benefit from them.

In a recent paper on improving thinking through instruction, Raymond Nickerson (in press) asserted that programs that address problem solving have as their major goal the *improvement* of thinking, rather than its *development*. Nickerson considers thinking as a spontaneously elicited process that therefore does not have to be produced; however, it must be improved. In his words, "While we do not have to be taught to think, most of us could use some help in learning to think better than we typically do. When we say we want to teach students to think, we really mean that we want to improve the quality of their thinking" (p. 2). This quotation makes clear the view that many programs designed for critical thinking, problem solving, and creative thinking serve individuals who possess these functions but make little or inefficient use of them.

Further evidence of this view may be found in Nickerson's (in press) analysis of the areas of thinking typically covered by researchers in their efforts to teach thinking: basic operations or processes, domain-specific knowledge, knowledge of normative principles of reasoning, knowledge of informal principles and tools of thought, wills, attitudes, dispositions, styles, and beliefs.

ASSUMPTION OF PREREQUISITE COGNITIVE PROCESSES IN THINKING PROGRAMS

Many of these areas of thinking cover the content of mental functioning but do not emphasize the prerequisite cognitive and metacognitive conditions that make this kind of thinking possible. These conditions are taken for granted, just as Piaget, in his search for conservation of matter, took for granted the presence of the process of comparative behavior. The success or failure of programs teaching these thinking operations are rarely explained by the presence or absence of these prerequisite conditions. Similar comments may be made of the framework for dimensions of thinking developed by Marzano and colleagues (1988), which covers parallel aspects of thinking.

This point can also be made for the work of Piaget. The authors did not find the Piagetian concept of conservation of matter as a developmental, maturational phenomenon in the functioning of Moroccan children, despite the fact that they were 4 or 5 years older than the age suggested for this achievement in a Genevan population. When we started to look into the process responsible for this difficulty and to manipulate the assessment procedure, it became evident that the most important component of this mental operation—namely, comparative behavior—was missing, and therefore the conservation of matter could not be achieved. Assuming that this activity at this stage of the child's development was universally present, the absence of conservation seemed like a pathological phenomenon. However, when we oriented the children to compare the variations in the form of the plasticine with the constancy of its weight, we found that once this elementary cognitive prerequisite was established, the conservation of matter and even the conservation of volume (which represents an even higher level of operation) were acquired and adequately used (Feuerstein & Richelle, 1963).

Educational systems and intervention programs are replete with false assumptions as to the universal and obligatory presence of certain prerequisites of thinking. Conversely, whenever an inaccessibility to a given program is established or even anticipated, program planners conclude that the cognitive functions addressed in this program are simply not appropriate, not designed, or not necessary for the person who does not respond to them. One can see the circular nature of this assumption. On a most simple level, these programs are not made available as a matter of choice. Some educators even invoke the noble need to protect the children from the undue pressure with which they will be confronted if they are faced with a program whose set of goals is too high, and therefore their accessibility to the program is denied.

The senior author remembers the negative reaction of teachers and supervisors of Educable Mentally Retarded children when it was suggested that they introduce one of the Instrumental Enrichment program instruments that requires a high level of spatial functioning and hand–eye coordination. Teachers did not criticize the instrument for requiring a high level of information processing, but for requiring a level of visual–motor skills that was assumed to present particular difficulties for the Educable Mentally Retarded child. This did not prove to be true. The fact that, after adequate mediation, these children mastered the tasks on the instrument became proof to many teachers that indeed these children were much more modifiable in their cognitive performance than had been expected.

In order to make such modes of thinking available to the disadvantaged and to make them able to achieve what such programs require, a system-oriented approach must be implemented. Much more is required than offering some specific skills or mental operations. In a system-oriented approach, a single school system or school district is totally involved in (a) assessing the students' characteristics and their level of modifiability more dynamically; (b) offering the information obtained through this assessment to policy makers, teachers, parents, and last, but not least, to the children themselves; and then (c) establishing guidelines for intervention based on the preferred modes for increasing modifiability, as derived from the results of a dynamic assessment. In a system-oriented approach, emphasis is placed on the system that is the target for change, rather than on the individual. The environment is shaped so that it becomes a modifying environment. Ultimately, however, with the shaping of the environment, the modifiability of the individuals is increased.

In their thorough review, Resnick and Resnick (1977) pointed out that the current movement to teach thinking is distinctive in no longer addressing a small elite as in the past, but rather in its attempt to serve all learners in a truly democratic educational system. The question is: To what extent have the programs in current use been designed to make them accessible and beneficial to the masses of persons in need of development? It is our belief that these masses have been largely unable to benefit from whatever the school system offered them in curricular, content-oriented programs because they have been unprepared for this confrontation and limited in their use of cognitive skills necessary for mastering the curriculum (see chapter 9, this volume). These disadvantaged students were even less able to derive from their acquisition of basic school skills either higher mental processes or "good" thinking behaviors. To some extent, this failure is true even among students who are well prepared for their schooling and have benefited from instruction by becoming better achievers in school, although not necessarily better thinkers. This position accords with Nickerson's (in press) view: "In the aggregate, the findings from these studies force the conclusion that it is possible to finish 12 or 13 years of public education in the USA without developing much competence as a thinker" (p. 3).

PREREQUISITES FOR LEARNING:
TARGETS FOR INTERVENTION

Feuerstein and his colleagues (1980) have emphasized the decisive role played by the presence of prerequisites of thinking in the capacity of the learner to benefit from learning opportunities. Specifically, three levels of cognitive deficiencies found in retarded performers have been defined. Input level deficiencies concern the quantity and quality of data gathered by the individual. Elaboration level deficiencies include those factors that impede efficient use of available data and existing cues. Output level deficiencies include those factors that lead to an inadequate communication of final solutions. Examples of deficiencies at each level are shown in Table 5.1. Deficiencies at the input, elaboration, and output levels markedly reduce the accessibility of the content of thinking. We explain what this means for each level of deficiency.

The Effects of Input Deficiencies

A blurred perception that renders the gathering of data laborious, fragmented, partial, and imprecise will set strict limits on the individual's interaction with the stimuli, necessary for the process of thinking itself. Similarly, a lack of systematic exploration of the data at the input level will expose the individual to the hazards of a probabilistic perceptual encounter with stimuli and will not be conducive to the elaboration of all of the available data. Failure to use two or more sources of information will limit the individual's cognitive processes to the simple act of recognition and will not be conducive to the higher order conceptual thinking. The various objects that are thus perceived will not be coordinated. Such deficient functions on the input level will both affect and be affected by inadequate elaborative processes. Inadequate elaboration will follow an inadequacy in perceiving and registering a problem, because the individ-

TABLE 5.1
Deficient Cognitive Functions on Input, Elaboration, and Output Levels

Impaired cognitive functions affecting the Input level include those impairments concerning the quantity and quality of data gathered by the individual as he or she is confronted by a given problem, object, or experience. They include:

(1) Blurred and sweeping perception.
(2) Unplanned, impulsive, and unsystematic exploratory behavior.
(3) Lack of, or impaired, receptive verbal tools that affect discrimination (e.g., objects, events, relationships, etc. do not have appropriate labels).
(4) Lack of, or impaired, spatial orientation; the lack of stable systems of reference impairs the establishment of topological and Euclidian organization of space.
(5) Lack of, or impaired, temporal concepts.
(6) Lack of, or impaired, conservation of constancies (size, shape, quantity, orientation) across variation in these factors.
(7) Lack of, or deficient, need for precision and accuracy in data gathering.
(8) Lack of capacity for considering two or more sources of information at once; this is reflected in dealing with data in a piecemeal fashion, rather than as a unit of organized facts.

Impaired cognitive functions affecting the Elaborational level include those factors that impede the efficient use of available data and existing cues:

(1) Inadequacy in the perception of the existence and definition of an actual problem.
(2) Inability to select relevant versus nonrelevant cues in defining a problem.
(3) Lack of spontaneous comparative behavior or limitation of its application by a restricted need system.
(4) Narrowness of the mental field.
(5) Episodic grasp of reality.
(6) Lack of, or impaired, need for pursuing logical evidence.
(7) Lack of, or impaired, interiorization.
(8) Lack of, or impaired, inferential-hypothetical, "iffy" thinking.
(9) Lack of, or impaired, strategies for hypothesis testing.
(10) Lack of, or impaired, ability to define the framework necessary for problem-solving behavior.
(11) Lack of, or impaired, planning behavior.
(12) Non-elaboration of certain cognitive categories because the verbal concepts are not a part of the individual's verbal inventory on a receptive level, or they are not mobilized at the expressive level.

Impaired cognitive functions on the Output level include those factors that lead to an inadequate communiction of final solutions. It should be noted that even adequately perceived data and appropriate elaboration can be expressed as an incorrect or haphazard solution of difficulties exist at this level.

(1) Egocentric communicational modalities.
(2) Difficulties in projecting virtual relationships.
(3) Blocking.
(4) Trial and error responses.
(5) Lack of, or impaired, tools for communicating adequately elaborated responses.
(6) Lack of, or impaired, need for precision and accuracy in communicating one's responses.
(7) Deficiency of visual transport.
(8) Impulsive, acting-out behavior.

Note: The three disparate levels were conceived so as to bring some order into the array of impaired cognitive functions seen in the culturally deprived. Yet, there is interaction occurring between and among the levels that is of vital significance in understanding the extent and pervasiveness of cognitive impairment.

ual will not ascertain the incompatibility between the stimuli that are perceived.

The failure to adequately register and define a problem, which may be due to blurred perception or to a lack of relevant data (with consequent insufficient information processing about the characteristics of the stimuli), will meaningfully limit any motivation to search for additional data. As a consequence, the learner will not experience the disequilibrium produced by a perceived incompleteness, incompatibility, or controversiality of data. A lack of curiosity, reflecting a lack of motivation to know more, is often the outcome of a deficiency on the input level.

The Effects of Elaborative Deficiencies

In many cases, deficiencies on the elaborative level, such as lack of need for logical evidence or a lack of need to compare, are responsible for a lack of critical thinking behavior. In turn, elaborative deficiencies often create insufficiency in the input processes. Gathering data not only determines the nature of thinking but, to a very large extent, is determined by it. The goals set by elaboration for the perceptual apparatus during the input phase—such as creating relationships between discrete units of information through their comparison, creating substitutes, or producing groups through categorization—all these operations and elaborative activities result in a greater need for accuracy and precision, a more systematic exploration, and a meaningful reduction in the individual's impulsivity. These are conditions of thinking itself that affect the disposition and orientation of an individual's interaction with reality, with external or internal sources of information, and with formal or informal opportunities to learn. As a result, the individual benefits from experiences by developing higher level cognitive processes. Presenting low-functioning individuals with tasks that aim at producing problem-solving behaviors, strategic thinking, and critical thinking without equipping them with the prerequisites of thinking leaves their deficiencies uncorrected and will necessarily render these efforts inefficient. Intervention programs that do not include the correction of these deficient functions are, of necessity, inaccessible to individuals with such deficiencies.

The Effects of Output Deficiencies

The output level, that phase of the mental act in which individuals communicate the product of their thoughts, also largely determines the efficiency of the mental processes. Impulsive responses and egocentricity (in the Piagetian sense of the term) may leave even an adequately elaborated answer without the attributes necessary to make it acceptable. Furthermore, imprecision, or the lack of need for precision on the output level, may, but need not always, result in limited needs for precision on the input or elaborational levels of the low-functioning individual. All mental processes will be affected by the confrontation with tasks to which the individual has not learned to respond with the required degree of precision. The result will be a failure to use such tasks for the development of meaningful learning processes.

GOALS OF REMEDIAL PROGRAMS

A number of goals can serve as guidelines in the selection and production of tasks to include in programs designed to develop cognitive processes, problem-solving behavior, creative thinking, critical thinking, philosophical modes of thinking, or even lateral thinking (such as is present in the de Bono program, 1973) when they are addressed to retarded performers, regardless of the distal determinants of their low functioning. In order to benefit from any program, students must have the capacity to learn from experiences, whether those experiences are intentionally produced for developing thinking or emerge from informal circumstances that individuals may be exposed to in their daily life. The capacity to learn cannot be considered as universally and equally present in all individuals. Some people benefit from each exposure, be it accidental or incidental, no matter how organized the experience is or whether or not it is meant to be a learning situation. Others have an extremely limited capacity to benefit from such learning opportunities. These individuals are exposed to experiences, are confronted with many and often powerful sources of stimuli, and yet are affected by them very little. For disadvantaged learners, it is not sufficient to make these stimuli available; they need help in rendering stimuli accessible to them.

These individuals need to enhance their propensity to use their encounters with stimuli in order to become modified and more experienced by this exposure. They must be rendered more flexible so that their previous ways of thinking and the established schemata can interact with the new data by new ways of perceiving them, new modes of elaborating them, and new and more adequate ways of responding to them. Through this process of assimilating the novel and the more complex and becoming modified by this very process of assimilation in the direction of a better accommodation to the new situation, they will become better able to benefit from experience. Without this process of enhanced assimilation and accommodation, the simple presentation of data will affect the population of low-functioning individuals very little, if at all.

In other words, the first goal of a program that aims at enriching low-functioning individuals will be to render them permeable to the program by creating in them the prerequisites for learning, that is by increasing their modifiability. To this end, a number of subgoals are necessary. These subgoals must guide the construction of the program and the selection of its materials and its content. Even more, they must be considered in determining the program's presentation, didactics, and techniques that shape the interaction between the teacher (turned mediator) and the learner (turned mediatee). In the following subsections, we present the six subgoals that we chose as the basis for an intervention program whose major goal is to enable individuals to better learn what is being offered them by life or by education.

Correction of Deficient Cognitive Functions

The first subgoal is to correct the deficient cognitive functions referred to previously (see Table 5.1). What we presented as prerequisites of learning we now define as goals. The overarching goal aims at correcting the deficient functions that characterize the individual with learning problems and reduced modifiability. This goal requires that the program be designed and applied both implicitly, in the way that tasks are structured, and explicitly, in the way the tasks are presented. The program is, therefore, designed to correct those deficient cognitive functions that are responsible for the reduced learning propensity of the individual.

Thus, in the Instrumental Enrichment program, tasks are shaped so as to compel the learner to invest much more meaningfully in their perception. For instance, the learner is compelled to search at great length for a given figure in a cloud of dots in which the figure is superimposed among others. The act of segregating a given shape in a cloud of dots requires that the perceptual activity be regulated, that impulsivity be inhibited, and that the number of dots identified as belonging to the sought-after shape be kept constant until the other dots that belong to it are found. Learners will have to look for strategies to facilitate their search, such as keeping their fingers on two of the dots while looking for the other two missing dots of the square, or finding certain systems of references that facilitate greater efficiency in the process of searching. Perception must be much more accurate than when it is confronted with unequivocal stimuli. Furthermore, by making the task require more than sheer perceptual processes, the learner must actively use cognitive processes to solve the problem.

Thus, in the search for the hidden square, individuals will have to gather more precise data about the model figure. The square's attributes will have to be compared with the attributes of a triangle or quadrangle.

For this end, learners will have to use numerical criteria, such as four sides and four angles. The concept of equilaterality will have to be applied, as opposed to the differences in size of the sides of the rectangle. They will have to use the concepts of distance, length, and size. The constancy of the object across changes in its orientation will have to be maintained. From the presence of a given set of dots, the presence of another set must be inferred. From the absence of one particular dot, conclusions will be reached as to the inadequacy of the set under consideration (see Fig. 5.1).

The elaborational process is initiated by confrontation with incompatibilities inherent in the task, which are intended to produce a state of disequilibrium. The immediate feedback of the outcome of their activities will correct many deficiencies on the output level and will create a greater readiness in individuals to control their impulsivity and to check on their hypotheses, restructuring them according to the outcomes of previous trials. Instrumental Enrichment has been shaped by this need to confront the learners with stimuli, experiences, and tasks that correct their specific deficient functions. The list of deficient cognitive functions has been very important in the development of tasks designed to reach this particular goal (see Table 5.1).

Acquisition of Prerequisite Repertoire

The second subgoal is to equip the learners systematically and intentionally with the prerequisite information, verbal labels, types of relationships, and modes of operation that they need to do the exercises. Terms such as *square, triangle, parallel, equilateral, central, peripheral, before, after,*

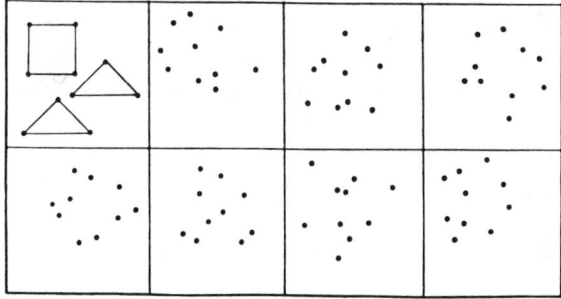

FIG. 5.1.   Selected tasks from Organization of Dots, page 2. The individual must seek the necessary dots in an irregular, amorphous cloud so as to project figures identical in size and form to the given model. Successful completion involves segregation of the dots and articulation of the field. Tasks of Organization of Dots become more difficult with increased density of dots, complexity of figures, overlapping, and changes in orientation.

simultaneous, identical, similar, and *opposite* are necessary prerequisites whose presence in the individual's repertoire should not be taken for granted, even though, in practice, there may be evidence of their application even by the most low-functioning individual (Bryant, 1974). For purposes of learning and generalizing, however, the explicit meaning of such terms is a precondition for adequate learning. Similarly, operations such as analogical reasoning, logical multiplication, permutations, substitutions, and elisions will have to become active and explicit components of the repertoire of the individual's mental functioning (see Fig. 5.2).

This second subgoal is achieved mostly through the active intervention of teachers/mediators who interpose themselves between the learner and the task and, according to their knowledge of the individual's need, introduce the vocabulary, operations, and strategies necessary for the mastery of the tasks. This subgoal should not be seen as the specific content of learning, even though it represents the content aspect of the program, which itself is not content-oriented.

Production of Generalization and Transfer

The third subgoal is to build into the program itself a propensity for generalization and transfer as a dimension of the learning process. This subgoal, the most neglected in many other programs, is mainly achieved through the creation of insight and opportunities to activate this propensity immediately. Teachers/mediators interpose themselves between the learners and the tasks and help in the analysis of the processes involved in solving a specific task. The mediator interprets to the learners the meaning of these processes and the way such processes can be applied in a variety of situations. Insight enables the learner to recognize that the functions that have been applied in a given task are relevant and applicable in others. Insight is also oriented towards discovering (through a self-reflective process) the kinds of changes produced in one's own cognitive

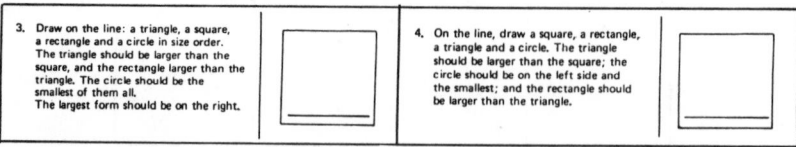

3. Draw on the line: a triangle, a square, a rectangle and a circle in size order. The triangle should be larger than the square, and the rectangle larger than the triangle. The circle should be the smallest of them all. The largest form should be on the right.

4. On the line, draw a square, a rectangle, a triangle and a circle. The triangle should be larger than the square; the circle should be on the left side and the smallest; and the rectangle should be larger than the triangle.

FIG. 5.2.   Selected tasks from Instructions, page 11. Vocabulary, concepts, and relationships previously acquired in earlier instruments are applied in the tasks of later instruments. Operations, such as inferential thinking and logical reasoning, are elicited in Instructions. Tasks require encoding, decoding, and translation from a verbal to a graphic modality.

structure by exposure to given experiences. These will be the source of new strategies applicable to other situations. Thus, insight will become an effective and powerful tool in producing transfer of the acquired elements and their generalization over situations differing from those to which the individual has been exposed.

Insightful learning, leading to generalization and transfer, relies heavily on the concept of transcendence, taken from the mediated learning experience. Mediators do not interact with the learner only to the extent that the current task requires; they go beyond the immediacy of the needs of the current situation into other areas of functioning that the individual may be called upon to fulfill. Many of the programs that fail to generalize and transfer to other tasks have failed because there was no provision for those elements that would ensure that such generalization and transfer would occur; they relied heavily on what the processes themselves would do. It was supposed that individuals who were given a set of principles would apply them spontaneously, by themselves, because development was assumed to be spontaneous and from within, outwards. The social origins of generalization and transfer have been neglected very badly. They originate in a mediated orientation toward such processes. Through the transcendent nature of their interactions, the mediators orient individuals toward a process of generalization.

In Instrumental Enrichment, for instance, the passage from learned rules, principles, strategies, and habits to other areas that are unrelated to the initial task is accomplished through what we refer to as *bridging*. The process of bridging consists in creating a certain orientation of the individual's mental activities. The individual is constantly oriented to seek areas of affinity between situations that warrant the application of the same principle. Transfer is ensured by the individual's acquired propensity toward comparing situations in terms of their commonality and difference; by an orientation toward facilitating problem-solving behavior by referring to previous experiences; by the use of the solutions of previous experiences; and by the selection of specific strategies, or modes, or styles (see Fig. 5.3).

The teacher as mediator not only activates one particular individual in the classroom, but enriches that person's propensity to generalize through the participation of the whole group, which offers the variety and diversity of its particular experiences, thus fostering divergent thinking. Insight, defined here largely as metacognition, orients the individual toward the search for the mental process to master a given task. This metacognitive activity, involving self-reflection and control, leads to activating a variety of cognitive processes that will enhance meaningfully the structural nature of the changes produced by learning. For example, the current task may be compared to a past task in which difficulty was

In the following progression, fill in the relationships, and the relationship between the relationships.

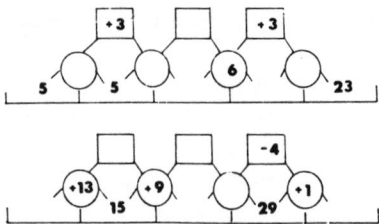

FIG. 5.3. Selected tasks from Numerical Progressions, page 21. The tasks of Numerical Progressions, presented in a numerical and graphic modality, deal with establishing the rule governing the relationship between objects and events and using that rule to explain the past and anticipate the future. The preceding tasks illustrate higher order relationships that are not readily discerned. The principle that is revealed is readily bridged to family relationships, or divisions of the atom, or the phenomenon of chain letters.

experienced. Following this comparative behavior, the current task will be solved more easily by the application of a strategy that was found to be efficient in the previous situation.

Development of Intrinsic Motivation

The development of an intrinsic motivational system is the fourth subgoal that must be kept in mind in developing programs for the disadvantaged learner. This intrinsic motivation is necessary in order to ensure that the learner will apply those learned rules, principles, sets, strategies, and problem-solving behaviors to situations in which there is no explicit demand to do so, as in the classroom (in particular), or in life situations (in general), it is not enough to know that there is a strategy. In order for it to be applied, one must also be motivated to use it. Such motivation may be extrinsic, as when one is specifically asked to implement the strategy; but such situations are rarely present in the life of disadvantaged individuals, whose encounters with situations that demand higher order thinking may be very limited (at least as long as they function as disadvantaged, both in school and at home).

The motivation to use adequate cognitive processes may become possible through an internalization and an intrinsically determined activation of part of the repertoire of functioning. One disadvantage of many available programs is that intrinsic motivation as a determinant of behavior is not addressed. Producing intrinsic motivation is especially important for disadvantaged learners. The great problem is how intrinsic motivation can be produced where it does not exist. The disadvantaged learner is often very much of a "realist," seeking types of skills or information that can best serve in immediate encounters with situations. When it comes to intellectual higher order mental processes, internal needs rarely animate. There is a pragmatism in grasping at the easiest way to perform and achieve immediate goals.

How, then, can we produce intrinsic motivation towards types of functioning that are not always needed and not necessarily economical? What types of investment are required in order to endow the low-functioning individual with a motivation that is detached from the immediately experienced, extrinsically generated need? To deal directly with low-functioning individuals, we must confront this question. Our answer is that intrinsic motivation can be equated with habit formation. A habit is an intrinsic way of determining behavior. In certain cases, the habit is not contingent on any situational constraints. In some extreme cases, it is even incompatible with extrinsic needs. When we are habituated to do something, we do not do it because it is necessary; but because we have the habit of doing it. The habit itself makes it necessary that an act be performed in a specific way.

Habit formation has been badly neglected in an era when everything has had to rely on internal reconstruction, on discovery learning, and on a spontaneous and fluid kind of approach. Many educators have fought against habit formation, which has been considered—and rightly so—as too mechanical, less thought-through, and as having no requirement for the fluid intelligence that is applied in operational thinking. Habit formation, therefore, has been totally neglected in programs in which thinking rules and problem solving are the major goals. Principles that are taught are applied to a situation in the immediate experience episodically and spuriously, leaving place for another principle to be taught. All that is taught remains on the level of fluid intelligence. There is no purposeful, intentional way of producing a crystallized form of thinking in the learner.

Habit formation usually relies heavily on a repetitive, rote type of learning. It requires repeating the same thing until it gets applied mechanically. The question, therefore, is to what extent should rote, mechanical learning be used in order to form habits of thinking and functioning? The damage that may be produced in the motivation of individuals (in having them do things they do not like to do), and to the fluidity of their thinking (by making them do things without having to think) may be greater than the benefit derived from forming habits of cognitive functioning.

In attempting to solve this problem, which sounds very much like "squaring the circle," we have used a Piagetian concept initially termed by Baldwin (1925) as the "circular reactions." We have made sure that habit formation through repetition of the same principle will never become purely mechanical. We achieved this by designing tasks that repeat themselves in one or two of the parameters they have in common but change in other parameters. A need has always been created to rediscover the familiar, the mastered part of certain skills in situations that constantly become different, more complex, more novel. Even when the same rule is applied, it will always be done with the help of more fluid types of thinking, by rediscovery, and by shaping the known element so it will fit the situation that was previously unknown. This need to create habits is addressed in Instrumental Enrichment by producing numerous repetitions of the same principle, but never applying it mechanically or blindly nor using exactly the same situation. The repetitive tasks require a great effort of discovery and restructuring. The goal of producing intrinsic motivation through habit formation makes the program require more time than does a usual enrichment program in which principles and rules are taught in a hit-and-run fashion, with hopes that by hitting and running the goal will be attained (see Fig. 5.4).

The need to crystallize the acquired cognitive processes is felt mostly in the input and output phases of the mental act, which are more resistant to change than the elaborative phase and, therefore, require much more investment in order to reach higher levels of automatization and efficiency. Thus, in order to make individuals with blurred, sweeping perception invest more and focus longer in order to reach a greater level of clarity and accuracy in the perceived, many situations must be created in which this will be imposed by the nature of the task. The same is true in the output phase. Inhibiting impulsivity in the output level is not achieved by imparting to the individual the meaning of control of impulsivity. It will require a neutralization of the original determinant of impulsivity and then the undoing of the habit that has become established through long years of practice. Undoing a habit is best achieved by substituting another and more desirable one for it. Formation of a new habit requires more effort and is spread over longer periods of time.

Follow-up research (Rand, Mintzker, Miller, & Hoffman, 1981) found an increase in the effects of Instrumental Enrichment with time elapsed after cessation of the program, a fact at least partially explained by the process of consolidation and crystallization of the cognitive habits. Time has thus acted as a reinforcer rather than as a weakening determinant of the acquired cognitive functions (see Fig. 5.5).

Habit formation adds the dimension of efficiency to the mental act. Efficiency (defined later as the "rapidity–precision" complex and the feeling of ease by which a given task is performed) is strongly dependent on whether the program allows for habit formation. The more habit

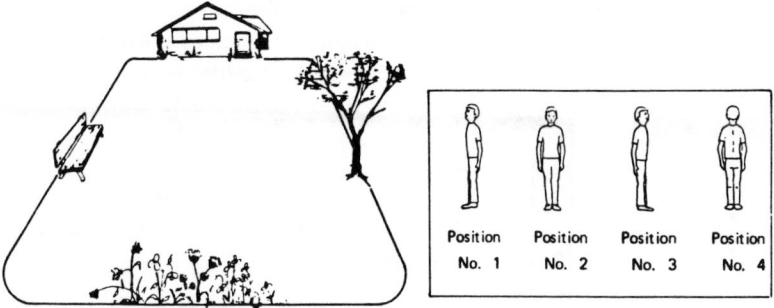

Fill in what is missing:

Position	Object	Direction in Relation to the Boy
1	The tree	
4		right
2		back
	The house	front
3	The bench	
2	The house	
	The tree	left
4		back
	The bench	
		left
3		back
4	The tree	
		right

FIG. 5.4. Orientation in Space I, page 5. The preceding task illustrates the controlled repetition of the same principle. The field must be constantly restructured for mastery. The instrument, Orientation in Space I, introduces a personal, stable system of reference by which to describe spatial relationships. It also seeks to develop and enhance the use of representation and the ability "to put oneself in the shoes of the other." A transcendent goal of the instrument is to develop an understanding and tolerance for ideas and attitudes that stem from perspectives different from one's own.

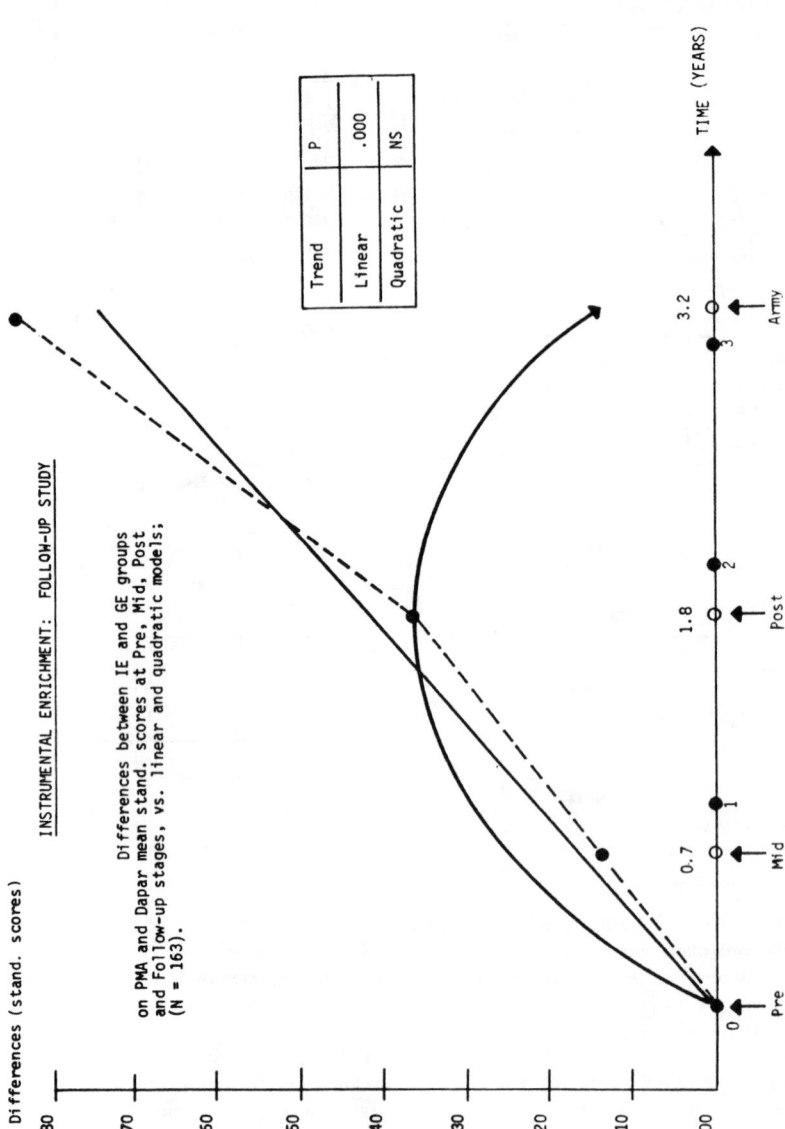

FIG. 5.5. Divergent Effects of Instrumental Enrichment. Differences between Instrumental Enrichment and general enrichment groups on PMA and Army Dapar mean standard scores at pre, mid, post, and follow-up stages indicate that nearly 2 years after the cessation of intervention, the positive effects of IE intervention continue to grow. Differences between the two groups closely resemble a linear, rather than a quadratic, model.

formation, the greater the efficiency. The greater the efficiency, the more chances that the individual will use the acquired cognitive functions, because it will be easier, require less investment, and hence be more economical.

The Piagetian concept of assimilation and accommodation has been used in shaping the formation of habits. We create a schema through repetitive behavior. But then, in order to make this schema able to accommodate to the new elements that the schema assimilates, we create conditions by which to keep the schema flexible and plastic. Thus, in Instrumental Enrichment, we have made sure that the rules and principles, strategies, modes of search, and the various subgoals that deal with the correction of cognitive deficiencies will be spread over the whole program, and that individuals will again and again have the opportunities to apply what they have learned to other areas and in a large variety of tasks. Bridging and insight will render explicit the applicability of certain automatized strategies implicit in other situations (see Fig. 5.6).

Correct the errors.
Do the separate parts in each frame fit together so that they form the complete design? If they do not, correct.

FIG. 5.6. Selected tasks from Analytic Perception, page 10. Cognitive operations, such as identification, differentiation, discrimination, categorization, representation, hypothetical thinking, and logical reasoning are elicited by tasks in Analytic Perception and will be used over and over in coping with tasks of other instruments. The sources of errors of commission and omission illustrated in the preceding tasks will be discussed and bridged into errors occurring in academic and vocational areas, daily life experiences, world affairs, and interpersonal relationships.

Development of Task-Intrinsic Motivation

The fifth subgoal is the creation of task-intrinsic motivation. This requires producing types of tasks that will entice the disadvantaged learner and stimulate a readiness to act in response to the appeal of the task itself. To be stimulating, Instrumental Enrichment uses rather complex and difficult tasks. Instrumental Enrichment makes these tasks accessible to learners by offering them the necessary mediation, carefully gauged to individual needs, to help them succeed. Once the learners are successful, the mediator leaves them to work independently. The task may be complex, but the learners' competency is not based on their previous experiences. We have carefully avoided making success contingent on previously known units of information. The complexity of the task relates only to the mental act that the individual will have to perform to solve the problem, with very little reference to previous experiences. Of course, some individuals will be more advantaged when confronted with these tasks because of their greater generalized or specific experience. However, even the advantaged must invest again and again when they are confronted with the same task. Teachers themselves must invest and make an effort when presented with our materials. In certain cases, their effort is even accompanied by their feeling, "How is it possible that I cannot do what the children are supposed to learn, and I must make an effort to do what the children will have to learn with ease?" Usually, programs used in training for problem-solving behavior are easily mastered by the teachers themselves. By the nature of the complexity of its tasks, and its independence from demands for previous learning, this program becomes a target worthy of mastery by individuals with a proficient education, as well as being interesting and appealing to the disadvantaged who have had very little or very inefficient modes of learning (see Fig. 5.7).

This task-intrinsic motivation, which is produced by the very nature of the tasks, has both a substantive and a social aspect. The substantive aspect is, of course, the nature of the mental operation in which the individual becomes engaged while doing the tasks, which tends to become "addictive" because it is both challenging and a source of success. Some of the children cannot stop doing the exercises. Some adults, as well, experience this because of the challenge of the exercise and the prospects of success. In many instances, low-functioning individuals may initially be frustrated when they see themselves caught in a task in which they have to invest, because they have never done anything requiring from them more than a very fleeting, sweeping kind of perception and attention. They may actually tear up the page of exercises. But if the mediator has enabled them to experience a first success, they come back slowly, so

Look at the sample. In each of the two frames, make a drawing that is the same as the sample ONLY in those aspects indicated by the encircled words.

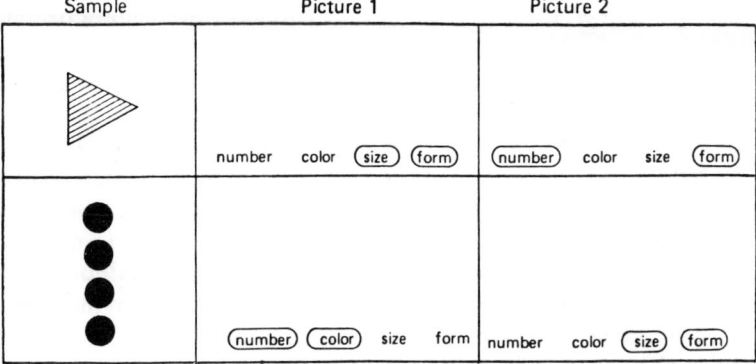

FIG. 5.7. Selected tasks from Comparisons, page 12. The preceding exercises from Comparisons illustrate the level of difficulty posed by the tasks for even advantaged learners. In order to draw items that are similar to the given model in only a few aspects, it is necessary to process information from several sources simultaneously and to devise a strategy for checking the completed work. The instrument, Comparisons, teaches the student to find and describe the similarities and differences between two or more objects or events. It also aims at enriching the verbal repertoire of parameters to direct clear, precise and accurate perception.

that what was initially a source of frustration becomes enticing. Then the task-intrinsic motivation and the curiosity emerge, not only about the task but also about themselves ("How will I be able to do it?," "How much better will I be able to do it at a later stage?," "How much more difficult will the tasks be that I will be able to do later?"). Indeed, some of the learners, having once experienced success, request more difficult tasks. This kind of task-intrinsic motivation is very seldom experienced with disadvantaged, dysfunctional learners. They usually avoid learning. They also avoid anything that is new because of the difficulties it presents to them. This behavior is followed by the evasion and lack of persistence that so strongly mark the disabled learner.

Another positive aspect of task-intrinsic motivation is the social meaning that the mastery of such tasks bears for the learner. The learner—child or adult—learns the worth of this type of activity as a socially valued and appreciated experience. Many of the children in the classroom situation who have experienced constant failure learn through Instrumental Enrichment for the first time that they can do as well as the more successful students do in subject-matter areas. Furthermore, the nature of the tasks is such that they require a constant rediscovery when they are presented to even initiated, experienced learners, including the teacher, who have performed the tasks before. A constant need exists for investment each time they are confronted with similar tasks. Even if, admittedly, they will need less investment, nevertheless they will not be able to perform just by looking at the task. Learners cannot solve the problem by simple recognition, they must restructure and rediscover the problem. The tasks have been shaped in a way that will make such discovery possible, but it requires a reinvestment. Teachers and students then realize that they are very close to each other in doing these tasks and that the relationship in the teacher/mediator–task–student triangle is much more equilateral than in any other instructional experience (see Fig. 5.8).

A new social status emerges when a disadvantaged student becomes involved in Instrumental Enrichment. Opportunities are created for the individual to succeed and to feel competent in areas in which even adults have to work hard in order to succeed. Students feel an attraction to tasks that are so effective in changing their status.

Changing the Role of the Learner

The sixth subgoal, probably the most important in dealing with the disadvantaged, is to create a feeling of not being just passive reproducers of units of information that are offered to them ready-made, but as people who are called on to generate new information that would not

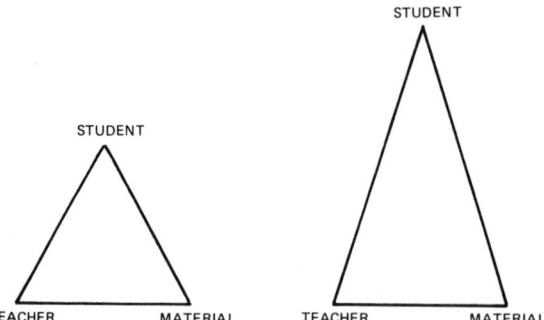

FIG. 5.8.   Teacher–Student–Material Relationship. In teaching curriculum material, the teacher is usually very familiar with the lesson's content. Students perceive the teacher and material as a unit and feel very distant from both. In Instrumental Enrichment, however, the teacher-mediator and student confront the tasks together. This cooperative relationship makes the distance from the material the same for both. The teacher–student–material interactions more closely resemble an equilateral triangle.

come into existence without their direct contribution. In many instances, deficiencies in the functioning of the disadvantaged, deficiencies in their learning process, are the direct result of a view of themselves as the recipients of information and, at best, the reproducers of the received information, without any pretense or even readiness to see themselves in the role of those who are called on and able to produce information. In many instances, programs designed to create higher mental processes offer the learner problems that are matched to the presumed repertoire of prerequisites of thinking, the componential skills, and the motivation to solve them.

Success in such programs is built on the conditions for solving the tasks, which presuppose certain prerequisites. However, low-functioning learners do not possess these prerequisites. They will not be able to solve such problems unless they are properly and systematically prepared for them and unless they are equipped, through previous focused intervention, with the necessary conditions for such problem-solving behavior. Presenting tasks that require the production of new modes of thinking, new strategies, and the discovery of rules in situations not previously experienced leads towards their perception and awareness of themselves as generators and creators of new information, which is essential in solving problems (see Fig. 5.9). Many of the individuals experience this change as having a significant impact on their lives.

Low-functioning students often attribute their failure to that to which they have not been exposed. If they do not function properly, they comment: "I have never learned it. Nobody taught me. I have never been

Every day Joan bought a tuna sandwich and a cup of coffee for lunch. She usually ate at Joe's Cafe, but one day she decided to eat at Tip's Tea Room, a place that had just opened. The total bill for her egg sandwich and cup of tea was exactly the same as it usually was at Joe's for her regular lunch; however, she noticed that the price of the sandwich at Tip's was higher than at Joe's. She immediately concluded that:

The coffee at Joe's ☐ the tea at Tip's Tea room

When A + B $=$ C + D	When A + B $=$ C + D
And A $<$ C	And A $>$ C
Then B $>$ D	Then B $<$ D

FIG. 5.9.   Selected task from Transitive Relations, page 17. The transitivity of the relationships in the preceding task permits students to generate information and arrive at conclusions otherwise unavailable to them. The instrument deals with logicoverbal reasoning and requires the use of functions, operations, and strategies acquired in earlier instruments.

told to learn it," as if everything one knows depends on external sources of information. It is noteworthy that outer-directedness is described by Zigler and Butterfield (1986) as a typical phenomenon of the mentally disadvantaged individual. This affects the output phase of the mental act, turning even a properly elaborated problem into a failing response, just because the students do not dare think they will ever be able to respond to something about which they have never been told. Programs addressing themselves to the low-functioning learners have to create the situations, the modes of presentation, and the interpretation that will convey to that learner, "Yes, you are the generator of information and thereby can be engaged in the processes of discovery and creativity, and in more efficient learning." Processes of generalization and transfer to situations other than those that have been learned will then take place.

THE DILEMMA: EMBEDDING OR ISOLATION

The literature is replete with questions about the nature of a program aimed at developing cognitive processes or enhancing problem-solving skills. Should it be given as an independent type of activity? Or should the ingredients and components of the program be intermingled and entwined as interstitial tissues in an otherwise content-oriented academic studies curriculum? (Resnick, 1987; Jones, Palincsar, Ogle, & Carr, 1987).

Those who advocate the latter approach would say that teaching intelligence without a specific content to which it is applied may leave it totally isolated from the areas of performance in which the individual is called to function. What is learned may remain isolated without any effect on the performance of the individual in a real-life or academic situation. Other arguments pertain to the structure of the intellect and to some theoretical considerations about the specificity of certain modes and types of thinking operations that are not considered to be freely and easily generalized, but must be taught, learned, and applied to specific content. The question is, therefore, to what extent will creating cognitive skills outside of, or free from, specific content be as efficient as when they are taught within their specific context? This argument is, of course, valid when we deal with higher mental processes in a direct way. However, it cannot be considered a valid argument once we deal with prerequisites of thinking, such as adequate data gathering on the input level through proper focusing, through sharpened perception, through prolonged and persistent investment, and through systematic search for data. It is not valid when we must equip the individual with the most elementary type of mental functions, such as comparative behavior, or when we deal with the episodic grasp of reality that is characteristic of the learning disabled.

An episodic grasp of reality hampers the individuals' orientation and readiness to create relationships between things, and keeps them from organizing the experienced events in a sequence that permits the perception of causal relationships, the means-and-goal relationship, or the types of associations that are necessary when one is involved in such higher order thought processes as categorization and inductive and deductive reasoning.

When one deals with elementary cognitive functions that have not been established, for whatever reason, in the individual's cognitive apparatus, then the issue of specificity is much less important. These basic cognitive functions have to be mediated and consolidated in order to render them efficient, especially when dealing with the peripheral phases of the mental act (the input and the output phases; see Table 5.1). They must be dealt with in a very focused way in situations that permit the exercise of these functions in a systematic, repetitive, and crystallizing way. This cannot be done when one deals with the curricular content-oriented programs that require a particular strategy or a particular type of function. Therefore, in attempting to increase the cognitive modifiability of the low-functioning individual with deficient cognitive functions on the input, elaboration, and output levels, the usefulness of the curricular, content-oriented approach is very doubtful.

The controversy around the question as to which is the preferable approach to the development of cognitive skills is best resolved when one refers to the broader goal of learning to learn, notably to increase the modifiability of individuals by rendering them more sensitive to opportunities for learning in a formal and informal manner. Learning to learn may then become the source of the acquisition of new strategies, the development of specific cognitive skills, the acquisition and retention of information, and the organization of sets or units of information in a way that will permit easy access and retrievability whenever required. This goal is to be considered as a precondition for any attempt to involve low-functioning individuals in more specific types of objectives that would render them accessible to content-oriented goals of learning.

REASONS FOR CONTENT-FREE PROGRAMS

In addition to the preceding arguments, four specific reasons in favor of using a specially designed content-free program for these goals, rather than making them a derivative of curricular content-oriented approach are as follows.

Resistance of the Student

The first difficulty in using curriculum materials for creating prerequisites of thinking resides in the resistance of the student. When these students are involved in learning and acquiring units of information of any nature, they usually show very little readiness to allow themselves to be "led off" or "taken away" from the subject matter with which they are dealing in order to elaborate on the relationship between units of information to which they are exposed or to deal with certain molecular components of the mental act. Low-functioning learners are often marked by a materialistic approach. They want to master the presented material. They are not interested in going beyond the stimuli, the data, or the events with which they are dealing in order to speak about the relationship between these events, the way they are organized, the way they are grouped, substituted, generalized, and conceptualized as accomplished by using higher mental processes. Some of the learners claim their right to finish a given number of pages or a given number of exercises. Never mind how much comprehension accompanies this "mastery." Teachers who attempt to derive from the acquired information the supraordinate inferences (the "moral of the story") are met with the resistance of the learners whose orientation is focused very little on the relationships and much more on the facts themselves.

The detachment from the content to the more formal aspects of thinking that can be derived from it is to be considered as an end product of a process of mediation and training, rather than as a primary goal. It is only after the program has created a state of accessibility in the disadvantaged learners that they will be able to use content-oriented learning, as well as any other event they directly experience as a source of rule learning and conceptualization. The two programs, content-laden and content-free, have to run parallel to each other with the teacher as mediator, building bridges between the two streams of learning. In this way, the resistance of the learner will be more neutralized. Once equipped with the orientation and the proper tools for the acquired information, there are much greater chances that the learner will be ready to invest in organizing, planning, encoding, categorizing, judging situational conflicts, searching for criteria for truth and falsehood and the "objective" logical evidence within it. Hopefully, then, the way of learning the curriculum content materials will prove to be much more effective and mean more than when the learning is devoid of the principles, rules, and efficient modes of input and output.

Resistance of the Teacher

A second source of resistance to the use of curriculum learning for training toward higher mental processes (such as critical thinking and problem solving) are the teachers. The teachers' materialistic orientation is encouraged by the educational system and its supervisors as well as by the children themselves. Teachers become very reluctant to spend too much time on formal aspects of learning, because this interferes with the possibility of dispensing the amount of information the learners are supposed to acquire during a given period in their school activities. Teachers often jealously guard the time allocated for teaching content even when they know how little of what is offered the children reaches them. Asking teachers to stop the flow of information or the learning of basic school skills in favor of teaching formal elements of thinking is considered to be a true loss of time, especially if they do not believe in the modifiability of the learner and when their teaching efforts are not found to lead to measurable, palpable academic achievements.

Teacher resistance is even more difficult to counteract, because teachers are little aware of the prerequisites of thinking that are responsible for adequate cognitive processes. This lack of awareness is due to their training or orientation, or their interest and motivation. They take for granted certain conditions of thinking that do not necessarily exist in each student; or, even when they do exist, they are not always used efficiently by the student. Thus, teachers base their instructional strategies on false assumptions.

For all these reasons, teachers trained in the traditional manner do not use the content of their teaching for the broader goal of teaching how to learn. However, according to our experience, a program that uses mediational interaction and "bridging" to content is more acceptable to teachers. When the program's major goals and subgoals focus on the learning-to-learn strategies, teachers will be more likely to use even content-oriented learning in a way that is compatible with this broader objective of education.

Resistance of the Subject Matter

A third reason for not combining instruction in prerequisite skills with subject-matter instruction is that the structure of the subject matter may compete with the enhancement of the process of learning. The subject matter (e.g., literature, geography, history, biology, mathematics, physics) resists the imposition of a structure of learning that is alien to the content's nature. For example, consider an attempt to use a poem written in an associative way in order to derive from it the cognitive dimensions of organization and succession. Trying to create types of grouping of events that are totally inadequate in order to learn categorization or classification may render the learning of the content extremely difficult, if not impossible. Changing the flow of a given set of data in order to reflect upon it, as required by the more formal goals of learning, may again seriously disturb the learning of the subject matter. This may result in a double loss, with the subject matter and the process of learning neutralizing, rather than reinforcing, each other.

As previously described, a program designed to produce the prerequisites of thinking has its own rhythm and rationale, and cannot follow the natural succession of the events required by the subject matter. Indeed, some programs fuse the two goals, with the consequence being that neither one is adequately reached. Therefore, we consider it much more appropriate to keep the programs of teaching subject matter and teaching thinking parallel to each other, rather than to have them mixed and integrated. The two streams of learning can be integrated by the active interpretation of the teacher and amplified by the participation of the students in the classroom.

Resistance Associated with Failure

Finally, another danger in the use of content-oriented material lies in the fact that some of this content was experienced as a source of failure and negative experiences by many of the dysfunctional students. Any attempt, therefore, to use this content as the way to provide a more positive, more optimistic experience may be met with great student resistance. Some of them say quite openly, "I won't try again," "I have failed so many times to learn this," "I give up." The use of a neutral program that is not content-oriented is much less conducive to such negative attitudes.

Even difficult tasks, but those that the students have no reason to believe they are supposed to know without learning, are more appealing and easier for the learners than engaging in something with which they have a repeated history of failure. The conditions of mediation that accompany the Instrumental Enrichment program ensure successful mastery by varying the amount and nature of the mediation that is offered. This may offset the negative orientation and enhance in the learners a readiness to re-engage in the process that they previously adamantly rejected.

In conclusion, a program mainly designed to help students acquire the prerequisites of learning will be required to make accessible to individuals those cognitive processes that are necessary for their greater adaptability.

EXPECTED OUTCOMES OF INTERVENTION

Another consideration in constructing programs for low-functioning individuals is deciding upon which areas to place the greatest emphasis. Such decisions cannot be made simply as a function of the individual's greater or lesser strengths. Because the goal of an intervention program is to create a greater facility for benefiting from learning processes, the decision as to which dimensions to choose for greater investment must be guided by conceptual, theoretical considerations.

Our own work has been guided by the "cognitive map," a conceptual framework that has enabled us to analyze tasks that require mental operations. The cognitive map is not limited to the construction of intervention programs, but it is an important tool for understanding the differential responses of individuals to different tasks in various universes of information and domains of skills. Through its parameters, it is possible to analyze and pinpoint the anticipated sources of failure inherent in the nature and characteristics of a particular task. With this information, a teacher or mediator is able to devise strategies and techniques by which to overcome or bypass the difficulties a particular individual (with a specific cognitive structure and level of information) will encounter.

The cognitive map, as opposed to the list of deficient cognitive functions, does not describe the individual; it describes the tasks and its requisites. Analysis of tasks according to the cognitive map contributes significantly to the teaching of all curricular materials. It not only permits a differential diagnosis of possible pitfalls, it also orients the teacher to the particular elements students must acquire in order to cope efficiently with the demands of the material of a lesson. It also becomes a powerful guide in decisions concerning the choice of one or another type of task, or mode of presentation, as suitable for attaining the goals set by a program.

Each cognitive task, each mental activity, can be analyzed by the following seven dimensions:

1. Universe of content.
2. Language of presentation.
3. Phase of mental act.
4. Type of operation.

5. Level of abstraction.

6. Level of complexity.

7. Degree of efficiency.

Universe of Content

The first, the universe of content, is the least relevant to the area of cognitive functions and operations. Categorization, permutation, or logical multiplication can be literally applied to any universe of information. A task's content has the least relevance to the individual's mental capacity and also probably the least influence on the nature of teaching. A very simple story may illustrate an elaborate array, and the most complex content may be used to reach a very pedestrian, illogical, irrational understanding.

Although each universe may have its own rules, they are not necessarily exclusive. Therefore, when we deal with the prerequisites of thinking, content learning should be the last component of concern. To a certain extent, anchoring the thinking process in a specific content may either cause too strong an attachment to it or narrow it too much.

As previously mentioned, this is one of the reasons why we suggest making the intervention program as content-free as possible. This means choosing the content that is best fitted to teaching a given principle or mode of thinking, rather than choosing the latter and adapting it to a given content. In evaluating functioning, one must be extremely careful not to judge an individual on the basis of a content that, for a variety of reasons, may be unfamiliar. By the same token, teaching thinking (or reading) with content that is too familiar may become so boring that it obstructs learning, because the necessary orienting process and alertness are not produced.

Language of Presentation

The second parameter of the "cognitive map," the language of presentation, is also a relatively peripheral component as compared to the cognitive processes. Of course, verbal language is the most economical and adequate modality for conceptual, abstract thinking. However, there are many languages by which problems and concepts can be presented for learning and elaboration. Symbolic language (symbols and signs as in algebraic and mathematical thinking) or figural, spatial elements may be woven into a logical network no less complex than when words are used as the major modality of presentation and communication. Failing in one modality may not necessarily obstruct the more successful use of another.

A linguistic modality may be better for training individuals who may then be able to apply what they have learned in another modality. In one of our research studies, we offered training of analogies in a figural modality; then we looked for the effects of this training in the verbal modality of presentation (Feuerstein, Rand & Hoffman, 1979).

In planning a program for an individual or a group with certain deficiencies, one must consider using a language that will not, at least in the beginning, arouse too many resistances on the part of the learners because of their specific deficiencies. Thus, the first instruments of Instrumental Enrichment require very little, if any, literacy. Verbal components are introduced only following a thorough preparation with nonverbal exercises. Similar planning decisions may be necessary in dealing with people with low levels of literacy, reading comprehension, and decoding ability. To wait until they are literate before they acquire the prerequisites of thinking and of learning may result in a very costly delay that will negatively affect their learning capacity and achievement.

Too many intervention programs and measurements of intelligence and achievement use verbal, literate behavior as the sole criterion for success and totally neglect other modalities of communication, interaction, comprehension, and problem solving. This does not mean that the verbal element should not be given a very important role in the education processes; however, it should be considered as a goal to be achieved through intervention, rather than as a means.

Phase of Mental Act

The third parameter is the phase of the mental act. As previously mentioned, we used the information-processing model of input, elaboration, and output as the major phases of the mental act. The choice of a program for the disadvantaged learner or its development should clearly define its goals at a given stage of intervention in order to choose deficient functions in one or two of the three phases for special emphasis.

The elaborative phase, responsible for the data's transformation, their categorization, classification, labeling, and other operations by which new information is generated, is certainly the essential goal of a program that aims at developing thought processes. However, for increasing the individual's capacity to learn through a learning-to-learn program, mediating the input (i.e., increasing the efficiency by which the individual gathers the data, makes use of the perceptual apparatus, and registers information) and, at a later stage, the output level (i.e., defining the results of elaboration in order to convey them to oneself or to a partner) may be crucial. Choosing programs that emphasize only the elaboration of data may not necessarily enhance the learning process. In certain cases, they may even miss the major goal itself if the peripheral input and output phases have not been corrected through adequate investment.

Instrumental Enrichment emphasizes correcting deficiencies on the input and output levels, and exercises are structured so as to confront the learners with the need to gather data systematically and to be precise and to elaborate events using a spatiotemporal grid. Through the nature of the task and the mediated learning experience, which is the prevalent mode of interaction, learners search for modalities of presentation, learners search for modalities of presentation that are most responsive to the need for logical evidence as the way to make the conveyed response acceptable to partners. If the elaboration phase represents the core of the thought processes, the peripheral phases of input and output represent those means that make the elaboration possible and the output acceptable.

Analyzing the mental act according to phases permits the ascription of a differential weight to the success or failure of functioning and achievement instead of the global evaluation that results from a product-oriented measurement.

Type of Operation

The type of operation is the fourth parameter to be considered when constructing tasks of an intervention program. Operations may range from purely perceptual and reproductive, such as the process employed in "re-cognition," or may reach the upper levels of formal and abstract thinking, such as inferential, inductive, and deductive reasoning. A certain number of basic operations, monitored by a taxonomy of operations requisite for further learning, must be imparted to the learner in the course of any enrichment program.

In Instrumental Enrichment, a number of such operations have been dispersed over the entire program. These operations include tasks that can only be accomplished by representational thinking, tasks that require inferential and hypothetical thinking, seriation of events according to rules, transitive relationships, logical multiplication, analogical thinking, eduction of rules, deductive and inductive processes, and so on. Whenever the operations are not explicit, they are evoked and shaped in the mediational interaction of the classroom. Thus, inferring the presence of a little square from a cluster of dots allows us also to infer the presence of other figures intermingled in an amorphous cloud (see Fig. 5.1). The co-existence of two conditions permits us to infer the existence of one condition from the presence of the other. The same is true for inductive and deductive modes of thinking and transitive relationships (see Fig. 5.9). It is most interesting to see how operations from hierarchically higher levels of thinking can be implemented in programs that address otherwise low-functioning individuals. This is done by choosing appropriate content, language, and phase without necessarily renouncing the operation itself.

Level of Abstraction

The fifth parameter that must be considered in choosing or constructing a program is its level of abstraction. The level of abstraction is a very ambiguous concept, especially when it is used by educators to define certain tasks and the failure to achieve them. Thus, the ability to count or to compute is considered a higher level of abstraction, although we know that learning to compute may be based on a purely reproductive, technical memorization process and serial learning and need not rely on abstract thinking. By the same token, certain verbal interactions are considered abstract when very little operational thinking is either necessary or used during their generation.

It is, therefore, necessary to define the level of abstraction operationally (very much in line with the Piagetian approach) as the distance between a mental act and its concrete component. Piaget, who relates to mental behavior as an interaction ("conduit"), describes the sensorial concrete interaction as marked by a zero distance between the act/"conduit"/behavior and the reality upon which it is effected. Touching a table represents an interaction of zero distance between organism and the object. Zero distance also defines an interaction between a star and the eye that sees it. It does not really matter whether the light of the star reaches the eye or whether the finger touches the table. In both examples, the interaction is limited to a sensorial experience, and the distance is zero.

Calling an object "a table" immediately sets a great distance between the object itself and the mental act that results in its labeling. Think of the considerable differences in size, color, material, function, and so forth that are included in "table." From what distance will the labeler perceive the common traits of all these objects and be able to ignore the number of differences among them? The distance is increased even more when two objects that exist in isolation are brought together by a mental act and grouped by the words, "two tables." When "furniture" is used, conceptualizers climb up a number of steps, and the distance between them and the specific objects to which they relate is increased even more. The concept of distance is very useful in gauging the modalities by which abstract thinking can be introduced and evaluated.

Thus analyzed, the mental acts of various levels of retarded performers may actually be far more abstract than one would tend to believe, so that barriers considered as unsurpassable are actually much less so. Abstract thinking may be considered more accessible and, wherever necessary, more economical to the individual's adaptation.

Level of Complexity

The level of complexity is also a parameter that must be borne in mind in attaining a well-defined goal of creating the prerequisites of thinking. We define the level of complexity as the number of units of information required to elaborate a given task. The absolute number may be corrected and even reduced significantly by certain cognitive processes. Categorizing a list of units or bytes of information may reduce the number by simply using categories instead of units. By the same token, the degree of an individual's familiarity with certain units of information may reduce the level of complexity of certain tasks. Deciding and selecting the desirable level of complexity at a given point in the development of an individual or a program may have an important bearing on the efficiency of the intervention.

It is clear that disadvantaged learners are accustomed to dealing with very limited levels of complexity. In certain cases, due to their episodic grasp of reality, they ignore whatever is beyond their threshold. Therefore, it is important to endow them with adequate cognitive strategies to enlarge their capacity to deal with complexity, teaching them how to group, to categorize, to generalize, and to use other cognitive approaches.

Level of Efficiency

The seventh parameter, and probably the most controversial one, is the level of efficiency. The reader must take note that the concept of efficiency refers to the level of efficiency required for a given task to be mastered; it is neither the individuals nor their functioning that is the target of analysis. Tasks differ in the amount and degree of efficiency required for their mastery.

Efficiency is defined by two measurable dimensions. One is referred to as the "rapidity–precision" complex. The other, an imponderable but still important dimension, is the subjectively experienced effort involved in working on a given task. Rapidity can be measured by the time required to do the task. Precision can be scored by simply counting the number of errors. The effort can be evaluated indirectly by the statements of subjects about their feelings, their readiness to continue, their fatigue, or from other cues. Tasks that require efficiency for their mastery may require special investment, lest the achievement be very poor.

Efficiency may best be acquired through automatization and habit formation, which, in turn, are produced by repetitive, mechanical, rote kinds of learning. Any reluctance to use rote repetitive learning may deleteriously affect the mastery of tasks that strongly depend on high levels of efficiency. By illustration, reading is one of the activities whose mastery depends mostly on efficiency. Somebody who reads too slowly may understand very little of what has been read because of a broken gestalt and an overload on the mnemonic functions due to the dispersion of the data over time. Somebody who takes a year to read a book may have very little understanding of the basic denouement of the story because the beginning may have been forgotten by the time the end is reached. This also occurs with sentences. Children who have difficulty in decoding forget the beginning of a sentence by the time they reach its end. Also, without a satisfactory level of precision in reading, comprehension will be very limited. Rapidity attained at the expense of precision, or precision to the detriment of rapidity, may render reading extremely inefficient. By the same token, when accompanied by a subjective feeling of effort, reading will be very limited, even if it is rapid and precise. Efficiency, therefore, is a dimension that must be purposefully, systematically developed, particularly with tasks that require efficiency as a precondition.

Certain new modes of learning, such as discovery learning and critical thinking, have totally ignored the development of efficiency. We suspect that many of the difficulties in learning may be due to the inefficiency of individuals in their interactions with the new elements they must learn.

In summary, as described by both the discussions of the deficient cognitive functions and the cognitive map, the types of tasks to be offered in a program designed to increase the modifiability of individuals, that is, to render them more sensitive to learning experiences, must be guided and purposefully related to the combined needs of the learner and the tasks.

TEACHER TRAINING

Another characteristic of programs addressing disadvantaged and low-functioning individuals is their strong dependence on training the teacher to act as a mediator and not merely as a dispenser of information. Mediated Learning Experience (MLE), a pivotal component of the theory of Structural Cognitive Modifiability, is defined as a quality of the organ-ism–environment interactions that are characteristic of human beings and responsible for their modifiability. It serves as a powerful guideline for structuring programs for the enhancement of Structural Cognitive Modifiability.

To turn teachers into mediators instead of conveyors and dispensers of units of information requires a very meaningful change in both the perception of the child as a modifiable entity and in the belief that, indeed, education can play a significant role in this process. Furthermore, turning teachers into mediators means equipping them with the skills and motivation to produce such changes. Additionally, teachers must reach mastery of the program they offer the child, a mastery that will be buffered by a good knowledge of its theory and a full understanding of the "whys, the hows, the whens, and the when nots." The more theoreti-cally based the teaching activity, the more modifying the interactions and the greater the degree of freedom teachers will have in structuring the learning experiences of their students.

MLE is characterized by closing the loop between the teacher as an emitter of a message (the proximal partner of the interaction), the re-ceiver of the message (the distal partner of the interaction), and finally, the emitted message itself. The three partners involved in the interaction (mediator, stimuli/message, and mediatee) are manipulated and trans-formed so that, indeed, the emitted message will be received and have the desired effect on the receiver.

By way of contrast, consider the regular modality of teaching. The teacher emits a message, presents a unit of information to a classroom of children or even to a single individual, and is contented with the process of emission, without considering the need to ensure that what was trans-mitted was truly registered, received, and eventually integrated into the receiver's system. Regular teaching often neglects to ensure that the communication loop is closed. In many cases, teachers ignore the need to change all three partners in this interaction so as to guarantee that the mediational process has been accomplished.

The intention of the mediators is recognized by the way they transform the message, amplifying it, detailing it, substituting language to make it better understood, and increasing its appeal so that it will penetrate the system of the mediatee. By manipulating the mediatee's state and rendering them more attentive, more eager, more affected by the unit of information, they are transformed and rendered more accessible and sensitive to the particular element mediated to them. By the same token, mediators are changed by their intention to mediate to the child. By the intentionality of the mediators, the teaching interaction receives the quality of a mediational experience (see Fig. 5.10).

MEDIATED LEARNING EXPERIENCE MODEL (M. L. E.)

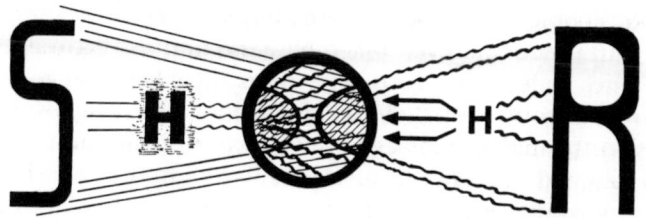

FIG. 5.10. Mediated Learning Experience. The human mediator (H) interposes himself/herself between the stimulus (S) and the organism (O) and between the organism and the response (R) in order to change the quality of the interaction. In MLE there is a change in the nature of the stimulus, an increased vigilance and alertness on the part of the organism, and change in the mediator as well. As illustrated, the mediator does not block out stimuli that reach the organism by direct exposure, nor does he/ she control all response to stimuli. One of the mediator's functions is to filter, frame, and focus incoming stimuli in the input phase. At the output level, among other functions, the mediator attempts to restrain impulsivity or to help initiate a response.

It is for these reasons that teacher training is a condition sine qua non for making any program accessible to the disadvantaged. We consider that teacher training is a necessary condition for many of the required qualities of any instruction. However, programs for advantaged individuals whose functioning allows them to benefit from direct exposure to stimuli and learning opportunities are less dependent on Mediated Learning Experience interactions. On the other hand, disadvantaged learners can benefit very little from even the most powerful programs if there is not adequate mediation. Teacher training, though it may be costly and problematic logistically, should therefore be considered as an integral quality of the program. Without it, the program's value may be extremely limited, even though it may be attractive and easy to implement.

Many evaluators of intervention programs consider dependence on teacher training as a costly burden and, to a certain extent, a negative feature. We contend, however, that programs that are carried out without teacher training as a condition of their application may do more damage than good, even if they show some effects. As strong as this assertion sounds, it highlights our belief that disadvantaged learners do not simply need tasks to master nor principles to learn. A disposition must be produced in them that will change their cognitive structure, their way of interacting with new aspects of information, and the way they perceive themselves as changing entities affected by experience in the direction of a higher level of efficiency. Exercises and activity alone, even if they are efficient and very meaningful, do not always lead to this state of awareness. People may repetitively experience certain events, become familiar with them, and even reach mastery, and still have a feeling of incompetence unless a mediator interprets their behavior to them and turns it into a source of their self-perception of being producers of information through processes of inference, of being decision makers through planned exploration of alternatives, and of choosing among priorities by comparing various processes. In fact, they must perceive themselves as contributors to reality rather than as being subdued by it.

For this end, direct experience is not enough. This is borne out by the great number of people who do not derive these cognitive and emotional structures from their direct experience. A mediator is needed for much of what makes us human. The fact that we are dependent on mediators does not reduce our status as independent autonomous thinkers. It only interprets the story of our autonomy as a product of millenia of cultural transmission through our Mediated Learning Experiences. Teacher must be mediators. To turn teachers into people who believe and who are sufficiently skilled, training is a must. In addition to its role in increasing the efficiency of any program, a vital by-product of teacher training is the large body of information on human modifiability and the most efficacious ways in which it can be achieved. Through such training, a teacher will acquire a better understanding of cognitive processes, the prerequisites of learning, and the deficient cognitive functions responsible for learning disabilities, thereby becoming more aware of the skills by which to turn the student into a willing and efficient learner.

SUMMARY

In this chapter, we have attempted to show that the tendency today is to produce programs with built-in conditions for accessibility, but that the conditions do not exist in the most needy population. The "creaming up" phenomenon then becomes a natural selection process that renders those who cannot "make it" unable to benefit from such programs. We have outlined a number of conditions that may make programs accessible and beneficial to such individuals, even when their own conditions seem to show no promise of benefit. These suggested conditions become especially useful for programs deemed essential to modify the individual's course of life. The modifiability of individuals, in turn, is dependent on the cognitive processes, their capacity to learn from formal and informal experiences, and their disposition or readiness to adapt to more novel and complicated life situations.

The mass of disadvantaged learners represent an untapped reservoir of human resources. In these days when life requires a constant adaptation through the process of learning, we cannot afford to turn these neglected human resources into a danger to themselves or society, nor to offer them a menial, restrictive life. Investment in intervention and enrichment programs must not be considered a luxury but a vital instrument for personal and societal progress.

REFERENCES

Baldwin, J. M. (1925). *Mental development in the child and the race.* London: Macmillan.
Bourdieu, P., & Passeron, J. C. (1964). *Les heritiers: Les etudiants et culture.* Paris: Les Editions de Minuit.
Bryant, P. E. (1974). *Perception and understanding in young children.* London: Methuen.
de Bono, E. (1973). *CORT thinking.* New York: Pergamon Press.
Feuerstein, R., Rand, Y., & Hoffman, M. B. (1979). The dynamic assessment of retarded performers. In R. Feuerstein, Y. Rand, & M. B. Hoffman (Eds.), *The Learning Potential Assessment Device: Instruments and techniques.* Baltimore: University Park Press.
Feuerstein, R., Rand, Y., Hoffman, M. B., & Miller, R. (1980). *Instrumental Enrichment: An intervention program for cognitive modifiability.* Baltimore: University Park Press.
Feuerstein, R., & Richelle, M. (1963). *Children of the Mellah.* Jerusalem: Mossad Szold Press.
Harvard University; Bolt, Beranek and Newman, Inc.; & The Ministry of Education of the Republic of Venezuela. (1983). *Odyssey: A curriculum for thinking (Foundations of reasoning; understanding language; verbal reasoning; problem solving; decision making; innovative thinking).* Watertown, MA: Mastery Education.
Jones, B. F., Palincsar, A. S., Ogle, D. S., & Carr, E. G. (Eds.) (1987). *Strategic thinking and learning: Cognitive instruction in the content areas.* Alexandria, VA and Elmhurst, IL: Association for Supervision and Curriculum Development in cooperation with the North Central Regional Educational Laboratory.
Lipman, M., Sharp, A. M., & Oscanyan, F. S. (1980). *Philosophy in the classroom.* Philadelphia, PA: Temple University Press.
Marzano, R. J., & Arrendondo, D. E. (1986). *Tactics for thinking.* Aurora, CO: Mid-continental Regional Educational Laboratory.
Marzano, R. J., Brandt, R. S., Hughes, C. W., Jones, B. F., Presseisen, B. Z., Rankin, S. C., & Suhor, C. (1988). *Dimensions of thinking: A framework for curriculum and instruction.* Aurora, CO: Association for the Supervision and Curriculum Development in cooperation with the Mid-Continental Regional Educational Laboratory.
Meeker, M. N. (1969). *The structure of the intellect: Its interpretation and uses.* Columbus, OH: Charles Merrill.
Nickerson, R. (in press). On improving thinking through instruction. *Review of Research in Education.*
Rand, Y., Mintzker, Y., Miller, R., & Hoffman, M. B. (1981). Instrumental Enrichment: Immediate and long-term effects. In P. Mittler (Ed.), Frontiers of knowledge in mental retardation: Vol. 1 (pp. 141–152). Baltimore: University Park Press.
Resnick, D. P. and Resnick, L. B. (1977). The nature of literacy: A historical explanation. *Harvard Educational Review, 47,* 370–385.
Resnick, L. B. (1987). *Education and learning to think.* Washington, DC: National Academy Press.

Sternberg, R. J. (1986). *Intelligence applied.* New York: Harcourt Brace Jovanovich.

Whimbey, A., & Lockhead, J. (1980). *Problem solving and comprehension: A short course in analytical reasoning.* Philadelphia, PA: Franklin Institute Press.

Zigler, E., & Butterfield, E. C. (1986). Motivational aspects of changes in IQ test performances of culturally deprived nursery school children. *Child Development, 39,* 1–14.

Dimensions of Thinking: Implications for Testing

Robert L. Linn
Center for Research on Evaluation, Standards, and Student Testing
University of Colorado, Boulder

This book and the associated efforts by the Association for Supervision and Curriculum Development and the North Central Educational Laboratory to encourage the teaching of thinking attest to the fact that there is great interest in the topic of thinking, especially in the skills and processes that have come to be called "higher order thinking skills." Pleas for greater emphasis on higher order thinking skills are plentiful. This is apparent not only in the rash of reports on the status of education that have appeared in the past 5 years (e.g., National Assessment of Education Progress, 1985; The National Commission on Excellence in Education, 1983); but also in the wide array of educational journals and periodicals. Partially as a result, a wide variety of instructional materials and teaching approaches devoted to improving the teaching of problem solving, comprehension, critical thinking, metacognitive skills, and other higher level thinking processes have been developed.

Testing and assessment have not been ignored in the recent emphasis on thinking. The Alexander and James (1987) report of the Study Group on the Nation's Report Card, for example, strongly urged that the National Assessment of Educational Progress place greater emphasis on the assessment of higher order thinking skills. It is apparent, from even a cursory review of the brochures of test publishers or a visit to their exhibit booths at a professional meeting, that the message that testing needs to include higher order thinking skills has not been missed by the test publishers.

CONCERNS ABOUT CURRENT APPROACHES

When testing or assessment is mentioned in discussions of ways to improve the teaching of thinking skills, however, three themes are most common. First, dissatisfaction with current tests is frequently expressed, because they are seen as placing too much emphasis on simple factual knowledge. Second, suggestions are made that the approaches to assessment need to be expanded beyond paper-and-pencil tests, in general, or more forcefully and specifically, beyond standardized multiple-choice tests. Finally, the notion is often expressed that tests, or more broadly conceived assessment systems, signal what is held to be important to teachers, parents, and students, Thus, for the teaching of thinking to be recognized as important and given enough emphasis, it is necessary to develop assessment procedures that do justice to the goals.

The third concern, that tests are devices that direct instruction, is critical to the interpretation of criticisms of tests and to discussions about needed changes. The degree to which tests influence what teachers do and what students learn depends heavily on the uses that are made of test results. Regardless of one's position in the long-standing debate about whether tests should follow or lead instruction, it is clear that tests can be an important factor in shaping instruction and learning.

"Will this be on the test?" is a question that is too familiar to teachers. Although it is not a question that most teachers like to hear, it is easily understood in terms of Walker's (1983) observation that "the things that are really important, as every student knows, are the things that appear on tests and are used in grading" (p. 173).

Traditionally, of course, it is teacher-made tests, not standardized tests, that determine student grades. In the past, most standardized tests had little influence on learning and instruction, because they did not influence student grades, and because most schools made relatively little use of the results, they had little impact on teachers. Certainly, there are exceptions, such as the New York State Regents Examinations or the College Board Advanced Placement Tests; however, before the start of the minimum-competency test movement and the great expansion in the use of tests as a means of gaining greater accountability, most uses of standardized achievement tests were relatively benign.

Today, however, there are examples throughout the country of testing programs that have been introduced for the explicit purpose of directing education. Tests have become the major tool of policy makers in implementing educational reform (see, e.g., Linn, 1987; Madaus, 1985; Pipho, 1985). By their actions, policy makers have taken the affirmative position on the role of tests in directing teaching and learning.

This changed context is important for considering the concern that tests overemphasize factual knowledge and the concern that the multiple-choice format is inadequate for testing more important, higher order thinking skills. Research, for example, that shows that multiple-choice tests correlate as well or better with essay tests as the latter do with each other, or that multiple-choice tests are better predictors of grades than are essay tests, is relevant when the goal is prediction. Such evidence is not convincing, however, when the purpose of the test is to direct instruction and learning. Similarly, the content validity evidence that shows the match between the questions on a test and the content and exercises in, for example, science textbooks is not sufficient for the person who is dissatisfied with the textbooks and argues for the importance of hands-on experience.

In the following sections of this chapter, the concerns about the over-emphasis on factual knowledge, the constraints of multiple-choice tests, and the inadequacy of current tests as targets that will enhance thinking are discussed. That discussion is followed by a consideration of alternatives to current approaches to assessment and changes in testing that are needed in order have tests and other assessment procedures contribute more to the teaching of thinking.

Factual Knowledge

Dissatisfaction with current tests has a variety of sources. For the focus of this discussion, however, a primary concern is the emphasis that both teacher-constructed and standardized tests place on the simple recall of factual knowledge. Analyses of teacher-constructed tests (e.g., Fleming & Chambers, 1983; Stiggins, Griswald, & Green, 1988) indicate that questions that require the use of higher order thinking skills are the exception, rather than the rule. Questions that ask students to recall information are much more common than questions that require comparison, inferences, or evaluation.

As has been highlighted in several reviews, the emphasis on factual knowledge is not limited to teacher-constructed tests. The classification of questions on standardized tests by level of skill required is equally discouraging. Frank (1978), for example, classified 765 items from 12 standardized science tests using the first four developmental levels in Bloom's (1956) taxonomy. Only 2% of the items were placed in the two higher categories: application and analysis. In contrast, 78% of the items were placed in the lowest category, the simple recall of factual information. In another review of science achievement tests, Morgenstern and Renner (1984) found that 90% of the items on the tests that they reviewed required only the recall of factual information. Others, such as Bowman and Peng (1972) and Levine, McGuire, and Nattress (1970), have reported similarly discouraging results even for standardized tests used at the graduate and professional school level.

The perceived overemphasis on low-level skills is not limited to science tests. Similar concerns have been expressed, for example, by critics of standardized reading tests. According to the report of the National Academy of Education Commission on Reading (1985), "reading is the process of constructing meaning from written words" (p. 7). Skilled reading requires thinking and interrelating information from the printed page with prior knowledge to construct meaning. It requires self-monitoring of understanding. Component skills of decoding and fluency of word recognition are certainly important, but they alone are insufficient.

Reviews of standardized reading tests (e.g., Cross & Paris, 1987; Linn & Valencia, 1986; Valencia & Pearson, 1986), however, reveal a heavy emphasis on the component skills. Items that require the recognition of word meanings and literal comprehension make up a majority of the questions on many standardized tests. Items that attempt to assess the test taker's ability to derive meaning from a passage and to make inferences are often limited to questions such as the following: What is the main idea in this story? What is this story mostly about? What is the best title for this story? How did the character probably feel? These are not bad questions; however, a close inspection often reveals that such questions can be answered using information that is explicitly stated in the text.

For survey tests that are not used to make decisions about students, teachers, or programs, and that are not used to rank-order schools, there is less reason to be concerned about the number of items placed at various levels of Bloom's taxonomy or the limited degree of integration of information across different segments of a text or the limited nature of inferences that a student must make to answer reading comprehension questions. Scores based on such items are apt to correlate quite highly with scores based on tests that critics would judge to require greater amounts of integration of information, more complicated inferences, and the solution of novel problems. Thus, if the test is only used as a proxy for the more difficult-to-measure, albeit more important, outcomes of instruction, then the high correlations between the two types of measures are reassuring.

When schools can, and do, purchase materials specifically designed to increase scores on specific standardized achievement tests because of the increased importance that policy makers, the press, and the general public are placing on the test scores, however, then predictive validity is not satisfying. As Brown (1987) has argued,

> . . . insecure teachers and schools under pressure to raise achievement levels blatantly teach to the tests. Since the tests require little thoughtfulness, the instructions and curriculum that revolve around them remain stuck at a very basic level. Under such circumstances, the demands for accountability intrude on teaching and learning time and warp instruction in ways that may often raise test scores even as they lower the quality of the education being delivered. (p. 51)

Constraints of Standardized, Paper-and-Pencil Tests

Even under the best of circumstances, it is difficult to write good questions to assess deeper understanding. However, the difficulty is exacerbated by the constraints of standardized testing. Among the more important constraints are the need for efficiency, the desire to represent the test results by a single number that places each test taker on a common scale, and the emphasis on the use of test results for purposes of accountability. The emphasis on accountability limits the domain of the test and, I argue, also reduces the instructional utility. The desire for a single score contributes to the emphasis on well-structured problems with a single right answer. The need for efficiency limits tests to machine-scorable formats, which usually means multiple-choice test items.

Multiple-choice questions can be written that require much more than simple recognition. Consider, for example, the following illustrative item from Ebel and Frisbie (1986):

> If the radius of the earth were increased by 3 feet, its circumference at the equator would be increased by about how much?
> a. 9 feet
> b. 12 feet
> c. 19 feet
> d. 28 feet (p. 171).

Ebel and Frisbie (1986) argued that items such that one, which present "novel problem situations reward the critical-minded student who has sought to understand what he/she was taught and penalize the superficial learner" (p. 171). The key is that the problem is novel.

Students obviously could be given a formula for calculating the increase in the circumference as a function of an increase in the radius.

Memorization of the formula and practice with similar problems would destroy the novelty of Ebel and Frisbie's problem and turn what was once an item that was sensitive to degree to which students understand fundamental principles and can use those principles to solve problems into a problem that simply requires the recognition of a problem type and the application of a memorized formula with or without understanding the reasons why the formula works.

Problem Structure.   Norman Frederiksen (1984) provided an excellent discussion of these constraints in an article entitled "The Real Test Bias: Influences of Testing on Teaching and Learning." Frederiksen argued that items on standardized tests typically present well-structured problems, that is, ones that "are clearly stated, all the information needed to solve the problem is available in the problem (or presumably in the head of the student) and an algorithm exists that guarantees a correct solution if properly applied" (p. 199). He went on to argue that most important problems, both in and out of school, are ill-structured in the sense defined by Simon (1978). They may not have a single correct answer, much less provide all the information needed to solve the problem or be solvable by applying a previously learned algorithm. Ill-structured problems often contain ambiguities. Problem identification and representation, the generation of hypotheses, planning, and the exploration of solution strategies are of central importance.

Although, as the prior example item from Ebel and Frisbie (1986) illustrates, multiple-choice items can tap higher order thinking and problem-solving skills, such items are difficult to write and usually involve well-structured problems. Multiple-choice items that get at the thinking processes that are crucial in the solution of ill-structured problems are even rarer. Even if multiple-choice items that are effective at measuring the thinking processes required to solve ill-structured problems can be obtained, the problems themselves are apt to be considered to be unacceptable on a test that is used to hold students accountable. As Frederiksen (1984) noted, such problems could almost certainly be attacked as unfair. Challenges to minimum competency tests support this conclusion. In the Debra P. case, for example, the Fifth Circuit Court of Appeals ruled that "fundamental fairness requires that the state be put to test on the issue of whether the students were tested on material they were or were not taught" (644 F.2d at 404). Although thinking skills and strategies can be taught, teaching a correct solution path for a particular ill-structured problem that might be included on a test would destroy the purpose by converting the problem into a simple recall question.

The report of the National Academy of Education's Committee that reviewed the recommendations of the Alexander-James study group on the Nation's Report Card (National Academy of Education, 1987) provided the following important caution in this regard:

> It is all too easy to think of higher-order skills as involving only difficult subject matter as, for example, learning calculus. Yet one can memorize the formulas for derivatives just as easily as those for computing areas of various geometric shapes, while remaining equally confused about the overall goals of both activities. All subjects have a basic knowledge component that can be taught by drill and practice. This basic knowledge, while prerequisite to competence, is also distinct from the intellectual skills of gathering relevant information, evaluating evidence, weighing alternative courses of action, and articulating reasoned arguments. (p. 54)

The obvious implication of this caution is that it is important not to confuse apparent difficulty of subject matter with the demands that a test problem makes for the exercise of thinking skills as conceived of by the National Academy of Education Committee.

Efficiency.   Efficiency looms as another major obstacle to the development of assessment procedures that will better serve the goals of teaching thinking skills. As Frederiksen (1984) noted, "efficient tests tend to drive out less efficient tests, leaving many important abilities untested—and untaught" (p. 201). Multiple-choice tests are certainly efficient, but, as has already been stated, they tend to emphasize factual knowledge at the expense of inference, analytical thinking, problem solving, and the application of knowledge to novel situations.

The area of writing provides an excellent example of the tendency for efficiency to govern the nature of testing. The most recent National Assessment results on the performance of students in writing suggest that all is not well (Applebee, Langer, & Mullis, 1986). This should be no surprise, given the amount of writing most students are required to do in school and the nature of the tests that are most often used to assess writing skills. Linn and Palmer (1985) discussed the role of testing in relationship to teaching writing, a skill that clearly requires the application of thinking skills, along the following lines.

Chall's (1977) analysis suggests that textbooks, even those in grammar and composition, give little emphasis to writing. Assignments are more apt to require "underlining, circling, and filling in single words" (Chall, 1977, p. 64). Multiple-choice tests do little to emphasize the importance of writing. Only one of the two College Board Achievement Tests in English composition requires any actual writing, and that one allocates only 20 minutes to writing an essay and the remaining 40 minutes to multiple-choice items (paraphrased from Linn & Palmer, 1985).

There are, of course, many reasons for the scarcity of tests that require actual writing rather than choosing among alternative sentences or the identification of grammatical errors. Essays are expensive to score, and they yield lower reliabilities than can be achieved in a fixed period of time using multiple-choice items. Research has shown that multiple-choice tests can be constructed to correlate relatively well with essay tests; indeed, the correlations sometimes approach the limits set by the reliabilities of the tests. Essay tests are also unlikely to enhance the predictive validity that is provided by a multiple-choice test. Thus, it is difficult to justify such tests in terms of traditional criteria of reliability and predictive validity, particularly if the substantial difference in efficiency is given any weight. However, as has been noted previously, those should not be the only, or even the primary, considerations for tests that are being used to direct instruction and learning.

Adequacy of Instructional Targets

Writing, like other applications of thinking to solve problems, requires practice. It deserves to be emphasized by students and teachers. But tests send messages to students and teachers regarding the importance of mastering particular skills. To convey the message that writing is of great importance, more emphasis needs to given to tests that actually require students to write, even at the expense of some reduction in reliability (Linn & Palmer, 1985).

Some progress has been made in this area in recent years. Writing samples are included in a number of state and district assessment systems. The scores that are derived, however, are often of less interest than the examples of the essays that students produce. Certainly, from an instructional perspective, the comments and suggestions that a teacher makes on a student's written work are apt to be more useful in helping students improve their writing than the summary grade that is assigned. That is also apt to be true of other assessments of student thinking skills.

Consider, for example, the relatively simple case of story problems in arithmetic. I say "relatively simple" because the problems are well structured and yield a single correct answer. Furthermore, an effective job of testing a student's ability to solve such problems can be done using multiple-choice items. However, the instructional utility of the global score provided by a standardized test is limited. It can provide a reasonable indication of a student's overall proficiency level, but a low score doesn't reveal where a student's difficulty lies. The arithmetic operations needed to solve most story problems are less likely to be the major source of difficulty than other aspects of the problem.

Often, the most difficult step in solving a story problem is the formation of a coherent representation of the problem. As Mayer (1985; see also Snow & Lohman, 1989) has suggested problem representation requires translation, that is, the use of linguistic and factual knowledge to understand the problem statement, and integration, or use of schema knowledge to create a representation of the problem. The distinction is illustrated by Riley, Greeno, and Heller's (1983) review of research using story problems. Consider, for example, the following two versions of what Riley, Greeno, and Heller referred to as a combine problem:

Version 1: Joe and Tom have eight marbles altogether.
Joe has five marbles.
How many marbles does Tom have?
Version 2: Together, Tom and Joe have eight marbles.
Three of these marbles belong to Tom.
How many of them belong to Joe? (1983, p. 173).

Although the two versions of the problem require the same formal operations, many students who are unable to solve problems like the first version give the correct answer when the problems are stated in the form of the second version. These children clearly have the procedural knowledge necessary to perform the subtraction, but they apparently have difficulty in being able to "represent the relationships among the quantities described in the problem situations in a way that relates to available solution procedures" (Riley et al., 1983, p. 173). Understanding the reasoning processes used by the student would be of much greater value to a teacher than simply knowing that he or she got a low score on the problem-solving section of a standardized test containing story problems.

According to Glaser (1986), "novices recognize the surface features of a problem or task situation and more proficient individuals go beyond surface features and identify inferences or principles that subsume the surface structure" (p. 55). Thus, in the assessment of a student's problem-solving skills, it may be more important to attempt to understand the student's representation of problems or mental models than it is to determine whether a correct answer is selected on a multiple-choice test.

ALTERNATIVE APPROACHES TO ASSESSMENT

Standardized achievement tests are quite efficient at measuring a student's accumulation of declarative knowledge. They also can efficiently measure a student's success in applying established procedures to solve problems with specified characteristics. For purposes of comparing the general level of knowledge in a given subject domain or predicting future performance, current standardized tests are quite effective. The assessment of a student's general achievement level is useful, but there are serious doubts about the degree to which these tests assess higher order thinking skills, such as creative thinking, skills of planning, problem solving, and metacognition. Moreover, current standardized tests do not provide information about thinking processes that a student is using or help in the diagnosis of misconceptions or particular sources of difficulty. Alternative assessment procedures are needed that focus on specific higher order thinking skills and that provide information about such thinking processes as the formation of problem representation, the construction of a mental model, the generation of hypotheses, the planning of steps to solve problems, and the self-monitoring of the application of a solution strategy. Alternative approaches that yield diagnostic information that can help guide instruction are also needed.

There are a number of efforts that have recently been undertaken that attempt to overcome some of the limitations that have been discussed. The remainder of this chapter is focused on a few such efforts that appear particularly promising.

Teacher-Directed Assessment

Although the focus in the following section of this chapter is on assessment procedures that are intended for large-scale use by districts or states, it should be recognized that externally imposed assessment represents only a fraction of the total amount of time and effort that goes into student assessment. More time and effort is devoted to teacher-constructed and teacher-selected assessment (e.g., tests and exercises accompanying curriculum materials) than to assessments required by districts and states. More importantly, it is the teacher-directed assessments, according to Stiggins (1988), "that most strongly influence student learning and academic self-concept" (p. 368). Thus, it is essential that attention be given not only to ways of improving the assessment of thinking skills by commercial publishers, districts, and states, but also to ways of helping teachers develop and select assessment procedures that encourage thinking.

Many of the concepts and ideas that are discussed in the following sections could be useful as general principles to consider when teachers develop or select their own assessments. However, it is clear that much more than these general ideas is needed. As Stiggins (1988) has convincingly argued, there is a need to give assessment issues much higher priority in both preservice and inservice teacher training. As stated by

Gullickson and Hopkins (1987), "The available research suggests that preservice instruction/curriculum in educational assessment is not adequate to develop the desired skills" (p. 15).

Materials and workshops provided by researchers at the Northwest Regional Educational Laboratory (Stiggins, 1987; Stiggins, Rubel, & Quellmalz, 1986) represent one significant effort to help teachers improve their assessment procedures, in general, and their assessment of thinking skills, in particular. The materials and workshops provide a framework for planning oral, paper-and- pencil, and performance forms of assessment that include five defined levels of thinking skills: recall, analysis, comparison, inference, and evaluation (Quellmalz, 1985).

The simple creation of a chart with three rows for the forms of assessment and five columns for the levels of thinking skills encourages the planning of assessments that do more than cover the "recall" row of the matrix. Good examples are provided of questions that require the higher level skills of analysis, comparison, inference, and evaluation (Stiggins et al., 1986). Together with the practice provided by the workshop, the program has been found to have a positive impact on teacher attitudes toward, and self-reports of, use of procedures in assessing higher order thinking skills (Stiggins, no date).

Reading Assessment

There has been a renewed interest in alternative approaches to the measurement of reading comprehension during the past few years. This interest has been stimulated by research that has led to changes in the conception of the reading process. As stated by Wixson and Peters (1987):

> . . . current research suggests that reading is a process of constructing meaning through the dynamic interaction of the reader, the text, and the context of the reading situation (Wixson & Peters, 1984). This view of reading focuses on how the reader builds meaning from print; what the reader brings to the reading situation in terms of experience, knowledge, skills, and motivation; how information is presented in written text; and the effects of context on reading performance. (pp. 333–334)

This conception of reading, which is consistent with that expressed by the National Academy of Education's Commission on Reading (1985) and a number of other authors (e.g., Curtis & Glaser, 1983; Valencia & Pearson, 1986), places heavy emphasis on the reader as an active agent and stresses the importance of prior knowledge (Bransford & Johnson, 1973; Johnston, 1983; Pearson & Spiro, 1980). It also focuses on the "coordination of a number of interrelated sources of information" (Commission on Reading, National Academy of Education, 1985, p. 7) and the use of higher level integrative and metacognitive skills. Consistent with this view of reading, the recent efforts to develop alternative approaches to assessing reading place more emphasis on the holistic process of constructing meaning and less emphasis on the interrelated component skills.

Two important examples of current efforts to develop reading assessments that are consistent with this emerging view of the reading process are the ongoing efforts for the state assessment programs in Illinois and in Michigan. These two efforts, together with an earlier effort in New York that led to the development of the Degrees of Reading Power (DRP) test (College Board, 1986; Koslin, Zeno, & Koslin, 1987), provide illustrations of alternative approaches to the measurement of reading comprehension that emphasize understanding and the integration of information in written text.

The DRP tests are intended to provide "holistic measures of how well the messages within a text are understood" (College Board, 1986, p. 1), rather than a measure of isolated skills. On the surface, the test appears to be similar to a simple cloze test, because, as is true of the latter, words are deleted from a passage, and the test taker's task is to choose from the available options the word that has been deleted. There are, as Linn and Palmer (1985) have previously noted, a number of important differences between the DRP and the traditional cloze test, however. The choice of words to delete is based on a theoretical conception that dictates that the difficulty of identifying the missing word should depend on the difficulty of understanding the surrounding text, not on the difficulty of the word that is deleted. Thus, only a small number of deletions are made per passage (usually only one or two words per paragraph), and the deletions are selected from words that have a higher frequency of occurrence in written text and a greater familiarity than much of the vocabulary in the passage that must be understood to comprehend the surrounding text.

The design of the DRP is intended to assure that "processing the surrounding prose is both necessary and sufficient for choosing the right answer" (Koslin, Koslin, & Zeno, 1979, p. 316). To assure that processing involves integration of information across sentences and not simply the processing of the individual sentence from which a word is deleted, distractors are carefully selected to be appropriate responses when the sentence is considered in isolation. Thus, in order to distinguish between the right answer and the distractors, the test taker "is required to integrate the meaning across several sentences" (Linn & Palmer, 1985, p. 94).

Although it is much shorter and less demanding in terms of the amount of text that a test taker must be able to integrate on the actual test, the following sample item from Form PX-1 of the DRP can be used to illustrate the need to rely on more than the single sentence from which a word is deleted:

It had been sunny and hot for days.
Then the s-1 changed.
It turned cloudy and cool. (College Board, 1986, p. PX–1).

The five options for this sample item ("price, road, job, weather, and size") are all acceptable if only the second sentence is considered. "When integrated with the information in the preceding and subsequent sentence, however, only 'weather' leads to a coherent set" (Linn & Valencia, 1986, pp. 27–28).

Although the DRP is consistent with the concept of reading as an integrative process, it does not attempt to measure more than "the ability to make inferences concerning the surface meaning of messages in English prose" (Koslin et al., 1987, p. 13). It does not attempt to measure, for example, the ability of a test taker to integrate information from the text with prior experience or background knowledge in order to draw inferences that go beyond the text. Nor is an attempt made to assess metacognitive skills or the degree to which a test taker is able to form "a coherent cognitive model of the text meaning" (Johnston, 1984, p. 236).

The more recent efforts to develop measures of reading comprehension that are currently being undertaken for both the Illinois and the Michigan State Departments of Education seek to bring the measurement of reading performance closer to the current theoretical conceptions of the reading process. Although there are a number of differences between the Illinois and Michigan efforts, they share a common conceptual framework, and the assessments have many parallels. An excellent description of the work related to the Michigan Educational Assessment Program has been provided by Wixson and Peters (1987; see also Cross & Paris, 1987; Wixson & Peters, 1984; Wixson, Peters, Weber, & Roeber, 1987). Partial descriptions of the Illinois assessment work are provided by Valencia (1988) and by Kerins (1988), and a comprehensive report by the four principal developers of the assessment (Sheila Valencia, P. David Pearson, Robert Reeve, and Timothy Shanahan) is in preparation.

Both the Illinois and Michigan assessments use passages that are several times as long as those found on typical standardized reading tests. The passages consist of full-length text of the sort that children might be expected to encounter in the classroom or to read outside of school. In both assessment programs, the narrative passages are short stories written for children that were selected from such sources as "children's magazines and grade-appropriate literature anthologies" (Wixson & Peters, 1987, p. 340). The expository passages were selected from textbooks and provide information and explanations of the type that students are expected to read and comprehend as part of their school work. The longer, more coherent passages were selected because it was expected that they would provide a better basis for constructing questions that require test takers to integrate information from various parts of the passage and to draw inferences. Of course, length alone assures neither that the text lends itself to questions requiring integration and the drawing of inferences nor that the questions will require these abilities. Systematic procedures are needed to analyze the text and guide the construction of questions. The Illinois and Michigan efforts both rely on the construction of story maps that display the structure of the text and serve as guides to the construction of questions (see Wixson & Peters, 1987, for a description and illustration of the story mapping used in Michigan).

The Illinois and Michigan assessments emphasize integrative processing and the role of the reader in constructing meaning from the text. Questions for the assessments are even referred to as "constructing meaning" questions to highlight this perspective. Test takers are required to use information from various parts of the passage to draw inferences. They are also expected to use the information in situations or contexts other than that presented in the particular passage. These characteristics are illustrated by the three types of processing that Wixson and Peters (1987) described as required by the constructing meaning questions. The three types are:

> . . . *intersentence,* which requires the reader to construct meaning from text of one to three contiguous sentences in length, *text,* which requires the reader to integrate information within sections of text larger than several sentences as well as across the entire text; and *beyond text,* which requires readers to rely heavily on information from their own experiences in addition to information in the text. (p. 346)

In addition to the constructing meaning scores, the two assessment systems attempt to assess the test taker's prior knowledge that is specific to the passage (referred to as "topic familiarity" in both programs) and metacognitive skills (referred to as "reading strategies" in Illinois and "knowledge about reading" in Michigan). There are differences in the approaches to the measurement of these two components, but the similarity of intent is clear.

One notable difference in the constructing meaning measures is that the Illinois assessment uses a multiple-right-answer question format rather than the more traditional single-right-answer multiple-choice format that is used in Michigan. As Snow and Lohman (1989) have noted, "most comprehension problems in school and the world involve multiple or alternative or optional correct answers, depending on contextual circumstances" (p. 96 of typescript). The use of questions that have one, two, or three of the options keyed as correct in the Illinois assessment reflects this perspective and encourages test takers to consider more than one interpretation.

Although the Illinois and Michigan assessment procedures have many appealing features, it is important to recognize that many questions about the procedures remain to be answered and that the instruments are designed for group assessment rather than for making decisions about individual students. The use of long passages means that the sampling of topics for a given student is more limited than on a test with several short passages. For group assessment, different passages can be administered to different subsamples of students so that the coverage is broader for the group as a whole, but, for individual student measurement, the generalizability of the results across passages is an open question, and it should not be concluded that what works well for group assessment will necessarily meet the needs of individual student assessment.

The topic familiarity and reading strategy (or knowledge about reading) sections of the assessments break new ground. Until a good deal more research has been completed that leads to a better understanding of the properties of these measures and their construct validity, however, they are best viewed as promising experimental approaches.

Critical Thinking Skills: History-Social Science

The assessment of critical-thinking skills in various content areas has received increasing attention in the past few years. Programs such as the California statewide assessment in history-social science illustrate the importance that is being attached to the use of critical-thinking skills in a subject matter domain. The statewide assessment of history-social science in California was developed as the result of a mandate from the State Board of Education in 1982. In response to that mandate, a statewide committee of teachers and curriculum leaders was formed to identify areas for assessment and establish assessment priorities. According to Kneedler (1985), "The committee placed a high priority on critical thinking—a priority supported by teachers and history-social science curriculum specialists throughout the state" (p. v).

In keeping with the high priority, 40% of the grade 8 assessment that began in 1985 is devoted to the measurement of critical-thinking skills in history-social science. Three general measurement approaches (multiple-choice questions, knowledge of vocabulary that is associated with critical thinking, student writing) are used in the assessment. Together, these three measurement approaches are intended to assess 12 critical-thinking skills that are classified in three broad areas: (a) problem definition and clarification (e.g., determination of central issues and formulation of appropriate questions), (b) evaluation of information related to the problem (e.g., distinguishing fact, opinion, and reasoned judgment, recognizing stereotypes, and identifying unstated assumptions), and (c) problem solution and the formation of conclusions (e.g., determining the adequacy of data and predicting probable consequences) (Kneedler, 1985).

A description of each of the critical-thinking skills, along with illustrative items, is provided by Kneedler (1985). Although not unlike items that can be found on some of the better standardized tests, the illustrative multiple-choice items demonstrate that this format can be used to do more than measure recall of historical or social science facts. Consider, for example, the following illustrative item (from Kneedler, 1985) that is intended to assess that student's ability to check the consistency of information in a political argument:

> Women should have the same job opportunities as men. Whether it be cook, fire fighter, executive, marine, or astronaut, no position should be denied a woman, except, of course, those positions requiring considerable physical strength.
>
> Is the speaker being consistent?
> A. No, because he fails to mention the Constitution, which guarantees equal rights to all men and women.
> B. Yes, because the speaker does not stray from the topic of equal rights.
> C. Yes, because the E.R.A. guarantees equal rights for all men and women.
> D. No, because he speaks of equal opportunity at the beginning and excludes women on the basis of physical strength at the end. (p. 17)

The limitations of multiple-choice questions for assessing student ability to think critically and solve complex problems is recognized by the program. Certain skills, such as the ability to "identify reasonable alternatives" are not addressed by the multiple-choice portion of the assessment. Written responses are needed not only to assess these skills, but to probe the depth of student understanding of arguments and their ability to think critically about more complex messages than are used for stems of multiple-choice items.

Constructed Response

Although research has generally shown that item format makes little, if any, difference when "existing multiple-choice tests [are compared] with their free-answer counterparts" (Frederiksen, 1984, p. 199), the converse is not true. That is, stated Frederiksen (1984), "when we begin with existing free-response tests designed to measure more complex cognitive problem-solving skills, different results are found" (p. 199). The formulating hypotheses test developed by Frederiksen and Ward (1978; Ward, Frederiksen, & Carlson, 1980) demonstrates that a paper-and-pencil test with open-ended responses can be used effectively to assess certain abilities that are crucial to scientific reasoning and that are not readily tapped in a multiple-choice testing format.

Ennis (1987; see also chapter 1 of this volume) has provided some compelling examples of the difficulty of constructing fixed-response tests of critical thinking. Using illustrative items from the *Watson-Glaser Critical Thinking Appraisal* (Watson & Glaser, 1980) that are intended to measure a test taker's ability to identify assumptions needed to support a statement, Ennis (1987) has provided clear explanations of how test takers "can get an item wrong when thinking critically" (p. 416). As Ennis has indicated, a major difficulty in defending the keyed answer and assuring that the person who is thinking critically *should* select the keyed answer is that "different test takers bring different background beliefs to bear on an item" (p. 416). Thus, whether a response should be considered right or wrong may depend on the reasons for the choice.

Consider, for example, the following illustrative item from Kneedler's (1985) description of the assessment of the critical-thinking skill "predict probable consequences" as part of the California grade 8 assessment of history-social science:

> When strawberries first appear on the market, their price is quite high. At the height of the season, their price goes down. As the season nears its end, their price goes up again.
>
>   The most probable reason for these changes in the price of strawberries is that
>
> A. strawberries are more plentiful at the middle of the season.
>
> B. strawberries are lower in quality at the middle of the season.
>
> C. the first and last crops of the season cost more to grow.
>
> D. strawberry pickers are paid more at the beginning and end of the season. (p. 26)

Although "A," the keyed answer, is what would be expected from anyone who used a supply-and-demand notion to support their reasoning, it is not inconceivable that some of the 29% of the 15,000 students in the field test sample who chose "C" or some of the 29% who chose "B" or "D" brought different beliefs or assumptions to bear on the item and got the wrong answer while thinking critically.

Ennis suggested several possible ways of dealing with this problem, including the use of open-ended questions that ask "Why" a given multi-ple-choice option was selected, the use of essay tests of critical thinking (e.g., *The Ennis-Weir Critical Thinking Essay Test,* Ennis & Weir, 1985), and the use of interviews. He concluded that "Open-endedness in critical thinking testing seems to be a good way to deal with the problems, but open-endedness in testing is expensive" (Ennis, 1987, p. 419).

Essay Tests of Subject-Matter Understanding

Research that is currently being conducted at the Center for Research on Evaluation, Standards, and Student Testing (CRESST) as part of a project co-directed by Eva Baker and Joan Herman is investigating the use of essays and other constructed response formats as ways of assessing the depth of a student's understanding in the area of social studies. A series of interviews of political scientists, historians, social studies educa-tors, and high school social studies teachers were conducted as part of the overall project to explore ways of identifying key concepts that could be used to define the content domain for social studies tests (House, 1988). Although the interviews did not suggest that there was much consensus regarding the content that was most critical, there was consid-erable agreement on two issues. First, there was considerable agreement that "one should not teach facts alone or primarily" (House, 1988, p. 78). Rather, the focus should be on concepts and the development of thinking critically about the content. Second, there was strong agreement that essay tests, rather than multiple-choice tests, are needed to assess depth of student understanding.

CRESST's studies (Baker & Herman, 1988) of measuring deep under-standing of history content are in keeping with the opinions expressed in the interviews conducted by House. The research is exploring ways of using essay tests of history content that "move beyond both molecular multiple choice assessments or global content quality judgments of stu-dents' writing" (Baker & Herman, 1988, p. 1). The approach that is being explored uses primary-source materials rather than textbook or specially written materials as the test stimuli. For example, in one of the initial experimental versions of the measure, students were given speeches from the Lincoln-Douglas debates and asked to analyze how Lincoln and Douglas interpreted Lincoln's statement, "A house divided against itself cannot stand . . . It will become all one thing or all the other." The students were instructed (Baker & Herman, 1988) that their analyses should:

> . . . be sure to clearly identify the issue(s) or problems which threaten to "divide the house"; summarize how each politician believes that the issue(s)

would best be resolved; explain what you consider to be the most convincing evidence each man uses to support his position; indicate what you consider to be the greatest strength(s) and the greatest weakness(es) of each man's argument.

A central issue in the research program is the development of scoring procedures that will yield reliable scores that reflect the depth of a student's understanding rather than a global measure of his or her writing. The approach being investigated follows the lead of work in cognitive psychology comparing expert and novice performance (e.g., Voss, 1986; Voss, Green, Post, & Penner, 1983). According to Glaser (1987), past work comparing expert and novice performance suggests that the features of the essays that are apt to distinguish superior performance from average performance include coherence, the degree to which information is interrelated, the use of underlying principle rather than only the surface features of the speeches, and the use of background knowledge about that period of history and about the two men.

Although it is still in its early stages, the work on assessment in history builds on a substantial experience with research on writing assessment (e.g., Baker, 1987). The demands of the task are more in line with the judgments of what is required to evaluate the important goals of social studies that were expressed by the subject matter experts and educators in the interviews conducted by House (1988).

Diagnostic Testing

Regardless of the format of a test, it should contribute to student learning. The nature of the contribution could take a variety of forms, but one that is often proposed is to provide teachers with diagnostic information that will lead to improved instructional decisions about individual students.

There are a number of standardized achievement tests that have been labeled "diagnostic." There is relatively little research evidence to support the diagnostic interpretation of such tests (Bejar, 1984; Linn, 1986); that is, there is little evidence that students with a particular pattern of scores on a set of skills measured by given "diagnostic" test battery would benefit most from a particular series of instructional experiences. Educational tests currently do a much better job of prediction of future achievement than of diagnosis and prescription. According to Glaser (1986), current "tests (with the exception of the important informal assessment of the good classroom teacher) typically are not designed to guide the specifics of instruction" (p. 45).

There are a variety of reasons that diagnostic achievement testing has not been more successful. One reason is that diagnosis often requires quite detailed information about what a student can and cannot do and, more importantly, about the types of misunderstandings and the nature of his or her mental model. In a one-on-one teaching situation, a skilled tutor may be able to probe the areas of strength and weakness and the ways in which the student conceptualizes and attacks problems and, thusly, come to an understanding of the student's misconceptions and the types of errors that the student is likely to make. From this information the tutor may also be able to prescribe a set of instructional activities that will be especially effective for that student at that particular stage of development. When faced with a classroom of, say, 30 students, however, a teacher does not have the time to obtain such detailed information about each individual student. The tasks of collecting, analyzing, and prescribing a set of instructional activities suited to each individual student's needs is just too labor-intensive.

Computers have the potential of providing the support needed to deal with the labor-intensive aspects of keeping track of the types of errors that each student makes and searching for consistencies that suggest particular misunderstandings. Researchers such as Brown and Burton (1978) and Tatsuoka (1983) have demonstrated that the errors that students make in solving problems are often systematic. The identification of systematic errors and the use of that information to draw conclusions about the nature of a student's misconception, however, requires detailed analysis of patterns of response to numerous problems.

Brown and Burton's (1978) research and that of Tatsuoka (1983) have demonstrated that computerized tests can be designed to do the labor-intensive tasks of keeping track of the student responses and testing hypotheses that the errors are the result of particular misconception or the consistent application of a faulty algorithm. Furthermore, the tests can obtain the needed information more efficiently than paper-and-pencil tests by tailoring the choice of problems that are presented to the previous performance of the student and the current hypotheses about the student's current source of difficulty. Once a systematic error or misconception is identified, the computer can also suggest the instructional activities that are designed to remedy the specific difficulty.

Although computers can reduce the labor by keeping track of detailed information about student responses to problems, the development of an effective diagnostic testing technology will require much more than a delivery system. As Ward (1984) has noted, diagnostic testing needs to be based on both a theory of knowledge and a theory of instruction. Diagnostic testing is also likely to require a different type of psychometric theory. As stated by Linn (1986), "Neither classical test theory nor item response theory is well suited for diagnostic testing problems. Both approaches rely on an assumption of unidimensionality and treat deviations as noise. It is precisely those deviations from a single dominant dimension, however, that are of central concern in diagnostic testing" (p. 159).

These are challenging demands. Considerable progress toward these ends has been made in the past decade, however. Research in cognitive psychology and artificial intelligence has made great progress toward providing a theoretical foundation for diagnostic testing. This work suggests, as was indicated previously, that the mental models or theories that students have and the ways in which they represent problems are central to student learning. As Glaser (1986) has noted, with the right instructions, "students test, evaluate, and modify their current theories on the basis of new information, and as a result, develop new schema that facilitate more advanced thinking" (p. 55).

A challenge for effective instruction, according to this conceptualization, is to decide on the information that will be most useful at a given stage of learning in helping a student "test, evaluate, and modify" their current mental models. This suggests that effective diagnostic testing needs not only to identify students' errors but also to assess their mental models.

Assessment of Students' Metacognition and Specific Cognitive Strategies

In addition to alternative assessments that tap cognition, there are instruments that measure metacognition and specific cognitive strategies. Traditionally, programs designed to serve the educationally disadvantaged at all levels of the educational system have focused on basic skills remediation. However, a growing body of research indicates that at-risk students perform poorly because of an impoverished or underdeveloped repertoire of learning and study strategies. To diagnose these deficits better, researchers and practitioners have constructed paper-and-pencil assessments of students' employment of metacognitive strategies in planning, monitoring, and revising their learning performance.

Weinstein, Zimmerman, and Palmer (1988), for example, have surveyed the materials available to assess and teach study strategies, generated categories covering the range of study strategies through a modified Delphi technique, and then constructed an assessment that included all categories and had items that met standards of reliability and validity according to expert judgment. The resulting instrument is called the Learning and Study Strategies Inventory (LASSI). LASSI is intended for use with postsecondary students to identify weaknesses and tailor interventions accordingly. It also can provide data to evaluate the effectiveness of training programs in learning strategies (Weinstein, Zimmerman, & Palmer, 1988). A high school version is currently being developed, and is scheduled to be available in 1989.

LASSI has ten scales that measure attitude, motivation, time management, anxiety, concentration, information processing, study aids, self-testing, and test strategies. More specifically, the scales include items that were intended to assess the following modifiable behaviors, both covert and overt, related to learning:

- Attitude: e.g., interest in college; educational values
- Motivation: e.g., incentives for college achievement; diligence; self-discipline; willingness to work hard
- Time management: e.g., systematic in planning the use of time; productive use of study periods; mindful of deadlines
- Anxiety: e.g., worrying interferes with ability to concentrate; nervous about test performance even when well prepared
- Concentration: e.g., easily distracted; ability to attend to the task at hand
- Information processing: e.g., linkages made relating prior knowledge to new learning; use of imaginal and verbal elaboration; translation of information into one's own words
- Study aids: good use of key words, sample problems, diagrams, headings, etc.
- Self-testing: e.g., frequent and on-going review of information learned; adequate preparation for classes
- Test strategies: e.g., prioritizing of material to review; integration of learning into a coherent whole.

By using this instrument, it is anticipated that educators can design targeted educational intervention to remediate students' deficiencies in using learning and study strategies. The instrument is supposed to be both diagnostic and prescriptive. The ultimate goal is to develop in students the thoughts and covert behaviors they need to direct and manage their own learning.

Dynamic Assessment

In traditional assessment, the teacher usually plays a more passive role than in instruction. The teacher generally stops instruction while the students "show" their learning in a paper-and-pencil assessment. However, some assessment techniques require that the teacher assume a more active role and the student undergo mediation in the process of assessment. Two such techniques include Feuerstein's (1979) assessment of learning potential and Campione and Brown's (1987) dynamic assessment.

Feuerstein (this volume) originated the idea of dynamic assessment, and operationalized that idea in an instrument called the Learning Potential Assessment Device (LPAD). The LPAD includes such tasks as the organization of dots, the representation of stencil designs, and the completion of syllogisms and numerical progressions. The tasks are intended to mediate such skills as orientation in space and time, the perception of part-whole relationships, systematic comparison, and hypothetical thinking.

According to Feuerstein, tasks are done across three phases of the mental act (input, elaboration, output), each of which has a set of prerequisite skills associated with it. The input phase requires that the learner scan the environment with accuracy and precision to gather relevant data. The elaboration phase entails the encoding and transforming of information necessary to carry out a problem-solving process. The output phase consists of the communication of elaborated responses to tasks. The phases are not necessarily performed in a linear sequence; they often recur and feed forward and back as a cyclical process.

With the LPAD, diagnosis of weaknesses occurs simultaneously with instruction—in fact, one could say instruction (or mediation, as it is conceptualized by Feuerstein), and the readiness to learn revealed by the examinee's response to mediation, constitute the assessment. This is to insure, by Feuerstein's own account "the closing of the loop between the teacher [examiner, in this case] as an emittor of a message, the receiver of the message, and finally, the emitted message itself." The examiner using the LPAD instrument assures that the examinee receives and integrates the conveyed message by providing on-going feedback in mediating the performance of the task by, for example, focusing the student's attention or modeling the problem-solving behavior. The purpose of the instrument, then, is not to have the examinee become proficient in performing a particular set of tasks, but to provide experiences that modify the cognitive structure of the examinee. The LPAD becomes merely a means to this end.

To use the LPAD, the examiner must relate to the examinee in a way that differs markedly from the conventional psychometric approach. In traditional test administration, the examiner is only permitted to record and catalogue responses to standardized test answers. The LPAD, on the other hand, requires that the examiner focus the assessment upon the identification and removal of the cognitive deficiencies that presently prevent the individual from functioning at higher levels. Delivering dynamic assessment procedures requires extensive training and a shift to a process orientation to testing (Jensen & Feuerstein, 1987).

Campione and Brown are working on an alternative dynamic assessment technique. A person employing their version of dynamic assessment presents examinees with increasingly explicit cues and prompts for performing a task. Unlike Feuerstein, Campione and Brown conceptualize the aid given according to the structure of the task itself, rather than the phase of learning and the deficits that often occur in the phases. The support is guided by a task analysis that proceeds from hints about the general approach to a particular problem type to a specific blueprint for solving a problem. The number of hints required for the student to solve each problem serves as a measure of learning efficiency. The fewer the cues given, the higher the learning efficiency; the greater the number of cues given, the lower the learning efficiency. The assessment of learning efficiency then focuses on how much help is needed for a student's potential to learn in a particular domain, rather than a static measure of what has already been acquired.

Campione and Brown also structure their assessment procedure to measure disposition to transfer skills to novel problems. To study this, they use the notion of transfer distance, defined in terms of the number of transformations distinguishing the transfer probes from the learning items. (This operational definition is, of course, suited best to formal tasks such as series completion, manipulation of Raven's matrices, and problems in formal logic.) Tasks are classified into maintenance, near transfer, far transfer, and very far transfer. Transfer efficiency is measured by determining the amount of aid necessary to perform a task. Correlations between IQ scores and number of hints given are not significant for maintenance and near transfer items, but they are statistically significant for far transfer and very far transfer items. In other words, low-performing students may require the same number of prompts as high-performing students on the identical task, but they often fail to transfer their knowledge to distantly similar tasks. Thus, this assessment procedure is instrumental in pinpointing transfer deficiencies that distinguish low-performing from high-performing students.

It seems that if teachers are to capture the open-ended, iterative process of thinking in their assessments of student performance, they will need to move away from static, paper-and-pencil assessments that stand alone from the learning process and toward the dynamic assessment procedures of Feuerstein and Campione and Brown. Standardized testing does not reveal the process by which a response to a problem or question is constructed and, thus, gives no insight into the student's cognition. In the words of Resnick (1985), standardized test scores and even course grades "do not reveal the quality of thinking, and they offer no indications of transfer beyond purely academic settings"(p. 33). She further argues that most current classroom tests favor students who have merely amassed factual knowledge, and they often fail to assess whether the student has a coherent grasp of that knowledge or whether students can use that knowledge in solving problems, making decisions, or constructing arguments. Presseisen (1986) adds that "paper-and-pencil assessments may not be the best way to address the assessment of the varied modalities that thinking can encompass" (p. 25).

For these reasons and others, Costa (1988) recommends a variety of alternatives to assessing students' thinking. To tap and mediate the cognitive process of students, teachers will need to explore the use of interviews, journals, observation of students in problem-solving situations, student dialogue, role playing, individual or group student projects, and intelligent testing systems. Collins (this volume) envisions a completely integrated learning and testing environment where students are given precisely specified cognitive feedback as part of testing procedures built into intelligent tutoring systems. Thus, such dynamic assessment becomes an integral part of the learning experience itself. Dynamic assessment may come to serve as the concept giving coherence to all viable alternatives to traditional assessment.

Computer Simulations

Assessments are incorporated as a necessary part of intelligent tutor systems. Simulations such as the patient management problems that have been used in the training and certification of physicians for a number of years incorporate many of these features. Patient management problems simulate the interaction between a physician and a patient. The test taker is initially presented with a limited set of information about a patient, such as a verbal description of symptoms of the type that a patient might provide at the start of a visit. The test taker then has a variety of options such as getting a patient history, ordering laboratory tests, or deciding on a course of treatment. Requested information is provided and new options can be followed by the test taker until a diagnosis is made and a course of treatment is prescribed.

As Ward (1984, p. 19) has indicated, patient management "problems are attractive because they offer greater realism than do standard 'one-shot' examination questions, and because they provide samples of performance that can be scored in example, how efficiently did the examinee attack the problem, how many serious errors were made, what was the cost to the patient in dollars and in pain and suffering, and so on." A computer can contribute to the realism of the simulations and can facilitate the scoring along different dimensions such as the ones suggested by Ward.

Computer-administered problem simulations have a number of potential advantages over current paper-and-pencil tests in all areas of the curriculum. They can provide a means of going beyond the sort of factual recall questions that too often dominate paper-and-pencil tests. Instead, they focus attention on a student's ability to use information to solve problems. Unlike multiple-choice questions which only reveal the product of a student's thinking, computerized simulations can assess the process that a student uses to solve a problem, including the way in which the problem is attacked, the efficiency of the solution, and the number of hints that may be needed to solve the problem. The process information may also be used to assess a student's mental representation of a problem, which, as was indicated above, may be more important to identify than whether or not a correct answer is produced.

Simulations are an important part of a number of computer-based instructional programs, especially ones that are called "intelligent tutors." As Collins (in press) has pointed out, such systems have great promise as intelligent testers. He identified three important benefits of developing intelligent tutors as intelligent testers: "(a) testing would be focused on problem solving and planning skills, (b) their ability to learn in a domain as well as their prior knowledge could be tested, and (c) the tests could be adaptive to the student's prior knowledge, and would test their generative abilities instead of their recognition abilities" (Collins, Chapter 4).

CONCLUSION

Constructing valid assessment procedures to tap thinking processes and metacognition is certainly not an easy task, but the difficulty of the task is not the major barrier. Practical concerns about cost and efficiency, the seemingly insatiable demand to boil everything down to single number, and the over-reliance on standard psychometric criteria to judge test reliability and validity present much more formidable barriers. As in the instance of writing assessment, *the case will have to be made that the form of the assessment represents an important part of the specification of educational goals which in turn influence what is taught and what is learned.* The case must also be made that thinking skills and processes are essential educational goals that go well beyond the accumulation of factual knowledge. Furthermore, the reliance solely on multiple-choice test items distorts the goals and frustrates their achievement. Hence, it is worth the added expense and complexity that such assessment will require.

ACKNOWLEDGMENTS

I thank Beau Jones and Lorna Idol for their comments on drafts of this chapter. I also thank Todd Fennimore for his assistance with the sections of the chapter dealing with dynamic assessment and the assessment of metacognition and specific cognitive strategies.

REFERENCES

Alexander, L., & James H. T. (1987). *The nation's report card: Improving the assessment of student achievement.* Cambridge, MA: National Academy of Education.

Applebee, A. N., Langer, J. A., & Mullis, I. V. S. (1986). *Writing: Trends across the decade, 1974–84.* Princeton, NJ: Educational Testing Service.

Baker, E. L. (1987, September). *Time to write: Report of the US-IEA study of written composition.* Paper presented at the International Association for the Evaluation of Educational Achievement General Assembly, New York.

Baker, E. L., & Herman, J. L. (1988). *Content assessment: Assessing deep understanding of social studies.* Proposal for years 4 and 5 to the Office of Educational Research and Improvement from the UCLA Center for Research on Evaluation, Standards, and Student Testing. Los Angeles: UCLA.

Bejar, I. I. (1984). Educational diagnostic assessment. *Journal of Educational Measurement, 21,* 175–189.

Bloom, B. S. (1956). *Taxonomy of educational objectives.* Ann Arbor, MI: Edwards Brothers.

Bowman, C. M., & Peng, S. S. (1972). *A preliminary investigation of recent advanced psychology tests—an application of a cognitive classification system.* Princeton, NJ: Educational Testing Service.

Bransford, J. D., & Johnson, M. K. (1973). Consideration of some problems in comprehension. In W. G. Chase (Ed.), *Visual information processing* (pp. 383–438). New York: Academic Press.

Brown, J. A., & Burton, R. R. (1978). Diagnostic models for procedural bugs in basic mathematical skills. *Cognitive Science, 2,* 155–192.

Brown, R. (1987). Who is accountable for "thoughtfulness"? *Phi Delta Kappan, 69,* (1), 49–52.

Campione, J. C., & Brown, A. L. (1987). Linking dynamic assessment with school achievement. In C. S. Lidz (Ed.), *Dynamic assessment: An interactional approach to evaluation learning potential* (pp. 82–115). New York: Guilford Publications, Inc.

Chall, J. S. (1977). *An analysis of textbooks in relation to declining SAT scores.* New York: College Board.

College Board. (1986). *DRP handbook.* New York: College Entrance Examination Board.

Collins, A. (in press). Reformulating testing to measure learning and thinking. In N. Frederiksen, R. Glaser, A. Lesgold, & M. Shafto (Eds.), *Diagnostic monitoring of skills and knowledge acquisition.* Hillsdale, NJ: Lawrence Erlbaum Associates.

Commission on Reading, National Academy of Education. (1985). *Becoming a nation of readers: The report of the commission on reading.* Washington, DC: National Institute of Education.

Costa, A. L. (1988, June). *Teaching for intelligent behavior: An awareness workshop.* Paper presented at a workshop at the Center for Critical and Creative Thinking, Wellesley, MA.

Cross, E. R., & Paris, S. G. (1987). Assessment of reading comprehension: Matching test purposes and test properties. *Educational Psychologist, 22,* 313–332.

Curtis, M. E. & Glaser, R. (1983). Reading theory and the assessment of reading skill. *Journal of Educational Measurement, 20,* 133–147.

Ebel, R. L., & Frisbie, D. A. (1986). *Essentials of educational measurement* (4th ed.). Englewood Cliffs, NJ: Prentice-Hall.

Ennis, R. H. (1987). Testing teachers' competence, including their critical thinking. *Proceedings of the 43rd Annual Meeting of the Philosophy of Education Society* (pp. 413–420). Cambridge, MA: Philosophy of Education Society.

Ennis, R. H., & Weir, E. (1985). *The Ennis-Weir Critical Thinking Essay Test.* Pacific Grove: Midwest Publications.

Feuerstein, R. (1979). *The dynamic assessment of retarded performers: The learning potential assessment device, theory, instruments, and techniques.* Baltimore: University Park Press.

Fleming, M., & Chambers, B (1983). Teacher-made tests: Windows to the classroom. In W. E. Hathaway (Ed.), *New directions for testing and measurement: Testing in the schools* (pp. 29–38). San Francisco, CA: Jossey-Bass.

Frank, H. J. (1978). An examination of the levels of questions on standardized tests of elementary science. *Science and Children, 14,* 30–32.

Frederiksen, N. (1984). The real test bias: Influences of testing on teaching and learning. *American Psychologist, 39,* 193–202.

Frederiksen, N., & Ward, W. C. (1978). Measures for the study of creativity in scientific problem solving. *Applied Psychological Measurement, 2,* 1–24.

Glaser, R. (1986). The integration of instruction and testing. *The redesign of testing for the 21st century: Proceedings of the 1985 ETS Invitational Conference* (pp. 45–58). Princeton, NJ: Educational Testing Service.

Glaser, R. (1987, December). *Expertise and assessment.* Paper presented at the Approaches to Subject Matter Assessment Conference, Los Angeles: UCLA Center for Research on Evaluation, Standards, and Student Testing.

Gullickson, A. R., & Hopkins, K. D. (1987). Perspectives on educational measurement instruction for preservice teachers. *Educational Measurement: Issues and Practice, 6,* (3), 12–16.

House, E. R. (1988). *Definition of content in social studies testing.* Technical Report, Grant Number OERI-G-86-0003. Los Angeles: UCLA Center for Evaluation, Standards, and Student Testing.

Jensen, M. R., & Feuerstein, R. (1987). The learning potential assessment device: From philosophy to practice. In. C. S. Lidz (Ed.), *Dynamic assessment: An interactional approach to evaluating learning potential* (pp. 379–402). New York: Guilford Publications, Inc.

Johnston, P. H. (1983). *Reading comprehension: A cognitive basis.* Newark, DE: International Reading Association.

Johnston, P. H. (1984). Prior knowledge and reading comprehension test bias. *Reading Research Quarterly, 19,* 219–239.

Kerins, T. (1988, April). *Changing the assessment program to respond to research on reading: The Illinois experience.* Paper presented at the 1988 Annual meeting of the American Educational Research Association, New Orleans, LA.

Kneedler, P. E. (1985). *Assessment of critical thinking skills in history-social science.* Sacramento, CA: California State Department of Education.

Koslin, B. L., Koslin, S., & Zeno, S. (1979). Towards an effectiveness measure in reading. In R. W. Tyler & S. H. White (Eds.), *Testing, teaching, and learning: Report of a conference on research on testing* (pp. 311–334). Washington, DC: National Institute of Education.

Koslin, B. L., Zeno, S., & Koslin, S. (1987). *The DRP: An effectiveness measure of reading.* New York: College Entrance Examination Board.

Levine, A. G., McGuire, C. H., & Nattress, L. W. (1970). The validity of multiple-choice achievement tests as measures of competence in medicine. *American Educational Research Journal, 7,* 69–82.

Linn, R. L. (1986). Barriers to new test design. *The redesign of testing for the 21st century: Proceedings of the 1985 ETS Invitational Conference* (pp. 69–79). Princeton, NJ: Educational Testing Service.

Linn, R. L. (1987). Accountability: The Comparison of educational systems and the quality of tests results. *Educational Policy, 1,* 181–198.

Linn, R. L., & Palmer, C. N. (1985). Standards and expectations: The role of testing. *Excellence in our schools: Making it happen* (pp. 88–95). New York: College Board.

Linn, R. L., & Valencia, S. W. (1986). *Reading assessment: Practice and theoretical perspectives.* Technical Report, Grant Number OERI-G-86-0003. Los Angeles, CA: UCLA Center for Research on Evaluation, Standards, and Student Testing.

Madaus, G. F. (1985). Public policy and the testing profession — You've never had it so good. *Educational Measurement: Issues and Practice, 4,* (4), 5–11.

Mayer, R. E. (1985). *Thinking, problem solving, and cognition.* San Francisco: Freeman.

Morgenstern, C. F., & Renner, J. W. (1984). Measuring thinking with standardized tests. *Journal of Research in Science Teaching, 21,* 639–648.

National Academy of Education. (1987). [Commentary by the National Academy of Education on *The Nation's Report Card.*] Cambridge, MA: Author.

National Assessment of Educational Progress. (1985). *The reading report card: Progress toward excellence in our schools, Trends in reading over four National Assessments. 1971–1984.* Princeton, NJ: Educational Testing Service.

National Commission on Excellence in Education. (1983). *A nation at risk: The imperative for educational reform.* Washington, DC: U.S. Printing Office.

Pearson, P. D., & Spiro, R. J. (1980). Toward a theory of reading comprehension instruction. *Topics in Language Disorders, 1,* 71–88.

Pipho, C. (1985, May 22). Tracking the reforms, Part 5: Testing—Can it measure the success of the reform movement? *Education Week,* p. 19.

Presseisen, B. Z. (1986). *Thinking skills: Research and practice.* Washington, DC: National Education Association.

Quellmalz, E. (1985). Needed: Better methods for testing higher-order thinking skills. *Educational Leadership, 43,* 2.

Resnick, L. B. (1987). *Education and learning to think.* Washington, DC: National Academy Press.

Riley, M. S., Greeno, J. G., & Heller, J. I. (1983). Development of children's problem-solving ability in arithmetic. In H. P. Ginsburg (Ed.), *The development of mathematical thinking* (pp. 153–196). New York: Academic Press.

Simon, H. A. (1978). Information-processing theory of human problem solving. In W. K. Estes (Ed.), *Handbook of learning and cognitive process: Vol. 5, Human information processing* (pp. 271–295). Hillsdale, NJ: Lawrence Erlbaum Associates.

Snow, R. E., & Lohman, D. F. (1989). Implications of cognitive psychology for educational measurement (pp. 263–331). In R. L. Linn (Ed.), *Educational measurement* (3rd ed.). New York: Macmillan.

Stiggins, R. J. (1987). Design and development of performance assessment. *Educational Measurement: Issues and Practice, 6,* (3), 33–42.

Stiggins, R. J. (1988). Revitalizing classroom assessment: The highest instructional priority. *Phi Delta Kappan, 69,* (5), 363–368.

Stiggins, R. J. (no date). *High impact teacher training in classroom assessment.* Portland, OR: Northwest Regional Educational Laboratory.

Stiggins, R. J., Griswald, M., & Green, K. R. (1988, April). *Measuring thinking skills through classroom assessment.* Paper presented at the 1988 annual meeting of the National Council on Measurement in Education, New Orleans, LA.

Stiggins, R. J., Rubel, E., & Quellmalz, E. (1986). *Measuring thinking skills in the classroom.* Washington, DC: National Education Association.

Tatsuoka, K. K. (1983). Rule space: An approach for dealing with misconceptions based on item response theory. *Journal of Educational Measurement, 20,* 221–230.

Valencia, S. (1988, April). *Research for reforming the assessment of reading comprehension.* Paper presented at the 1988 annual meeting of the American Educational Research Association, New Orleans, LA.

Valencia, S., & Pearson, P. D. (1986). *Reading assessment: Time for change.* Unpublished manuscript, University of Illinois, Center for the Study of Reading, Champaign.

Voss, J. F. (1986). Social studies. In R. F. Dillon & R. J. Sternberg (Eds.), *Cognition and instruction* (pp. 205–298). Orlando, FL: Academic Press.

Voss, J. F., Greene, T. R., Post, T. A., & Penner, B. C. (1983). Problem solving skills in the social sciences. In G. Bower (Ed.), *The psychology of leaning and motivation: Advances in research and theory* (Vol. 17, pp. 165–213). New York: Academic Press.

Walker, D. F. (1983). What constitutes curricular validity in a high school leaving examination? In G. F. Madaus (Ed.), *The courts, validity and minimum competency testing* (pp. 171–181). Hingman, MA: Kluwer Nijhoff.

Ward, W. C. (1984). Using microcomputers to administer tests. *Educational Measurement: Issues and Practice, 3,* 16–20.

Ward, W. C., Frederiksen, N., & Carlson, S. (1980). Construct validity of free-response and multiple-choice versions of a test. *Journal of Educational Measurement, 17,* 11–29.

Watson, G., & Glaser, W. M. (1980). *The Watson-Glaser Critical Thinking Appraisal.* San Antonio, TX: The Psychological Corporation.

Wixson, K. K., & Peters, C. W. (1984). Reading redefined: A Michigan Reading Association position paper. *Michigan Reading Journal, 17,* 4–7.

Weinstein, C. E., Zimmerman, S. A., & Palmer, D. R. (1988). Assessing learning strategies: The design and development of the LASSI. In C. E. Weinstein, E. T. Goetz, and P. A. Alexander, *Learning and study strategies: Issues in assessment, instruction, and evaluation.* San Diego: Academic Press, Inc.

Wixson, K. K., & Peters, C. W. (1987). Comprehension assessment: Implementing an integrative view of reading. *Educational Psychologist, 22,* 333–356.

Wixson, K. K., Peters, C. W., Weber, E. M. & Roeber, E. D. (1987). New directions in statewide reading assessment. *The Reading Teacher, 40,* 749–754.

7

Grouping Students for Instruction in Elementary Schools

Rebecca Barr
National College of Education

Carolyn S. Anderson
Niles Township High Schools

How should children be grouped for instruction in elementary schools? Many teachers and administrators are considering this question. In this chapter, we describe an interactive approach that professionals in elementary school districts may use to establish sound policies for instructional grouping. By "interactive" we mean one in which teachers and administrators jointly explore alternatives and establish policy. This approach is more time-consuming than policy established through administrative directive, because time is required to consider alternatives and to agree on policy. It has the advantage, however, of increasing knowledge and commitment of those involved to the policies developed.

We describe this complex decision-making process through a case study of a hypothetical elementary school district that is evaluating its current grouping and teaching practices[1]. We discuss the steps undertaken by these teachers and administrators to learn more about what is known about grouping, examine their own grouping practices, delineate their shared beliefs about grouping, and develop a district policy on grouping.

Decisions about how to group students occur at several points in schools: when catchment areas for schools are defined, when students are assigned to grades and to classes, and when they are assigned by teachers to groups for instruction. There is a long tradition of assigning students to classes and groups on the basis of ability or achievement

---

[1]The description of District 999 is a composite profile based on eight districts that the authors worked in during the past 10 years.

in order to create groups of students that are more homogeneous in achievement than they would be on the basis of random assignment.

Although ability grouping is frequently defended on the basis of ease in teaching and higher achievement, negative consequences have also been attributed to grouping, such as its detrimental effect on the achievement and attitudes of students at risk of failure. Many different issues must be considered in determining whether and when to ability-group students for instruction. We focus on these issues by showing how they were involved in the decision-making processes of the hypothetical elementary school district.

The chapter is not intended to be a scholarly review of the research literature on grouping, although a brief summary of this literature is included as one factor that influences district decision making. Many excellent reviews currently exist (see, e.g., Borg, 1965; Calfee & Piontkowski, 1987; Esposito, 1973; Findley & Bryan, 1971; Good & Marshall, 1984; Hiebert, 1983; Rosenbaum, 1980; Slavin, 1987; and Sorensen & Hallinan, 1986). Further, because the focus is on elementary schools, we do not consider the high school literature on tracking (see, e.g., Gamoran & Berends, 1987; Oakes, 1985; Persell, 1977; Rosenbaum, 1976). Similarly, the chapter is not primarily concerned with students at risk (see, e.g., Allington, 1983; Good & Marshall, 1984; Oakes, 1985), although this is a group of students that must be considered in establishing sound grouping policy. It does not treat cooperative forms of grouping (see Johnson & Johnson, 1975; Slavin, 1983) except to recommend them as alternatives to grouping based on ability. It does not examine the instructional and interactional processes that occur for groups of different ability levels (see Barr, 1989), although it considers how group composition may bear on the amount of academic work that groups accomplish. Finally, it does not consider research on grouping for affective and social purposes (see, e.g., Marsh, 1984), although the affective and social consequences of alternative forms of grouping must be considered by districts in establishing formal policies on grouping.

The chapter is organized in four parts. In the first, we discuss some of the assumptions that underlie our view of grouping and definitions of alternative forms of grouping. In the second, we describe the composite elementary school district used to illustrate decisions underlying the development of sound grouping policies and the conditions that led them to reconsider their grouping policy. The interactive decision-making process undertaken by the district occurs on two levels: On one level, a representative committee studies the issue of grouping and develops grouping policy; on the other, the committee interacts with teachers and administrators in the district to learn their views about grouping and grouping policy. In the third section of the chapter, we describe the committee work, how it considered the advantages and limitations of alternative grouping procedures, studied the characteristics of students in the district, considered the nature of reading and mathematics development, and reflected on their own beliefs about education, in general, and grouping, in particular. Concurrently, members of the school community were made a part of the interactive decision process. The committee actively solicited the views of staff members, shared what they were learning about grouping, and obtained their reactions to recommendations for a district policy on grouping. This district-wide interaction is described in the fourth and final section of the chapter.

ASSUMPTIONS AND DEFINITIONS

We view work in schools as characterized by a division of labor among levels of school organization, each with its own productive activities and outcomes (Barr & Dreeben, 1983; Dreeben & Barr, 1987). Although levels of school organization are distinguished by different sorts of activity, they are also interconnected, in that the decisions made at one level bear directly on the work of adjacent levels. The view emphasizes the conditional nature of events in schools and the manner in which decisions made at one level of school organization influence those at other levels.

District Level

With respect to the problem of grouping, district policies range from the extreme of no policy to the other extreme of a uniform, mandated policy to be followed by all schools. The existence of no policy is, in fact, policy by default and has the consequence of divulging power and responsibility for setting policy to schools or teachers. At the opposite extreme, a uniform, mandated policy may be inappropriate for some schools and classes. According to our view of school organization, one characteristic of effective grouping policy is that it enables sound decisions to be made at the school level, in assigning students to classes, and at the classroom level, in grouping students and developing appropriate instruction for them. Because conditions vary from school to school within districts, district level policy must permit variation in decision making at the school level that is responsive to the conditions of each school.

School Level

Two types of decisions may be made about grouping at the school level. The first is the assignment of students to classes, and the second involves grouping arrangements across teachers in one or several grade levels. One consideration in both forms of grouping is whether students should be assigned on the basis of ability or not and whether other characteristics such as gender, ethnic or racial background, and friendship patterns should have a bearing. Whatever the basis for grouping, decisions about grouping made at the school level have implications for related school-level decisions, such as scheduling, curriculum, and teacher planning.

With respect to class assignment on the basis of ability, when the composition of classes represents that of a grade as a whole, they are said to be *heterogeneous* in achievement. The extent to which grades differ in achievement will, of course, differ from school to school; some heterogeneous classes will be more diverse than others. But a class is called "heterogeneous" when the achievement variation of classes reflects that of the grade. When children are assigned to classes on the basis of their achievement, they are said to be *homogeneously* grouped, even though considerable variation in achievement may still exist in each class. What a "homogeneous class" denotes is that a given class is more homogeneous than the grade as a whole. If a grade is divided into three homogeneous classes, the achievement range of each class will be narrower than that of the grade, though there may be some overlap.

Cross-class or "departmentalized" grouping is frequently employed for reading instruction and sometimes for mathematics instruction. Students within a grade are regrouped for reading and/or mathematics instruction, and during the time for instruction in these areas, they may go to another class for instruction. Because groups are drawn from all students in a grade, they are more homogeneous than is typically possible in heterogeneous self-contained classes. After departmentalized instruction in given subjects, students return to their homeroom classes for instruction in other subjects. Cross-grade grouping is similar in conception, except that it involves students from two or more grades, which expands the number of levels possible.

Classroom Level

An initial activity of teachers in preparing for instruction is to consider the class, its distributive properties, and the characteristics of individual participants and to determine the appropriate social arrangement for instruction (Barr & Dreeben, 1983). Groups formed within classes on the basis of ability are referred to as "homogeneous" or "ability" groups; alternatively, they may be formed on some other basis, such as interest, a specific need, or team teaching. Some grouping is even random, simply to create groups that are small in size. The term *ability* group may be a misnomer, inasmuch as the most common way to form "ability" groups is on the basis of achievement: reading achievement when groups for reading instruction are formed and mathematics achievement when groups for math instruction are formed.

Whether the teacher decides to group students for instruction or to instruct the class as a whole has implications for the design of instruction. If teachers group children for instruction on the basis of ability, to some extent they solve the problem of matching the difficulty of materials with the ability of children. But this solution makes teachers less available to work directly with pupils who are not in the immediate subgroup they are teaching. Correspondingly, the solution of total class instruction may solve the problem of teacher availability, but, because it typically involves use of a single set of materials, the work is usually inappropriate for a number of students.

Related Decisions

Grouping for instructions has characteristics that make existing structures, habits, and attitudes resistent to change. First, changes in grouping strategies require major adjustments in scheduling, curriculum, teacher planning, and teaching strategies. Current grouping practices occur within well-coordinated systems, and changing one aspect may create pressures or undesirable consequences for another. Second, teachers tend to hold strong beliefs, if for different reasons, that ability- grouping is beneficial for all students. Grouping patterns are, therefore, likely to continue in their present form unless there is some initial directive to change, followed by incentives to change.

Because of the complexities involved in changing grouping policy, a district should not consider evaluating existing procedures in an interactive manner, such as is described in this chapter, unless it is prepared to devote considerable time and energy to the process. The advantage of such a thorough process is that teachers and administrators have the opportunity to examine their own values and actions and to consider alternatives. A major advantage inherent in this process is that it develops staff knowledge of grouping and instruction.

THE ELEMENTARY SCHOOL DISTRICT

In order to illustrate the decision-making process suggested in this chapter, a composite profile of an elementary district was developed. The district, which we refer to as "District 999," is a kindergarten through grade 6 district, including six elementary schools with a total of about 2,600 students. As shown in Table 7.1, the number of students per grade in each school ranges from about 23 to 74. The district is racially integrated, with schools varying in composition from about 40–85% White, with a mean proportion of 68%.

The original decision to study instructional grouping was made by the superintendent, with agreement from the curriculum staff. Several concerns led to this action. For instance, it was felt that homogeneous grouping was curtailing options for students, by making later instruction contingent on earlier group placement. Similarly, whether or not a student was placed in a high-, middle-, or low-ability reading group was dependent on the basal level in use at the end of the previous grade. There also were equity concerns, in that Black students were overrepresented in low groups and underrepresented in high ones. Other equity concerns focused on the fact that curriculum differed substantially for students at different ability levels, especially in reading, where high-ability students received a more enriched, and in some cases accelerated, program. Finally, there was no consistency among schools in the kind of grouping that was used or the justification for it, despite some consistency in populations served.

The committee that was charged with studying the issue and recommending a policy document consisted of three primary teachers, three intermediate teachers, two principals, the curriculum coordinator of the district, and the assistant superintendent. The committee was representative of teachers and administrators and served as a microcosm of the larger social system in reflecting diverse views toward grouping. Attitudes of the 10 members ranged from total opposition to total enthusiasm for heterogeneous grouping.

Work on this assignment began on two fronts: reviewing the professional literature to determine what grouping policies were recommended and describing grouping practices currently being followed in the six schools. Research was read and subjected to heated debate within the committee. As is shown in the following section, this process of dialogue within the committee concerning the meaning of the research led to a measure of consensus on the set of values or beliefs.

On the basis of their self-study, the committee confirmed that the district had no uniform policy on grouping; instead, the teachers and administrative staff in each of the six schools in the district determined their own policies. Table 7.1 describes the grouping practices followed in each of the six schools. The grouping approaches followed in the schools of District 999 represent a range of grouping alternatives.

The grouping approach in Schools A and B is a fairly typical pattern: Students are randomly assigned to classes (heterogeneous classes), and students are grouped on the basis of ability for reading within classes (homogeneous groups). Other subjects are, however, taught to the "heterogeneous" class as a whole.

Classes in Schools C and D are also heterogeneous in composition. In School C, students in first and second grade are ability-grouped for reading instruction, similar to students in Schools A and B. Beyond second grade, students within a grade are regrouped for "departmentalized" reading and "departmentalized" mathematics instruction, and during the time for reading and for mathematics, most go to another class for instruction. Following departmentalized instruction, students return to their heterogeneous homeroom classes for instruction in other subjects.

First-grade classes in School D are also grouped similarly to those in Schools A and B. From grade 2 on, students from as many as three grade

TABLE 7.1

Average Grade Size, Percentage of White Students, and Description of Grouping in District 999 Schools.

School	Avg. Grade Size	% of White Students	Description of Grouping
A	23	75	Heterogeneous classes; two to three ability groups for reading in classes; no ability grouping for other subjects.
B	52	60	Heterogeneous classes; two to four ability groups for reading in classes; no ability grouping for other subjects.
C	59	80	Heterogeneous classes; two to three ability groups for reading in grades 1–2; departmentalized ability grouping for reading and math in grades 3–6; no ability grouping for other subjects.
D	74	65	Hetergeneous classes; two to three ability groups for reading in grade 1; cross-grade ability grouping for reading and math in grades 2–6; no ability grouping for other subjects.
E	68	85	Homogeneous classes; two ability groups for reading in grades 1–6; optional ability groups for math in grades 4–6; class ability groups for other subjects.
F	63	40	Homogeneous classes; two ability groups for reading in grades 1–6; two ability groups for math in grades 3–6; class ability groups for other subjects.

levels are grouped into relatively homogeneous "cross-grade" reading and math groups. Students typically leave their homeroom classes for reading and math. Instruction in social studies, science, and areas other than reading and mathematics are taught in the heterogeneous homeroom classes.

Students in Schools E and F are assigned to classes on the basis of reading achievement. In addition, these "homogeneous" classes are further subdivided into ability groups for reading. Although the classes are fairly homogeneous in reading, they are diverse in mathematics because achievement in the two areas is only moderately related. Because of the diversity of the classes in math, some teachers also group students by ability for mathematics instruction. Social studies, science, and other subjects are taught to the class as a whole; because the class is homogeneous in terms of reading achievement, however, students only have the opportunity to interact with other students in the same achievement range.

Within the six schools, concerns about grouping differed somewhat according to the role of personnel. Table 7.2 describes the initial views of administrators and teachers and the problems that these views created at each level. Principals all tended to expect that teachers would group within a class, on the basis of some measure (objective or subjective) of ability. However, although four out of six were overtly opposed to assigning students to teachers on the basis of ability (homogeneous class grouping), most, in fact, admitted using it occasionally. All of them liked their current freedom to group as they saw fit and feared that a district-wide grouping policy would lead to a loss of principal autonomy. Some also anticipated negative teacher and parent reaction.

Teachers held widely mixed views, somewhat dependent on their current practice. For instance, teachers in School C strongly favored a departmentalized grouping approach within a single grade. Teachers who had taught "transition" classes at the primary level also favored this form of homogeneous grouping. There was also considerable fear that change would be imposed on them and that adequate support and training would not be available. Another fear expressed during the early phase of the grouping study by the teachers association was that class size would increase. On the other hand, there was also recognition of equity issues among some teachers and the fact that homogeneous grouping often created de facto segregation. Many of these teachers viewed the grouping dialogue as long overdue.

Finally, although parents were not involved in the process directly, their views were indirectly heard through administrators and teachers on the committee. Homogeneous classes tended to be favored by those whose children were in the high groups or levels, whereas parents of average- or low-ability children viewed homogeneous grouping as elitist and racist. The result was an interesting dichotomy between those who

TABLE 7.2
Addressing Belief Systems of Different Organizational Levels

	Subgroup	Initial View(s) of Grouping	Problem(s) Created by Grouping Study
High			
	Central Office Administrators	Concern for negative impact of homogeneous grouping	Diversity of views within and among subgroups
	Program Committee	Diverse views: —skeptical about homogeneous grouping —supportive of homogeneous grouping	Need to achieve consensus Intense disagreement within the committee
	Principals	—expect teachers to group with class —opposed to homogeneous assignment to teachers, but most use it occasionally —like current autonomy in grouping	Fear of change: —loss of autonomy —teacher reaction —parent reaction
	Teachers	Widely mixed views: —departmentalized approach favored by School C —transition classes (primary) favored —benefit of change to minority children	Fear of change: —without support and training —with increase in class size
	Parents	—Homogeneous classes favored by those involved (vocal parents) —homogeneous classes viewed as racist and elitist by those not involved	—fear of losing high or accelerated programs —hope for more equity
Low			

Level of Involvement in Study

feared the loss of a high-ability track and those who hoped for such a loss.

The job of the committee was to determine whether the patterns of grouping in the six schools were appropriate and effective. In the following section, we describe some of the issues that the school committee addressed in considering that appropriateness and effectiveness.

STUDY UNDERTAKEN BY THE COMMITTEE

How should a district committee evaluate the effectiveness of their grouping practices? On what basis can they establish a sound policy on grouping? A traditional criterion used in educational research has been the influence of grouping on achievement; if learning is enhanced, then a grouping system is recommended. Although we believe that achievement outcomes represent one important consideration, grouping policies must be understood in broader terms than this. Grouping decisions must be responsive to the characteristics of students in the schools, the nature of learning, particularly in the areas of reading and mathematics, and values and goals for schooling. Although other considerations may arise from the conditions of particular settings, the four considered in this section represent a basic set that we believe district personnel who are evaluating their grouping policy must examine. We consider these four issues in two parts each: First, we describe what is known in each area, and second, we discuss the implications that the District 999 committee drew about grouping policy.

Achievement Outcomes

Findings from Research

Studies of Grouping.   All of the grouping approaches undertaken in District 999 schools create homogeneous groups for reading instruction and sometimes for mathematics instruction. How does a pattern of grouping influence achievement? A vast number of studies has been conducted to answer this question, and yet, no clear answer has emerged. As summarized by Rosenbaum (1984), "Reviewers who have charted the pattern of findings in studies of the effects of ability-grouping on achievement have found almost equal numbers of studies finding positive effects as negative effects" (p. 53). Different conclusions emerge depending on the set of studies reviewers examine. For example, some reviewers have concluded that there is a tendency for high achievers in homogeneous groups to achieve more than comparable students in heterogeneous groups (see, e.g., Borg, 1965; Dahllof, 1971; Findley & Bryan, 1971). Reciprocally, they discern a tendency for low achievers to do less well in homogeneous than in heterogeneous groups. These results would be predicted if instruction were closely matched to the mean achievement levels of students. Unfortunately, most research on grouping fails to document instruction, so it is difficult to know for certain whether the difficulty of the curricular tasks accounts for the findings.

The grouping literature includes a wide assortment of studies that vary in the grouping arrangements, subject matter, and the age and range of students studied. In most reviews, a general question is posed: Does homogeneous or heterogeneous grouping lead to higher achievement? The analyses may fail to find consistent findings, because too many different levels and forms of grouping are treated together. A recent analysis of the grouping literature (Slavin, 1987) is of particular interest for school-based personnel, because in it the findings from research studies are organized in terms of the forms of grouping frequently employed in elementary schools (for further discussion of Slavin's analysis, see Gamoran, 1987).

Several trends emerge from Slavin's review with respect to grouping *between* classes. First, he found that assignment to classes based on ability did not lead to higher achievement; this conclusion was based on the mixed results from 13 well-designed studies. He found no support for the assertion that high achievers benefit from being streamed into homogeneous-ability classes or that low achievers suffer from it. Second, he found that the results from three studies comparing departmentalized instruction with that in heterogeneously grouped classes were similarly equivocal. Third, in contrast, he found that students grouped across grades for reading instruction learned more than comparable students in self-contained classes in 9 of 11 studies; one study of math instruction showed similar results. Low achieving students, as well as higher achieving ones, learned more when instructed in cross-grade groups than did similar students instructed in groups in self-contained classrooms.

Finally, with respect to grouping *within* classes, Slavin identified seven well-designed studies in which math instruction with ability was compared to ungrouped instruction in heterogeneous, self-contained classes. Each of these involved students in the upper elementary grades, and all reported greater achievement for ability-grouped than for ungrouped classes. Further, the gains were somewhat larger for low than for average or high achievers in ability-grouped classes. These results seem to indicate that grouping within heterogeneous classes is advantageous for upper elementary school mathematics. However, Eddleman (1971) compared a grouping pattern involving three heterogeneous and three homogeneous math groups within classes and found that the heterogeneous groups achieved as well or better than the homogeneous groups. Although the findings may reflect the limited extent to which instruction was differentiated, it raises the important question of whether small groups are effective because of their size or their composition. That is, it may turn out that the effectiveness of ability groups within classes over total class instruction derives from the small size of the group rather than its homogeneous composition.

It is interesting to note that Slavin found no studies in which ability-grouped reading instruction was compared to ungrouped instruction in heterogeneous, self-contained classes. This is probably because of the widespread practice of grouping students for reading instruction on the basis of achievement. Consequently, although the advantage of ability-grouped instruction may also hold for reading, we lack research evidence on this point.

Failure to Document Instruction. A grouping pattern does not lead directly to achievement; rather, the nature of the instruction that groups receive influences their achievement. Yet, most research on grouping fails to describe instruction. The few studies documenting instruction have shown two things: First, instruction is responsive to the characteristics of the group for which it is designed; in general, more able groups are assigned more demanding work than less able ones (Anderson, Evertson, & Brophy, 1979; Barr, 1974; Barr & Dreeben, 1983). Second, groups of comparable ability vary greatly in instruction, and those exposed to more demanding instruction achieve more. For example, when first-grade groups of comparable ability were exposed to different amounts of reading, those exposed to more learned more than those exposed to less of their basal reading programs (Barr & Dreeben, 1983; Dreeben & Gamoran, 1986). The curriculum introduced during instruction and the time devoted to reading strongly influenced what and how much students learned.

This research and other related work (Dahllof, 1971) provide the basis for thinking about how the composition of a group and its instruction interact to influence learning. When students are highly diverse in achievement, teachers may limit the pace of instruction so that most students in the class will master the concepts presented. This has the effect of not challenging the more able students in the class, and, because the work is less than they are capable of doing, they learn less than might be expected. If, on the other hand, the teacher proceeds at a more rapid pace, the more able students will learn more, but the less able students will evidence frustration and partial learning. In contrast, when students are more homogeneous in achievement, it is easier for teachers to pace instruction in such a way that is appropriate for all students.

The effectiveness of cross-grade grouping (Slavin, 1987) may come about through two conditions. The groups resulting from cross-grade patterns of grouping are likely to be more homogeneous than those from other patterns. This is because students from grade to grade overlap considerably in achievement; consequently, when the same number of groups are established, cross-grade grouping results in narrower ranges of proficiency than single-grade groupings. This greater homogeniety, in turn, should make it easier for teachers to design instruction that is appropriate for students. Beyond this, achievement is influenced by the difficulty of the curricular tasks assigned. Typically, a greater range of curricular materials, usually two or more grade levels, is available in cross-grade grouping than in other forms of grouping, which typically involve a single grade level. Thus, a greater opportunity exists for high achievers to be given work that is sufficiently demanding and lower achievers to be met at their precise reading level.

The lower achievement of low reading groups may, in part, reflect an undemanding curriculum and narrow instructional support. An extensive literature compares the reading instruction of students in low groups within classes with that of higher groups (see Allington, 1983, for a general review of this literature). Although it is clear that comparisons of the instruction of low and high groups fail to address the question of the most effective grouping arrangements for low achievers, the descriptions are useful in alerting us to the nature of instruction typically received by low-group members. Their instruction tends to be characterized by a greater number of intrusions (Eder, 1981), less time on-task (Gambrell, 1984; Gambrell, Wilson, & Ganatt, 1981; Good & Beckerman, 1978; Martin & Evertson, 1980), less demanding curricular tasks (Barr & Dreeben, 1983), more skillwork and oral reading (Collins, 1986; DeStephano, Pepinsky, & Sanders, 1982), and lower level questions (Seltzer, 1976) than that of higher groups. That the instruction of high and low groups should differ is not unexpected; indeed, one of the reasons for ability-grouping in reading is so that instruction can be more appropriate. At the same time, reading fewer stories and more isolated letters and words and responding to informational rather than higher level questions would seem to constitute neither appropriate nor effective instruction.

It is important to acknowledge that this way of thinking about grouping composition, curriculum demand, and learning may apply better to some content areas than others. It applies most clearly to content domains that can be divided into hierarchically related areas of learning, with earlier learning serving as the basis for more advanced later work. For example, instruction in mathematics is typically ordered hierarchically, so if students lack basic knowledge, it is difficult for them to profit from more advanced instruction. Similarly, beginning reading is characterized by a developmental progression such that children in the beginning stages are unable to read more advanced materials. Other subject matter areas may not demand instruction as closely matched to the abilities of group members; that is, if instruction is sufficiently broad and meaningful, most students can benefit from it at some level. For example, a story read to children can be understood and appreciated by them on a number of different levels. Ability-grouping would seem to be effective for tasks to achieve specific objectives that are hierarchical in organization, but unnecessary for tasks that can be approached in different ways.

In thinking about grouping, it is also useful to consider the findings from studies of classroom instruction that indicate that students in elementary schools learn more when they spend more time directly engaged in reading and math activities under the direct supervision of teachers (see, e.g., Brophy & Good, 1986; Rosenshine & Stevens, 1986). Two implications follow. First, teachers who form many ability groups within classes spend less time directly instructing each group than those who form fewer; therefore, it would seem to be advisable to form as few groups within classes as possible. Second, the nature of instruction, its quality and duration, may be more important for learning than attempts to narrow the achievement of instructional groups through ability-grouping.

Implications for Grouping in District 999

After considering the research findings, the committee derived some tentative conclusions about the effectiveness of the grouping approaches in the six schools. The research findings suggest that the ability groups within heterogeneous classes in Schools A and B are no less effective in promoting general achievement than the departmentalized groups in School C and the homogeneous class groups in Schools E and F. For those grouping patterns involving single grade levels, the range of curricular options are similar. Because the results suggest that homogeneous class grouping cannot be justified on the basis of higher achievement, teachers and administrators in Schools E and F may wish to rethink their grouping approach.

The cross-grade grouping of School D would likely result in more homogeneous groups than the grouping approaches in the other schools, with a greater range of curricular tasks. The more limited diversity of School D groups should make it easier for the teachers to design more appropriate instruction for all students; and for the high achievers, it should be possible to design more demanding instruction than might be true for the other schools. These conditions, according to the research finding, result in higher overall or mean school achievement.

Ultimately, if higher achievement were the sole criterion for setting grouping policy, cross-grade grouping would appear to be the most effective approach. As discussed earlier in the chapter, however, achievement results are not the only factor that should be considered when a district establishes grouping policy. Other conditions, considered in subsequent sections of this chapter, include characteristics of the students derived through self-study, the nature of reading and mathematics, and values and goals.

The Characteristics of Students

Self-Study Results

In some districts, a policy mandating either heterogeneous or homogeneous classes determines the approach followed by all schools in the district. The policy is followed whether or not the student composition is diverse in achievement or not. As we argued earlier, however, it is not necessarily appropriate for all schools in a district to follow the same plan. If the purpose of grouping is to reduce the variation among students so that instruction is more appropriate, then it follows that the composition of grades should have a bearing on how classes are composed. For example, schools with students that range from the 1st to the 99th percentiles may need to address the problem of group diversity in some manner, whereas those characterized by a narrower range may find instruction viable without special grouping arrangements.

Grouping, whether into grades on the basis of age or into classes on the basis of ability or other criteria, involves partitioning a diverse group of students in particular ways that educators believe will enhance instruction. Although grouping on the basis of age does not usually affect such characteristics as the gender, ethnicity, or racial representation of grades in predictable ways, grouping on the basis of ability may influence the ethnic, racial, or gender composition of groups. For example, in grouping for mathematics instruction on the basis of ability, high groups may tend to have a disproportionate number of males (Hallinan & Sorensen, 1987). Similarly, in some districts, grouping on the basis of ability in mathematics or reading may lead to a disproportionate number of White students in the high groups (Sorensen & Hallinan, 1984).

Self-study of student achievement can be used to determine whether or not a need for ability grouping exists. For example, Fig. 7.1 includes five graphs representing different achievement distributions. Most randomly assigned classes conform to profile A; there are many students concentrated in the middle of the distribution and few at the extremes. Distributions like this should require very little homogeneous grouping, because students already are quite similar. In contrast, profile B represents a wide range in achievement with many low and high, as well as average achievers. In areas of learning that are hierarchically or developmentally organized, some ability-grouping may be necessary. Profile C reflects a concentration of low achievers in the class, with few high achievers. This is the sort of "low-class" distribution that is created when students are grouped into classes on the basis of ability. Although no grouping for differential instruction may be necessary because students are, for the most part, similar in achievement, individualized assignments to challenge the top segment in the class may be necessary. Profile D represents a class with a concentration of high achievers. If the instruction is geared to the learning of this segment of the class, it will likely overshoot the competencies of the lower segment. Either total class instruction, followed by small group work with the lower contingent, or ability-grouped instruction within classes is appropriate. Finally, profile E with concentrations of students at both extremes rarely occurs. It is difficult to teach this class as a whole, because if instruction is geared to the higher achievers, it overshoots the needs of the lower achievers. On the other hand, if instruction is geared to the lower achievers, the higher achievers will not be challenged. For hierarchically organized subjects, some form of ability-groping will probably be necessary to maximize learning.

In addition to examining class composition to determine whether ability-grouping may be necessary, districts that practice ability-grouping should determine the influence that it has on the gender and racial or ethnic composition of classes. Examination of these characteristics may reveal that grouping on the basis of ability biases against the inclusion of certain children in higher ability classes.

Implications for Grouping in District 999

The variation in grouping approaches followed in District 999 schools reflects the fact that principals and their teachers have been free to differ in their grouping decisions. One reason underlying these differences may be the diversity of the student population in each school. To explore the influence of achievement composition of a grade on grouping in the elementary schools of District 999, we compare the achievement compositions of the two elementary schools (E and F) that assigned students to classes on the basis of achievement with the four that did not. Figure 7.2 shows stanine profiles of reading achievement in grades 2 and 5 for each school (the profiles for other grade levels are similar). The compositional profiles of the six schools are similar with one exception: School F. Because of the wide variation among students in School F, some form of achievement grouping may be necessary. However, given the prior discussion of the research literature, a cross-grade grouping pattern would be preferable to homogeneous class grouping or even a departmentalized form of grouping.

The size of the grade, rather than its achievement composition, has a bearing on the grouping in School A. It is not surprising that School A, with an average grade size of between 20 and 30, would need to form single heterogeneous classes at each grade level. Because the achievement distributions of students in School A are similar to those of schools other than School F, compositional considerations do not account for the differences observed in grouping.

Because of the possibility that de facto segregation issues were involved, the racial composition of the schools was also considered. As shown in Table 7.1, the schools ranged in composition from about 40–85% White, with a mean proportion of 68%. The two schools assigning students to classes on the basis of achievement differed widely in racial composition. School E enrolled about 85% White students, whereas school F enrolled about 40% While. De facto segregation did not occur

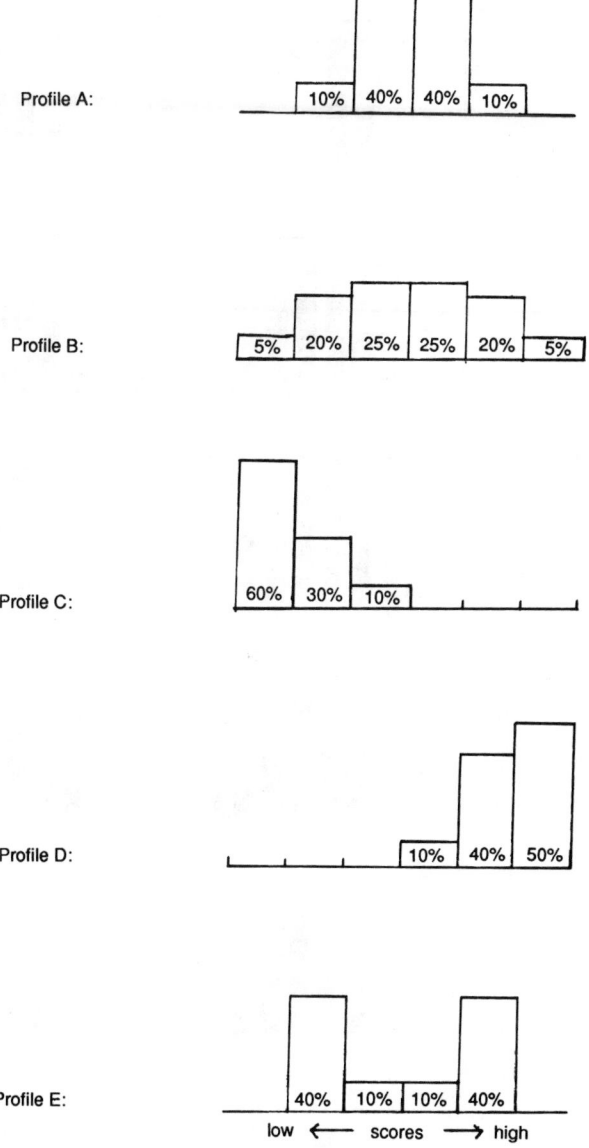

FIG. 7.1. Profiles representing different achievement distributions.

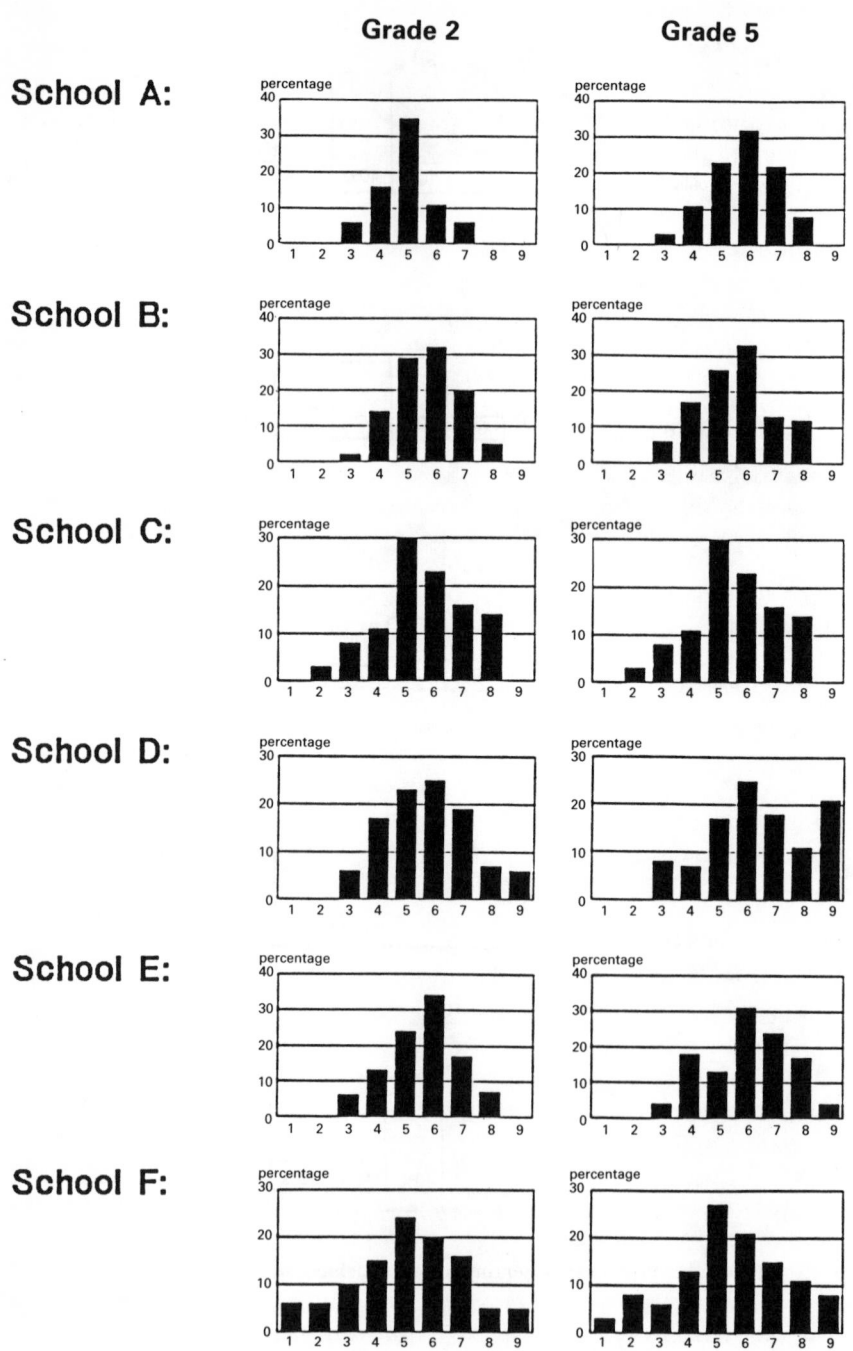

FIG. 7.2. Stanine reading achievement profiles for grades 2 and 5 in District 999 schools.

in school E, in part because Black and White students were from similar socioeconomic backgrounds. It did in School F because of the disproportionate number of Black, lower-socioeconomic-status students enrolled in the school. Some classes were composed only of Black students and other, mainly of White students. Because of the use of homogenous class grouping, students interacted *only* with students assigned to their classes.

Schools A, B, C, and D, with approximately 60–80% White students enrolled, used grouping arrangements that allowed interaction among students in groups that were heterogeneous in achievement and race for at least some portion of each day in subjects other than reading and sometimes mathematics. Because of the disproportionate number of Black students in the lower ability classes in School F, the committee concluded that it was inappropriate to assign students to classes on the basis of ability in any of the schools for fear that a similar bias would occur.

Reading and Mathematics Development

Discussion of Research Findings

Although the committee had previously examined the results from studies of instruction in general, it decided to consider reading and mathematics development in greater depth, because the self-study revealed that these were the areas of study for which ability grouping was used. Generally, ability-grouping has been used for these subjects, although the reason for this "preferential" treatment is not clear. It may reflect the extent to which reading and computing are necessary for academic work in other subject areas and for life in our society. The tendency may also arise from the nature of the subject matter. Reading and mathematics are often described as subjects that are developmentally organized with one area of learning building directly on prior learning. If this is true, then it is important to understand the nature of reading and mathematics development and to consider which aspects of them are developmentally organized and which are less clearly so.

Reading Development. Most reading researchers agree that the beginning stages of reading differ in fundamental ways from subsequent stages. Most important, beginning readers must learn about the nature of print and how print relates to their spoken language. Chall (1983), for example, described the initial stages of reading as learning to decode and then learning to read fluently. Typically, this focus on reading occurs in the first two or three grades of elementary school. The developmental nature of learning to read during this period becomes obvious in several ways. Children who read at a beginning first-grade level have extreme difficulty reading second- or third-grade level materials, because they have not yet acquired the needed sight vocabulary nor the skill to identify unknown words. Further, studies of reading development show that the achievement of first graders is closely tied to the content of the materials they read during instruction; the words they learn and the phonics concepts they acquire accurately predict their ability to read graded passages and to perform well on standardized reading tests (Barr & Dreeben, 1983).

As children learn a substantial number of words and can identify them easily, they consolidate this learning to become fluent readers. For most children, this integration occurs during the second or third grade. Learning about print is no longer a major emphasis of subsequent instruction; instead, reading instruction focuses on the strategies that children must acquire to comprehend effectively and critically. The materials that children encounter in the intermediate grades pose many new problems for them: Often, the vocabulary is unfamiliar; the structure of reading in science and social studies differs from the narrative forms experienced in the basal series; children are expected to read longer selections silently.

Most important to our discussion here, what children need to learn to become effective readers is no longer developmentally organized. Whereas skill with print relates directly to the level of the material that children can read in the early stages, in later stages interest in and prior knowledge about the topic are more determinant (Anderson & Davison, 1989). Accordingly, in the intermediate grades and beyond, it becomes much more difficult to predict whether or not a child can comprehend a particular story or article. The results from reading research support the conclusion that intermediate and upper elementary instruction should focus on the development of strategies for the comprehension of stories and articles, rather than on isolated skill practice (Anderson, Hiebert, Scott, & Wilkinson, 1985). Through prereading discussions that encourage students to share their knowledge about the topic of a selection, students are better prepared to comprehend the selection. Several useful teaching strategies have been developed to encourage students to think about what they may learn from the text and what they already know about the topic (see, e.g., Ogle, 1986; Raphael, 1982; Stauffer, 1975). It must be remembered, however, that word identification and fluency will still have a bearing on the reading of low-achieving students, and they may require special instructional provisions.

In sum, learning to read print fluently in the primary grade can be described as developmental in nature, but once students have achieved fluency, reading cannot be characterized in this way. Given this change in the nature of reading instruction and learning, grouping children in the primary grades to achieve a closer match between their ability to deal with print and the demands of printed material would seem to be desirable. In contrast, ability-grouping in the intermediate grades, once fluency has been achieved, finds little support because of the difficulty we encounter in accurately predicting what will be easy or difficult for students to comprehend. The principle being developed here is that grouping may be justified when subject matter is developmental in nature and a close match between learner proficiency and task demands facilitates learning. It is not appropriate to group students on the basis of ability, however, when a variety of different prerequisite experiences support comprehension. In short, it may be useful to ability-group students for reading in the primary grades but not in the intermediate grades.

Unfortunately, group assignments in the primary grades often determine those in the intermediate grades. That is, the level where students read in the basal at the end of the school year determines, in some schools, their group placement and basal level at the beginning of the subsequent grade (Gamoran, 1989). One consequence of this practice is that groups formed on the basis of decoding ability may be homogeneous in the primary grades; these same groups in the intermediate grades may be quite diverse in reading comprehension. Barr and Sadow (1989) examined the degree to which fourth-grade reading groups overlapped in reading comprehension as measured by a standardized test. Once single outliers were eliminated from consideration, the low and high groups in classes or schools were extremely similar in their range of comprehension. That is, there were many strong comprehenders in the low groups and many poor comprehenders in the high groups. Because the nature of reading in the primary grades differs from that in the intermediate, primary group placement is not an appropriate basis for establishing intermediate grade groups. Rather, recent research suggests that alternative forms of grouping, such as total class instruction followed by small-group support for those who need it or by heterogeneous peer-group work, lend themselves to strategy development and are effective in increasing comprehension (Barr, 1987; Stevens, Madden, Slavin, & Farnish, 1987).

Mathematics Development. Many areas of mathematics include hierarchically related concepts. It is generally believed that children must master basic operations of addition and subtraction before they can apply them to multiplication and division. Furthermore, in multiplication and division, simpler forms precede more complex ones. There may even be a logical basis for introducing fractions after division. At the same time, there seems to be no logical basis for the position of some areas, such a geometry and measurement, in the hierarchical sequence. There is, moreover, growing consensus among mathematics researchers concerning the role of children in actively constructing knowledge about mathematical relations (Resnick, 1982; Romberg & Carpenter, 1986). The strategies that they invent to solve addition and subtraction problems are often more efficient and powerful conceptually than the more mechanical procedures typically taught them. Instruction must be designed not only to build on the existing concepts and strategies of children, but to move beyond them in successive stages (Case, 1983).

In spite of the essentially developmental nature of mathematics, rarely are students ability-grouped within classes for instruction, and departmentalized forms of organization exist only in some schools (Gerleman, 1987; Good, Grouws, & Mason, 1987; Good, Mason, & Grouws, 1987). Failure to individualize instruction occurs in spite of the fact that inadequate mastery of prerequisite material may seriously interfere with learning higher order concepts. Some teachers resolve this difficulty by spending a substantial portion of each year reviewing previously introduced concepts and proceeding through new math material at a slow pace (Barr, 1988). One consequence of this strategy is a failure to challenge students who possess a talent for mathematics. The research evidence is clear in showing that ability-grouped math instruction in the intermediate grades leads to enhanced achievement (Slavin, 1987). Thus, some form of ability-grouping should be considered in the intermediate grades. Beyond this, cooperative forms of problem solving in heterogeneous small groups have been found to be effective in promoting mathematics learning in the elementary (Cobb, 1987) and intermediate grades (Slavin, 1983; Webb, 1982).

Implications for Grouping in District 999

With respect to reading instruction, the committee concurred with the research literature that suggests that initial reading development is enhanced when children of similar reading proficiency are grouped and instructed together. Primary teachers in all six schools employ some form of ability-grouping for reading instruction. The committee concluded that there was justification for this practice.

The committee viewed the interpretation of the research literature pertaining to intermediate-level reading instruction as being more controversial. Because all intermediate and upper-grade teachers ability-grouped students for reading instruction, and because the research literature supports the efficacy of cross-grade forms of grouping, the committee felt that it was inappropriate to recommend that ability-grouping be abandoned. On the other hand, the committee was convinced that it should be possible to undertake more total class instruction once students had achieved reading fluency. To further this end, they agreed that pilot experimentation with alternative forms of grouping, including total class instruction and cooperative groupwork, should be encouraged through summer planning grants to teachers who were willing to implement such alternatives.

With respect to mathematics, the research literature shows various forms of ability-grouping to be effective in enhancing intermediate-level mathematics development. Because schools differed in whether they had grouped students for math instruction in the past, the committee recommended that additional compositional studies of math achievement be undertaken to determine whether ability-grouping had been effective in increasing the achievement of those students who were talented in mathematics. They tentatively concluded that some form of ability-grouping would enhance mathematics development in the intermediate grades.

At the same time, the committee concluded that other instructional formats should also be considered for mathematics instruction, such as permitting lower achieving students to spend 2 years or a double period mastering math concepts instead of a single year or period (Beagle, 1973), providing differentiated assignments for students, and cooperative group work. The committee concluded that summer planning grants should also be made available to teachers who proposed modified forms of grouping students for mathematics instruction.

Beliefs

Consideration of Beliefs

Beliefs that bear on grouping can be divided into two main areas. First are those about the purposes of grouping and instruction. On one end of the continuum, some teachers believe that grouping serves a developmental purpose of establishing a sound learning basis from which students can move to more demanding work; at the other end, some believe that grouping serves a sorting function: Some students will always do high-quality or low-quality work regardless of the degree of instructional support; a group level denotes what can be expected. In a related vein, some teachers believe that all students need a balance in learning, including both basic work and higher order skills, and that higher achieving students need enrichment, rather than acceleration; others believe that lower achieving students profit from drill but are unable to benefit from instruction in higher order skills. The evidence on the instruction of low reading groups suggests that some teachers view low-group members as capable only of concrete thinking, who profit mainly from clearly focused tasks and drill.

Second are beliefs about social interaction and learning. On one end of the continuum, some teachers believe that in a democratic society it is important for students from different backgrounds and with different talents to learn to interact productively to solve problems; others believe that the development of talent overrides considerations of social learning. Relatedly, some believe that each student has a right to educational opportunities that are of high quality and supportive of social development; others believe that inferior educational opportunities for some can be justified on the basis of the general good achieved through the development of talent in a few.

Grouping on the basis of achievement is consistent with the belief that the main goal of schooling is the development of talent. Stratification of students in terms of what they know permits the development of more focused instruction and enhances learning, at least in developmentally organized subjects. Those who disagree with this position argue that the goal of schooling is multifaceted and includes social and emotional, as well as conceptual development. Further, they dispute whether most academic areas need be treated as being hierarchical in organization. To the extent that instructional tasks are meaningful and students have control over their mode of responding, the tasks becomes appropriate for a wider range of students.

Implications for Grouping in District 999

Although it is clear that student composition is not a primary influence on grouping in District 999, principal and teacher beliefs have considerable bearing. The assignment of students to heterogeneous classes in Schools A, B, C, and D results from the strongly held, shared beliefs of the principal and teachers about the negative effects of homogeneous classes and the positive benefits derived from children of varying backgrounds and abilities learning from each other. At the same time, teachers and the principals of Schools C and D are convinced that reading instruction is easier in departmentalized or cross-grade groups, because teachers then have to manage the instruction of only one or two different groups. Consequently, students spend more time interacting with others and less time on independent seatwork than is true when the teacher works with more groups. Providing a similar rationale, the principals and teachers of Schools E and F justified homogeneous classes on the basis that teachers worked more effectively with fewer instructional groups than are possible in heterogeneous classes.

These differences in beliefs were also represented in the committee. As the committee attempted to reach agreement on their recommendations for grouping policy, it became clear that a consensus about beliefs and values concerning the relationship of grouping and instruction had to be achieved. Grouping policy does not derive simply from what the research literature shows to be efficatious, from a self-study of composition, or from an understanding of the nature of reading and mathematics development. Although policy can be informed by these considerations, in the end, policy is a matter of goals. The committee had to rise above their own strong biases and experiences in order to consider the responsibility of the district in assuring quality education for all of its students.

A cornerstone for the District 999 committee in coalescing its beliefs about grouping was the existing district philosophy. From the broad district goal, that "all children can learn and should be given opportunities to fulfill their highest potential," they made explicit their assumptions about students and instruction that would affect the policy and practices of grouping:

1. Instructional Goals for Low and High Achievers. Students functioning at basic levels need higher order skills as well as remediation; they can learn higher order skills and concepts, with enough motivation, time, and quality instruction. The goal of instruction for low achievers is to move them to a higher level. High achievers need enrichment more than acceleration.

2. Social Interaction. Low achievers and high achievers benefit from interacting during instruction each day. Minority children should be integrated with other students in academic classes.

3. Criteria for Grouping. Different subjects and grade levels need different numbers and types of groups. There are many characteristics in addition to academic ability that are useful for grouping.

These beliefs were discussed in depth by the committee. Because there was very little variance in opinion in these three areas (despite the fact that they are not empirically provable), they served to show the committee how much in agreement they were.

Conclusions About Grouping Policy

The committee agreed on five main conclusions following from their consideration of the professional literature, their self-study, and their delineation of beliefs:

1. Mainly on the basis of their beliefs about the goals of education, they concluded that all students must receive some instruction in heterogeneous classes, balanced in terms of gender, race, and ethnicity.

2. On the basis of the research results and their compositional self-study, they concluded that homogeneous ability-grouping may facilitate instruction in some settings and in the content areas of reading and mathematics. However, they agreed that the implementation of ability-grouping should be based on more than teacher belief as to its efficacy. Compositional studies should be undertaken to demonstrate the need for ability-grouping. Further, they agreed that when ability grouping was used, the fewest number of groups feasible should be established.

3. The stability of group membership from year to year, in spite of the changing nature of task demands, was viewed as a problem with any form of grouping. Thus, the committee concluded that when ability-grouping is used, placement criteria must be valid and assignment must be reviewed at least annually.

4. Based on their stated values and on the research evidence concerning the instruction of low-ability groups, the committee concluded that all instruction, but particularly instruction of homogeneously grouped lower achieving students, must be of high quality with a balance between conceptual development and practice tasks.

5. Finally, based on the analysis of intermediate-level reading, the results from alternative forms of reading and math instruction, and the research on cooperative work groups, the committee concluded that some of these alternatives should be tried out on a limited basis in one or two classes and that teacher "grants" should be available to support this work.

Once the committee had reached consensus on these conclusions, their next step was to seek support within the system. In the next and final section of the chapter, we discuss the interaction of the committee with district teachers and administrators and the development of a policy on grouping.

INTERACTION WITH
STAFF AND DEVELOPMENT OF POLICY

The groundwork for the second phase of the process must begin at the same time that the committee begins its work[2]. The channels established with teachers and administrators during the first phase of the committee's study are what enable effective communication to occur during the sec-

---

[2]The description of interactions between the committee and district personnel draws heavily on the experience of the authors working with the administrators and faculty of District 201 in Crete-Monee, Illinois. We gratefully acknowledge our debt to them.

ond phase. After considering their own beliefs, it became clear that change would not happen in an area of established belief and practice, such as grouping, merely because a set of administrative procedures was issued. Through their study, the committee determined that several factors must be present for changes to be made in grouping practices (see, e.g., Rutherford & Murphy 1985; Sarason 1971; Sarason & Klaber 1985; Sirotnik, Goldenberg, & Oakes 1986).

Interaction with Staff

Initially, it is important to set the stage for change by assuring teachers and administrators that grouping in various forms will continue. From the beginning, many questions will arise; thus, two-way communication between the central planning committee and others must be kept open. Once the committee has developed a consensus on grouping issues, the feelings and beliefs of teachers and principals must be considered. Finally, teachers and administrators must be aware that they have some control over the change process and that support for change is forthcoming. In the following sections, we elaborate on these factors that influence effective change in grouping.

Open Communication

Accept the Existence of Grouping.   The real question for any district is rarely *whether* to group (it is an ingrained habit for most educators), but rather *how* and *when* to group. The process of change must begin with this assumption. The goal is not to eliminate the use of groups for instruction, but rather to consider how the use of groups can be improved and options for grouping strategies expanded so that the educational needs of all students can be met.

Establish Two-Way Communication.   With inherently volatile topics like grouping there is likely to be considerable suspicion and fear. It is critical that those involved in proposing change create an atmosphere in which questions and concerns are welcomed. While the committee was reading and studying the grouping issues, they distributed their minutes (which included anecdotal summaries of the discussion) and briefly discussed them at faculty meetings. In addition, they encouraged teachers and administrators to send their ideas about grouping to the committee. In some cases, members of the committee met (on request) with small groups of teachers who had concerns about changes that were in the offing.
   Formal communication within the district as a whole began after the committee had considered grouping issues for a year. At the beginning

of the second year, the committee developed inservices to inform administrators on the status of their study of the research and their consideration of beliefs and values. In order to avoid misunderstanding and provide similar communication to teachers through the principals, they developed a model for a school staff meeting, including a detailed outline and overhead transparencies[3]. In order to judge the response of the staff to the information, a representative from the committee attended the meeting to identify the nature of concerns and misunderstandings.

During the second year, the committee developed an inservice meeting focused on values and beliefs. They obtained reactions from teachers and administrators informally: Staff members were asked to think about the beliefs they shared and to contact the committee if they were interested in or concerned about any of the ideas shared.

This same type of inservice occurred at the end of the second year, after the committee wrote the first draft of guidelines for grouping. This time the inservice was more informal, and the principal had fewer responsibilities for communication. Teachers at the same level (for example, grade 1) were asked to react to the document in writing. Consideration of the guidelines through inservice discussion provided an opportunity for reflection and feedback. Teachers were consulted as professional colleagues. In addition to the formal response, they were invited to phone committee members or discuss their reactions with committee members in small groups.

Feelings and Beliefs

Mitigate Fear. There were initially two main sources of fear among the staff. The teachers association had expressed concern about the effect of proposed changes on class size. Teachers in School C were afraid that changes would cost them their departmentalized structure. When the grouping guidelines were submitted to the faculty for feedback at the end of the second year, a couple of other concerns emerged, in addition to these. The largest (most frequently mentioned) issue was the question of standards for identification and evaluation of students, including entrance and exit criteria for different ability levels. Another concern was that instructional materials currently available were not appropriate for heterogeneous groups in some subject areas, and that increased inservice and teacher preparation time would be needed if substantial changes were to be made in instructional strategies. In both cases, face-to-face discussion helped to allay some of these fears. In addition, important changes were made in the document that addressed these concerns.

---

[3]Samples of inservices planned for principals and faculty are available upon request from the second author.

Deal with Beliefs and Values Before Policy. Because teachers and administrators consider the question of grouping with strong biases, and because the evidence from research does not lead directly to policy without a consideration of values and goals, it was important to begin the process of change by discussing what those involved believed about grouping and instruction. In District 999, it was helpful for the committee to begin this discussion and arrive at some consensus before the topic was open to wider discussion. This group then became a unified force in molding wider district opinion and garnering support for ideas to which they themselves were already committed. Even after initial discussion occurred in multiple sites, there was still the need for the committee to identify the common themes and to suggest areas of consensus.

Generate Interest. If change is to be made nonthreatening, it is essential that a small core of people at the classroom and building administration level become enthusiastic and interested in trying out some alternatives. An inservice that encourages sharing and discussion of common values plays an important role in generating interest among teachers. Also important is the availability of resources and support for teachers who indicate some interest in piloting the ideas being discussed.

In District 999, the initial enthusiasm came from within the committee. One principal began to encourage teachers to move students to higher levels in some subject areas during the year, when students were functioning above the placement level. An intermediate teacher asked permission to teach the fifth-grade reading curriculum to all her students, including those who achieved at the fourth-grade level. Another intermediate teacher from School F, which had implemented ability-grouped classes in the past, agreed to teach a heterogeneous class using cooperative learning strategies (Johnson & Johnson, 1975).

Outside the committee, others also became interested. Conversations with teachers at School C resulted in some interest in team-teaching and flexible grouping of students at the intermediate level. A principal agreed to look at the distribution of test data for his building and to use his findings when talking with teachers about how to place students in groups for the coming year. An intermediate teacher requested and received assistance in enriching the basic-level curriculum with higher order reading and thinking skills. Another principal designed and taught a program in which a heterogeneous group of intermediate students met three times a week to read and discuss literature, using higher order questions (Hillocks, 1980).

The use of such pilot programs, in which teachers and principals volunteered to try out alternative grouping strategies, was effective in generating interest. The pilot projects also provided information about potential problems in the implementation process, as well as some encouraging success stories. These projects were expected to continue in the future, involving more teachers and administrators, either as participants or as observers.

The Process of Change

Assure Some Control over Change by Teachers and Administrators. Research suggests that this factor is critical for successful change. Although, in District 999, teachers were not the source of the decision to study grouping, they were involved at many levels in the process. More than half of the committee were teachers, selected to represent each level (primary and intermediate) of the district. In addition, teacher opinion was not only accepted continuously, but also solicited formally at several points. Teachers were encouraged to consider alternative instructional strategies, particularly those that facilitated teaching more heterogeneous groups of students or increased the chance that students would achieve on grade level faster. Teachers interested in such alternatives were given special training, resources, and other means of visible support. At no point in the process were teachers told exactly what specific grouping procedures to use.

Similarly, principals needed assurances that they had sufficient latitude to establish grouping procedures that were responsive to their goals and the needs of their students. In its final form, the document on grouping in District 999 was expected to provide this latitude so that grouping procedures could vary across schools in response to the needs of children in each building.

Introduce Change Gradually and Without Threat. The committee was careful at all points to indicate that its work was tentative, evolving, and open to input and critique. Participation in pilot programs involving alternatives to current grouping strategies was voluntary. It was assumed that teachers who volunteered to participate would be more positive than those who were told to do so. Volunteers would also be more inclined to share their enthusiasm with peers. It was expected from the beginning that change would be a gradual and organic process, in which both teachers and administrators would be involved. Furthermore, a cornerstone of the policy was its flexibility. It was designed to delineate the limits within which any form of grouping could be judged acceptable, rather than to prescribe specific behaviors.

Make Resources and Support Available. Effective change must be supported by the allocation of resources: time, training, materials, ideas for alternative approaches, and professional support and interest. Administrative support for volunteer teachers using alternative approaches was critical because of the risk they assumed in stepping outside of comfortable and familiar habits.

Where support was communicated in direct and visible ways in District 999, teachers became interested in and open to change. Teachers experimenting with alternatives were most positive when they received ongoing and effective support in scheduling, student assignment, materials, training, and moral support. Frustration resulted when teachers were encouraged to try alternatives and then not given appropriate building and central office support. The greatest levels of support for teachers in District 999 came in schools where the principal had been involved as a committee member in the process of studying grouping or had viewed the committee's work as applicable to some unique need of that building. It was important for district administrators and committee members to maintain their encouragement and support of building principals, as well as of teachers directly.

Grouping Guidelines: Questions to Address

In District 999, the value statements presented earlier were used as the basis for developing the grouping policy. The document was referred to as "guidelines" because it was intended to establish the criteria by which acceptable grouping practices could be identified. It was not the intention of the committee to establish a single uniform set of practices to be followed by all schools. Rather, the guidelines were designed to provide flexibility so that buildings could meet their own needs for grouping within broader common district standards.

The following elements are recommended for inclusion in a grouping policy statement. Questions that a grouping policy must address are indicated, and examples from the District 999 policy are used as illustrations. Another district may identify different values and therefore make different decisions on these questions.

Introduction

The introduction should spell out the purpose of the document and define any terms used in the document. Distinctions in terminology discussed earlier in this chapter are helpful here. In District 999, the introduction was used to explain that guidelines were intended to be flexible, and that although homogeneous grouping was in no way forbidden, it "must be based on a demonstrated need and must meet certain conditions."

Decisions about When to Group

This section of the document should indicate the conditions under which grouping (both within class and assignment to classes) is warranted. The District 999 document assumes that homogeneous grouping must be necessary in order to be acceptable. Specifically, the document proposed that a self-study of class composition as described earlier be made to demonstrate need. Grades with extreme heterogeneity may require some degree of ability grouping to restrict the variability and allow teachers to match instruction more closely to student needs.

This is also the place in the guidelines to address differences in subject areas and grade levels that affect the necessity for homogeneous grouping. For example, the existence of a developmental curriculum may justify grouping in some subjects at some grade levels. This section should also specify the data that will be available for assessing when to group.

District Restrictions on Grouping

Rather than spell out specific grouping strategies that are acceptable, this section should explain any conditions that must be present when a given strategy is used. For instance, the District 999 policy specifies that whenever students are to be grouped homogeneously, it must be done in such a way as to (a) allow students to have some experience learning academic subjects in heterogeneous groups each day and (b) use the fewest possible groups (no more than three) in a class.

Decisions About How to Place Students in Groups Appropriately

This section should specify characteristics of the criteria that allow students to be grouped (when ability-grouping is done) fairly and effectively. In the District 999 document, nine such recommendations were made:

1. Use objective criteria where possible, and find ways to make open-ended criteria like "teacher recommendation" more specific.

2. Use at least two sets of criteria, including teacher recommendation (made formal and objective) and academic performance.

3. Avoid criteria that determine future placement based on past experiences (e.g., prior basal reading level) or that prevent movement to higher levels.

4. Avoid establishing groups that are homogeneous in cultural background and gender.

5. Provide for flexible movement, so that students who achieve can work at a higher level as soon as possible.
6. Provide thorough screening for new students.
7. In case of doubt, provide placement at the higher level.
8. Do not allow background experiences that are remediable within a subject to be used to place students at a level lower than appropriate.
9. Develop exit goals that relate basic-level programs to average-level program entry skills.

Decisions about Providing Quality Instruction for Groups

This section should address the need to expand the range of tasks for all groups, so that all students receive appropriate instruction. As part of this process of developing guidelines, the committee on grouping must meet with the curricular committees in the district to clarify the implications of the Grouping Guidelines for curriculum development and program evaluation. This section should also specify considerations that apply to particular groups when ability-grouped. These considerations serve to assure that interests of each group are protected and well served whether or not ability-grouping is used. In the District 999 document, the following considerations were emphasized:

1. All students, basic as well as advanced, should be taught critical-thinking and problem-solving skills.
2. All students should be given enrichment activities.
3. Instructor skill (not tenure) should be matched to the needs of students, so that new teachers are not assigned all the lower achieving students.
4. Class size should be lowered when ability-grouping is used for basic-level students.
5. Instruction of special services personnel should be coordinated with that provided by classroom teachers.

Decisions about Inservice Training

A policy document should provide options for training and procedures for accessing such training. Appropriate support must be provided for the pilot projects undertaken by teachers and principals. Once teachers and administrators within schools incorporate new grouping patterns and instructional strategies more generally, they must be supported with inservice money, time, and other relevant resources.

Implementation of Grouping Policy

Once faculty and administrative reaction to the guidelines have been considered and needed modifications have been made, the policy must be put into effect. The superintendent must determine the time when principals and their teachers will specify the nature of grouping plans and procedures to be followed in their schools and when the plans are to be implemented. The committee must be available to respond to questions of interpretation during this period of implementation. Once implementation of the new policy on grouping is begun, feedback from teachers and principals must be gathered by the committee to determine if there is need for further modification or clarification in the document. Decisions about grouping cannot be settled once and for all. Refinement of documents such as the Grouping Guidelines Document must be ongoing, responding to shifts in population and to modification of goals and values.

SUMMARY

The preceding discussion reveals the complexities of school district policy development that is interactive and comprehensive in nature. The development is interactive in that it involves teachers and administrators actively in reviewing and evaluating existing grouping practices and in establishing new patterns. It is comprehensive in that it involves a consideration of the values and goals that underlie grouping practices, the needs of students, the nature of learning in different content areas, and the findings from the research literature on grouping. Although administratively mandated modes of establishing grouping policy may be more efficient in terms of time and money, the interactive process described herein assumes that professionals at all levels of school organizations must be involved in establishing policy. The experience of studying existing practice and experimenting with new alternatives provides for growth and renewal on the part of teachers and administrators, at the same time that a more responsive and a better understood policy is forged.

ACKNOWLEDGMENTS

We gratefully acknowledge the useful comments of Jean Bernstein, Robert Dreeben, Lawrence Friedman, Thomas Good, Laurie Nelson, William Pink, and Beverly Walker on earlier drafts of this chapter.

REFERENCES

Allington, R. (1983). The reading instruction provided readers of differing reading ability. *Elementary School Journal, 83*, 548–559.

Anderson, L. M., Evertson, C. M., & Brophy, J. E. (1979). An experimental study of effective teaching in first-grade reading groups. *Elementary School Journal, 74*(4), 193–223.

Anderson, R. C., & Davison, A. (1989). Conceptual and empirical bases of readability formulas. In G. Green & A. Davison (Eds.), *Linguistic complexity and text comprehension* (pp. 23–53). Hillsdale, NJ: Lawrence Erlbaum Associates.

Anderson, R. C., Hiebert, E. H., Scott, J. A., & Wilkinson, I. A. G. (1985). *Becoming a nation of readers*. Washington, DC: The National Institute of Education.

Barr, R. (1974). Instructional pace differences and their effect on reading acquisition. *Reading Research Quarterly, 9*(4), 526–554.

Barr, R. (1987). Classroom interaction and curricular content. In D. Bloome (Ed.), *Literacy and schooling* (pp. 150–168). Norwood, NJ: Ablex.

Barr, R. (1988). Conditions influencing content taught in nine fourth-grade mathematics classrooms. *Elementary School Journal, 88*, 387–411.

Barr, R., & Sadow, M. (1989). The influence of basal programs on fourth grade reading instruction. *Reading Research Quarterly, 24*, 44–71.

Barr, R. (1989). Social organization of reading instruction. In C. Emilhovich (Ed.), *Locating literacy across the curriculum: Ethnographic perspectives on classroom research* (pp. 57–86). Norword, NJ: Ablex.

Barr, R., & Dreeben, R. (1983). *How schools work*. Chicago: University of Chicago Press.

Beagle, E. G. (1973). Some lessons learned by SMSG. *Mathematics Teacher, 66*, 207–214.

Borg, W. R. (1965). Ability grouping in the public schools: A field study. *Journal of Experimental Education, 34*, 1–97.

Brophy, J., & Good, T. (1986). Teacher behavior and student achievement. In M. C. Wittrock (Ed.), *Handbook of research on teaching* (3rd ed., pp. 328–375). Chicago: Rand McNally.

Calfee, R. C., & Piontkowski, D. C. (1987). Grouping for teaching. In M. J. Dunkin (Ed.), *The international encyclopedia of teaching and teacher education* (pp. 225–232). New York: Pergamon.

Case, R. (1983). *Intellectual development: A systematic reinterpretation*. New York: Academic.

Chall, J. S. (1983). *Stages of reading development*. New York: McGraw-Hill.

Cobb, P. (1987). Young children's academic arithmetic contexts. *Educational Studies in Mathematics, 18*, 109–124.

Collins, J. (1986). Differential instruction in reading groups. In J. Cook-Gumperz (Ed.), *The social construction of literacy* (pp. 117–137). Cambridge: Cambridge University Press.

Dahllof, U. (1971). *Ability grouping, content validity, and curriculum process analysis*. New York: Teachers College Press.

DeStefano, J., Pepinsky, J., & Sanders, T. (1982). Discourse rules for literacy learning in a first grade classroom. In L. C. Wilkinson (Ed.), *Communicating in the classroom* (pp. 101–129). New York, NY: Academic.

Dreeben, R., & Barr, R. (1987). An organizational analysis of curriculum and instruction. In M. T. Hallinan (Ed.), *The social organization of schools. New conceptualizations of the learning process* (pp. 13–39). New York: Plenum.

Dreeben, R., & Gamoran, A. (1986). Race, instruction, and learning. *American Sociological Review, 51*(5), 660–669.

Eddleman, V. K. (1971). A comparison of the effectiveness of two methods of class organization for arithmetic instruction in grade five. *Dissertation Abstracts International, 32,* 1744A (University Microfilms No. 71-25035).

Eder, D. (1981). Ability grouping as a self-fulfilling prophecy: A microanalysis of teacher-student interaction. *Sociology of Education, 54,* 151–162.

Esposito, D. (1973). Homogeneous and heterogeneous ability grouping: Principal findings and implications for evaluating and designing more effective educational environments. *Review of Educational Research, 43,* 163–179.

Findley, W. G., & Bryan, M. (1971). *Ability grouping: 1970. Status, impact, and alternatives.* Athens: University of Georgia, Center for Educational Improvement. (ERIC Document Reproduction Service No. ED 060 595).

Gambrell, L. (1984). How much time do children spend reading during teacher-directed reading instruction? In J. Niles & L. Harris (Eds.), *Thirty-third yearbook of the National Reading Conference, Changing perspectives on research in reading/language processing and instruction* (pp. 193–198). Rochester, NY: National Reading Conference.

Gambrell, L., Wilson, R., & Ganatt, W. (1981). Classroom observations of task-attending behaviors of good and poor readers. *Journal of Educational Research, 74,* 400–404.

Gamoran, A. (1987). Organization, instruction, and the effects of ability grouping: Comment on Slavin's "best-evidence synthesis." *Review of Educational Research, 57,* 341–345.

Gamoran, A. (1989). Rank, performance, and mobility in elementary school grouping. *Sociological Quarterly, 30,* 109–123.

Gamoran, A., & Berends, M. (1987). The effects of stratification in the secondary schools: Synthesis of survey and ethnographic research. *Review of Educational Research, 57,* 415–435.

Gerleman, S. (1987). An observational study of small-group instruction in fourth-grade mathematics classrooms. *Elementary School Journal, 88,* 3–28.

Good, T. L., & Beckerman, T. M. (1978). Time on task: A naturalistic study in sixth grade classrooms. *Elementary School Journal, 78,* 192–201.

Good, T., Grouws, D., & Mason, D. (1987). *Teachers' beliefs about small-group instruction in elementary school mathematics* (Tech. Rep. No. 426). Columbia: University of Missouri, Center for Research in Social Behavior.

Good, T., & Marshall, S. (1984). Do students learn more in heterogeneous or homogenous groups? In P. L. Peterson, L. C. Wilkinson, & M. Hallinan (Eds.), *The social context of instruction* (pp. 15–38). New York: Academic.

Good, T., Mason, D., & Grouws, D. (1987). *Administrators' beliefs about teacher autonomy in organizing for mathematics instruction* (Tech. Rep. No. 426). Columbia: University of Missouri, Center for Research in Social Behavior.

Hallinan, M. T., & Sorensen, A. B. (1987). Ability grouping and sex differences in mathematics achievement. *Sociology of Education, 60,* 63–72.

Hiebert, E. (1983). An examination of ability grouping for reading instruction. *Reading Research Quarterly, 18*(2), 231–255.

Hillocks, G., Jr. (1980). Toward a hierarchy of skills in the comprehension of literature. *English Journal, 10,* 54–59.

Johnson, D., & Johnson, R. (1975). *Learning together and alone: Cooperation, competition, and individualization.* Englewood Cliffs, NJ: Prentice-Hall.

Marsh, H. W. (1984). Self-concept, social comparison, and ability grouping: A reply to Kulik and Kulik. *American Educational Research Journal, 21,* 799–806.

Martin, J., & Evertson, C. M. (1980). *Teachers' interactions with reading groups of differing ability levels.* (Tech. Rep. No. R-4903). Austin: University of Texas, Research and Development Center for Teacher Education.

Oakes, J. (1985). *Keeping track: How schools structure inequality.* New Haven, CT: Yale University Press.

Ogle, D. M. (1986). K-W-L: A teaching model that develops active reading of expository text. *Reading Teacher, 39*(6), 564–570.

Persell, C. (1977). *Education and inequality: The roots and results of stratification in America's schools*. New York: Free Press.

Raphael, T. E. (1982). Question-answering strategies for children. *Reading Teacher, 36*(2), 186–191.

Resnick, L. B. (1982). Syntax and semantics in learning to subtract. In T. P. Carpenter, J. M. Moser, & T. A. Romberg (Eds.), *Addition and subtraction: A cognitive perspective* (pp. 136–155). Hillsdale, NJ: Lawrence Erlbaum Associates.

Romberg, T. A., & Carpenter, T. P. (1986). Research on teaching and learning mathematics: Two disciplines of scientific inquiry. In M. C. Wittrock (Ed.), *Handbook of research on teaching* (3rd ed., pp. 850–873). New York: Rand McNally.

Rosenbaum, J. (1976). *Making inequality: The hidden curriculum of high school tracking*. New York: John Wiley and Sons.

Rosenbaum, J. E. (1980). Social implications of educational grouping. *Review of Research in Education, 8*, 361–401.

Rosenbaum, J. E. (1984). The social organization of instructional grouping. In P. L. Peterson, L. C. Wilkinson, & M. Hallinan (Eds.), *The social context of instruction* (pp. 53–68). Orlando, FL: Academic Press.

Rosenshine, B., & Stevens, R. (1986). Teaching functions. In M. C. Wittrock (Ed.), *Handbook of research on teaching* (3rd ed., pp. 328–375). Chicago: Rand McNally.

Rutherford, W. L., & Murphy, S. C. (1985, April). *Change in high schools: Roles and reactions of teachers*. Paper presented at the annual meeting of the American Educational Research Association, Chicago. (ERIC Document Reproduction Service No. ED 271 805).

Sarason, S. B. (1971). *The culture of the school and the problem of change*. Boston: Allyn & Bacon.

Sarason, S. B., & Klaber, M. (1985). The school as a social situation. *Annual Review of Psychology, 36*, 115–140.

Seltzer, D. A. (1976). A descriptive study of third grade reading groups. *Dissertation Abstracts, 36*, 5811 (University Microfilms No. 76-6345).

Sirotnik, K. A., Goldenberg, C., & Oakes, J. (1986). Teachers meet technology: Computer courseware authoring in schools. *Journal of Curriculum and Supervision, 1*(4), 316–330.

Slavin, R. E. (1983). *Cooperative learning*. New York, NY: Longman, Inc.

Slavin, R. E. (1987). Ability grouping: A best-evidence synthesis. *Review of Educational Research, 57*, 293–336.

Sorensen, A. B., & Hallinan, M. T. (1984). Effects of race on assignment to ability groups. In P. L. Peterson, L. C. Wilkinson, & M. Hallinan (Eds.), *The social context of instruction* (pp. 85–103). Orlando, FL: Academic.

Sorenson, A. B., & Hallinan, M. T. (1986). The effects of ability grouping on growth of academic achievement. *American Educational Research Journal, 23*, 519–542.

Stauffer, R. (1975). *Directing the reading-thinking process*. New York: Harper & Row.

Stevens, R. J., Madden, N. A., Slavin, R. E., & Farnish, A. M. (1987). Cooperative integrated reading and composition: Two field experiments. *Reading Research Quarterly, 12*, 433–454.

Webb, N. (1982). Student interation and learning in small groups. *Review of Educational Research, 52*, 421–445.

8

Motivation and Effective Teaching

Russell Ames
Carole Ames
University of Illinois at Urbana-Champaign

The purpose of this chapter is to uncover some of the mystery of negative student motivation. We hope that such understanding will help teachers eliminate some factors that commonly elicit negative student motivation in the classroom by providing them with strategies to enhance positive motivation in students.

Negative motivation is characterized by a perception that one does not have a strategy for getting from the beginning to the end of a task, and it entails a belief that the task, therefore, cannot be completed. When this happens, students often engage in behaviors associated with negative motivation. That is, they do not persist on the task, they engage in activities that distract others in the classroom, or they simply sit lethargically and engage in off-task thinking.

Our view of motivation focuses on certain qualitative aspects of how students think about the learning process. In particular, we are interested in how students place different values on various goals, in the ways they process and attend to information, and the different beliefs and evaluations they have about themselves and their performance. Thus, in order to understand negative motivation and to engage in corrective actions to enhance positive motivation, we believe it is necessary to understand what the student is thinking about as he or she is engaged in what we typically call "negative motivational behavior," such as procrastination, inability to make a decision, avoiding risk taking, or daydreaming. This chapter is divided into two major parts: first, student motivation and, second, effective teaching practices to enhance student motivation.

STUDENT MOTIVATION

A student's motivational thoughts typically involve a sense of self-worth, self-concept of ability, goals, efficacy beliefs, attribution for success and failure, and beliefs about effective and ineffective learning strategies.

Student Self-Worth

Self-worth is defined as the value a student places on his or her perceived abilities, qualities, and attributes (Covington & Beery, 1976). A positive sense of self-worth is derived from possessing attributes that are perceived by oneself and others as having high value. Such values are derived from society, parents, teachers, and other important adult role models, peers, and direct experiences with the environment. Students strive to possess—or at least appear as though they possess—these valued attributes, qualities, or abilities. Short of such a positive demonstration, they strive to avoid looking like they possess undesired attributes. One of the most valued attributes in our society is high ability. Although students might think it most virtuous to be both able *and* effortful, they are often caught in the difficult bind of looking able *or* being effortful.

Martin Covington and his colleagues, in a series of research studies (Covington, 1984, 1985; Covington & Omelich, 1979a, 1979b, 1984), have shown that being an effortful student is frought with all sorts of psychological risks, because, in our society, a student who is able at something is the most highly valued. Trying hard and failing demonstrates to oneself and to others that one is *not* able, at least with respect to the particular task at hand. If demonstrating a high sense of ability is necessary to maintaining a high sense of self-worth, then engaging in effortful behavior places one's positive sense of self-worth in jeopardy. A common practice for students, then, is to avoid such risky business by not trying. They might procrastinate, give up, or engage in off-task behavior. Although, ultimately, these negative behaviors increase the probability of future failure, they immediately serve as excuses for failure; excuses that allow the student to protect his or her sense of worth.

Self-Concept of Ability

Self-concept of ability has been studied as a global concept and in relation to specific abilities in math, art, sports, reading, and so on (Stipek, 1984). White (1960) introduced the concept of competence motivation, in which he hypothesized that persons were motivated to feel that they were behaving competently within their environment. Self-concept of ability is the judgment of whether or not one is able or competent at something. It is distinguished from self-worth in that one may be able or competent at something that is not perceived as very worthwhile.

Children's self-perceptions of ability change over time as children get older. In the first grade, children often hold unrealistically high evaluations of their competence. As children progress through school, their self-expectations decline and become more in line with their actual performance. Self-perceptions of competence decline especially during the elementary school years; and by the middle-school grades, self-evaluations are consistent with others' (teacher and parent) evaluations. Until about age 11, children view ability as a relatively unstable factor; something that changes with effort and practice. The concept of ability then takes on the status of a stable factor and is clearly differentiated from effort in the sense that ability limits the effectiveness of effort in obtaining desired outcomes (Stipek, 1984).

Closely related to children's conceptions of ability are their conceptions of intelligence. One view of intelligence is an incremental one, in which intelligence is seen as having a dynamic, increasing quality; something that grows and changes over time with experience and learning. The other view is a static one, in which intelligence is viewed as crystallized and fixed—an inherent or inborn trait. The research of Dweck (1984), Nicholls (1984), and Stipek (1984) has shown that children generally hold an incremental view that shifts to a more crystallized view in early adolescence. Dweck, however, has shown that these views of intelligence do vary among individuals; some tend to hold a more incremental view and others, a more static view. The incremental view of intelligence can be equated with the unstable or "immature," pre-age-11 view of ability, whereas the static view can be equated with the more mature, post-age-11 view of ability. Nicholls' work suggests that intrinsic motivation and significant task engagement are only likely to occur when the student takes the more incremental view during a learning task.

Goals

Recent research (Ames & Archer, 1987, 1988; Dweck, 1984, 1986; Maehr, 1984; Nicholls, 1984) on achievement motivation has focused on identifying different types of goal orientations among students. Two types of goal orientations have received a great deal of attention recently in the literature: (a) learning or mastery goals, in which individuals strive to acquire new skills and expand and develop their competence, and (b) ego or performance goals, in which individuals strive to obtain positive judgments of their ability, avoid negative judgments of ability, and generally document and validate their competence to themselves and to others. A performance goal orientation reflects a valuing of ability and doing better than others. With a mastery goal, the process of learning itself is valued, and the attainment of mastery is seen as dependent on effort utilization. Table 8.1 shows an analysis of these achievement goal orientations along dimensions of success, values, satisfaction, teacher orientation, incentives, view of errors, attention, and reasons for effort. The difference between these two goal orientations is perhaps best captured in two different children's responses to an interviewer's probe about the types of problems or materials they would like to work on (Dweck, 1985):

> Mastery response: ". . . problems that I'll learn something from, even if they're so hard, I'll get a lot wrong."
> Performance response: ". . . problems that aren't too hard, so I don't get any wrong. Problems that are hard enough to show I'm smart." (p. 292)

The pursuit of a mastery goal assumes an incremental view of intelligence. In contrast, a performance goal orientation is congruent with a static view of intelligence (Dweck, 1985).

Student Self-Efficacy

According to Schunk (1989), self-efficacy is a student's judgment that he or she is capable of organizing and implementing actions in specific situations that may contain novel, unpredictable, and possibly stressful features. For example, in his research on self-efficacy in mathematics,

TABLE 8.1
Achievement Goal Analysis: Mastery versus Performance Goals

Dimensions	Mastery	Performance
Success defined as . . .	improvement, progress	high grades, high normative performance
Value place on . . .	effort, learning	normatively high ability
Reason for satisfaction . . .	working hard, challenge	doing better than others
Teacher oriented toward . . .	how students are learning	how students are performing
Perceived incentives . . .	learn something new	grades, perform better than others
View of errors/ mistakes	part of learning	anxiety eliciting
Focus of attention . . .	process of learning	own performance relative to others
Reason for effort . . .	learn new things	high grades

Note: Adapted from Ames and Archer (1988).

Schunk shows children sample arithmetic problems for a few seconds, and asks them to indicate how sure they are that they could solve problems like those shown. Children then rate the certainty that they could solve such problems on a 10-point scale ranging from high to low certainty. Schunk's work on self-efficacy has shown that efficacy judgments affect choice of activities, effort expenditure, task persistence, and persistence in the face of obstacles.

In contrast to a student's global self-concept of ability, efficacy refers to a rather specific judgment of ability; a judgment that one knows how to do certain kinds of problems or tasks. Thus, a student could have a relatively high self-concept of mathematic ability but, never having been introduced to the quadratic equation in algebra, could also have a low sense of self-efficacy for solving quadratic equation problems. Further, the student might have a rather high sense of self-efficacy for learning how to solve such problems given proper instruction. Thus, efficacy beliefs are the "how-to" beliefs involved in any sense of competence, for example, the knowledge that one knows how to solve certain kinds of problems.

Attributions for Success and Failure

Attribution theory posits that students seek to explain why they have done well or poorly on some task or exam (Weiner, 1984). These explanations are typically described in terms of four basic causes: ability, effort, task difficulty, and luck. Ability attributions for success lead students to believe that they can succeed again in the future and are related to such emotional reactions as pride, positive self-esteem, and hopefulness. A low-ability attribution for failure leads a student to have a low expectancy of future success, a sense of hopelessness, shame, and low self-concept of ability. An effort attribution for success contributes to feelings of pleasure and pride and a belief that continued effort is necessary for future success. When a student explains his or her lack of failure in terms of low effort, he or she usually feels guilty and chastises himself or herself to try harder in the future. When students make external attributions (a hard or easy task and good or bad luck), they avoid taking responsibility for either success or failure. Such a lack of responsibility is usually associated with low-effort behaviors. Thus, whether or not students try depends on how they explain their past performance. Low ability, task, and luck attributions are usually related to low persistence and intensity. High ability and effort attributions usually relate to continued or increased effort.

Belief About Effective and Ineffective
Learning Strategies

Ames and Archer (1988) have recently completed work on students' use of effective and ineffective learning strategies. Learning strategies are the skills of studying, learning, and thinking that students use to master new material. Table 8.2 lists typical learning strategies that we have investigated in our recent research. There are two critical factors involved in whether or not students use learning strategies. One is whether or not they know the strategy and how to use it, and the other is whether they choose to use it. The latter question is the motivational issue. A student may know a strategy and how to deploy it, but may not use it because he or she does not want to put forth the effort to apply the strategy. For example, a student may know that it is a good strategy to reread material, check over math problems before turning them in, or review notes daily, but may not use these strategies. Ames & Archer (1988) have found that when students perceive their classroom as emphasizing mastery, rather than performance goals (see Table 8.1), they are more likely to use effective learning strategies. In fact, this work has shown that when students are pursuing mastery goals, they are also more likely to attribute their performance to effort, have a higher sense of efficacy (i.e., believe they know how to use a strategy to complete the task successfully), are less worried about whether or not they are able or unable, and are more likely to choose challenging tasks than when they are pursuing performance goals.

Target Behaviors Associated with Negative Motivation

Examining Table 8.3, we can see more clearly some of the student thought patterns that are associated with negative motivation. When a student attributes failure to a lack of ability, he or she comes away with a low sense of self-worth and low opinions about his or her own ability.

TABLE 8.2
Learning Strategies

Plan study schedule
Set goals
Pull out main ideas
Pull together information
Persistence when uninteresting
Make charts, diagrams, or tables
Cover extra, nonrequired material
Relate new information to other knowledge
Fit topics together logically
Reread material
Do sample problems, practice exercises

Note: Adapted from Ames and Archer (1988).

The student expects to do poorly in the future and, therefore, tends to give up easily. Although it is clear that the student has made a low or negative ability attribution, more importantly, the student has not focused on strategies for solving a particular task. Usually, the student is focused on evaluating his or her ability, when, in fact, he or she needs to be thinking about specific strategies that might be used to overcome a particular difficulty in a learning situation. Research (Ames, 1984; Ames & Archer, 1988) suggests that a specific strategy focus would increase the student's sense of efficacy for success.

Students who are concerned about their ability may hold different goals in a teaching situation than the teacher. For example, we recently had occasion to observe spelling lessons in an elementary school classroom. Each Tuesday, the students would copy the spelling words from the blackboard and write each word out five times. The teacher carefully checked to see that the student had spelled the words correctly, and then the student took the words home to study. On Friday, when the students took the spelling test, they got a star, and a football was placed on a goalpost on a public class chart if all 10 words were correct. However, the teacher also included three challenge words (unknown until Friday) each week. The teacher complained that students rarely chose to try these challenge words. When questioning the students about why they did not try the challenge words, it became clear that if they chose the challenge word and got it wrong, they did not get their name on a football placed on the goalpost chart—even if they had gotten the 10 other words right!

Thus, the goal for the students was to get a football with their name displayed on the wall, but the teacher was more interested in having the students take on challenge words. The teacher was completely unaware of how this reward structure had contributed to the negative motivation of the students. In fact, she thought that she was enhancing the intrinsic

TABLE 8.3
Target Behaviors Associated With Negative Motivation

Attribute failure to a lack of ability—low opinions of own ability
Tend to give up easily
Procrastination
Deny that they can do something—don't want to try
Low participation level—takes the easy way out
Deny that they have tried even when they have
Have difficulty making decisions
Set unrealistically high or low goals for themselves
Self-punitive when they fail
Anxious or nervous about schoolwork
Negative or low expectations
Many off-task behaviors

motivation of students to select a challenge word because she was not offering a reward for it.

Teachers in another school were concerned that students were selecting too easy material for independent reading. Further examination revealed that the school had recently instituted an incentive program for reading. If students wrote four book reports a month, they received a certificate for a special treat at a local restaurant. This treat was very enticing to most of these elementary school students. Of course, from the students' perspective, the most efficient strategy was to read four relatively easy selections so that the reports could be done quickly. There was no mechanism in this system for rewarding more difficult or longer books or for encouraging students to set their own, more challenging goals. As a result, many students were faced with agonizing dilemmas about what books to read (easy but uninteresting ones or more difficult and lengthy books). Clearly, the program had severe undermining effects for children who enjoyed reading and who were avid readers before the program began.

When students are concerned about whether or not they are going to demonstrate high ability, they often set unrealistically high or low goals for themselves. By setting an unrealistically high goal, a failing student can say "Well, it was such a difficult task, nobody could have achieved it, and therefore I don't really lack ability," and if the student has set a low goal, he or she fully expects to succeed and, again, to avoid the demonstration of low ability. Such behaviors are commonly associated with negative or low expectations, anxiety, or nervousness about one's school work.

In another example of an actual classroom practice, students in a second-grade class were practicing addition and subtraction facts. The teacher was using a procedure in which, once a week, students took a timed math test. If a student got all the problems correct in 5 minutes or less, his or her name was put on a wall chart. There were three categories in which the name could go: under 2 minutes, under 3 minutes, and under 5 minutes. Did this practice lead to increased learning of math facts, and did it enhance self-concept of ability about math, or did it increase their math anxiety? Observations lead us to believe that many more students became anxious about their performance, and, as the pressure for completion within shorter time periods increased, students regressed in their strategies for solving math problems. A number of students were concluding that they were not very good at math. Even the student who had achieved the fastest time in the class on subtraction skills, namely 2 minutes and 55 seconds, said he was not any good in math because he could not get under the 2-minute level that that teacher had set as the highest goal. Even though this student continued to be the top performer, he exhibited some severe self-doubts.

These examples have been provided to demonstrate that negative motivation is a set of thoughts related to goals, self-concept, self-perceptions, and explanations for behavior, and that negative motivation is related to various kinds of teacher practices that are occurring on a moment-to-moment basis in the classroom. We now turn to a consideration of some of the factors in the classroom that contribute to a pattern of negative motivation.

Factors That Contribute to a Negative Motivation Pattern

In this section, we discuss nine factors that contribute to a negative motivation pattern. These factors are listed in Table 8.4. Our research (Ames, 1978, 1984; Ames & Ames, 1977, 1984; Ames & Felker, 1979) completed over the last 10 years in experimental and classroom settings has shown that many classroom environments focus students on their ability to perform. These classrooms are characterized by a competitive orientation where performing better than others, a scarcity of rewards, and public evaluation are salient features. It may prove illustrative here to describe the experimental paradigm used in some of this research.

In one study, for example, students were assigned to competitive and noncompetitive experimental conditions. In the competitive setting (Ames & Ames, 1977), students working side-by-side were told that the student successfully completing the task first would receive a prize. (In other studies, no rewards or prizes have been given; instead, students were told who performed best.) The actual performance of the students was predetermined by the experimenters. Immediately following the award of the prize, the children were asked to respond to a number of

TABLE 8.4
Factors That Contribute to a Negative Motivation Pattern

Competition and social comparison in the classroom
Public evaluation
Reinforcing ability, instead of effort
Communicating low expectations
Permitting students to be uninvolved in learning
Reinforcing performance, instead of learning
Excessive emphasis on success and grades
Lack of recognition (can't get it)
Poor working/learning conditions (noise level, over-crowding, etc.)

questions about themselves and the other student. The responses of successful students showed that they had a very positive view of their own ability, but a negative view of the other student. In contrast, the failing students showed a very negative view of their own ability, had low expectations for the future, and saw the other student as superior to themselves.

In the noncompetitive setting, the students worked on a similar task, and one student performed well and the other student performed poorly. In contrast to the competitive setting, however, the students were told that they would each be able to select a prize at the end of the session for their participation. (Again, in other studies, they were asked to improve their performance or merely to try hard.) Instead of focusing on ability, as in the competitive setting, the successful students focused on effort and held a positive view of themselves *and* the low performing student. Although the failing students showed evidence of some negative feelings, they believed that effort was the cause of their poor performance and expected to perform better on subsequent tasks.

In a competitive goal structure, rewards are restricted so that only the few who are the best or highest performers are acknowledged as being successful or are rewarded in some way. Social comparison is emphasized in classroom practices such as grouping by ability, using comparative information to determine grades, publicly charting student progress, and calling attention to those students who are exhibiting specific exemplary behavior. It is an empirical reality that competition produces irreverent and sometimes even irrational behaviors when we find, for example, that children value winning over fairness (Kleiber & Roberts, 1981), believe that being happy and deserving a reward is more related to winning than to performing well (Ames & Felker, 1979), will deny themselves of rewards to prevent another from getting any rewards (Nelson & Kagan, 1972), and spontaneously engage in besting (Pepitone, 1972) and self-enhancing (Bryant, 1977) behaviors.

Competitive structures depict situations of "forced social comparison," in that students are faced with information about their peers' performance, and this comparison information is both salient and obtrusive (Levine, 1983). Because social comparison information is made salient, students focus on this information. As a result, self-ascriptions of high versus low ability follow success and failure respectively. In a competitive setting, students are focused on demonstrating high, or avoiding the demonstration of low, ability, because ability is highly salient. The student's sense of self-worth is closely tied to this concern about ability, such that if the student is successful, he or she is worried about whether he or she will be able to maintain the success. Even students who usually show high ability are quite concerned about the continual threat of failure, which would show that they have low ability (Kohn, 1986). Thus, even though they may be successful, they are continually struggling with whether or not it is better to engage in behavior that would lead to success and demonstrate high ability or engage in behavior that would avoid the demonstration of low ability: namely, drop out, not participate, avoid trying very hard, or select easy goals.

Effort in this context is truly the "double-edged sword." Trying is necessary for success, but it also implicates one's ability in the occasion of failure. Covington and Beery (1976) have chronicled the failure-avoiding strategies that help students avoid the negative implication of failing in a competitive situation. Failure resulting from not trying is referred to as "failure with honor" and is often seen as procrastination; it becomes a way of coping for the student with a low self-concept of ability.

The following chronicle demonstrates the operation of these psychological processes in a real classroom setting. In a class of fourth graders, the teacher had students write stories for a youth essay contest. The teacher brought in parents and an aide to help the students work on their stories, and each student wrote a story about something that interested him or her. One student who had rarely written much, was observed to have written a very clever story about his dog getting lost and finding a friend and then having an encounter with some people who were trying to steal dogs. It was the longest and most elaborate story this student had written to date in the class. The next day, the teacher decided to have the students vote on which stories were the best stories in the class. The teacher read each story and then the students were asked to vote on whether they liked the story or not. The teacher made sure that students did not see who was voting for each story. The three stories receiving the highest number of votes were selected as the winners. Before the vote, the student who wrote the clever story about his dog was quite excited about his story. After losing the class vote, he reported no longer liking the story and did not want to even have the story read to him again.

Public Evaluation

Casual observation of many elementary school classrooms shows that many teachers use public display of students' work as a motivational strategy. In these public displays, teachers use various kinds of charts and graphs to show which students have accomplished or met various goals. Such public evaluation tends to focus students on comparing their performance with their peers and tends to lead them into a set of motivational thoughts associated with competitive learning environments. Are

these public evaluations really motivating, and for whom are they motivating?

Recently, we heard two fifth-grade teachers make a presentation about
the intrinsically motivating practices that they had been using based on
the work of Edward Deci (Deci & Ryan, 1985). After describing at some
length all of the various practices they were using to enhance intrinsic
motivation, they noted that they used one chart on the wall to motivate
their fifth-grade students to learn their multiplication tables. They noted,
however, that they placed this chart in an inconspicuous spot in the back
of the room. The chart listed all the students' names in the class, and
stars were placed next to the students' name for each time they obtained
a perfect score on their multiplication tables test. After the teachers made
this fine presentation on intrinsic motivation, we inquired about who
went back and looked at this "time tables" chart. The response was "Oh,
very few students . . . In fact, the only students who go back and look at
it are the two students who are at the top and have the most stars."
Clearly, this anecdote demonstrates the impact of public evaluation on
student motivation. It has very little positive impact, perhaps affecting
one or two students at the most, and it has considerable negative impact.
Again, the public chart tends to focus students on either demonstrating
high, or avoiding the demonstration of low, ability. By not looking at the
chart, students were avoiding the awareness, at least, of having publicly
demonstrated low ability as compared to others.

Many classrooms, both elementary and secondary, have too much
evaluation. Almost every activity and performance in the classroom is
tied to a grade. For example, a high school social studies teacher gives
three or four homework assignments per week, and every single one of
them is graded "A" through "F." She claimed that students will not
complete the assignment unless they are graded. In other words, students
complete the assignments for extrinsic reasons, and not for intrinsic
reasons. And, without some radical shift in the teachers' reward structure,
the students will not complete assignments in the absence of these extrinsic factors. If our goal is to enhance intrinsic motivation, it is not being
achieved through these methods.

In another example involves two junior high teachers who taught
similar students at similar a grade level: One had considerable trouble
getting students to complete homework, and the other rarely had a
student miss turning in a piece of homework. Their respective homework
grading policies were revealing. The teacher who had difficulty getting
students to turn in homework had a grade structure in which each piece
of homework was graded "A" through "F," and if problems were not
completed, they were counted against the grade; further, the total homework grade was approximately 30% of the quarter grade. In contrast,

the teacher who had almost all of her students completing their daily homework told the students to spend no more than 30 minutes per night on their homework, and if they had difficulty completing a problem to leave it and bring it up for question in class the next day. Further, the homework was graded as satisfactory or unsatisfactory and returned for students to redo and complete. Finally, homework counted approximately 10% of the quarter grade.

The heavy emphasis on grades in the former case was actually leading students to withdraw from even trying the homework. Why? Because the "A" through "F," heavily weighted homework policy focused them on ability and self-worth concerns. To complete the homework at the level that the teacher desired often required too much effort from the students' perspective. Some students gave up trying altogether, rather than risk a low evaluation. At least in this way, they did not have to risk a demonstration of low math ability. In the case of the second teacher, mistakes were viewed as acceptable, and as long as students appeared to the teacher to be making a reasonable effort at completing the homework, the teacher accepted it. These practices allowed students to learn from their errors and to bring questions to class. Thus, the homework became a *process of learning*. Students were not "risking a sense of their ability" each time they worked on homework, but rather they were attempting to learn. They now could see homework as part of learning, and they could see strategies to use in their homework, and such strategies were salient to them. In the case of the first teacher, the strategies for learning were not salient, but the strategies to avoid looking stupid were quite salient. Where there is excessive emphasis on performance and grades, we often find students dropping out, not completing work, or using ineffective learning strategies and generally avoiding higher order or critical thinking.

TEACHER GUIDELINES FOR ENHANCING MOTIVATION IN THE CLASSROOM

In this section, we discuss variety of specific strategies that teachers can use to enhance motivation in the classroom. Table 8.5 shows five broad areas of strategies that are discussed in this section.

Reduce Social Comparison

Perhaps the most important set of strategies that teachers can focus on are those that reduce students' tendencies to compare themselves to each other, particularly with respect to their performance on classroom tasks, tests, and report cards. In elementary schools, teachers need to examine

TABLE 8.5
Guidelines for Enhancing Motivation

I.   REDUCE SOCIAL COMPARISON
     a. Avoid social comparison
     b. Reduce public evaluation/emphasis on success and grades
     c. Communicate performance expectations in advance
     d. Use variety of grading practices
II. INCREASE INVOLVEMENT IN LEARNING
     a. Use cooperative learning methods
     b. Use peer tutoring
     c. Use games and simulations
     d. Allow student choices—method, pace, content
III. FOCUS ON EFFORT
     a. Emphasize student progress
     b. Reinforce learning/effort
     c. Make known that mistakes and errors are a part of learning
     d. Require "reasonable" effort
IV. PROMOTE BELIEFS IN COMPETENCE
     a. Focus on role of effort and strategy in learning
     b. Make grades contingent on reaching goals
     c. Communicate positive expectations
     d. Make plans with students for improvement
V.   INCREASE CHANCES FOR SUCCESS
     a. Provide skill training
     b. Use peer tutoring
     c. Use cooperative team learning
     d. Use individualized instruction

---

the ways in which charts and other public pronouncements focus students on positive or negative comparisons with each other. Public displays, as has been noted, tend to increase the students' focus on a performance versus mastery.

Teachers also need to look for ways to reduce public evaluation. Public evaluation normally leads to social comparison. In high school, we may not find much on walls in the form of charts that compare students, but we do find that teachers frequently post test grades, announce high and low scores, and grade on a norm-referenced curve. Students are aware of these grading systems, and they compare their grades on tests as well as their grades on report cards.

If teachers want students to keep a record of how they are doing in elementary school (e.g., on spelling words, math quizzes, etc.), they can have each student maintain a chart of his or her own progress in a folder kept in the student's desk. This chart would be the private information of the student, and it would provide the student with a record of how he or she is doing, avoiding public evaluation and social comparison. Additionally, we suggest that teachers talk to students about their expectations in terms of learning goals, rather than as grade or performance goals. For example, in a recent class of seventh-grade students, we asked students to think about an upcoming week of school and to list their goals for that week. Almost without exception, every student put down that their goal was to get high grades. For the next 2 weeks, we instructed the students in how to write goals with respect to what they were going to learn that week, that is, content and objective to be mastered, not what grade they were going to get. At first, students found it difficult to write learning goals, but after a few days of instruction, they mastered the task. Their goal statements showed that they were now thinking quite differently about their school goals.

Increased Involvement in Learning

Providing students with choices may seem like a reasonable suggestion, but it is difficult to implement. For example, the teacher offers a student a choice to read one of two books, one on Africa and the other on India. However, from the student's perspective it is not a choice at all, because the book on Africa is much more difficult than the one on India. A student faced with a choice of whether to read an easy book or a hard book will often choose the easy book, particularly if he or she has to write a report on it or be tested on it. In fact, we suggest that teachers develop some formal or informal rating system for the alternatives involved in choices that they are providing to students to ensure that they are giving students options that are equally difficult and equally attractive. Along with choices, teachers can vary the number of alternatives in any assignment. They can give students choice over the content, time for completion, and even method of learning or for demonstrating their mastery. The important point is that the choices that an individual student is given must be seen by him or her as equally attractive and equally difficult.

In addition to providing students with choices, involvement can also be enhanced through games, simulations, small-group teaching, cooperative learning (DeVries & Edward, 1973; Johnson & Johnson, 1975, 1984, 1985; Slavin, 1977, 1978), and whole class discussions when at least 80% of the class contributes to the discussion (Rosenshine & Stevens, 1986).

A third category of involvement techniques involves peer tutoring (Slavin, 1978, 1983). Peer tutoring is most effective when students in one class tutor students in a lower grade. Do not just let your "best" third-grade readers read to kindergarteners or first graders, for example. Instead, let a cooperative but below average student work with the youngest students; let your best readers work with second graders. In other words, there are ways to involve all students in peer tutoring, not just the "best" students.

Focus on Effort

Recall that we initially defined effortful behavior as knowing and using strategies to accomplish goals. Thus, when trying to get a student to expend effort, it is very important for us, as teachers, to focus on what the student is thinking and not on our own thoughts and goals. What goal is the student pursuing? Is it the same as ours? Does the student have a strategy for accomplishing the goal we have assigned? If the student is not consciously aware of a strategy to accomplish the assigned goal, he or she will often pursue a different goal or use a familiar but wholly ineffective strategy. For example, instead of writing in his or her daily journal, a student may daydream about what he or she will do after school; the goal is to put oneself into a pleasant state of mind; the strategy is to allow thoughts and images about after-school activities to enter one's mind. In math, a student who is unaware, at least momentarily, of alternative strategies may use his fingers to subtract 36 from 57—a highly ineffective and slow-going approach.

The noted philosopher William James (1899) once referred to pulses of effort, which others (see Kirby & Grimely, 1986) have come to call strings of loosely connected self-statements, as an internal dialogue. The effortful student monitors and controls internal dialogue that relates to:

1. Defining and clarifying the nature of tasks.
2. Generating means of solution.
3. Monitoring process and errors.
4. Anticipating success.

Students who lack skill in deliberate use of internal dialogue tend to have problems on tasks and situations that require sustained effort, self-regulation, and self-control. Thus, we must develop teaching strategies to help students self- instruct, self-monitor, and self-evaluate in a variety of academic and social situations in the classroom.

Helping students focus on effort is much more than exhortations to try harder; rather, it involves developing activities that help students define and clarify tasks, generate means to solutions, monitor process and errors, and anticipate success. In emphasizing progress, teachers must help students focus on their improvement and help them recall the specific strategies they are using to make these improvement. They must reinforce the students' use of specific learning strategies by having them verbalize their internal dialogue. They must use an evaluation/grading system that encourages risk-taking, for example, trying strategies on new or difficult problems, making errors and mistakes, analyzing the errors in terms of use of ineffective strategies, and encouraging students to try again. Reasonable effort in middle or high school, for example, may involve asking students to engage in their math homework for 30 minutes per night and no more, bringing in unsolved problems to class for discussion and analysis of strategies.

Promote Beliefs in Competence

Beliefs in competence and a focus on effort are closely related, in that a student who believes he or she can accomplish a goal usually is aware of a strategy for reaching the goal and engages in strategic effort to accomplish the goal. One way that has been found to be effective in helping students relate effort, strategy in learning, and competence beliefs is to teach them a set of academic problem-solving skills. If students can internalize these problem-solving steps so that they become the content of their internal strategic effort dialogue, they are likely to be more effective learners. By directly teaching students the following 10 problem-solving steps and helping students practice these steps on various academic tasks, teachers can help students focus on the role of effort and strategy in learning. The following list consists of 10 sequential effort-related thoughts or strategies that effective and effortful students use routinely:

1. Understand the task and goals
2. Awareness of confusion about task and goals
3. Generate plan or strategy
4. Estimate feasibility of plan or strategy
5. Monitor progress to task solution; start over as necessary
6. Break distant goals into sub-goals
7. Estimate time requirements for task and budget available time
8. Cope with being stuck; avoid negative emotional interference
9. Engage in means–ends thinking
10. Consult self as a resource when stuck—memory search and retrieval of solutions to past problems.

Research has shown that these 10 thought patterns are involved in sustained strategic effort (Covington, 1985; Kirby & Grimley, 1986). Although we know that effective learners use these sustained strategic thoughts, we are not sure how these thoughts can best be taught to less effective learners.

In addition to helping students focus on such strategic thinking, teachers need to avoid using classroom practices that interfere with the use of this strategic thinking. Many of these interfering classroom practices have been discussed elsewhere in this chapter; they include structuring competitive learning environments, an emphasis on performance rather than mastery or learning, public evaluation, and rigid or inflexible grade systems that require everyone to perform at the same level. Alternatives to these classroom practices have also been discussed elsewhere in this chapter.

It is important to emphasize, however, that the teachers' grading practices and policies have dramatic impact on promoting students' beliefs in competence and their use of strategic thinking. The grading system must have flexibility, rewarding students for improvement, progress, and reaching individually set goals. In such a system, one student might get an "A" for obtaining a 10 out of 10 on a spelling quiz. Another student should receive recognition for getting 6 out of 10, if the student has improved from the last quiz. Such an emphasis on progress and improvement allows the teacher to communicate positive expectations to all students by helping them focus on how they can improve in incremental steps. Additionally, the teacher can work with each student in making plans for improvement. Such plans should include a direct and explicit discussion of the strategic thoughts needed to make improvements.

Increase Chances for Success

From our point of view, increasing chances for success does not mean giving students easy tasks; rather, it means teaching them strategic thinking and giving them practice in using strategic thinking on different academic tasks. At first, the teacher may have to help the students make the problems or tasks easier by breaking them down into subtasks. Later on, the students may be able to break the tasks down into subparts themselves. Weinstein's (1989) research has shown that success obtained under false pretenses contributes to negative, rather than positive, motivation. If a teacher tells one student that he or she did well and another student that he or she tried hard, the latter student often concludes that he or she is incompetent because he or she tried hard and failed. Instead, the teacher should focus the student on replacing the ineffective strategies with more effective ones.

Students often feel successful and honored when they have the opportunity to tutor another student. Use of cooperative team learning environments, developed by Johnson and Johnson (1985) and Slavin (1983), also lead to overall perceptions of success. Finally, individualized instruction that focuses students on setting their own progress goals and strategies for accomplishing these goals can aid students in obtaining success and increasing beliefs in competence associated with the success.

Teaching Strategies for Enhancing Students' Self- Determination

It is our belief that teachers can and should set goals for teaching students how to be self-motivated, or self-determined (Ryan, Connell, & Deci 1985). Much of what we have already recommended will lead to student self-motivation. In the remaining part of this chapter, we outline an overall framework for how teachers can help students become motivationally mature. A motivationally mature student is one who can set his or her own academic goals, identify strategies, correct ineffective strategies, and make improvements in performance. We would expect that as students proceed from early elementary grades to high school that they would improve in general motivational maturity. However, we view motivational maturity from a situational perspective. That is, a student may demonstrate motivational maturity in one content area but not another, or on one task in a particular content area but not another task.

Examination of Fig. 8.1 shows that for students judged high in motivational maturity, the teacher provides relatively little direction and monitoring, allowing for a high degree of autonomy and self-determination. These teaching strategies have been derived from the work of Hersey and Blanchard (1982) on situational leadership, and from the work of Kirby & Grimley (1986) and Meichenbaum (1977) on cognitive motivation training. In contrast, a student who has been judged low in motivational maturity for a particular task or content area needs a great deal of structure, task organization, direction, and teacher monitoring, providing for little autonomy or self-determination.

The question is: How does the teacher move the student from a low motivational state to a high state of motivational maturity? Figure 8.1 suggests that the teacher needs to teach the student how to think strategically by teaching strategies of self-organization, self-direction, and self-monitoring and at the same time removing, in small steps, the amount of teacher direction and monitoring. Qualitatively different sets of teacher behaviors should be associated with each level of motivational maturity: low motivational maturity, moderately low motivational maturity, moderately high motivational maturity, and high motivational maturity. When teacher begin a new task or content area, most students are probably at a low or moderately low state of motivational maturity. Here, teachers must initially provide a great deal of direction, but they should also be teaching students how to apply strategic thinking to this content area or task. As students become more facile with general strategic thinking and the specific strategic thoughts associated with the tasks, the teacher gradually removes directional and organizational supports, providing feedback to students on their own self-direction, organization, and monitoring. In this way, students develop greater motivational maturity in this content area. Careful examination of Table 8.6 shows specific sets of teacher behaviors associated with each level of motivational maturity.

SUMMARY

In this chapter, we have described motivation as a set of thoughts involving a sense of self-worth, self-concept of ability, goals, efficacy beliefs, attributions for success and failure, and beliefs about effective and inef-

Low	Mod. Low	Mod. High	High
define goals	discuss past	allow involvement	allow student to
supervise carefully	performance and	in setting goals	formulate own
emphasize	look at future	and defining	direction
deadlines	open for changes	standards	encourage student
take steps to	but maintain	make student feel	to work out own
assure students	focus on task	involved and	problems
working in a	meet with student	important avoid	be available on an
well-defined	and contract	being directive	informal basis
manner	maintain what and	be encouraging	
uniform	how of task	focus on	
procedures	vary when and	motivation and	
specify what is to	where	interest	
be done	increase		
when	responsibility		
where task			
accomplished			
how			

HIGH _____ organization _____ LO
HIGH _____ direction _____ LO
HIGH _____ monitoring _____ LO
LO _____ autonomy _____ HIGH
LO _____ self-determination _____ HIGH

FIG. 8.1.   Teacher behaviors related to student motivational maturity.

TABLE 8.6a
An Incomplete List of Teacher Behaviors
For Low Motivational Maturity

1. Begin lesson with short statement of goals.
2. Review previous, prerequisite learnings.
3. Present new material in small steps.
4. Give detailed instructions and explanations; break assignments into small steps.
5. Have high level of active practice with continuous reinforcement.
6. Frequently check for student understanding.
7. Frequent and systematic positive feedback and reinforcement and corrections.
8. Close guidance during initial practice.

Note: Attributional Assumptions: Teacher is responsible for motivating and developing ability of student. Student believes he or she has little motivation of ability to complete the task.

TABLE 8.6b
An Incomplete List of Teacher Behaviors For Low–Moderate
Motivational Maturity

1. Show students how to break a task down into subgoals.
2. Have students practice breaking a task down into subgoals.
3. Model for students how to break tasks down into subgoals.
4. Help students make a plan for completing specific projects. Start with short 15-minute projects; move up to longer time frames.
5. Encourage students to feel good about successful completion of a project or step towards completion of a project.
6. Hold discussions with students about the role effort plays in their productive work.
7. When making an assignment, help students brainstorm lists of strategies for getting the project done. Help them analyze the effectiveness of these strategies.
8. Give students a list of criteria for evaluating an assignment, and have them practice using the assignment.
9. Give students practice in setting realistic goals and devising strategies to accomplish those goals.
10. Monitor somewhat closely, but give feedback first by asking them to examine their work, cueing them to relevant information as necessary.
11. Confront students directly about misbehavior; engage them in a discussion about what they can do to engage in more positve behavior.
12. Keep problem focused, and help students identify strategies they can use to solve the problems—both learning and behavior problems.

Note: Attributional Assumptions: Teacher is responsible for teaching and coaching specific steps of self-motivation and involving student in process of improving his or her ability. Student believes he or she has some ability but needs help in acquiring skill and in maintaining motivation.

TABLE 8.6c
Teacher Behaviors for High-Motivational Maturity

1. Be available to help students set goals if they need help.
2. Generally, let students initiate requests for help.
3. If students come for help, help them identify the problem, allow them to develop solutions to the problem, and encourage them to continue working on their own.
4. Reinforce students for working independently. Tell them you like it when they can work for a longer period on their own.
5. Remind students that they already know how to break a task down into subgoals, make plans for accomplishing these goals, and monitor their own progress. Encourage them to engage in these motivational behaviors.
6. When students misbehave, ask them to describe what they are doing, to evaluate their behavior, and encourage them to follow through on their plan for improvement.
7. When students need feedback, ask them for their own self-evaluation first, and ask them to give good reasons for that self-evaluation.
8. Encourage students to keep trying; tell them you know that they know how to do it.
9. Remind students that they know how to do it, and that they just need to build their confidence by trying on their own.

Note: Attributional Assumption: Student is responsible for using acquired ability to solve problems and for maintaining motivation and enthusiasm for assignment with stronger encouragement from the teacher. Student believes he or she has ability and motivation as long as supportive environment is available.

Note: With younger students, use smaller units of instruction than with older students.

TABLE 8.6d
An Incomplete List of Teacher Behaviors
for High Motivational Maturity

1. Let student set own short- and long-term goals.
1. Expect students to review on their own what they already have learned.
2. Allow students to set own action plan for how they will complete projects and assignments.
3. Let students work through difficulties they have on an assignment on their own.
4. Expect students to monitor their own progress, work through difficulties themselves, and only call on you as a last resort.
5. Expect students to reward themselves for intermediate and long-term goal accomplishment.
6. Provide little or no teacher guidance.
7. Give infrequent feedback—only at the conclusion of assignments.
8. Be comfortable knowing that students desire to do well, will think about success, and will feel bad if they fail.

Attributional Assumptions: Student is responsible for own motivation and using his or her ability to solve problems; believes he or she has motivation and ability to do work.

Note: You are working towards task-specific independence. You may very well allow for this kind of independence for your top reader in 1st and 2nd grade, yet use a low motivational maturity style with this same student in math.

fective learning strategies. Negative motivation is characterized by a desire to protect one's sense of self-worth by avoiding the appearance of being unable, avoidance of situations that require effort because failure under high effort expenditure leads to a conclusion of low ability, low efficacy beliefs, attributions for success and failure to ability rather than effort, and lack of use of effective learning strategies.

After describing the negative motivation thought pattern, we identified and described nine factors that contribute to a negative motivation pattern. Our research suggests that the most significant of these factors are evaluation and reward systems that emphasize competition, social comparison, and public evaluation.

In the second section of the chapter, we identified five guidelines for enhancing motivation. These five guidelines suggest that student motivation can be enhanced by reducing social comparison, increasing involvement in learning, focusing student attention on effort-related strategies, promoting student beliefs in their own competence and increasing the student's chances of success.

In the final sequence of the chapter, we identified specific teaching strategies that can be used to help students move from a relatively low state of motivational maturity, or low self determination for a task, to a relatively high state of motivational maturity, or high self determination for a task. These teaching recommendations focus on teaching the student how to think strategically about self-organization, self-direction, and self-monitoring.

REFERENCES

Ames. C. (1978). Children's achievement attributions and self-reinforcement: Effects of self-concept and competitive reward structure. *Journal of Educational Psychology, 70,* 345–355.

Ames, C. (1984). Competitive, cooperative, and individualistic goal structures: A cognitive motivational analysis. In R. Ames & C Ames (Eds.), *Research on motivation in education: Vol. 1. Student motivation* (pp. 177–208). New York: Academic Press.

Ames C., & Ames, R. (1977). Competitive versus individualistic goal structures: The salience of past performance information for causal attributions and affect. *Journal of Educational Psychology, 69,* 1–8.

Ames, C., & Ames, R. (1984). Systems of student and teacher motivation: Toward a qualitative definition. *Journal of Educational Psychology, 76,* 535–556.

Ames, C., & Archer, J. (1987). Mothers' beliefs about the role of ability and effort in school learning. *Journal of Educational Psychology, 18,* 409–414.

Ames, C., & Archer, J. (1988). Achievement goals in the classroom: Student learning strategies and achievement motivation. *Journal of Educational Psychology, 80,* 260–267.

Ames, C., & Felker, D. (1979). An examination of children's attributions and achievement-related evaluations in competition, cooperative, and individualistic reward structures. *Journal of Educational Psychology, 71,* 413–420.

Bryant, B. (1977). The effects of the interpersonal context of evaluation on self- and other-enhancement behavior. *Child Development, 48,* 885–892.

Covington, M. V. (1984). The motive for self-worth. In R. Ames & C. Ames (Eds.), *Research on motivation in education: Vol. 1. Student motivation* (pp. 77–113). New York: Academic Press.

Covington, M. V. (1985). Strategic thinking and fear of failure. In J. Segal, S. Chipman, & R. Glaser (Eds.), *Thinking and learning skills: Relating instruction to research* (pp. 389–416). Hillsdale, NJ: Lawrence Erlbaum Associates.

Covington, M. V., & Beery, R., (1976). *Self-worth and school learning.* New York: Holt, Rinehart & Winston.

Covington, M. V., & Omelich, C. L. (1979a). It's best to be able and virtuous too: Student and teacher evaluative responses to successful effort. *Journal of Educational Psychology, 71,* 688–700.

Covington, M. V., & Omelich, C. L. (1979b). Effort: The double-edged sword in school achievement. *Journal of Educational Psychology, 71,* 169–182.

Covington, M. V., & Omelich, C. L. (1984). Task-oriented versus competitive learning structures: Motivational and performance consequences. *Journal of Educational Psychology, 76,* 1038–1050.

Deci, E. L., & Ryan, R. M. (1985). *Intrinsic motivation and self-determination in human behavior.* New York: Plenum.

DeVries, D., & Edward, K. (1973). Learning games and student teams: Their effects on classroom process. *American Educational Research Journal, 10,* 307–318.

Dweck, C. (1984). Motivation. In R. Glaser & A. Lesgold (Eds.), *The handbook of psychology and education, 1,* (pp. 87–136). Hillsdale, NJ: Lawrence Erlbaum Associates.

Dweck, C. (1985). Intrinsic motivation, perceived control, and self-evaluation maintenance: An achievement goal analysis. In C. Ames & R. Ames (Eds.), *Research on motivation in education: Vol. 2. The classroom milieu* (pp. 289–303). New York: Academic Press.

Dweck, C. S. (1986). Motivational processes affecting learning. *American Psychologist, 41,* 1040–1048.

Hersey, P., & Blanchard, K. (1982). *Management of organizational behavior, utilizing human resources* (4th ed.). Englewood Cliffs, NJ: Prentice-Hall.

James, W. (1899). *Talks to teachers on psychology: And to students on some of life's ideals.* New York: Holt.

Johnson, D. W., & Johnson, R. (1975). *Learning together and alone.* Englewood Cliffs, NJ: Prentice-Hall.

Johnson, D. W., & Johnson, R. (1984). Building acceptance of differences between handicapped and non-handicapped students. *Journal of Social Psychology, 122,* 257–267.

Johnson, D., & Johnson, R. (1985). Motivational processes in cooperative, competitive, and individualistic learning situations. In C. Ames & R. Ames (Eds.), *Research on motivation in education: Vol. 2. The classroom milieu* (pp. 249–277). New York: Academic Press.

Kirby, E. A., & Grimley, L. K. (1986). *Understanding and treating attention deficit disorder.* New York: Pergamon Press.

Kleiber, D. A. & Roberts, G. (1981). Sport experience in childhood and the development of social character: A preliminary investigation. *Journal of Sports Psychology, 3,* 114–122.

Kohn, A. (1986). *No contest: The case against competition.* New York: Houghton Mifflin.

Levine, J. (1983). Social comparison and education. In J. Levine & M. Wang (Eds.), *Teachers and student perceptions: Implications for learning* (pp. 105–124). Hillsdale, NJ: Lawrence Erlbaum Associates.

Maehr, M. L. (1984). Meaning and motivation: Toward a theory of personal investment. In R. Ames & C. Ames (Eds.), *Research on motivation and education: Vol. 1. Student motivation* (pp. 115–144). New York: Academic Press.

Meitchenbaum, D. (1977). *Cognitive behavior modification.* New York: Plenum.

Nelson, L. L., & Kagan, S. (1972, September). Competition: The star-spangled scramble. *Psychology Today*, 53–56, 90–91.

Nicholls, J. G. (1984). Conceptions of ability and achievement motivation. In C. Ames & R. Ames (Eds.), *Research on motivation in education: Vol. 1. Student motivation* (pp. 39–73). New York: Academic Press.

Pepitone, E. A. (1972). Comparison behavior in elementary school children. *American Educational Research Journal, 9*, 45–63.

Rosenshine, B., & Stevens, R. (1986). Teaching functions. In M. C. Wittrock (Ed.), *Handbook of research on teaching* (pp. 376–391). New York: Macmillan Publishing Company.

Ryan, R. M., Connell, J. P., & Deci, E. L. (1985). A motivational analysis of self-determination and self-regulation in education. In C. Ames & R. Ames (Eds.), *Research on motivation in education: Vol. 2. The classroom milieu* (pp. 13–51). New York: Academic Press.

Schunk, D. H. (1989). Self-efficacy and cognitive skill learning. In C. Ames & R. Ames (Eds.), *Research on motivation in education: Vol. 3. Goals and cognition* (pp. 13–44). New York: Academic Press.

Slavin, R. (1977). Classroom reward structure: Analytical and practical review. *Review of Educational Research, 47*, 633–650.

Slavin, R. (1978). Student teams and achievement divisions. *Journal of Research and Development in Education, 12*, 39–49.

Slavin, R. (1983). *Cooperative learning*. New York: Longman.

Stipek, D. J. (1984). The development of achievement motivation. In C. Ames & R. Ames (Eds.), *Research on motivation in education: Vol. 1. Student motivation* (pp. 145–174). New York: Academic Press.

Weiner, B. (1984). Principles for a theory of student motivation and their application within an attributional framework. In C. Ames & R. Ames (Eds.), *Research on motivation in education: Vol. 1. Student motivation* (pp. 15–38). New York: Academic Press.

Weinstein, R. S. (1989). Perceptions of classroom processes and student motivation: Children's views of self-fulfilling prophecies. In C. Ames & R. Ames (Eds.), *Research on motivation in education: Vol. 3. Goals and cognition* (pp. 187–221). New York: Academic Press.

White, R. W. (1960). Competence and psychological stages. In M. R. Jones (Ed.), *Nebraska symposium on motivation*. Lincoln, NE: University of Nebraska Press.

How Policy and Regulation Influence Instruction for at-Risk Learners or Why Poor Readers Rarely Comprehend Well and Probably Never Will

Richard L. Allington
State University of New York at Albany

Children who fail to learn on schedule share a number of characteristics, even though they are served by a variety of programs that assume that distinct groups can be identified and that these groups have identifiable and distinct instructional needs (Allington & Johnston, 1989; McGill-Franzen, 1987). Regardless of which categorical instructional support program these children are assigned to (e.g., Chapter 1, special education, migrant education, etc.) the instructional intervention rarely accomplishes a return of the learner to on-schedule reading acquisition. In addition, little evidence is available to suggest that participants in these instructional support programs ever develop into readers who demonstrate adequate abilities to extract meaning from text efficiently and effectively. Even less is available to suggest that the participants develop refined higher order thinking skills, strategies, and abilities.

This chapter offers an explanation for this rather dismal state of affairs, an explanation that is rooted in the instruction offered to low-achievement children, especially the reading instruction provided. This explanation assumes that *children are more likely to learn that which they are taught than that which they are not.* An attempt is also made to explain why low-achievement children are taught certain things (and not others) and why instructional intervention programs are most often designed in ways that are unlikely to facilitate either learning to read well or learning to think critically. This explanation is rooted in an analysis of the conventional wisdom that shaped the policies and regulations that constrain the instructional interventions that low-achievement children participate in.

In this chapter, then, I first review current instructional practices in the education of low-achievement learners and attempt to illustrate how these practices affect the learning of the participants. In the second section, I offer an interpretation of how the policies and regulations that constrain these programs shape the nature of the instruction offered. In the conclusion, I argue that, until beliefs, policies, and programs are substantially altered, we have little reason to expect the situation to change and little reason to expect that low-achievement learners will ever read well or think critically in school settings.

CURRENT INSTRUCTIONAL PRACTICES

There are a number of attributes of instructional settings that one might elect to explore in an attempt to describe current instructional practices in the education of low-achievement children. In this chapter, I have elected to review just three broad, but critical, aspects of instructional settings. These three are (a) instructional time allocations; (b) the instructional tasks that are set; and (c) the nature of the teaching offered to low-achievement children.

Instructional Time

The relationship of various measures of instructional time (e.g., allocated time, engaged time, academic learning time) to learning has been well documented (Denham & Lieberman, 1980; Fisher & Berliner, 1985; Kiesling, 1978). In our interpretation of the role of instructional time in the instruction of low-achievement learners, my colleagues and I (Allington & Johnston; 1989; Allington & McGill-Franzen, 1989b; Johnston, Allington, & Afflerbach, 1985) have suggested that low achievement primarily results when learners have insufficient time or opportunity to learn. We have argued, following Carroll (1963), that learning can be estimated by comparing the amount of time spent to the amount of time needed to acquire the learning desired. In the case of low-achievement learners then, insufficient learning time results in achievement that falls behind schedule (the most commonly accepted schedule being 1 year's growth for each year of schooling). Following this interpretation of the influence of instructional time on learning, I examine hereafter the evidence available on whether current instructional programs serving low-achievement learners typically expand the opportunity to learn.

Low-achievement learners are most often served by remedial programs funded under Chapter 1 of the Educational Consolidation and Improvement Act of 1980 (ECIA) or special education programs mandated by PL 94-142, the Education of Handicapped Children Act of 1975 (EHA). Virtually every school system offers a variety of instructional support services under the auspices of both of these federally initiated attempts to enhance the instruction, and hence the achievement of low-achievement children. The instruction that participants in both programs experience has been studied, with instructional time issues often central to that inquiry. Unfortunately, there exists scant evidence that either remedial or special education programs normally enhance the quantity of instruction for participants.

School differs in the amount of instructional time they allocate to reading instruction, and these differences contribute to achievement differences in the aggregate (Wiley & Harnischfeger, 1974). An important, but puzzling, finding of several studies is that schools with high levels of Chapter 1 participants and high levels of poverty often allocate less instructional time for reading than do schools that report fewer Chapter 1 participants and lower rates of poverty. For instance, Vanecko Ames, and Archambault (1980) reported that, in two thirds of the school districts they studied, schools without Title 1 (the precursor to Chapter 1) remedial programs offered significantly larger amounts of classroom reading instruction than did districts with Title 1 programs. In addition, in 90% of the districts, Title 1 participants received less classroom reading instruction than did nonparticipants. Stanley and Greenwood (1983) also reported less instructional time allocated to reading in Chapter 1 schools, compared to schools without Chapter 1 programs. Birman and her colleagues (1987), drawing upon the data available from a national evaluation of Chapter 1, reported that schools with lower levels of poverty among the students schedule significantly larger amounts of classroom reading instruction (nearly 20 minutes more per day).

Rowan, Guthrie, Lee, and Guthrie (1986) reported that the combination of classroom and Chapter 1 instructional time had little impact on the total amount of instructional time allocated for reading instruction and, likewise, Haynes and Jenkins (1986) reported that the combination of classroom and resource room instruction did not result in increased reading instructional time for mainstreamed learning-disabled students. These findings are similar to those reported by Ligon and Doss (1982) for Chapter 1 and by Ysseldyke, Thurlow, Mecklenburg, and Graden (1984) for mildly handicapped students. In a direct comparison of the instructional experiences of Chapter 1 and mainstreamed mildly handicapped students, (Allington & McGill-Franzen, 1989b) found that mainstreamed special-education students received less reading instruction than Chapter 1 participants; no regular education students were observed, however, and comparisons between those students and students participating in these instructional support programs could not be drawn.

Finally, Leinhardt (1980) offered a report that explains the lack of success that primary-grade transition rooms have had in producing on-schedule reading growth. She found that children assigned to transition rooms (rooms with fewer pupils, more aides, and better trained teachers) experienced about 150 minutes less reading instruction per week than did similar children who had been simply promoted to the next grade. This situation would hardly lead one to expect enhanced achievement.

The critical aspect of these studies is that little evidence exists that participation in either instructional support program (Chapter 1 or special education) is likely to enhance the amount of time allocated for reading instruction. A second important, but little discussed, feature of these studies is the enormous variability in the instructional time data across subjects (Allington & McGill-Franzen, 1989b; Zigmond, Vallecorsa, & Leinhardt, 1980). In these studies, is not uncommon to find time allocations for reading instruction that range from less than 10 minutes per day to over 120 minutes per day. Although variability is the hallmark of classroom-based research, the differences reported in these studies of low-achievement learners suggest a reduced sense of accountability on the part of those who design, deliver, and monitor such efforts. Nonetheless, in our conceptualization of reading failure, instructional treatments must include enhanced opportunities to learn to read, and, on average, current programs fail to deliver such. As Levine and Leibert (1987) noted, until such "strategic instructional issues" are addressed, it is unlikely that our efforts will produce results much different from the very small effects reported to date.

Allocated instructional time, however, is a slippery creature. Obviously, the most effective strategy for enhancing reading development would not be one that simply increased the amount of inappropriate instruction offered! On the other hand, inadequate allocations of instructional time affect both teaching and learning. For instance, relatively short blocks of time influences the types of instructional activities selected (Doyle, 1984). Small blocks of instructional time make some activities and tasks more manageable and others less so. Instructional activities are selected that "fit" the time allocated. It is clear that completion of either extended reading or composing activities (e.g., stories) requires more instructional time than completion of activities that require the reading or production of shorter texts (e.g., a paragraph). Insufficient time to provide sufficient modeling and explanations, as well as opportunities to practice, leads to either a slower pacing through curriculum materials or less learning on the part of students, or both. Although adequacy of allocations of instructional time are important, the content of instruction and the tasks presented to students are also critical and intermingled.

Instructional Tasks

If one accepts the previously noted premise that children are more likely to learn that which they are taught than that which they are not, then consideration of the instructional tasks that children complete during instructional sessions is important. Marx and Walsh (1988) took this one step further and argued that it is the thinking that children do while engaged in academic work that is the crux of the matter. Unfortunately, children's thinking—especially the thinking of low-achievement children—during instructional sessions has rarely been studied. Thus, in this section I rely primarily on reports of the types of instructional tasks that low-achievement children most often engage in during reading instructional sessions. At the same time, inferences can be drawn about the cognition necessary to complete the tasks that are assigned. An examination of instructional tasks could be ordered in a number of ways, and, here, I simply attempt to depict the most common tasks, and their characteristics, that confront low-achievement children. From this presentation, I conclude with the suggestion that there seems to be little reason to expect that low-achievement children should be able to read with comprehension, particularly comprehension beyond remembering a few facts from the material read.

One of the characteristics of the reading instruction experienced by low-achievement learners that we first noted was the differential distribution of both opportunities to read text and opportunities to read text silently (Allington, 1983). Simply put, poor readers are far less likely than better readers to have an opportunity to read text during reading instructional sessions, and, when they do read, they are far more likely to read aloud, round-robin style, and, resultantly, will read far fewer words, stories, and books than better readers. This pattern of preference for oral reading continues in remedial and special-education settings (Allington, Stuetzel, Shake, & Lamarche, 1986; Haynes & Jenkins, 1986; Quirk, Trisman, Weinberg, & Nalin, 1976; Thurlow, Graden, Ysseldyke, & Algozzine, 1984; Ysseldyke et al., 1984). In oral reading activities, the instructional emphasis is more likely to be the accurate oral rendition of the text than accessing meaning. In oral reading, one can only be sure that one child, the reader, is actually engaging in the reading task. The lack of instructional moves that would signal an emphasis on meaning (e.g., schema activation prior to reading, purpose setting, hypothesis generation, postreading questions, or discussion) also communicates an orientation to the reader that accessing meaning is not the critical goal (Cole & Griffin, 1986). Additionally, silent reading activities foster self-regulation, because the reading performance is private, whereas oral reading fosters other-dependent behavior; looking to the external monitor for verification of oral reading accuracy (Allington, 1980). The common description of instructional tasks set for poor readers in reading groups suggests that one might expect poor readers to be better at reading aloud, with little self-monitoring of responses, than at silent reading comprehension tasks.

The classroom and support-program reading instruction of low-achievement children also emphasizes isolated drill and practice activities, particularly activities that center on letter–sound relationships and word pronunciation, although, by the upper grades, the focus of instruction has expanded to sentences and paragraphs in isolation (Allington et al., 1986; Allington & McGill-Franzen, 1989a; Morsink, Soar, & Thomas, 1986; Quirk et al., 1976; Rowan et al., 1986). Reading extended text, orally or silently, is an infrequent aspect of the instructional tasks set for poor readers. If, as Clay (1979) argues, acceleration, or the substantially enhanced opportunities to engage in text-reading tasks are central to resolving reading difficulties, then the current situation holds little promise for accomplishing this feat. In the rare case where abundant opportunities to read text are available in remedial and special-education programs, reported success rates are substantially above the norm (Boehnlein, 1987; Lyons, 1987).

Given the nature of the available descriptions of instructional tasks commonly set for low-achievement children, one should not be surprised that another consistent finding of studies of the instruction offered to poor readers is that there is little emphasis on higher order comprehension, or thinking skills. Although Crawford, Kimball, and Patrick (1984) found little emphasis on higher order skills, they did find that more successful teachers offered some higher order questions and tasks to their Chapter 1 students. Likewise, Morsink et al., (1986) examined instruction for mildly handicapped children and noted that one critical flaw in the instruction offered in special-education classrooms was that "there is almost no instruction . . . that might be classified as involving high-level cognitive skills" (p. 38). Similarly, Rowan et al. (1986) reported that "most Chapter 1 projects provided students with few opportunities to engage in higher-order skills" (p. 5.13). Similar findings are reported in our work (Allington, et al., 1986; Allington & McGill-Franzen, 1989a) and others, (Birman et al., 1987; Cole & Griffin, 1986). Collectively, these reports suggest two things: (a) when it is present, low-achievement learners benefit from instruction that includes comprehension and higher-order thinking tasks, and (b) current instruction for poor readers, whether in classroom or support program, rarely include such opportunities.

Because text reading seems to play only a small role in the instruction offered to low-achievement children, one might ask, "What tasks do they frequently encounter?" The answer is, of course, seatwork. The standard garden-variety seatwork (skillsheets, workbooks, and dittos) dominates the instructional time of low-achievement readers, just as it does that of better performing peers. There are differences, however; better readers spend more of their instructional time involved in reading text, especially silently, and more often have comprehension tasks set for them. The mainstreamed special-education students in our study (Allington & Mc-Gill-Franzen, 1989b) spent substantially larger proportions of the allocated reading instructional time involved in independent seatwork activities than did the Chapter 1 participants. Both Chapter 1 and special-education participants spent time doing seatwork in both their regular classroom and in the support program setting, but the special-education setting had the greatest proportion of time filled with seatwork tasks. Rowan et al. (1986) reported that the Chapter 1 students they observed spent two thirds of their allocated time on seatwork tasks, an allocation similar to what we reported in an earlier study (Allington et al., 1986). Haynes and Jenkins (1986) reported that over half the allocated time was spent seatwork by the special-education students they observed.

Seatwork tasks, in and of themselves, are not necessarily inappropriate, although time spent on such tasks seems less predictive of reading growth than one might hope (Leinhardt, Zigmond, & Cooley, 1981). More important than the type of instructional task, it seems, is the nature of student cognition while completing the work (Marx & Walsh, 1988). This aspect of the instruction has received little attention, but the work of Anderson, Brubaker, Alleman-Brooks, and Duffy (1985) perhaps indicates why seatwork seems to be a relatively unprofitable way to expend available instructional time. Anderson and her colleagues studied first-grade students' responses to seatwork in four Chapter 1 schools. Low-achievement students experienced much difficulty with these tasks; too often, they simply did not have the necessary skills or strategies to complete the work independently. These children completed the tasks, more often than not, by applying several strategies that were undoubtedly different than those that the teacher and curriculum developers had in mind. They copied, cheated, and guessed, but they got the tasks done and up to the teachers desk to be corrected. When queried about the seatwork tasks, neither the low-achievers nor the better readers could provide much evidence that they understood the content-related purpose of these tasks. We found a similar situation in our interviews (Johnston, et al., 1985) with children participating in instructional support programs.

McGill-Franzen and Allington (1990) added two other concerns about the seatwork tasks that Chapter 1 and special-education students experience. Here the seatwork assigned in both the classroom and in the support instruction was compared. However, no consistent pattern of task difficulty between the two settings was found. That is, one could not predict whether the seatwork assigned in the classroom or support program seemed more appropriate for the students. In some cases, the classroom work elicited few errors, whereas the support-program task elicited many. Some children had the reverse situation, and some experienced success and some failure in both settings. The point is that there was little predictability concerning the appropriateness of the tasks presented. A second feature noted was the widespread assignment of "undifferentiated" seatwork tasks by both classroom and specialist teachers. In both settings, there was little evidence that seatwork was differentiated by individual needs; instead, more often than not, all participants were held accountable for completing the same seatwork tasks. Children who participated in remedial and resource-room programs were often held accountable for completing seatwork tasks in the regular classroom, even though the relevant instruction had occurred while they were out of the room attending the support instruction session. Low-achievement pupils spend larger amounts of instructional time doing more seatwork tasks, which are more likely to be more difficult, than do achieving pupils. Because time is always finite, they have less time available to engage in text-reading activities.

The problem with much of the seatwork assigned is that it presents fragments of text and fragments of the reading process. In our analyses of instructional tasks, we have attempted to estimate the "proximity" of the task presented to the end goals of independent text reading and text composing. For instance, the traditional teacher-directed silent reading of a basal reader selection would typically be considered more proximal to the end goal than would teacher-monitored completion of a main idea skillsheet (student reads a single paragraph and selects from a list of possible best titles, and teacher provides feedback on correctness of response). Similarly, pupil construction of a summary statement after reading an article on off-shore oil exploration would be more proximal than would supplying randomly deleted words for a cloze version of the same article. In the first case, the proximity is influenced primarily by the text length and the postreading task demands. Outside of skillsheet tasks and standardized test formats, readers rarely encounter the reading of single paragraphs, followed by a multiple-choice recognition task, with the text present. Likewise, in the second case, outside of school few readers will ever encounter a reading task that requires supplying words randomly deleted from a text, especially in comparison to the likelihood of being asked to supply a coherent summary of the text read. Even in school, the less proximal tasks described are unlikely to occur outside of reading instructional sessions. In this view, then, the most common seatwork tasks are more often distal than proximal to the end goal of reading instruction.

Substantial allocations of time to seatwork activity seem potentially more damaging to low-achievement learners than to achieving students for two reasons. First, low-achievement students already have less exposure to text reading (while needing exposure in excess of that required by achieving students), and seatwork activities replace text-reading opportunities. Second, decreased exposure to text reading, accompanied by increased exposure to fragments of text (especially the smallest fragments: letter, word, and sentence tasks), seems unlikely to facilitate the acquisition of text-reading abilities. Perhaps Cole and Griffin (1986) made this argument more clearly:

> Children are drilled on these "lower-order-skills" on the assumption that automaticity will lead them up the ladder of complexity . . . [but reading] requires that both top-down and bottom-up factors be present and coordinated to make reading possible . . . any curriculum that requires children to work resolutely at one level at a time would be minimizing the possibilities of producing adequate reading . . . instead of using print to help them mediate future activity, they conform as closely as possible to the precise level of the system that their educational experience encourages them to concentrate on. The very tenacity with which they subordinate themselves to instruction fatally cuts them off from the insight that reading means comprehension. (p. 119)

For instance, the substantially increased emphasis on word-level skills that characterizes the instruction of low-achievement readers may, not so subtly, influence the strategies they select when attempting to read. Rather than attending to the semantic and syntactic information inherent in text, these children seem to overrely on word structure and employ strategies that seem to ensure slow recognition processes and disruption of syntactic parsing. The most commonly emphasized decoding strategy seems to be left-to-right single letter sounding out, an inefficient procedure even when it can be used successfully. This strategy obscures larger invariant word structures that efficient readers employ in more mature decoding strategies. The inefficiency of the letter-by-letter sounding interferes with the effective use of contextual information, and continued insistence that such sounding-out strategies be used seems a potential source of impedance. None of this is to suggest that low-achieving readers have adequately developed word structure skills and strategies; in fact, the argument is quite the opposite. The point is that these children have learned, and adhere to the single inefficient strategy taught, and that continued emphasis on such skills and strategies will simply reinforce their current instructionally induced misconceptions about the process of reading. These children will often benefit from additional word structure training but not of the type we have most commonly observed—teacher insistence that the words be "sounded out," understood by the children to mean letter by letter.

This brief review of descriptive reports on the nature of instructional tasks that are most commonly presented to low-achieving readers suggests that, if children are more likely to learn those skills, strategies, and knowledges that are presented in the academic work they complete, then we should not be surprised that few low-achievement learners ever acquire effective and efficient strategies for the independent reading of extended pieces of textual material (e.g., stories, chapters, articles, and books). However, there is a final aspect of the instructional environment that further exacerbates the problems of the low-achievement child.

In a series of reports, my colleagues and I have examined the nature of the curriculum tasks presented to children who participate in instructional support programs (Allington et al., 1986; Allington & Johnston, 1989; Allington, Boxer, & Broikou, 1987; Allington & McGill-Franzen, 1989a & b; Johnston, Allington, & Afflerbach, 1985, McGill-Franzen & Allington, 1990). These reports have been analyses of the consistency of the curriculum tasks that these children experience across the several instructional settings they encounter in a typical school day. A single finding, that of extensive fragmentation and incoherence of curriculum, has dominated our reports. Our investigations assumed that a curriculum was a coherent and organized set of instructional activities that were designed to facilitate that acquisition of skills, strategies, and knowledge. We further assumed that children who experienced difficulty learning needed larger amounts of higher quality instruction in order to master the curriculum as planned.

Low-achievement learners were more likely to be confronted with several different curricula, often curricula that were derived from competing philosophies concerning how reading proficiency is acquired. We commonly found poor readers experiencing two distinct curricula, one in the classroom and the other in the support program, and being successful in neither. The competing curricula presented no parsimonious view of the reading process, and the less able the reader, the greater the conflict, because programs differ markedly at the beginning levels. For instance, the Scott, Foresman and Company's, *Reading: An American Tradition* and Science Research Associate's, *DISTAR* present such a conflict. The former attempts to control difficulty through standard syntax and familiar topics accompanied by pictures relevant to the text base, whereas the latter presents an original orthography and minimally informative artwork, with difficulty control attempted through restricting the letter–sound patterns presented. These differences literally preclude the application of common strategies by beginning readers assigned both texts. Beyond the differences in the textual material, there also exists appropriate, but substantial, differences in the strategies emphasized and the suggested format of the teacher–pupil exchanges. In such cases of curriculum conflict, we have argued (Allington & Johnson, 1989), learners are more likely to develop cognitive confusion about the nature of the activity we call reading and confusion about how to proceed. With the development of a consistent set of text-reading strategies thwarted by the curriculum conflict, the learner relies more heavily on external cues to guide strategy selection, and self-monitoring is lessened, if not eliminated.

Even when the two curricula presented no strong philosophical differences, the low-achievement learner typically was confronted with mastering twice as many vocabulary words, twice the number of decoding skills, and so on, but had less instructional time allocated for this than the normally achieving reader had to master a single curriculum. Children who are experiencing difficulty in learning are unlikely, we have argued, to be best served by curriculum fragmentation and reduced opportunity to learn.

Perhaps the various studies of the instructional experiences of low-achievement learners provide some insight into why so few children, once they have fallen off-schedule in reading acquisition, ever become proficient on-schedule readers. As Cole and Griffin (1986) have suggested, most poor readers "do not have the slightest notion of what the system of mediation we call reading is about. The system of remediation most commonly used does not re-mediate the overall understanding of what reading is or is for . . ." (p. 129). From our perspective, the instruction that most poor readers experience is neither of sufficient quantity nor quality to alter their status. The instructional tasks that are most commonly set for these children seem unlikely candidates to facilitate the development of proficient reading comprehension, and the fragmentation of the learning activity is similarly damaging.

Teaching

Much of what we commonly refer to as teaching involves setting and monitoring the instructional tasks described heretofore. This section focuses on two other aspects of teaching, (a) a general discussion of the evidence on what constitutes effective teaching for low-achievement learners, and (b) instructional explanation, or the actual teaching tasks that accompany developing proficient readers.

As Slavin (1987) has noted, we know substantially more about the effects, or the lack of them, in compensatory and special education than we know about how exemplary programs actually teach children to read. He attributed this to the enormous expenditure of funds to prove that programs are useful and the neglect of funds for attempting to figure why some programs work reasonably well but most do not. Leinhardt and Pallay (1982) offered a similar argument, that attention needs to be directed at identifying effective instructional practices, though their analysis suggests that effective practice for one group is likely to be effective practice for any other.

This finding is reflected in virtually every study of effective instruction for low-achievement children. Good (1983), in his summary of a number of studies, made three arguments: (a) teachers make a difference in student learning, (b) low achievers benefit from appropriate instruction, and (c) positive teacher expectations, good management, and active teaching are the key features of instruction that promote learning. These points have been reiterated, by and large, in studies of effective practice in remedial and special-education classes (Crawford et al., 1984; Englert, 1983; Larrivee, 1985; Morsink et al., 1986). In short, it is difficult to locate evidence that low-achievement learners benefit from instruction that differs in any substantial way from the instruction that other learners benefit from. Poor readers do seem less able to tolerate instruction that is not of high quality, and, as Good (1983) pointed out, "It seems unfortunate that students who have the least adaptive capacity may be asked to make the greatest adjustments as they move from room to room" (p. 49) and from year to year.

Although we have, then, a general description of effective teaching, what we have lacked are more careful descriptions of just what effective teachers do when they teach skills, strategies, and knowledge to developing readers. Although they are still inadequate, recent descriptions of effective teacher strategy explanations break new ground and provide us with a substantially clearer picture of how we might facilitate the acquisition of reading in low-achievement learners. Duffy and his colleagues (Duffy, Roehler, Meloth, & Vavrus, 1986; Duffy, Roehler, & Rackliffe, 1986) provided clear description of the differences between teachers who can effectively explain, or model, the cognitive process associated with comprehending text and those who cannot. They found that quite subtle differences in what teachers say can have profound effects on low-achievement students' understanding of a task and, particularly, on their understanding of effective strategies for accomplishing the task. Two points seem especially relevant here: Less successful teachers (a) offered students sets of rules, or a series of steps or procedures to be followed, but failed to explain the cognitive processes involved, and

(b) failed to make the link between the instructional task and real reading activity. Potentially more damaging is the general absence of any modeling or strategy explanation in the instruction provided to low-achievement readers (Allington, 1986; Haynes & Jenkins, 1986).

Although the work of Duffy and his colleagues has focused on strategies for developing text comprehension in low-achieving learners during regular education reading instruction, there exists, in addition, a substantial set of experimental and clinical studies that demonstrate the efficacy of various procedures for enhancing the text comprehension of remedial and special education participants (e.g., Brown & Palincsar, 1984; Garner, Hare, Alexander, Haynes, & Winograd, 1984; Idol, 1987). Low-achievement pupils can be taught effective and efficient strategies for reading with comprehension; it just seems that such strategies are rarely the focus of the instruction they experience.

In many respects, we are woefully ignorant when it comes to teaching, particularly when it comes to effectively initiating young children into the world of literateness and especially when we begin to discuss specifics of precisely what teachers need to know and attend to as they plan and deliver instruction. However, even those general things we do know seem difficult to locate in descriptions of instructional programs that currently serve low-achievement children. That distressing conclusion led us to begin to examine why current programs so rarely seem to implement much of the little we know.

HOW POLICIES AND REGULATIONS SHAPE
SCHOOL RESPONSE TO LEARNING DIFFICULTY

Mehan, Hartweck, and Meihls (1986) noted that "the view that status is, and should be, attained on the basis of hard work, effort, and merit, and not passed on from one generation to another through inheritance, is inherent in the American egalitarian credo" (p. 4). Schools, then, have been appointed the agent for ensuring that all children have the opportunity to acquire the cognitive skills necessary to attain improved status but currently they seem unable, or unwilling, to meet the challenge. As described in the previous section, schools seem to be organized more along the lines of the "Matthew effect" (Stanovich, 1986), in that those that need the most and best instruction in order to acquire the necessary cognitive skills are more likely to get the least and worst. Coles (1987) differed with Mehan and his colleagues in arguing that "school personnel by and large reflect society's assumption that success is stratified and thus they are likely to expect that it is the destiny of some children to end up at the bottom" (p. 153). Johnston (1987) addressed both issues when he noted that the American public is prepared to accept a normal distribution of IQ scores and physical abilities, neither of which is the province of schools, but is unwilling to accept a normal distribution of reading achievement scores. I begin this section with a brief examination of professional and societal beliefs about schools and learning. Beliefs and conventional wisdom seem appropriate beginning points because, we have argued, it is these beliefs that shape policy (Allington & Johnston, 1989), not the policy that shapes our beliefs, although it undoubtedly can perpetuate archaic beliefs past their prime and it obviously affects our actions.

Conventional Wisdom, Schools, Learning, and Low-Achievement Children

The programs that were described earlier are designed and staffed by educated, well-meaning professionals, so, one might ask, "What leads good folks to such unsatisfactory ends?" One can never be completely sure in such cases, but I argue that conventional wisdom has become problematic and that until we reject and replace critical assumptions about learners, learning, and schools, we will be hardpressed to solve the problem of low-achieving children. Instead, we will simply go through the motions of helping and rarely consider the outcomes or alternatives.

Our instructional efforts in the name of helping poor readers are trapped in an archaic paradigm—that of reductionism. As suggested with the Cole and Griffin (1986) quotation earlier, we seem to have reached the point where participation in the instructional support programs offered to "assist" the low-achievement learner is more likely to perpetuate the problem than to resolve it. Rohwer (1980) raised the relevant issue a decade ago:

> What if the procedure followed by the smart student was incompatible with the procedure I imposed upon the slower student? If so, the more effective my instruction in inducing the slow student to adopt the recommended procedure, the greater its potential for retarding his progress. At least in principle, then, instruction that is indisputably well-intentioned can nevertheless set a student on a dead-end road . . . (p. 37).

The conventional wisdom that undergirds instruction for low-achievement children is steeped with the notion of explicit instructional goals, small steps through a curriculum, and frequent tests and feedback. This conceptualization limits the kinds of knowledge and performance that can be conveyed to students (Doyle, 1986). Walmsley (1986) echoed this notion:

Nowhere has the hierarchical view dominated so completely than in the strategies used to diagnose and remediate childrens' reading and writing difficulties. The poor reader is known (via testing) to be deficient in reading skills, and therefore is given additional skills in remedial classes. Since it is assumed that skills development is a necessary prerequisite to reading literature, little attempt is made to have poor readers read literature ... Similarly in writing, remedial writers spend much time being instructed in prerequisite skills (e.g., fine motor exercises, spelling, handwriting) assumed to precede actual composition. (p. 3)

The traditionally accepted diagnostic/prescriptive subskills approach has never generated much empirical support (Alter & Jenkins, 1979; Coles, 1987), although it has dominated conventional wisdom and, thus, traditional practice. Concommitant with the acceptance of this view was the era of content-free approaches to reading remediation. Content-free materials offer no useful curricular information or knowledge, as exemplified by specially designed remedial materials with topics drawn, it seems, from the *Inquirer*. Bigfoot, killer bees, and the Loch Ness monster are such topics and are frequently the content of choice in the materials marketed for poor-reader consumption. These texts are rarely well written, unlikely candidates to win awards for their stylistic merit and unlikely to foster success in the remainder of the school curriculum.

In a discussion of how one might teach higher order thinking skills to poor readers, Adams (1986) suggested that "for maximum impact, the course must be content-rich ... the provision of content is of utmost importance in itself . . . the more you know, the more you learn" (p. 103). Walmsley (1986) made a similar argument in advocacy of increased use of childrens' literature as curriculum materials for the low-achievement child. Conventional wisdom has trivialized the reading process and the process of learning to read, reducing each to an array of easily mastered discrete objectives. This, in turn, has trivialized instruction to the point where reading activity is but a scant part of the instructional experience, especially for the poorest readers (Allington et al., 1986; Thurlow, Ysseldyke, Graden, & Algozzine, 1984). When text reading is accomplished during reading instruction, it is most likely to be round-robin renditions of poorly written content on topics of no utility.

Finally, conventional wisdom has proffered individualized instruction, meeting each learner's unique instructional needs. Fraatz (1987) reported that virtually all teachers she interviewed indicated that the purpose of reading instruction was to meet individual needs. As with the McGill-Franzen and Allington (1990) study however, most of these same teachers assigned the same seatwork tasks to all students. Dreeben and Barr (1983), like Fraatz; noted the contradiction in expecting schools, as collective enterprises, to be concerned with individuals' specific needs. Instruction that actually focuses on individual learners seems to be a good idea, but individualization as currently practiced means placing large numbers of students at computer terminals to spend 20 minutes doing decontextualized vocabulary drill and practice tasks 3 days a week with no instruction, in the best traditional sense, and no reading, in any traditional sense, offered (Allington et al., 1987).

These aspects of conventional wisdom shape not only our practice but also our policy and our regulatory language. As conventional wisdom is discarded, or replaced, best practice can come into conflict with policy and regulation, a situation now too common (Slavin, 1987).

Federal and State Policies and Regulations

As noted earlier, we have argued that policy is shaped from conventional wisdom and professional beliefs (Allington & Johnston, 1989). Policies are established by governmental agencies based on the conventional wisdom of the era. Once in place, however, policies reinforce conventional wisdom and provide justification for that wisdom, even in the face of information and ideas that undermine convention. Three examples of how the conventional wisdom has shaped governmental policies and how these policies have constrained, or influenced, the instructional programs described earlier now follow.

McGill-Franzen (1987) provided an analysis of the shifting conventional wisdom concerning reading failure. She linked the emergence of Title 1/Chapter 1 with the civil rights movement and the "war on poverty" of the 1960s. Disadvantage, both economic and experiential, were understood as primary contributors to low school achievement, and a variety of federal initiatives were established on these understandings. As it became clear that these programs were only marginally successful in alleviating the problems they were designed to address, and as a new problem, recognition that reading failure extended beyond the populations that were targeted by existing programs, another set of understandings emerged. Thus, "learning disabilities," an explanation of primarily middle-class reading failure developed and, in 1975, was codified into a legally recognized disability with attendant legal protections.

In order to establish district eligibility for fiscal support from federal programs, Congress created general categories (e.g., poverty indices) and procedures (e.g., local Committees on the Handicapped). These were refined into regulations that created reimbursable categories (Allington, 1986). In the case of both federal programs, then, categorical classification was required and the classification procedures were driven by the dominant diagnostic/prescriptive wisdom and a focus on individualized instruction. State regulatory agencies typically accepted these federal guidelines or refined them further. The Individualized Educational Plan (IEP) required for each learning-disabled child and New York State's Pupil Educational Plan (PEP) for Chapter 1 participants are operationalized definitions required by regulation and derived from conventional wisdom.

As noted previously, however, acceptance of the reductionist/hierarchical wisdom limits the description of skills, knowledges, and strategies that learners are to require. Budoff (1975), commenting on the then new IEP plan, went a step further:

> Specification, however, does not necessarily lead to the identification of the most appropriate goals . . . Moreover, excessive pressure for specification may result in trivial, pseudo- mathematical statements that give the appearance of progress when, in fact, the changes demonstrated by the child may not relate to longer-term goals for that child. (p. 523)

Given the recent evidence offered by Mehan et al., (1986) and others, the concern that Budoff expressed seems well-founded. With computer software for generating listings of specific learning objectives and the scant evidence of individualization of instruction, in the traditional sense, in either Chapter 1 or special education (McGill-Franzen & Allington, 1990; Fraatz, 1987), and the trivialization of reading instruction in both programs, we have instructional programs that are shaped by and that meet the regulatory criteria but fail to adequately address the learning failure.

Classification for categorical program eligibility is influenced by fiscal incentives, or disincentives, that are inherent in regulations (McGill-Franzen, 1987; Nelson, 1983). Although there is no common standard for reimbursement of excess costs associated with remedial or special education interventions, both state and federal policies offer fiscal incentives to school districts establishing such programs. The lack of a common standard for reimbursement has allowed for comparisons of the effects of different policies on the classification of students into one categorical program or another. The most common finding is that of substantial influence of fiscal incentives with high reimbursement rates resulting in substantially greater classification than low reimbursement. McGill-Franzen (1987) argued that, between 1975 and 1985, roughly 1.5 million low-achievement learners were shifted from Chapter 1 remedial programs to learning disability programs, primarily as a result of the substantially enhanced reimbursements available for special-education placements compared to allocations for remedial services under Chapter 1.

Fiscal policies, then, seem to shape the nature of the intervention offered to low-achievement learners, or at least how the problem is defined by educators.

Differences in the regulations of Chapter 1 and special education influence the reading instruction that low-achievement readers experience, once the classifications are in place. In our recent analysis of the educational experiences of participants in these two programs, we found that Chapter 1 participants were more likely to participate in classroom reading instruction than were their mainstreamed mildly handicapped peers (Allington & McGill-Franzen, 1989b). However, Chapter 1 regulations require that the intervention supplement, as opposed to supplant, instruction offered in the regular education program. No similar requirement exists in the EHA or the state regulations governing special education programs. As a result of this influence, Chapter 1 participants were more likely to receive increased quantities of reading instruction than were their mainstreamed mildly handicapped peers.

The differences in program regulations influence more than just the quantity of instruction, however. Different organizational arrangements accrue under the differing regulations governing minimum contact time necessary for fiscal reimbursement, maximum client loads, and the permanence of the classification. For instance, Chapter 1 participants attend intervention classes for shorter time periods in larger groups with greater homogeneity of achievement levels than do their mildly handicapped peers (Allington & McGill-Franzen, 1989a). Chapter 1 interventions offer more teacher-directed instruction, in no small part because of these differences. Chapter 1 instruction is more often small-group instruction, whereas special education sessions were individualized as a result of the homogeneity/heterogeneity differences. An unexpected result of the increased individualization, however, was the decrease in teacher-directed instruction and the increase in assignment of low-level seatwork tasks during the resource-room instruction.

District and Building Policies

Although federal and state policies constrain the development of district and school policies, a myriad of instructional support program variations exist in both Chapter 1 and special education. These variations reflect school district and building administrator decisions about the design of instructional support programs. The most common program design in both remedial and special education is a "pull-out," whereby low-achievement children are removed from the regular education classroom for instructional support services. Although regulations for neither program require such distancing of support instruction (and not all districts organized their programs in this manner), such a design facilitates the administrative tasks of accounting for the expenditure of excess funds received from external sources. This program design feature, then, seems to be derived more from auditing concerns than from an analysis of appropriate educational interventions. This very segregation works against coherence and consistency of the instruction offered in the two locations and against collaboration among the teachers who work with the same children (Allington, 1986). In a similar vein, most districts mandate, or suggest, the use of different commercial curriculum materials in the classroom and support program instruction, again easing accountability tasks but enhancing curriculum fragmentation.

Districts tended to employ a set psychometric procedure for determining eligibility for services, but these procedures and the resultant entry criteria varied by district, depending on the availability of external fiscal support and average district achievement levels. In some districts, children scoring, for example, below the 50th percentile were eligible for remedial services, and, in others, children were served only when they scored below the 23rd percentile. Generally, the lower the achievement level in a district the lower one had to score to receive instructional support services. Regardless of the entry criteria, we concluded that most school districts scheduled low-achievement children with an eye on fiscal issues more than on instructional needs (Allington & McGill-Franzen, 1989a). We reached this conclusion by noting that most children served by either Chapter 1 or special education resource-room programs were scheduled for the minimum minutes required to achieve maximum fiscal reimbursements from external agencies. A 12-year-old child in grade 5 with a grade 2 reading level typically received the same number of minutes of support instruction, in a similarly sized group, as did a 9-year-old grade 3 child with the same achievement level. Thurlow, Ysseldyke, Graden, & Algozzine (1984) also found little evidence that schools differentiated instructional opportunity by instructional needs, inasmuch as no clear pattern of differences in instructional intensity were observed for children receiving different levels of special education services.

Some districts attempted to maximize the number of children served while minimizing the cost by using teacher aides extensively and, in some cases, exclusively. The net result, however, was a substantial increase in the variability of instruction. Most common was an increase in the quantity of low-level tasks assigned to low-achievement children (Rowan et al., 1986). The irony of one assigning the least well trained adults to work with the children with the most serious difficulties in learning seemed to have escaped those who made such decisions.

Some districts explicitly noted that reading instruction for main-streamed mildly handicapped children was the responsibility of the special education teacher, yet, these students were routinely scheduled for resource-room instructional periods that were substantially shorter than the classroom reading instructional period (but long enough to qualify for reimbursement of costs). In some cases, the resource-room instruction would have had to have been seven times as effective as the classroom instruction in order to maintain the child's learning rate at the pace that had been established before intervention. Yet, resource-room instruction offered less teacher-directed activity and more low-level seatwork (Allington & McGill-Franzen, 1989b).

Conventional wisdom, governmental regulations, and district policy all work to shape the instructional experiences of low-achievement children. The fiscal incentives that are linked to different categorical classifications, the regulations governing maximum client load, minimum time allocations, and the development of the IEP/PEP objectives, the decisions about program design and curricula, when coupled with conventional wisdom that adheres to hierarchical conceptualizations of the reading process, produce the instructional offerings that have been described herein. Conventional wisdom and governmental regulation work together to impede the implementation of other, more satisfactory programs, as Slavin (1987) pointed out. So, until there comes a time when conventional wisdom is wiser and regulations are less regulatory, we may see only what Singer and Butler (1987) saw as a result of EHA—widespread shifts in school organization but little evidence of the enhancement of education for children.

SUMMARY AND CONCLUSIONS

There seems to be consensus that low-achievement children rarely read well, rarely read with comprehension, and rarely exhibit higher order thinking during or after reading. Much has been written about the deficits, deficiencies, and disabilities of these children, but less has been written about their instructional experiences. In this chapter, I have proposed that current instructional practices are as likely a source of their disabling as any inherent psychological, physiological, or out-of-school experiential deficits. My argument is simply that some children will require reading instruction in substantially enhanced quantities and of substantially enhanced quality in order to develop into independent, comprehending readers. Current programs typically fail on both accounts.

In an attempt to explain the current situation, I provided a brief sketch of how conventional wisdom influences the development of educational programs and policies, and how these programs and policies constrain and influence the instruction offered to low-achieving children. If the research community is to have an effect in the immediate future, researchers will necessarily have to increase their sophistication in policy matters and the conduct of schooling. There seems to exist little debate about whether low-achievement children can become comprehenders and critical thinkers, although it may take time and expertise. The question left to ponder is: Who will deliver the necessary instruction, and when can we expect it to begin?

REFERENCES

Adams, M. J. (1986). Teaching thinking to Chapter I students. In B. William, P. Richmond, B. Mason (Eds.), *Designs for compensatory education: Conference proceedings and papers* (pp. IV-85–IV-119). Washington, D.C.: Research and Evaluation Associates.

Allington, R. L. (1980). Teacher interruption behaviors during primary grade oral reading. *Journal of Educational Psychology, 72*, 371–377.

Allington, R. L. (1983). The reading instruction provided readers of different reading abilities. *Elementary School Journal, 83*, 549–559.

Allington, R. L. (1986). Policy constraints and effective compensatory reading instruction: A review. In J. Hoffman (Ed.), *The effective teaching of reading: From research to practice.* Newark, DE: International Reading Association.

Allington, R. L., Boxer, N., & Broikou, K. (1987). Jeremy, remedial reading and subject area classes. *Journal of Reading, 30*, 643–647.

Allington, R. L., & Johnston, P. (1989). Coordination, collaboration, and consistency: The redesign of compensatory and special education interventions. In R. E. Slavin, N. L. Karweit, & N. A. Madden (Eds.). *Effective programs for students at risk.* Boston: Allyn-Bacon. (pp. 320–354).

Allington, R. L., & McGill-Franzen, A. (1989a). Different programs, in different instruction. In D. Lipsky & A. Gartner (Eds.), *Beyond separate education: Quality education for all.* Baltimore: Brookes. (pp. 75–97).

Allington, R. L., & McGill-Franzen, A. (1989b). School response to reading failure: Chapter 1 and special education students in grades 2, 4, and 8. *Elementary School Journal, 89*, 529–542.

Allington, R. L., Stuetzel, H., Shake, M., Lamarche, S. (1986). What is remedial reading? A descriptive study. *Reading Research and Instruction, 26*, 15–30.

Anderson, L. M., Brubaker, N. L., Alleman-Brooks, J., & Duffy, G. G. (1985). A qualitative study of seatwork in first-grade classrooms. *Elementary School Journal, 86*, 123–140.

Arter, J. A., & Jenkins, J. R. (1979). Differential diagnosis-prescriptive teaching: A critical appraisal. *Review of Educational Research, 49*, 517–555.

Birman, B. F., Orland, M. E., Jung, R. K., Anson, R. J., Garcia, G. N., Moore, M. T., Funkhouser, J. E., Morrison, D. R., Turnbull, B. J., & Reisner, E. R. (1987). *The current operation of the Chapter I program: Final report from the National Assessment of Chapter I.* Washington, DC: U.S. Government Printing Office.

Boehnlein, M. (1987). Reading intervention for high-risk first graders. *Educational Leadership, 44,* 32–37.

Brown, A. L., & Palincsar, A. S. (1984). Inducing strategic learning from texts by means of informed, self-control training. *Topics in Learning and Learning Disabilities, 1982, 2,* 1–17.

Budoff, M. (1975). Engendering change in special education practices, *Harvard Educational Review, 45,* 507–526.

Carroll, J. B. (1963). A model for school learning. *Teachers College Record, 64,* 723–733.

Clay, M. (1979). *The early detection of reading difficulties.* Exeter, NH: Heinemann.

Cole, M., & Griffin, P. (1986). A sociohistorical approach to remediation. In S. deCastell, A. Luke, & K. Egan (Eds.,) *Literacy, Society and Schooling: A reader* (pp. 110–131). New York: Cambridge University Press.

Coles, G. (1987). *The learning mystique: A critical look at learning disabilities.* New York: Pantheon.

Crawford, J., Kimball, G. H., & Patrick, A. (1984, April). *Differences and similarities in teaching effectiveness findings between regular classroom instruction and Chapter I compensatory instruction.* Paper presented at the AERA annual meeting, New Orleans.

Denham, C., & Lieberman, A. (1980). *Time to learn.* Washington, DC: U.S. Government Printing Office (1980-695–717).

Doyle, W. (1984). How order is achieved in classrooms: An interim report. *Journal of Curriculum Studies, 16,* 259–277.

Doyle, W. (1986). Vision and reality: A reaction to issues in curriculum and instruction for compensatory education: In B. Williams, P. Richmond, & B. Mason (Eds.), *Designs for compensatory education: Conference proceedings and papers* (pp.–). Washington, DC: Research and Evaluation Associates.

Dreeben, R., & Barr, R. (1983). Educational policy and the working of schools. In S. S. Shulman & G. Sykes (Eds.), *Handbook of teaching and policy* (pp. 81–96). NY: Longmans.

Duffy, G. G., Roehler, L. R., Meloth, M. S., & Vavrus, L. G. (1986). Conceptualizing instructional explanation. *Teaching and Teacher Education, 2,* 197–214.

Duffy, G. G., Roehler, L. R., & Rackliffe, G. (1986). How teachers' instructional talk influences students' understanding of lesson content. *Elementary School Journal, 87,* 4–16.

Englert, C. S. (1983). Measuring special education teacher effectiveness. *Exceptional Children, 50,* 247–254.

Fisher, C. W., & Berliner, D. C. (1985). *Perspectives on instructional time.* New York: Longmans.

Fraatz, J. M. B. (1987). *The politics of reading: Power, opportunity, and prospects for change in America's public schools.* New York: Teachers College.

Garner, R., Hare, V., Alexander, P., Haynes, J., & Winograd, P. (1984). Inducing the use of a text lookback strategy among unsuccessful readers. *American Educational Research Journal, 21,* 789–798.

Good, T. (1983). Research on classroom teaching. In L. S. Shulman & G. Sykes (Eds.), *Handbook of Teaching and Policy* (pp. 42–8C). New York: Longmans.

Haynes, M. C., & Jenkins, J. R. (1986). Reading instruction in special education resource rooms. *American Educational Research Journal, 23,* 161–190.

Idol, L. (1987). Group story mapping: A comprehension strategy for both skilled and unskilled readers. *Journal of Learning Disabilities, 20,* 196–205.

Johnston, P. H. (1987). Assessing the process and process of assessment in the language arts. In J. Squire (Eds.), *The dynamics of language learning: Research in the language arts* (pp. 335–357). Urbana, IL: National Council of Teachers of English.

Johnston, P. H., Allington, R. L., & Afflerbach, P. (1985). The congruence of classroom and remedial reading instruction. *Elementary School Journal, 85,* 465–478.

Kiesling, H. (1978). Productivity of instructional time by mode of instruction for students at varying levels of reading skill. *Reading Research Quarterly, 13,* 554–582.

Larrivee, B. (1985). *Effective teaching for successful mainstreaming.* New York: Longmans.

Leinhardt, G. (1980). Transition rooms: Promoting maturation or reducing education? *Journal of Educational Psychology, 72,* 55–61.

Leinhardt, G., & Pallay, A. (1982). Restrictive educational settings: Exile or haven? *Review of Educational Research, 52,* 557–578.

Leinhardt, G., Zigmond, N., & Cooley, W. (1981). Reading instruction and its effects. *American Educational Research Journal, 18,* 343–361.

Levine, D. U., & Leibert, R. E. (1987). Improving school improvement plans. *Elementary School Journal, 87,* 397–412.

Ligon, G. D., & Doss, D. A. (1982). *Some lessons we have learned from 6500 hours of classroom observations* (Pub. 81.56). Austin, TX: Office of Research and Evaluation, Austin Independent School District.

Lyons, C. (1978, April). *Reading recovery: An effective intervention program for learning disabled first graders.* Paper presented at the annual meeting of the American Educational Research Association, Washington, DC.

Marx, R. W., & Walsh, J. (1988). Learning from academic tasks. *Elementary School Journal, 88,* 207–219.

McGill-Franzen, A. (1987). Failure to learn to read: Formulating a policy problem. *Reading Research Quarterly, 22,* 475–490.

McGill-Franzen, A., & Allington, R. L. (1990). Comprehension and coherence: Neglected elements of literacy instruction in remedial and resource rooms. *Journal of Reading, Writing, and Learning Disabilities: International, 6,* 149–180.

Mehan, H., Hartweck, A., & Meihls, J. L. (1986). *Handicapping the handicapped: Decision making in students' educational careers.* Stanford, CA: Stanford University Press.

Morsink, C. V., Soar, R. S., Soar, R. M., & Thomas, R. (1986). Research on teaching: Opening the door to special education classrooms. *Exceptional Children, 53,* 32–40.

Nelson, F. (1983). School district response to labeling, cost, and programmatic incentives in special education. *Journal of Educational Finance, 8,* 380–398.

Quirk, T. J., Trismen, D. A., Weinberg, S. F., & Nalin, K. B. (1976). Attending behavior during reading instruction, *Reading Teacher, 29,* 640–646.

Rohwer, W. D. (1980). How the smart get smarter. *The Quarterly Newsletter of the Laboratory of Comparative Human Cognition, 2,* 35–39.

Rowan, B., Guthrie, L. F., Lee, G. V., & Guthrie, G. P. (1986). *The design and implementation of Chapter I instructional services: A study of 24 schools.* San Francisco, CA: Far West Laboratory for Educational Research and Development.

Singer, J. D., & Butler, J. A. (1987). The Education for All Handicapped Children Act: Schools as agents of social reform. *Harvard Educational Review, 57,* 125–152.

Slavin, R. E. (1987). Making Chapter I make a difference. *Phi Delta Kappan,* 110–119.

Stanley, S. O., & Greenwood, C. R. (1983). How much "opportunity to respond" does the minority disadvantaged student receive in school? *Exceptional Children, 50,* 370–373.

Stanovich, K. E. (1986). Matthew effects in reading: Some consequences of individual differences in the acquisition of literacy. *Reading Research Quarterly, 21,* 360–407.

Thurlow, M., Graden, J., Ysseldyke, J., & Algozzine, R. (1984). Student reading during reading class: The lost activity in reading instruction. *Journal of Educational Research, 77,* 267–272.

Thurlow, M. L., Ysseldyke, J. E., Graden, J., & Algozzine, B. (1984). Opportunity to learn for LD students receiving different levels of special education services. *Learning Disability Quarterly, 7,* 55–67.

Vanecko, J. J., Ames, N. L., & Archambault, F. X. (1980). *Who benefits from federal education dollars?* Cambridge, MA: ABT Books.

Walmsley, S. A. (1986). *Toward an integrated language arts program: The North Warren Project.* Unpublished manuscript, State University of New York at Albany.

Wiley, D. E., & Harnischfeger, A. (1974). Explosion of a myth: Quantity of schooling and exposure to instruction, major educational vehicles. *Educational Researchers, 3*, 7–12.

Ysseldyke, J. E., Thurlow, M. L., Mecklenburg, C., & Graden, J. (1984). Opportunity to learn for regular and special education students during reading instruction. *Remedial and Special Education, 5*, 29–37.

Zigmond, N., Vallecorsa, A., & Leinhardt, G. (1980). Reading instruction for students with learning disabilities. *Topics in Language Disorders, 1*, 89–98.

Student Diversity and Mathematics Education Reform

Walter G. Secada
University of Wisconsin—Madison

Other chapters in these two volumes have presented topics in learning and cognitive instruction from psychological points of view; they have drawn implications from the general literature on learning and teaching; and they have focused on specific content domains, such as reading and mathematics. The advances in our knowledge of these areas are truly impressive. Yet, as we read these and similar accounts of learning and instruction, we should be struck by how issues of affect and of student diversity are missing from the pictures that are drawn (see McLeod, 1988; Secada, 1988a). Such omissions are unfortunate, not only because they represent important forces that are known to have effects on course taking, achievement, careers, and students' later life opportunities to participate in our society; they are also dangerous because our efforts at educational reform are likely to misfire, because the knowledge base on which those reforms are built will be overly narrow and may be biased against non-White, non-male, and non-middle-class students.

The purpose of this chapter is to reintroduce issues of student diversity into the discourse of these volumes. The content domain is mathematics education, an area that is embarking on a reform of what should be taught and how it should be taught. This reform movement has drawn extensively from work that is similar to what is found in these volumes (see National Council of Teachers of Mathematics, 1987; Romberg & Stewart, 1987). Yet, for the comprehensiveness of its efforts, that movement also has failed to address issues of student diversity.

The first section of this chapter provides an overview of the current educational status of minorities in mathematics. That literature has reported the existence of broad-based disparities among groups defined by demographic characteristics along various indicators. The intuitions behind that literature are well known to most people—researchers and practitioners alike—who are involved in the education of minorities. These indicators set the stage for what follows.

A complex set of economic and social forces is changing our world. Schools are charged with helping empower *all* students to gain entree into that changing world and its workforce. Mathematics education itself is undergoing a period of change in an effort to respond to the changing demands of society. On the other hand, demographic projections show that our schools will become increasingly diverse in terms of their social makeup. Unfortunately, the agenda for change has failed to address the changing nature of the student population. Socially enlightened self-interest, if nothing else, would assert the need to take the educational status of minorities more seriously than in the past. In the second section of this chapter, I quickly review the forces of change and try to place the review on indicators within that context.

Research does suggest some ways in which we might revision current research and practice to set the stage for deeper and more lasting reform and school improvement. In the third section of the chapter, I take the position that the discontinuity between current indicators of mathematics participation for diverse student populations and social demands for a mathematically and scientifically literate populace in the future should lead to a fundamental questioning and rethinking of many of our assumptions about the mathematics education that is provided to minority students. This rethinking can be focused on four areas: the learner, curriculum, classroom practice, and teacher attitudes and beliefs about minority students. In each of these areas, I review some selected research that should lead us to question commonly accepted views.

This chapter ends with a short discussion of how practice might change, but with a caveat. Too often we ask research to specify what should be done in great detail. My personal reading of the situation is that research might serve practice better by providing conceptual ways of viewing practice and then by nudging practitioners to address, in a serious manner, how their own actions might change as a result of their changed understandings of what they are doing. The final section of this chapter is written in that spirit.

THE CURRENT MATHEMATICS EDUCATIONAL
STATUS OF MINORITIES

Along a broad range of indicators, we can find disparities between men and women (boys and girls), between Whites and Asian Americans on the one hand versus Blacks, Hispanics, and American Indians on the other, and among people of different socioeconomic status (SES) and language proficiency characteristics. Differences have been found using a wide variety of indicators: course taking, affect, academic achievement, academic degrees, and careers related to mathematics. They are located along the length of what is considered the pipeline of mathematics and science education—beginning with elementary school, through high school, undergraduate, and graduate school, and ending in careers (Oakes, 1987). The following narrative is organized around achievement, course taking, and other indicators.

Mathematics Achievement

In terms of mathematics achievement, gender-based discrepancies first appear in middle school. In contrast, those based on race and/or ethnicity start as early as third grade, when children are first assessed systematically. Gender-based achievement discrepancies increase mainly on measures of problem solving and other forms of higher order thinking; in contrast, those based on race and/or ethnicity are pervasive across basic skills as well as higher order applications. Finally, discrepancies based on gender seem not to be as great as those based on race and/or ethnicity (Anick, Carpenter, & Smith, 1981; Dossey, Mullis, Lindquist, & Chambers, 1988; Lockheed, Thorpe, Brooks-Gunn, Casserly, & McAloon, 1985; Matthews, Carpenter, Lindquist, & Silver, 1984; Oakes, 1987, in press).

Some gender-based discrepancies are similar across different ethnic groups. Jones, Burton, and Davenport (1984), in an analysis of the 1973 NAEP data, reported significant race differences favoring 13-year-old Whites over Blacks, but no gender differences, nor interaction of gender with race. For 17-year olds, they found significant race and gender differences, but no interaction.

On the other hand, there is evidence to suggest that the patterns of achievement differences are more complex than we might suspect. For example, in an analysis of the High School and Beyond data set, Del Harnisch and I followed the lead suggested by Grant and Sleeter (1986a) and considered total mathematics achievement as a function of SES, gender, and ethnic/racial group membership (Figs. 10.1 and 10.2). For 7 of 10 gender-by-ethnicity groups, one can see a steady improvement in achievement as a function of SES. For Asian females, high SES students performed no better than, if not less well than,[1] the next lower quartile. For American Indian females, SES differences were virtually nonexistent. For American Indian males, SES based differences appeared only between the highest and next highest quartiles.

Differences ranging from slight to substantial, favoring males over females, can be seen for 12 of the 20 SES-by-ethnicity groups. The classic pattern of achievement disparity favoring males over females can be found, in a consistent manner, only for Whites and Hispanics; the differences are more pronounced for Hispanics. Among Asian students, for two SES groups, gender differences favor females over males; in one case, the difference is so slight as to be nonexistent; only at the highest SES level do clear differences favoring males over females appear. Among American Indians, only at the highest SES level do clear differences favoring males over females appear; in the other cases, the large standard error of measurement suggests that differences are unreliable. For all four SES groups among Blacks, differences are small. In two cases, they favor females; only in the case of the highest SES groups do they favor the males.

Asian males at all four SES quartiles outperformed their White peers, who outperformed Hispanic males. Hispanic males outperformed Black males, who outperformed American Indian males in all but the highest SES quartile. This last group of American Indian students outperformed both their Black and Hispanic peers. On the other hand, Asian females outperformed their White counterparts in all but the highest SES group, where the two groups were equivalent. There is a clear break between Asian and White females and Indian, Black, and Hispanic females across all SES groups. American Indian females outperformed Hispanic and Black females at the two lowest quartiles, but they fell behind at the two highest. Hispanic and Black females were essentially equivalent at the three low SES quartiles. At the highest SES quartile, achievement differences favored the Hispanics. Hence, gender differences tend to be smaller than ethnic and SES differences in the High School and Beyond data set, but the pattern of differences varies from group to group.

There is some reason to believe that the major assessments of student academic achievement might overestimate the mathematics performance of various groups based on race, ethnicity, and social class. First, NAEP and many state assessments routinely exclude students whose English proficiency is deemed insufficient for purposes of taking tests. One of

---

[1]Note the size of the standard error of measurement.

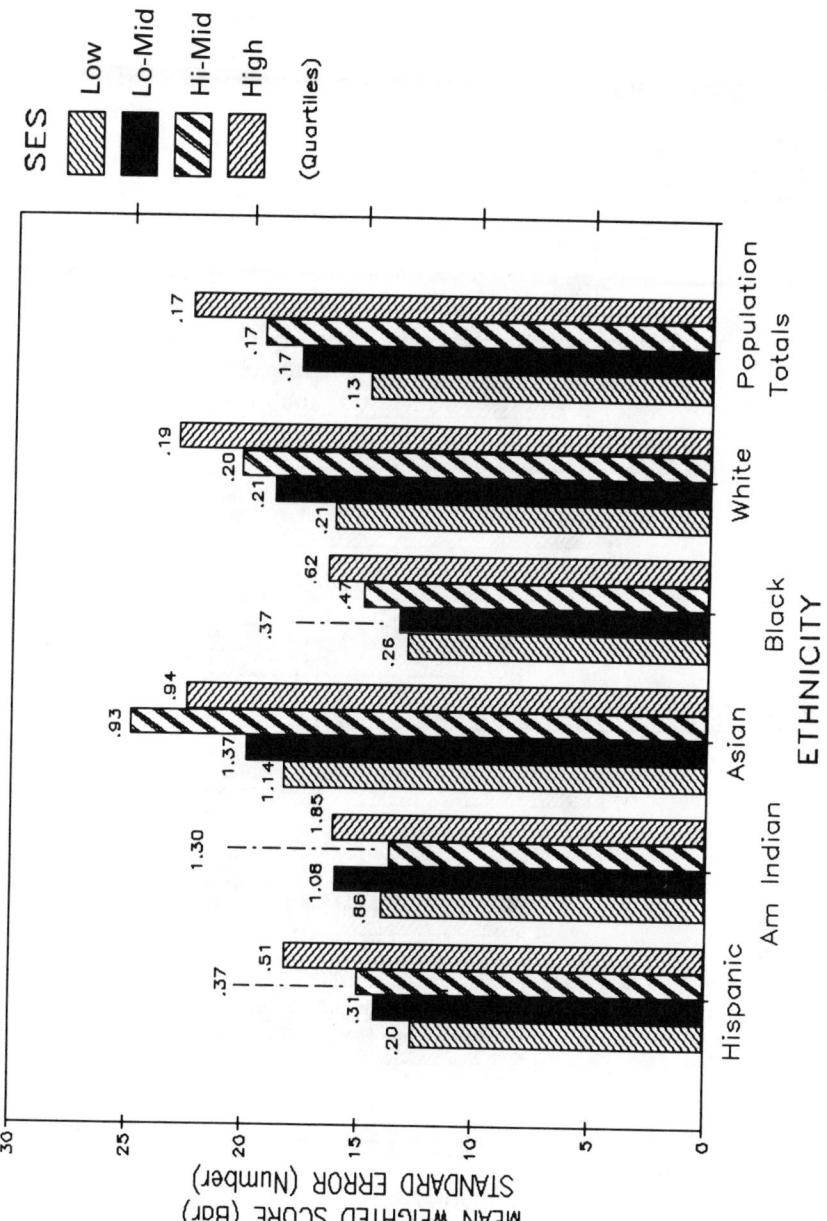

FIG. 10.1. Total math scores for tenth grade females: SES within ethnicity.

High School & Beyond 1980 Sophomore Cohort.

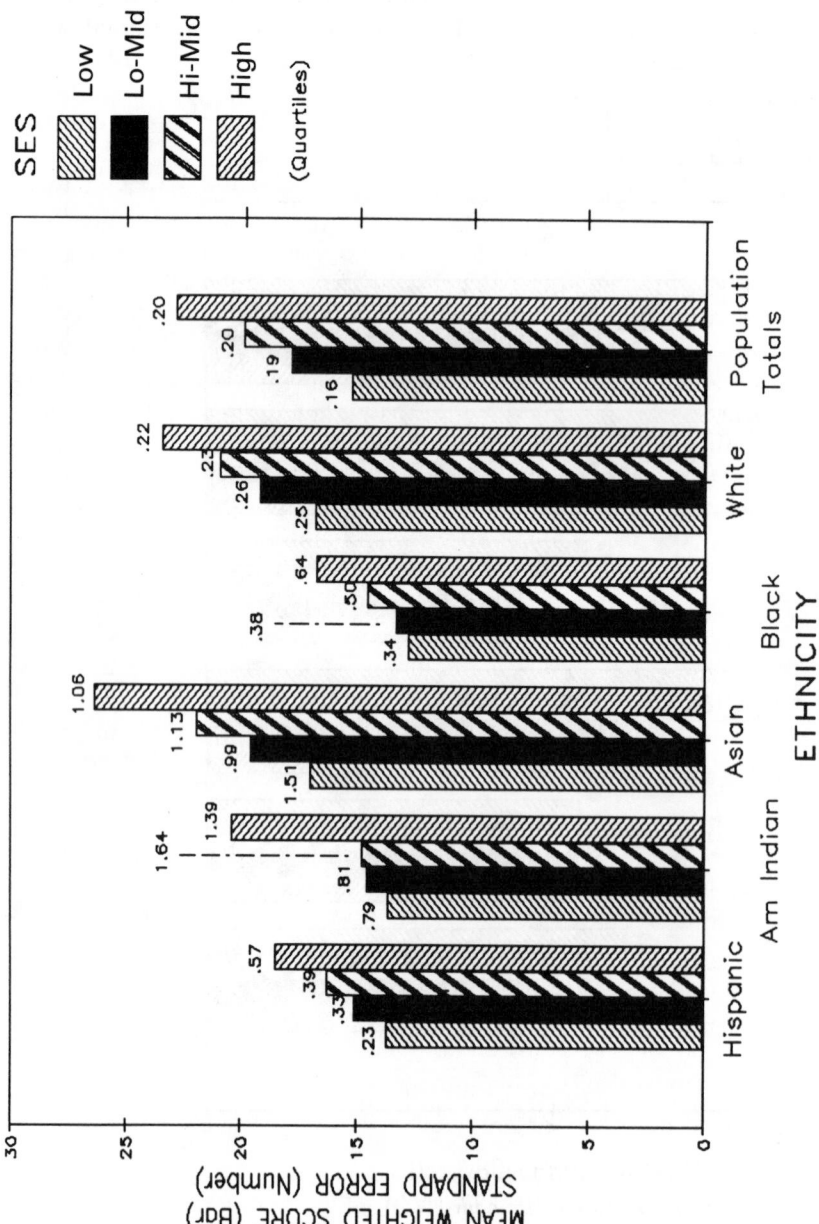

FIG. 10.2. Total math scores for tenth grade males: SES within ethnicity.

the defining characteristics of being limited English proficient (LEP) is low academic achievement, usually including reading and mathematics. Hence, large-scale assessments will omit the lowest achieving members from minority language groups (i.e., Hispanics, Asians, and American Indians).

Second, Blacks, American Indians, Hispanics, and the poor are known to drop out of high school—if not before—in numbers that exceed their representation in the school age population, and low academic achievement is correlated to dropping out (California Department of Education, 1986; Rock, Ekstrom, Goertz, & Pollack, 1986; Steinberg, Blinde, & Chan, 1984). Rock et al. (1986, chapters 9 and 10) have computed estimates of the effects of dropping out on student academic performance in a variety of academic areas. Dropping out of school affects subsequent mathematics achievement more than achievement in any other area—vocabulary, reading, writing, or science. Hence, again, for older students, national and state assessments might overestimate population performance. Because Hispanic children drop out of school at an earlier age and in greater numbers than many other groups (Arias, 1986, p. 38), even data for the High School and Beyond Tenth Grade Cohort may represent an inflated population estimate.

Course Taking

In high school, the taking of mathematics courses has been called (Oakes, in press) the "strongest school related predictor of student achievement" (p. 26; see also, Myers & Milne, 1988; Rock et al., 1986; West, Miller, & Diodato, 1985). On the other hand, data from the 1986 NAEP suggest that although course taking results in greatly improved academic performance, it does little to reduce achievement differences based on gender or on race/ethnicity. If anything, group differences are exacerbated.

For example, females who had not taken Algebra outperformed their male counterparts by an average of three points on the Algebra Subtest, although females who *had* taken Algebra scored one point below their male counterparts. A 16-point Black/White gap among students not taking Algebra increased to a 22-point gap, favoring Whites. A 13-point Hispanic/White gap also increased to 18 points. In Geometry, the differential rates of improvement were worse; a four-point male/female discrepancy increased to eight points; a 10- point Hispanic/White difference became a 17-point difference; and a 20-point Black/White difference increased to 27 points (Dossey et al., 1988, Table 3.1, p. 60). Whether this increasing gap is a function of course content, of teaching quality, or of preexisting achievement differences is not clear.

Course taking is important in its own right. One cannot take advanced mathematics courses—and presumably enter mathematics postsecondary courses and gain access to careers—unless one has taken prerequisite high school mathematics courses. Differential course taking and the pervasiveness of tracking based on gender, race, ethnicity, and SES have been well documented in the literature (Nielsen & Fernandez, 1981; Oakes, 1985; West et al., 1985). Unfortunately, we do not know enough about the interrelationships among preexisting achievement differences, student choice to enter less demanding tracks, and the sources of how tracking works to reduce educational opportunity to make really strong recommendations.

What little research there is concerning the relationship of course taking to gender and ethnicity indicates that the relationship is not a simple one. In a study of mathematics course taking among Mexican American males and females, MacCorquodale (1988) found different patterns of gender versus ethnic differences. Proportionately more males than females enrolled in Pre-Algebra and Geometry; more Whites than Hispanics enrolled in Algebra 1 and Geometry; and, more Hispanics than Whites enrolled in General Math. In the most advanced mathematics courses, differences among the groups were minimal. What such differential course taking means in terms of student demographics is not fully understood.

Other Indicators

Gender-based differences on affect and mathematics have been studied extensively (Fennema, 1984; Fennema & Meyer, 1989; Reyes, 1984). I have not found similar lines of research involving minorities or the poor. Interestingly, the 1986 NAEP results (Dossey et al., 1988) found some small group-based differences along various indicators of affects, including usefulness of mathematics, intent to pursue a mathematics-related career, confidence, and so forth. In general, the NAEP data show that positive attitudes about mathematics are related to better performance. NAEP's failure to replicate prior research that found strong gender differences in affect should caution us against accepting similar results with respect to race and ethnicity. Questions tended to be rather direct, when more subtle questions might reveal differences. What student, when asked about the importance of a subject for which he or she is constantly tested, will respond that the subject is not important?

Gaps in high school course taking and academic achievement become chasms when we consider college course taking, the receipt of mathematics and related degrees, and careers in related fields (Crowley, 1986; Dix,

1987; Duran, 1983; National Science Foundation, 1986; Thomas, 1986). As would be expected, males more than females, Whites and Asians more than Hispanics, Blacks, and Indians take courses, receive degrees, and enter professions involving mathematics. I could locate only one study, by Leggon (1987), that tried to integrate gender with ethnicity for Blacks, Hispanics, and Asian Americans. Interestingly, the rate of participation for Black and Hispanic women is greater than for men at the bachelor's and master's degree levels; the reverse is true for all ethnic groups at the doctorate; and Asian American men have greater rates of participation than women across all levels. Although Leggon (1987) concluded that "minority women share the fate of those in their gender group as well as those in their ethnic group" (pp. 152–153), the data she reported paint a much more complex picture.

Summary Comments

The literature on indicators does suggest some ways of improving the mathematics achievement of minorities. The most obvious suggestion is for them to take more courses, and, indeed, much of the current reform mandates more course taking for everyone. Yet there is more to course taking than that. The taking of additional courses seems to exacerbate, rather than alleviate, differences. Oakes (1987, in press) hypothesized that course content, teacher quality, and classroom processes might help explain this phenomenon. But we still need better knowledge of what occurs in classes that may result in differential learning, why some students choose to embark on a specific sequence of courses in order to counsel them to take more advanced courses, and how to overcome the existence of structural barriers to advanced course taking, such as tracking.

Indicators take meaning within specific contexts. Hence, before making responses based on the preceding information, we need to consider the context within which we are trying to improve the educational opportunity of diverse learners. A review of what these indicators might mean within current educational research and practice lies beyond the scope of this chapter; I hope to do so at some future time. What I wish to do in the remainder of this chapter is look toward the future more than at the present.

Educational reform for minorities has tended to lag behind reform aimed at improving the mathematics education of the mainstream (Cole & Griffin, 1987). For example, we have invested great resources in the development of basic computational skills among Blacks, Hispanics, American Indians, and the poor, and we seem to have been moderately successful in improving those skills (Dossey et al., 1988; Kennedy, Jung, & Orland, 1986). Yet, ongoing educational change might make such efforts insufficient, if not superfluous. One must question the efficacy of developing computational wizardry among such groups while other children use pocket calculators, engage in problem solving, and have extensive access to computers in their mathematics education, as recommended by the National Council of Teachers of Mathematics (1987). Moreover, compensatory programs are resistant to change (Cole & Griffin, 1987); we must be concerned about their adapting to, or at least not interfering with, educational reform for children in their programs. For this reason, the discussion next turns to the challenge that is facing us in terms of evolving forces: the demographic shifts in our population, the changing nature of society and of the job market, and how mathematics education reform is responding to those forces.

THE CHALLENGE OF THE FUTURE

Social, employment, and demographic projections for the United States into the 21st century indicate a mixture of opportunity and challenge with respect to the mathematics education of minority students. On the one hand, the entry-level workforce is shrinking in absolute terms while non-White minorities, especially Hispanics, are increasing their numbers. Industry and the military are being forced to look at these groups, as never before, to fill their workforce needs.

On the other hand, participation in the workforce and in our society in general will entail greater levels of mathematics and science literacy than are presently needed. Our society is becoming increasingly technological in aspects ranging from home to employment. Social problems will become increasingly complex and will require the cooperative efforts of individuals bringing to bear varying knowledge and skills. Information and its management are becoming a primary form of production. New jobs will be, primarily, in the service sector of the economy. Currently, jobs filled by minorities tend to be in manufacturing or agriculture; they require lower levels of mathematics and science literacy than will be required by jobs in the developing sectors of the economy. Even low-skill jobs are being transformed by the use of computers and by the introduction of other technological advances into the work place. How these forces interact to create the mixture of hope and crisis is the focus of the following sections.

The Changing Demographics

In 1976, 24% of the total student enrollment in United States schools was non-White; by 1984, the figure had risen to 29%; by the year 2000, between 30% and 40% of the country's school population will be minority (Center for Education Statistics, 1987a, p. 64; Hispanic Policy Development Project, 1988; Hodgkinson, 1985). In the country's 20 largest school districts, the respective figures for 1976 and 1984 were 60% and 70% (Center for Education Statistics, 1987a, p. 64). One in four students is poor (Kennedy et al., 1986, p. 71); one in five students lives in a single-parent home (Center for Education Statistics, 1987b, p. 21). The intercorrelation among various demographic characteristics has been well documented in the literature. For example, poverty, ethnicity and race, and family structure are correlated. Among White children living in households with an adult male present, 11.9% are poor; among Black and Hispanic children similarly situated, the respective figures rise to 23.8% and to 27.3%. On the other hand, among children living in female-headed households, the rates of poverty rise to 47.6%, 68.5%, and 70.5% for Whites, Blacks, and Hispanics, respectively (Kennedy et al., 1986, Figure 3.3, p. 36).

Increasing numbers of children from minority language backgrounds are entering school with little or no competence in the English language (Hispanic Policy Development Project, 1988; O'Malley, 1981). Although Spanish is the predominant first language for such children—and it is likely to remain so into the next century—increasing numbers are entering school with non-Spanish language backgrounds, such as Arabic, Chinese, Hmong, Khmer, Lao, Thai, and Vietnamese (Oxford-Carpenter, Pol, Gendall, & Peng, 1984).

Hispanics are the fastest growing group in the United States. From 1982 to 1985, the Hispanic population grew an average of 3.0% per year; the Black population grew 1.6% per year; and, the White, non-Hispanic population grew by 0.6%. Depending on assumed rate of growth, Hispanics are projected to become the largest minority group in the United States sometime between the years 2000 and 2050 (U.S. Bureau of the Census, 1986). Although Hispanics have shifted from rural to urban population centers and are found throughout the United States, over 60% of them live in California, New York, and Texas. Adding Florida and Illinois raises the total to 75% (Arias, 1986, p. 29). Hispanics increasingly are being segregated in school (Arias, 1986; Espinosa & Ochoa, 1986).

Hence, not only are there correlations among various characteristics—such as poverty, family structure, and ethnicity—for each of which indicators of participation in mathematics are distressingly low, but also the projected growth is precisely for those populations for whom the school system has not worked as well as it might. Needless to say, this has caused serious concern in many quarters (Hodgkinson, 1985; Hispanic Policy Development Project, 1988). Cole and Griffin (1987) sounded the alarm:

> The problem of underrepresentation in higher levels of the educational system has reached disastrous proportions in this country. In southern California, for example, more than half the Hispanic-American children who enter the school system drop out before they complete high school. ... Yet in many areas of southern California, Hispanic-Americans are an absolute majority of the citizens whose educational needs serve as the *raison d'etre* for the public support of a university. This situation is so obviously dangerous from a political and economic point of view that it deserves the serious concern of policymakers and the academic community, as well as the military and the business community. (p. 1)

In the next two sections, those concerns are viewed in terms of projected social and employment changes.

The Changing Nature of Society

A vision that relates school mathematics to our changing society was articulated in a three-volume set of papers edited by Romberg and Stewart (1987). The need for reform of school mathematics received support from a variety of fields. Mathematicians provided their views of their discipline, educational and cognitive psychologists wrote about how children learn mathematics, and curriculum theorists drew implications for what mathematics should be taught and how instruction should be delivered from these other sources. Cornbleth (1987) expressed concerns about the pervasive nature of myth-making in curriculum reform as a caveat against excessive zeal.

Romberg and his colleagues (Romberg & Smith, 1987; Romberg & Zarinnia, 1987; Zarinnia & Romberg, 1987) drew heavily on projections for the economic growth and development of the United States into the next century in creating their vision. They tried to move beyond economics in an effort to situate the current reform movement within a world view of mathematics. According to that view, the United States is entering a postindustrial age in which "information is the new capital and the new raw material" (p. 22). The newly developing economic system will be based on information and its management. Hence, the United States faces dislocations in the employment of much of its population, as manufacturing and similar jobs will move to other countries during the transition to that system.

Although driven, in large part, by economic forces, Zarinnia and Romberg's vision of a changing social order tries to be broader. Information may be the new capital; but the world itself will become increasingly complex. Easily available natural resources will be depleted; the development of a worldwide economy and the movement of specific kinds of jobs from some countries to others in that economic system will lead to stress on national political systems and the need to manage that stress; computers and computer-related technologies will pervade not just industry but many other niches of our everyday lives. These changes in the fabric of our society point to a need for a population who can think in more interrelated ways than what is currently in vogue. Zarinnia and Romberg (1987) summarized the educational implications of their new world view:

> Accelerating change in the rezoning of world economic activity has drastically changed educational expectations. . . . Among the results of these new educational expectations are:
>
> 1. A stress on integrative, intuitive, expert thinking.
>
> 2. The notion that evaluation should be measured against a goal rather than against past performance.
>
> 3. A stress on an educated populace, rather than selecting an elite for educating, and training the remainder. (p. 36)

The economic system is but part of the social whole. For example, the mathematical literacy necessary to gain access to basic services in our society might be very low; but understanding how those services are allocated, and hence gaining the ability to *control* the services, requires much higher levels of literacy. For example, decisions about who qualifies for compensatory educational services are based on some rather complex standards for the concentration of poverty in specific areas (Kennedy et al., 1986). Access to such services might seem simple. But for parents to understand why their children receive different levels of service under different conditions would require their understanding how that funding was determined. Insofar as parents do not have the mathematical knowledge that might give them access to *how* those decision are made, their ability to improve the educational opportunities of their children is commensurately constrained.

Similarly, buying food in a market is easy; understanding the forces that lead to higher food prices in specific neighborhoods, and deciding where to buy based on such information, requires mathematical literacy.

One can think of various examples in which low levels of mathematical literacy do not rule out receiving a particular service—all one must do is go to a broker—but in which, nonetheless, such low literacy would effectively rule out the possibility of individuals' gaining *control* of that service. This is but one way by which individual participation in our society becomes increasingly limited for people whose mathematical literacy is low. There are others, which are related to our political and democratic institutions.

The Changing Job Market

A more narrow focus on the job market also links mathematical and scientific literacy to a changing world. Industry and the military are concerned about the demographic projections that portend major changes in the composition of the school-age population in the 1990s and, by extension, of the entry-level workforce in the next century. If our country is to survive as an economic and military power, it must attend to the implications of those changes in terms of the education of its diverse student populations so that industry and the military can meet the demand for a technologically literate workforce.

The National Alliance for Business (NAB, 1986a, 1986b) has been one of the most vocal advocates in this area. The size of the 16- to 24-year-old labor force is expected to decline, whereas the number of minorities is expected to increase in absolute terms and, hence, in percentage. These youth will be asked to enter a radically changing work place. Of 20 million new jobs created during the late 1970s and early 1980s, 90% were in service and information industries; in contrast, previous employment opportunities could be found in manufacturing, which required lower levels of mathematical literacy. By the end of the century, technology will alter not only developing job opportunities, but also how many current jobs are performed. According to the NAB (1986a), "Computer skills will comprise only a small part of the skill requirement, but basic academic skills, problem solving, and interpersonal skills will be increasingly important. . . . Jobs that rely on computer based information will offer greater mobility" (p. 4).

In a manner that echoed Zarinnia and Romberg's (1987) "stress on an educated populace, rather than selecting an elite for educating, and training the remainder" (p. 36), the NAB (1986a) placed enlightened self-interest at the intersection of our country's changing demographics and the increasing skill levels needed for employment: "Programs to improve the effectiveness of schools cannot sacrifice or lose large segments of young people by concentrating their efforts to serve 'the best and brightest.' With the total number of new entɪ·· ɩ ɹ the work force declining, business will need to rely on all youth, not just certain segments of the youth population" (p. 7).

But whereas Zarinnia and Romberg couched the need for increased mathematical literacy in terms of participation in the larger society, the NAB has placed that need solely in terms of labor.

In *Youth 2000,* the NAB (1986b) again articulated a similar range of concerns. A delicate balance between a challenge and an opportunity may be irretrievably lost and, hence, it may take on crisis proportions. Thomas Bell, President of the Hudson Institute, gave particular urgency to this mix of opportunity cum crisis: "We have a unique opportunity . . . but it's fleeting. . . . The problem of youth unemployment can be solved by the turn of the century. That is something we have never been able to say before, and perhaps will never be able to say again" (p. 15).

Admiral James D. Watkins (NAB, 1986b), then Chief of Naval Operations, asserted that:

There is a confluence of national thought right now, there's an opportunity that presents itself to all us, and if we don't grasp the opportunity, we're going to plunge the nation into economic and military crisis. By the end of this decade, the military will require one out every two qualified males. Industry, business, will all be clamoring with us [the military] for the same resources that simply are not going to be there in the kinds of numbers this nation needs. (p. 23)

The opportunity lies in the shrinking size of the entry labor force tied to an increasing demand for labor. This is the promise of full employment, provided that the labor pool has been adequately trained. The danger lies in the missed opportunity, and it has multiple facets.

First, the creation of a pool of people who are illiterate and will remain a permanently unemployable underclass, regardless of industry's and the military's need for workers, represents an economic drain and political danger to the country's well-being. Second, if supply does not meet demand for trained workers, the United States will lose its economic and military prestige and position as it watches other, more prepared nations take advantage of the opportunity that is presented to them. A third danger is implicit in those projections. This concerns the overall ability and willingness of today's youth to support an aging society that failed to educate them in the first place and thereby condemned them to a life of second-class power, economically and militarily, both as a nation and individually. In response to the second danger, the NAB (1986a) has called for a review of United States immigration policy so that industry can meet its demand for skilled workers from abroad. There is no ready response to the first and third dangers.

Support for the projections on which industry and the military's concerns are based can be found in a study by Johnston and Packer (1987). They placed the changing demographic nature of the American workforce as the first and most important issue to be drawn from future labor projections. Of a net 25 million *new* jobs to be created in the period 1985–2000, 15% are projected to be filled by White males, 43% by White females; 7% and 13% will be filled by native non-White males and females, respectively; 13% and 9% by immigrant males and females (Johnston & Packer, 1987, p. xxxi). Yet, the fastest growing job areas will require highly skilled workers: natural scientists, lawyers, engineers, managers, teachers, technicians (Johnston & Packer, 1987, p. xxii). The small number of *new* jobs to be filled by White males, as well as increased skill demands of those new jobs, support the view that we must educate women and minorities, if for no other reason than because of the needs of the work place.

Echoing the concerns of the NAB, Johnston and Packer (1987) paid special attention to the mixture of opportunity and danger inherent in the case for Blacks and Hispanics in this changing economy. Moreover, where they located that challenge reveals the limits of enlightened self-interest: "Minority workers are not only less likely to have had satisfactory schooling and on-the-job training, *they* may have language, attitude, and cultural problems that prevent them from taking advantage of the jobs that will exist" (p. xxvi, emphasis added).

Employment is not just an issue of adapting the work place to these new demographics[2]; it is one of addressing the "problems" that belong to minorities. Johnston and Packer (1987) warned:

> If the policies and employment patterns of the present continue, it is likely that the demographic opportunity of the 1990s will be missed and that by the year 2000 the problems of minority unemployment, crime and dependency will be worse than they are today. Without substantial adjustments, blacks and Hispanics will have a smaller fraction of the jobs of the year 2000 than they have today, while their share of those seeking work will have risen. (p. xxvi)

We need not accept such a narrow vision that would shift the burden for employment to schools and, by extension, to minorities in a new and subtle way of blaming the victim. Yet we must accept that schooling has

---

[2]Interestingly, the NAB (1986a) does grant that changes in the workplace will be necessary in order to accommodate the demands of child rearing.

some role to play and that our larger society does have a need for a mathematically literate population. Moreover, mathematics might be used to serve the interests of minorities if it could be applied to helping them analyze their own situations and take some control of them (see, e.g., Grant & Sleeter, 1986b). The general mathematics education curriculum reform movement provides an additional context within which to view the mathematics education of minorities.

Mathematics Education Curriculum Reform

The rationales for radically changing the mathematics school curriculum found in Romberg and Stewart (1987) are recapitulated and acted on in a recently published set of *Curriculum and Evaluation Standards for School Mathematics* (National Council of Teachers of Mathematics, 1987). On the down side, the current curriculum has failed in terms of national assessments, international comparisons (McKnight et al., 1987), and the opportunities for women and minorities to participate in mathematics education and careers. On the positive side, developments in mathematics, in psychology, and in the new world combine to require major reforms in mathematics education. Taken together, they suggest that the mathematics curriculum should focus on developing the knowledge and skills that people will need to possess in order to function within that new world.

That knowledge is tied to the fact that the United States is becoming an increasingly complex society. Both the ability to obtain work and participation in that society will require higher levels of mathematical literacy than are currently necessary. Literacy will take on the most advanced forms of thought studied by psychology and taught in the schools: problem solving, innovative thinking, and thinking across disciplines. Hence, covering a broad range of mathematics, much of which is obsolete, is outmoded. In its place, the school curriculum should stress covering a few important topics, covering them well, and encouraging students to work together and to develop new knowledge as needed. Schooling will have to prepare students for change, rapid and constant. Finally, the changing economy that students will enter requires that they view education as a lifelong process and learn how to learn.

Intended to guide curriculum developers in their efforts, the *Standards* (NCTM, 1987) call for some radical restructuring of what and how mathematics gets taught in the schools. The *Standards* propose five sets of interrelated goals for the student: (a) to become a mathematical problem solver; (b) to communicate mathematically; (c) to learn to reason mathematically; (d) to value mathematics; and (e) to become confident in his or her own ability to do mathematics. In achieving these goals, students should examine mathematical contexts; they should represent and transform those contexts in a variety of ways; students should make and prove their own conjectures, apply what they have learned, solve problems, and, finally, students should communicate with one another using mathematical symbols and language.

The *Standards* provide a basis from which to severely question current practices in the mathematics education of most minority students who are known to be overrepresented in schools' compensatory programs (Cole & Griffin, 1987; Kennedy et al., 1986). Computational skills should be deemphasized in light of the widespread availability of calculators and computers; ability-group tracking in elementary and secondary school mathematics should be abolished. Unfortunately, the *Standards* fail to address other issues that should also be of concern to educators of minority students: Equity and the use of multicultural materials in the curriculum receive scant attention.

The Moving Target

One reaction to the disparities reviewed in the first section of narrative is to argue that low-achieving students should receive support by "sheltering" them within compensatory programs—ranging from Chapter 1 to bilingual education. These programs are judged based on their ability to curtail student dropout and on improved scores measured by standardized achievement tests. On those criteria, compensatory programs seem to have been moderately successful over the past years (Congressional Budget Office, 1987).

Hence, one might ask, why not more of the same? Because the target is moving. The mathematics that gets taught in these programs tends to focus precisely on the lower level and computational skills that are tested in standardized tests, which the current reform movement is trying to replace, and which projections for living and working in the future are questioning. Even computers, when available in compensatory education programs, tend to be used for drill and practice. It is very unlikely that reform will trickle down to students in these programs without specific attention given to their educational condition. Cole and Griffin (1987) characterized the situation thusly:

> Educators of minority students are pressured to "do the basics" better and leave innovative educational practices to others. However, a continued imbalance in the educational mandates that guide the education of minorities and of white middle-class children deepens the problem: as schools

serving minority children focus their resources on increasing the use of well-known methods for drilling the basics, they decrease the opportunities for those children to participate in the higher level activities needed to excel in mathematics and science. (pp. 4–5)

The *Standards* (NCTM, 1987) acknowledged a similar danger:

Affluent suburban school districts already provide their students more opportunities and resources for the study of mathematics, and they are likely to be the first to react to the current crisis and recommendation. They are already spending more money on computers and teacher inservice, thus widening further the opportunity gap between affluent suburban students and their poor, urban counterparts. (p. 10)

More of the same simply will not do. Changes in our society, in our economy, and in job opportunities are leading to changes in what mathematics needs to be taught to *all* students, not just to those for whom mathematics education has succeeded. Unfortunately, changing curriculum has not resulted in concerted efforts to change the mathematics that is taught to minorities. The educational experiences of low achieving students—overrepresented by Blacks, Hispanics, Indians, the poor—have been and will continue to be constrained by the press of mastering basics. It would be bitterly ironic if we succeeded in making our low-achieving children computational wizards while their middle class peers developed other, more important competencies. It requires little cynicism to predict that, unless *proactive steps* are taken to ensure that diverse learners are included in the current mathematics education reform movement, the next wave of educational reform will bemoan—as this one so eloquently does—the low achievement of precisely those students who are most in danger of being omitted from today's reforms.

We need to develop strategies not for achieving a better version of what we do today—though we should not ignore what we have learned and accomplished. To achieve today's educational goals, however, is to leave the education of minorities, at best, chasing a target that will have moved. We need to develop strategies that build on the successes we have had and that aim for where the future will be. Research can help develop some strategies in two ways. First, it might suggest alternative ways for practice to proceed. Second, it may cause us to rethink some of the basic assumptions with which we approach current educational practices. In the next section of this chapter, I hope to expand on those themes by discussing how research has served to challenge some of our past views of the mainstream and how it might be used to challenge the same views with respect to diverse learners.

CURRENT RESEARCH AND PRACTICE: THE
NEED TO RETHINK OUR BASIC ASSUMPTIONS

The need to rethink the mathematics education of minorities encompasses at least four conceptual areas: the learner, curriculum, classroom practice, and teacher attitudes.

How We View the Learner

Most of the research involving members of marginalized groups can be characterized as an effort to relate student deficiencies to one another. The view is that, because students from one group do not perform as well as students from another, there must be something deficient or wrong either with the students or with their background experiences. For females, deficiencies have been sought in spatial skills, in affect, or in learned behaviors (Fennema, 1987); for minorities and the poor, in cultural deprivation and disadvantage; and for students from language minority backgrounds, in their limited English proficiency.

Limited English Proficiency. Efforts to explain the mathematical deficiencies of minority language students through appeals to linguistic deficiencies are particularly strong. For example, Mestre (1988) presented a detailed analysis of how Hispanic college students missolve the students-and-professor problem. He argued that their error patterns are qualitatively different from those of monolingual English-speaking students and, hence, that those errors are due to the students' Spanish-speaking backgrounds. Cuevas (1984) has developed a teacher training effort based on mathematical English that bilingual children are hypothesized to be missing. Crandall and her associates (Crandall, Dale, Rhodes, & Spanos, 1987, in press; Spanos, Rhodes, Dale, & Crandall, 1988) have engaged in validating an extensive curriculum based on teaching Limited English Proficiency (LEP) students to analyze the linguistic features of mathematical word problems. Recently, the view that language-based deficiencies cause problems in the learning of mathematics has been extended to the case of students who speak Black English Vernacular (Orr, 1987; Secada, 1988b).

Such efforts legitimate the view of LEP students as deficient, but now they are doubly so. An alternative view might be to consider LEP students as students who are becoming bilingual. From this view, we could draw on two bodies of literature. The first suggests that bilingualism has cognitive advantages tied to language proficiency (see, e.g., Diaz, 1983). The second suggests that children enter school able to solve a broad range of word problems, that the problem-solving strategies that children use are tied to the semantic structures of word problems, and that problem difficulty is a function of logical, semantic, and syntactic structures as well as of the repertoire of strategies at a child's disposal (see Carpenter & Moser, 1983, 1984; Nesher, 1982; Secada, 1988a). Together, this literature suggests that we might use word problems to develop arithmetic competence and that children, as a function of degree of bilingualism, will show varying initial levels of competence in solving such problems. I am currently researching this hypothesis.

Further support for the notion that degree of bilingualism is related to students' performance and learning of mathematics is provided by Duran (1988) and De Avila and his associates (De Avila, 1988; De Avila, Cohen, & Intili, 1981; De Avila & Duncan, 1981). Duran (1988) found that reading proficiency in Spanish, over and above reading proficiency in English, was predictive of performance on a set of logical reasoning tasks administered in English to a group of Puerto Rican adults. Although De Avila and Duncan (1981) did demonstrate a strong relationship between degree of English proficiency and mathematics achievement among various ethnolinguistic groups, later work by De Avila (De Avila, 1988; De Avila et al., 1981) demonstrated that middle school children's participation in cooperative groups while involved in mathematics and science activities is related not only to degree of English proficiency, but also to degree of bilingualism.

Cultural Deprivation. Another view of the minority mathematics learner that needs rethinking is that of cultural deprivation. According to this view, something in the background of the child makes it difficult for him or her to adjust to the demands of schooling. In its most absolute form, this view provides little or no room for interpretations of schooling as a source to the problem; few people really hold it to such an extreme. Yet it is worth noting that cultural deprivation was the basis for the Great Society's education programs.

In place of cultural deprivation, some researchers have proposed the notion of cultural discontinuity, which means that there is a mismatch between what is valued in the child's home culture and what is needed in his or her school. Unfortunately, there have been few analyses that link that mismatch to the learning and teaching of mathematics. I have seen just one, by Lily Wong Fillmore (1987).

Fillmore reviewed research involving diverse cultural styles of child rearing and socialization vis à vis work. Children from traditional Hispanic households are given relatively large tasks to manage—such as setting the table, or helping with cooking and cleaning, or taking care of siblings. Though supervised by adults, children are expected to try such tasks, even if they don't get them right. A "large" task may be too difficult, but with help and over time, the child will get closer and closer to mastery. The task is meaningful: It is well situated within the child's home environment, and it is adultlike. Indeed, mastery is a sign of becoming more and more mature. Chinese children, on the other hand, receive small tasks to master—setting just the silverware and not the whole table, or preventing a sibling from doing just one thing—before moving on to other, more advanced tasks. The cultural belief is that Chinese children should master such small and meaningless (Fillmore's terms) tasks before they can progress to larger, more adultlike and more meaningful work. Finally, traditional American Indian children are expected to observe adults and to assume tasks independently. Moreover, American Indian children do not display their efforts until they feel that they have mastered the tasks.

The praise that children receive also seems to vary. Hispanic parents praise their children for trying hard—after all, the tasks are usually beyond their reach. The contingency is that they do the task better next time. Chinese parents, on the other hand, praise only when the task is perfect, and then praise in moderation. Much more common seems to be criticism of failure; after all, the task was pitched well within the child's reach. American Indian parents acknowledge a child's display of mastery, but mute their praise somewhat to ensure that the child does not get a swollen head.

Fillmore's observations of children from these ethnic groups support her analysis. In one task, first-grade children were told to write as many numbers as they could on a piece of paper. Chinese children competed with themselves and with each other to see who could fit the most numbers on the page. Their writing became smaller and smaller in this competition. Hispanic children wrote normal sized numbers, but really did not make more out of the task than what had been requested—that is, to fill the page with numbers in as systematic a manner as possible. Anyone familiar with first-grade arithmetic would likely agree with Fillmore's observation that, as designed and implemented, it is replete with such small tasks that are easily disposed of and that require very little additional interpretation. This mismatch between children's cultures and arithmetic on how meaningful and large tasks are, on expectations of work and success, and on rewards given as a function of success may be sources of the disparate learning and achievement experienced by many minorities in mathematics.

We cannot deny that students may be deficient in some skills and knowledge. But there is good reason to develop a view of the minority student that is more complex than one based solely on deficiency. Research evidence suggests that there is more proficiency than suspected, and that we might build on that proficiency if we could figure out how to tap it.

Needed Curriculum Reform

As noted earlier, Hispanic and other minority students are overrepresented in compensatory education programs (Cole & Griffin, 1987; Kennedy et al., 1986). Such programs are characterized by their stress on low-level basic skills. Although simple inertia would make efforts to change the focus of such programs difficult, one can find two added views that support such an educational arrangement and, hence, that need to be rethought. The first notion is that of prerequisite knowledge: Before students progress to a given piece of knowledge, they must master the prerequisite skills and knowledge. For example, basic computational skills are thought to precede problem solving and higher order skills. Hence, students in compensatory programs must master basic skills before they can solve problems.

The second view is that mathematics learning is a zero-sum game, and especially so for low-achieving students. According to such a view, we can teach either basic skills or higher order skills, but not both. Given that basic skills are usually thought to be prerequisite to more advanced work, and given the difficulty in teaching those advanced skills anyway, programs end up focusing on basic skills so that low-achieving students at least have something.

Both of these views are being successfully challenged in the case of mainstream students. For example, knowledge of number facts need not preclude arithmetic problem solving; if anything, the relationship seems to be the reverse. Children enter first grade able to solve a wide range of word problems, and they invent strategies for solving both word problems and number–fact combinations. Over time—lasting into third grade for some cases—children replace these strategies with memorized number facts (Carpenter, 1985; Carpenter & Moser, 1983, 1984). Hence, Carpenter (1985) suggested that the teaching of number facts need not preclude arithmetic problem solving.

Moreover, Carpenter, Fennema, Peterson, Chiang, and Loef (1988) presented evidence to suggest that the teaching of number facts is *not* a zero-sum game. Twenty first-grade teachers received instruction of the core findings of the work conducted by Carpenter and Moser (1984). These teachers spent 26% of mathematics class time on number facts, compared to 47% spent by a group of 20 control teachers. In contrast, experimental teachers spent 55% of class time on word problems, compared to 36% spent by controls.

Vis à vis comparisons of *student* performance, on the ITBS test of computation, there were no significant group differences for experimental versus control classes. On a number facts test developed by Carpenter and colleagues (1988), significant group differences favored the experimental group, *that is, those children who spent less time on basic facts, and more on problem solving learned their basic facts better.* In problem solving as measured by the ITBS, on a test of simple word problems,[3] and on a test of advanced word problems,[4] no group differences were found. On tests of complex word problems, which are more difficult than the simple, yet easier than the advanced, word problems, and on an individualized interview measure, group differences favored the experimental group.

More interesting, and potentially more important with respect to the education of low achieving students, are the results of a regression analysis from pre- to post-test on the test of simple word problems. Students in the control group showed the classic pattern of growth in which pretest scores predicted posttest achievement. For the experimental group, however, the regression line was almost horizontal, that is, performance at pretest did *not* predict performance at posttest. One of the most salient goals for compensatory education programs has been to *reduce* the predictive power of early achievement for later success in school (Coleman, 1975). Carpenter and colleagues' results suggest that, by focusing on computational skills to the exclusion of problem solving, compensatory programs may have been exacerbating, rather than reducing, that phenomenon.

Evidence based on the education of minorities is beginning to accumulate to challenge the prerequisite and zero-sum notions of education for this case as well. I am finding that first-grade Hispanic, bilingual children can solve many of the word problems—in both Spanish and English— used by Carpenter and Moser (1984). The combined, math/science program known as *Finding Out/Descubrimiento* has been used successfully in fostering both computational and conceptual development for Hispanic middle-school children (De Avila, 1988; De Avila et al., 1981). Orr (1987) has shown that Black students whose pre-high school mathematics education was based on rote memorization of computational skills can develop problem solving in algebra and geometry through instruction that focuses on the meaning of the problem and the relationship of that meaning to symbolic representations.

A very compelling counter-example to basic skills as prerequisite to successful learning has been provided by Roy (1988). In a Magnet High

---

[3]First-grade children *should* be able to solve *these* particular problems (Carpenter & Moser, 1984).

[4]These were multistep problems, which are beyond the ability of many older children.

School, Black students spend one day per week in field settings where scientific research is conducted, with health care personnel including surgeons, or in some other scientific setting. Students have been successful in science competitions and have gone on to enter scientific fields. By no stretch of the imagination could we claim that students in this program entered with the traditionally accepted prerequisite basic skills to participate in such settings. Not only did they participate, they succeeded.

Classroom Practice

Direct Instruction. There is ample evidence that basic skills can be taught by means of what is known as *direct instruction* or *active teaching*. In mathematics education, the best known form of direct instruction was developed by Good and Grouws (1979; see also, Rosenshine, 1987). Direct instruction is a highly structured delivery system; in Good and Grouws, it includes specified amounts of time for daily review, development, seat work, homework, and special reviews. Results from studies of direct instruction with low-achieving students in mathematics, as well as reading, have consistently reported enhanced student performance.

Typically, suggestions are made for modifying direct instructional approaches based on students' home cultural norms or on their languages. For example, Tikunoff and his colleagues (e.g., Tikunoff, 1983) have developed and validated a model of effective instruction in bilingual settings based on direct instruction, but also including cultural and linguistic considerations:

> In effective instruction, teachers must accomplish four clusters of teaching behaviors. They must: communicate clearly, obtain and maintain the engagement of students, monitor students' progress, and provide immediate feedback to students with regards to their performances. . . . Bilingual instructional mediation is accomplished in three ways: through the use of both [languages] during instructions; through a focus on [dual] language development.) . . during instruction; and through response to and use of cultural cues from the students' native culture. . . . The organization of instruction includes instructional activities through which teachers establish and maintain task demands and institutional demands. (p. 40)

Cole and Griffin (1987) reviewed a series of studies conducted in classrooms with large numbers of American Indian, Hawaiian, and Hispanic students. These studies included the adapting of behavior norms in the classroom to mimic what children expect based on their home cultures.

Research on the development of problem solving, higher order thinking and other mathematics knowledge, however, has not systematically investigated the efficacy of direct instruction. Moreover, Doyle (1983) suggested that higher forms of thinking, what are termed control and executive functions, might not be amenable to direct instruction. Rather, teachers might have to model their own thought processes, to have children discuss how they thought particular tasks through, to maintain ambiguity in assigned tasks in order to force students to think about what they should be doing, and to engage in other forms of indirect instruction.

Student Talk. Having students talk about what they are doing, and why, seems to be a promising instructional strategy. Student self-reports about how problems were solved was a prominent feature of the instruction implemented by the experimental teachers in the Carpenter and colleagues (1988) study reviewed earlier. The success of small-group instructional strategies seems tied, at least in part, to the need for students to talk among themselves (see De Avila's, 1988, description of the classroom processes during the development of *Finding Out/Descubrimiento*). Orr (1987) had her students think aloud while they were solving algebra and geometry problems.

Pimm (1987) discussed two functions that student talk served in the mathematics classroom. First, it forces students to form their thoughts more fully than if they do not speak. Talking requires that students follow norms for communication to ensure that their peers understand them. Second, student talk creates a public record of student thinking. That public record becomes available for scrutiny by others. Insights become available for other students, and misconceptions can be addressed.

If student talk is encouraged in the mathematics classroom, it needs to be on task. Commonly accepted notions of classroom management—such as students working silently at their seats—will need to be reconsidered. Finally, some cultures discourage the correction of one's peers. Hence, teachers might need to engage students through other means; for example, they might make mistakes on purpose to elicit correction and subsequent discussion (Cole & Griffin, 1987).

Cooperative Learning. The use of cooperative learning has shown promise for the development of higher order thinking among children from diverse SES and ethnic backgrounds (De Avila, 1988; Slavin, 1983a, 1983b). The role of the teacher in cooperative learning shifts. From being a dispenser of knowledge and from having to maintain whole class or individualized instruction, the teacher becomes more of a coach who forms groups by assigning students to them,[5] assigns group activities and helps monitor on-task group behaviors, assesses group and individual performance on tasks, and, in general, helps the group's members work with each other.

Care must be taken in the formation and maintenance of cooperative groups. Stratification based on status might take place if some students dominate the group. Cole and Griffin (1987, pp. 32–35) warned that cooperative group learning may result in dominant students' increasing their status at the expense of others. Students must have some idea of how to work cooperatively, and the teacher must act to reinforce norms that support the group. Moreover, in some cases the teacher might need to coach a student to help him or her overcome differential status participation in a cooperative group.

The use of rewards is also contingent on how the group has been organized to perform a task. For example, if focus is on the completion of a single task, it is a simple matter for the group to assign the task to its most able member. In this case, rewards should be based on how each individual in the group performs, and the group must be encouraged to ensure that everyone has achieved mastery. Alternatively, if a task is multifaceted, complex, and requires the completion of subtasks by individual members of the group, then rewards should be based on how the group as a whole performs (Mergendoller & Marchman, 1987, p. 310). In other words, care must be taken to ensure that *each* student learns all of the material. This entails that rewards be based on different task and group contingencies.

Finally, Slavin (in verbal communication) reported that, although low-achieving children do improve their academic achievement under cooperative group arrangements, they do not close the gap between themselves and higher achieving students.

The Zone of Proximal Development.   An intriguing idea for the development of higher order thinking skills is drawn from the work of Vygotsky (1978; Wertsch, 1985). This is the notion of the Zone of Proximal Development, which was defined in translation (Vygotsky, 1978) as "The distance between the actual developmental level as determined by independent problem solving and the level of potential development as determined through problem solving under adult guidance or in collaboration with more capable peers" (p. 86).

The notion is that adults can help a child perform tasks and solve

---

[5]Many believe groups should not be based on ability, unless it is a short term arrangement for a very specific purpose. For example, it would be all right to form a group to reteach material missed on a test when a small group of students need the review.

problems meaningfully by asking questions, directing attention, providing cues, monitoring performance, and, in general, serving as an executive function for the duration of the task. Over time, children come to perform the task in question by themselves. Moreover, they do so by internalizing the roles taken by their adult helpers, and hence, children develop the higher order functions that were performed by the adults (Wertsch, 1985). Bruner (1985) extended this idea to include the notion of scaffolding, by which an adult—or a more capable peer—provides help that is pitched at a level within the child's reach but is removed, bit by bit, as the child comes to master the task in question.

Fennema (in personal communication) provided an example from her observations of a classroom in which Cognitively Guided Instruction (Carpenter et al., 1988) was being implemented. Students in this classroom were all first graders who had been identified as having learning difficulties. The teacher told the children to work on individually assigned problems that could be found in each child's work folder. One boy in particular did not seem enthralled with working the problems. One of his problems went something like this: Your father cooks you 16 pancakes for breakfast. He thinks you might be very hungry, so he makes you 10 more. But you only eat half of them. How many pancakes did you eat?[6]

At first, the child looked to the adult to provide the solution. Instead, she suggested that maybe some counting objects might help. The boy went and got them. Slowly, he counted out 16 counters, and then, 10 more. Becoming increasingly frustrated, he appealed to the adult for the answer. Instead, Fennema asked, "Do you know what one-half is?". Immediately the child responded, "Don't help me anymore." He proceeded to split the 26 into two sets and to count one of them.

It seems unlikely that this child would have solved the problem by himself. At two critical junctures, an adult intervened to provide focus and support. The first was to suggest that he stay on task and get some counters to help him. The second intervention would seem to represent the kind of "scaffolding" referred to by Bruner. The adult could have told the child to split the 26 counters into two sets; instead, she pitched a question at a level where the child had to think a bit. Over time, this scaffolding could be removed.

I am not aware of any systematic research into the notion of Zone of Proximal Development for instruction in mathematics, although Feuerstein (1979, 1980) has based his work on this notion and seems to have had some success in teaching cognitive strategies.

---

[6]This was during April, in a first-grade classroom of children identified as low achievers!

Teachers' Attitudes and Beliefs About Students

That teacher expectancies are related to student achievement is a well-established fact (Dusek, 1985). The literature, folklore, and personal experiences provide many examples of how teachers communicate expectations to their students about success or failure and its causes in mathematics. Moreover, we even have some sense of how different formats for providing information about students can lead to expectations: Written information about student social class and verbal information about race elicit stereotypical expectations from teachers about their students (Baron, Tom, & Cooper, 1985).

Teachers have attended numerous workshops intended to combat stereotyping of students. These have had varying degrees of success. For example, Fennema, Wolleat, Pedro, and Becker (1981) conducted a comprehensive intervention study, which included inservice for mathematics teachers about discrimination of girls in classrooms. And male teachers' attitudes did show some improvement. Yet Grant and Secada (in press) have found few research studies on this topic, and fewer still that could claim success. Sanders (1989) provided one possible reason:

> In the heyday of schools' attention to the sex equity issue in the mid- to late 70s, many sex equity trainers fell into the new convert trap: our passion and our anger at the injustices came through clearly to the teachers who were required to attend these in-service sessions. With hindsight, the result was predictable. Since no one likes to be yelled at or blamed for oppressing poor defenseless little girls, teachers who had been neutral about sex equity distanced themselves from it, and teachers who had been actively sexist found their resentment justification for being so. (p. 163)

A difference between the Fennema group (1981) effort and those alluded to by Sanders is that, in the former, research evidence linking mathematics course taking to achievement, and linking attitudes to course taking, was presented to participants. Moreover, Fennema (in personal communication) has noted that teachers who received Cognitively Guided Instruction training (Carpenter et al., 1988) have engaged in fewer gender-based stereotypical behaviors than teachers who did not. The question is: Why?

Stereotyping may serve a function for initial classroom management and for teachers to make initial pedagogic decisions. It is an article of faith that we should teach based on what children know and can do. Yet, at the start and through any school year, teachers must organize their classrooms by communicating standards of behavior to students; they must enforce those norms and plan and implement instruction; and they must attend to the myriad details that go into the life of a classroom (Doyle, 1985; Emmer, 1987). It may be that teachers make judgments about students as a way of organizing their classrooms initially. They use race, gender, social class, ethnicity, or language background as an initial proxy for student ability—after all, they have been bombarded with information that links these characteristics to student achievement in mathematics, reading, and other areas. At first, the teacher simply does not have the time to obtain evidence from each student concerning his or her level of functioning. By the time the teacher has had time to obtain direct information about each student, the expectations of behavior and achievement have already been communicated, and the students act to fulfill them.

If this analysis is correct, then we need to rethink teachers' beliefs and attitudes about their students. It is not enough to exhort them to stop being sexist or racist. We must provide them with ways of gaining direct information about student competence earlier during the school year. The Carpenter group (1988) workshop did this for teachers.

Moreover, if mathematical problem solving is considered to require higher order thinking, which we think is best taught through a variety of strategies, then we should consider that teaching itself requires no less advanced forms of thinking. Our training of mathematics teachers should take account of that fact as well.

DISCUSSION

In the first sections of this chapter, I tried to describe the current state of affairs regarding the mathematics education of diverse students. I purposely called these "indicators," in an effort to resist any attempt to assign cause or to lay blame. Rather, those data were meant to provide a descriptive lay of the land.

In the second section, I sketched out, in broad strokes, what the future might hold in terms of social and economic changes that would influence what mathematics should be taught in the schools. I argued that it is to the future that we should target efforts at improving the education of diverse learners.

In the third section, I presented some needed research that might be used for creating a vision of the possible. I selected lines of work that seem promising, but also I tried to present speculation and caveats as I thought necessary. Throughout this chapter, I have tried to communicate a sense of challenge that is tied to a real danger that reform will omit an increasingly large segment of our population. Enlightened self-interest as tied to our social, economic, and democratic institutions would argue that we cannot fail to meet this challenge. Equity argues that our failure to do so would be a miscarriage of justice. Orr (1987) described, in rather bleak terms, how many mathematics teachers get overwhelmed by their inability to teach some of their students:

> I hear more and more about situations where teachers, understandably discouraged with high failure rates, gradually, and more often than not unconsciously, modify what they do and require. It is painful to face unremitting large numbers of students who do not understand and not to be able to get them to understand; good teachers blame themselves and try again and again. . . . The current pressures are, perhaps understandably, resulting in focus on the memorizable, the replicable: in math, computation becomes the first priority. (pp. 201–202)

Yet, Orr also described how she and her staff have tried to meet those challenges:

> We chose to focus first on breaking the habit of depending on patterns. . . . Not only did these students become aware of their own abilities as they became involved in figuring out what to do when they worked with these irregular number systems, but their teachers in other courses, whom we asked to tackle the same problems the students were successfully handling, discovered, some with near disbelief, that the students were far more capable than had previously been apparent. When this happens the notion that higher expectations will produce the sought-after improvement in performance becomes more than just a good idea: teachers really do expect more of these students because they really believe the students can do more. (pp. 206–208)

I cannot express the distinction between a challenge and an excuse any more eloquently than did Orr. It is imperative that we begin to draw that distinction for ourselves, as researchers, teachers, and administrators. As much needed work in this area begins, it is important to realize that there are no magic cures to the problems that beset the mathematics education of diverse student populations. Their educational status has suffered from neglect—malign as well as benign. As we think about cognitive instruction, we should think broadly enough to encompass *all* our students.

ACKNOWLEDGMENT

The Upper Great Lakes Multifunctional Resource Center is operated under contract no. 300860050 with the U.S. Department of Education, Office of Bilingual Education and Minority Language Affairs, and also is supported by the Wisconsin Center for Education Research, School of

Education, University of Wisconsin—Madison. Findings, opinions, and recommendations in this chapter are the author's and do not reflect the official positions of either OBEMLA or WCER.

An earlier version of this chapter was presented at the Symposium sponsored by the Southwest Center for Educational Equity: Equity Issues in Mathematics and Science Achievement, May 27–28, 1988, Culver City, California. Reprinted by permission of ARC Associates.

REFERENCES

Anick, C. M., Carpenter, T. P., & Smith, C. (1981). Minorities and mathematics: Results from the National Assessment of Educational Progress. *Mathematics Teacher, 73,* 560–566.

Arias, M. B. (1986). The context of education for Hispanic students: An overview. *American Journal of Education, 95*(1), 26–57.

Baron, R. M., Tom, D. Y. H., & Cooper, H. M. (1985). Social class, race and teacher expectations. In J. B. Dusek (Ed.), *Teacher expectancies* (pp. 251–269). Hillsdale, NJ: Lawrence Erlbaum Associates.

Bruner, J. (1985). Vygotsky: A historical and conceptual perspective. In J. V. Wertsch (Ed.), *Culture, communication and cognition: Vygotskian perspectives* (pp. 21–34). London: Cambridge University Press.

California Department of Education. (1986). *California dropouts* (A status report). Sacramento: Author.

Carpenter, T. P. (1985). Learning to add and subtract: An exercise in problem solving. In E. A. Silver (Ed.), *Teaching and learning mathematical problem solving: Multiple research perspectives* (pp. 17–40). Hillsdale, NJ: Lawrence Erlbaum Associates.

Carpenter, T. P., Fennema, E., Peterson, P. L., Chiang, C., & Loef, M. (1988, April). *Using knowledge of children's mathematical thinking in classroom teaching: An experimental study.* Paper presented at the annual meeting of the American Educational Research Association, New Orleans.

Carpenter, T. P., & Moser, J. M. (1983). The acquisition of addition and subtraction concepts. In R. Lesh & M. Landau (Eds.), *The acquisition of mathematical concepts and processes* (pp. 7–44). New York: Academic Press.

Carpenter, T. P., & Moser, J. M. (1984). The acquisition of addition and subtraction. *Journal for Research in Mathematics Education, 15,* 179–202.

Center for Education Statistics. (1987a). *The condition of education.* Washington, DC: Government Printing Office.

Center for Education Statistics. (1987b). *Digest of education statistics.* Washington, DC: Government Printing Office.

Cole, M., & Griffin, P. (Eds.). (1987). *Contextual factors in education: Improving science and mathematics education for minorities and women.* Madison: Wisconsin Center for Education Research, University of Wisconsin—Madison.

Coleman, J. (1975). What is meant by an "equal educational opportunity"? *Oxford Review of Education, 1*(1), 27–29.

Congressional Budget Office. (1987, August). *Educational achievement: Explanation and implications of recent trends.* Washington, DC: Government Printing Office.

Cornbleth, C. (1987). The persistence of myth in curriculum discourse. In T. A. Romberg & D. M. Stewart (Eds.), *The monitoring of school mathematics: Background papers: Vol. 3. Teaching and future directions.* (chapter 25, pp. 27–58). Madison: Wisconsin Center for Education Research, University of Wisconsin—Madison.

Crandall, J., Dale, T. C., Rhodes, N. C., & Spanos, G. (1987). *English language skills for basic algebra.* Englewood Cliffs: Prentice-Hall.

Crandall, J., Dale, T. C., Rhodes, N. C., & Spanos, G. (in press). The language of mathematics: The English barrier. *Proceedings of the 1985 Delaware Symposium on Language Studies* (VII). Newark: University of Delaware Press.

Crowley, M. F. (1986, November). *Minorities in science and engineering.* Paper presented at the National Science Foundation Workshop on Minorities in Science and Engineering, Washington, DC.

Cuevas, G. (1984). Mathematical learning in English as a second language. *Journal for Research in Mathematics Education, 15,* 134–144.

De Avila, E. A. (1988). Bilingualism, cognitive function, and language minority group membership. In R. R. Cocking & J. P. Mestre (Eds.), *Linguistic and cultural influences on learning mathematics* (pp. 101–121). Hillsdale, NJ: Lawrence Erlbaum Associates.

De Avila, E. A., Cohen, E. G., & Intili, J. K. (1981, August). *Multicultural improvement of cognitive abilities* (Final report, Contract no. 9372). Sacramento: California Department of Education.

De Avila, E. A., & Duncan, S. E. (1981). *A convergent approach to oral language assessment: Theoretical and technical specification on the Language Assessment Scales (LAS) Form A* (Stock 621). San Rafael, CA: Linguametrics Group.

Diaz, R. M. (1983). Thought and two languages: The impact of bilingualism on cognitive development. *Review of Research in Education, 10,* 23–54.

Dix, L. S. (Ed.). (1987). *Minorities: Their under-representation and career differentials in science and engineering* (Proceedings of a workshop). Washington, DC: National Academy Press.

Dossey, J. A., Mullis, I. V. S., Lindquist, M. M., & Chambers, D. L. (1988). *The mathematics report card: Are we measuring up?* (Trends and achievement based on the 1986 National Assessment, Report no. 17-M-01). Princeton, NJ: National Assessment of Educational Progress, Educational Testing Service.

Doyle, W. (1983). Academic work. *Review of Educational Research, 53,* 159–199.

Doyle, W. (1986). Classroom management. In M. C. Wittrock (Ed.), *Handbook of research on teaching* (pp. 392–431). New York: Macmillan.

Duran, R. P. (1983). *Hispanics' education and background* (Predictors of college achievement). New York: College Entrance Examination Board.

Duran, R. P. (1988). Bilinguals' logical reasoning aptitude: A construct validity study. In R. R. Cocking & J. P. Mestre (Eds.), *Linguistic and cultural influences on learning mathematics* (pp. 241–258). Hillsdale, NJ: Lawrence Erlbaum Associates.

Dusek, J. B. (Ed.). (1985). *Teacher expectancies.* Hillsdale, NJ: Lawrence Erlbaum Associates.

Emmer, E. T. (1987). Classroom management and discipline. In V. Richardson-Koehler (Ed.), *Educators' handbook: A research perspective* (pp. 233–258). New York: Longman.

Espinosa, R., & Ochoa, A. (1986). Concentration of California Hispanic students in schools with low achievement: A research note. *American Journal of Education, 95*(1), 77–95.

Fennema, E. (1984). Girls, women and mathematics. In E. Fennema & M. J. Ayer (Eds.), *Women and education: Equity or equality?* (pp. 137–164). Berkeley: McCutchan.

Fennema, E. (1987). Sex-related differences in education: Myths, realities, and interventions. In V. Richardson-Koehler (Ed.), *Educators' handbook: A research perspective* (pp. 329–347). New York: Longman.

Fennema, E., & Meyer, M. R. (1989). Gender, equity, and mathematics. In W. G. Secada (Ed.), *Equity in education* (pp. 146–157). London: Falmer Press.

Fennema, E., Wolleat, P. L., Pedro, J. D., & Becker, A. D. (1981). Increasing women's participation in mathematics: An intervention study. *Journal for Research in Mathematics Education, 12*(1), 3–14.

Feuerstein, R. (1979). *The dynamic assessment of retarded performers: The learning potential assessment device, theory, instruments, and techniques.* Baltimore, MD: University Park Press.

Feuerstein, R. (1980). *Instrumental enrichment: An intervention program for cognitive modifiability*. Baltimore, MD: University Park Press.

Fillmore, L. W. (1987, September 24). *Is effective teaching equally effective across diverse cultural learning styles?* Presentation made at the Upper Great Lakes Multifunctional Resource Center, Wisconsin Center for Education Research, University of Wisconsin—Madison.

Good, T. L., & Grouws, D. A. (1979). The Missouri mathematics effectiveness project: An experimental study in fourth-grade classrooms. *Journal of Educational Psychology, 71*, 355–362.

Grant, C. A., & Secada, W. G. (in press). *Preparing teachers for diversity*. In W. R. Houston, M. Haberman, & J. P. Sikula (Eds.), *Handbook of research on teacher education*. New York: Macmillan.

Grant, C. A., & Sleeter, C. E. (1986a). Race, class, and gender effects in education: An argument for integrative analysis. *Review of Educational Research, 56*(2), 195–211.

Grant, C. A., & Sleeter, C. E. (1986b). Educational equity: Education that is multicultural and social reconstructionist. *Journal of Educational Equity and Leadership, 6*, 105–118.

Hispanic Policy Development Project. (1988). *Closing the gap for U.S. Hispanic youth: Public/private strategies*. Washington, DC: Author.

Hodgkinson, H. L. (1985, June). *All one system: Demographics of education, kindergarten through graduate school*. Washington, DC: Institute for Educational Leadership.

Johnston, W. B., & Packer, A. E. (1987, June). *Workforce 2000: Work and workers for the twenty-first century*. Indianapolis: Hudson Institute.

Jones, L. V., Burton, N. W., & Davenport, E. C. (1984). Monitoring the mathematics achievement of Black students. *Journal for Research in Mathematics Education, 15*(2), 154–164.

Kennedy, M. M., Jung, R. K., & Orland, M. E. (1986, January). *Poverty, achievement and the distribution of compensatory education services* (An interim report from the National Assessment of Chapter 1, OERI). Washington, DC: Government Printing Office.

Leggon, C. B. (1987). Minority under-representation in science and engineering graduate education and careers: A critique. In L. S. Dix (Ed.), *Minorities: Their underrepresentation and career differentials in science and engineering* (Proceedings of a workshop, pp. 151–157). Washington, DC: National Academy Press.

Lockheed, M. E., Thorpe, M., Brooks-Gunn, J., Casserly, P., & McAloon, A. (1985). *Sex & ethnic differences in middle school mathematics, science and computer science: What do we know?* (A report submitted to The Ford Foundation). Princeton, NJ: Educational Testing Service.

MacCorquodale, P. (1988). Mexican-American women and mathematics: Participation, aspirations, and achievement. In R. R. Cocking & J. P. Mestre (Eds.), *Linguistic and cultural influences on learning mathematics* (pp. 137–160). Hillsdale, NJ: Lawrence Erlbaum Associates.

Matthews, W., Carpenter, T. P., Lindquist, M. M., & Silver, E. A. (1984). The third national assessment: Minorities and mathematics. *Journal for Research in Mathematics Education, 15*(2), 165–171.

McKnight, C. C., Crosswhite, F. J., Dossey, J. A., Kifer, E., Swafford, J. O., Travers, K. J., & Cooney, T. J. (1987). *The underachieving curriculum: Assessing U.S. school mathematics from an international perspective*. Champaign, IL: Stipes.

McLeod, D. B. (1988, May). *Research on learning and instruction in mathematics: The role of affect*. Paper presented at the First Wisconsin Symposium for Research on Teaching and Learning Mathematics, sponsored by the National Center for Research in Mathematical Sciences Education, Wisconsin Center for Education Research, University of Wisconsin—Madison.

Mergendoller, J. R., & Marchman, V. A. (1987). Friends and associates. In V. Richardson-Koehler (Eds.), *Educator's handbook: A research perspective* (pp. 297–328). New York: Longman.

Mestre, J. (1988). The role of language comprehension in mathematics problem solving. In R. R. Cocking, & J. P. Mestre (Eds.), *Linguistic and cultural influences on learning mathematics* (pp. 201–220). Hillsdale, NJ: Lawrence Erlbaum Associates.

Myers, D. E., & Milne, A. M. (1988). Effects of home language and primary language on mathematics achievement. In R. R. Cocking & J. P. Mestre (Eds.), *Linguistic and cultural influences on learning mathematics* (pp. 259–293). Hillsdale, NJ: Lawrence Erlbaum Associates.

National Alliance for Business. (1986a). *Employment policies: Looking to the year 2000.* Washington, DC: Author.

National Alliance for Business. (1986b). *Youth: 2000. A call to action* (Report to a National Leadership Meeting, June 10, 1986. Washington, DC). Washington, DC: Author.

National Council of Teachers of Mathematics, Commission on Standards for School Mathematics. (1987). *Curriculum and evaluation standards for school mathematics* (Working draft). Reston, VA: Author.

National Science Foundation (1986, January). *Women and minorities in science and engineering* (Report no. NSF-86-301). Washington, DC: Author.

Nesher, P. (1982). Levels of description in the analysis of addition and subtraction. In T. P. Carpenter, J. M. Moser, & T. A. Romberg (Eds.), *Addition and subtraction: A cognitive perspective.* Hillsdale, NJ: Lawrence Erlbaum Associates.

Nielsen, F., & Fernandez, R. M. (1981). *Hispanic students in American high schools: Background characteristics and achievement* (Contractor report to the National Center for Education Statistics). Washington, DC: Government Printing Office.

Oakes, J. (1985). *Keeping track: How schools structure inequality.* New Haven, CT: Yale University Press.

Oakes, J. (1987). *Opportunities, achievement, and choice: Issues in the participation of women, minorities and the disabled in science* (Paper prepared for the National Science Foundation). Santa Monica, CA: Rand.

Oakes, J. (in press). The distribution of excellence. Indicators of equity in precollege mathematics, science and technology education. In R. Shavelson, L. McDonnell, & J. Oakes (Eds.), *Indicators of math & science education: A source book.* Santa Monica, CA: The Rand Corporation.

O'Malley, J. M. (1981). *Children's English services study: Language minority children with limited English proficiency in the United States.* Rosslyn, VA: National Clearinghouse for Bilingual Education, InterAmerica Research Associates.

Orr, E. W. (1987). *Twice as less: Black English and the performance of black students in mathematics and science.* New York: Basic Books.

Oxford-Carpenter, R., Pol, L., Gendell, M., & Peng, S. (1984). *Demographic projections of non-English-background and limited-English-proficient persons in the United States to the year 2000 by state, age, and language group.* Rosslyn, VA: National Clearinghouse for Bilingual Education, InterAmerica Research Associates.

Pimm, D. (1987). *Speaking mathematically.* New York: Routledge and Kegan Paul.

Reyes, L. H. (1984). Affective variables and mathematics education. *The Elementary School Journal, 84*(5), 558–581.

Rock, D. A., Ekstrom, R. B., Goertz, M. E., & Pollack, J. (1986). *Study of excellence in high school education: Longitudinal study, 1980–82 final report* (Contractor report to OERI, Center for Statistics). Washington, DC: Government Printing Office.

Romberg, T. A., & Smith, M. S. (1987). The monitoring of school mathematics. In T. A. Romberg & D. M. Stewart (Eds.), *The monitoring of school mathematics: Background papers: Vol. 1. The monitoring project and school mathematics* (chapter 1, pp. 3–19). Wisconsin Center for Education Research, University of Wisconsin—Madison.

Romberg, T. A., & Stewart, D. M. (1987, March). *The monitoring of school mathematics: Background papers* (3 vols.). Madison: Wisconsin Center for Education Research, University of Wisconsin—Madison.

Romberg, T. A., & Zarinnia, A. (1987). Consequences of the new world view to assessment of students' knowledge of mathematics. In T. A. Romberg & D. M. Stewart (Eds.), *The monitoring of school mathematics: Background papers: vol. 2. Implications from psychology: Outcomes of instruction* (chapter 18, pp. 153–201). Madison: Wisconsin Center for Education Research, University of Wisconsin—Madison.

Rosenshine, B. V. (1987). Explicit teaching. In D. C. Berlinger & B. V. Rosenshine (Eds.), *Talk to teachers* (pp. 75–92). New York: Random House.

Roy, E. (1988, May). *King/Drew Medical Magnet High School.* Presentation at the Symposium: Equity Issues in Mathematics and Science Achievement, sponsored by the Southwest Center for Educational Equity, Culver City, CA.

Sanders, J. (1989). Equity and technology in education: An applied researcher talks to the theoreticians. In W. G. Secada (Ed.), *Equity in education* (pp. 158–179). London: Falmer.

Secada, W. G. (1988a, May). *Is equity served when we omit student diversity from cognitivist research on learning and teaching of mathematics?* Paper presented at the First Wisconsin Symposium for Research on Teaching and Learning Mathematics, sponsored by the National Center for Research in Mathematical Sciences Education, Wisconsin Center for Education Research, University of Wisconsin-Madison.

Secada, W. G. (1988b). Watching our language [Narrative review of *Twice as less* by Eleanor Wilson Orr and *Speaking mathematically* by David Pimm]. *Journal for Research in Mathematics Education, 19*(4), 362–366.

Slavin, R. E. (1983a). *Cooperative learning.* White Plains, NY: Longman.

Slavin, R. E. (1983b). When does cooperative learning increase student achievement? *Psychological Bulletin, 94,* 429–445.

Spanos, G., Rhodes, N. C., Dale, T. C., & Crandall, J. (1988). Linguistic features of mathematical problem solving: Insights and applications. In R. R. Cocking & J. P. Mestre (Eds.), *Linguistic and cultural influences on learning mathematics* (pp. 221–240). Hillsdale, NJ: Lawrence Erlbaum Associates.

Steinberg, L., Blinde, P. L., & Chan, K. S. (1984). Dropping out among language minority youth. *Review of Educational Research, 54,* 113–134.

Thomas, G. E. (1986). *The access and success of Blacks and Hispanics in U.S. graduate and professional education* (A working paper prepared for Office of Scientific and Engineering Personnel, National Research Council). Washington, DC: National Academy Press.

Tikunoff, W. J. (Ed.). (1983, March). *Teaching in successful bilingual instructional setting* (Part I of the study report, Vol. IV, Document SBIF-81-R.6-IV). San Francisco, CA: Far West Laboratory for Educational Research and Development.

U.S. Bureau of the Census, Gregory Spencer. (1986). *Projections of Hispanic population: 1983 to 2080* (Current population reports, Series P-25, No. 995). Washington, DC: Government Printing Office.

Vygotsky, L. S. (1978). *Mind in society* (Edited by M. Cole et al.). Cambridge, MA: Harvard University Press.

Wertsch, J. V. (Ed.). (1985). *Culture, communication and cognition: Vygotskian perspectives.* London: Cambridge University Press.

West, J., Miller, W., & Diodato, L. (1985, March). *An analysis of course-taking patterns in secondary school as related to student characteristics* (Contractor report to the National Center for Education Statistics). Washington, DC: Government Printing Office.

Zarinnia, E. A., & Romberg, T. A. (1987). A new world view and its impact on school mathematics. In T. A. Romberg & D. M. Stewart (Eds.), *The monitoring of school mathematics: Background papers: Vol. 1. The monitoring project and mathematics curriculum* (chapter 2, pp. 21–61). Madison: Wisconsin Center for Education Research, University of Wisconsin—Madison.

Exploring the Complexity of Language and Learning in Classroom Contexts

Judith L. Green
Rebecca M. Kantor
Theresa Rogers
The Ohio State University

In the last two decades, an extensive body of literature has developed about language learning and, to a lesser extent, the influence of language on learning. This body of knowledge reflects an international commitment to the understanding of language learning with a special focus on school settings. Drawing on work in language-related disciplines, such as anthropology, linguistics, literary theory, psychology, and sociology, educators concerned with language in educational settings have provided clear insights into the ways in which children learn language and use language to learn.

What is unique about this body of scholarship is that it has led to changes in curriculum simultaneously with the generation of the knowledge base. Thus, theory and practice have been, and will continue to be, inextricably linked for those working in the area of language and schooling. This is because the work on language and schooling has been a shared enterprise in two senses: First, teachers, curriculum developers, researchers, and policy makers share a common body of knowledge on which to base their work; and second, those involved in the enterprise often share each others' roles. For example, teachers are often researchers of student learning or classroom practice while they are also developing curriculum. Researchers are often involved in curriculum development as they engage in collaborative research with teachers. What joins these people and makes their roles interactive is more than just a concern for language; it is a concern for learning in educational settings.

What we hope to do in this chapter is to locate our perspective within the conversation of this community of educators. To do this, we explore how our perspective builds on the extant knowledge about language and learning and suggest how it might extend the conversation.

EXTENDING THE BOUNDARIES OF THE CONVERSATION

The conversation that currently exists about language and learning can be characterized in different ways, because members of the community vary in the questions they ask, the theories they draw on, and thus, the way they go about research and practice. The major themes of the conversation to date are best captured by Halliday (1982). His argument is that children learn language, learn about language, and learn through language. The first, he argued, happens naturally as part of the everyday interactions of children with significant others in their various environments. The second is the focus of the school, where language is viewed primarily as an object of study. The third reflects a social-semiotic perspective of language in which language is related to the social structure of the learning context, including the type of lesson or event, the social relationships, the patterns of interaction, and the purposes and requirements of the event. It is this latter perspective that nearly reflects the complex relationship between the social actions of teachers and students and what is learned from participating in such actions.

This characterization of children's language experiences can also be used to characterize the areas of research on language and learning. That is, researchers have focused on one of these themes: language learning, learning about language as an object, or learning through language. And although researchers have acknowledged the interrelatedness of these themes, they have tended to focus primarily on one. In this chapter, we attempt to develop a perspective that embeds the study of language and learning in the study of social action; that is, we view language as a social process embedded in and influenced by everyday social life. This perspective draws on work in interactive sociolinguists, ethnography of communication in educational settings, ethnomethodology, and social semiotics and demonstrates that, rather than simply co-occurring, the various language themes mentioned previously are fundamentally interconnected. From this perspective, it becomes clear that to consider language without considering how it contributes to and is influenced by everyday life is to decontextualize it and to ignore the situated and interpretive nature of language in use.

Consider the following example of language in use. The simple word "okay" is often heard in conversation. However, just what this term means depends on the situation in which it occurs, how it is delivered, how it functions, the role relationships of participants, and the ways in which they interpret its meaning as reflected in their actions. For example, okay can be used to confirm a date with someone or to provide feedback about the accuracy of an answer. Both of these uses are confirmations, but they serve different purposes. The difference in purpose becomes visible when the role relationships of the participants are considered. In the first instance, the people may be friends, and thus, okay is a signal that they have agreed to meet at a particular time. It said in a rising tone, it functions as a request for confirmation. In classrooms, though it might serve these two functions, the more common use of okay is its confirming function; that is, okay provides feedback about the accuracy of a student's response. This function is primarily the domain of the teacher, for it would not be appropriate in most classrooms for students to confirm a teacher's response.

Okay can also serve a variety of other functions (Green & Weade, 1985). In classrooms, okay can serve a management function, as in the case of the teacher who says okay in a public voice to signal the need for the group to quiet down and to refocus on the task. The delivery and placement of the stress, as well as the placement of the item in the stream of activity, are the cues that contextualize this use (cf. Gumperz, 1984). Okay can also be used to hold the speaker's place. If the teacher is talking and then pauses and looks around, he or she may also use okay to signal to the students that he or she still has the floor, wants students to "hold on for a minute", and is going to continue telling them something. Teachers also use okay as a marker or "frame" (Sinclair & Coulthard, 1975) that signals, "Listen carefully. I am going to say something important.", as in "Okay, now who can tell me what to do next?".

Okay can also be used as a signal for change of turns, as in "Okay, Rebecca." This latter uses co-occurs with a visual scan of the reading group, with a pattern of turn distribution that involves one turn per student in a random fashion, with an intonational contour that elongates both the "o" and the "a," with a rising tone at the end of the word, and with a staccato delivery of the person's name. It can also be used as a strategy to keep the conversation going (backchanneling) and to signal the listener's attentiveness. In this instance, the listener inserts okay into the stream of conversation in a voice that is quiet and encouraging but does not interrupt the speaker's turn.

Thus, what appears to be a simple and somewhat innocuous lexical item on the surface is, in fact, an important and complex conversational device as well as a lexical item. Just what okay means can only be determined by situating it in the flow of conversation, by considering the nature of the event, by examining the relationships and roles of the participants, by listening to its delivery, and by seeing how the people are responding to and interpreting its use. Whether the okay becomes a shorthand way of signaling a routine (e.g., clean up; get quiet) in a recurrent event (e.g., reading group; nap time) can only be determined by examining when it occurs, with whom, under what conditions, for what purposes, and with what expected outcomes (cf. Hymes, 1974). The meaning of any word or "bit of language" depends on its use (Gumperz, 1984). Although the example focused on a single word, similar arguments can be made for longer stretches of discourse and for recurrent types of discourse events.

If we return now to the distinctions about learning language, learning about language, and learning through language, the complexity of the task for the learner becomes self-evident. Children must learn when to use the word, the multiple meanings that it can have, how to use it to accomplish particular aspects of conversational participation, how to interpret its use by others, and so forth.

Schooling adds to the complexity of the task facing children, because they may need to invoke the various functions of the term in a written narrative in subtle ways. Although children may extract the functions of the term from the oral language context, the use of it in written form may require studying this type of lexical item and its functions in a formal language sense, in which language becomes the object of examination. Thus, whereas the latter is a marked event that is especially constructed for instructional purposes, the other dimensions of language learning are not overtly taught but are left to the student to extract from the ongoing flow of conversation that is part of the daily life in classrooms and beyond.

The preceding discussion demonstrates the need to locate language in the stream of everyday life and explore its influence on both learning and participation in this life. Therefore, in the remainder of this chapter, we construct a conceptual framework for considering the role and place of language in the flow of everyday social life that will make visible the complex relationships between language and learning.

LANGUAGE IN THE FLOW OF EVERYDAY LIFE

We argue that the framework we present in the following sections can be applied to any social situation; however, because we are ultimately interested in addressing the issues of language and learning in school, we focus on language in the special lifeworld of classrooms. Our approach is based, to a large extent, on an understanding of social life from three complementary perspectives: an anthropological view of culture (Geertz, 1973; 1983; Goodenough, 1971; Hymes, 1982; Spradley, 1980); an interactive sociolinguistic conceptualization of face-to-face interaction (Erickson & Shultz, 1981; Gumperz, 1984, 1986; Gumperz & Hymes, 1972; Hymes, 1974), and a sociological perspective on the social accomplishment of everyday life (Garfinkel, 1967; Goffman, 1981; Heap, 1988; Mehan, 1979; Mehan & Wood, 1975). The first two have been used extensively in our work on communication in classrooms to date; the contributions of the latter to understanding the accomplishment of classroom life and its influence on learning are currently being explored. Thus, the conceptualization that follows should be viewed as evolving, and not as complete or static.[1]

UNDERSTANDING SCHOOL AS A SOCIAL SETTING: THE CONSTRUCTED NATURE OF CLASSROOM LIFE

Before we can understand the relationship between language and learning in the school setting, we must understand school as more than a setting or mere context for language use and language learning. We must understand school as a social setting, where people construct and conduct daily life together. Once we understand the nature of schools— or, more precisely, classrooms—as social systems, we can locate the place, role, and influence of language on what occurs there and the outcomes or products of such life. We argue that, without this step, we cannot know whether the language that was produced and observed is a result of the student's ability or an artifact of the social expectations for participating in the daily life of the classroom. Thus, we are arguing that to ignore the patterned ways of "doing life" in classrooms is analogous to decontextualizing print in the study of literacy.

The classroom, before students and teachers enter it, is simply a room in a place called school. Knowing that it is a room in a school marks it in our culture as a room with special purposes. This common cultural knowledge also leads to expectations about: the types of materials that will be there (artifacts); the roles and relationships, and rights and obligations, of the members of the classroom (the actors); the ways in which time will be scheduled (the rituals and routines); the ways in which space will be organized; the types of events that can and will occur; and the

---

[1]In fact, we recently have found that work in other areas (e.g., information processing, cognitive development, literary theory, text analysis, and social theory) will need to be incorporated if we are to understand the relationship of the social and the task demands of school in the construction of meaning (Green & Harker, 1988) and, ultimately, of knowledge.

types of outcomes that will be generated (Spradley, 1980). In other words, because we are members of a group with a common culture, a group that uses a formal institution for schooling, we have expectations about who can do what with whom, when, where, under what conditions, for what purposes, and with what outcomes (Hymes, 1974; Green, 1983).

However, although these are common cultural themes within schooling, they do not predict the specific nature of life in individual classrooms or even of groups within the classroom. To be able to interpret what occurs within any given classroom requires an understanding of that classroom as a "mini" society with norms and expectations, rights and obligations, and roles and relationships for its members. In other words, a classroom must be conceived of as a social system in which life is constructed over time by members interacting with and building on each other's actions, intentions, and messages (Gumperz, 1981). Such life becomes patterned over time as routines and rituals develop, events recur, norms become established, and a common set of expectations and common language develops for "doing life" in classrooms.

This patterned way of being in a social group is referred to in cognitive anthropology as the "culture" of the group (Goodenough, 1971; Spradley, 1980). From this perspective, the culture of each classroom is constructed by participants as they work together to meet the expected goals of schooling. This perspective on classroom culture does not negate the existence of larger social groups that have their own culture (e.g., the school, the community, the nation) or social groups that transcend the classroom and school (e.g., the peer group; the family). Further, it assumes that individuals within the classroom society are also simultaneously members of these other social groups, each of which has its own ways of "doing life." Thus, participation in classrooms, both verbally and nonverbally, is influenced not only by what students learn to expect and do in that setting but also by the expectations they bring from other settings.

In addition, schooling involves more than life in a single classroom. During their educational careers, students will be members of a wide variety of classrooms, each with its own norms and expectations, rights and obligations, and roles and relationships for participating and demonstrating knowledge in and through language and social actions. Thus, students bring to each new classroom sets of expectations for participating, demonstrating group membership, and interpreting life. These expectations reflect the accumulation of knowledge from each of their previous experiences, in and out of schools. This knowledge, when joined with the knowledge from other aspects of daily life, forms a frame of reference (Heap, 1980; Goffman, 1974, 1981; Green, 1983; Mehan, 1979; Tannen, 1979) that students use to perceive, interpret, contribute, and orient to the ordinary aspects of the social world in the face-to-face situation.

By viewing members as living within co-occurring, and often embedded, social groups or lifeworlds, we are arguing that there are multiple sets of cultural patterns: cultural patterns constructed in the local social world of the classroom; and cultural patterns brought to this world from "outside" experiences and group memberships. Thus, we must consider the "inside" culture of the classroom and the cultural patterns of the "outside" world as interacting and providing resources for the students. If we acknowledge the coexistence of different cultural patterns within the frame of reference of an individual, then we can better understand why, at times, an individual does not appear to act appropriately or why "breakdowns" (frame clashes) in events and interpretations occur (Mehan, 1979; Green, 1983). From this perspective, then, culture in classrooms is not a predictable or given entity. It is a dynamic, unfolding, constructed product of the patterned ways of perceiving, believing, acting, and evaluating that develop over time (cf. Goodenough, 1971) in that classroom.

The emphasis here is on the constructed nature of the classroom culture as opposed to the view of *Culture* as transmitted. Culture in the latter sense suggests an object that can be acquired directly from others. Culture in the former sense suggests that culture is reflected in the norms and expectations for the conduct of everyday life and influences what can and will occur verbally and nonverbally in the face-to-face interactions of participants and in the interactions of the participants with the social world of objects and artifacts (e.g., books, paper, pencils, science equipment).

Culture, therefore, is not "out there" created by others to be obtained (learned); rather, culture is created by people as part of their ordinary actions and is similar to language in that it is learned and constructed in the "doing." All classrooms have unique cultural characteristics as well as characteristics in common with other classrooms. For example, one way to view the difference among classrooms is to place them on a continuum that reflects the role relationships in the construction of everyday life and teaching–learning events. In some classrooms, the teacher may involve students in the decisions about what to do, when, where, with whom, and in what ways. In these kinds of classrooms, the teacher has elected to "share" the role of decisionmaker with the students; the students are more equal participants than in other classrooms, where the teacher assumes the principle role of architect and foreman, and students become the construction gang. That is, these students have little public "voice" about what can and cannot occur. In yet other classrooms, students (and the teacher) may be required to fit into a prefabricated structure (e.g., a reading laboratory) with predefined rules set by "architects" outside of the classroom (e.g., curriculum developers and textbook writers).

In each of these classrooms, different patterned ways of life develop, along with different requirements for participation that lead to differences in learning (Cazden, 1986; Edwards & Furlong, 1978; Green, Weade, & Graham, 1988; Kantor, 1988; Marshall, 1987; Marshall & Weinstein, 1988). What leads to the differences in the cultures of each of these classrooms are the ways in which the rights and obligations are constructed, interpreted, and enacted by participants. What we argue, then, is that in each of these classrooms, language use will be elicited, supported, or constrained in different ways and that these ways influence what teachers and observers see as "language communicative competence," or learning. Language that is produced in these contexts, then, reflects the social life that has been constructed and may not reflect the "competencies of individuals" (DeStefano, Pepinsky, & Sanders, 1982) or what they have learned.

An example of the way classroom culture is constructed can be seen in the following examples from the study of two kindergarten classrooms at the beginning of school (Green & Harker, 1982; Wallat & Green, 1979, 1982; Wallat, Green, Conlin, & Haramis, 1981). In both classrooms, students entered to a free choice time (arrival time) and then moved to a group discussion/group lesson time. Although the events were similar in type, the ways of participating and the norms and expectations for "doing" the event differed, as did the artifacts that were available for use and the ways in which they could be used. In one classroom, students "shared" the right to construct the ways to do "news and views." That is, they determined who would talk, when, and where. The teacher retained the right to establish with the students the ways in which the event was constructed (e.g., turn distribution, topic maintenance, and the duration of the event). In the other teacher's classroom, the teacher retained all of those rights and placed obligations on students to enact her goals and directions.

The impact of the different expectations for and ways of "doing" discussion time could be seen when each teacher interrupted the ordinary flow of the day and brought in a special event in the time slot ordinarily reserved for discussion. In the first teacher's classroom, the students adapted to the change in event with a minimum of observable disruption and engaged actively in the new event. In contrast, the students in the second teacher's classroom became confused and distressed. They did not know what to do, and the ordinary smooth flow of life became tense and unpredictable, and the novel event was not completed. In other words, the two groups reacted to a change in the ordinary ways of doing life (a frame clash) in dramatically different ways because of the difference in the way life was constructed in the two classrooms.

That patterned ways of "doing" life in classrooms develop over time has been shown by a variety of classroom ethnographers (e.g., Bloome, 1987; Bloome, Puro, & Theodorou (1989); Cochran-Smith, 1984; Collins, 1986; Cook-Gumperz, 1986; Dorr-Bremme, 1982; Florio & Shultz, 1979; Gilmore & Glatthorn, 1981; Green & Harker, 1982; Kantor, Elgas, & Fernie, 1989; McDermott, 1976; Wallat & Green, 1979; 1982; Wilkinson, 1982) and other classroom researchers (e.g., Marshall, 1987; Marshall & Weinstein, 1988). What becomes evident when this body of work is taken as a whole is that life is patterned and, thus, generally predictable but not rigid or invariable. It may be possible to predict that an event will occur, but even if the event is highly ritualistic (e.g., a church service; the opening pledge), it will not be possible to predict with assurance *exactly* how it will unfold or what will be said. Therefore, members of the social group participating in the construction of the event, as well as researchers observing it, will need to monitor the actions of those involved as the event unfolds in time. Thus, some aspects of life in classrooms become stable over time, but other aspects evolve in the "doing." In other words, participants cannot know what events will "look like" or require until they have occurred.

This work has direct implications for those concerned with how language use in classrooms influences student learning. If life in classrooms becomes patterned, and such life is constructed by participants, then the social world must be considered as more than a background variable or simple context for language use. From this perspective, then, social actions are both constructed through and influenced by language use, and language use is influenced and constrained by the social actions and expectations that develop within and across the events of classroom life. These interrelationships will become visible in the examples that follow, taken from preschool and junior high school classrooms.

THE INFLUENCE OF LANGUAGE ON LEARNING

In the previous sections, we have argued that classroom life is constructed by teachers and students as they interact with and build on each others' behaviors, actions, messages, and intentions. On a practical level, this means that teachers and students must observe, monitor, and interpret the moment-by-moment actions of those involved in the event; an event, from this perspective, is an outcome of these interactions. Language is one of the primary resources for the participants to use in constructing events through face-to-face interaction. Thus, to explore what influence language has on learning, we must first define what is meant by language in this particular context of use.

To answer the question, "What is language?", we must once again return to Halliday (1973), who stated that the answer to this question depends on why you are asking the question. We are asking the question here to understand the place and role of language as a resource for participants as they work at accomplishing classroom events. Therefore, we focus on language as discourse among participants and as one element of social action. Such a focus necessitates consideration of: the delivery of the discourse (i.e., contextualization cues: pitch, stress, intonation, juncture, gesture, eye gaze, proxemics, kinesics); the semantic content of the messages; the roles and relationships of conversational participants; the history of the discourse (e.g., other similar occurrences across time); the history of the relationships among participants; and the cultural expectations within the setting for engaging in conversation and social life (nonverbal activity).

In addition, because discourse does not occur in scripted form, we must also consider the actions of participants that indicate how they have interpreted what is occurring, what they are holding each other accountable to and for, and how they are "working" with or failing to work with the actions and messages of others. By considering these elements of discourse in action, we can observe and identify: the work of participants as they build topic and negotiate the rules for participating in the conversation (e.g., turn taking, turn distribution); the negotiation of meanings within the unfolding event; the consequences of action or lack of action for the participants; instances of frame clash and how participants repair or fail to repair such clashes; the outcome of the event, and the goals of the various participants that are reflected in their actions. Thus, for our purpose, we must define language as involving more than semantic, lexical, or syntactic components. Language at the discourse level is language in use and, thus, it involves the discourse strategies and social actions employed by participants as they work together verbally and nonverbally to accomplish their goals for this "bit of social life."

Just how this definition of language as discourse helps us can be seen in the examples of event construction and classroom life that follow. In each instance, we focus on a local event and also on the place of this event in the historical perspective within the lifeworld of the classroom in order to develop a contextualized interpretation of the meanings of the life being observed. These examples were selected to illustrate how the ways in which discourse is constructed influence what students do during the event, as well as what they display as knowledge, both during and after the event. The examples represent two different age ranges (preschool and junior high school) to illustrate how the framework that is being developed applies to any level of schooling.

In the first example (preschool circle time), language is both a social process and an informal object of study; that is, students are learning how to "do circle time," including learning group conversation skills. Thus, this example shows the interrelatedness of learning language, learning about language, and learning through language in a very early school experience. In addition, this example illustrates the role of language in the construction of everyday classroom life.

Preschool Circle Time: Learning to Talk in Group

Circle time is one of the most ordinary events in preschool and primary-grade classrooms (Michaels, 1984). This event is referred to in a variety of ways: rug time, group time, show and tell, bring and brag, news and views, sharing time, discussion time, and so forth (e.g., Wallat & Green, 1979; Dorr-Bremme, 1982). The purpose of this activity is to help students learn to share information with their classmates in socially appropriate ways and, thus, to develop group conversation skills.

The following example of circle time demonstrates how: learning to converse in group settings is developed over time; the teacher and student roles shift as students learn to initiate topic and build on each others' contributions; the social organization of the event shifts over time; the norms and expectations for participation are constructed through the interactions and actions of participants; and these norms and expectations shift over time as students develop the ability to construct collaborative conversation.

The circle time example was drawn from a year-long study of socialization to schooling in the preschool with 3- to 4-year-olds (Fernie, Kantor, Klein, Meyer, & Elgas, 1989). To obtain information, Kantor and her colleagues had to consider each instance of circle time and then explore the evolving picture over time. Thus, for each individual event, the researchers had to explore what was happening and consider how the past history of the event influenced and/or was indicated in the particular speech event that was being considered. They also maintained the linkages between language and the broader social actions that accompanied its use and in which language was embedded.

Circle time was a daily event that occurred in the same place, at a specified time, with the same groups of participants (the teacher, the assistant teacher, and eighteen 3- and 4-year- olds). Circle time had five parts: milling time, transition to circle, talking, singing, and dismissal

(Kantor, 1988; Kantor & Elgas, 1987). The event was defined by the teacher as serving multiple purposes: to interact with the group to have collaborative conversation; to provide a transition from playground activities to classroom activities; and to provide opportunities to build on or work from children's ideas and interests to encourage divergent thought and problem solving.

An analysis of 12 circle time sessions throughout the year (fall, winter, and spring) showed that this event evolved over time in both structure and substance. The first accomplishment of teacher and students was the "look of the circle"—students had to learn the social expectations for getting into and remaining part of the circle shape. Figure 11.1 displays the social action rules for creating the "look of the circle" identified across the school year. As indicated in Fig. 11.1, students had to learn to put their playthings and belongings away in the designated place, to join the circle and wait until all students were in the circle to begin the event, to negotiate their own space, to sit attentively at the circle, and then to share in appropriate ways. The look of the circle was accomplished during the pre- and post-discussion phases: milling time, transition time, and

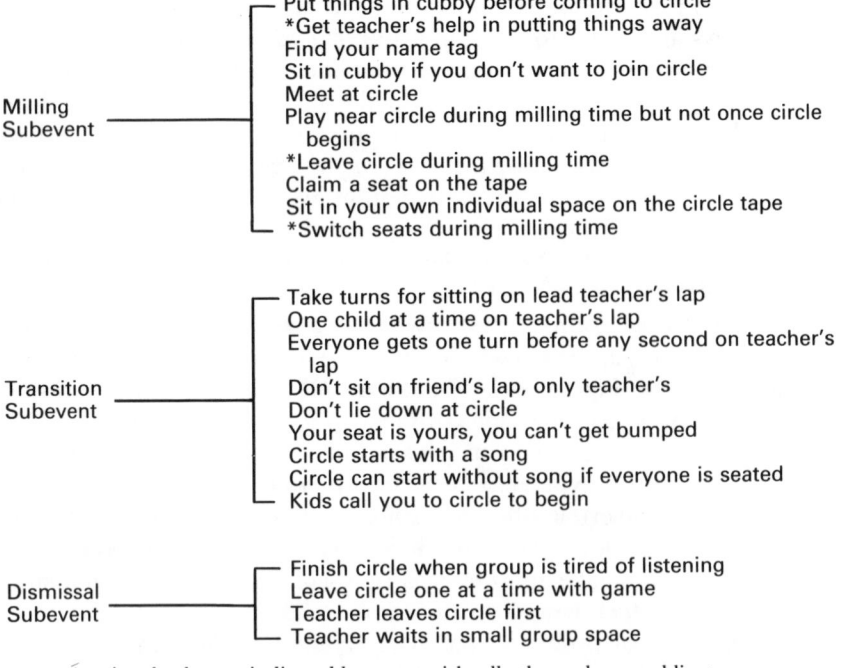

Milling
Subevent
- Put things in cubby before coming to circle
- *Get teacher's help in putting things away
- Find your name tag
- Sit in cubby if you don't want to join circle
- Meet at circle
- Play near circle during milling time but not once circle begins
- *Leave circle during milling time
- Claim a seat on the tape
- Sit in your own individual space on the circle tape
- *Switch seats during milling time

Transition
Subevent
- Take turns for sitting on lead teacher's lap
- One child at a time on teacher's lap
- Everyone gets one turn before any second on teacher's lap
- Don't sit on friend's lap, only teacher's
- Don't lie down at circle
- Your seat is yours, you can't get bumped
- Circle starts with a song
- Circle can start without song if everyone is seated
- Kids call you to circle to begin

Dismissal
Subevent
- Finish circle when group is tired of listening
- Leave circle one at a time with game
- Teacher leaves circle first
- Teacher waits in small group space

*optional rules are indicated by an asterisk; all other rules are obligatory.

FIG. 11.1.   Establishing "the look of the circle": Social Action Rules Guiding Participation The Milling Time, Transition, Dismissal Subevents.

dismissal time. Thus, to understand how the students formed the group in which discussion occurred, it was necessary to consider the actual boundaries of the circle time event, not just the part in which discussion occurred. In other words, the speech event labeled as discussion (circle time) was part of a larger "piece of social and academic life."

To understand the discussion part without considering how students learn to get to the circle or leave the circle is to decontextualize it from the overall demands of classroom life that influence what students know and do. What became evident during the analysis of this event was that students had to acquire the "look of the circle" before they could attend to the "sound of the group."

Similar findings have been reported for junior high school students in well-managed classrooms and poorly managed classrooms. Evertson, Weade, Green, & Crawford (1985) found that in classrooms that were poorly managed, students focused on what they were to do and not on what they were to know. These examples, therefore, help identify factors from the broader social life that influence what can and will occur in any given speech event.

The preceding discussion has focused on the physical structuring and organizing of the event. The "look of the circle," however, was not the goal of the lesson. Rather, the purpose of the lesson was to provide a systematic and supportive time for students to learn to converse together. This part of the lesson was defined during analysis as the "sound of the group." Figure 11.2 details the rules for conversational participation that developed across time in the classroom. However, as is shown hereafter, appropriate participation was not rigid; rather, it developed and changed over time as students developed their skills in collaborative discourse.

To explore the development of collaborative conversation, Kantor (1988) and her colleagues (Kantor & Elgas, 1987) explored the direction of the conversational engagement between teacher and students and among participants: who initiated topic, who did the talking (teacher or student) over time, and the ability of the individuals and the group to build topic across turns within a given day.

The change of the "sound of the group" over time reflected the students' development of collaborative discourse skills. That is, the ways in which the students engaged in conversation, the types of roles they assumed, and the source of the topic shifted across the school year. Table 11.1 provides a summary of the development of these discourse skills as they were observed during conversations over the school year.

As indicated in Table 11.1, there is a clear shift in all of these areas from fall to spring. For instance, the direction of conversational exchange shifts from primarily between teacher and student and teacher and group toward other kinds of exchanges, such as child with child. There is also

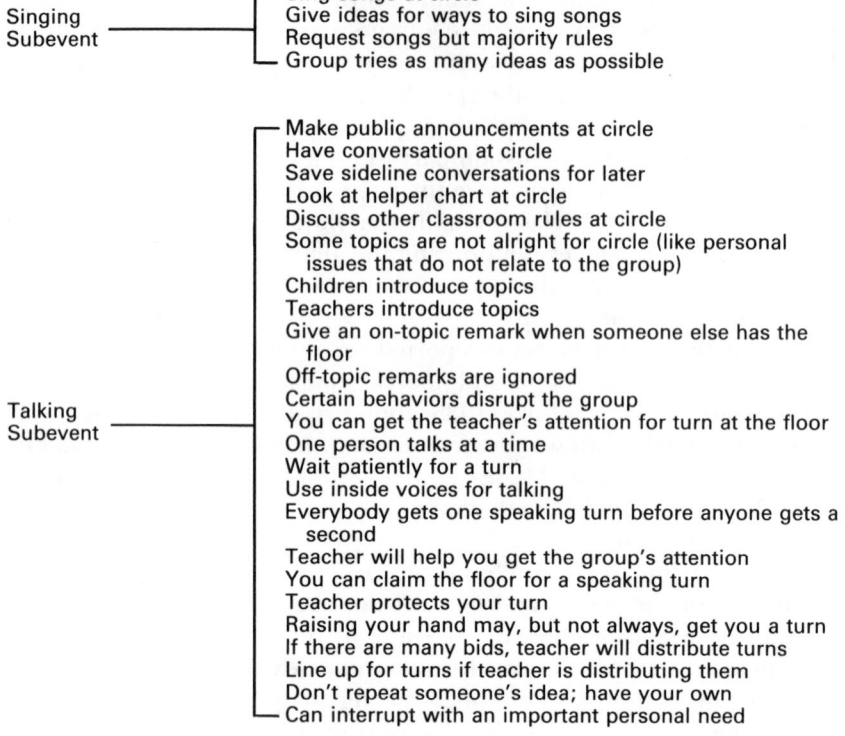

Singing
Subevent
- Sing songs at circle
- Give ideas for ways to sing songs
- Request songs but majority rules
- Group tries as many ideas as possible

Talking
Subevent
- Make public announcements at circle
- Have conversation at circle
- Save sideline conversations for later
- Look at helper chart at circle
- Discuss other classroom rules at circle
- Some topics are not alright for circle (like personal issues that do not relate to the group)
- Children introduce topics
- Teachers introduce topics
- Give an on-topic remark when someone else has the floor
- Off-topic remarks are ignored
- Certain behaviors disrupt the group
- You can get the teacher's attention for turn at the floor
- One person talks at a time
- Wait patiently for a turn
- Use inside voices for talking
- Everybody gets one speaking turn before anyone gets a second
- Teacher will help you get the group's attention
- You can claim the floor for a speaking turn
- Teacher protects your turn
- Raising your hand may, but not always, get you a turn
- If there are many bids, teacher will distribute turns
- Line up for turns if teacher is distributing them
- Don't repeat someone's idea; have your own
- Can interrupt with an important personal need

FIG. 11.2. Establishing the "sound of the group": Social Action ruled
Guiding Participation in the Talking and Singing Subevents.

a shift indicating a movement from the dependence on the teacher at the beginning of the year to introduce topic and to talk toward the greater involvement of student participants. At the end of the year, the 3- and 4-year-old students were responsible for the introduction of topic, for topic elaboration, and for the majority of the talk that occurred.

With the emergence of more child-initiated talk, competition for a "turn at talk" became greater. To examine the impact of this on group participation requirements, Kantor examined the strategies students had for "getting the floor" and how the strategies were established by the group. As reflected in Table 11.2, over the school year, the types of strategies changed. For example, at the beginning of the year students used strategies that did not maintain the "look of the circle" or the "sound of the group"; that is, they were often nonverbal. These strategies included: getting out of their seat, tapping teacher on the shoulder, leaning into or moving into the teacher's space, and physically moving the teacher's face in order to gain eye contact. These strategies were

TABLE 11.1
Development of Conversation at the Preschool Circle
Over 12 Events

	Fall	Winter	Spring
Direction of conversational exchange in average number of turns per circle over 12 circles			
Teacher with Child	30	89	63
Teacher with Group	14	16	16
Child with Group	—	1	3
Child with Child	—	—	16
Group with Child	—	—	2
Group with Teacher	—	—	1
Introduction of topic, total # over 12 circles	8T	12T	8T
	3C	12C	30C
Percent overall teacher–child talk by turns per circle	63%T	51%T	45%T
	37%C	49%C	55%C
Average number conversational turns per circle	44	106	153
Number of on-topic to off-topic remarks by children in a single circle	6 on	5 on	45 on
	0 off	19 off	14 off

never used in the circle time sessions that were explored in winter and spring. As time went on, students began to use a greater variety of strategies, including: claims, attentional devices, and requests for turn. In other words, students moved from a dependence on nonverbal communication to verbal interactions. This shift, then, indicates that students learned what was appropriate as established by the group for this event.

Once again, to explore language without considering the social actions tells us a limited story. What becomes evident when language and social action are explored simultaneously are the ways in which the teacher, and conversely the students, worked together to maintain the group. Table 11.3 presents a summary of the group rules for social participation across the year. Included in these data are explicit references by the teacher to the rules, as well as indicators of adherence by teachers and students. Whereas the former are verbally signaled in the talk during the

TABLE 11.2
Child Strategies for Floor-Taking During Circle Time (Total Number
Over 12 Circles)

	Fall	Winter	Spring
Physical strategies (i.e., getting out of seat to tap)	11	0	0
Claims (speaking out with statement, questions, etc.)	52	82	133
Attention devices ("Hey! Guess what!")	2	50	54
Distributed by teacher ("first Rachel then Sean")	0	14	38

event, the latter were inferred from the nonverbal actions of students that indicate that both the teacher and students are acting as if they are adhering to the rule. Once again, we see a shift in the frequency of occurrence that showed a shift from a focus on the rules that guide the "look of the circle" to those that guide the "sound of the group." In addition, there is a shift toward more tacit adherence to the rules.

The preceding discussion makes visible the complexity of the task of talking to learn and learning to talk. This seemingly simple task is highly complex; it becomes rule-governed and patterned, has shifted norms and expectations, and has evolving roles and relationships and rights and obligations. In addition, this example shows that students and teachers are continually working together to construct the events (circle time) that themselves have different phases. Each of these phases (e.g., milling, transition, talk, singing, dismissal), in turn, has distinct roles and relationships, norms and expectations, and rights and obligations.

This construction process, however, changes as students learn how to talk, what to talk about, who to talk to, who talks when, how to get a turn, and so forth. On a broader scale, the students are actually learning more than learning how to talk; they are also learning how to accomplish life through talk and social actions. They are learning how to accomplish a social event, how to "read" the shifting requirements for participation, and how to adapt their performance and participation to the demands of the event. In the following examples, we show how this process is one that crosses ages and types of classrooms. What differ are the ways in which the participants are expected to work together, the content of their talk, the types of tasks that are being constructed, and the expected academic outcomes of such participation.

TABLE 11.3
Explicitly Stated and Implicitly Operating Social
Action Rules Guiding Participation in Circle Time Over the Year

Subevent	Fall		Winter		Spring	
	Explicit	Implicit	Explicit	Implicit	Explicit	Implicit
Milling	23	11	8	15	0	8
Transition	10	7	9	2	0	8
Dismissal	0	4	1	3	2	3
Total	33	22	18	20	2	19
Singing	0	7	0	20	0	3
Talking	5	35	46	85	28	116
Total	5	42	46	105	28	119

Junior High Grammar Lesson:
Learning to Read the Task

In the preschool example, the social and academic tasks were one in the same in circle time. That is, the goal of the "lesson" is to help students learn to accomplish group through talk (language) and to develop language through participating in the group. The content of the talk is not predefined; rather, it is negotiated by the students and the teachers in ways that are similar to conversations outside of school. Appropriate discourse, use of discourse strategies, and social actions are outcomes that are expected; topic is incidental. Topic is important, in that students need to learn to develop the topic and learn to contribute to the topic of others.

In the junior high school example that follows, knowing how to talk and act appropriately is assumed after the first days of class. The goal of the lesson, then, becomes the academic content—in this case grammar review, in which language is the object of study as well as a social process. However, as we demonstrate, this assumption is not totally accurate. Although life in the classroom becomes routine, it is not a static script. Rather, the social and academic demands are never fixed but are established, checked, modified, suspended, and reestablished within a lesson, as well as over time (Green & Wallat, 1981). Thus, to participate verbally and nonverbally in lessons, to contribute to the construction of the lesson, and to have one's knowledge "counted," students and teachers must constantly monitor what is occurring in face-to-face interaction on a moment-by-moment basis. Lesson, from this perspective, can be likened to a composition that is being collaboratively written by teacher and students through their verbal and nonverbal actions (Green, Weade, & Graham, 1988). In this group composition, teacher and students must: read the actions and messages of others; interpret these messages; select from their repertoire appropriate information to be added or to be negotiated; "slot in" the information in socially and structurally appropriate ways; and contribute to the structure as well as the content of the lesson. To do this, students and teachers must also use knowledge from beyond the lesson to help them interpret what is occurring, what is appropriate, and what is expected. That is, as teachers and students interact with each other over time in classrooms, routines develop, common meanings for ordinary ways of doing life develop, and a history of events is constructed that guides how they read, interpret, and act in other situations, as was shown in the earlier section of this chapter in the example of the circle time.

This previous knowledge and the prior common actions from other segments of life in the classroom is often reflected in the actions and talk of the teachers and students as they construct a particular lesson, as is shown in the grammar review example. Thus, participation in a given lesson is not a unique occurrence but an embedded one in which the past, present, and future are often signalled and, thus, available to participants and observers alike. The key to uncovering these elements is threefold: to ask questions about what participants are referring to; to understand that this event has a history that can and will influence what students and teachers do together in the current lesson; and to explore discourse and social actions that appear ordinary to the participants but are unclear to the observer (e.g., elliptical references, "shorthand talk," nonverbal rituals and routines). For example, in the middle of the grammar review lesson described hereafter, the teacher said, "Now I think we've all decided that 'ain't' is not acceptable." No prior reference to this decision exists within the lesson. However, exploration of the themes developed in other lessons over time in the classroom suggest that this decision occurred at a previous point in time and is simply being reestablished here. Thus, to interpret what this statement meant required going beyond the local lesson and considering the lesson in the broader context and history of life in this classroom.

The grammar review lesson that follows occurred in November of the school year (Weade & Green, 1989). This lesson was similar to others that occurred in August, September, October, and May in terms of both content and structure (Weade & Evertson, 1988; Evertson et al., 1985). Although the particular task was review, the content that was presented was representative of the curriculum of this classroom. Table 11.4 reflects the academic, social, and literacy demands by phase of the lesson. Just as there were five parts, or phases, in circle time, there are five phases to this lesson as defined by the rights and obligations, norms and expectations, and roles and relationships. In addition, content or ways in which content (academic task) varied helped to further define the differentiated nature and boundaries of each phase.

As indicated in Table 11.4, the five parts of the lesson were related to five sections of a grammar text taken on a previous day. The teacher in this lesson has returned the test, and the class is reviewing the test on an item-by-item basis. As indicated in this table, academic, social, and literacy demands changed by phase in an integral fashion. That is, as the type of content shifted so did the amount and type of "written" text. Thus, the literacy or reading demands and the academic demands are tightly interrelated. However, the shifts in the social demands could not be predicted from the academic and text information in the same manner as shifts in academic and reading demands. The teacher shifted the ways

TABLE 11.4
Academic, Social, and Reading Demands, by Phase,
in a Grammar Review Lesson

Phase	Academic Demand	Social Demand	Reading Demand
1	Name past and past participle of given verb.	Respond when called on (at random)	Read each verb; recognize each as present tense form.
2	Name tense for given verb.	Volunteer by raising hand; respond when called on.	Identify each verb or verb phrase; recognize "helping" verbs as part of verb phrase.
3	Given present tense verb and a sentence without a verb, place verb form in correct tense in the sentence.	Respond when called on (at random).	Read given sentence, placing verb form in *context* of sentence.
4	Given sentence with incorrect verb usage, read the sentence, correcting the usage.	Respond when called on (at random); then volunteer another response (more than one correct answer) by raising hand; then respond when called on.	Read sentence to identify incorrect usage, repair usage, then read in correct form.
5	Check paper as T. gives answers—identifying given verbs as active or passive.	Listen as T. gives answers; ask questions at end, if any.	Match work (active/passive) with teacher's dictation.

in which she called on students and thus the ways in which each phase of the task was accomplished. She began by calling on students in a random fashion (phase 1), then moved to asking for volunteers (phase 2). She then returned to calling on students in a random fashion (phase 3 and, in part, in phase 4). In phase 4, she combined random calling with volunteering.

The constructed nature of this event becomes evident in phase 5. In this phase, the teacher signals to students that they are "running out of time" and that she wants to change the social structure and simply read the answers to them. The teacher is not completely successful in accomplishing this shift as indicated by student actions: students continue to volunteer answers. She does eventually succeed and then ends by asking students if they have any questions. Phase 5, therefore, is dramatically different in social, academic, and reading demands from those in previous phases. In the previous phases, the teacher elicits student interactions, requires students to read items, and uses the discussion of the review of the item to "teach" about grammar and to "tie" to themes she has been developing across the year. Table 11.5 displays the process in the first phase of this process.

This table is a "map" of the lesson and it shows the content themes that were signalled in the talk between teacher and students. In it, we see a structure for the test that shows 15 verbs—13 irregular verbs and 2 regular verbs. What is important to note is that the regular verbs occur at the end of this phase of the test. The talk between the teacher and the students indicated that the teacher was surprised at the number of students who missed these two items. As discussed elsewhere (Weade & Green, 1989), the reason for these errors can be attributed to the "frame of reference" that students develop within a lesson. That is, as students begin to participate in task, they "read" and interpret the expectations from the information available. In this instance, the information was the items on a printed test (the irregular verbs). The students then use these interpretations to predict what will occur. They do not read each item as a novel item; rather, they develop an expectation set or frame of reference for what is required in this task.

The structure of phase 1 of the test led students to expect irregular verbs throughout the phase. Thus, the errors that were observed by the teacher (that the students spelled the word "drown" wrong and gave the past and past participle for "rise" instead of "raise") might actually be seen as logical answers, prompted by the structure of the task and not reflecting students' actual ability. The teacher's comments during the lesson supported this conclusion. In the content themes of the entire lesson, which are summarized in Table 11.6, we can see further evidence of why the error might have occurred.

The teacher constantly signals ways of obtaining the correct verb form, one of which is "We don't just add "ed" to irregular verbs" in phase 4. The spelling error on drown then begins to make sense if we assume that the students have interpreted the task as one of doing irregular verbs. Thus, by working through the test and by using prior knowledge obtained from previous lessons, students construct interpretations about what is expected and how to do task that may override the directions at the beginning of the test section. Performance on tests, therefore, is a constructed and interpretive process. In other words, social and academic demands are signalled throughout the lesson and are constructed by the "doing" of the lesson.

That lessons have social and academic demands is evident from the preceding discussion. However, we have argued that the demands of a given lesson are also embedded in the history of this event over time. To illustrate the relationship of the grammar review lesson to other kinds of English lessons in this classroom, Weade & Green (1989) extracted the

TABLE 11.5
Content and Theme Distribution by Time
Phase 1

Instructional Sequence Unit (ISU)	Topic	Content	Themes Signalled	Interaction Units (IU)	Time (Seconds)
				Length of ISU	
1	(a verb)[a]			2	8.2
2	rise	irregular verb	spelling	2	8.0
3	lie	irregular verb	meanings	9	70.2
4	be	irregular verb	principal parts	7	59.2
5	(procedural statement: Skip C, she wasn't here)			1	4.8
6	have, has	irregular verb		3	13.2
7	Using have, has in sentences	irregular verb		13	98.6
8	choose	irregular verb	spelling	3	13.1
9	see	irregular verb		1	5.0
10	swim	irregular verb	principal parts	4	24.0
11	drew	irregular verb		1	6.3
12	lay	irregular verb	meanings	7	25.0
13	give	irregular verb		1	4.5
14	bring	irregular verb		8	37.5
15	ring	irregular verb		1	7.1
16	inaudible interaction			1	3.3
17	take	irregular verb		5	30.6
18	drown	regular verb		9	51.9
19	raise	regular verb		9	52.5
20	Questions on part 1	Conclude	part 1	1	4.9

[a] Students's response was inaudible. The teacher signalled that the response was correct.

TABLE 11.6
Frequency of Themes by Lesson Phase

	I	II	III	IV	V
Memorize principal parts	4				
Think of the verb in a little sentence	1				
Spelling	4	1	1	2	
Meaning	2		5	5	
"Sound" is a clue			1	5	
Think about principal parts		1	1		
Algorithm-like grammar rules, e.g.:					
present tense + will = future tense		1			
"ing" form = progressive		1			
present participle + "be" verb helper = progressive		1			1
past participle + "have" = present perfect		1			
"shall have", "will have" = future perfect helpers		1			
past participle + "be" verb helper = passive		7			3
"had" means past perfect		1			
"does", "did" = emphatic		1			
singular verbs end in "s"		1			
Don't change tense midsentence				1	
Don't just add "ed"; to irregular verbs				1	
Use "up" with "rose" when you need to show direction				1	
Think of an alternative [verb]				1	
When the subject is acted on, the tense is *passive*					2
When the subject acts, the tense is *active*					4
Totals by Lesson Phase	11	17	8	16	10

social and academic demands across time and contrasted these to demands in the grammar review lesson. Figures 11.3 and 11.4 portray this contrast.

The historical aspects of life in classrooms and the existence of the past and present in the current lesson were most evident when the issue of text was considered. Although the students had a text (the graded grammar test) in front of them during most of the lesson, the teacher often referred to other texts, those not present in the lesson being constructed. That is, she referred to information she obtained during the grading of the test and by watching students take the test as well as from observing what students were doing in the current lesson. Figure 11.5 presents a taxonomy of the various types of text that were identified by considering the referents made by the teacher to other texts read at other

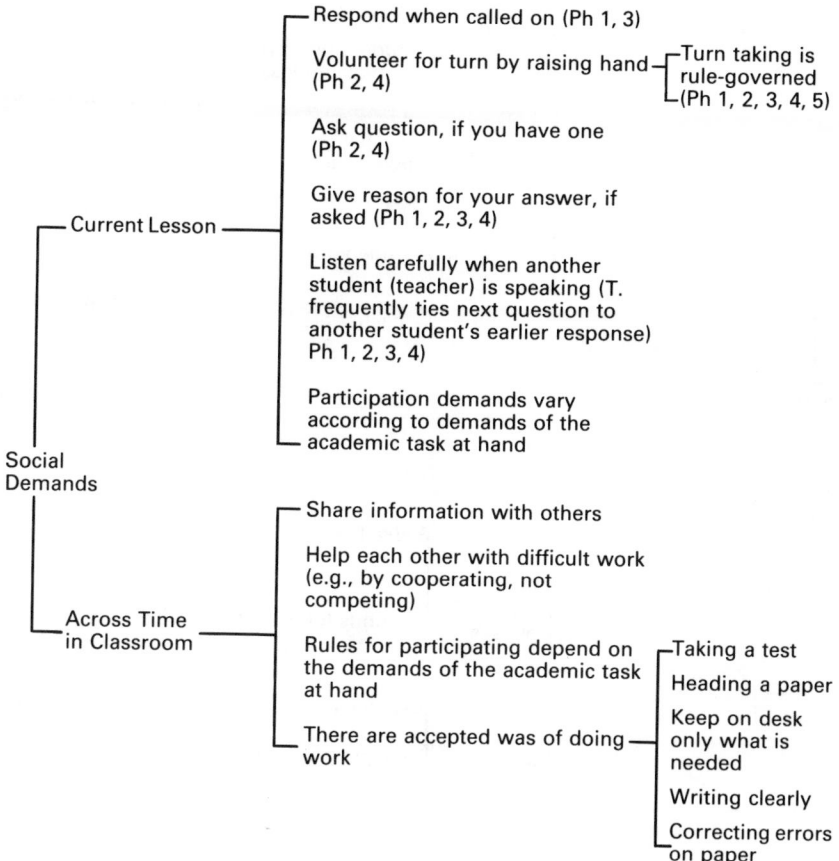

Ph = Phase

FIG. 11.3. Taxonomy of social demands.

times. As indicated in this figure, the graded text had many phases in its life.

Thus, what appeared to be a simple artifact in the setting and a simple task—"reading the test"—was, in actuality, a complex process that required prior knowledge of earlier engagements with the test and a shared history of life in that particular classroom. Analysis of this event from an exploration of only what occurred in that event, without considering its ties to previous events, would distort the interpretation and lead to a limited understanding of the social, academic, and reading demands of the lesson. In addition, without considering the meanings being signalled in the oral and written language within the event would distort the interpretation. The error on the two regular verbs could only be

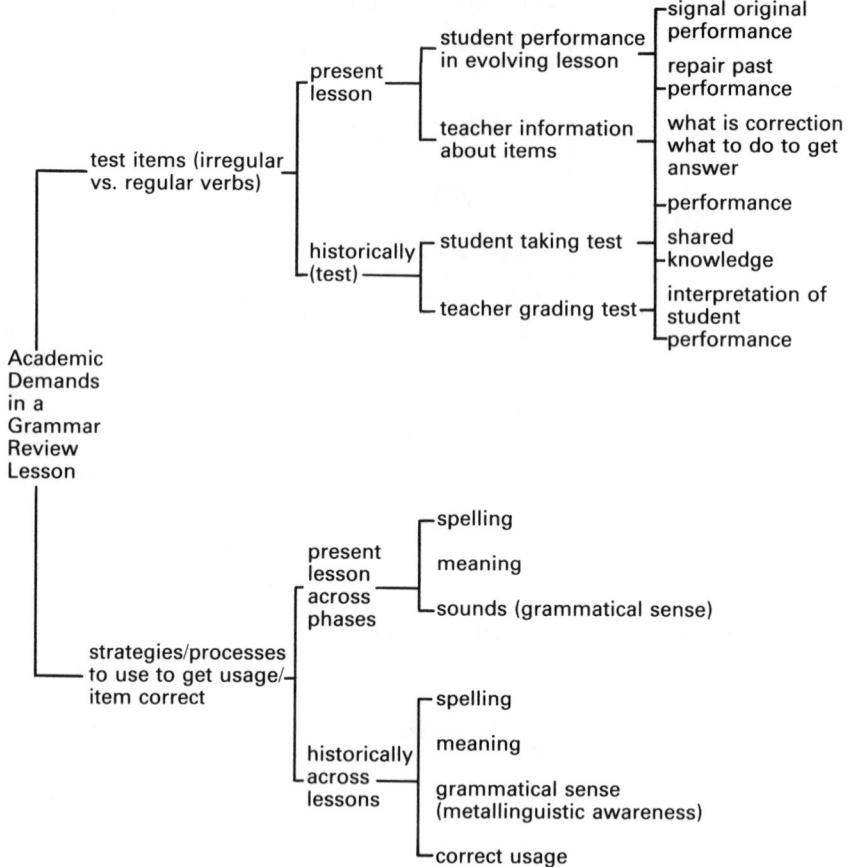

FIG. 11.4.   Taxonomy of academic demands.

determined by considering how the language used on the test influenced the unfolding of the event and, therefore, student performance.

Junior High Literature Lesson: Learning to Read the Academic Norms and Expectations

In the previous example of the grammar review lesson, the students' performance did not necessarily reflect their competence, but instead reflected their reading of the task demands. In the following example of a literature lesson, students' performance is related to their reading of the academic norms or expectations that are negotiated during the lesson or

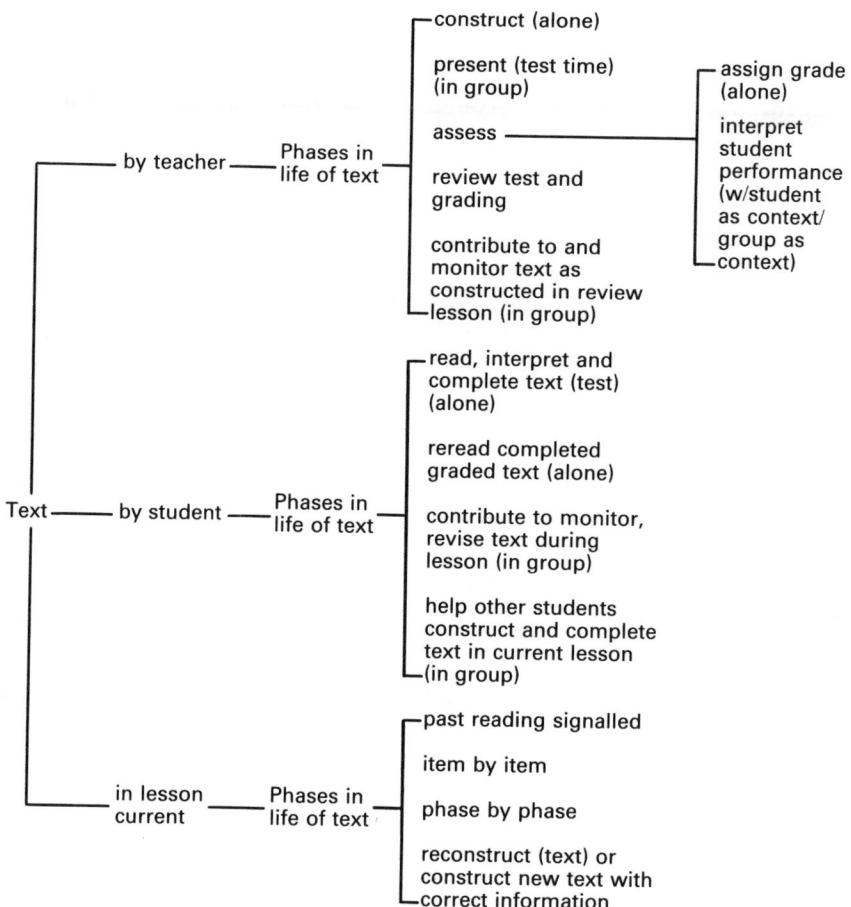

FIG. 11.5. Taxonomy of text and text interpretation.

that have been negotiated in past lessons. Although the apparent task in the lesson is to interpret a previously read short story by participating in a "discussion" of that story, the actual norms or expectations for participating in the interpretation of the story are very different. This difference is reflected in the students' comments about their literature lessons.

This lesson was observed as part of a larger study of the teaching of literature in junior high and high school classrooms (Rogers, 1987; 1988). This lesson was a discussion of the story "Flowers for Algernon" by Daniel Keyes (1966). The excerpt in Table 11.7 was chosen because it focused on the theme of the story. This is one of 22 episodes (each having its own "topic") of the discussion. An analysis of the entire discussion revealed that this episode is typical in terms of the kinds of interaction patterns that took place during this and other lessons (Rogers, 1987).

In this excerpt, the teacher attempts to signal to Karl the preferred interpretation of the story through her use of questions. For example, when she asks Karl to characterize the restaurant scene in the story, Karl responds with the word, "sympathetic." The teacher then asks if there is a theme of sympathy in the story. Karl responds by saying there is a theme of sympathy in that scene. At this point, Karl struggles to maintain his own interpretation without breaking the flow of the lesson. For instance, he partially agrees with the teacher's interpretation and restates his own interpretation in a modified form. Ultimately, the teacher accepts Karl's interpretation of the story, and another student (Anne) supports that interpretation, and what looks like a true discussion begins to develop. However, at that point, the teacher retakes the floor by calling on yet another student.

Several students in this class were interviewed to find out how they perceived the academic norms and expectations relating to the study of literature in their classroom. Their comments reflect their "reading" of the academic norms and expectations, which support the description of the lesson just provided:

Susan: Basically, everyone's theme gets changed a little bit so we all have one idea of what the theme is, and that's a lot easier for the teacher also. So when she grades something, she can just say she has established the main theme.

Gary: Usually, there is a class theme. Everyone gets the same idea.

Bob: Usually, you find out what the themes are from the teacher. They have to tell you before a test. In class discussions, we sort of have our own opinions, but they sort of get pushed aside. When the teacher focuses on something, we usually pay attention to her.

These comments reveal the students' awareness of the academic norms or expectations that are signalled to them through the teacher's talk and actions. That is, the students are aware of their limited role in the development of story themes or interpretations in this class. They are also aware that they are expected to provide *the* "class theme" on tests. Perhaps Karl's own comment, made during an interview a year later, is the most remarkable, because he was able to trace the shifting patterns of expectations for students participating in reading or literature lessons over the course of his schooling:

TABLE 11.7

Excerpt of A Junior High School Literature Discussion

At the start of this lesson excerpt, the students are referring to a scene in which Charlie, now intelligent, defends a retarded bus boy in a restaurant.

TEACHER: OKAY, KARL? (The teacher is responding to Karl's bid to speak).

Karl: Well, He [Charlie] jumped up and he made a scene and said, "Leave him alone." He tried to defend the boy and then ran out of the restaurant.

TEACHER: WHAT CHARACTERISTICS WOULD YOU ATTACH TO THIS SCENE—IN TERMS OF CHARLIE? IF YOU HAD ONE WORD THAT YOU HAD TO PICK THAT REFLECTS THE WAY CHARLIE REACTED TO THE SITUATION, WHAT WOULD THAT WORD BE?

Karl: Sympathetic.

TEACHER: OKAY, DO YOU THINK THERE IS A THEME OF SYMPATHY IN THIS STORY?

Karl: Well, in that particular scene.

TEACHER: OR DO YOU THINK THERE IS A SYMPATHETIC THEME THAT RUNS THROUGH THE STORY? DO YOU THINK PEOPLE REACT WITH A SENSE OF CARING TOWARD OTHER PEOPLE IN THE STORY?

Karl: Well, that's not the main theme I got out of the story.

TEACHER: WELL, DO YOU THINK IT COULD BE A THEME? NOT NECESSARILY THE MAIN THEME?

Karl: Well, it could be, but there are other themes.

TEACHER: YOU DON'T THINK IT IS A THEME AT ALL IN THIS STORY?

Karl: Well, it is a theme. I don't think it is a main theme.

TEACHER: OKAY, WHAT DO YOU THINK IS THE MAIN THEME?

Karl: I think that people like you for what you are, not how smart you are. I got that from quite a few examples.

TEACHER: OKAY, GIVE ME AN EXAMPLE.

Karl: Like, he was not happier when he was intelligent and his friends were starting to leave him.

TEACHER: DO YOU THINK THAT WAS BECAUSE HE WAS SMART?

Karl: Well, his friends were so used to treating him like an inferior being, so used to laughing at him, and now he is smarter than they are and they're kind of afraid of him.

TEACHER: OKAY, ANNE?

Anne: Like when they say, Oh, don't you know what time it is, or whatever.

TEACHER: DO YOU THINK THEY ARE LAUGHING AT HIM WHEN THEY SAY THAT, ANNE?

Anne: No. He just—now he thinks that when he was mentally retarded, he thought everyone was really smart.

TEACHER: UH HUH. OKAY, TONY?

Karl: In the first grade, they teach you, they ask you, "How did you like this story?", and then you tell them you don't have to give them evidence, so from the second grade on they say, "I want you to give hard evidence and support your ideas," and before you know it you're writing five paragraph essays and they say, "well, don't use your opinions in your thesis, now." And gradually they allow you to use less and less of your emotions until it's not allowed. That's where we are now. I don't get any emotional reaction out of my reading anymore. All teachers want you to do is tell them how this relates to the theme they've given you. What the tests essentially say is, "This is the theme, give me evidence." It's like, okay, that was fun. Instead of saying, "How did you feel about the story? Give examples in your answer."

In this comment, Karl traces the shifting expectations he has experienced from grade to grade in terms of whose "voice" is heard in the classroom and on tests. What this comment reveals is that, through their talk and actions, teachers clearly signal to students what "counts" and whose ideas "count" in school. Students such as Karl, who are successful students, have learned how to read the academic norms and expectations that are signalled through the language and social actions that make up classroom life.

CLOSINGS AND OPENINGS

In this chapter, we have tried to illustrate our perspective on the relationship between language and learning in classroom life. We have argued that the everyday social life of classrooms is constructed during face-to-face interactions of students and teachers. There are both similarities and differences in the kinds of events that get constructed within and across classrooms in terms of how teachers and students work together, what they say and do, the types of tasks that are created, the expected academic outcomes, and the broader social and academic contexts that form the history of the event. Within classrooms, the social life becomes patterned and predictable, but not rigid and invariable. Finally, we have argued that, to study the relationship between language and learning, it is necessary to study language as a social process, because language is both embedded in and influenced by everyday social life.

Through this kind of study, we can see what "counts" as schooling, whose knowledge counts in the construction of classroom events, and what students display as learning. That is, we can make visible what the curriculum world refers to as the "hidden curriculum"—the curriculum

that is constructed by students and teachers during the face-to-face interactions of classroom events (Eisner, 1979; Weade, 1987).

We decided to call this section "closings and openings"—a phrase
borrowed from conversational analysis—because it captures what we
hope will occur. That is, we have come to the end of our part of this
particular conversation about this way of viewing classroom life, the role
of language in this life, and ultimately, the influence of language on
learning. We also chose this phrase because it suggests new directions
that may be opened by this way of viewing the relationship of language,
classroom life, and learning.

In addition, in this chapter, we have raised a variety of issues that must
be considered if we are to understand student performance in classroom
lessons. That is, what we see students do in classroom lessons may not
reflect what students actually know and can do, but rather their interpretation of the social and academic requirements of the task. Questions that
teachers and administrators might ask about what "learning" is in their
classrooms and schools include:

- What do students have to know and do to participate in socially and
  academically appropriate ways in the classroom?
- How are students assessed who do not "read" the requirements and
  act in preferred ways?
- Are some students who are defined as learning disabled or special
  students competent academically but not socially?
- How does the social history of the event influence what can be "seen"
  in the given event?
- How does the life beyond the classroom influence what occurs in
  the classroom and the ways in which classroom events will be interpreted and constructed?
- What is the cumulative effect of the types of social and academic
  demands permitted in classrooms on future learning?
- What "counts" as knowledge, performance, and appropriate participation, and whose knowledge counts?
- How is life in classrooms constructed through and influenced by the
  language and social actions of participants?
- What are the social and academic consequences for students of
  participating in the daily life of classrooms across their educational
  careers?

Finally, as indicated in this chapter, there is a community of educators
who are concerned about the accomplishment of social life through

language as well as its influence on subsequent language learning and learning in general. The information presented in this chapter represents only the "tip of the iceberg." Although the examples discussed were drawn from our own work so that we could develop an argument and illustrate the concepts in depth, there is a vast body of literature that has developed over the past 15 years that contributes to the framework presented. (For summaries of this work, see Cazden, 1986; 1988; Erickson, 1986; and Green, 1983.)

We hope that we have shown in this chapter that much can be gained by constructing a conversation between members of this community and the larger community of those who are interested in language learning that will benefit teachers and students as they participate in the complex world of life in classrooms.

ACKNOWLEDGMENT

A version of this chapter was presented at the Language in Learning Symposium, University of Queensland, Brisbane, Australia, July 10–15, 1988.

REFERENCES

Bloome, D. (1987). *Literacy & schooling.* Norwood, NJ: Ablex.
Bloome, D., Puro, P., & Theodorou, E. (1989). Procedural display and classroom lessons. *Curriculum Inquiry.* 19(3), pp. 265–291.
Cazden (1986). Classroom discourse. In M. C. Wittrock (Ed.), *Handbook of research on teaching* (3rd ed.), pp. 432–436. NY: MacMillan.
Cazden, C. (1988). *Classroom discourse.* Portsmouth, NH: Heinemann.
Cochran-Smith, M. (1984). *The making of a reader.* Norwood, NJ: Ablex.
Cook-Gumperz, J. (Ed.) (1986). *The social construction of literacy.* Cambridge, MA: Cambridge University Press.
Collins, J. (1986). Differential instruction in reading. In J. Cook Gumperz (Ed.), *The social construction of literacy* (pp. 117–137). Cambridge, MA: Cambridge University Press.
DeStefano, J., Pepinski, H., & Sanders, T. (1982). Discourse rules for literacy learning in the classroom. In L. C. Wilkinson (Ed.), *Communicating in the classroom,* (pp. 101–128). New York: Academic Press.
Dorr-Bremme, D. (1982). *Behaving and making sense: Creating social organization in the classroom.* Unpublished doctoral dissertation, Harvard University, Cambridge, MA.
Edwards, A. & Furlong, V. (1978). *The language of teaching.* London: Heinemann.
Eisner, E. (1979). *The educational imagination: On the design and evaluation of school programs.* New York: MacMillan.
Erickson, F. (1986). Tasks in times: Objects of study in a natural history of teaching. In K. K. Zumwalt (Ed.), *Improving teaching* (pp. 131–148). Alexandria, VA: Association for Supervision and Curriculum Development.
Erickson, F., & Schultz, J. (1981). When is a context? Some issues and methods in the

analysis of social competence. In J. Green & C. Wallat (Eds.), *Ethnography and language in educational settings* (pp. 147–160). Norwood, NJ: Ablex.

Evertson, C., Weade, R., Green, J., & Crawford, J. (1985). *Effective classroom management and instruction: An exploration of models* (Report No. N.E.G-83-0063). Washington, DC: National Institute of Education.

Fernie, D., Kantor, R., Klein, E., Meyer, C., & Elgas, P. (1988). Becoming students and becoming ethnographers in preschool. *Journal of Research in Childhood Education, 3*(2), 132–141.

Florio, S., & Schultz, J. (1979). Social competence at home and at school. *Theory into Practice, 18,* 234–243.

Garfinkel, H. (1967). *Studies in ethnomethodology.* Englewood Cliffs, NJ: Prentice-Hall.

Geertz, C. (1973). *The interpretation of cultures.* New York: Random House.

Geertz, C. (1983). *Local knowledge: Further essays in interpretive anthropology.* New York: Basic Books.

Gilmore, P., & Glatthorn, A. (1981). *Children in and out of School: Ethnography and education.* Washington, DC: Center for Applied Linguistics.

Goffman, E. (1974). *Frame analysis: An essay on the organization of experience.* New York: Harper & Row.

Goffman, E. (1981). *Forms of talk.* Philadelphia: University of Pennsylvania Press.

Goodenough, W. (1971). *Culture language, and society.* Reading, MA: Addison-Wesley.

Green, J. (1983). Research on teaching as a linguistic process: A state of the art. In E. Gordon (Ed.), *Review of research in education,* 10, (pp. 151–252). Washington, DC: American Educational Research Association.

Green, J., & Harker, J. (1982). Gaining access to learning: Conversational, social, and cognitive demands of group participation. In L. C. Wilkinson (Ed.), *Communicating in the classroom* (pp. 183–222). New York: Academic Press.

Green, J., & Harker, J. (1988). *Multiple perspective analysis of classroom discourse.* Norwood, NJ: Ablex.

Green, J., & Wallat, C. (1981). *Ethnography and language in educational settings.* Norwood, NJ: Ablex.

Green, J., & Weade, R. (1985). Reading between the words: Social cues to lesson participation. *Theory into Practice, 14*(1), 14–21.

Green, J., & Weade, R., & Graham, K. (1988). Lesson construction and student participation: A sociolinguistic and analysis. In J. Green & J. Harker (Eds.), *Multiple perspective analysis of classroom discourse* (pp. 11–48). Norwood, NJ: Ablex.

Gumperz, J. (1981). Conversational inference and classroom learning. In J. Green & C. Wallat (Eds.), *Ethnography and language in educational settings* (pp. 3–24). Norwood, NJ: Ablex.

Gumperz, J. (1984). *Discourse strategies.* London: Cambridge University Press.

Gumperz, J. (1986). Interactive sociolinguistics in the study of schooling. In J. Cook-Gumperz (Ed.), *The social construction of literacy* (pp. 45–68). London: Cambridge University Press.

Gumperz, J., & Hymes, D. (1972a). *Directions in sociolinguistics.* New York: Holt, Rinehart and Winston.

Halliday, M. (1982). Three aspects of children's language development: Learning language, learning through language, learning about language. Paper presented at the National Council of Teachers of English, Impact Pre-convention Institute, Atlanta, GA.

Heap, J. (1989). On task in classroom discourse. *Linguistics & Education, 1*(1), 177–198.

Heap, J. (1980). What counts as reading? Limits to certainty in assessment. *Curriculum Inquiry, 10*(3), 265–292.

Hymes, D. (1974). *Foundations of sociolinguistics: An ethnographic approach.* Philadelphia: University of Philadelphia Pres.

Hymes, D. (1982). What is ethnography? In P. Gilmore & A. Glatthorn (Eds.), *Children in and out of school* (pp. 21–32). Washington, DC: Center for Applied Linguistics.

Kantor, R. (1988). Creating school meaning in preschool curriculum. *Theory into Practice, 27,* 25–35.

Kantor, R., & Elgas, P. (1987, April). *First the look and then the sound: Creating conversations at circletime.* Paper presented at the annual meeting of the American Educational Research Association, Washington, DC.

Kantor, R., Elgas, P., & Fernie, D. (1989). First the look and then the sound: Creating conversations at circle time. *Early Childhood Research Quarterly, 4*(4), 433–448.

Keyes, D. (1966). Flowers for Algernon. In J. Moffat & K. R. McElheny (Eds.), *Points of view* (pp. 111–139). New York: New American Library.

Marshall, H. (1987). Building a learning orientation. *Theory into Practice, 26,* 8–15.

Marshall, H., & Weinstein, R. (1988). Beyond quantitative analysis: Recontextualization of classroom factors contributing to the communication of teacher expectations. In J. Green & J. Harker (Eds.), *Multiple perspective analyses of classroom discourse* (pp. 249–280). Norwood, NJ: Ablex Publishing Corp.

McDermott, R. (1976). *Kids make sense: An ethnographic account of the interactional management of success and failure in one first grade classroom.* Unpublished doctoral dissertation, Stanford University, Stanford, CA.

Mehan, H. (1974). Accomplishing classroom lessons. In A. V. Cicourel (Ed.), *Language and school performance* (pp. 76–142). New York: Academic Press.

Mehan, H. (1979). *Learning lessons: The social organization of classroom behavior.* Cambridge: Harvard University Press.

Mehan, H., & Wood, H. (1975). *The reality of ethnomethology.* New York: John Wiley and Sons.

Michaels, S. (1984). Listening and responding: Hearing the logic in children's classroom narratives. *Theory into Practice, 28,* 218–225.

Rogers, T. (1987). Exploring a socio-cognitive perspective on the interpretive processes of junior high school students. *English Quarterly, 20*(3), 218–230.

Rogers, T. (1988). *Students as literary critics: The interpretive theories, processes and experiences of ninth grade students.* Dissertation, University of Illinois at Urbana-Champaign.

Sinclair, J., & Coulthard, R. (1975). *Towards an analysis of discourse: The English used by teachers and pupils.* London: Oxford University Press.

Spradley, J. (1980). *Participant observation.* New York: Holt, Rinehard, and Winston.

Tannen, D. (1979). What's in a frame? Surface evidence for underlying expectations. In R. Freedle (Ed.), *Advances in discourse processing* (Vol. 2, pp. 137–181). Norwood, NJ: Ablex.

Wallat, C., & Green, J. (1979). Social rules and communicative contexts in kindergarten. *Theory into Practice, 18,* 275–284.

Wallat, C., & Green, J. (1982). Construction of social norms. In K. Borman (Ed.), *The social life of children in a changing society.* Norwood, NJ: Ablex.

Wallat, C., Green, J., Conlins, S., & Haramis, M. (1981). Issues related to action research in the classroom: The teacher and researcher as a team. In J. Green & C. Wallat (Eds.), *Ethnography and language in educational settings* (pp. 87–116). Norwood, NJ: Ablex.

Weade, R. (1987). Curriculum instruction: The construction of meaning in *Theory into Practice, 26,* (1), 15–25.

Weade, R., & Evertson, C. (1988). The construction of lessons in effective and less effective classrooms, *Teaching and Teacher Education, 4* (3), 189–213.

Weade, R., & Green, J. (1989). Reading in the instructional context. In C. Eimihovich (Ed.), *Locating learning across the curriculum.* Norwood, NJ: Ablex.

Wilkinson, L. (1982). *Communicating in the classroom.* New York: Academic Press.

Instructional Conversations in Learning to Write and Learning to Teach

Susan Florio-Ruane
Michigan State University

This chapter is about instructional conversations between teachers and students. The issues in question are learning to write and learning to teach. The chapter explores some instructional limits of conversations typically held by teachers and students in the classroom. Examples are drawn from two strategic sites—the conversations held between young writers and their classroom teachers and those between beginning teachers and teacher educators. These are rich conversational situations to examine in tandem. What we learn in one can help us understand the other. This is so, not only because both sites depend on conversation to support learning and development, but because, as Donald Graves (1983) has aptly stated, writing and teaching are "twin crafts" in the sense that "the teaching of writing demands the control of two crafts, teaching and writing. They can neither be avoided, nor separated."

The chapter begins with an exploration of two popular images in cognitive science: the expert/novice conversation as the heart of cognitive development and the metaphor of the instructional "scaffold" that supports and extends the learner's intellectual growth. These ideas are explored with specific reference to the teaching and learning of writing in school and to the process of learning to teach.

The chapter continues with an examination of the instructional conversation of a teacher educator and a novice teacher. Like a play within a play, this vignette portrays their conversational struggle to discover how the novice teacher should best respond to the writing of one of her young pupils. This vignette sets the stage for an exploration of the limits and possibilities of instructional talk about text and about teaching.

Based on consideration of instructional conversations situated in the elementary school and the university, the chapter concludes by describing issues of authority, intimacy, meaning, and purpose as they operate to shape the talk that occurs between experts and novices and the learning mediated by that talk. Implications for school policy and curriculum are suggested.

LANGUAGE INSTRUCTION AS TALK ABOUT TEXT

At the heart of a great deal of contemporary research on text composition and comprehension is a model of learning in which the novice's development is supported by dialogue with a more experienced person (Bruner, 1966; Wertsch, 1980). Many scholars seeking metaphors for how beginners learn to compose or comprehend turn to research on oral language acquisition. Here, they find evidence that the conversations of care-givers and young children play an important part in language development (see, e.g., Halliday, 1975; Ninio & Bruner, 1976). Bruner (1975), for example, argued that as children learn language in the family, "mothers most often see their role as supporting the child in achieving an intended outcome, entering only to assist, reciprocate, or 'scaffold' the interaction" (p. 12).

Many of those applying Bruner's "scaffold" metaphor to language instruction cite the developmental theories of Vygotsky (1978) in support of their work. Here, too, dialogue between novice and experienced cultural members plays a fundamental role in intellectual development. Extending Vygotsky's theoretical work to problem-solving experiments with mothers and young children, Wertsch (1980), for example, found that in dialogue with their mothers, children operate just beyond, but in anticipation of, competence. With conversational support, children participate in solving problems before they can solve them unassisted. Over time, and with models and practice, children gradually internalize the knowledge represented in conversations with adults and become independent problem solvers. By analogy, educational psychologists hypothesize that if teachers engage in scaffolded dialogues with students to solve problems of text comprehension or composition, they can provide information and models that are supportive of growth in school literacy skills (Applebee & Langer, 1983; Calkins, 1983; Palincsar & Brown, 1984).

Application to Classroom Instruction and Research

Application of developmental research on mother–child interaction to classroom instruction and research depends, at least in part, on the assumption that a dialogic model of language learning can be generalized across settings, purposes, and relationships. Educational psychologists are not alone in making this assumption. Sociolinguistic and ethnographic studies of the differential treatment of children from diverse ethnic backgrounds hold this assumption as well. In arguing that, at least for White, middle-class children, ways of learning about language in school are strongly associated with language learning and use at home, researchers assume strong contextual similarities between middle-class homes and classrooms (Philips, 1983; Shultz, Florio, & Erickson, 1982). Heath (1982), for example, asserted that "close analysis of how mainstream school-oriented children come to learn to take meaning from books at home suggest that such children learn not only how to take meaning from books, but also how to talk about it. In doing the latter, they repeatedly practice routines which parallel closely those of classroom interaction" (p. 56).

This research is intuitively appealing, because it seems to help us understand the interactional nature of differential treatment in school. It can, however, be criticized for assuming a direct relationship between middle-class values and school norms and practices or for tacitly reifying that relationship (Delpit, 1988; Bernstein, 1977). The argument that, in theory (or, at least for some economically privileged children, in practice), learning at home resembles learning at school obscures important differences and points of conflict between the two settings and begs the question of effectiveness of ordinary classroom talk to support the development of higher order literary skills in any children.

Despite the limits of research that assumes a family resemblance between school talk and middle-class family talk about text, we can safely draw one conclusion from this work. Language learning in both the home and the school is a socially mediated process. However, to the extent that conversation is constrained by social contexts and roles, we have reason to expect that the language learning conversations children have with their teachers will be unique ones, different from any others they have with adults in their families or neighborhoods. It remains to be seen what instructional role teacher–student conversation can play in students' learning of higher order skills involved in literacy. Brown and Palincsar (1986) made this point, with reference to typical classroom recitations in which the teacher initiates, students reply, and the teacher evaluates, when they noted that:

Certain participant structures have been amply demonstrated as culturally inappropriate for a variety of ethnically different groups. What has not been proven is that simple reciprocation is culturally appropriate in the dominant culture. Indeed, many have argued against this claim (Mehan, 1979), particularly when the children in question are young, poor, or academically delayed (Brown, Palincsar, and Purcell, 1985). Collaboration may be the preferred mode for many children. (p. 16)

The remainder of this chapter takes a closer look at the social contexts and relationships that shape classroom instructional conversations. It focuses on the specific problem of teachers' responses to student writers in the literacy event commonly known as the "writing conference." In analyzing conferences, it examines their inherent problems and promise with examples from two kinds of novices: those learning to write and those learning to teach.

WRITING CONFERENCES AS SCHOOL
LITERACY EVENTS: IDEALS AND REALITIES

The writing conference, as popularized especially by Murray (1968; 1979), Graves (1983), and Calkins (1983), is both a conversational setting and, according to Graves (1983), a "form of language" (p. 97). As such, the ideal conference has certain distinctive conversational features. Chief among them is the participation of a reader/listener who helps an author plan or revise his or her text by means of questions and responses about that text. Certainly, conferences can occur with or without teachers and in groups as well as dyads. In all instances, however, conferences require a responsive other with whom an author can discuss a text. Where beginning writers are concerned, the other's participation leads not only to the revision of a draft, but, gradually, to the author's internalization of the reader/writer dialogue. This internalization heralds the mature writing process in which an author can engage in planning and revision with greater independence (Murray, 1979).

Writing conferences occur at all grade levels, from preschool to university, and are strongly encouraged in some school buildings and districts. Their popularity is related to a contemporary shift in interest from evaluation of isolated student texts to dialogic support of the composing process and its development (Beach & Bridwell, 1984). This shift in emphasis potentially transforms the teacher's role from task master and evaluator to reader and respondent (Shaw, Pettigrew, & Van Nostrand, 1983) and opens the door to greater peer interaction in literacy learning (Gere & Stevens, 1985).

However liberating these changes seem for teachers and students, the promise of writing conferences as scaffolded dialogue between teacher/experts and student/novices is tempered by the realities of classroom life as described in classroom discourse research (summarized in Green, 1983, and Cazden, 1986). According to this research, teachers ordinarily dominate instructional talk. Not only do they speak far more than students, but they generally control topic and access to the floor. In addition, teacher talk is powerful. It interweaves referential and social information with public assessment (Heap, 1985). Because schools inculcate propositional, procedural, and normative knowledge, teachers evaluate student talk for evidence of learning in all three areas. Typically, teachers initiate instructional talk, students respond, and teachers evaluate those responses (Mehan, 1979).

Research on classroom writing suggests that its structure and functions are quite similar to those of classroom talk. Teachers routinely initiate writing tasks and topics, students write in response, and their writing is evaluated by teachers (Applebee, 1981; Staton, Shuy, Kreeft, & Reed, 1982). As with student talk, when teachers evaluate student texts, they appear to seek evidence of propositional, procedural, and normative knowledge. Just as student talk is shaped by the social and cognitive demands of schooling, so are student texts and the talk that surrounds them (Street, 1984; Stubbs, 1980; 1982).

In the ideal writing conference, however, students and teachers are practically free to trade conversational places. Students have the right to initiate talk and determine topic. Teachers are obliged to respond to student concerns. Students take from those responses useful information about revision. Even when teachers actively instruct about writing, that instruction is offered in the service of the student's current writing needs and concerns. Thus, writing conferences potentially alter the conversational rights and duties of teacher and students and, in so doing, change the range of language strategies available to students for learning (Barnes, 1976). Given what we know about the norms organizing routine classroom talk, however, it seems appropriate to question the possibility of such a profound and localized shift in classroom task, talk, and text.

WRITING INSTRUCTION AS TALK ABOUT TEXT

The research and teaching literature about writing conferences offers little help in our understanding the limits and possibilities of conversation as a means to teach and learn writing. Consisting primarily of descriptions of successful conferences and prescriptions for practice (see, e.g., Calkins, 1983; Graves, 1983; Murray, 1968), the work is very attractive to educators. However, claims about the widespread feasibility of writing conferences remain untested. We know little about the kind of pedagogical knowledge it takes to achieve successful conferences. In addition, there is little research on conferences across different genres or among students of varying ability or background. Finally, there have been few analyses of conferences as literacy events that are, according to Heath (1983), "occasions in which written language is integral to the nature of participants' interactions and their interpretive processes and strategies" (p. 50). Thus, we do not know the extent to which the norms organizing school's routine definitions of situation, status, and role continue to operate within writing conferences. We have not studied sufficiently the ways teachers' and children's experience of these conversations are connected to pedagogy, social relations, and learning (Barnes, 1976; Searle, 1984).

Insights from Current Research

From the few extant studies of writing conferences as literacy events come troubling findings. These studies suggest that prevailing school norms limit the conference's possibilities as scaffolded dialogue. They also suggest that considerable attention must be paid to pedagogy if teachers are to help students learn to write by reading and discussing their work with them. Current research finds that much conference talk tends to resemble the unilateral communication found in lessons. Largely teacher-driven, this talk lacks the conversational structure or content that might ultimately, in Freedman's (1985) words, "(a) help students identify and solve composing problems; (b) stimulate practice; and (c) in that practice, transfer their skills to new writings" (p. xi).

Freedman and Sperling (1985), for example, studied the writing conferences of one college teacher and four of her students. The students differed in ability and ethnicity, and the researchers found that although the teacher intended to treat all students equally, what she taught, how she taught it, the synchrony of conference talk, and the teacher's openness to further conferences differed in relation to students' writing abilities, ways of presenting themselves, and chosen topics.

In a study of 32 junior college writing conferences, Jacob (1982) expected to find that conferences were conversations driven by student authors' interests and concerns. Instead, he found that they were far more like lessons than conversations. In most instances, Jacob (1982) found that communication was "unilateral, from instructor to student, that most instructors shaped and directed the conversation, that students didn't mind the teacher dominance, in fact, they wanted it." (p. 386).

In research on conferences in an upper elementary classroom, Michaels, Ulichney, & Watson-Gegeo (1986) and Ulichney and Watson-Gegeo (1989) found that teacher response and student revision seem geared not to students' articulation of their audiences, purposes, and problems but to their attainment of a match with the teacher's implicit schema for an adequate textual representation of a class field trip. How the conference proceeds and the kind of response a student receives seem related to how well the student's text already matches the teacher's schema and to the interpersonal relationship between teacher and student predicting whether a match (or a mismatch) is likely.

Michaels and her colleagues made two key assertions about the conferences they researched: first, that conferences are motivated by the teacher's desire to make specific corrections or improvements in the text (and to coproduce these alterations with the students by getting them to acknowledge, accept, or display the teacher's solution) and, second, that this display occurs within a language game that looks remarkably like other teaching events in the classroom (i.e., lessons). Within this language game, the teacher holds the dominant interpretive framework. He or she decides what should be corrected, what the corrections should look like, and how the student should make them. Additionally, the teacher tends not to state this information directly or explicitly—perhaps owing to his or her sense that a conference should be nondirective. This leads, however, to the following sort of exchange, cited by Ulichney and Watson-Gegeo (1989) from a conference in which a student was attempting to revise her description of her favorite part of a circus act:

T:* MY FAVORITE PART WAS WHEN THE KIDS . . . WENT ON THE TRAPEZE///(softly)
Okay . . . how 'bout a better word than *went*/
That's kind of a boring word//
What . . . what are you talkin about?/

L: (fly up on/

T: -that went up on the-
(1 sec)
flying way up high on the=

L: =uh huh/

T: =thing?//
Now *think* of a better word//
Instead of just *went* on it/
What did they do?/Maybe they/ . . .
Think about how they looked when they were goin' up/

---

*"T" refers to teacher; "L" refers to Laura; see Ulichney & Watson-Gegeo (1989) for details on transcription conventions.

and give me a better word//
L: Um colorful?//
T: Colorful//
     THE BEST PART WAS WHEN THE KIDS *COLOR*FUL?/ON THE
     TRAPEZE?/
L: No=
T: =No that doesn't sound right/
L: Jumped on the trapeze/=
T: =Jumped on it?/
     Okay//think of how they looked when they went up// . . .
     Remember they had a . . . (. . .) up like this?//
     Didn't they have a rope they had to go on like?//
     Go look at the circus book and see if you can . . . remember/
     How did they get up there?// (p.319–320)

The researchers argued that the teacher and student do not share a
sense of the intended meaning. Whereas the teacher interprets Laura's
"went" to refer to climbing up onto the trapeze, Laura intends it to
mean "performing" on the trapeze. Additionally, Laura misinterprets the
teacher's strategy for repair when she responds with "colorful" to the
teacher's request that she think of a better word to describe how they
looked when they were going up. This mismatch of interpretive frames
is compounded by the teacher's authoritative role. Her representation of
the task dominates, and her interpretation of the student text overwhelms
the conference talk. Laura, appropriately, does not resist. The researchers further argued that it is likely that students who are less able writers
at the outset will experience mismatches of this sort more often than
students assessed who write well.

Flower (1987) has recently observed that, in typical academic assignments, tasks may be specified in a manner that is clear to the teacher but
not so clear to the writer. Students must learn not only how to write,
but how and when to match interpretations of tasks (and subsequent
composing strategies) with the teacher's. Conferences that rule out talk
about how the task was or is to be construed—and what strategies may
lead to the realization of the task—fail to help students learn important
aspects of written language, such as audience awareness and task representation.

Limits on Instructional Talk About Text

If we reflect on the findings of the research reported heretofore, we find
that some of the conference's limitations arise precisely because it is
instructional talk. Barnes (1976) observed that theories of instruction usually assume talk between experts and novices. The expert/novice distinc-

tion in classrooms reinforces ordinary conversational norms in which teachers hold the right to determine tasks and standards. Thus, it is extremely difficult for participants to hold instructional conversations in which students can assume rights to initiate talk, determine topic, or serve as "experts" even about their own writing problems and purposes.

Other limitations of conferences appear to be related to the knowledge that teachers and students bring—knowledge about the writing process, schooling, and one another. Because classroom talk typically interweaves knowledge in these three domains, it is not surprising that some researchers find conferences faltering because of confusion or conflict along interpersonal lines, whereas others locate problems in the absence of shared knowledge about writing and the text.

Still other limits on the writing conference as a scaffold for the learner's development may arise from the demands of time, mandated curricula, and the school's evaluative climate. In this regard, Erickson (1984) argued that, although in some aspects of classroom life, "the press toward scaffolding work by both teacher and student seems ubiquitous" (p. 534), formal assessment and scripted or partly scripted lessons virtually preclude interactional scaffolding. Thus, in some of the more central instructional events, Erickson (1984) wrote, "not only does the learner not have rights to shape the learning task, but neither does the teacher" (p. 534).

THE ROLE OF TEACHER KNOWLEDGE IN INSTRUCTIONAL TALK

Learning to teach writing is clearly more than a technical problem of learning how to speak with learners. It is also a problem of one's image of those learners, one's knowledge of the trajectory of their writing and social development, one's understanding of the writing process, and one's sharing with them a meaningful writing goal. These contextual conditions profoundly shape how teachers and students organize themselves to speak and work together—and it is these conditions that are within the teacher's power to influence. Thus, it is these conditions about which teachers must learn if they are to hold conversations with youngsters that are genuinely supportive of writing growth. The forthcoming vignette illustrates the complexity of this process for one novice teacher.

I have worked for a number of years trying to help beginners teach in ways that are responsive to the plans, drafts, and revisions of youngsters learning to write. In this effort, I was initially captivated by the metaphor of the conversational scaffold. I encouraged beginning teachers to hold writing conferences with their students. However, my students and I found that it was very difficult to learn to respond to young writers and their texts.

Although other aspects of teaching seemed easily reduced to procedure, response eluded many of the beginning teachers. Each year, I watched even those who enthusiastically claimed to "love children" struggle to let those children speak, to find meaning in their texts, and to support their plans and revisions through talk. Often, writing conferences became not conversations about student writing but empty rituals or opportunities for the beginning teachers to edit the children's texts. In addition, although the conferences were intended to deal with the writing process as well as its product, "process" quickly became the sole "product" of the young teachers' efforts.

The following vignette comes from my experience as a teacher of writing instruction to university juniors preparing to become teachers. As my students learned to teach writing, I kept a journal of the challenges that they and I faced. I quickly found that watching novice teachers illuminated not only problems of learning to teach writing but also a great deal about the normative nature of the teacher's role and classroom talk.

The vignette demonstrates some of the ways in which writing conferences differ from mother–child talk about text. On one hand, it locates some of the sources of writing instruction's difficulty in the functions of schooling and the nature of the teacher's role. On the other, it identifies some of the special opportunities teachers have to teach by taking children's work seriously and responding to it. Thus, it offers new ways of thinking about the education of young writers and young teachers as conceptual and conversational.

Kristen and Matt: A Vignette

Kristen, a junior in my language arts teaching class, wanted to practice what she had learned to call "the process approach to teaching writing." She planned to add a "free writing activity" to the end of her second grade basal reading group. To get her young writers started, she selected a color drawing from a part of the basal reader that they had not yet read. The drawing contained two panels. In the first, children are pictured looking at the books in a school library. In the second, a child is reading at a table while other children are talking at the book shelf. One child is handing a book to another who is seated in a wheelchair. Showing them the picture, she asked them to write as much as they could describing its contents.

Matt, one of Kristen's young students, was slow in getting started.

When she asked him why he was not writing, he said, "Is it okay to write names for the kids in the picture?" Kristen said it was. With that reply, Matt wrote busily for what was left of the 10 minutes that Kristen had allotted for the writing task.

Kristen collected the writing of her six students. All of them but Matt had written strings of declarative sentences dutifully describing the picture. Only Matt elected to name the children in the picture. His text is reproduced in Fig. 12.1.

Kristen did not have time to talk with the students about their writing that day. She planned to hold individual conferences with them 2 days later on her next visit to the classroom. Kristen knew that young writers have few opportunities to learn and practice revision, so she planned to talk with the children about their drafts, encouraging each one to "improve it by adding more details."

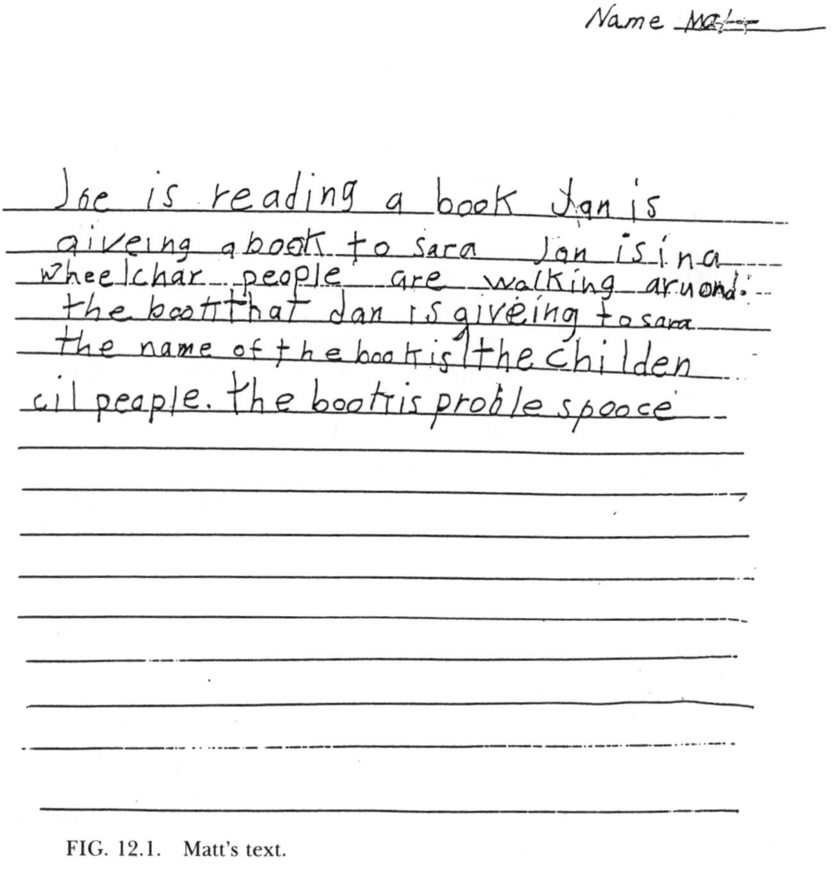

Name _Matt_

Joe is reading a book Jan is giveing a book to Sara Jon is in a wheelchar people are walking aruond the boot that dan is giveing to Sara the name of the book is the childen cil peaple. the boot is proble spooce

FIG. 12.1. Matt's text.

Back at the university, Kristen looked over the drafts. She was stunned when she saw Matt's, and she brought it to me, pleading, "Help! There's so much wrong with this paper, I don't know where to begin." I asked her what was wrong with it, and a litany of "errors" poured forth. "Look," she said, "he can hardly spell. He also doesn't understand about punctuation. There are only two periods in this paragraph. It is like two long sentences. Also, he didn't put a capital letter at the beginning of the second sentence."

"Anything else?" I asked, hoping to get all of Kristen's concerns on the table. "Well," she said, "he didn't do what I asked him to do. This was supposed to be a description. I was looking for details, color words. Matt didn't write a description. I think when I told him it was okay to give the kids names, he thought it was okay to write a story instead of a description. I just don't know how I can conference with Matt about all this without turning him off to writing."

Kristen is a beginner herself. Her situation may seem extreme to experienced teachers, but it is not atypical among the many young people whom I teach. Moreover, I believe it underscores some of the reasons why we must take a closer look at our assumptions about school talk, tasks, and text if we are to create in classrooms congenial environments for writing growth. If we put context around the talk and texts of teacher and students, we begin to see that changes in the surface features of classroom organization or discourse do not necessarily reflect changes in the nature of classrooms as environments for learning. With this in mind, let us return to Kristen and Matt.

Unpacking Kristen and Matt's situation, we find that, on the surface, it does not look very different from the instance of scaffolded language learning described in the seminal and oft-cited research of Ninio and Bruner (1976). Like a mother, Kristen initiated a naming task. Students, like the young child, had a response slot. In that slot, however, students would write, rather than say, what they saw in the picture. Like the mother, Kristen already knew the answer to her "what's that?" question, and, like a mother, she would make some sort of response to the child's picture naming.

Despite surface feature similarities, however, there are profound differences between Kristen's writing lesson and mother and child conversing about a picture book. These differences are interpretable in terms of the differences between the two literacy events and the speech communities in which they occur. Although in both cases the name of the game may have been describing pictures, the school writing task differs from talk on mother's knee in its purpose, conversational organization, knowledge required for appropriate participation, and in the learning that might accrue from the talk.

How was the encounter of Kristen and Matt different from the scaffolded dialogue of mother and child? First, mothers engage children in conversation with the assumption of children's competence. In contrast, when I asked Kristen to tell me what evidence of competence or potential she saw in Matt's text, she was nonplussed. Second, whereas mother or teacher may initiate a task, mother and child work, in Ninio and Bruner's (1976) words, "toward a shared format and mutually clear set of expectations" (p. 8). Kristen and Matt did not appear to achieve such consensus.

Teacher and student had a brief negotiation about the writing task when Matt asked if he could name the children in the picture; to Kristen, in retrospect, her answer opened the door to Matt's construing the task to be one of narration rather than description. Teacher and student failed to coordinate purposes, and in this light, Newman (1985) argued that, in an "idealized application of Vygotsky's work," such coordination is essential because the child internalizes not specifically what the adult says but a heuristic version of their interaction.

One can only imagine that the failure of Kristen and Matt to reach consensus about the task—Is it describing? Is it story telling?—might continue when they met again. Thus, a sort of instructional "schizmogenesis" would be set in motion, with conflict, rather than consensus, the result (Erickson, 1984). Indeed, Kristen anticipated this when she worried that her upcoming conference with Matt might "turn him off to writing."

There are other aspects of the picture-describing event at school that stand in sharp contrast to what mothers do with children. In school tasks, learning is not incidental to the completion of another activity—it is the primary activity. As such, school tasks carry heavy baggage. Mothers may desire and enjoy growth of their children as speakers, but teachers have mandatory curricular goals for such skills as "writing descriptively." In fact, the children in Matt's school district are expected to demonstrate that they can write simple descriptions by the end of second grade.

The burden of such an instructional agenda increases the likelihood that teacher and student purposes in picture naming may never really converge. Compounding the problem of needing to teach and assess skills in isolated writing tasks is the fact that, unlike a mother, the teacher has brief periods of contact with individual students and enjoys only limited knowledge of their prior learning and experience with the task at hand. Although for Kristen, as a student teacher, this problem is extreme, Jackson (1974) argued persuasively that lack of intimacy and the press of time and tasks in classrooms truncate relationships between teachers and children, thus limiting what they can know about each other as they transact.

Additionally, given the press of time, lack of intimacy, and the drive to achieve predetermined learning goals, the teacher is most unlikely to do something that mothers often do—that is, she is unlikely to follow the learner's lead. Ninio and Bruner found that mothers were more likely to respond to a child's turn if it constituted the initiation of a new dialogue cycle rather than the recycling of what had been said in a previous maternal turn. In short, although mothers initiate naming tasks, there is room, perhaps even preference, for mothers to move with the child. This movement, along with opportunity for extended talk and access to the child's prior knowledge, increases the likelihood that a scaffold will be not static and rigid but dynamic and self-destructing as the child moves toward more independent problem solving.

Finally, mother–child conversations seem to be genuine. They are about what they are about. Classroom lessons are more like plays within plays. Ninio and Bruner reported for example, that mothers make no gross modifications in their customary use of language to carry out book reading with children. Yet, the education literature is replete with scripted or semiscripted scenarios for how to talk with children about text. In other words, ordinary and spontaneous conversation between adults and children is apparently insufficient when participants toil in crowds and short time periods, across gaps in background knowledge, and with rigid learning goals. Kristen came to me for advice precisely because she felt she did not know how to respond to Matt. Her problem did not stem from an inability to speak with children, but from the conversational demands imposed on her and Matt in classroom literacy events.

Kristen squirmed in her seat when I asked her to tell me about Matt's writing competence and show me examples of potential learning in his paper. "I don't know what you want from me," she said in frustration. In the moment, I was painfully aware that my own role and institutional place made it difficult for me, as well, to have a scaffolded dialogue with my student. "Forget about what I want," I said, "What do you see? Can you play archaeologist with Matt's text?"

Kristen began by reading Matt's paper aloud. Until this moment, she had not thought to do so. As she read, she paused for a breath at the end of each idea unit: "Joe is reading a book (pause) Jan is giving a book to Sarah (pause) Jan is in a wheelchair (pause) people are walking around (pause) the book that Jan is giving to Sarah the name of the book is . . ." Here, Kristen stopped and said, "Oops. Here he as a run-on sentence."

Interrupting her, I exclaimed, "What did you say?" She looked up at me. "I said that, well, its not a run-on sentence, but it looks like Matt started this sentence twice." "Sentence?", I inquired. "I thought you said there were only two long sentences in this whole text." "Oh, that's only if you go by punctuation," she replied. "Really, there are a whole bunch of sentences. They just don't have periods and capital letters."

I suggested that we go back and mark the sentences off one at a time. As we did, Kristen made a remarkable observation. Although Matt had not marked the boundaries between sentences with conventional punctuation, it seemed to her that he had increased the space between idea units almost twofold. In addition, Kristen noted, "He does have capital letters at lots of places where sentences begin. Its just that I didn't notice them before because they were for people's names." In fact, it seemed to Kristen that every "sentence" was either marked by extra space and a capital letter or by a period and a capital letter (See Fig. 12.2).

We talked about how Kristen had marked idea units as she read aloud. "With breaths mostly," she said, "and sometimes with tone of voice." I

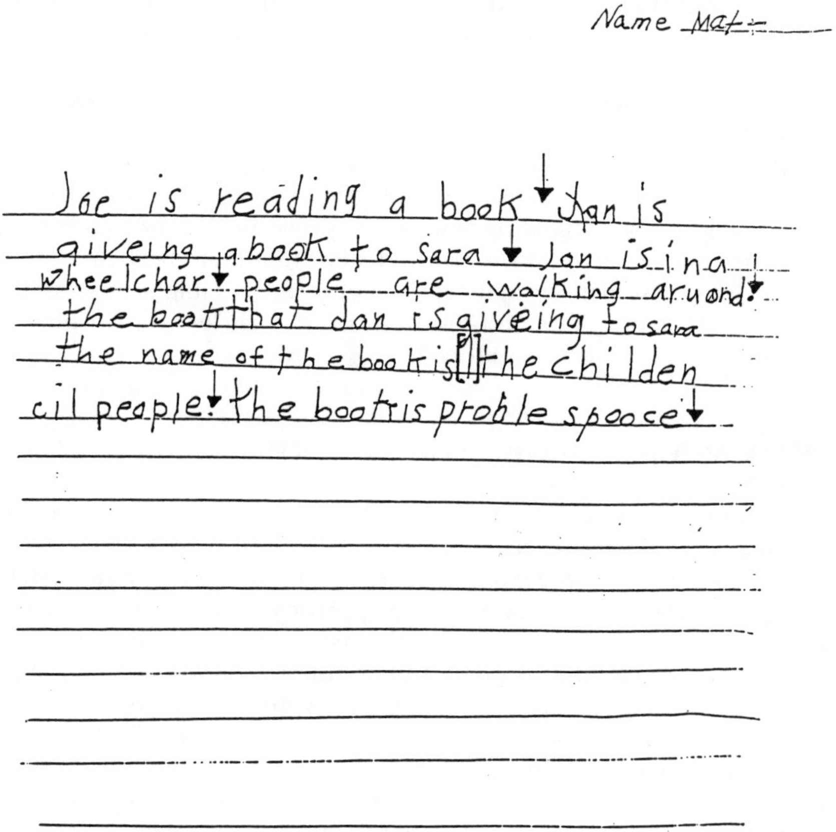
Name Matt

Joe is reading a book ↓ Dan is giveing a book to sara ↓ Jon is in a wheelchar ↓ people are walking aruond ↓ the boot that dan is giveing to sara the name of the book is [ ] the childen cil people ↓ the book is proble spooce ↓

FIG. 12.2 Matt's text noting sentence boundaries and book title.

observed that writers need graphic ways to replace such cues. "Leaving space on the paper is sort of like taking a breath," she said.

Once started on the search for Matt's ways of making meaning, it was hard for us to stop. We found more clues to his thinking as we combed the text. Kristen pointed out that there was a slash mark in front of the name of the book. She wondered how he knew to set off a book title. "I don't think they've learned that yet," she said. "But he knows about books and that titles are in big letters, special." We also observed that Matt's spellings were so close to the actual pronunciation of words that, while they had originally disarmed Kristen, they certainly did not get in the way of her knowing what Matt's words meant.

Finally, I asked Kristen, "Does what Matt wrote hang together? Can you follow it?" Shrugging, she replied, "Sure. He really did more than I asked. It doesn't say in the picture what the name of the book is. He made that up by himself. And he said it was probably spooky. Their teacher is working on prediction in reading comprehension." Kristen smiled as she packed up her papers and prepared to leave, "I can't wait to talk to Matt tomorrow. I want to ask him some questions about why Jan is giving Sarah a scary book. Maybe he can write more about why Jan is in a wheelchair, too."

"What about punctuation?" I asked. "Well, he's getting the idea. He already knows about the different groups of words, and he's trying out ways to separate them. Maybe I could show him that and help him to learn why we use periods and capital letters. Spaces might be okay for him, but other people might not understand what he means when he leaves extra spaces between ideas."

CHANGING THE CONDITIONS FOR LEARNING

Pondering why conferences might be so difficult for beginning teachers has helped me to realize that a great deal more than "talk" goes into a teacher–learner dialogue if it is to be truly educative. As we have seen in the preceding example, a laissez-faire approach to classroom talk about text is likely to lead novice and experienced teachers to reproduce ordinary conversational norms in ways unhelpful to the young writer. Yet, we have also seen in these examples that knowing how to scaffold a learner's development by means of response to his or her words and his or her work is not simply a technical matter of knowing "what to say when." The problems bedeviling Kristen, the novice teacher, cast in sharp relief issues of teacher knowledge, pedagogy, and social context that we must all confront if we hope that, in conversations with us, students will be helped to become more independent thinkers and self-regulated learners (Brophy, 1990). In the concluding section of this chapter, I review some of these issues as they present themselves in teaching and teacher education.

Challenging Pervasive Ideas About Teaching

In the case of Kristen and Matt, the ideal of the scaffolded dialogue made havoc with some basic, normative assumptions about teaching acquired by beginning teachers during their prior socialization to schools (Florio-Ruane, 1989). The successful conference depends on student initiation and teacher response in the service of students' writing growth. Yet, this apparent reversal of conversational rights and obligations challenges the beginner's assumptions about (a) what experts have to offer novices; (b) what teachers need to be "expert" about; and (c) the nature of the teaching/learning encounter.

On the first matter, many beginning teachers assume a vision of knowledge as a commodity to be transferred. Clearly, the theory of cognitive development underlying dialogic approaches to teaching assumes, in contrast, a view of knowledge development as a continuing process of negotiation and transformation. This difference has profound implications for teaching by conference. As we have seen herein, showing, telling, and evaluating are transformed into diagnostic listening, asking, and responding.

On the second matter of "expertise," beginners are typically and appropriately concerned with "getting through" and they therefore tend to emphasize procedure over content in their early lessons. Yet, writing conferences are not procedures; they are conversations—ones in which, paradoxically, greater rather than less reciprocity between teacher and learner is required for them to be truly instructive. Thus, in conference, if students have rights to initiate talk or determine topic, teachers need to be able and free to relinquish or reshape their putative rights and responsibilities to determine the content and pace of student learning. Moreover, if teachers serve not as explainers and evaluators so much as respondents and audiences, they cannot rely on procedure to "get them through." They need to be not so much "expert" managers and technicians, but listeners and diagnosticians.

Each young author and nascent text presents a somewhat unique problem and opportunity for teaching about writing. However, to recognize and seize such an instructional moment requires that the teacher know a good deal about writing development (in general terms as well as in the specific instance of a particular student author), the way written language works to produce texts, and alternative ways to help young writers frame their writing problems and tackle them in drafting and revision. Research currently suggests that these kinds of teacher knowledge and disposition tend not to be fostered in teacher education or in the daily life of classrooms (Buchmann, 1982; Jackson, 1974).

As if the first and second areas of new knowledge were not a sufficiently tall order, teachers who want to teach responsively need to reexamine their assumptions about the nature of the teaching–learning encounter in school. Too easily we assume that the encounter in brief, evaluative, public (or semipublic), and friendly-but-businesslike. Yet, these social conditions seem antithetical to the ones demonstrated to produce powerful language learning in home settings. And it is here, perhaps more than anywhere else, that sensitivity to children's nonschool lives can offer keys to enhancing learning in school.

If we return to the problem with which this chapter began—the possibility of generalizing from research on the learning of oral language at home to the teaching of language (and literacy) in school—we can begin to think about social conditions that might preclude or improve classroom language learning. For the purpose of this comparison, I distilled from studies of mother–child conversation the following five maxims that teachers might draw from nonschool learning to help them support language learning in school. These maxims represent not only what care-givers say and do but what they know and the social resources they draw on in conversations with young children:

- Assume competence
- Know the learner
- Share interest in the task at hand
- Follow the learner
- Capitalize on uncertainty.

Ninio and Bruner (1976), Halliday (1975), and Wertsch (1980) are among a growing number of scholars who have shown in experimental and descriptive work that the setting, purposes, and relationships of children to their care-givers are tied to learning by conversation. Although these maxims seems almost trivially self-evident on first glance, their application in school settings is thorny and requires not only particular pedagogical knowledge and dispositions, but changes in the contextual factors within which teachers work.

Classrooms, in disturbing contrast to many learning situations outside school, tend to be typified in Jackson's (1974) words, by "crowds, praise, and power" (p. 10). These conditions discourage, and may even prevent, teachers from following a simple set of maxims to enhance learning by conversation. Ironically, these conditions for learning are hardest to create in school—precisely that place where social life exists explicitly for the business of learning and teaching.

The enormous power inherent in the teacher role from the point of view of students limits the possibility for reciprocity in teacher–student talk. Yet, cross-cutting this power is another reality—that the teacher's power is greatly tempered by institutional forces outside the classroom. Lack of sufficient time, materials, or space may impeded intimate teacher–student communication. In addition, the pressure on teachers to serve the school's sorting and evaluation functions to cover the mandated curriculum can preclude the teacher's "assuming competence" or "following the learner." Large classes, too, work against intimacy and flexibility. "Uncertainty"—far from being viewed as an essential feature of learning, is avoided by the imposition of rigid instructional procedures and rituals. Lastly, teachers' relative lack of subject matter preparation and the vacuousness of much elementary curricula in the area of writing instruction (Florio & Clark, 1982) often preclude teachers and students from genuinely "sharing interest" in challenging learning tasks.

CONCLUSION

Mothers are not teachers; schools are not homes. Many homes fall short of meeting children's learning needs; many schools do so as well. Despite all this, a great deal can be drawn from the study of how novices come to learn by communication with interested and caring adults. In this chapter, we have seen that a simplistic mapping of mother–child discourse research onto the teacher–student relationship does not get us very far. We have also seen that the potential for talk to be educative in either setting depends on features of context, activity, and relationship that are often overlooked in the informal learning of the household—and in the crowded, hurried, and impersonal learning of the school. These insights are of greatest importance to educators, because their classrooms, unlike families, exist explicitly for the purpose of the education of the young.

By looking at beginners and how they might learn from adults, this chapter has attempted to argue that it is neither particular instructional techniques nor discourse strategies and moves that make the difference in learning at home—or at school. And it is not a family resemblance at this level that is important to the child trying to make sense of learning in each of the settings.

What is more important for teachers to draw from research on the talk of mothers and children is insight into the conditions under which social life serves to support intellectual development. This insight, as we have seen in the experience of young Kristen, leads teachers to a need to know. Teachers want and need to know more about their learners, more about the processes by which their learners are developing the capacity to make meaning in talk and in text. They need knowledge of pedagogy that allows them to take a greater hand in shaping learning environments. Finally, they need to learn to create with learners, in Hawkins' (1974) words, "worthy interests and pursuits . . . through a community of subject matter" (p. 29) so that literacy learning can be socially mediated in ways that ultimately set the learner free to become his or her own teacher.

ACKNOWLEDGMENTS

The author thanks Jere Brophy, Margret Buchmann, Magdalene Lampert, Timothy Lensmire, Sarah Michaels, and Paul Naso and Polly Ulichney for their helpful comments on earlier versions of this chapter.

REFERENCES

Applebee, A. L. (1981). *Writing in the secondary school: English and the content areas* (Research Rep. No. 21). Urbana, IL: National Council of Teachers of English.
Applebee, A. L., & Langer, J. A. (1983). Instructional scaffolding: Reading and writing as natural language activities. *Language Arts, 60,* 168–175.
Barnes, D. (1976). *From communication to curriculum.* New York: Penguin.
Beach, R., & Bridwell, L. S. (Eds.). (1984). *New directions in composition research.* New York: Guilford Press.
Bernstein, B. (1977). Class and pedagogies: Visible and invisible. In J. Karabel & A. H. Halsey (Eds.), *Power and ideology in education* (pp. 511–534). New York: Oxford University Press.
Brophy, J. (Ed.). (1990). *Advances in research on teaching.* Greenwich, CT: JAI Press.
Brown, A. L., & Palincsar, A. S. (1986). Guided, cooperative learning and individual knowledge acquisition. In L. Resnick (Ed.), *Knowing, learning, and instruction: Essays in honor of Robert Glaser.* Hillsdale, NJ: Lawrence Erlbaum Associates.
Bruner, J. S. (1966). *Toward a theory of instruction.* Cambridge: Belknap Press.
Bruner, J. S. (1975). The ontogenesis of speech acts. *Journal of Child Language, 2,* 1–19.
Buchmann, M. (1982). The flight away from content in teacher education. *Journal of Curriculum Studies, 14,* 61–68.
Calkins, L. (1983). *Lessons from a child: On the teaching and learning of writing.* Portsmouth, NH: Heinemann.
Cazden, C. B. (1986). Classroom discourse. In M. C. Wittrock (Ed.), *Handbook of research on teaching* (3rd ed., pp. 432–463). New York: MacMillan.
Delpit, L. (1988). The silenced dialogue: Power and pedagogy in educating other people's children. *Harvard Educational Review, 59,* (3), 280–298.
Erickson, F. (1984). School literacy, reasoning, and civility: An anthropologist's perspective. *Review of Research in Education, 54,* 525–546.

Florio, S., & Clark, C. M. (1982). The functions of writing in an elementary school classroom. *Research in the teaching of English, 16*(2), 115–130.

Florio-Ruane, S. (1989). Social organization of schools and classrooms. In M. Reynolds (Ed.), *Knowledge base for beginning teachers: A handbook* (pp. 163–172). Oxford, UK: Pergamon Press.

Flower, L. (1987). The role of task representation in reading-to-write. (Tech. Rep. No. 6). Berkeley, CA: University of California—Berkeley.

Freedman, S. W. (Ed.). (1985). *The acquisition of written language: Response and revision.* Norwood, NJ: Ablex.

Freedman, S. W., & Sperling, M. (1985). Written language acquisition: The role of response and the writing conference. In S. W. Freedman (Ed.), *The acquisition of written language: Response and revision* (pp. 106–130). Norwood, NJ: Ablex.

Gere, A. R., & Stevens, R. S. (1985). The language of writing groups: How oral response shapes revision. In S. W. Freedman (Ed.), *The acquisition of written language: Response and revision* (pp. 85–105). Norwood, NJ: Ablex.

Graves, D. W. (1983). *Writing: Teachers and children at work.* Exeter, NH: Heinemann.

Green, J. (1983). Research on teaching as a linguistic process: A state of the art. In E. W. Gordon (Ed.), *Review of research in education* (Vol. 10, pp. 151–252). Washington: American Educational Research Association.

Halliday, M. A. K. (1975). *Learning how to mean: Explorations in the development of language.* London: Edward Arnold.

Hawkins, D. (1974). *The informed vision: Essays on learning and human nature.* New York: Agathon Press.

Heap, J. L. (1985). Discourse in the production of classroom knowledge: Reading lessons. *Curriculum Inquiry, 15*(3), 245–279.

Heath, S. B. (1982). What no bedtime story means: Narrative skills at home and school. *Language in Society, 11,* 49–76.

Jackson, P. (1974). *Life in classrooms.* New York: Holt, Reinhart, and Winston.

Jacob, G. P. (1982). An ethnographic study of the writing conference: The degree of student involvement in the writing process. *Dissertation Abstracts International, 43,* 386A. (University Microfilms No. 8216050).

Mehan, H. (1979). *Learning lessons.* Cambridge, MA: Harvard University Press.

Michaels, S., Ulichney, P., & Watson-Gegeo, K. (1986, April). *Social processes and written products: Teacher expectations, writing conferences, and student texts.* Paper presented at the annual meeting of the American Educational Research Association, San Francisco.

Murray, D. M. (1968). *A writer teaches writing.* Boston: Houghton Mifflin.

Murray, D. M. (1979). The listening eye: Reflections on the writing conference. *College English, 41,* 13–18.

Newman, D. (1985, April). Functional environments for microcomputers in education. *The Quarterly Newsletter of the Laboratory of Comparative Human Cognition, 7,* 51–57.

Ninio, A., & Bruner, J. S. (1976). The achievement and antecedents of labelling. *Journal of Child Language, 5,* 1–15.

Palincsar, A. S., & Brown, A. L. (1984). Reciprocal teaching of comprehension-fostering and comprehension-monitoring activities. *Cognition and Instruction, 1,* 117–175.

Philips, S. U. (1983). *The invisible culture: Communication in the classroom and community on the Warm Springs Indian Reservation.* New York: Longman.

Searle, D. (1984). Who's building whose building? *Language Arts, 61,* 480–483.

Shaw, R., Pettigrew, J., & Van Nostrand, A. D. (1983). Tactical planning of writing instruction. *The Elementary School Journal, 84,* 45–51.

Shultz, J. J., Florio, S., & Erickson, F. (1982). Where's the floor?: Aspects of social relationships in communication at home and at school. In P. Gilmore, & A. Glatthorn (Eds.), *Children in and out of school: Ethnography and education* (pp. 88–123). Washington: Center for Applied Linguistics.

Staton, J., Shuy, R. W., Kreeft, J., & Reed, L. (1982). *The analysis of dialogue journal writing as a communicative event.* (Final report to the National Institute of Education, NIE-G-80-0122). Washington, DC: Center for Applied Linguistics.

Street, B. V. (1984). *Literacy in theory and practice.* Cambridge, England: Cambridge University Press.

Stubbs, M. (1980). *Language and literacy.* London: Routledge & Kegan Paul.

Stubbs, M. (1982). Written language and society: Some particular cases and general observations. In M. Nystrand (Ed.), *What writers know: The language process, and structure of written discourse* (pp. 31–55). New York: Academic Press.

Ulichney, P., & Watson-Gegeo, K. (1989). Interactions and Authority: The Dominant Interpretive Framework in Writing Conferences. *Discourse Processes,* 12–30, Vol. 12, No. 3, July–September, 1988. pp. 309–328.

Vygotsky, L. S. (1978). *Mind in society: The development of higher psychological processes.* Cambridge: MA: Harvard University Press.

Wertsch, J. (1980). The significance of dialogue in Vygotsky's account of social, egocentric, and inner speech. *Contemporary Educational Psychology, 5,* 150–162.

13

The Change Process and Its Implications in Teaching Thinking

Daniel U. Levine
University of Missouri-Kansas City

Eric J. Cooper
Simon and Schuster

After the editors of this volume asked us to review the literature on successful implementation of innovations in schools and other organizations, our major task was to identify the most important conclusions and generalizations from this enormous body of knowledge. In doing so, we tried to give particular attention to material that may be most relevant for educators who are initiating, or who plan to initiate, projects to improve student performance with respect to thinking and other higher order mental processes.

Research and analysis that deals with implementation of change and the change process constitute too large a field to summarize comprehensively in one relatively short chapter. Distinct subareas can be identified that deal with differing stages, such as adoption, implementation, and institutionalization, and with a variety of related topics, such as the role of change agents, linkage with external resources, dissemination of new knowledge, assessment of organizational structures and cultures, feedback of data to facilitate change, and planning for change. Observers such as Fullan (1982) and Schmuck and Runkel (1985) have provided summaries of research in these and other subareas. Rather than simply summarizing the results of major studies and research reviews, which sometimes differ substantially from one author to another, we begin by discussing four fundamental issues that should be considered when undertaking a significant innovation. Then, we briefly review 10 types of prerequisites and antecedents for successful change. The final sections deal with manageability and implementability of innovations and with general conclusions that are particularly pertinent for projects to improve students' performance in thinking and other higher order skills. The general conclusions can be summarized as follows:

- Successful innovations to improve instruction in thinking and other higher order skills will generally have to be relatively large and complex.

- If educators select a thinking-skills approach that utilizes specific teaching materials in order to enhance manageability for teachers or for other reasons, care should be taken to allow, encourage, and assist participating teachers to adapt the materials to the realities of their classrooms.

- Whether or not the thinking-skills approach that is selected utilizes specific sets of teaching materials, project administrators should attempt to identify core components that require fidelity in implementation, and they should work with teachers to ensure that these components are stressed and implemented well.

- Because thinking-skills approaches require large, complex, and difficult changes in the behaviors and attitudes of teachers and students, even more stress than usual should be placed on ensuring that innovations are manageable and implementable for teachers and that prerequisites and antecedents of successful implementation are firmly in place. Concern for manageability and prerequisites should include attention to such considerations as planning time, class size, change overload, amount of paperwork, adaptability in participating classrooms, compatibility with other demands, capacity for inspiring commitment, and large-scale staff development.

- Predictable obstacles that should be addressed in advance include school realities that stress classroom order and passive learning, students' preferences for lower order skills, student/teacher compromises that trade obedience for undemanding instruction; low-level learning scripts for low achievers, and teacher preferences for easy-to-teach lessons.

- Projects to improve students' thinking are likely to be greatly hampered when student assessment focuses on low-level skills.

- Successful implementation of approaches for improving thinking skills will require unusual stress on revising organizational and institutional arrangements and structures.

- Initiation of effective projects for improving thinking skills is an imposing challenge not to be undertaken lightly.

FOUR FUNDAMENTAL ISSUES

The four fundamental issues discussed in this section involve the following themes: (a) adaptation versus fidelity; (b) top-down versus bottom-up mandates; (c) packaged versus locally developed materials and procedures; and (d) scope and phasing.

Adaptation Versus Fidelity

A well-known study that Berman and McLaughlin (1978) conducted for the Rand Corporation provided widely cited and influential conclusions regarding the importance of adapting innovative approaches to local school settings. Based on a 2-year study of 293 local projects funded by four federal programs in 18 states, Berman and McLaughlin distinguished between unsuccessful projects, which were *non-implemented* or *co-opted,* and those that attained some success through *mutual adaptation.* Non-implementation was associated with projects that were overly planned and highly prescribed, and/or were applied in a pro forma way with little change in teaching or student performance. Co-optation occurred, as stated by Berman and McLaughlin (1978), where the staff "adapted the project, usually emasculating it, to meet their own needs, without any corresponding change in traditional institutional behavior or practices" (p. 16–17). By way of contrast, mutual adaptation involved change in both the project and the setting, and frequently involved a variety of adjustments, such as "reduction or modification of idealistic project goals, amendment or simplification of project treatment, [and] downward revision of ambitious expectations" (p.). The authors concluded that although projects characterized by mutual adaptation were not invariably successful, they had a "better chance of being effectively implemented" (pp. 16–17).

Granted that mutual adaptation may be more likely to succeed than either rigidly adhering to initial project design or largely ignoring fidelity in favor of flexible site-level implementation, should fidelity or adaptation receive more emphasis? Crandall, Eiseman, and Louis (1986) recently considered this issue under the heading "Replication versus Adaptation" as part of their systematic analysis of strategic planning issues that have implications for the success of school improvement efforts. After citing several studies indicating that users sometimes can successfully implement innovations faithfully (also see Hall & Hord, 1987, p. 129), and that mutual adaptation is sometimes negatively associated with personal and organizational change, these authors concluded that one must examine both the clarity of the innovation and the extent to which it has been field-tested and debugged: when innovations are both focused and debugged, as well as technically challenging, users permitted to make significant adaptations are, according to Crandall and his colleagues (1986), "unlikely to achieve the effects . . . achieved by the developers" (p. 31) because they tend to omit challenging components that may be the "key to success" (p. 31). By way of contrast, when "administrators both insisted that teachers faithfully implement well-designed and technically challenging innovations *and* provided the requisite support, the implementation outcomes were positive" (p. 31).

Thus, research can be interpreted as supporting an emphasis on fidelity in the case of well-designed and field-tested innovations, but some adaptation generally still seems necessary to fit local circumstances, as indicated by Berman and McLaughlin and other researchers (e.g., Fullan, 1982; Goodlad, 1987). In considering this issue further, Crandall and his colleagues (1986) recommended that distinctions be made as follows between innovation components and requirements: (a) *core components* that "developers believe are required if the desired results are to be obtained"; (b) *related components* that "either enhance the operation of core changes or increase the likelihood" of success; and (c) *implementation requirements* necessary for successful implementation (p. 31). They also concluded, however, that identifying the aspects of a change program that belong in the three categories is "much more difficult than one would intuitively expect" (p. 31). Their overall conclusion regarding the difficult task of finding the appropriate balance between fidelity and adaptation is as follows (Crandall, Eiseman, and Louis, 1986):

> First, core components of any improvement programs should be clearly identified in advance. No changes should be made in those programs without careful analysis of the effects of the change on goal achievement. Second, strategic, organizationwide planning should be carried out to identify any additional changes that need to be made . . . Third, early planning should explicitly identify both short and long-term resources that will be needed to maintain the change program. (pp. 32–33)

Top-Down Versus Bottom-Up Mandates

A second overriding issue that has been addressed frequently in research and analysis on the change process involves the extent to which initiative and decision making should emphasize "top-down" mandates or "bottom-up" participation. This issue is somewhat related to the fidelity/adaptation question, inasmuch as top-down approaches probably tend to emphasize fidelity to a mandate, as compared with an adaptation emphasis that places relatively greater stress on widespread participation in determining the nature and details of implementation. And parallel to recent movement toward acceptance of the possibilities for faithful implementation of core components in a predetermined approach to innovation, research and analysis seem to be moving toward more stress on the importance and value of appropriate top-down initiative. During the 1960s and 1970s, many researchers and academic observers placed most of their emphasis on the need for teacher participation in initiating and guiding innovation, but some research reported in the 1980s has shifted to some extent toward a more balanced conclusion.

Probably the best example of recent recognition of the role and possibilities of top-down leadership in bringing about successful change has been provided in longitudinal studies conducted by Miles and his colleagues. Miles (1983) summarized much of this research in an article in which he outlined the forces leading to "institutionalization"[1] of innovations as follows:

> . . . high administrative commitment tends to lead to both *administrative pressure* on users to implement the innovation, along with *administrative support,* which often shows up in the form of *assistance* to users. Both the pressure and the assistance tend to lead to increased *user effort. . . .* the harder people worked at an innovation, the more *committed* they grew; that commitment was also fueled by increasing technical *mastery* of the innovation.
>
> Commitment and mastery both lead toward increasing *stabilization of use* . . . [which is] aided if administrators decide to *mandate* the innovation, which also naturally increases the *percentage of use* . . . [that in turn] decisively encourages *institutionalization.* (p. 18)

Emphasizing top-down action in bringing about change is not necessarily the same, of course, as de-emphasizing bottom-up participation. For one thing, the conclusions just quoted were concerned with institutionalization, not just initial mastery and implementation, and certainly Miles and his colleagues would be among the last researchers anywhere to ignore or play down the importance of teacher participation and commitment in designing and implementing innovation. In addition, their conclusions continue to emphasize the importance of "teacher-administrator harmony" and of "both teacher mastery/commitment and

---

[1]Miles (1983) provided the following examples of institutionalized change: "altering the structure and approach of inservice training, writing the innovation's requirements into job descriptions, making new budget lines, appointing permanent coordinators for the innovation, and making sure that needed materials and equipment would continue to be available" (p. 18).

administrative action" (Miles, 1983, p. 19). Nevertheless, their data and conclusions do provide an important balance to the work of some others who have tended to minimize the necessity for and possibilities of strong top-down mandates and action in carrying out innovation successfully.

Hall and Hord (1987) and Crandall, Eiseman, and Louis (1986) also have reviewed research related to the top-down/bottom-up issue and reached conclusions that are similar to those of Miles and his colleagues. Elaborating on some of the important considerations involved in devising and implementing innovations, Hall and Hord (1987) stressed that "mandates and decrees" (p. 208) are helpful in providing clear indications of priority, and Crandall, Eiseman, and Louis (1986) concluded that a strategy based on mandates by strong leaders "appears to require five elements: absence of debilitating conflict; an effective, debugged innovation; continuity of leadership; frequent reminders that successful and faithful implementation is important; and adequate resources and support" (pp. 40–41).

Packaged Versus Locally Developed Mandates

The third issue that we briefly consider involves the question of whether or not innovations that consist largely or substantially of materials and/ or procedures developed or defined in advance (i.e., "packaged") are more successful than those that are mostly developed during implementation. On the one hand, innovations that have been developed prior to implementation should enhance their manageability by reducing the demands made on participants, but materials and procedures prepared in advance may not fit the requirements of a particular school or classroom and may provide too little scope for encouraging participants' sense of ownership of a change.

In considering this issue, one should keep in mind that schools seem to have an almost inexhaustible capacity for misimplementing innovations, no matter how much has been done to prepare usable materials and procedures thought to be valuable in working for effective change. This seems to be true even in cases where the decision to participate was made at the building level, with little or no coercion from external forces. Thus, researchers reporting on years of experience in implementing Individually Guided Education (IGE) concluded that a number of schools implementing this approach were "illusory" sites that on the surface, appeared to be using many of the project's materials and procedures but actually had made little progress in improving the underlying patterns they were intended to influence (Romberg, 1985).

Perhaps the issue involved here is appropriately viewed as a combination of the fidelity/adaptation and top-down/bottom-up dilemmas, with the contrast in this case frequently being between introduction of externally developed and mandated packages, on the one hand, and local-site selection and development on the other. We have not found much in the literature that adds substantially to consideration of the issue beyond material already cited and summarized herein. For some further guidance in deciding between selection and imposition of relatively packaged approaches versus local selection and development, however, analysis by Crandall, Eiseman, and Louis (1986) may be helpful. Under the heading "Development by Teachers Versus Nonteachers," these authors have stressed the importance of considering the heavy demands already made on teachers as part of the standard "classroom press" in schools. Given the intensity and variety of everyday pressures and demands, the "local teacher development" approach has numerous "documented problems . . . including fatigue and inability to produce 'usable' programs without outside assistance" (p. 29). Thus, these authors have focused attention on the extent to which proposed innovations are manageable for teachers. We return to this critically important consideration in the next sections of this chapter.

Scope and Phasing

A fourth major issue that should be addressed explicitly in designing and implementing a substantial innovation project involves its scope and phasing. Should one try to keep a change effort relatively small, so as to maintain more control over its implementation and ensure that sufficient resources are available to carry it out, or should relatively large plans and goals be pursued to enhance the likelihood that most or all pertinent variables and obstacles have been addressed and the change really can make a noticeable difference? Some observers (e.g., Goodlad, 1987) have cautioned that changes that least disturb a school's existing routines and arrangements may have the best chance to win acceptance, but others (e.g., Fullan, 1982) point out that smaller rather than larger changes may not have much impact in the face of strong tendencies toward maintenance of existing arrangements. Hall and Hord (1987) considered some aspects of this issue and pointed out that many sizeable innovations (such as IGE) consist not so much of a single innovation as of "large, complex, and multifaceted innovation bundles" (p. 135). The authors proceeded to make the useful point that change facilitators working with large innovations are likely to be more successful if they distinguish among the main components and work out appropriate staff development and other "facilitative supports" (p. 135) for each one. This type of conclusion implies that one can realistically consider implementing relatively large changes, provided that care is taken to provide appropriate and large-scale assistance and support in keeping with the broad scope of the goals being pursued in such cases.

On the central issue of whether to lean toward larger or smaller innovations, Crandall, Eiseman, and Louis (1986) again provided useful guidance; based on their review of the literature, they offered a sensible generalization, stating that the:

> "greatest success is likely to occur when the size of the change is large enough to require noticeable, sustained effort, but not so massive that typical users find it necessary to adopt a coping strategy that seriously distorts the change . . . if extensive effort is going to be put forward, it should be channeled toward making changes that are large enough to justify the human and financial costs of such efforts" (pp. 26–27).

Under the heading "The Scope of Initial Implementation," they made the additional point that the initial scope of a project should depend to some extent on whether it has been fundamentally "debugged"; innovations that are not yet fully developed should not be implemented on a large scale. But if the innovation has been debugged, they further concluded, the implementor still must determine whether to initiate a project in stages or implement it on a large scale all at once. They suggested that this decision should take into account such factors as receptivity and capability of potential users, extent of the demands made on users, congruence with the prevailing organizational culture, competition from other projects, and availability of requisite resources.

PREREQUISITES AND ANTECEDENTS AND OTHER NONISSUES

Material in the preceding pages has pointed several times toward some of the antecedent conditions and prerequisites that must be attended to and put in place in order to implement innovation successfully. For example, Hall and Hord (1987) stressed the conclusion that success in implementing an external provision faithfully depends on provision of "requisite support" for participants; Miles (1983) identified "administrative support" and "organizational change" as prerequisites in turning administrative "pressure" into institutionalized outcomes, and Crandall, Eiseman, and Louis (1986) cited outside assistance and numerous other forms of support required to help teachers implement an innovation successfully.

Differing analysts have classified and subclassified prerequisites for success in a variety of ways. We do not have the space or inclination to review all of these classifications; instead, we identify several prerequisites that, in one form or another, have been cited either frequently or centrally in recent studies or papers. These prerequisites for success appear to us to be nonissues in the sense that they are well established in the work of researchers and/or the experience of persons who spend a lot of time working to bring about change in elementary and secondary schools. This is not to say, of course, that such prerequisites are usually provided, or even recognized, in most or many improvement efforts in the schools. In fact, in our experience, the great majority of innovative projects neglect or ignore the kinds of prerequisites for success that are discussed in the remainder of this section.

1. Site-level Emphasis. The necessity to focus on the school building level in working to bring about substantial improvement has been widely recognized in recent years. Observers who have stressed this point include Fullan (1982), Goodlad (1984, 1987), Henshaw, Wilson, and Morefield (1987), Hopkins (1987), and Sarason (1982).

2. Continuing Training and Staff Development Focusing on Classroom-Level Implementation. Under the heading "Concrete, teacher-specific, and on-going training," Berman and McLaughlin (1978) listed this prerequisite first among the "elements" that, when "well executed," have "major, positive effects on project outcomes and continuation" (p. 29). Among the many others who since have stressed on-going training and assistance delivered at the school and classroom levels are Crandall, Eiseman, and Louis (1986), Fullan (1982), Janowitz (1969), Loucks-Horsley and Cox (1984), Loucks-Horsley and Hergert (1985), and Miles (1983, 1987).

3. Incentives for Participation. The importance of incentives to participate in a serious change effort has been emphasized by many studies and observers. Included among the incentives most often cited are provision of additional resources and access to outside assistance (e.g., Crandall et al., 1986), intrinsic motivators associated with career plans and the approbation of significant others (Huberman & Miles, 1984), the opportunity to become more effective (Berman & McLaughlin, 1978), chances to visit other schools and districts (Berman & McLaughlin, 1978), and public recognition for good work (Miles, 1987).

4. Avoidance of Change Overload. This aspect of manageability involves the need to limit the scope and number of innovations being introduced at one point in time, in accordance with the fact that, except in rare and unusual circumstances, teachers and schools cannot successfully implement a multitude of extensive and simultaneous changes. Among the observers who have stressed this point are Corbett and D'Amico (1986), Corbett and Rossman (1986), Fullan (1982), Levine (1985), and Loucks-Horsley and Cox (1984).

5. *Stability in Leadership and Participating Personnel.* Among the researchers and observers who have reported that innovative projects frequently fail in part due to instability in leadership at the district and school levels or among teachers participating in an improvement effort, are Corbett and D'Amico (1986), Loucks-Horsley and Hergert (1985), and Kenney and Roberts (1986). Closely related to the need for stability is the fact that significant innovations take a long time to introduce and refine (Crandall et al., 1986; Loucks-Horsley & Hergert, 1985). Hall and Hord (1987) described the stages that teachers typically pass through in utilizing an innovation as beginning with "orientation," and then proceeding (ideally) through "preparation," "mechanical use," "routine," "refinement," "integration," and, ultimately, "renewal" (p. 84).

6. *Clarity in Objectives and Procedures.* Clear specification and definition of goals and procedures are important in helping participants understand what is involved in an innovation and what their own responsibilities will be. Conversely, change efforts emphasizing overly general goals seldom have much impact on schools. Partly for this reason, change efforts should aim at, or at least include, specific instructional and/or curricular goals (Crandall et al., 1986; Gottfredson & Gottfredson, 1987; Loucks-Horsley & Cox, 1984; Louis & Rosenblum, 1982).

7. *Change in Organizational Procedures, Routines, and Arrangements.* Almost by definition, important innovations cannot be carried out without some significant change in the procedures, routines, and arrangements of the organization that is attempting to implement them. Among the authors who have provided documentation for or otherwise stressed this generalization are Corbett and D'Amico (1986), Corbett and Rossman (1986), and Miles (1987). The types of organizational changes needed to implement change successfully are difficult, if not impossible, to generalize about, because they depend so much on current practices in the school, the nature of the innovation being pursued, the level of education and the characteristics of students involved, and other idiosyncratic variables.

8. *Leadership.* Along with administrative initiative and support, leadership—particularly by the building principal—has long been recognized as a key aspect of successful change as well as of school effectiveness in

general. The literature on leadership in schools or in other organizations is too voluminous to attempt to summarize here; instead we mention several recent studies and papers that appear to provide some particularly useful information regarding what administrators of successful change efforts actually do and how they go about doing it. Inescapably, the behaviors and attitudes of leaders who implement change effectively are intimately related to concepts and themes discussed throughout this chapter.

One of these studies, an ongoing examination of successful implementation of improvement efforts in urban high schools, is being conducted by Miles (1987) and his colleagues. Preliminary results (Miles, 1987) indicate that successful leadership appears to function, in part, through its effects in selecting and initiating an approach that is well designed (in terms of "training and technical support; reasonable planning and monitoring procedures, etc.") and constitutes a "reasonably good fit" with the school and its culture; in promoting a vision of "what the school should look like" and the "nature of the change process" that will get it there; and in "rewarding staff for participation" (pp. 7, 11). Among the leadership and management skills that, according to Miles (1987) appear to contribute to successful implementation of innovations are the following: "creative invention"; "supporting; 'dreaming' by others"; "communicating intentions clearly"; "developing ownership of visions by others"; "deriving implications from data"; "supporting others' initiative without subtle benevolent control"; "clear decision allocation"; "active initiation without imposing"; "developing local assistance capacity, linking to outsiders"; "brokering"; and "imaginative design of strategies" (p. 11).

Several of the leadership skills and qualities cited by Miles and his colleagues have been documented in a study that Taylor (1984, 1986) conducted of unusually effective elementary schools. Although Taylor's study was not strictly an investigation of implementation of a particular innovation or set of innovations, it did examine schools that were making, or had made, impressive gains in achievement, and it concentrated on the role of principals in bringing about improved achievement. Taylor found that the principals of unusually successful schools were particularly adept at establishing and maintaining positive organizational directions (i.e., "meta-sensemaking") through continuous dialogue and communications episodes focusing on strategic goals and actions critical to effective implementation of instruction. Partly through generating "units of strategic dialogue," Taylor (1984) concluded (p. 70), the effective principal not only gains knowledge of daily implementation problems but also bounds the environment to make it more manageable, negotiates agreements with staff to focus attention and effort on the attainment of central priorities, and reduces ambiguity in roles. Important leadership variables, as described by Taylor, are similar to characteristics such as vision, creative invention, clear decision allocation, brokering, and several other qualities described by Miles and his colleagues.

Another set of studies that directly assessed relationships between principals' leadership styles and implementation of innovations was conducted by Hall, Hord, Huling, and other researchers at the University of Texas at Austin (Hall & Hord, 1987; Huling, Hall, Hord, & Rutherford, 1983). Defining successful implementation in terms of resolution of teachers' concerns about innovations they were introducing and the extent to which they actually utilized important aspects of the innovations, these researchers found that principals who were initiators were much more likely to implement change successfully than were principals classified as responders or managers. Principals who utilized an "initiator change facilitator style" were defined and characterized by Hall and Hord (1987) in terms that are somewhat similar to those utilized by Taylor and by Miles and his colleagues:

> Initiators hold clear, decisive, long-range goals for their schools that transcend, but include, implementation of current innovations. They have a well-defined vision of what their school should be like and of what teachers, parents, students, and the principal should be doing to help the school move in that direction . . . They listen to their teachers, then make decisions . . . Initiators push . . . to see that all are moving in goal-oriented directions. They convey and monitor these high expectations through frequent contact with teachers and clear explication of how the school is to operate and how teachers are to teach. (p. 230)

9. Problem Identification and Resolution and Coping. Personnel who successfully implement a significant educational innovation necessarily must overcome a multiplicity of problems and obstacles that are present initially or that arise thereafter to threaten the effectiveness of the innovation. Among the researchers who have reported that organizational problem identification and resolution are crucial in successful change efforts are Herriott and Gross (1979), who described leadership tasks in implementing planned change as constituting an "Expanded Leadership Obstacle Course" (p. 11), and Miles (1987), who described the centrality of "problem-coping" (p. 11) in serious change efforts and identified requisite actions and skills that involve "recurrent problem listing"; "generation of coping alternatives before decision"; "routine problem/coping tracking"; "problem-stating in . . . non-defense-arousing terms"; and "imaginative design of strategies" (p. 11). As mentioned previously, Taylor (1984) and others have underlined the importance of administrators' capacity to identify problems and communicate solutions as part of their efforts to address key obstacles through utilization of "knowledge-in-action" (p. 66) in complex situations.

10. Productive Organizational Culture. Aspects of the organizational culture in a school or district play an important part in determining whether instruction is effective or ineffective and whether innovations are successful or unsuccessful. (Parish & Krueger, in press). However, there does not seem to be much agreement among researchers concerning the definition of organizational culture, the aspects that are most important, or the specific ways in which it influences effectiveness and the change process.

Among the many useful definitions and analyses of organizational culture applicable to elementary and secondary schools are those formulated by Taylor (1984, 1986), who defined school culture in terms of the beliefs that "people who work in the building share about their work and the cause–effect relationships of the tasks in their work" (1984, p. 140). Taylor's study of elementary schools that had increased in effectiveness concluded that key cultural elements include the dissemination of shared "criteria of effectiveness" (e.g., "all kids can learn"), common understandings regarding working relationships among principal, staff, and students (e.g., "the needs of kids come first"), and acceptance of agreed-on standards (e.g., strong academic emphasis on basic skills and independent learning skills). In the elementary schools studied by Taylor, the principal played the most important part in developing a productive culture in which. appropriate innovations could flourish and succeed, partly through such means as buffering the school from external forces, establishing and enforcing a code of discipline, planning for and implementing curriculum improvements, and coordinating work rules, operating procedures, and curriculum objectives (Taylor, 1984, p. 151).

Another useful recent analysis of school culture has been provided by Heckman (1987). Based on data collected as part of *A Study of Schooling*, Heckman (1987) concluded that norms in "renewing" schools emphasized such considerations as a "take-care-of-business" attitude, staff attention to key problems rather than "drift from one problem to another without solving the initial problem," and interaction and cooperation among teachers in addressing key problems (p. 69). However, Heckman also found that positive renewing schools that were addressing fundamental problems were not particularly successful in changing classroom instruction; consequently, he and his colleagues concluded that staff collaboration to identify and solve problems should focus more directly on improvement of culture and instruction at the classroom level. Other observers who have emphasized the importance of collaborative/collegial problem solving or decision making in bringing about culture change include Fullan (1982, 1985), Goodlad (1984), Hopkins (1987), Lieberman and Rosenholtz (1987), Little (1984), and Sarason (1982).

Some observers have gone beyond analysis of organizational culture to identify stages of change through which organizations move in becoming more productive. For example, Allen (1985) has identified the following four phases for bringing about planned cultural change:

1. *Analysis and Objective Setting,* in which planning gives particular attention to rewards, modeling behavior, information and communication systems, interactions and relationships, management and supervisory skills, organizational structures, policies, and procedures, training, orientation, and allocation of resources;

2. *Systems Introduction and Involvement,* in which work teams and individuals are involved in the change process to build ownership;

3. *Systems Implementation and Change,* in which participants begin to modify work environments based on analysis and experience in the first two phases; and

4. *Evaluation and Renewal,* in which information is regularly collected and analyzed to identify and address emerging problems (Allen, 1985, pp. 340–346). Particular attention throughout is given to overcoming negative "barrier" norms such as blame placing, win–lose behavior, simplistic problem-resolution habits, and learned helplessness (pp. 346–347). As is apparent from this summary, approaches for improving organizational culture can and frequently do aim at revising and rebuilding the entire organization and all its most important policies and practices.

Other authors who have provided important analysis related to organizational culture and the change process include Argyris (1980) and Vaill (1984). Argyris has emphasized the role of trust and open communications in working to identify and overcome forces that cause problems to be not just ignored but "undiscussable", whereas Vaill has described how leaders' behaviors and attitudes with respect to "time," "feeling," and "focus" affect the culture of high- versus low-performing organizations. Argyris and Vaill, along with many other researchers and analysts, have produced a substantial body of knowledge concerning the nature and dynamics of cultural impediments to change in schools and other organizations. This literature provides much useful advice and guidance, as in the following generalizations summarized by Fullan (1982):

— Significant change involves a certain amount of ambiguity, ambivalence, and uncertainty for the individual about the meaning of the change. Thus, effective implementation is a *process of clarification.*

Assume that conflict and disagreement are not only inevitable but fundamental to successful change.

— Assume that no amount of knowledge will ever make it totally clear what action should be taken. Action decisions are a combination of valid knowledge, political considerations, on-the- spot decisions, and intuition. (pp. 91–92)

Unfortunately, much more seems to be known about the characteristics of productive organizational cultures in which innovations can be implemented effectively than about specific actions that should be taken to improve organizational culture in particular situations. Many valuable sources are available that provide assessment instruments and suggestions for undertaking culture improvement and other organization development activities (e.g., Kilmann, 1984; Schmuck & Runkel, 1985), but how and when to use them in actual reform efforts usually is unclear, particularly when one does not have the resources or opportunity to aim at full-scale reform of the entire organization. As recently concluded by Lieberman and Rosenholtz (1987), we are "just beginning to understand *how* to mobilize and organize school improvement efforts at the local level" (p. 86).

MANAGEABILITY AND IMPLEMENTABILITY

Among the themes and topics that appear most frequently in the literature on successful change in educational organizations are those that involve the necessity for innovations to be manageable for teachers and "implementable" in the real world of schools and classrooms. These aspects of innovations are, of course, closely related to the recurrent emphases among researchers and other observers cited earlier, who concluded that successful innovation requires substantial resources and administrative support as well as clarity in goals, role definitions, and technical procedures.

Whether or not innovations are manageable in participating classrooms or schools could be assessed in a variety of ways, using various definitions of manageability; widely accepted definitions or typologies isolating the most critical aspects do not appear to be available. However, several sources do suggest that concern for manageability should place some stress on whether innovations generate overly burdensome paperwork requirements for teachers (e.g., Romberg, 1985), on whether they have adequate time for instructional planning (Zahorik, 1975), and on whether they are feasible for participating teachers.

The manageability of *paperwork* requirements appears to be a particular concern with respect to innovations aimed at improving thinking and higher order skills in general, because some efforts to improve student performance in this regard have attempted to do so through elaborate record keeping on students' progress in mastering a plethora of skills. Thus, mastery learning programs, for example, frequently have failed partly or largely because of the unrealistic record keeping burden they placed on teachers (Levine, 1985).

Instructional planning time also seems to be emerging as a particularly critical concern in implementing innovations intended to improve students' thinking skills. Although planning time is important in implementing any significant instructional innovation, it may be especially important with respect to thinking skills, because most teachers are neither trained nor experienced in designing or implementing instruction for this purpose (MacGinitie & MacGinitie, 1986) and because growth in thinking skills is a more complex and difficult goal than are the passive-learning objectives that are typically emphasized in classrooms. Thus, Ryan (1985) has pointed out that successful implementation of mastery learning focused on important learning skills requires teachers to engage in a variety of "preactive" and "proactive" planning activities, and Johnson, Knight, and Waxman (1987) found evidence that "Instructional Planning may be a greater factor in students' higher-level, problem-solving achievement than the effects of planning indicated in previous research examining achievement in lower-level skills" (p. 4).

Feasibility is a less specific aspect of manageability than are paperwork and planning time. Whether or to what extent an innovation can be realistically implemented might well be analyzed with reference to a variety of considerations, such as class size and class load in relation to the demands being made on teachers and students, provision of staff development and instructional materials, structural change to accommodate the innovation, and other considerations cited earlier in this chapter. Proposals for innovation are likely to be more feasible if the proposed change requires less, rather than more, disturbance in existing arrangements (Goodlad, 1984) and if it provides detailed and specific directions and guidelines for teachers (Gottfredson & Gottfredson, 1987). But, as pointed out earlier, small changes may inspire insufficient commitment or may not be worth initiating in the first place, whereas "packaged" innovations may leave too little room for adaptation and development of ownership among participating teachers and administrators.

Another particularly important aspect of manageability of innovations stressing higher order learning involves the extent to which students have been prepared for and are accustomed to working independently in a self-directed fashion. Because effective teaching of higher order skills requires students to become more active learners, some stress must be placed on development of self-directed learning. This emphasis often generates severe management problems for teachers whose students have not been prepared to function independently. Many instructional innovations have failed due to management problems resulting from failure to prepare students for self-directed learning.

Although "implementability" is not a term that has been used widely in research on the change process, Louis, Dentler, and Kell (quoted in Crandall et al., 1986) concluded that this concept is useful in calling attention to and summarizing some of the following "key dimensions of innovations and materials" that determine whether proposed changes are "implementable and attractive" to teachers (Crandall et al., 1986):

- Craft legitimization: Is there evidence of reality testing in the construction of the materials, for example, were practitioners involved as consultants or developers, and was the product field-tested?

- Compatibility: Is the social context of prospective users, particularly in regard to their opportunities and incentives for action, incorporated into the innovation or materials? . . .

- Adaptability: Do the innovation and materials encourage local adaptation, and were they designed for local adaptation?

- Inspiration: Does the innovation have a strong inspirational thrust? Are idealistic-altruistic values an important component of the message?

Aspects of implementability, as identified by Louis, Dentler, and Kell, obviously overlap with concepts and issues such as manageability, feasibility, and replicability, which have been introduced and discussed briefly in the preceding pages. However, we believe that the term "implementability" is very useful in calling attention to several additional aspects, such as "craft legitimization" and "inspiration," and in extending issues involving adaptation/fidelity/local development to a consideration of the "adaptability" of proposed innovations.

Other aspects of innovation that might be considered under the heading of "attractiveness" involve the extent to which proposed changes create doubts among teachers, challenge their sense of competence and self-worth, or appear to be complex and, hence, difficult to implement. As pointed out by Fullan (1982), changes that do not appear to be complex or otherwise unattractive to promoters of change may seem so to teachers who subsequently retreat into a "self-protective cocoon" (p. 37).

CONCLUSION

The purpose of the preceding discussion has been to review research on successful implementation of innovations in schools and other organizations for consideration by educators who are, or will be, implementing changes to improve students' performance in thinking and other higher order skills. Necessarily, our review could not be a comprehensive summary of all conclusions and issues in the change literature; instead, we highlighted some of the findings and considerations that we believe are most important and relevant for educators initiating projects to improve students' higher order mental processing.

In considering the material introduced in this chapter, readers should keep in mind the likelihood that innovations to improve instruction in thinking and other higher order skills generally will have to be relatively large and complex. Teachers have not been well prepared in the past to offer effective instruction to enhance higher order skills (e.g., MacGinitie & MacGinitie, 1986), the knowledge base for teaching thinking is still relatively small and undeveloped (Marzano, et al., 1987), emphasizing higher order skills will constitute a major change in many or most classrooms and schools (Goodlad, 1984), and many students will need close guidance and assistance (i.e., mediation) from highly skilled teachers (Marzano, et al., 1987).

The general complexity and large magnitude of change involved in innovative projects to improve instruction in thinking was underlined in a recent analysis of teaching thinking skills prepared by Nickerson, Perkins, and Smith (1985). Although the authors first pointed out (pp. 308–309) that thinking-skills approaches vary considerably with respect to considerations such as amount of class time devoted to instruction, specific skills addressed, and amount of special training for teachers, they also emphasized the general conclusions that teachers of thinking need to be facilitators of knowledge, that students must explore and discover knowledge rather than passively absorb it, that many teachers resist approaches that do not yet offer a clear and definite technology, that assessment of thinking skills is still relatively primitive, and that significant time-on-task opportunity will have to be available to students. They further concluded that implementation of *any* thinking-skills program should make sure that tasks generally are intrinsically interesting to students, that objectives and exercises should be "calibrated" to "students' current level of knowledge and abilities," that reasons for students' success or failure should be explicitly assessed, that considerable feedback should be provided for students, and that practice should be provided in "a variety of problem contexts" (pp. 342–343)—no small job for any classroom teacher.

The reader also should keep in mind that change in schools and other organizations is itself a complex and difficult process that cannot be guided effectively by simple prescriptions and preconceived formulae. Successfully implementing an innovation of any significant magnitude requires constant assessment and reassessment of what one has accomplished to date, of immediate and long-range obstacles blocking effective implementation, and of the various strategies and tactics that might be most appropriate at each step. As Fullan (1982) has eloquently pointed out, successful change requires that one deal continuously with "countless" dilemmas and subdilemmas involving issues such as the appropriate emphasis on "top-down" direction and "bottom-up" participation, and adaptation at the local site versus fidelity to initial plans and specified techniques. But, however individuals responsible for an innovation decide to respond to such interrelated dilemmas, significant emphasis must always be placed, as Fullan (1982) has insisted, on "planning change in such a way that groups of people must interact and make choices," and there must be "particular involvement on the part of those who have the most at stake in sorting out the nature of change according to individual and collective choices about the ends and means of education" (p. 291).

Taking into account the preceding generalizations and caveats, as well as others offered earlier in this chapter, we believe that several useful conclusions regarding implementation of projects to improve students' higher order skills can be derived from our discussion and the literature on which it is based. Six such conclusions are presented hereafter.

1. If educators select a thinking-skills approach that utilizes specific teaching materials in order to enhance manageability for teachers or for other reasons, care should be taken to allow, encourage, and assist participating teachers to adapt the materials to the realities of their classrooms. Encouragement and assistance in adapting materials serve several major purposes: to help build ownership, to enhance opportunities for teachers to figure out what the project means as part of their instructional program, and to increase the likelihood that implementation will take account of practical problems in the classroom.

2. Whether or not the thinking-skills approach selected utilizes specific sets of teaching materials, project administrators should attempt to identify core components that require fidelity in implementation (Crandall et al., 1986) and should work with teachers to ensure that these components are stressed and implemented in line with the intentions and suggestions of the developers. However, relatively little is known at present concerning the ways in which teachers should proceed to develop, sequence, or assess thinking skills, how to coordinate content instruction with emphasis on thinking, and methods for adapting higher order instruction to the needs of individual students or groups of students

(Marzano, et al., 1987); this, in turn, probably means that relatively more stress should be placed on mutual adaptation than on fidelity during the next decade.

3. Because thinking-skills approaches require relatively large, complex, and difficult changes in the behaviors and attitudes of teachers and students, even more stress than usual should be placed on ensuring that innovations are manageable and implementable for teachers, and that prerequisites and antecedents (discussed earlier in this chapter) of successful implementation are firmly in place. Concern for manageability and implementability should include attention to such considerations as planning time, class size, change overload, amount of paperwork, adaptability in participating classrooms, compatibility with demands already placed on teachers, and capacity of the innovation for inspiring enthusiasm and commitment among teachers and students. Regarding staff-development requirements in helping teachers learn to deliver higher order instruction effectively, Kurth and Stromberg (1984) have reported that the staff development required is "Herculean" (p. 22). Similarly, research conducted by Putnam, Roehler, and Duffy (1987) indicated that "the staff development effort must be quite elaborate when the goal is to develop cognitive understanding . . . and independent decision making" among teachers, rather than technical prescriptions (p. 24).

4. Related to manageability issues and to the importance of problem identification and resolution in implementing innovations successfully, educators implementing thinking-skills projects should identify in advance the obstacles likely to impede implementation and take definite steps to overcome them. Among the obstacles that generally impede efforts to center instruction on the development of thinking and other higher order skills are: institutional realities of schools that stress classroom order and passive learning (Goodlad, 1984); students' preferences for lower order skills (Doyle, 1985); compromises between students and faculty who trade obedience for undemanding instruction (Sedlak, Wheeler, Pullin, & Cusick, 1986); low-level learning scripts teachers utilize with low achievers (Payne, 1984; Shavelson, 1985); and teacher preferences for easy-to-teach lessons (Levine & Havighurst, 1989).

5. As indicated previously, clarity of goals is an important consideration in successful implementation of change. One particularly important aspect of goal setting in projects to improve students' higher order skills involves the measures used to assess the performance of students, teachers, or schools. Analysis of the school reform movement during the past decade indicates that it frequently has stressed assessment of student performance with respect to low-level, mechanical skills, and thereby has tended to "drive" instruction still further away from development of

higher order skills (e.g., McNeil, 1986; Rosenholtz, 1987). Although such analysis has not explicitly examined prerequisites for successful implementation of change, it does suggest that projects to improve students' thinking are likely to be greatly hampered when student assessment focuses on low-level skills.

6. Special considerations and problems regarding approaches for improving students' thinking skills suggest that successful implementation will require unusual stress on revising organizational and institutional arrangements and structures. Preceding sections of this chapter cited research (e.g., Crandall et al., 1986; Corbett & D'Amico, 1986; Miles, 1987) pointing to the importance of change in organizational procedures and arrangements in successful implementation of significant innovations. This is likely to be particularly true with respect to thinking skills projects, because they generally will require considerable cooperation and coordination across teachers and classrooms, and because there is much current uncertainty regarding the integration of subject-matter and process objectives, the sequencing of skills across grades and levels, allocation and reallocation of time throughout the school day and school year, and other issues that have implications for organizational structure and arrangements in schools.

If the conclusions just outlined make it appear that initiation of thinking skills projects is an imposing challenge not to be undertaken lightly, we have succeeded in communicating our most important overall conclusion. Making sure that such projects are manageable for teachers and that fundamental realities and characteristics of elementary and secondary schools are addressed and modified as part of a thinking skills project is, indeed, an enormous burden. Similarly, the need to deal with basic problems in leadership, organizational culture, and related matters as part of a thinking skills project also means that one should think many more times than twice before deciding to launch an effort to improve instruction aimed at improving thinking and other higher order skills.

Absent the foresight, resources, and commitment required to fundamentally reform instruction in order to implement thinking-skills projects successfully, educators interested in this type of change would be well advised to move very slowly, if at all, until such time as these prerequisites can be put in place. Educational history already provides numerous instances of promising instructional innovations that have failed in part, at least, because they were initiated without adequate attention to the considerations discussed in this chapter. For example, Popkewitz, Tabachnick, and Wehlage (1982) have described how IGE frequently was an "illusory" innovation in schools that manifested the form and language of change while accomplishing almost nothing in terms of improving instructional practices and arrangements, and Pogrow (1983) has described how new technologies frequently have been implemented "conceptually" but not "physically" because they tended to complicate instruction and thereby "victimize" teachers, rather than simplifying tasks and enhancing teachers' effectiveness (p. 73). Efforts to improve the performance of students with respect to thinking and other higher order skills will produce the same sad result and will soon be discredited and forgotten if they ignore the lessons and cautions derivable from the literature on how to implement change successfully in schools and classrooms.

REFERENCES

Allen, R. F. (1985). Four phases for bringing about cultural change. In R. H. Kilmann, M. J. Saxton, & R. Serpa (Eds.), *Gaining Control of the corporate culture* (pp. 332–350). San Francisco: Jossey-Bass.

Argyris, C. (1980). Making the undiscussable and its undiscussability discussible. *Public Administration Review, 40*(3), 205–213.

Berman, P., & McLaughlin, M. W. (1978). *Federal programs supporting educational change. Vol. VIII: Implementing and sustaining interventions.* Santa Monica, CA: Rand.

Corbett, H. D., & D'Amico, J. J. (1986). No more heroes: Creating systems to support change. *Educational Leadership, 44*(1), 70–72.

Corbett, H. D., & Rossman, G. B. (1986, April) *Fanfare and failure: Path ways to implementing change.* Paper presented at the annual meeting of the American Educational Research Association, San Francisco.

Crandall, D. P., Eiseman, J. W., & Louis, K. S. (1986). Strategic planning issues that bear on the success of school improvement efforts. *Educational Administration Quarterly, 22*(3), 21–53.

Doyle, W. (1985). Academic work. *Review of Educational Research, 53,* 159–199.

Fullan, M. (1982). *The meaning of educational change.* New York: Teachers College Press.

Fullan, M. (1985). Change processes and strategies at the local level. *Elementary School Journal, 85*(3), 391–421.

Goodlad, J. I. (1984). *A place called school.* New York: McGraw-Hill.

Goodlad, J. I. (1987). A comprehensive view of school improvement. In J. I. Goodlad (Ed.), *The ecology of school renewal* (pp. 1–19). Chicago: University of Chicago Press.

Gottfredson, G. D., & Gottfredson, D. C. (1987, April). *Organization development approaches for change in school climate.* Paper presented at the annual meeting of the American Educational Research Association, Washington, DC.

Hall, G. E., & Hord, S. M. (1987). *Change in schools.* Albany: State University of New York Press.

Heckman, P. (1987). Understanding school culture. In J. I. Goodlad (Ed.), *The ecology of school renewal* (pp. 63–78). Chicago: University of Chicago Press.

Henshaw, J., Wilson, C., & Morefield, J. (1987). Seeing Clearly: The school as the unit of change. In J. I. Goodlad (Ed.), *The ecology of school renewal* (pp. 134–151). Chicago: University of Chicago Press.

Herriott, R. E., & Gross, N. (1979). *The dynamics of planned educational change.* Berkeley, CA: McCutchan.

Hopkins, D. (Ed.) (1987). *Improving the quality of schooling.* London: Falmer.

Huberman, A. M., & Miles, M. B. (1984). *Innovation up close.* New York: Plenum.

Huling, L. L., Hall, G. E., Hord, S. M., & Rutherford, W. L. (1983). *A multidimensional approach for assessing implementation success* (Rep. No. 3157). Austin: University of Texas Press.

Janowitz, M. (1969). *Institution building in urban education.* New York: Russell Sage.

Johnson, L. C., Knight, S. L., & Waxman, H. C. (1987, April). *Investigating the influence of teacher behaviors on students' achievement in mathematical problem solving.* Paper presented at the annual meeting of the American Educational Research Association, Washington, DC.

Kenney, J. L., & Roberts, J. M. E. (1986 April). *Characteristics and predictors of institutionalization.* Paper presented at the annual meeting of the American Educational Research Association, San Francisco, April.

Kilmann, R. H. (1984). *Beyond the quick fix: Managing five tracks to organizational success.* San Francisco: Jossey-Bass.

Kurth, R. J., & Stromberg, L. J. (1984, April). *Improving the teaching of comprehension in elementary schools.* Paper presented at the annual meeting of the American Educational Research Association, New Orleans.

Levine, D. U., & Havighurst, R. J. (1989). *Society and Education* (7th ed.). Newton, MA: Allyn and Bacon.

Levine, D. U. (1985). Key considerations for achieving success in mastery learning programs. In D. U. Levine (Ed.), *Improving student achievement through mastery learning programs* (pp. 273–294). San Francisco: Jossey-Bass.

Lieberman, A., & Rosenholtz, S. (1987). The road to school improvement: Barriers and bridges. In J. I. Goodlad (Ed.), *The ecology of school renewal* (pp. 79–98). Chicago: University of Chicago Press.

Little, J. (1984). Seductive images and organizational realities in professional development. *Teachers College Record,* Fall, 84–102.

Loucks Horsley, S., & Cox, P. L. (1984, April). *It's all in the doing: What recent research says about implementation.* Paper presented at the annual meeting of the American Educational Research Association, New Orleans.

Loucks Horsley, S., & Hergert, L. F. (1985). *An action guide to school improvement.* Alexandria, VA: Association for Supervision and Curriculum Development/The Network.

Louis, K., & Rosenblum, S. (1982). *Linking R&D with schools.* Cambridge, MA; Abt.

MacGinitie, W. H., & MacGinitie, R. K. (1986). Teaching students not to read. In S. DeCastell, A. Luke, & K. Egan, (Eds.), *Literacy, society, and schooling,* (pp. 256–269). Cambridge: Cambridge University Press.

Marzano, R. J., Brandt, R. S., Hughes, C. S., Jones, B. F., Pressesen, B. Z., Rankin, S. C., & Suhor, C. 1987. *Dimensions of thinking. A framework for curriculum and instruction.* Alexandria, VA: Association for Supervision and Curriculum Development.

McNeil, L. M. (1986). *Contradictions of control.* New York: Routledge and Kegan Paul.

Miles, M. B. (1983). Unraveling the mysteries of institutionalization. *Educational Leadership,* 41(2), 14–19.

Miles, M. B. (1987, April). *Practical guidelines for school administrators: How to get there.* Paper presented at the annual meeting of the American Educational Research Association, Washington, DC.

Nickerson, R. S., Perkins, D. N., & Smith, E. E. (1985). *The teaching of thinking.* Hillsdale, NJ: Lawrence Erlbaum Associates.

Parish, R., & Krueger, J. (in press). The face of change. *Planning and changing.*

Payne, C. M. (1984). *Getting what we ask for.* Westport, CA: Greenwood.

Pogrow, S. (1983). *Education in the computer age.* Beverly Hills, CA: Sage.

Popkewitz, T. S., Tabachnick, R. B., & Wehlage, G. (1982). *The myth of educational reform.* Madison: University of Wisconsin Press.

Putnam, J., Roehler, L. E., & Duffy, G. R. (1987). The staff development model of the teacher explanation project (Occasional Paper No. 108). East Lansing: Michigan State University Institute of Research on Teaching.

Romberg, T. A. (1985). *Toward effective schooling.* Lanham, MD: University Press of America.

Rosenholtz, S. J. (1987). Education reform strategies: Will they increase teacher commitment? *American Journal of Education, 95*(4), 534–562.

Ryan, D. W. (1985). Preactive and proactive supervision of mastery learning programs. In D. U. Levine (Ed.), *Improving student achievement through mastery learning programs* (pp. 45–67). San Francisco: Jossey-Bass.

Sarason, S. B. (1982). *The culture of the school and the problem of change.* Boston: Allyn and Bacon.

Schmuck, R. A., & Runkel, P. J. (1985). *The handbook of organizational development in schools* (3rd ed.). Palo Alto, CA: Mayfield.

Sedlak, M. W., Wheeler, C. W., Pullin, D. C., & Cusick, P. S. (1986). *Selling students short.* New York: Teachers College Press.

Shavelson, R. J. (1985, April). *Schemata and teaching routines: A historic perspective.* Paper presented at the annual meeting of the American Educational Research Association, Chicago.

Taylor, B. O. (1984). *Implementing what works: Elementary principals and school improvement programs.* Unpublished doctoral dissertations, Northwestern University, Evanston, IL.

Taylor, B. O. (1986, April). *How and why effective elementary principals address strategic issues.* Paper presented at the annual meeting of the American Educational Research Association, San Francisco.

Vaill, P. B. (1984). The purposing of high performing systems. In T. J. Sergiovanni & J. E. Corbally (Eds.), *Leadership and organizational culture* (pp. 85–104). Urbana: University of Illinois Press.

Zahorik, J. (1975, April). *Teachers' planning models.* Paper presented at the annual meeting of the American Educational Research Association, Washington, DC.

Creating an Educational Paradigm Centered on Learning Through Teacher-Directed, Naturalistic Inquiry

Robert J. Marzano
Mid-Continent Regional Educational Laboratory
Aurora, Colorado

One of the constants within education is that someone is always trying to change it. Yet many seemingly powerful change-oriented innovations are short-lived. Cuban (1987) has chronicled the fate of a number of educational innovations over the last three decades. Some of the more visible ones that have not endured include: programmed instruction, open classrooms, the Platoon System, differentiated staffing, and flexible scheduling. An important question relative to these defunct innovations is "Why did they fail?". All seemed quite logical at their conception. Many were researched based. The answer proposed by Watzlawick, Weakland, and Fisch (1974) is that an innovation within any system must not challenge the existing paradigms of the system. If it does, then the innovation must be accompanied by a paradigm shift—the introduction of a new paradigm that supports the innovation. As shall be explained, a paradigm within a social system is represented by a set of beliefs about how the system operates, or as Deal and Kennedy (1982) noted, the paradigms within a social system are found in the culture of that system. Any proposed educational innovation, then, must fit within the existing beliefs about education or it will not endure. From this perspective, the failure of at least some of the innovations on Cuban's list can be explained in terms of their lack of a concomitant paradigm shift. They simply did not fit within the predominant educational culture, and no new paradigm emerged that supported them.

Banathy (1980, 1984) has noted that education is currently organized around three paradigms, or three sets of beliefs. One paradigm views education from the broadest institutional level. The institutional paradigm is common in societies where educational authority is centralized (for example, a society that has a national system of education), in societies or situations where education is defined as part of a larger organization (such as a church), and in societies or situations where the only or primary purpose of education is enculturation.

A second paradigm views education as an administrative system. This paradigm is common in the United States and other cultures where control is semidecentralized. The primary purpose of systems organized around this paradigm is also to enculturate or indoctrinate; however, unlike systems organized around the institutional paradigm, the components of the culture or doctrine are determined at a local level.

A third paradigm, also common in the United States, views education as an instructional system. Such a paradigm is predominant in educational settings where instruction is viewed as a pedagogical system aided by technology. The purpose of systems organized around this paradigm is student learning, but the primary unit of study is the actions of the instructor with some attention paid to the characteristics of the learner.

All three paradigms bring a certain order to education, but all three also bring limitations. Banathy has asserted that all three are currently experiencing a "ceiling effect." They have been developed to their maximum potential; there is little significant change to be accomplished within their parameters. This is consistent with systems theory, which asserts that, to progress, a system must inevitably evolve out of its incumbent paradigms into one(s) that create(s) opportunities for change that is impossible within the existing paradigms (von Bertalanffy, 1968; Watzlawick, et al., 1974).

Currently, there is an innovation that is receiving growing national and international attention—the direct teaching of thinking. However, it too, warned Bereiter (1984), will end up on Cuban's list if it is not accompanied by a new set of beliefs—a new paradigm. At its core, this innovation attempts to translate research and theory on human cognition into a model (or metaphor) for what happens in the mind of the learner during optimal learning situations. In effect, the current emphases on the teaching of thinking answers Banathy's (1986) call for a learner-centered paradigm to replace the three current paradigms in education. More specifically, Banathy noted that if educational practice is to break through the limitations imposed by the current paradigms, it must develop a paradigm that is organized around the thought processes that occur during learning. The current emphasis on the teaching of thinking, then, is based on a set of beliefs that could effect significant change in education. Yet those beliefs must become part of the culture of education—become a new paradigm from which education operates.

This chapter attempts to describe the components of that new paradigm along with the processes by which it can become part of the culture of education. The chapter is divided into three major sections. The first deals with the nature of paradigms and the theory base underlying them. The second section describes an educational paradigm centered on learning. The third described the process of shifting to a new paradigm through the use of teacher-directed, naturalistic inquiry.

THE NATURE OF PARADIGMS

The concept of paradigm is commonly credited to Thomas Kuhn and his influential book, *The Structure of Scientific Revolutions* (1962). Kuhn first defined a paradigm in his description of the differences between normal science and revolutionary science. Normal science progresses by gradual additions to one's knowledge base. Revolutionary science progresses by discontinuous breakthroughs that demand a whole new "perspective" relative to the phenomena under study. Kuhn equated the commonly held perspectives relative to a phenomenon, with the paradigm relative to that phenomenon. For Kuhn, then, a paradigm was a mental perspective or "mental set" one took while engaged in scientific inquiry.

As it relates to everyday functioning, Lincoln and Guba (1985) defined a paradigm as a systematic set of beliefs that help one make sense of the world. A paradigm for Lincoln and Guba is a way of interpreting the world. Smith (1982) also viewed paradigms as interpretive structures used to organize experience. He referred to a paradigm, a "theory of the world in our heads" (p. 57)—a theory that is the basis of all our perceptions and understanding of the world. Our theory helps us organize reality. The concept of a paradigm as an organizer for reality is not new. For example, Kant described consciousness as an active ordering of otherwise chaotic impressions. The order we experience, asserted Kant, is not the "order of the world," passively received, but the order we perceive is very much a function of an active organization performed by the mind. Consequently, the same array of stimuli can be organized in different ways.

According to Schwartz and Ogilvy (1979), Hegel was the first to appreciate the fact that different paradigms create different interpretations of reality. To this extent, noted Patton (1978), a paradigm can be both enabling and constraining. It enables in that it provides a framework with which stimuli can be organized in meaningful ways. It constrains in that it limits perception. That is, the assumptions inherent within any paradigm automatically rule out other organizations of stimuli.

Sathe referred to the enabling and constraining nature of paradigms in the context of culture. He noted that culture appears to be a "box" within which individuals operate. On the positive side, this box constitutes a set of guiding principles on which individuals rely to make decisions about how to operate. However, just as the culture of a society enables, so does it delimit by creating blinders to realities that are outside of the culture. Sathe (1983) referred to this as the development of "cultural blind spots" (p. 74).

Education, then, operates within a certain set of assumptions about what can and can not be accomplished within the system. Banathy (1987) has noted that the assumptions underlying the current educational paradigms naturally lead to an emphasis on factors external to the process of learning, such as: the resources available, the time available, the provided curriculum, and performance on tests of low-level, factual information. A paradigm "centered on learning," asserted Banathy, would necessarily focus attention on the cognitive processes involved in learning and provide for educational changes not possible within the current paradigms.

A PARADIGM CENTERED ON LEARNING

A paradigm centered on learning cannot be fully described a priori, because the creation of a new paradigm is a dynamic, generative process. However, there has been enough research and theory on human learning to describe the probable components of such a paradigm.

Even though, historically, the majority of research and theory on learning has been behavioristic, the last 30 years have seen an explosion of more cognitively based endeavors. In fact, Shuell (1986) asserted that the time is becoming increasingly more ripe for a comprehensive, cognitively based theory of learning. Specifically, educational research and theory is providing powerful insights into the processes that occur in the mind of a learner during an effective learning experience. An "effective learning experience" includes that period of time from the initial introduction of content to the point at which the content has developed to a sophisticated level that is consistent with the maturity of the learner. There are five types of thinking that appear to be characteristic of an effective learning experience: (a) thinking that establishes and maintains the context for learning, (b) thinking that gives rise to the structuring of content, (c) thinking that generates the representation of content in long-term memory, (d) thinking that changes existing knowledge structures, and (e) dispositional thought. Parts of these five components are adapted from the framework developed by Marzano and Marzano (1988).

Thinking that Establishes and Maintains the Context for Learning

Learning any type of content, whether it be factual or skill related, takes place in a mental environment that either enables or inhibits learning. Simply stated, one is or is not "mentally set" for learning at any given point in time. Technically stated, one's thinking at any point in time can be mathemagenic (i.e., conducive to learning) or mathemathanic (i.e., detrimental to learning) (Loman, 1986; Rothkopf, 1970). Three aspects of thought that render one's mental set mathemagenic versus mathemathanic have been identified as (a) affect, (b) attitude, and (c) focus (Marzano & Marzano, 1987).

Affect. Most theories of cognition emphasize the strong connection between affect and intellect. For example, Piaget (1962) noted that "we must agree that at no level, at no stage even in the adult, can we find a behavior or a state which is purely cognitive without affect nor a purely affective state without a cognitive element involved" (p. 130). Similarly, Meichenbaum (1977) stated that the inseparably interactive relationship between cognition and affect attests to the need for control and monitoring of affect relative to specific tasks.

In general, the terms *affect* and *emotion* are used interchangeably when discussing responses of relatively short duration, whereas the term *mood* is used to describe a "disposition persisting over time" (Owens & Maxmen, 1979). From a physiological perspective, affect is generated by a set of related systems of the midbrain that regulate the general "backdrop of emotion" for a situation. This emotional backdrop determines the intensity with which one responds to situations—how strong or weak reactions will be (Mandler, 1983).

Research indicates that when one's emotional backdrop has high intensity, it is very difficult to change (Heliman & Satz, 1983). However, some researchers (Ellis, 1962; Meichenbaum, 1977; Santostefano, 1986) have shown that the intensity of one's emotional backdrop can be decreased via verbal mediation (selective self-talk) aimed at increasing awareness of the possible effects of high emotional intensity (e.g., "I know I'm emotional right now. I'm going to try not to let it affect what I'm doing.").

When one's emotional backdrop is low, it is more malleable and easier (although not easy) to change. Sometimes, a low-intensity backdrop is generated by physiological factors (e.g., an illness, not enough sleep). In such cases, it is difficult, if not impossible, to generate higher energy. However, when the emotional backdrop is low simply because of lack of interest or engagement in a task, a higher intensity can be effected by artificially generating some secondary characteristics of high intensity.

Specifically, Bettencourt, Gillett, Gall, and Hull (1983) found that by practicing such secondary characteristics of enthusiasm as animated gestures and an erect body position, a higher level of enthusiasm could be generated within a given situation.

In terms of thinking that establishes and maintains the context for learning, then, an important component is one's awareness and control of his or her emotional backdrop at a given time.

Attitudes.   An attitude includes "a mental position with regard to a general fact or state along with a strong negative or positive emotion (*Webster's Ninth New Collegiate Dictionary*, 1986, p. 114). Mental positions are statements of value that determine whether the emotion associated with the general fact or state is positive or negative. It is believed that mental positions are stored linguistically as propositions (Marzano & Marzano, 1988). Mental positions are generally specific to given situations, marking whether an individual considers an incident to be good, bad, or neutral. However, over time, a mental position can become an attitude via the process of generalization. As Anderson (1982, 1983) noted, when we generalize, we change a very specific mental position into a general one. In other words, an attitude is a mental position that is at a high level of generality and has strong associated emotion. Theorists, such as Glasser (1981) and Powers (1973), have asserted that human beings operate from a complex hierarchic structure of attitudes, with those at the very top functioning as basic operating principles that govern a great deal of our actions.

In terms of thinking which establishes and maintains the context for learning, then, another important component is the attitudes one has toward the learning tasks. In a series of studies, McCombs (1984, 1986, 1987) identified three attitudes that are important to a learning situation:

1. The extent to which the learner views the content as valuable.
2. The extent to which the learner believes he or she has control over the learning task.
3. The extent to which the learner believes he or she has the necessary abilities for the learning task.

A negative position on any of these attitudes decreases the learner's motivation for, and consequent engagement in, the learning task (Weiner, 1972, 1983). However, just as one's emotional backdrop for a particular situation can be changed by verbal mediation so, too, can negative attitudes be changed, or at least decreased, by affirming positive self-statements. Specifically, it has been shown that negative attitudes toward a learning situation can be changed by rehearsing positive self-talk relative to the situation (McCombs, 1984; Meichenbaum, 1977; Sokolov, 1972).

Focus.　Focus refers to the ability to attend to specific information at any point in time, whereas "attend" refers to the selective transfer of information from sensory information storage to working memory (Norman, 1969). Broadbent (1958) was one of the first to demonstrate that human beings selectively attend to the multitude of stimuli bombarding them at any time. That is, we process a small amount of information available at a given point in time due to the limited capacity of working memory.

At a very basic level, we attend to the stimuli that is most salient within the environment. This form of attention is commonly exhibited by infants. For example, Luria (1973) demonstrated that an infant will naturally turn his or her head in the direction of a loud noise. He likened this to what Pavlov termed *the orienting reflex.* However, a much more efficient form of attention is that which is focused because of a previously established goal. So important is goal-directed attention that a number of psychologists have postulated that it represents a unique cognitive state. For example, Neisser (1967) referred to goal-directed attention as a "controlled state"; Lindsay and Norman (1977) called it a "conscious state."

Focus, as defined by Marzano and Marzano (1987), is attention that is goal driven. The research on goal-directed learning is relatively clear. Over 40 years ago, Sears (1940) found that successful students tended to set explicit goals. More recently, Brophy (1982) found that successful students set increasingly more difficult goals in academic situations. Instructionally speaking, Bandura and Schunk (1981) found that it is best to introduce students to short-term (proximal) goals before presenting techniques for accomplishing long-term (distal) goals. Thinking that establishes and maintains a context for learning is goal directed, then. The learner sets or accepts goals and uses them to provide direction and focus for the learning process.

In summary, the extent to which learning occurs is, at least partially, a function of the learner's :

- Affective tone
- Attitudes about the learning task
- Awareness of explicit goals

These elements are the "context" on which the learner functions from moment to moment. Certain dispositions relative to these parameters

enable learning (are mathemagenic); others do not (are mathemathanic).

Thinking that Gives Rise to the
Structuring of Content

A number of theorists have either directly or indirectly asserted that
learning content of any type is fundamentally a constructive process (e.g.,
Wittrock, 1974). That is, the learner does not passively receive new
information as presented by a teacher or a textbook; rather, he or she
structures incoming information in ways that are compatible with his
existing knowledge base. This is referred to as "comprehension" (Raphael, 1987). As defined here comprehension involves the generation of
meaning for written and oral information. Therefore, it includes reading
and listening. Recent research has provided great insights into the manner in which a reader generates meaning. For example, van Dijk and
Kintsch (1983) have shown that meaning is generated by activating one's
prior knowledge of a topic and then using it to construct a rough outline,
or "macrostructure," of the salient information in the text. It is the
macrostructure that is retained by the learner. Interestingly, the macrostructure is always a hybrid of old and new information. That is, it
virtually never contains the information exactly as stated in the text.
Comprehending, then, is always a subjective, constructive process.

Clark and Haviland (1977) have illustrated that the process of comprehending and generating oral discourse involves this same tension between
old and new information. What is learned as a result of listening and
speaking results from an interplay between what is already known about
the topic and the information presented about the topic. The basic constructive nature of listening and speaking has also been discussed by
Moffett (1968) in his description of an interaction-based language arts
curriculum. (For other discussions of the constructive nature of listening
and speaking, see Staton, 1984, and Tough, 1974, 1976).

In summary, comprehension in its various forms gives rise to the
structuring of content in a way that is meaningful to the learner. Unfortunately, the effectiveness of the learner's structuring of content is commonly judged on the basis of its compatibility with external structures.
That is, the extent to which the learner's structures are compatible with
those considered important to the content being learned are determiners
of the effectiveness of the individual's learning (at least as judged by
standards within the discipline). From this perspective, it is important to
know the information structures commonly used to organize domain-
specific content (i.e., what is learned in school).

There have been a number of distinctions made as to the types of cognitive structures used to organize information (e.g., semantic versus episodic, linguistic versus nonlinguistic.). Relative to domain-specific content, one of the more useful distinctions is the one between declarative and procedural knowledge.

Declarative Information. Declarative information is descriptive in nature. It has been characterized as a knowledge *that* (Paris & Lindauer, 1982; Paris, Lispon & Wixson, 1983). For example, such information as the fact that "Columbus discovered America in 1492" and "Seattle is the largest city in Washington State" are forms of declarative knowledge. In terms of domain-specific content, declarative knowledge has been subdivided into a number of different types.

Perhaps at the lowest level of declarative knowledge are facts—statements of states and events related to specific animate entities, places, and things (e.g., "Seattle is the largest city in Washington State."). At a more complex level are structures such as: (a) time sequences (e.g., the events that occurred between two specific dates in history); (b) problems and solutions (e.g., the different possible ways of fixing a faulty distributor in an automobile engine); (c) causal networks (e.g., the events leading up to the bombing of Pearl Harbor); and (d) episodes (e.g., the circumstances surrounding Watergate). (For a discussion of the various structures used to organize declarative information, see Marzano, 1987, Shank & Abelson, 1977, van Dijk, 1980.)

An aspect of comprehending, then, is organizing the information read or heard into salient facts, time lines, episodes, and so on. However, these are relatively lower order organizational structures. Over time, and with the appropriate experiences, the learner transforms many of these structures into concepts and principles. Both are more general, relatively abstract organizers of content (Klausmeier, 1985). At the level of concept and principle, much of the specifics of the facts, time sequences, and episodes have been "decontextualized." For example, when the learner has attained the concept of *democracy,* he or she might include specific episodes, facts, and causal networks, but he or she will also include abstract characteristics of democracies generalized from those specific structures. Where concepts tend to be represented by single words within a society (e.g., *love, democracy, energy, equilibrium* are all examples of concepts), principles tend to be represented by entire statements (e.g, "Water seeks its own levels."). Smith and Medin (1981) have identified various categories and types of concepts within declarative knowledge; Katz (1976) has identified various types of principles.

Schemata represent the broadest and, perhaps, most subjective category of declarative information. Rumelhart (1980) described schemata as "packages" of information stored in long-term memory. A commonly used example of a schema is the knowledge associated with going to a restaurant. That is, people in our culture have an internalized restaurant schema that includes knowledge about reading a menu, ordering food, waiting for it to come, eating with an array of utensils, and paying the bill. Schemata can be viewed as the top of the hierarchy of declarative information. They contain facts, time sequences, concepts, principles, and so on about a given topic organized in ways that are meaningful to the learner. Although there is great commonality in the schemata within the people of a given culture, there is also great diversity, with one individual's schema for a given topic containing somewhat different and idiosyncratically organized information from that of another person's schema for the same topic.

Procedural Information.   Procedural information is sometimes characterized as knowledge of *how* (Paris & Lindauer, 1982; Paris, et al., 1983). For example, knowing how to read a bar graph or how to perform long division is procedural. Procedural knowledge includes process knowledge and conditional knowledge. Processes involve "steps" that are either ordered or unordered. For example, the process for reading a bar graph involves a relatively unordered set of steps. The process for performing long division, on the other hand, has a rather rigid order to the steps involved. A process that has a very rigid set of steps is commonly referred to as an algorithm. A process that has loosely ordered steps is sometimes referred to as a set of heuristics.

Processes can be very short or quite long, consisting of many subprocesses. A useful metaphor is that process knowledge is like a computer program (Lewis & Greene, 1982). Some programs are very simple and contain only a few steps. Others are quite complex and include subroutines nested within subroutines. So, too, can mental processes be relatively simple, containing a few steps, or quite complex, containing subprocesses within subprocesses.

Along with knowledge of process, procedural knowledge includes "conditional knowledge," or knowing when the process should be used. For example, along with knowledge of the process for performing long division, one should have an understanding of the situations in which it is useful (e.g., in certain types of problems and not in others).

Procedural knowledge, then, is comprised of both process knowledge and conditional knowledge. The extent to which a learner organizes information presented by the teacher, the textbook, or a learning experience into appropriate procedural structures determines the effectiveness of the learning.

The Interaction of Declarative and Procedural Information.   Although declarative and procedural knowledge have been discussed separately up to this point, they, of course, are not separate in long-term memory. In fact, procedural knowledge is highly dependent on declarative knowledge. Theorists in artificial intelligence (Anderson, 1983; Newell & Simon, 1972) represent the interaction of declarative and procedural knowledge as "productions"—*if/then* structures in long-term memory. For example, consider the following:

IF: 1. It is snowing,
        2. the time is before 9:00 a.m. on a work day,
        3. the snow accumulation is 6 inches or more, and
        4. the car is in the garage.
THEN: I shovel the driveway.

The process knowledge in this production is about shoveling the driveway. The conditional knowledge is represented in statements 1, 2, 3, and 4. Together, the process and conditional knowledge make up the procedural information. Yet, contained within that procedural information is such declarative information as the schema for "snowing," the schema for a "work day," the concept of "6 inches," and so on. Hence, this production contains both declarative and procedural information integrated in a unified whole.

In summary, learning content within any discipline involves the learner organizing the content into appropriate declarative and procedural structures. These structures, once they are perceived by the learner, are represented in long-term memory in a number of ways.

Thinking That Generates the Representation of Content in Long-Term Memory

There are a number of theories about how information is represented in long-term memory. One important distinction that is commonly made is the one between linguistic and nonlinguistic representations. Specifically, Paivio (1969, 1972) and Bower (1972) asserted that nonverbal imagery and verbal symbols are two distinct and major modes of knowledge representation. This has been referred to as the "dual coding" theory. In other words, knowledge is represented in long-term memory in linguistic and nonlinguistic codes.

Information stored linguistically is commonly realized as "inner speech." Both Vygotsky (1962) and Piaget (1959) emphasized the importance of inner speech to human cognition. It is a misconception, however, to think that linguistic thought is represented only as words. Linguistic thought is probably represented in its most basic form as highly abstract semantic units. For example, Slobin (1979), in his explanation of the semiotic theory of language processing, explained that human beings are predisposed to code information linguistically into basic forms, such as agents, objects, and relationships. We tend to separate our experience into persons, places, and things that act on or are acted on by other persons, places, or things. This occurs at a very deep or prelinguistic level that might be likened to a deep structure semantic level (Schlesinger, 1971). Of course, this is similar to the contention of case grammarians (e.g., Fillmore, 1968) who assert that all languages have a deep semantic regularity. The linguistic coding of information, then, contains abstract representations of information that are commonly expressed as words.

Information represented nonlinguistically is encoded as visual, auditory, kinesthetic, tactile, and olfactory components. Drawing from the hemispheric research, Gazzaniga (1985, Gazzaniga & LeDoux, 1978) explained that these forms of representation operate in a modular fashion. So strong are the modular components in determining human behavior that Gazzaniga characterized the human mind as comprised of "multiple selves." Sometimes a module or a "self" contains auditory information along with olfactory, tactile, visual and other types of information. Sometimes it is comprised primarily of one type of information (e.g., visual).

Perhaps the most powerful form of nonlinguistic coding for learning purposes is visual representation of information. Visual representations fall on a continuum that runs from episodic to symbolic. Episodic visual representations are the mental pictures that come from true-to-life episodes or fabricated episodes. Even when fabricated, the episodes are represented by true-to-life people, places, and things. Symbolic, visual, and mental representations are not true to life. They are not comprised of mental pictures of real people, places, and things organized as events. Instead, they are composed of abstract shapes and forms that convey meaning to the learner about the information being represented.

Relating the dual coding theory to the structure of knowledge discussed in the previous section, we might conclude that both declarative and procedural knowledge are stored (encoded) as images and as language symbols. Just as an effective learning experience involves the organizing of information into appropriate declarative and procedural structures, so does it involve the efficient storage of information. This is accomplished by the learner representing the information in linguistic and nonlinguistic ways.

Thinking That Changes Existing Knowledge Structures in Long-Term Memory

Declarative and procedural knowledge, once represented in long-term memory, are not static; they are developed in a number of ways, some of which are quite surprising and unpredictable (Vosniadou & Brewer, 1987). There are a number of different descriptions of the structural changes that occur to information in long-term memory. For example, Piaget (1959) characterized changes in one's knowledge structures as accommodation. Rumelhart and Norman (1981) described structural changes in terms of accretion, tuning, and restructuring. For educational purposes, however, it is probably more useful to identify the cognitive operations that create changes in knowledge structures. Such operations can be organized into two broad categories: macroprocesses and microprocesses.

Macroprocesses. Macroprocesses are broad, generally (although not always) time-consuming, cognitive operations that utilize and change existing knowledge structures. Included in this category are: (a) problem solving, (b) decision making, (c) scientific inquiry, and (d) composing. Each macroprocess has a relatively specific purpose. Consequently, each produces different changes in the knowledge in long-term memory.

Problem solving is the macroprocess of attempting to reach a goal, the progress to which is in some way constrained (Polya, 1957; Wickelgren, 1974). The end product of problem solving is commonly restructured procedural knowledge. The learner devises new ways of accomplishing a goal. Smolensky (1986) explained that new productions are dynamically created in problem-solving situations, productions that can be used for future problems.

Decision making has as its purpose selection among equally appearing alternatives (Halpern, 1984; Wales, 1979). The end product of decision making is commonly restructured declarative knowledge, especially that involving one's priorities and values concerning the alternatives considered.

Scientific inquiry is the macroprocess of explaining a phenomenon (Marzano et al., 1988). Products of scientific inquiry include restructured declarative knowledge (in the form of new concepts and principles) and restructured procedural knowledge (in the form of new heuristics or algorithms for accomplishing goals related to the phenomenon under study).

Composing is the macroprocess of conceiving and developing a new product, whether it be a piece of writing, a dance, a song, a painting, or a sculpture (Marzano et al., 1988). It provides restructured declarative information in the form of new concepts, principles, and schemata relative to the topic of the composition. It can also involve the creation of new procedural knowledge when something must be produced for which the composer has no readily available heuristics or algorithms (Flower & Hayes, 1980a, 1980b, 1981).

In summary, learners change their existing knowledge structures by engaging in such macroprocesses as problem solving, decision making, scientific inquiry, and composing. Additionally, they modify their knowledge structures by engaging in a series of microprocesses.

Microprocesses. There are many ways of describing the various microprocesses that are used to shape and sharpen knowledge. For example, Gubbins (in Sternberg, 1985) listed over 30 microprocesses. By definition, microprocesses typically take less time than the macroprocesses and are commonly used in the service of the macroprocesses. For example, while engaged in decision making (a macroprocess), an individual may have occasion to *compare* or *classify* alternatives (both of which are microprocesses). Although there is no set, prespecified order in which the microprocesses are applied (i.e., they tend to be used as needed by the individual in the accomplishment of a goal), it is useful to describe them by type. Marzano and colleagues (in press) listed 12 different microprocesses commonly used to shape and sharpen information (cf. Marzano et al., 1988). These can be organized under five major headings (see Fig. 14.1).

According to Fig. 14.1, learners can change their existing knowledge structures by engaging in cognitive operations that allow them to match new information in various ways, infer information not directly stated, evaluate information, examine the value of information, and extend information. Although these microprocesses can be used in isolation, they are most commonly used during the execution of more complex and time-consuming macroprocesses.

Dispositional Thought

A final type of thinking that affects learning is dispositional. Dispositions are habitual ways that we approach a learning situation (Resnick, 1987). There have been a number of attempts to identify various types of dispositions. Here, seventeen dispositions have been highlighted (see Fig. 14.2). They borrow heavily from, and, to some extent, can be considered a composite list from, the work of Amabile (1983), Ennis (1985), Lipman, Sharp, and Oscanyan (1980), Paris and his colleagues (Paris & Lindauer,

I. Matching Microprocesses
   1. Comparing: Identifying and articulating similarities and differences between information relative to specific attributes.
   2. Classifying: Grouping items into categories on the basis of their attributes.
II. Inferring Microprocess
   3. Elaborating: Inferring unstated but known information about familiar concepts, facts, principles, or schemata.
   4. Deducing: Inferring unknown examples from a known principle.
   5. Inducing: Inferring unknown generalizations or principles based on observation or analysis.
   6. Predicting: Anticipating the outcome of a situation and then checking the accuracy of the anticipated outcome.
III. Evaluating Microprocesses
   7. Verifying: Confirming or proving the truth of an idea via the construction of a rational argument.
   8. Identifying errors: Identifying and articulating mistakes in one's own thinking or that of others.
IV. Valuing
   9. Identifying personal value: Identifying and articulating the personal value assigned to information and the reasons for that value assignment.
   10. Dialectic thinking: Identifying and articulating values for information opposed to personally assigned value.
V. Extending Microprocesses
   11. Analogical reasoning: Identifying and articulating values for information opposed to personally assigned value.
   12. Extrapolating: Identifying and articulating how the pattern or component parts of two entities are related at an abstract level.

FIG. 14.1. Microprocesses.

1982; Paris et al., 1983), Perkins (1984, 1985), and Raudsepp (1983). These 17 dispositions, when activated, drastically change the nature of learning. In fact, critical thinking, creative thinking, and self-regulated thinking can be partially defined in terms of the dispositions listed in Fig. 14.2.

The concept of critical thinking is rooted in ancient philosophy. For example, Aristotle described the process of discerning truth through rational thought as grasping the design or *telos* of reality. Greene (1984) noted that, in the Western World, philosophy preceded by at least 2,000 years the growth of what we now call science. As old as its roots are, critical thinking is still found in many of the adopted educational goals of most states and school systems (Goodlad, 1984), primarily because critical thinking is considered essential for democratic citizenships (Remy, 1980).

Some of the aspects of critical thinking are realized as microprocesses. For example, the microprocesses of classifying, inducing, deducing, predicting, verifying, and identifying errors in one's logic are commonly

1. Seeking clarity and precision when information is unclear.
2. Trying to be well informed.
3. Seeking reasons for what you believe.
4. Taking into account the total situation.
5. Carefully analyzing information.
6. Remaining open-minded.
7. Taking a position (and changing it) when the evidence is sufficient to do so.
8. Showing sensitivity to the feelings, level of knowledge, and degree of sophistication of others.
9. Resisting impulsivity.
10. Engaging intensely in tasks even when answers or solutions are not immediately apparent.
11. Pushing the limits of one's knowledge and abilities to keep improving on one's knowledge and skills.
12. Generating, trusting, and maintaining one's own standards of evaluation.
13. Generating new ways of viewing a situation outside the boundaries of standard conventions.
14. Planning.
15. Being sensitive to feedback.
16. Evaluating progress.
17. Making use of available resources.

FIG. 14.2.   Dispositions.

considered critical-thinking skills (Ennis, 1985). However, at its core, critical thinking is dispositional in nature. Specifically, it is the activation of such dispositions as items 1 through 9 listed in Fig. 14.2 that renders one's thinking critical, rather than using specific mental processes, such as classifying or inducing. For example, an individual is engaged in critical thinking when he or she seeks clarity, tries to be well informed, remains open-minded, shows sensitivity to the feelings of others, and so on. However, an individual might not necessarily be involved in critical thinking while engaging in classification or induction.

Creative thinking is closely related to critical thinking; however, the emphasis is more on the generation of new and unique ways of conceiving information than on the thoughtful analysis of information. For example, Halpern (1984) stated that "creativity can be thought of as the ability to form new combinations of items to fulfill a need" (p. 324). Perkins (1984) described creativity as thinking patterned in a way that tends to lead to results that are new and unique, yet appropriate to the situation. Again, some of the microprocesses have been associated with creative thinking. For example, analogical reasoning and extrapolation have been considered creative-thinking skills (Torrance, 1986). However, dispositions such as items 10 through 13 in Fig. 14.2 form the basics for creative thought. For example, an individual behaves creatively when he or she continues to operate at the edge rather than the center of his or her competence, and when he or she seeks to restructure the task in unique ways. However, the individual may not be thinking creatively while forming analogies.

Finally, self-regulation can also be conceived of as dispositionally based. Specifically, many of the characteristics of metacognition (Flavell, 1978, 1979) are reflected in dispositions 14 through 17 in Fig. 14.2 That is, an individual is behaving in a self-regulated, metacognitive manner when he or she plans, is sensitive to feedback, evaluates progress, and uses available resources.

In summary, a paradigm centered in learning is one that is organized around what happens inside the mind of the learner. The model described in this subsidiary postulates five distinct forms of thinking that occur during effective learning:

1. Thinking that establishes and maintains the context for learning.
2. Thinking that gives rise to the structuring of content.
3. Thinking that generates the representation of content in long-term memory.
4. Thinking that changes existing knowledge structures.
5. Dispositional thought.

The consequences of an educational system that makes decisions based on a paradigm like the one just presented could be profound. Many of these implications are discussed in Marzano et al. (1988). Briefly, a paradigm centered on learning would affect curriculum, instruction, and assessment. Currently, the curriculum within most educational systems is conceived of as content- or domain-specific declarative and procedural information—the facts, concepts, principles, schemata, and processes that are important to various content areas. A paradigm centered on learning would necessarily expand this traditional notion of curriculum to include and emphasize such components as:

- A repertoire of strategies for setting the context for learning.
- A repertoire of strategies for structuring information.
- A repertoire of strategies for representing information.
- A repertoire of micro- and macrolevel strategies for changing existing knowledge structures.
- The dispositions toward critical, creative and self-regulated learning.

Curriculum, then, within any content area, can be conceptualized as in Fig. 14.3.

At the center of curriculum planning is still the declarative and procedural knowledge important to the content. However, also considered important to the content are various strategies for each component of the learning-centered paradigm. Thus, the content-area teacher, from this perspective, is more than a teacher of content. He or she is also a teacher of how to effectively learn and use the content.

Just as curriculum would be affected by a paradigm focused on learning, so would general instructional models. That is, instruction would be impacted, in that instructional models would necessarily become more robust to include all aspects of the learner-centered paradigm. As useful as current models are (e.g., Reigeluth, 1983), they do not include even a majority of the components described herein. Most models emphasize the structuring and representation of declarative and procedural information. Few detail the specifics of the various micro- and macroprocesses for changing existing knowledge structures, and fewer still deal with thinking that establishes and maintains the context for learning, or the dispositions toward critical, creative, and self-regulated learning.

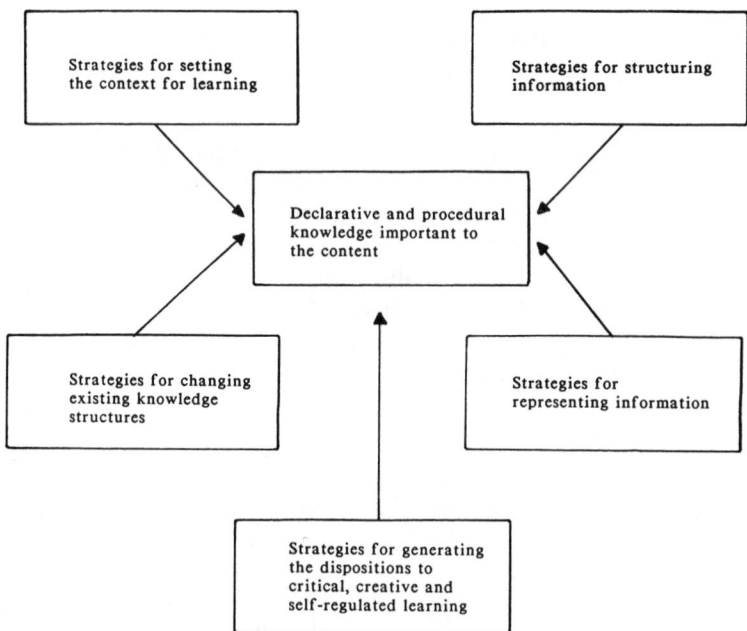

FIG. 14.3.   A learning-centered view of curriculum.

Finally, assessment strategies would necessarily shift from their current monolithic view of knowledge. Specifically, current testing procedures are heavily skewed toward domain-specific declarative knowledge (chapter 6 of this volume; Marzano & Costa, 1988; Marzano & Jesse, 1987), to a large extent because of the restrictive nature of multiple-choice formats. To assess process knowledge, (both domain-specific processes and the knowledge restructuring micro- and macroprocesses) assessment procedures would be expanded to include open-ended answers and essays. To assess dispositional thinking and that which establishes and maintains the context for learning, such strategies as informal observation and analysis of students' thinking via protocol analysis would be considered valid assessment techniques.

In short, a paradigm centered on learning would affect almost every aspect of schooling. Yet, for such a paradigm to develop there must be a shift from the existing paradigms.

SHIFTING TO A NEW PARADIGM

Sawada and Caley (1985) explained that new paradigms do not emerge in a linear fashion as a natural outgrowth of existing paradigms. Rather, new paradigms emerge via a radical restructuring of old paradigms (Schwartz & Ogilvy, 1979). Radical restructuring is called "bifurcation," and it occurs when a system maintains a state that is "far from equilibrium" for a prolonged period of time. To illustrate, Sawada and Caley noted that any system can exist in three states: (a) at equilibrium with respect to its environment, (b) near equilibrium with respect to its environment, or (c) far from equilibrium with respect to its environment. When systems approach a far-from-equilibrium state, which Sawada and Caley referred to as the "threshold of becoming," they are subject to spontaneous reorganization or bifurcation.

How, then, can a far-from-equilibrium state be reached relative to the current paradigms of education given that the current paradigms exist as a set of beliefs? Glasser (1981) and Powers (1973) have noted that, with belief-oriented systems, a far-from-equilibrium state can be reached and maintained by introducing "error" into the perceptions of the individuals within the system. Error refers to information that is contradictory or challenging to established beliefs. Herein lies the role of naturalistic inquiry in generating a new educational paradigm; it provides a vehicle for introducing error within the current set of beliefs about education—those beliefs in which the current paradigms exist.

Naturalistic Inquiry

Naturalistic inquiry itself represents a paradigm shift in the field of social science research. According to Lincoln and Guba (1985), naturalistic inquiry is an emerging research paradigm that follows two preceding paradigms. Specifically, naturalistic research is a reaction to the positivist paradigm for inquiry, which itself was an outgrowth of the prepositivist era.

Of the three paradigm eras, the prepositivist is the longest and least influential for modern research. It ranged over a period of two millennia from the time of Aristotle (384–322 B.C.) to that of, but not including, David Hume (1711–1776). Lincoln and Guba characterized this era of research as that of the passive observer. According to Wolf (1981), the mode of passive observer was largely due to the influence of Aristotle, who believed that human interference in "the natural order" produced discontinuity. Wolf (1981) noted that, "Scientists were passive then. It would take a while before they would attempt to reach out and touch, to try ideas and see if they worked" (p. 23).

It was this reaching out that ushered in the era of the researcher as active observer, which is referred to as the positivist era. Reese (1980) noted that positivism is most accurately defined as a family of philosophies that began in France and Germany under the title of logical positivism with guidance from such scholars as Gustav Bergman, Rudolf Carnap, and Moritz Schlick. There is considerable disagreement as to which scientist or group of scientists actually established the theoretical foundations for positivism. Some cite John Stuart Mill's *A System of Logic* in 1843 (in Herrnstein & Boring, 1965, p. 180) as the cornerstone of positivism. Wolf (1981) believed that Newtonion physics was the foundation of positivism.

Whereas there is disagreement about the beginnings of positivism, there is considerable agreement about the assumptions underlying positivism. At its core, positivism assumes that:

- Any event, any entity, can be broken apart into pieces that can be studied independently; the whole is simply the sum of the parts.
- The observer can be separated from what is being observed.
- Events at one time and place also may, under similar circumstances, occur at another time and place.
- All effects are products of causes.
- A methodology for research can be (and has been) established that is free of the influence of bias. (Lincoln & Guba, 1985)

Although this is still the predominant research paradigm in education and psychology, Lincoln and Guba (1985) asserted that it is gradually being replaced by a new paradigm: "Cracks have begun to appear in science's magnificent edifice as new 'facts' are uncovered with which the old paradigm cannot deal or explain. Normal science . . . is becoming more and more difficult to sustain. Serious challenges are being mounted from the perspective of alternative paradigms that suggest new and different answers" (p. 7).

This alternative research paradigm is referred to as the postpositivist era, or the era of naturalistic inquiry. A number of descriptions of the assumptions underlying the naturalistic paradigm have been articulated (e.g., Hesse, 1980; Schwartz & Ogilvy, 1979). Basically, many of the assumptions underlying postpositivism are directly counter to those underlying positivism:

- Whereas positivism assumes a reality in which the whole is a combination of the parts, postpositivism allows for entities and events that are more than the sum of their component parts.

- Whereas positivism assumes that the observer can be separated from what is observed, postpositivism assumes that the observer and observed always interact.

- Whereas positivism assumes that events can be replicated under appropriate conditions, postpositivism assumes that events are, to some extent, always unique.

- Whereas positivism assumes that effects are products of causes, postpositivism asserts that effects sometimes activate causes.

- Whereas positivism assumes that a research methodology can be devised that is free of bias, postpositivism asserts that research is always biased by the a priori beliefs of the researcher.

Operationally, naturalistic inquiry integrates the study of a specific phenomena with the study of the context in which the phenomenon occurs and the beliefs and assumptions of the investigator. Specifically, the very methodology of naturalistic inquiry encourages the investigation of both context and investigator beliefs, as well as the phenomenon under study. Patton (1978, 1980) has described a number of methodological principles of naturalistic inquiry that facilitate such investigation. These include: (a) use of natural setting, (b) use of a holistic viewpoint, (c) getting close to the data, and (d) development of emerging theory base.

Natural setting refers to the use of the environment and atmosphere in which the phenomenon under study usually occurs. Patton (1980) noted that: "The research setting is a naturally occurring event, program, relationship, or interaction, that has no predetermined course by or for the research. Rather, the point . . . is to understand naturally occurring phenomena in their naturally occurring roles" (p. 3). Similar descriptions have been offered by Willems and Rausch (1969) and by Guba (1978). The use of natural settings can be contrasted to an experimental approach, where the investigator attempts to completely control conditions of the study by manipulating, changing, or holding constant external influences and where a very limited set of outcomes variables are measured (Patton, 1980).

A *holistic view* refers to studying the phenomenon under investigators as a whole. According to Patton (1980), the researcher tries to understand the social, the totality, and the unifying nature of a phenomena. Such an approach assumes that the whole is greater than the sum of its parts; it also assumes that a description and understanding of a phenomenon's context is essential. In contrast to experimental designs that manipulate and measure the relationships among a few carefully selected and narrowly defined variables, the naturalistic approach is open to gathering data on a number of aspects of the research phenomenon.

Many times, a holistic perspective discloses effects that an experimental approach might miss. For example, during a study of the effects of an enriched Follow Through (FT) program modeled along the lines of open education, which produced no significant differences between control and experimental groups on a standardized test, Shapiro (1973) noted that a holistic perspective helped disclose some important qualitative differences between groups. Specifically, it was found that the Follow Through classrooms were, in the words of Shapiro (1973):

> . . . lively, vibrant, with a diversity of curricula projects and children's products, and an atmosphere of friendly, cooperative endeavor. The non-FT classrooms were characterized as relatively uneventful, with a narrow range of curriculum, uniform activity, a great deal of seat work and less equipment; teachers as well as children were quieter and more concerned with maintaining or submitting to discipline. (p. 529)

The principle of *getting close to the data* is a natural consequence of a holistic view. As Patton (1980) noted, the individual engaged in naturalistic research gets close to the phenomenon under study through physical proximity for a period of time, as well as through development of closeness in a social sense of intimacy and confidentiality. Lofland (1971) stated that, even though experimental researchers do not advocate getting close to the phenomenon under investigation, they utilize this principle in their day-to-day interactions. Asserting the importance of getting close to the data, Denzin (1978) noted that the process of naturalistic inquiry involves "the studied commitment to actively enter the world of interacting individuals" (pp. 8–9). Similarly, Bruyn (1963) stated that the inner perspective necessary to truly understand a phenomenon "assumes that understanding can only be achieved by actively participating in the life of the observed and gaining insight by means of introspection" (p. 226).

Finally, the principle of *emerging theory* refers to allowing a guiding substantive theory to emerge from the research process. Miles and Huberman (1984) referred to this as allowing a conceptual model to emerge. Guba (1978) noted that naturalistic inquiry is like a wave on which the investigator moves from varying degrees of a "discovering mode" to varying emphasis on a "verification mode" in attempting to understand the real world. As a study begins, the researcher is open to whatever emerges from the data. Then, as the inquiry reveals patterns, the investigation begins to focus on verifying and evaluating those that appear to be emerging. This, said Patton (1980), renders naturalistic inquiry a useful vehicle for both discovering and verifying what has been discovered. Experimental research, on the other hand, is skewed toward verification. Making the same point, Hesse (1980) stated that naturalistic inquiry is oriented toward a "context of discovery," whereas experimental research is oriented toward a "context of justification" (p. 82).

Three of the five principles described heretofore—using a natural setting, using a holistic perspective, and getting close to the date—naturally facilitate studying the context of a phenomenon. The principle of developing an emerging theory base facilitates investigation of the researcher's beliefs. When applied to education, these principles suggest a redefined role for the classroom teacher and a way of shifting from the current paradigm. Specifically, the paradigms from which education currently operate exist as beliefs in the minds of educators. Naturalistic inquiry, when practiced by teachers about the process of learning, should create a shift in emphasis from education as an institutional, administrative, or instructional system to an emphases on education as a set of interactions among teachers, students, and content that create changes in the minds of learners. One might conclude that the current emphasis on teaching thinking can be sustained by the adoption of a new research agenda—the study of the learning process—by a new and somewhat untapped population of researchers—teachers.

Teachers as Naturalistic Researchers

There is a rapidly growing number of models of teacher-directed naturalistic inquiry. For example, there have been many attempts to operationalize the research role of the classroom teacher. Michigan State University's Institute for Research on Teaching (IRT) has consistently used public school teachers as research collaborators (Eaton, 1984). Participating teachers are actively involved in all phases of research, from conceptualization and design to data collection, data analysis, and research dissemination. The Institute for Research on Teaching also uses a forum model to bring researchers and teachers together to discuss and analyze key issues relative to recent research findings. Within the IRT forum, educators utilize research findings as the bases for inquiry about current assumptions relative to schooling.

One disturbing finding from IRT's efforts is that teacher collaborators, after participating in field-based research, find it difficult to return to schools that do not value the inquiry process (Eaton, 1984). About one third of the IRT's former teacher collaborators return to teaching, another third only return part-time, and the remaining third leave the classroom entirely. It appears from the IRT experience that the process of inquiry is exciting and motivating to teachers. Unfortunately, it is also clear that many (perhaps most) schools do not value and foster inquiry as a standard practice. Those teachers who become educators/researchers find few traditional settings in which to practice their new-found role.

Taking down the boundaries between teaching and research is also the focus of the "academic alliance" model described by Gaudiani and Burnette (1985–1986). They asserted that academic alliances between school teaching staffs and university faculty can be a powerful tool in fostering naturalistic inquiry. Gaudiani and Burnette have identified a number of principles for success for such "communities of inquiry." These principles include: (a) discovering commonalties concerning major issues and a common language for addressing those issues, (b) erasing many of the status distinctions between school and college faculty, (c) focusing on common problems that need to be solved, (d) providing specific rewards and/or incentives for engaging in the community of inquiry, and (e) identifying tangible change as a result of the inquiry process. Gaudiani and Burnette noted that this model of inquiry creates a strong shared expertise, a new way of looking at academic subject areas, and a shared sense of power.

One example of teacher-directed naturalistic inquiry in education and its effect on the paradigms of those involved is Bussis, Chittenden, and Amarel's (1976) study of teacher beliefs and their effects on instructional practice. The researchers conducted in-depth interviews and extensive case studies of 60 teachers. At first, their intent was not so much to involve teachers directly in the research process as it was to identify the types of beliefs that were determinants of specific teacher behaviors. However, as the study progressed, the participating teachers, themselves, became engaged in the inquiry process. Teachers began to collect data and question the assumptions behind their behaviors. Bussis, Chittenden, and

Amarel found that the inquiry process did as much to change teacher beliefs (change their paradigms) as it did to disclose the beliefs from which they operated.

Perhaps the most direct attempt to create a paradigm shift via teacher-directed naturalistic inquiry is Gibboney and Gould's (1987) inquiry-based staff development model. Central to their model of staff development is the systematic analysis and questioning of the underlying assumptions about learning via informal studies conducted by teachers.

Effects of Teacher-Directed Naturalistic Inquiry

An assumption that is inherent in this chapter is that naturalistic inquiry, when used by teachers to study the learning process, will eventually engender a new educational paradigm centered on learning. But what of short-term effects of teacher-directed naturalistic inquiry? Although teacher-directed, naturalistic research is still in its infancy, its utility as a tool for change is already being noted. For example, Patterson and Stansell (1987), in their discussion of the effects of naturalistic inquiry in the classroom and the benefits of collaborative efforts between a researcher (Karen) and a teacher (Maura), noted:

> Maura had never before been asked by anyone to ask her own questions and to find her own answers. Although she had always asked questions about her teaching, her students, and her curriculum, she had never taken the time to answer her questions in any depth or to any degree of satisfaction. Because of the collaboration, she gave herself permission to take the time to reflect, analyze, and problem solve. With Karen's guidance, Maura involved herself not in traditional research methods but in an informal, yet logical and systematic, analysis of her curriculum. She did not concern herself with reporting the results of her research to an outside audience or institution. Maura was her own audience. She applied the results of her research immediately in her classroom. She was the immediate benefactor of her newfound sense of purpose, understanding, and direction. Naturally, her students became benefactors as well. (p. 719)

Burns (1983) described how teacher-directed naturalistic inquiry can produce powerful effects in student learning: "The English teacher who thinks like an ethnographer (naturalistic researcher) can create an environment where students are free to learn in a natural setting and in an interesting, effective and meaningful way" (p. 19). In addition, Burns (1983) asserted that naturalistic inquiry can be a powerful learning tool for teachers:

Ethnographic researchers must develop a dynamic tension between the supportive role of participant and the role of observer so that he [or she] is neither one entirely. The teacher must be careful to develop a similar sort of dynamic tension between the roles of classroom-community partici- pant and professional teacher, maintaining the objectivity needed to help our students learn. Participant observation can, however, help us gain vital new knowledge about our students and what they believe, the values they hold, the goals they have set and how they think (p. 19).

Finally, Applebee (1987) reinforced the paradigm shifting potential of teacher-directed naturalistic inquiry:

It is through the process of systematic reflection that teachers can most enrich the research process—reflection upon their own teaching, upon interpretations of data collected and upon the implications for practice of the questions and directions highlighted in discipline-based research. Based on their knowledge of the classroom, teachers can ask questions that help define new problems to study, provide evidence about what works and what does not and gain insights into the complex life of the school and classroom. Research in education has at times ignored the teacher's profes- sional knowledge, of course, and has inevitably suffered from it (p. 715).

CONCLUSION

It is an assumption of this chapter that teacher-directed, naturalistic inquiry about the learning process will lead to the development of a paradigm centered on learning. Once teachers systematically begin to ask and answer questions about how learning occurs, they will, quite naturally, note different types of thinking in the mind of the learner (five of which have been described herein) and make more powerful instructional decisions based on those distinctions. Yet, fostering this new research agenda and the changing role of the teacher is a difficult task. As Gideonse (1983) pointed out, educators do not feel the need to learn about the scientific bases of their profession because they believe they already know, they believe it is unimportant, they do not care what it is, or they are not aware of their need to know. Yet the journey appears worth the effort. It is my contention that teacher-directed, naturalistic inquiry about the learning process can engender one of the most power- ful education shifts in recent decades.

ACKNOWLEDGMENT

This publication is based on work sponsored wholly, or in part, by the Office of Educational Research and Improvement, Department of Education, under Contract Number 400-86-0002. The content of this publication does not necessarily reflect the views of OERI of any other agency of the U.S. Government.

REFERENCES

Amabile, T. M. (1983). *The social psychology of creativity.* New York:Springer-Verlag.

Anderson, J. (1982). Acquisition of cognitive skills. *Psychological Review, 89,* 369–406.

Anderson, J. (1983). *The architecture of cognition.* Cambridge, MA: Harvard University Press.

Applebee, A. (1987). Teachers and the process of research. *Language Arts, 64*(7), 714–716.

Banathy, B. (1980). The school: An autonomous or cooperating social agency. In L. Rubin (Ed.), *Critical issues in educational policy* (pp. 111–118). Boston: Allyn and Bacon.

Banathy, B. (1984). *Systems design in the context of human activity systems.* San Francisco: International Systems Institute.

Banathy, B. (1986). A systems view of institutionalizing change in education. In S. Majumbar (Ed.), *1985–86 Yearbook of the National Association of Academies of Science* (pp. 12–19). Columbus, OH: Ohio Academy of Science.

Banathy, B. (1987). Instructional systems design. In R. Gagne (Ed.), *Instructional technology: Foundations* (pp. 85–112). Hillsdale, NJ: Lawrence Erlbaum Associates.

Bandura, A., & Schunk, D. H. (1981). Developing competence, self- efficacy and intrinsic interest through proximal self-motivation. *Journal of Personality and Social Psychology, 41*(3) 586–598.

Bereiter, C. (1984). How to keep thinking skills from going the way of all frills. *Educational Leadership, 42,* 75–78.

Bettencourt, E. M., Gillet, M. H., Gall, M. D., & Hull, R. E. (1983). Effects of teacher enthusiasm training on student on task behavior and achievement. *American Educational Research Journal, 20,* 435–450.

Bower, G. (1972). Analysis of a mnemonic device. In M. Coltheart (Ed.), *Readings in cognitive psychology* (pp. 399–426). Toronto: Holt, Rinehart & Winston.

Broadbent, D., (1958). *Perception and communication.* London: Pergamon Press.

Brophy, J. (1982). *Classroom organization and management.* Washington, DC: National Institute of Education.

Bruyn, S. (1963). The methodology of participant observation. *Human Organization, 21,* 224–235.

Burns, W. (1983). The English teacher as ethnographer. *English Record, 34*(4), 19–21.

Bussis, A. M., Chittenden, E. A., & Amarel, M. (1976). *Beyond surface curriculum.* Boulder, CO: Westview Press.

Clark, H. H., & Haviland, S. E. (1977). Comprehension and the given-new contract. In R. O. Freedle (Ed.), *Discourse production and comprehension* (Vol. 1, pp. 1–40). Norwood, NJ: Ablex.

Cuban, L. (1987, July). *Constancy and change in schools (1880's to the present).* Paper presented at the Conference on Restructuring Education, Keystone. CO.

Deal, T. E., & Kennedy, A. A. (1982). *Corporate cultures: The rites and rituals of corporate life.* Reading, MA: Addision-Wesley.

Denzin, N. K. (1978). The logic of naturalistic inquiry. In N. K. Denzin (Ed.), *Sociological methods: A sourcebook.* New York: McGraw-Hill.

Eaton, J. (1984, Winter–Spring). Teachers participate in research dissemination. *Communication Quarterly* (pp. 2–4). East Lansing, MI: Institute for Research on Teaching, Michigan State University.

Ellis. A. (1962). *Reason and emotion in psychology.* New York: Lyle Stuart.

Ennis, R. H. (1985). Goals for a critical thinking curriculum. In A. Costa (Ed.), *Developing minds: A resource book for teaching thinking* (pp. 54–57). Alexandria, VA: Association for Supervision and Curriculum Development.

Fillmore, C. F. (1968). The case for case. In E. Beck & R. T. Harms (Eds.), *Universals in linguistic theory* (pp. 1–210). New York: Holt, Rinehart & Winston.

Flavell, J. H. (1978). Metacognitive development. In J. M. Scandura & C. J. Brainerd (Eds.), *Structural/process theories of complex human behavior* (pp. 213–245). The Netherlands: Sijthoff and Noordoff.

Flavell, J. H. (1979). Metacognition and cognition monitoring. *American Psychologist, 34,* 906–911.

Flower, L. A., & Hayes, J. R. (1980a). The cognition of discovery, defining a rhetorical problem. *College Composition and Communication, 13,* 21–32.

Flower, L. A., & Hayes, J. R. (1980b). The dynamics of composing: Making plans and juggling constraints. In L. W. Gregg & E. R. Steinburg (Eds.), *Cognitive processing in writing* (pp. 31–50). Hillsdale, NJ: Lawrence Erlbaum Associates.

Flower, L. A., & Hayes, J. R. (1981). A cognitive process theory of writing. *College Composition and Communication, 32,* 365–387.

Gaudiani, C. L., & Burnett, D. G. (1985–1986). *Academic alliances: A new approach to school/college collaboration.* Washington, DC: American Association for Higher Education.

Gazzaniga, M. S. (1985). *The social brain.* New York: Basic Books.

Gazzaniga, M.S., & LeDoux, J. E. (1978). *The integrated mind.* New York: Plenum Press.

Gibboney, R. A., & Gould, J. M. (1987). *Staff development and educational renewal through dialogue in two school systems: A conceptual and empirical assessment* (Tech. Rep.). Philadelphia: University of Pennsylvania, School of Education. (ERIC Document Reproduction Service No. ED 290 215).

Gideonse, H. D. (1983). *In search of more effective service: Inquiry as a guiding image for educational reform in America.* Cincinnati: S. Rosenthal and Company.

Glasser, W. (1981). *Stations of the mind.* New York: Harper and Row.

Goodlad, J. I. (1984). *A place called school.* New York: McGraw-Hill.

Greene, M. (1984). Philosophy, reason and literacy. *Review of Educational Research, 54*(4), 547–559.

Guba, E. (1978). *Toward a methodology of naturalistic inquiry in educational evaluation.* (CSE Monograph Series in Evaluation, No. 8) Center for the Study of Evaluation, University of California, Los Angeles.

Halpern, D. F. (1984). *Thought and knowledge: An introduction to critical thinking.* Hillsdale, NJ: Lawrence Erlbaum Associates.

Heliman, K. M., & Satz, P. (Eds.). (1983). *Neuropsychology of human emotions.* New York: Guilford Press.

Herrnstein, R. J., & Boring, E. G. (1965). *A sourcebook in the history of psychology.* Cambridge, MA: Harvard University Press.

Hesse, M. (1980). *Revolutions and reconstructions in the philosophy of science.* Bloomington: Indiana University Press.

Katz, S. E. (1976). *The effect of each of four instructional treatments on the learning of principles by children.* Madison: Wisconsin Research and Development Center for Cognitive Learning, The University of Wisconsin.

Klausmeier, H. J. (1985). *Educational psychology.* New York: Harper & Row.

Kuhn, T. (1962). *The structure of scientific revolutions.* Chicago: University of Chicago Press.

Lewis, D., & Greene, J. (1982). *Thinking better.* New York: Holt, Rhinehart & Winston.

Lincoln, Y. S., & Guba, E. G. (1985). *Naturalistic inquiry.* Beverly Hills, CA: Sage Publications.

Lindsay, P. H., & Norman, D. A. (1977). *Human information processing.* New York: Academic Press.

Lipman, M., Sharp, A. M., & Oscanyan, F. S. (1980). *Philosophy in the classroom* (2nd ed.). Philadelphia: Temple University Press.

Lofland, J. (1971). *Analyzing social settings.* Belmont, CA: Wasdworth.

Loman, D. F. (1986). *Predicting mathemathanic effects in the teaching of higher order thinking skills.* Unpublished manuscript, University of Iowa, School of Education, Iowa City.

Luria, A. (1973). *The working brain.* New York: Basic Books.

Mandler, G. (1983). The nature of emotion. In J. Miller (Ed.), *States of mind* (pp. 136–153). New York: Pantean Books, Inc.

Marzano, R. J. (1987). *Decomposing curricular objectives for specivity of instruction.* (Tech. Rep.) Aurora, CO: Mid-continent Regional Educational Laboratory. (ERIC Document Reproduction Service No. ED 290 220).

Marzano, R. J., Arredondo, D., Blackburn, G., Brooks, D., Ewy, R., & Pickering, D. (in press). Creating a learner-centered paradigm of instruction. *Educational Leadership.*

Marzano, R. J., Brandt, R. S., Hughes, C. S., Jones, B. F., Presseisen, B. Z., Rankin, S. C., & Suhor, C. (1988). *Dimensions of thinking: A framework for curriculum and instruction.* Alexandria, VA: Association for Supervision and Curriculum Development.

Marzano, R. J., & Costa, A. L. (1988). Question: Do standardized tests measure general cognitive skills? Answer: No. *Educational Leadership, 45,* 66–73.

Marzano, R. J., & Jesse, D. M. (1987). A study of general cognitive operations in two achievement test batteries and their relationship to item difficulty. (Tech. Rep.) Aurora, CO: Mid-continent Regional Educational Laboratory. (ERIC Document Reproduction Source No. ED 291 062).

Marzano, R. J., & Marzano, J. S. (1987). *Contextual thinking: The most basic of the cognitive skills.* (Tech. Rep.) Aurora, CO: Mid-continent Regional Educational Laboratory. (ERIC Document Reproduction Source No. ED 286 634).

Marzano, R. J., & Marzano, J. S. (1988). A cognitive model of commitment and its implications for therapy. *Psychotherapy in Private Practice, 6*(4), 69–81.

McCombs, B. (1984). Processes and skills underlying continuing intrinsic motivation to learn: Toward a definition of motivational skills training intervention. *Educational Psychologist, 19,* 197–218.

McCombs, B. (1986). The role of the self system in self-regulated learning. *Contemporary Educational Psychology, 11,* 314–332.

McCombs, B., (1987, April). *Issues in the measurement by standardized tests of primary motivation variables related to self-regulated learning.* Paper presented at the annual meeting of the American Educational Research Association, Washington, DC.

Meichenbaum, D. (1977). *Cognitive behavior modification: An integrated approach.* New York: Plenum Press.

Miles, M., & Huberman, A. M. (1984). *Qualitative data analysis.* Beverly Hills, CA: Sage Publications.

Moffett, J. (1968). *Teaching the universe of discourse.* Boston: Houghton-Mifflin.

Neisser, V. (1967). *Cognitive psychology.* New York: Appleton.

Newell, A., & Simon, H. A. (1972). *Human problem solving.* Englewood Cliffs, NJ: Prentice-Hall.

Norman, D. (1969). *Memory and attention.* New York: Wiley.

Owens, H., & Maxmen, J. S. (1979). Moods and affect: A semantic confusion. *American Journal of Psychiatry, 136,* 97–99.

Paivio, A. (1969). Mental imagery in associative learning and memory. *Psychological Review,* *76,* 241–263.

Paivio, A. (1971). *Imagery and verbal processing.* New York: Holt, Rhinehart and Winston.

Paris, S. G., & Lindauer, B. K. (1982). The development of cognitive skills during childhood. In B. W. Wolman (Ed.), *Handbook of developmental psychology* (pp. 333–349). Englewood Cliffs, NJ: Prentice-Hall.

Paris, S. G., Lipson, M. Y., & Wixson, K. K. (1983). Becoming a strategic reader. *Contemporary Educational Psychology, 8,* 293–316.

Patterson, L. & Stansell, J. C. (1987). Teachers and researchers: A new mutualism, *Language Arts, 64,* (7) 717–721.

Patton, M. Q. (1978). *Utilization-focused evaluation.* Beverly Hills, CA: Sage Publications.

Patton, M. Q. (1980). *Qualitative evaluation methods.* Beverly Hills, CA: Sage Publications.

Perkins, D. N. (1984). Creativity by design. *Educational Leadership, 42,* 18–25.

Perkins, D. N. (April, 1985). *Where is creativity?* Paper presented at University of Iowa Second Annual Humanities Symposium, Iowa City, IA.

Piaget, J. (1959). *Language and thought of the child.* Cleveland, OH: World.

Piaget, J. (1962). The relationship of affectivity to intelligence in the mental development of the child. *Bulletin of the Menninger Clinic, 26,* 129–137.

Polya, G. (1957). *How to solve it.* Princeton, NJ: University Press.

Powers, W. T. (1973). *Behavior: The control of perception.* Chicago, IL: Aldine.

Raphael, T. E. (1987). Research on reading: But what can I teach on Monday? In D. C. Berliner, U. Casanova, C. M. Clark, R. H. Hersh, & L. S. Shulman (Eds.), *Educator's handbook: A research perspective* (pp. 26–49). New York: Longman.

Raudsepp, E. (1983). Profile of the creative individual: Part I. *Creative Computing, 9,* 170–179.

Reese, W. L. (1980). *On becoming a social scientist.* Atlantic Highlands, NJ: Humanities.

Reigeluth, C. M. (1983). The elaboration theory of instruction. In C. M. Reigeluth (Ed.), *Instructional design theories and models: An overview of their current status* (pp. 315–381). Hillsdale, NJ: Lawrence Erlbaum Associates.

Remy, R. C. (1980). *Handbook of basic citizenship competencies: Guidelines for comparing materials, assessing instruction, and setting goals.* Alexandria, VA: Association for Supervision and Curriculum Development.

Resnick, L. B. (1987). *Education and learning to think.* Washington, DC: National Academy Press.

Rothkopf, E. Z. (1970). The concept of mathemagenic activities. *Review of Educational Research, 40,* 325–336.

Rumelhart, D. E. (1980). Schemata, the building blocks of cognition. In R. J. Spiro, B. C. Bertram, & W. I. Brewer (Eds.), *Theoretical issues in reading comprehension* (pp. 33–58). Hillsdale, NJ: Lawrence Erlbaum Associates.

Rumelhart, D. E., & Norman, D. A. (1981). Accretion, tuning and restructuring: Three modes of learning. In J. W. Colton & R. Klatzky (Eds.), *Semantic factors in cognition* (pp. 37–53). Hillsdale, NJ: Lawrence Erlbaum Associates.

Santostefano, S. (1986). Cognitive controls, metaphors and contexts. An approach to cognition and emotion. In D. J. Bearson & H. Zimiles (Eds.), *Thought and emotions: Developmental perspectives* (pp. 175–210). Hillsdale, NJ: Lawrence Erlbaum Associates.

Sathe, V. (1983). Implications of corporate culture: A manager's guide to action. *Organizational Dynamics, 5,* 73–84.

Sawada, D., & Caley, M. T. (1985). Dissipative structures: New metaphors for becoming in education. *Educational Researcher, 14,* 3–19.

Schank, R., & Abelson, R. (1977). *Scripts, plans, goals and understanding.* Hillsdale, NJ: Lawrence Erlbaum Associates.

Schlesinger, I. M. (1971). Production of utterances and language acquisition. In D. I. Slobin (Ed.), *The ontogenesis of grammar* (pp. 63–101). New York: Academic Press.

Schwartz, P., & Ogilvy, J. (1979). *The emergent paradigm: Changing patterns of thought and belief.* Menlo Park, CA: Values and Lifestyles Program.

Sears, P. S. (1940). Levels of aspiration in academically successful and unsuccessful children. *Journal of Abnormal and Social Psychology, 35,* 498–536.

Shapiro, E. (1973). Educational evaluation: Rethinking the criteria of competence. *School Review,* 523–549.

Shuell, T. J. (1986). Cognitive conceptions of learning. *Review of Educational Research, 56,* 411–436.

Slobin, D. I. (1979). *Psycholinguistics.* Glenview, IL: Scott, Foresman.

Smith, E. E., & Medin, D. L. (1981). *Categories and concepts.* Cambridge, MA: Harvard University Press.

Smith, F. (1982). *Understanding reading.* New York: Holt, Rhinehart and Winston.

Smolensky, P. C. (1986). Formal modeling of subsymbolic processes: An introduction to harmony theory. In N. E. Sharkey (Ed.), *Advances in Cognitive Science* (Vol 1, pp. 204–235). New York: Halsted Press.

Sokolov, A. N. (1972). *Inner speech and thought.* New York: Plenum Press.

Staton, J. (1984). Thinking together: Interaction in children's reasoning: In C. Thaiss & C. Suhor (Eds.), *Speaking and writing K–12* (pp. 144–187). Urbana, IL: National Council of Teachers of English.

Sternberg, R. J. (1985). Critical thinking: Its nature, measurement, and improvement. In F. Link (Ed.), *Essays on the intellect* (pp. 43–66). Alexandria, VA: Association for Supervision and Curriculum Development.

Torrance, E. P. (1986). Teaching creative and gifted learners. In M. C. Wittrock (Ed.), *Handbook of research on teaching* (3rd ed., pp. 630–647). New York: MacMillan Publishing Company.

Tough, J. (1974). *Talking, thinking and growing.* New York: Schocken Books.

Tough, J. (1976). *Listening to children.* London: Schools Council Publication.

van Dijk, T. A. (1980). *Macrostructures.* Hillsdale, NJ: Lawrence Erlbaum Associates.

van Dijk, T. A., & Kintsch, W. (1983). *Strategies of discourse comprehension.* New York: Academic Press.

von Bertalanffy, L. (1968). *General systems theory.* New York: George Braziller.

Vosniadou, S., & Brewer, W. F. (1987). Theories of knowledge restructuring in development. *Review of Educational Research, 51*(1), 51–67.

Vygotsky, L. S. (1962). *Thought and language.* Cambridge, MA: MIT Press.

Wales, C. E. (1979). Does how you teach make a difference? *Engineering Education, 69,* 394–398.

Watzlawick, P., Weakland, J., & Fisch, R., (1974). *Change: Principles of problem formation and problem resolution.* New York: W. W. Norton and Company.

Webster's ninth new collegiate dictionary. (1986). Springfield, MA: Merrian-Webster, Inc.

Weiner, B. (1972). Attribution theory, achievement motivation and the educational process. *Review of Educational Research, 42,* 203–215.

Weiner, B. (1983). Speculations regarding the role of affect in achievement-change programs guided by attributional principles. In J. M. Levine & M. C. Wang (Eds.), *Teaching and student perceptions: Implications for learning* (pp. 57–74). Hillsdale, NJ: Lawrence Erlbaum Associates.

Wickelgren, W. A. (1974). *How to solve problems.* San Francisco, CA: Walt Freeman.

Willems, E. P., & Rausch, H. L. (1969). *Naturalistic viewpoints in psychological research.* New York: Holt, Rhinehart & Winston.

Wittrock, M. C. (1974). Learning as a generative process. *Educational Psychologist, 11,* 87–95.

Wolf, F. A. (1981). *Taking the quantum leap.* San Francisco: Harper & Row.

Epilogue

Several key issues emerge from the chapters within this volume. They include:

1. Whether or not to teach thinking skills in a separate or an integrated curriculum.
2. Whether or not thinking skills taught separately will transfer or generalize to new and relevant contexts.
3. The influence of particular student characteristics on cognitive instruction.
4. The influence of the classroom atmosphere and other contextual factors on cognitive instruction.
5. The needs for the future preparation of teachers to teach thinking skills.
6. Critical areas to consider in bringing about change in American schooling.

SEPARATE OR INTEGRATED CURRICULA

The authors of both Volumes 1 and 2 have presented a convincing literature base for the efficacy of teaching thinking skills to novices. They have brought to the reader the debate of whether it is better to teach content-specific thinking skills or some general principles of critical thinking, taught in a separate curriculum. In particular, note the discussion of these issues in this volume in chapter 1, by Kennedy, Fisher, and Ennis, who favored a mixed approach using a little of both. Compare this to the conceptual framework or cognitive map used to teach students to analyze tasks that require mental operations in a separate context that is described in chapter 5 by Feuerstein, Rand, Hoffman, Egozi, and Shacharsegev.

Again, compare these approaches to that of O'Flahaven and Tierney who, in chapter 2, recommended integrating reading, writing, and thinking instruction. They have focused their chapter on how the reading and writing acts vary with respect to cognitive operations, using the convincing argument that writing is a way of focusing and organizing thoughts. They recommended that thinking skills be taught not only within a subject area, but also as integrated instruction for reading and writing so that a more holistic approach is taken to language arts instruction. Finally, refer to chapter 3, where Idol, Jones, and Mayer presented their analysis of curricular programs for teaching thinking skills separately versus some instructional strategies that can be used within reading and content area instruction.

The case for offering cognitive instruction is drawn out farther in several chapters that address the specifics of content area instruction (see chapters 2, 3, 6, 9, and 10).

TRANSFER

Critical to this discussion is the question of whether or not thinking skills taught in one context will generalize (or transfer) to another. Five different chapters contained relevant discussion of transferability of specific instruction (see chapters 3, 4, 5, and 6). Collins recommended that, via situated learning, skills and knowledge can be taught in contexts that reflect how the knowledge will be used in real life. In order to achieve transfer, Collins recommended that teaching occur in multiple contexts so that students can learn different ways that knowledge can be used, so that generalization can begin. Idol, Jones, and Mayer provided a summarization of whether or not consideration is given to teaching students to generalize in several commonly known curricula for teaching thinking skills separately, as well as a description of how this process occurs more naturally in some of the more recently developed approaches for teaching certain cognitive skills; their analysis revealed that there is considerable variability among the various programs and approaches for availability of transfer data.

In contrast, Feuerstein and his coauthors offered some worthwhile considerations for teaching in a content-free program; these considerations focus on various types of resistance to content area instruction raised by students, teachers, the subject matter itself, and previous student associations with failure.

Finally, in his analysis of problems related to testing, Linn described several important efforts to overcome the limitations of lack of match between current testing efforts and the teaching of thinking skills. He recommended that critical thinking skills be taught specifically in history and social science and that essay tests of particular subjects be used to test students' acquisition of these skills.

STUDENT CHARACTERISTICS

The various chapter authors have addressed some critical characteristics that students bring to the learning process that are especially likely to influence efforts in cognitive instruction: (a) developmental levels of students, (b) influence of students' prior knowledge, (c) culture, (d) gender, and (e) students' motivation.

Developmental Levels. Green, Kantor, and Rogers (chap. 11) provided a provocative discussion of the influence of language on learning. They constructed a conceptual framework for the role of language in everyday life. The interactions between language and intellectual development have profound implications for teaching of cognition. Related to this was Florio-Ruane's chapter (chap. 12) describing how instructional conversations are used in helping children develop both their language skills and their writing skills. She described how language learning takes place both in the home, via the influence of parents—particularly mothers, and in the schools, via the influence of teachers; with both types of influences taking place within the context of conversations. Particularly relevant to this is the impact of language within particular cultures and the problems with crosses in cultures between home and school as discussed in Secada's chapter (chap. 10).

Prior Knowledge. Although the relationship between prior knowledge and cognitive instruction is woven throughout both of the volumes in this series, four chapters in Volume 2 provided particularly relevant discussion of this important relationship (chapters 2, 6, 11, and 14, as well as Pearson and Raphael's chapter in Volume 1).

Culture. Whenever socioeconomic differences of students are discussed, discussion of cultural and ethic differences arise as well. Unfortunately, in America, social conditions are still such that races and cultures are frequently divided by socioeconomic lines. For this reason, as well as for reasons of reducing cultural biases and prejudices, it is probably best to think about making innovative instruction available to the economically disadvantaged, knowing that in many instances cultural differences as measured by school achievement will be increasingly reduced. However, the point remains that cultural values and mores must also be taken into consideration when constructing new educational curricula. Secada (chapter 10) reviewed the literature on mathematics achievement, pointing out that discrepancies based on gender are not nearly as great as those separating race and/or ethnicity. He placed emphasis on the changing nature of society and the need to make instruction relevant for the population, as well as for the changing demands of the job market. Secada's reminder to us to replace notions of cultural deprivation with observations of cultural differences are especially relevant in our efforts to reform education so that a positive impact is felt across cultures, impacting on the whole of America. Critical here is focus on examination of specific cultural differences that impact both positively and negatively on school learning.

Also related to this discussion is Barr's and Anderson's chapter (chap. 7) on practices of grouping students for instruction and the impact grouping practices can have on culturally different and/or economically disadvantaged students who often end up in low-ability groups with few opportunities to rise to higher functioning groups.

Gender Differences.   Statistics on gender differences are still evident in school achievement data pools, although certainly less than other sources of student differences. Walter Secada provided an excellent review of such differences and contributed significantly to the raising of our consciousness of the more important relationship between societal expectations for male versus female students. Efforts are needed to restructure not only the curricula, as examined by Secada, but also the attitudes and levels of consciousness of the teachers who offer the curricula.

Student Motivation.   Several of the authors addressed the contribution of students' motivation and attitudes toward school achievement, and particularly toward cognitive development (chapters 2, 5, and 8). In their chapter on student motivation (chap. 8), Ames and Ames identified several teaching practices that are likely to enhance student motivation for learning. These included: (a) reducing social comparisons among students, (b) increasing students' active involvement in learning, (c) placing focus on student effort, (d) promoting beliefs in consequences, (e) increasing student opportunities for success, and (f) teaching students self-determination strategies.

Related is the discussion in chapter 2 on self-initiated learning, in which O'Flahaven and Tierney contended that one's reasoning ability is best developed in conjunction with learning in situations that nurture student initiative. Feuerstein and his colleagues also wrote of the importance of intrinsic motivation for successful learning. In the Instrumental Enrichment Program, they have provided opportunities for students to begin to develop habits leading to intrinsic motivation, referred to as "habit formation."

Classroom Atmosphere. Contextual attributions of the classroom or learning environment itself are critical to successful cognitive instruction (see chapters 7, 9, 11, and 12). Barr and Anderson, in chapter 7, have provided us with an analysis of the assumptions that are made concerning the grouping of students for learning purposes. They described a school district that has schools with different grouping practices; they then go on to describe a process of how school committees can work to establish grouping policies and the interactions that occur at the district level.

Although grouping practices are a key factor in determining classroom atmosphere, other contextual factors also influence attempts to teach students thinking skills. As an example, Allington (chap. 9) provided us with a discussion of three critical aspects of instructional settings: (a) time allocated for instruction, (b) the types of instructional tasks that are set, and (c) the nature of the teaching of low-achieving students. At a very different level, both Florio-Ruane (chap. 12) and Green and her colleagues (chap. 11) described the language atmosphere that is created by the teacher and the students in the classroom.

TEACHER PREPARATION

All of these various contextual factors, as well as the other factors mentioned earlier, have tremendous implications for what kinds of preparation teachers need in order to offer effective classroom instruction that focuses on learning to think critically and to use problem-solving skills. Several authors (Allington; Collins; Feuerstein et al.; Idol et al.; Linn; Marzano) have offered guidance to us in this area. For instance, Collins, in his chapter on using the computer as a teacher (chap. 4), described a teaching process that might well be considered for use by human teachers as well as by computers. This process includes placing primary emphasis on teaching for transfer and is characterized by:

1. Teachers modeling and explaining.
2. Coaching.

3. Reflecting, or looking back and analyzing performance.
4. Articulating methods for forcing students to explain and think about what they are doing to make knowledge explicit.
5. Exploring and trying out different hypotheses, methods, and strategies to see their various effects.

This process could well be developed into one that is standardly taught to teachers as we move to developing more explicit pedagogical processes. Likewise, the conceptual framework that is discussed in chapter 5 (Feuerstein et al.) to teach students to analyze tasks that require mental operations is one that could be taught to teachers both for their own teaching and for their use in analyzing instructional tasks. Likewise, Marzano (chap. 14) wrote of teachers being taught to use naturalistic inquiry in the classroom to determine efficacious methods of teaching, again raising the consciousness and skill levels of teachers from merely being required to follow a prescribed curriculum to being actively involved in the problem-solving process of naturalistic inquiry, as well as in teaching such skills to their students. Linn also leaned toward giving the teacher more control in the classroom by recommending that assessments of student performance be teacher-directed. In chapter 3, Idol, Jones, and Mayer described a teaching process called "strategic teaching" that utilizes the teacher as a manager of the learning environment, as well as a guide and model for students in how thinking takes places in learning.

Such shifts would require a massive shift in preparatory programs moving to teaching teachers to solve their own problems, to conduct classroom-based evaluations, and to construct their own assessment instruments. This combination of proper preparation and mutual empowerment are necessary for both preservice teacher candidates and practitioning teachers.

BRINGING ABOUT CHANGE

Finally, this volume is about bringing about needed educational reform in both what and how students are taught (see chapters 7, 12, 13, and 14), as well as how they are assessed (see chapter 6). Both chapters 7 and 12 called our attention to the need to structure learning environments that foster maximal learning from both teachers and other students. Chapter 13 led us through a better understanding of the fundamental issues to be considered when bringing about school change. Chapter 14 spoke of teacher empowerment by shifting from the traditional development of theoretical paradigms that are presented to teachers to development of educational paradigms that are centered on learning in the classroom and that stem from naturalistic classroom observations by both teachers and researchers. Such efforts could be well-guided by the directions for future research, as offered by Ennis and colleagues.

THE NEED FOR
INTERDISCIPLINARY COLLABORATION

The works in both Volumes 1 and 2 reflect the obviously enriched outcomes that are produced from an interdisciplinary approach to thinking about a problem—in this case, the dimensions of thinking and cognitive instruction with need for educational reform. Production of these two volumes has been an effort to foster such interdisciplinary efforts. There are several important initiatives for such interdisciplinary groups to take in the future.

One is to develop further curricula for teaching thinking. Curriculum developers would be well advised to place emphasis on generalized learning and to be sensitive to individual student characteristics, such as developmental levels of learners, cultures of students, and student motivation.

A second initiative would be for some interdisciplinary groups to wrestle with the needs for teacher education. Efforts must be made to raise the conscious level of teachers so that more broad-minded approaches are taken to teaching both genders, as well as to being sensitive to cultural differences of students. Most critical to teacher education is for experimentation to develop in how best to teach teachers to offer cognitive instruction as discussed in these chapters, placing emphasis on (a) broadening the knowledge base of teachers and (b) teaching them how to model for students the various dimensions of thinking. Teachers must also be taught how to develop classroom atmospheres or learning environments that are conducive to teaching thinking.

A third initiative is for interdisciplinary groups to work closely with both teachers and policy makers in bringing about these needed changes in education. Such groups and policy makers must be willing to empower teachers to be involved in the establishment of educational policy so that the changes are relevant to the demands of the classroom and so that teachers are not only willing but anxious to take a leadership role in implementing the needed reform. Such efforts are more likely to be successful if a truly collaborative approach to problem solving is taken, rather than having some group members serve as experts to others in the policy-making groups, thus broadening the opportunity to use all possible expertise and knowledge in the decision making.

All groups must accept the challenge of providing a more relevant education for the students of today and tomorrow. We may not always be able to predict the kinds of jobs our children will encounter in the future world of work, but we would do well to help develop their cognitive abilities to the highest levels possible so that they may be better prepared for the demands of an ever-changing and increasingly more technological and complex world. Certainly, such efforts would help pave the way for offering equal learning and development opportunities to all students, regardless of race, creed, or socioeconomic status.

Lorna Idol
Beau F. Jones

Author Index

Subject Index